MALACHI

VOLUME 25D

THE ANCHOR BIBLE is a fresh approach to the world's greatest classic. Its object is to make the Bible accessible to the modern reader; its method is to arrive at the meaning of biblical literature through exact translation and extended exposition, and to reconstruct the ancient setting of the biblical story, as well as the circumstances of its transcription and the characteristics of its transcribers.

THE ANCHOR BIBLE is a project of international and interfaith scope: Protestant, Catholic, and Jewish scholars from many countries contribute individual volumes. The project is not sponsored by any ecclesiastical organization and is not intended to reflect any particular theological doctrine. Prepared under our joint supervision, THE ANCHOR BIBLE is an effort to make available all the significant historical and linguistic knowledge which bears on the interpretation of the biblical record.

THE ANCHOR BIBLE is aimed at the general reader with no special formal training in biblical studies; yet it is written with the most exacting standards of scholarship, reflecting the highest technical accomplishment.

This project marks the beginning of a new era of cooperation among scholars in biblical research, thus forming a common body of knowledge to be shared by all.

William Foxwell Albright
David Noel Freedman
GENERAL EDITORS

THE ANCHOR BIBLE

MALACHI

♦

A New Translation
with Introduction and Commentary

ANDREW E. HILL

THE ANCHOR YALE BIBLE

Yale University Press
New Haven & London

THE ANCHOR BIBLE
PUBLISHED BY DOUBLEDAY
a division of Random House, Inc.

THE ANCHOR BIBLE, DOUBLEDAY, and the portrayal of an anchor
with a dolphin are registered trademarks of Doubleday, a division of
Random House, Inc.

A hardcover edition of this book was published
in 1998 by Doubleday

Original Jacket Illustration by Margaret Chodos-Irvine

The Library of Congress has catalogued the hardcover edition as follows:

Library of Congress Cataloging-in-Publication Data
Bible. O.T. Malachi. English. Hill. 1998.
    Malachi : a new translation with introduction and commentary / by
Andrew E. Hill.
        p. cm. -- (The Anchor Bible reference library) (The Anchor
Bible ; v. 25D)
    Includes bibliographical references and indexes.
    1. Bible. O.T. Malachi — Commentaries.   I. Hill, Andrew E.
II. Title.   III. Series.   IV. Series: Bible.   English. Anchor
Bible.   1964 ; v. 25D.
BS192.2.A1   1964.G3   1998
[BS1673]
224′.99077 — dc21   96-50480
                                                        CIP

ISBN-978-0-300-13977-8

PRINTED IN THE UNITED STATES OF AMERICA

For
Jennifer Leah
May the *sun of righteousness* illumine your path always
Mal 3:20 [4:2]

CONTENTS

◆

Preface	xi
Acknowledgments	xv
List of Illustrations	xvii
Maps	xvii
Charts	xvii
Photographs and Drawings	xvii
List of Abbreviations	xix
Glossary of Terms	xxv
The Book of Malachi: Outlines and Translation	xxxiii
Thematic Outline of Malachi	xxxv
Rhetorical Outline of Malachi	xxxvi
Interrogative Elements Outline of the Haggai-Zechariah-Malachi Corpus	xxxvii
The Book of Malachi: A Translation	xl
I. INTRODUCTION	1
A. Textual Considerations	3
1. Hebrew Texts	3
2. Greek Translations	4
3. Syriac Translations	6
4. Aramaic Translations	8
5. Latin Translations	9
6. Present Translation	10
B. Canonical Considerations	12
C. Literary Considerations	15
1. Authorship	15
2. Unity	18
3. Genre	23

4. Structure 26
5. Form 34
6. Literary Features 38
7. Message 41
8. Theology 46

D. Historical Considerations 51
1. The Persian Period 51
2. Persian Palestine 57
3. Implications for Malachi 74

E. Dating the Oracles of Malachi 77
1. Historical Factors 77
2. Lexical and Literary Factors 79
3. Intertextual Dependence 79
4. Religious, Sociological, and Political Factors 80
5. Theological Factors 80
6. A Date for Malachi 80

F. The Study of Malachi 84
1. Malachi in the New Testament 84
2. The Liturgical Use of Malachi 88
A. Judaism 88
B. Christianity 90

II. BIBLIOGRAPHY 93

III. TRANSLATION, NOTES, AND COMMENTS 131

A. Superscription (1:1) 133

B. First Oracle: Yahweh's Covenant Love for Israel (1:2–5) 145

C. Second Oracle: Faithless Priests Rebuked (1:6–2:9) 170

D. Third Oracle: Faithless People Rebuked (2:10–16) 221

E. Fourth Oracle: Judgment and Purification (2:17–3:5) 259

F. Fifth Oracle: Call to Repentance (3:6–12) 291
Excursus: Divine Testing 311

G. Sixth Oracle: Judgment and Vindication (3:13–21 [4:3]) 326

H. Appendixes: Appeals to Ideal OT Figures 363
1. Moses (3:22 [4:4]) 366
2. Elijah (3:23–24 [4:5–6]) 374

IV. APPENDIXES   391

    A. von Bulmerincq's Categories for Dating Malachi   393

    B. Typological Analysis of the Postexilic Prophets   395
        1. Polzin's Grammatical and Syntactic Diagnostic
           Categories   395
        2. Distribution of Linguistic Features in Control and
           Target Corpora   396
        3. Typological Continuum of Control and Target Corpora   397

    C. Intertextuality in the Book of Malachi   401

    D. Vocabulary Richness in the Book of Malachi   412

V. INDEXES
    Index of Authors   415
    Index of Subjects   421
    Index of Scriptural and Other Ancient Sources   425
    Index of Hebrew and Other Languages   433

PREFACE

◆

The three tasks of religious scholarship, according to E. H. Harbison (pp. 4–5), include the "restudy" of the Hebraic-Christian tradition. The periodic reexamination of the biblical text and the related secondary literature is necessary for the purpose of refining or clarifying biblical interpretation. This volume of the *Anchor Bible* restudies the language, historical and sociopolitical background, and the literary structure and message of the book of Malachi for that express purpose. Such intermittent reevaluation of accrued biblical scholarship (on any topic) is warranted, given the continual advances registered in our knowledge and understanding of the biblical world and the languages of the Bible.

I acknowledge A. von Bulmerincq's classic two-volume work (1926, 1932) as the benchmark for exegetical commentaries on the book of Malachi. Thus, his copious, erudite, and systematic elucidation of the prophet's oracles provides a model for this study on three counts: first, with the gracious consent of the publisher and the encouragement of the general editor, the commentary treats every phrase and/or clause of the book (if not word as in the case of von Bulmerincq!); second, Malachi's message is analyzed within the larger canonical context of the OT/HB (and at times in the NT for the Christian reader); and third, the history of the interpretation of the book receives serious attention (through both comparative study in the ancient versions of the OT/HB and careful interaction with the train of Jewish and Christian biblical commentators who have produced expositions on Malachi — especially those writing during the seven decades spanning von Bulmerincq's classic and the recent publication of commentaries [in English] by Redditt [1995] and Petersen [1995]).

The encyclopedic approach imitates the pattern previously established in the series for the books of Haggai and Zechariah coauthored by Eric and Carol Meyers. I hope this comprehensive and eclectic collocation and review of the literature on Malachi subsequent to von Bulmerincq's epic tome will prove useful as a supplement to his study. In addition, I trust my contribution (to the ever-expanding numerical alphabet of the *Anchor Bible*) will prove a helpful resource for the serious student of the postexilic prophets as a companion volume to the Meyers' excellent work (AB 25B and 25C).

Admittedly, much of this commentary addressing the interpretation of the prophet's disputations is simply a "public reissue" of previous "confessions" summarizing and affirming the long-established scholarly consensus for much of the book of Malachi. Nonetheless, it is my desire that in those instances where I pose alternative interpretations or offer fresh insights my research will promote an even clearer understanding of these remarkable prophetic utterances. At the very least, perhaps this effort will make the next exegetical foray into the book of Malachi that much easier.

The description and analysis of the Hebrew language in the NOTES treating the Masoretic Text (MT) of the book of Malachi are informed primarily by the discussions found in the reference grammars of Joüon and Muraoka (JM, *A Grammar of Biblical Hebrew*) and Waltke and O'Connor (WO'C, *An Introduction to Biblical Hebrew Syntax*). I have also made a deliberate appeal to the other volumes of the *Anchor Bible* (both diachronically and synchronically) in a conscious effort to emphasize the value of the collection as a commentary series. In part, I have borrowed the format of J. M. Sasson's striking exemplar of the Bible commentary genre (*Jonah* [AB 24B]); namely, for the organization of introductory materials and the presentation of the biblical text (in transliteration) in the NOTES.

Given Bright's (1981: 463–64) discussion of the two "destinations" of ancient Israel's history, I have attempted to recognize both the Christian and the Jewish reader of the *AB* series by citing the Scriptures containing the book of Malachi as OT/HB (Old Testament/Hebrew Bible, after the pattern of Zvi, Hancock, and Beinert). Likewise references to biblical chronology are marked B.C./E. (Before Christ/Before Common Era) and A.D./C.E. (Anno Domini/Common Era). Biblical citations are ordered after the canonical contents of the OT/HB in the English versions for the benefit of the general reader. The constraints of inclusive language are everywhere in place except in the translation of Malachi, where "one cannot change or remove the masculine figurative representations of God without distorting the text of the Bible" (WO'C: 109).

Writing about the scholarly enterprise, W. S. LaSor (pp. 26–27) notes that "our problem is not with hidden motives, but with *a priori* convictions — and we all have them." I am hopeful that "showing my cards" here will enable the reader to better appreciate and understand the tack I have chosen in this assessment of Malachi. Further, I concur with LaSor that pointed difference of opinion, in any case, should be understood to imply nothing personal.

Matthews and Moyer (1991) have sorted samples of OT/HB studies by categories labeled "mainstream" and "conservative" scholarship. These designations (in theory) insinuate nothing as to particular religious faith and practice (pejorative or otherwise). Rather, they are "descriptors" of differing methodological approaches to the reading and understanding of the Bible. By conviction I accede to the classification of "conservative" (or "evangelical") biblical scholar, so tagged by Matthews and Moyer (p. 219).

By "conservative," I mean that approach to the study of the biblical documents that recognizes among other things the tradition of the divine origin of the Scriptures (i.e., in addition to the human authors the Bible has "one Author" following Levenson 1993: 6), a decided reluctance to emend the Masoretic Text (MT) apart from convincing evidence to the contrary (and hence a tendency to downplay speculation concerning the multiple redactional levels detected in the MT), and a preference for "substantiating" rather than "reconstructing" biblical history (cf. Hayes and Miller [pp. 65–66]; their discussion is useful as one example of pejorative typecasting of what they label "orthodoxy" or the "traditional approach").

Other assumptions serving as touchstones for my analysis of Malachi include a commitment to authorial intent in texts (disavowing the reader-oriented hermeneutic of postmodernism, cf. McKnight [1988: 263–64]), healthy awareness of the tension between "religious traditionalism" and "modern rationalism" with respect to the interpretation of the Bible (cf. Levenson 1993: xiv), adherence to a methodological approach for the study of the Bible known as "believing criticism" (i.e., the application of the various forms of biblical criticism of the so-called historical-critical method so long as they are not predicated on the denial of the basic tenets of "orthodoxy," cf. Noll [1986: 158]), and reliance on the conventional source-critical designations for the biblical documents (as catalogued by Soulen, but intending no prejudgment as to literary integrity or date of compilation).

Fyodor Dostoyevsky grasped the profound mystery that biblical texts transmit "revealed or inspired" knowledge, that they are "Word of God" and "human words" for the confessing faithful (cf. Patte in McKenzie and Haynes [p. 155]). Father Païssy urged his young charge Alyosha in *The Brothers Karamazov* to "remember . . . unceasingly" that despite the critical analysis of everything handed down in the "holy books" by the "science" of this world, "the whole" (i.e., the Bible) has lasted for centuries and is still a "living, a moving power in the individual soul and in the masses of the people" (Dostoyevsky [pp. 137–38]). I trust that the beauty of Malachi's rhetorical style and the force of the prophet's disputational message will remain "a living and moving power" as "Word of God" for the reader quite apart from yet another "scientific dismantling" of his ardent proclamation.

Andrew E. Hill
Wheaton, Illinois
Lent 1996

ACKNOWLEDGMENTS

◆

I am deeply indebted to David Noel Freedman, my former professor at the University of Michigan, for the opportunity to contribute to the *Anchor Bible* commentary series. I must confess a certain hesitation initially at the generous offer, couched as it was in an invitation to write "another dissertation." I think perhaps he failed to recall how "tortuous" writing that first one had been for me.

Nonetheless, I am indeed appreciative for this gesture of his confidence and can only say that the essay bears the imprint of my mentor at almost every turn of the page (as the discerning reader will readily notice). Any virtue inherent in the work should be equally attributed to this most remarkable biblical studies savant. The author willingly accepts full responsibility for those flaws and shortcomings that remain.

I "earned" a degree with that "first dissertation" treating the book of Malachi back in 1981. I have "learned" the degree with this "second dissertation" explicating the oracles of Yahweh's "angel" or "messenger" thanks to the tireless, scrupulous, and perspicacious help of the series General Editor. I trust the reader of this commentary will likewise benefit from that most illuminating exchange between author and editor.

Michael Iannazzi, Mark Fretz, and the rest of the staff at Bantam Doubleday Dell are to be commended for ably overseeing and coordinating every phase of production in the process of renovating the debris of a manuscript into the finely crafted artform of a published book.

I am grateful for the encouragement of those colleagues who found time to affirm me during the writing process, especially James K. Hoffmeier who ably facilitated my work on the Malachi commentary by his friendship, by the example of his scholarship, and by his charitable dispensations on my behalf as department chair. I profited as well from my interactions with Cynthia L. Miller and Gary A. Long, whose all too brief but significant contributions to the Biblical Studies Department at Wheaton College were providentially timed.

Thanks as well to freelance artist Hugh Claycombe. His collaboration on the design and layout of the photographic insert was invaluable. In addition, his excellent illustrations enhance that supplement to the commentary.

Three former graduate assistants, Judith Mankell, James Scott, and Diane Wakabayashi also deserve mention for the many hours of research and proofreading they contributed to this project.

I would be remiss if I failed to acknowledge my debt to Carol L. and Eric M. Meyers. Not only was my task made easier by their groundbreaking studies in the Second Temple prophets Haggai and Zechariah, but also my analysis of the language and message of Malachi directly benefited from their most ambitious and innovative *Anchor Bible* commentaries. I have aspired to complement their signal volumes on the postexilic prophets of Yehud with like-minded (if not equal) sensitive and meticulous scholarship. Any failure on my part in the matter of "quality control" should in no way discredit their achievement.

As always, my family remains my primary concern and my greatest source of inspiration apart from the Scriptures themselves. May God reward their patience and loyalty as accomplices in the weariness of writing and the vanity of publishing. I trust Malachi's exhortations to faithfulness and righteousness will long avail the companion of my youth, Terri, and me as we continue to encourage Jennifer, Jesse, and Jordan to revere Yahweh and esteem his name (Mal 3:16–17).

LIST OF ILLUSTRATIONS

◆

MAPS

    1. The Persian Empire   58

    2. The Satrapy of Beyond-the-River (Eber-Nahara)   59

    3. Yehud and Other Persian Provinces   63

    4. The Province of Yehud Under Persian Rule   64

CHARTS

    1. The Kings of Persia from Cyrus to Darius III   51

    2. Exilic and Postexilic Israelite Chronology   55

    3. Provincial Districts of Yehud   62

    4. Persian Period Governors of Yehud   71

PHOTOGRAPHS AND DRAWINGS

    1. King Darius I, Audience Scene from the Treasury Relief

    2. King Darius I

    3. Eastern Stairway of the Apadana

    4. Processional of Servants, Palace of Darius I

    5. Cylinder Seal of Darius I, with Impression

    6. Palace of Darius I

    7. Behistun Relief

    8. Behistun Inscription

    9. Winged Bull, Gate of Xerxes (Gate of All Nations)

    10. Fire Altar, Central Facade of the Tomb of Darius II

    11. Solomon's Temple

    12. Zerubbabel's Temple

    13. Ahuramazda Symbol, Persepolis Council Hall

    14. Foundation Documents of Xerxes (Harem Text)

LIST OF ABBREVIATIONS

◆

A	Aleppo Codex
א	Codex Sinaiticus
α	Aquila (LXX recension)
ABD	*Anchor Bible Dictionary*, D. N. Freedman, ed.
ʿAbodZar	*ʿAboda Zara*
A.D./C.E.	*anno domini* (year)/common (or Christian) era
Adv haer	*Adversus omnes haereses (Against All Heresies)*, Irenaeus
AdvJud	*Adversus Judaeos (Against the Jews)*, Tertullian
AgAp	*Contra Apionem (Against Apion)*, Josephus
AHW	*Akkadisches Handwörterbuch*, W. von Soden, ed.
ANE	Ancient Near East
Ant	*Antiquitates Judaicae (Jewish Antiquities)*, Josephus
AoF	*Altorientalische Forschungen*
ARAB	*Ancient Records of Assyria and Babylonia*, D. D. Luckenbill
ARW	*Archiv für Religionswissenschaft*
ATR	*Anglican Theological Review*
b.	Babylonian Talmud
BA	*Biblical Archaeologist*
BAR	*Biblical Archaeology Review*
BASOR	*Bulletin of the American Schools of Oriental Research*
BBat	*Baba Batra* ("The Last Gate")
B.C./E.	before Christ/before common (or Christian) era
BDB	Brown, Driver, and Briggs, *Hebrew and English Lexicon of the Old Testament*

xix

BeO	*Bibbia e oriente*
BH	Biblical Hebrew
BHK	*Biblia Hebraica*, R. Kittel and P. Kahle, eds.
BHS	*Biblia Hebraica Stuttgartensia*, K. Elliger and W. Rudolph, eds.
Bib	*Biblica*
Bib hist	*Bibliotheca historica* (*Library of History*), Diodorus Siculus
BibLeb	*Bibel und Leben*
BJRL	*Bulletin of the John Rylands University Library of Manchester*
BN	*Biblische Notizen*
BSac	*Bibliotheca Sacra*
BSV	*Biblia Sacra: Vulgatae*
BT	*Bible Translator*
BTB	*Biblical Theology Bulletin*
CAD	*The Assyrian Dictionary of the Oriental Institute of the University of Chicago*, I. J. Gelb, et al., eds.
CAH	*Cambridge Ancient History*, I.E.S. Edwards, et al., eds.
CBH	Classical Biblical Hebrew
CBQ	*Catholic Biblical Quarterly*
CC	*Cross Currents*
CChr	*Corpus Christianorum*
CDR	Cairo Damascus Rule (Zadokite Document)
CHAL	*A Concise Hebrew and Aramaic Lexicon of the Old Testament*, W. L. Holladay, ed.
CivDei	*De civitate Dei* (*The City of God*), Augustine
Comm in Jn	*In Johannem Commentarius* (*Commentary on John*), Origen
ConBOT	Coniectanea biblica, Old Testament
Conf	*Confessiones*, Augustine
ConstAp	*Constitutiones Apostolorum* (*Apostolic Constitutions*)
CR: BS	*Currents in Research: Biblical Studies*
CToday	*Christianity Today*
CTR	*Criswell Theological Review*

CurTM	*Currents in Theology and Mission*
D	"Deuteronomic" source
DDO	definite-direct object (marker)
DJD	*Discoveries in the Judaean Desert*
Dtr	Deuteronomic History corpus
DialTrypho	*Dialogus contra Tryphonem* (*Dialogue with Trypho*), Justin Martyr
Did	*Didache* (*Treatises*), Cyprian
'*Eduy*	'*Eduyyot* ("Testimonies")
EncJud	*Encyclopedia Judaica* (1971)
EvT	*Evangelische Theologie*
ExpTim	*Expository Times*
Giṭṭ	*Giṭṭin* ("Bills of Divorcement")
GKC	*Gesenius' Hebrew Grammar*, E. Kautsch, ed., A. E. Cowley, trans.
GTJ	*Grace Theological Journal*
HAR	*Hebrew Annual Review*
HB	Hebrew Bible
HBD	*Dictionary of the Bible*, J. Hastings, ed.
Hist	*Historiae* (*The Histories*), Herodotus
HTS	Harvard Theological Studies
IDB	*Interpreter's Dictionary of the Bible*, G. A. Buttrick, ed.
IDBSup	*Interpreter's Dictionary of the Bible Supplementary Volume*, K. Crim, ed.
IER	*Irish Ecclesiastical Review*
ISBE	*The International Standard Bible Encyclopedia: Revised.* G. W. Bromiley, ed.
Int	*Interpretation*
JAOS	*Journal of the American Oriental Society*
JBL	*Journal of Biblical Literature*
JETS	*Journal of the Evangelical Theological Society*
JJS	*Journal of Jewish Studies*

JM	P. Joüon and T. Muraoka, *A Grammar of Biblical Hebrew*
JNES	*Journal of Near Eastern Studies*
JNSL	*Journal of Northwest Semitic Languages*
JOTT	*Journal of Translation and Textlinguistics*
JPOS	*Journal of the Palestine Oriental Society*
JPSV	Jewish Publication Society Version (1985)
JQR	*Jewish Quarterly Review*
JSOT	*Journal for the Study of the Old Testament*
JSS	*Journal of Semitic Studies*
K	Kethib ("it is written")
KBL	Koehler, Baumgartner, and Stamm, eds. *The Hebrew and Aramaic Lexicon of the Old Testament.* 3rd ed.
KJV	King James Version
L	Leningrad Codex
LBH	Late Biblical Hebrew
LXX	*Septuaginta*, A. Rahlfs, ed. (Septuagint)
	LXX α — Aquila
	LXX A — Codex Alexandrinus
	LXX B — Codex Vaticanus
	LXX C — Codex Ephraemi Cyri rescriptus
	LXX G — Codex Colberto-Sarravianus
	LXX L — Lucian (textus Graecus ex recensione Luciani)
	LXX Q — Codex Marchalianus
	LXX S — Codex Sinaiticus
	LXX σ — Symmachus
	LXX θ — Theodotion
	LXX W — Codex Atheniensis
	LXX Y — Codex Taurinensis
Marc	*Adversus Marcionem (Against Marcion)*, Tertullian
MWCD	*Merriam-Webster's Collegiate Dictionary*, 10th Ed.
Meg	*Megilla* ("The Scroll of Esther")
Midr. Rab.	*Midrash Rabbah*
MT	Masoretic Text
NAB	New American Bible
NEB	New English Bible

NGTT	*Nederduits Gereformeerde Teologiese Tydskrif*
NIV	New International Version Bible
NJB	New Jerusalem Bible
NRSV	New Revised Standard Version Bible
NT	New Testament
OG	Old Greek
OL	Old Latin
OT	Old Testament
OTE	*Old Testament Essays*
OTS	*Oudtestamentische Studiën*
OTWSA	*Ou-Testamentiese Werkgemeenskap van Suid-Afrika*
P	"Priestly" source
Pg	"Priestly" base strand
Ps	"Priestly" extensions
PEQ	*Palestine Exploration Quarterly*
PG	*Patrologia graeca,* J. Migne
PH	Primary History
PL	*Patrologia latina,* J. Migne
Q	Qere ("to be read"); Qumran
Presb	*Presbyterion*
RB	*Revue biblique*
RevExp	*Review and Expositor*
RevQ	*Revue de Qumran*
RevSém	*Revue sémitique*
RTR	*Reformed Theological Review*
S	Samaritan Pentateuch
σ	Symmachus (LXX recension)
Sanh	*Sanhedrin* ("The Sanhedrin")
SBLSP	*Society of Biblical Literature Seminar Papers*
ScotJTh	*Scottish Journal of Theology*
SEÅ	*Svensk Exegetisk Årsbok*

SHA	Codex Syro-Hexaplaris Ambrosianus
SkrifK	*Skrif en Kerke*
ST	*Studia Theologica*
SwJT	*Southwestern Journal of Theology*
Syr	*Vetus Testamentum Syriace* (Peshitta), The Peshitta Institute
	SB — Codex Londini British Museum SC — Codex Leningradensis SL — S. Lee, versio Syriaca secundum SU — editio Urmiensis SW — Walton, *London Polyglot*
θ	Theodotion
T	*The Bible in Aramaic*, A. Sperber, ed. (Targum)
TB	*Tyndale Bulletin*
TBT	*The Bible Today*
TDOT	*Theological Dictionary of the Old Testament*, G. J. Botterweck and H. Ringgren, eds., D. E. Green, trans.
TE	*Theologica Evangelica*
TgNeb	*Targum (Jonathan) to the Prophets*
THAT	*Theologisches Handwörterbuch zum Alten Testament*, E. Jenni and C. Westermann, eds.
Them	*Themelios*
UBS	United Bible Societies
US News	*U.S. News & World Report*
UT	*Ugaritic Textbook*, C. H. Gordon, ed. (An Or 38. Rome; suppl. 1967)
V	*Biblia Sacra: Vulgata*, B. Fischer, et al., eds. (Vulgate)
VT	*Vetus Testamentum*
VTS	*Vetus Testamentum Syriace*
VTSup	*Vetus Testamentum Supplements*
WO'C	B. K. Waltke and M. O'Connor, *An Introduction to Biblical Hebrew Syntax*
x	(number of) times
ZAW	*Zeitschrift für die alttestamentliche Wissenschaft*
Zebaḥ	*Zebaḥim* ("Animal Offerings")

GLOSSARY OF TERMS

◆

ablative — denoting a noun case in inflected languages having among its functions indication of place, movement away from, manner, means, instrument, agent.

Achaemenid — term commonly applied to the Persian Empire (and/or Persian kings) established by Cyrus the Great, a descendant of Achaemenes, in the sixth century B.C./E. (See Chart 1.)

Aleppo Codex — a manuscript of the Masoretic Text (Codex A), and an important textual witness of the Hebrew Bible (dated ca. 925 A.D./C.E.).

allative — indicating direction or movement to or toward.

anacoenosis — a figure of speech by which a speaker appeals to opponents for their opinion, as having a common interest in the matter in question (common cause).

anaphora — reference of a grammatical element to something mentioned earlier, e.g., in "Moses fled and Jethro helped *him*," *him* is an anaphoric pronoun.

anarthrous — lacking the definite article.

anthropomorphic — having human characteristics.

anthropopathic — having human feelings.

aorist — (Greek "without + boundaries"), a verb form indicating a situation without regard to absolute time; the actual use of the aorist form in, e.g., Greek involves a variety of factors.

apocalyptic — literally "revelation," and often equated with literature forecasting the ultimate destiny of the world, forboding imminent disaster or final doom.

apodosis — the "then" clause of an "if-then" construction in case (or casuistic) law or a conditional sentence.

apologia — a defense of one's opinions, position, actions.

apostrophe — a type of personification in which words are addressed in an exclamatory tone to a thing (regarded as a person) or an actual person.

appellative — a common noun used as a proper name, a descriptive name.

apposition — juxtaposition of a noun (or noun phrase) to another noun (or noun phrase) with the same reference and in the same grammatical slot.

Unless otherwise noted, the definitions of terms in the glossary are based on similar items in *EncJud*, Hals 1989: 348–63, *MWCD*, Meyers and Meyers 1987: xxi–xxiv, Soulen, Tov, Würthwein, and WO'C: 689–94.

archaizing — a process by which the characteristics of an earlier time are imitated.

assertive speech — a speech act in which the speaker (or writer) affirms basic (and widely accepted) truth claims for the purpose of assuring the audience (or reader, see Watts [1987a]).

attributive (adjective) — an adjective that posits an attribute of the substantive it modifies (e.g., *hammā'ôr haggādôl*, "the *great* light").

Book of the Twelve — a designation for the twelve books of the Minor Prophets as a single collection in keeping with the Heb. canonical tradition.

bulla(e) — seal(s) affixed to a document.

canon — a closed or completed collection of authoritative (religious) writings.

cataphora — reference of a grammatical element to something mentioned later; e.g., in "When *he* fled, Moses was afraid," *he* is a cataphoric pronoun.

chiasm(us) — an inverted relationship between syntactic elements of parallel phrases.

cohortative — expressing a volitional mood (a lengthened form of the prefixing conjugation or imperfective used only in the first person and possessing the distinctive affix *-āh*).

coda — a concluding section of a literary or dramatic work, formally distinct from the main structure of the composition.

cognate forms — words that are ultimately derived from the same source; e.g., Hebrew *šēm*, Akkadian *šumu*, and Arabic *ism* are cognates.

colon — the basic unit of Hebrew verse (or "line" in WO'C: 691).

construct-genitive — a grammatical construction expressing a genitive function by the juxtaposition of two (or more) nouns, the first in the construct state (often a shortened form of that word) and the following noun in an absolute state.

copula — a word (e.g., the pronoun *hû'*, "he, that") that joins the subject and predicate of an equational verb clause.

cultic — formal religious expression, a system of religious beliefs and ritual.

dative — the case of indirect object (usually a recipient).

definite(ness) — possessing the definite article (or having a unique or particular reference).

deixis (deictic) — a system of words, in which their referents shift, depending on the speech situation (especially personal, temporal, and locational features), including prominently pronouns.

Deuteronomic — pertaining to the book of Deuteronomy.

Deuteronomistic — pertaining to the books (or characteristic features) of the so-called Deuteronomic History.

deutero-prophetic — later Hebrew prophetic books demonstrating characteristics of having been inserted or appended to earlier books attributed to Israel's classical prophets, dependency (even composite in character) upon earlier prophetic compositions, emphasizing eschatological scenarios, and evidencing exegetical, programmatic, or devotional purposes (see Petersen [1977: 14–16]).

diachronic — pertaining to historical development across chronological periods.

disputation — generally a term for a dispute or controversy between two or more parties in which differing points of view are expressed in a formal (and often confrontational) manner. Specifically in Malachi, the answering of implied or expressed charges made against God by his people or against the prophet (see March [1974: 168]).

dittography — accidental repetition of a letter, word, or larger unit of a text during the process of manuscript transmission.

divine or prophetic utterance formula — the phrase *nĕ'ūm YHWH* ("Oracle of Yahweh") labeling prophetic speech as the word of Israel's God.

envelope construction — see *inclusio*.

epiphany — an appearance or manifestation, especially of a divine being.

epithet — a characterizing word or phrase accompanying or occurring in place of the name of a person or thing.

eschatology — a branch of theology concerned with the final events in the history of the world, relating to the end of the world.

expressive speech — a speech act in which a speaker (or writer) voices concern over popular sentiments for the purpose of persuading the audience (or reader) to assess and/or change current patterns of belief and/or behavior (see Watts 1987a).

fientive — a verb describing motion or a change of state; see also *stative*.

Former Prophets — the books of Joshua, Judges, Samuel, and Kings in the OT/HB.

gapping — the omission of a word or phrase in the second of two adjacent clauses of similar structure (forward gapping), or the omission of a word or phrase in the first of two adjacent clauses of similar structure (backward gapping).

gloss — a scribal or editorial correction, addition, or explanation usually introduced in the text (MT) to clarify or expand an obscure or important point.

haplography — literally "single writing," haplography occurs when two identical or similar letters, groups of letters, or words are found together in immediate sequence, and one of them is omitted by error.

hendiadys — the expression of a single idea by the use of two independent words (connected by "and" instead of the usual combination of a noun and its modifier).

hierocracy (hierocratic) — pertaining to priestly rule or authority.

Hiphil — a Hebrew verb form, which usually carries a causative force.

Hithpael — a Hebrew verb form usually denoting a reflexive force.

homoeoarcton — literally "like beginning," homoeoarcton is the accidental omission of a letter(s), word(s), or phrase(s) by a copyist due to the repeated similarities in the initial formation of these words and phrases.

homoeoteleuton — literally "like ending," homoeoteleuton is the accidental omission of words or phrases by a copyist due to the repetition of identical or similar features in the final formation of these words and phrases.

Hophal — a Hebrew verb form usually marking a causative-passive form.

hortatory — pertaining to exhortation.

hypostasis — the substance or essential nature of an individual (to attribute real identity to a concept).

Ibn Ezra, Abraham — rabbinical poet, grammarian, biblical commentator, philosopher, astronomer, and physician (born in Tudela, Spain; lived A.D./C.E. 1089–1164). (See *EncJud* 8:1163–70.)

imperfective — an aspect in which a situation (verbal action) is understood as ongoing, whatever its temporal relation to the time of speaking.

incipit — heading or title for a literary work, often taken from the first word or words of the manuscript.

inclusio(n) — a special form of repetition marking structure in literary units by duplicating words, phrases, or whole clauses from the beginning of a poem or narrative at the end of a section to mark it as a completed whole.

interpolation — an alteration or insertion (by a later hand in the biblical text).

intertextual(ity) — similarities in lexicography and/or phraseology in literary texts suggesting a relationship of interdependence between the documents.

irony — a figure of speech in which the expression of a thought is cast in a form that naturally conveys its opposite (usually for dramatic effect or emphatic force).

judicial or trial speech — a prophetic speech-form patterned after legal procedure, often exhibiting formal structure, including: a summons, trial, and sentencing (see March [p. 165]; Westermann [1991: 129 ff.]).

jussive — a shortened third-person Hebrew verb form (imperfective), expressing a wish, command, or exhortation.

Kethib — (literally "it is written"), a term employed to distinguish the literal and uncorrected wording of the Masoretic Text from the corrected wording (see *Qere*) recorded in the margin. (See further *ABD* 4:24–30.)

Kimchi, David — rabbinical grammarian and exegete of Narbonne, France (lived A.D./C.E. 1160?–1235?). (See *EncJud* 10:1006–7.)

Latter Prophets — the prophetic books of Isaiah, Jeremiah, Ezekiel, and the Twelve Minor Prophets in the OT/HB.

lectionary — a list or book of readings (usually Scripture and prayers) used liturgically in worship services.

Leningrad Codex — a manuscript of the Masoretic Text (Codex L), and an important textual witness of the Hebrew Bible (dated A.D./C.E. 1008) and the basis for both the *BHK* and *BHS* editions of the Hebrew Bible.

Levant — the lands bordering the eastern shore of the Mediterranean Sea, especially Syria, Lebanon, and Israel.

line — see *colon*.

(literary) foil — a contrast or parallel heightening the dramatic effect of a narrative or discourse (see Ryken [1984: 54–55]).

mantological exegesis — the technique of (Jewish) scribal elucidation of prophetic oracles that are ominous or oracular in scope and content (see Fishbane [1985: 443–46]).

Masora(h) — broadly understood the term refers to the traditional rules governing the production of a handwritten copy of the biblical text. More narrowly, the word refers to the body of scribal notes included in copies of the Masoretic Text. (See further *ABD* 4:592–93.)

Masoretes — members of Jewish scribal schools responsible for maintaining the traditions governing the production of copies of the Hebrew Bible (Masoretic Text), especially active between the fifth and the ninth centuries A.D./C.E. (See further *ABD* 4:593–94.)

mater lectionis — (Latin "mother of reading"; plural *matres lectionis*), a letter used in a consonantal script to indicate a vowel.

merismus — a figure of speech enumerating the totality of a thing by the use of two contrasting parts, or by citing the first and last elements of a series (including by implication everything in between).

messenger formula — the clause [*kōh*] *'āmar YHWH* . . . ("so Yahweh [has] said"), introducing a messenger speech (or prophetic oracle) and signifying the oral transmission of a message by means of a third party.

metahistory — an approach to Israelite history assuming the cohesion of all reality as a single, all-embracing process, in which Israel and Yahweh form the two essential poles (see Koch [1983: 73]).

metonymy — a figure of speech using the name of one thing for that of another of which it is an attribute or with which it is associated.

midrash — the explanation or exposition of the Scripture (especially a rabbinic method of exegesis penetrating the meaning of the Scriptures beyond the literal sense and deriving interpretations not immediately obvious).

(midrash) haggadah — a midrashic exposition of a nonlegal, ethical, or devotional nature.

(midrash) halakah — a midrashic exposition yielding a legal teaching.

multivalency — the quality or state of having many values, meanings, or appeals.

mythopoeia (mythopoeic) — a creating of myth, giving rise to myths.

Niphal — a Hebrew verb form used in the simple stem, usually indicating a passive or reflexive meaning.

nonperfective — see *imperfective*.

oracle formula — the formula *ḥay YHWH* . . . ("as the Lord lives . . ."), usually introducing an oath.

paraphrastic — having the nature of or being a paraphrase.

paraenesis (parenetic) — a figure of speech employed when a direct statement is changed and recast in the form of an exhortation (exhortative).

(parallel) word pairs — common terms (e.g., "earth" [*'ereṣ*]/"world" [*tēbel*]) or prominent names and titles (e.g., "Israel" [*yiśrā'ēl*]/"Judah" [*yĕhûdâ*]; "Lord" [*YHWH*]/"God" [*'ēl*]) frequently coupled in a fixed relationship (as synonyms or antonyms) in rhetorical and poetic literature in the OT/HB (cf. Dahood [1965: xxxiii–xxxiv]; *IDBSup*: 669).

particle — a class of words that connects and subjoins nouns and verbs (including prepositions, some adverbs, the article, etc.) or exists on the margins of utterances (e.g., exclamations and interjections).

perfective — an aspect in which a situation (verbal action) is understood as complete, as a whole.

pericope — a distinct literary unit.

pesher — (Aramaic *pšr*, literally "solution" or "interpretation"), a method of (Jewish) exposition of or commentary on biblical texts.

Peshitta — (Syriac "simple"), the authorized Bible of the Syrian Church dating from the fourth or fifth century A.D./C.E.

Piel — a Hebrew verb form, commonly called the "intensive" stem, but also having other nuances of meaning.

polar questions — "yes-no" questions addressing an entire proposition rather than just one feature of a proposition.

preterit(e) — a verbal form describing simple past action.

Primary History — a literary convention designating the single longest continuous narrative in the Hebrew Bible, combining of the Torah (the books of Genesis, Exodus, Leviticus, Numbers, Deuteronomy) and the books of the Former Prophets (Joshua, Judges, Samuel, and Kings). The PH constitutes one-half of the OT/HB and relates the *story* of Israel. The second half of the OT/HB (i.e., the Latter Prophets and books of poetry and wisdom) serves practically as both elaboration and commentary on the *story* of Israel.

prolepsis — the representation or assumption of a future act or development as if presently existing or accomplished.

Pual — a Hebrew verb form, usually marking the passive stem of the Piel.

Qal — the simple form or stem of the Hebrew verb.

Qere — (literally "to be read"), a term employed to distinguish a variance in the MT between "what is written" (*Kethib*) in the consonantal text and "what is read" (Hebrew *qĕrê*) according to the tradition of vocalization. These variances arose because the traditional text was considered to be unsatisfactory by the Masoretes on grammatical, aesthetic, or doctrinal grounds. The *Qere* suggests an orthography or spelling different from that in the consonantal text of the MT. It marks the distinction made between the written form, which could not be altered (*Kethib*), and the corrected form to be read (with its consonants in the margin and its vowel points written with the consonants of the *Kethib*). A *Qere* required but not written in the margin because of frequency is called a *Qere Perpetuum* (see further *ABD* 4:24–30.)

Rashi, Solomon ben Isaac — leading rabbinical commentator on the Hebrew Bible and Talmud (born Troyes, France; lived A.D./C.E. 1040–1105). (See *EncJud* 13:1558–67.)

recursive(ness) — referring to itself (for the purpose of congruency, see Hendrix).

reported speech formula — the distinctive use of the verb *'āmar* ("to say") coupled with *bammâ* or *bammeh* ("in what [thing]") in the oracles of Malachi to introduce the (hypothetical?) audience's rebuttal of the prophet's initial declaration.

satrap — the governor of a province in ancient Persia, appointed by the emperor.

satrapy — a large administrative territory or province under the jurisdiction of a *satrap* during the time of the Persian Empire.

scripture — authoritative (religious) writings.

Scripture — a synonym for the Holy Bible.

self-introduction formula — a formula by which a speaker reveals his or her identity to an addressee by announcing his or her name (e.g., *'ǎnî YHWH* . . . , "I am Yahweh").

Shaharit — the early morning prayer or the daily morning service of Judaism, the most elaborate of the three prescribed daily prayers, from the Hebrew *šahar* ("dawn").

simile — a figure of speech making a comparison, introduced by *like* or *as*.

substantive — a word or word group functioning as a noun.

superscription — a statement of classification and/or identification prefixed to a literary work.

synchronic — pertaining to one well-defined chronological period.

synecdoche — a figure of speech which represents the whole by one of its constituent parts.

Targum — (Aramaic "translation, interpretation"), broadly speaking the word refers to an Aramaic translation or interpretive commentary on scriptural books (originally delivered orally in the Second Temple period). More narrowly, the term refers to the various Aramaic renderings of the OT/HB.

tautological — true by virtue of its logical form alone (rhetorical repetition).

telic — possessing a goal or endpoint.

terminus a quo — a point of origin.

terminus ad quem — a final limiting point in time.

theodicy — defense of God's goodness and omnipotence in view of the existence of evil.

theophany — a visible manifestation of a deity.

theophoric — derived from or bearing the name of a deity.

typological analysis — a linguistic approach to the (literary and chronological) assessment of documents that differentiates among written texts on the basis of grammatical and syntactic categories.

univalency — the quality or state of having a single meaning, value, or appeal.

Vorlage — prototype, forerunner.

Vulgate — Jerome's Latin translation of the Bible.

word-event formula — the construction of the phrase *děbar YHWH* ("the word of Yahweh") as subject with the verb *hāyâ* ("the word of Yahweh came . . ."), emphasizing the historical character of the word of God and its character as an event (see *TDOT* 3:112–14).

Yehud — subunit of the ancient Persian satrapy of "Beyond the River," a smaller approximation of the preexilic kingdom of Judah.

THE BOOK OF MALACHI: OUTLINES AND TRANSLATION

◆

THEMATIC OUTLINE OF MALACHI

I. Superscription: Malachi — Yahweh's Messenger (1:1)

II. Yahweh's Love for Israel (1:2–5)

    A. Yahweh's Love Challenged, 1:2a

    B. Yahweh's Love Vindicated in Edom's Judgment, 1:2b–4

    C. Yahweh's Greatness, 1:5

III. Indictment of Corrupt Priesthood (1:6–2:9)

    A. Yahweh Dishonored by Improper Ritual, 1:6–10

    B. Yahweh's Greatness Denied by Insolence, 1:7–11

    C. Threat of Curse for Neglect of Yahweh's Glory, 2:1–3

    D. Yahweh's Covenant Defiled by Self-Serving Instruction, 2:4–9

IV. Indictment of Faithless People (2:10–16)

    A. Yahweh's Covenant Profaned by Disobedience, 2:10–12

    B. Covenant of Marriage Profaned by Divorce, 2:13–16

V. Yahweh's Messenger of Justice and Judgment (2:17–3:5)

    A. Yahweh's Justice Challenged, 2:17

    B. Yahweh's Justice Vindicated by the Messenger of the Covenant, 3:1–4

    C. Yahweh's Judgment, 3:5

VI. The Call to Serve Yahweh (3:6–12)

    A. Call to Repentance, 3:6–7

    B. People Indicted for Robbing Yahweh in the Tithe, 3:8–12

VII. The Day of Yahweh (3:13–21 [4:3])

    A. Obedience to Yahweh Challenged, 3:13–15

    B. Obedience to Yahweh Vindicated in the Reward of the Faithful, 3:16–18

    C. The Day of Yahweh: Judgment and Vindication, 3:19–21 [4:1–3]

VIII. Appendixes (3:22–24 [4:4–6])

    A. Challenge to Obey the Law of Moses, 3:22 [4:4]

    B. Elijah and the Day of Yahweh, 3:23–24 [4:5–6]

RHETORICAL OUTLINE OF MALACHI

Superscription (1:1)

A. Thesis Disputation: Yahweh's Covenant Love for Israel (1:2–5)

  Declaration — *I loved you* . . . (1:2)

  Refutation — *How have you loved us?* (1:2)

  Rebuttal — *But Esau I hated!* (1:3)

  B. Disputation Indicting Faithless Priests (1:6–2:9)

   Declaration — *If I am [your] father, where is my honor? If I am [your] master, where is my respect?* (1:6ab)

   Refutation — *How have we despised your name? How have we defiled you?* (1:6c–7a)

   Rebuttal — *And when you present a blind [animal] for sacrifice, there is no evil! Or when you present crippled or diseased [animal], there is no evil!* (1:8)

   C. Disputation Indicting Faithless People (2:10–16)

    Declaration — *Yehud has broken faith* . . . (2:11)

    Refutation — *But you say, Why?* (2:14)

    Rebuttal — *Indeed [The One] hates divorce!* (2:16)

    D. Disputation Averring Yahweh's Judgment (2:17–3:5)

     Declaration — *You have wearied Yahweh with your talk.* (2:17a)

     Refutation — *How have we wearied [him]?* (2:17b)

     Rebuttal — *See! I am sending my messenger* . . . (3:1)

   C'. Disputation Indicting Faithless People (3:6–12)

    Declaration — *Return to me, so that I may return to you.* (3:6–7ab)

    Refutation — *How can we return?* (3:7c)

    Rebuttal — *Surely you are robbing me!* (3:8a)

    2nd Refutation — *How have we robbed you?* (3:8b)

    2nd Rebuttal — *Bring the full tithe into the [Temple] storehouse!* (3:10a)

  B'. Final Disputation Indicting the Faithless and Acquitting the Faithful (3:13–21 [4:3])

   Declaration — *Your words against me have been harsh.* (3:13a)

   Refutation — *How have we spoken against you?* (3:13b)

   Rebuttal — *It is futile to serve God!* (3:14a)

   2nd Refutation — *What profit [is there] that we have kept his charge?* (3:14–15)

   2nd Rebuttal — *Once again you will see the difference between a righteous and wicked one* . . . (3:18–19 [4:1])

E. Appendixes: Concluding Exhortations (3:22–24 [4:4–6])

  1. *Remember the Law of Moses* . . . (3:22 [4:4])

  2. *See! I am sending Elijah* . . . (3:23–24 [4:5–6])

INTERROGATIVE ELEMENTS OUTLINE OF THE HAGGAI-ZECHARIAH-MALACHI CORPUS

A. Haggai's Sermons:
    1. The Charge to Rebuild the Temple, 1:1–15
        Is it a time for you yourselves to live in your finished houses, while this house lies desolate? (1:4)
        Why? Oracle of Yahweh of Hosts. (1:9)
    2. The Glory of the First and Second Temples Compared, 2:1–9
        Who remains among you who saw this house in its former glory? How are you seeing it now? Surely it must seem like nothing in your eyes? (2:3)
    3. The Promise to Purify and Bless, 2:10–19
        If someone carries consecrated meat in the fold of his garment, and with his fold he touches bread or stew or wine or oil or any foodstuff, do any of these become holy? (2:12)
        ·   *If anyone who is [ritually] unclean by contact with a corpse touches any of these, does it become [ritually] unclean?* (2:13)
        Before a stone was set upon stone in the temple of Yahweh, how was it with you? (2:15)
        Is there still seed in the granary? Even the [grape] vine, the fig tree, the pomegranate, and the olive trees have not yielded [fruit, have they]? (2:19)
    4. The Oracle to Zerubbabel, 2:20–24
        No interrogative element
B. Zechariah's Sermons and Visions:
    1. Introductory Challenge, 1:1–6
        Your patriarchs, where are they? And the prophets, do they live forever? (1:5)
        But my words and my statutes, [by] which I charged my servants the prophets, surely they have overtaken your patriarchs? (1:6)
    2. First Vision: The Horsemen, 1:7–17
        What are these, my lord? (1:9)
        O Lord of hosts, how long will you suppress compassion for Jerusalem and the cities of Judah, which you cursed these seventy years? (1:12)

The interrogative outline has been adapted from Pierce 1984a: 281–82. A consistent interrogative element is demonstrated throughout the Haggai-Zechariah-Malachi corpus, with the notable exception of Zechariah 9–14. Pierce (p. 282) attributes the sudden break in the flow of the interrogative element of the corpus to deliberate authorial intent in calling the reader's attention to the focal point of the Haggai-Zechariah-Malachi corpus, the vivid picture of Yahweh's flock doomed for slaughter.

3. Second Vision: The Horns and the Blacksmiths, 2:1–4 [1:18–21]
What are these? (2:2 [1:19])
What are they coming to do? (2:4 [1:21])
4. Third Vision: The Man with a Measuring Line, 2:5–9 [2:1–5]
Where are you going? (2:6 [2:2])
5. First Interlude: Yahweh's Prophet Authenticated, 2:10–17 [2:6–13]
No interrogative element
6. Fourth Vision: Joshua the Priest and Satan, 3:1–10
Surely this [man] is a brand rescued from the fire? (3:2)
7. Fifth Vision: The Lampstand and Olive Trees, 4:1–14
What do you see? (4:2)
What are these [things], my lord? (4:4)
Surely you know what these are? (4:5)
Who are you, O great mountain? (4:7)
What are these two olive trees, on the right of the lampstand, and on the left? (4:11)
What are these two branches of the olive trees, which are in the hand of the two golden pipes emptying the gold[en oil] from them? (4:12)
Surely you know what these are? (4:13)
8. Sixth Vision: The Flying Scroll, 5:1–5
What do you see? (5:2)
9. Seventh Vision: Women and a Basket, 5:5–11
What is it? (5:6)
Where are they taking the ephah basket? (5:10)
10. Eighth Vision: Four Chariots of Judgment, 6:1–8
What are these [things], my lord? (6:4)
11. Second Interlude: Crowning of Joshua the Priest, 6:9–15
No interrogative element
12. Justice and Mercy vs. Fasting, 7:1–14
Should I mourn and practice abstinence in the fifth month, fasting as I have practiced for so many years? (7:3)
When you fasted and lamented in the fifth month and the seventh month even for these seventy years, did you really fast for my sake? (7:5)
And when you eat and when you drink, surely you were eating and drinking only for yourselves? (7:6)
Surely [these] are the words that Yahweh proclaimed through [his agents] the earlier prophets, when Jerusalem was populated and secure along with the towns around it, and when the Negev and the Shephelah were inhabited? (7:7)
13. Promise of Restoration to Zion, 8:1–23
If it is miraculous in the eyes of the remnant of this people, in those days [how much] more will it be miraculous in my eyes, Oracle of Yahweh? (8:6)

14. Oracle against Hadrach and Damascus, 9:1–11:17
　　No interrogative element
15. Oracle against Jerusalem, 12:1–14:21
　　What are these wounds between your hands? (13:6)
C. Malachi's Sermons:
　　1. Yahweh's Love for Israel, 1:1–5
　　　　How have you loved us? (1:2)
　　2. Indictment of Corrupt Priesthood, 1:6–2:9
　　　　So then, if I am a father, where is my honor? And if I am a master,
　　　　　where is my respect? (1:6a)
　　　　How have we despised your name? (1:6b)
　　　　How have we defiled you? (1:7)
　　　　And when you present a blind [animal] for sacrifice, there is no
　　　　　evil![?] Or when you present a crippled or diseased [animal],
　　　　　there is no evil![?] Bring it to your governor! Will he be pleased
　　　　　with you or grant you favor? (1:8)
　　　　Will he accept any of you? Yahweh of hosts has said. (1:9)
　　3. Indictment of Faithless People, 2:10–16
　　　　Surely, we all have one father? Surely one God created us? Why
　　　　　then do we break faith with each other, thereby profaning the
　　　　　covenant of our forefathers? (2:10)
　　　　But you say, 'Why?' (2:14)
　　　　Surely [The] One made [everything]! And what does The One seek?
　　　　　(2:15)
　　4. Yahweh's Messenger of Justice and Judgment, 2:17–3:5
　　　　How have we wearied [him]? Where is the God of judgment? (2:17)
　　5. The Call to Serve Yahweh, 3:6–12
　　　　How can we return? (3:7)
　　　　Will anyone rob God? How have we robbed you? (3:8)
　　6. The Day of Yahweh, 3:13–21 [4:3]
　　　　How have we spoken against you? (3:13)
　　　　What profit [is there] because we have kept his charge, or because
　　　　　we have paraded mournfully before Yahweh of Hosts? (3:14)

THE BOOK OF MALACHI: A TRANSLATION

Superscription

1 ¹An Oracle: the word of Yahweh to Israel through Malachi.

First Oracle: Yahweh's Covenant Love for Israel

²"I have loved you," Yahweh has said. But you have said, "How have you loved us?" "Surely Esau was Jacob's brother?" Oracle of Yahweh. "Yet I loved Jacob; ³but Esau I hated. So I made his mountains a wasteland and his ancestral homeland a desert [haunt] for jackals." ⁴"If Edom [should] say, "We have been demolished, but we will again build the ruins." Thus Yahweh of Hosts has said, "As for them, let them rebuild! But as for me, I will destroy. Then they will call them [the] 'Territory of Evil,' and the people whom Yahweh has cursed perpetually. ⁵And then your eyes will see, and [as for] you, you will say, 'May Yahweh be great over the territory of Israel!'"

Second Oracle: Faithless Priests Rebuked

⁶"A son honors [his] father, and a servant [respects] his master. If I am [your] father, where is my honor? If I am [your] master, where is my respect?" Yahweh of Hosts has said to you, "O priests — despisers of my name." But you say, "How have we despised your name?" ⁷"[By] offering upon my altar defiled food." But you reply, "How have we defiled you?" When you say, "The table of Yahweh is despicable." ⁸"And when you present a blind [animal] for sacrifice, there is no evil! Or when you present a crippled or diseased [animal], there is no evil! Bring it to your governor! Will he be pleased with you or grant you favor?" Yahweh of Hosts has said.

⁹"And now, [earnestly] entreat the favor of God, so that he may be gracious to us! From your hand this [thing] has come. Will he accept any of you?" Yahweh of Hosts has said. ¹⁰"Oh that one from among you might shut the doors, so that you would not kindle fire on my altar in vain! I take no delight in you," Yahweh of Hosts has said. "Indeed, I will not accept [any] offering from your hand. ¹¹Indeed, from the rising of the sun to its setting, 'Great' is my name among the nations! And everywhere incense is being offered to my name, even a pure offering. For 'Great' is my name among the nations!" Yahweh of Hosts has said. ¹²But you are profaning it when you say, "The table of the Lord is defiled, and its fruit, its food, is despised!" ¹³And you say, "What weariness!" "And you sniff at it," Yahweh of Hosts has said. "You bring stolen or crippled or diseased animals — and so you bring the offering. Shall I accept it from your hand?" Yahweh has said.

¹⁴"Accursed is the cheat who has a male in his flock, and he vows but sacrifices a blemished [animal] to the Lord. For I am a great king," Yahweh of Hosts has said, "and my name is revered among the nations."

2 [1]"And now, this charge to you, O priests! [2]If you will not listen, if you will not lay it to heart to give glory to my name," Yahweh of Hosts has said; "then, I will let loose the curse upon you, and I will curse your blessings. Indeed, I have already cursed it because you do not lay it to heart. [3]See! I am rebuking your seed! And I will spread offal upon your faces — offal of your feasts. And so he will lift you up to it!"

[4]"Then you will know that I [myself] have delivered this charge to you, in order to revive my covenant with Levi," Yahweh of Hosts has said. [5]"My covenant was with him, life itself and peace itself; and I gave them to him. [One of] reverence, and he revered me; and he stood in awe before my name. [6]True instruction was in his mouth, and no deceit was found on his lips. In peace and uprightness he walked with me, and he turned many from iniquity."

[7]"Surely [from] the lips of the priest they safeguard knowledge; and Torah they seek from his mouth; since he is the messenger of Yahweh of Hosts. [8]But you yourselves have turned from the way. You have caused many to stumble over Torah. You have corrupted the covenant of Levi," Yahweh of Hosts has said. [9]"So indeed, I myself will make you despised and abased before all the people. Inasmuch as you are not observing my ways, and [you are not] acting graciously in [matters of] Torah."

Third Oracle: Faithless People Rebuked

[10]Surely we all have one father? Surely one God created us? Why then do we break faith with each other, thereby profaning the covenant of our forefathers? [11]Yehud has broken faith, and an abomination has been committed in Israel and Jerusalem; for Yehud has profaned the holiness of Yahweh, because he loved and married the daughter of a strange El. [12]May Yahweh cut off any man who does this — witness or respondent — from the tents of Jacob, even the one who brings an offering to Yahweh of Hosts!

[13]And this second [thing] you do: tears cover the altar of Yahweh — weeping and wailing; because there is no longer a turning to the offering, nor receiving a favor from your hand. [14]But you say, "Why?" Because Yahweh, he serves as a witness between you and the wife of your youth; with whom you [even you] have broken faith, though she is your marriage partner, and the wife of your covenant. [15]Surely [The] One made [everything]! Even a residue of spirit belongs to him. And what does The One seek? A seed of God. So guard yourselves in your spirit! Stop breaking faith with the wife of your youth!

[16]"Indeed, [The One] hates divorce!" Yahweh, the God of Israel, has said. "For he covers his clothing with violence," Yahweh of Hosts has said. So guard yourselves in your spirit! You shall not break faith!

Fourth Oracle: Judgment and Purification

[17]You have wearied Yahweh with your talk. Yet you say, "How have we wearied [him]?" When you say, "Everyone practicing evil is good in Yahweh's eyes, and in them he takes pleasure." Or "Where is the God of judgment?"

3 ¹"See! I am sending my messenger, and he will clear a way before me. Then suddenly he will enter his temple — the Lord, whom you seek; and the angel of the covenant, whom you desire. See! [He] is coming," Yahweh of Hosts has said.

²But who is able to endure the day of his coming? And who can survive at his appearance? Because he is like the smelter's fire and like the launderer's soda powder. ³And he will remain a refiner and purifier of silver, and he will purify the Levites and refine them like gold and like silver — until they belong to Yahweh, bearers of an offering in righteousness. ⁴Then the offering of Yehud and Jerusalem will be pleasing to Yahweh, as in the days of old — like the former years.

⁵"Yes, I will draw near to you for judgment; then I will be a ready witness against the sorcerers, against the adulterers, against those swearing falsely, against those withholding the wage of the laborer — the widow and the orphan, and those who turn away the sojourner — that is, [all] who do not revere me," Yahweh of Hosts has said.

Fifth Oracle: Call to Repentance

⁶"Indeed, I am Yahweh; I have not changed. And so you, O descendants of Jacob, you have not been destroyed. ⁷Since the days of your forefathers, you have spurned my statutes, and you have not kept [them]. Return to me, so that I may return to you," Yahweh of Hosts has said.

But you say, "How can we return?" ⁸"Will anyone rob God? Surely you are robbing me!" But you say, "How have we robbed you?" "The tithe! The tithe tax! ⁹[So] with the curse you are being cursed; yea, it is me you are robbing — the whole nation! ¹⁰Bring the full tithe into the [Temple] storehouse, so that there may be food in my house! Test me outright in this [thing]," Yahweh of Hosts has said; "[see] if I will not open for you the windows of heaven, and then I will pour out for you a blessing without measure. ¹¹I will repulse for you the devourer so that it may not ravage for you the produce of the land, and so the grapevine in the field may not be [utterly] barren for you," Yahweh of Hosts has said.

¹²"Then all the nations will call you happy. Indeed, you yourselves shall become a land of [his] favor!" Yahweh of Hosts has said.

Sixth Oracle: Judgment and Vindication

¹³"Your words against me have been harsh," Yahweh said. But you have said, "How have we spoken against you?" ¹⁴You have said, "It is futile to serve God! What profit [is there] because we have kept his charge, or because we have paraded mournfully before Yahweh of Hosts? ¹⁵So now we consider the arrogant fortunate. Not only have those doing evil been built up, but also they have tested God and escaped!"

¹⁶Then the fearers of Yahweh spoke together, each one with his companion. And so Yahweh took notice and he listened. A book of remembrance was recorded in his presence, [enrolling] the fearers of Yahweh and those esteeming

his name. [17]"They will be mine," Yahweh of Hosts has said, "a prized possession during the day when I act. Then I will show compassion upon them, even as a man shows compassion for his son, the one who serves him. [18]Once again you will see the difference between a righteous and a wicked one, between one who serves God, and one who has not served him."

[19 [4:1]]"For indeed, the day is coming, burning like an oven, when all [the] arrogant and all evildoers will be stubble. And this coming day will devour them," Yahweh of Hosts has said, "so that it will leave them neither a root nor a branch. [20 [4:2]]But a sun of righteousness will arise for you, those revering my name; and healing [is] in her wings. And so you will go out and you will frisk about like stall-fed calves. [21 [4:3]]And you will trample the wicked, indeed they will be ashes beneath the soles of your feet, during the day I am preparing," Yahweh of Hosts has said.

First Appendix

[22 [4:4]]Remember the Torah of Moses my servant, whom I commanded at Horeb on behalf of all Israel — [the] statutes and [the] ordinances!

Second Appendix

[23 [4:5]]See! I am sending Elijah the prophet to you before the coming Day of Yahweh — the great and the terrible [day]! [24 [4:6]]And he will turn the heart of the forefathers toward the[ir] descendants and the heart of the descendants toward their forefathers; or else [when] I come I will strike the land [with] a curse [for destruction].

INTRODUCTION

◆

I. A. TEXTUAL CONSIDERATIONS

This catalog of the significant variant readings in the primary versions of the text of Malachi serves as an introduction and an orientation to the Translation and Notes advanced in the commentary. The arrangement of the ancient versions follows the order of importance established by McCarter (1986: 20) and R. W. Klein (1974: 74; who echoes Würthwein) and prioritizes in this manner: Hebrew, Greek (LXX, Aquila, Symmachus, Theodotion), Syriac, Aramaic, and Latin (note the two sources differ as to the precedence of Syriac and Aramaic). The subsequent textual discussion includes, but is not necessarily restricted to those textual variants cited in the critical apparatus of the standard editions of the Hebrew Bible (see Hebrew Texts below).

The secondary witnesses to the text of Malachi, including Coptic, Ethiopic, Arabic, and Armenian (see R. W. Klein [1974: 74]; McCarter [1986: 20]), have received only scant attention. While this omission does expose my limitations as a scholar, it should not be regarded as an indictment of the merit of these later versions. They do represent an important exegetical tradition of the text of Malachi, although Tov (p. 15) has maintained these secondary translations are of only limited value for the textual criticism of the Hebrew Bible.

In accord with Tov's (p. 372) observation that both scholar and student need help in locating and evaluating textual evidence, I have included this list of the more useful resources treating the text of Malachi: Budde (1906), Fuller (1991), Gelston (1987), Kruse-Blinkenberg (1966, 1967), Sebök, and J.M.P. Smith (1912). By way of general discussion, including basic bibliographies, see "Textual Criticism, OT" (ABD 6:393–412); and "Versions, Ancient" (ABD 6:787–813).

1. Hebrew Texts

The textual discussion and translation of Malachi offered herein is based upon the Masoretic Text (MT) of the Hebrew Bible as represented in the *Biblia Hebraica Stuttgartensia* (*BHS*), ed. K. Elliger and W. Rudolph (Stuttgart: Deutsche Bibelgesellschaft, 1967/77). In addition, the textual discussion is supplemented by occasional reference to the *Biblia Hebraica* (*BHK*3), ed. R. Kittel and P. Kahle (Stuttgart: Württembergische Bibelanstalt, 1951). Both the *BHS* and the *BHK* editions of the Hebrew Bible are based on the Leningrad Codex (L). The textual apparatus of both the *BHS* and the *BHK* for the book of Malachi also cites the

Hebrew manuscripts of the Kennicott, de Rossi, and Ginsburg editions of the Hebrew Bible (see further Tov [1992: 374–77] and Würthwein [1979: 37–41]). Though given only scant attention in the BHK and BHS due to its incompleteness, this discussion of the MT of Malachi includes references to the complete text and Masorah of the Aleppo Codex (A, generally regarded as an older and better witness than the Leningrad Codex; cf. Tov [1992: 46–47]).

The Dead Sea Scrolls or Qumran (Q) manuscripts are currently of limited value for the study of Malachi. The cache yielded one fragment with a reference to and commentary on Mal 1:13–14 (cf. DJD 3:180). Additional fragments (twenty-one) known as 4QXIIa–g were recovered from Cave 4 at Qumran. They preserve parts of the book of Malachi from 2:10 through the appendixes (3:24 [4:6]). Preliminary investigation reveals that portions of 4QXIIa agree with the LXX against the MT of Malachi (see Fuller; cf. Petersen [1995: 34–35]). Specific examples of this correspondence between Q and the LXX of Mal 2:10–16 cited by Fuller are discussed in the commentary NOTES addressing Malachi's third oracle. No doubt the eventual publication and assessment of the 4QXII fragments of the Minor Prophets will shed further light on the textual character of the book of Malachi (see the forthcoming volume of DJD by R. Fuller devoted to 4QXII). A quotation of Mal 1:10 (apart from the omission of gam and the reading of dltw for dltym) has also been identified (CDR 6:11) in the previously known Zadokite Document or Cairo Damascus Rule.

2. Greek Translations

The Notes to the Translation and Commentary of this study cite the standard edition of the Greek Old Testament or Septuagint (LXX) edited by A. Rahlfs, Septuaginta (Stuttgart: Württembergische Bibelanstalt, 1935). This edition of the LXX is based primarily upon three ancient Greek manuscripts of the Old Testament, Codex Vaticanus (B), Codex Sinaiticus (S or ℵ), and Codex Alexandrinus (LXXA). The textual apparatus of Malachi in both the BHK and the BHS makes substantial appeal to several other ancient Greek versions, including Aquila (α), Symmachus (σ), Theodotion (θ), Ephraemi Syri (C), Purpureus Vindobonesis (L), Marchalianus (Q), and Freer (W). The standard critical edition of Malachi in Greek is the Septuaginta: Vetus Testamentum Graecum, Vol. 13, J. Ziegler, ed. (Göttingen: Vandenhoeck & Ruprecht, 1943). (See further Würthwein [1979: 68–72].)

The critical apparatus of the BHS identifies thirty textual variants in twenty-one separate verses of the book of Malachi (1:1, 7, 8, 13; 2:2, 3 [3x], 4, 9, 10, 12 [2x], 13, 15 [2x], 17; 3:2, 5 [2x], 8 [4x], 9, 13, 16, 19 [2x], 22). The critical apparatus of the BHK lists thirty-three textual variants in twenty-three separate verses of Malachi (1:1, 3, 4, 6, 7, 8, 13; 2:2, 3 [4x], 4 [2x], 5, 13, 15; 3:2, 5, 6, 8 [4x], 9, 10, 15, 16 [3x], 19 [2x], 22). This selective appeal to the differing readings of the LXX in the book of Malachi does accentuate the most significant variants, but represents only a small portion of the textual data available. The NOTES and COMMENTS introduce additional material from the LXX where pertinent.

By way of overview, the LXX does constitute an important witness to the MT of the book of Malachi and represents, for the greater part, a faithful translation of the Hebrew text(s) preserving the prophet's oracles. Exceptions to this generalization include what J.M.P. Smith (1912: 45, 68) has cited as "verbose expansions" in the LXX (e.g., 1:1, 7; 2:2, 4; 3:2, 5, 8, 19 [4:1]) and the tendency of the LXX toward a midrashic interpretation or loose paraphrasing of difficult Hebrew words and phrases (e.g., 1:3, 7, 9, 10; 2:2, 3, 4, 10, 11, 12, 13, 16; 3:5, 6–7, 8, 9, 10, 11, 15, 16, 17, 19 [4:1], 23 [4:5], and 24 [4:6]; cf. Verhoef [1987: 170]).

In addition, some versions of the LXX reorder the last three verses of Malachi so as not to conclude the oracle on the harsh note of divine threat (3:23, 24, 22 [4:5, 6, 4]; cf. Baldwin [1972a: 251]). Later Jewish liturgical tradition introduced the repetition of Mal 3:23 [4:5] after the reading of 3:24 [4:6] in the *shabbat gadol haftarah* (the Masorah appended to Malachi instructs the reader to repeat the next to last verse of the book after the pattern of reading for the books of Isaiah, Lamentations, and Ecclesiastes; cf. Hirsch [1966: 575–76]). Elsewhere, some versions of the LXX introduce further paragraphing of the text of Malachi (e.g., 1:5, 14; 3:5 [or 6]), or offer alternative textual divisions to the MT (e.g., MT 2:16 // LXX 2:17a [or 17b]; MT 3:5 // LXX 3:6 [or 7]), thus delineating a new configuration for certain of the MT pericopes (e.g., MT 1:1–13 // LXX 1:2–14; MT 2:13–16 // LXX 2:10–17; MT 2:17–3:12 // LXX 3:1–12).

Like the other ancient versions, the LXX represents both a translation of the HB and an early exegetical tradition or interpretive approach to the Hebrew text. For instance, the LXX demonstrates internal stylistic harmonizations (e.g., *légei Kýrios* for *nĕ'ūm YHWH* in 1:2; and the addition of *pantokrátōr* [= *ṣĕbā'ōt*] in 1:13), as well as intratestamental harmonization (note here the translation of 2:16 permitting divorce in view of Deut 24:1–4 and the insertion of "the Tishbite" in 3:23 [LXX 3:22] after 1 Kgs 17:1).

There are also examples of paraphrastic or interpretive translation in an attempt to clarify perplexing words and phrases in Malachi's oracles (e.g., reading *dōmata* ["houses"] for the unique MT *tannōt* ["jackals"] in 1:3, specifying idolatry as the issue in 2:11 with the rendering *theous allotríous* ["other gods"], and the addition of *meth' hymōn eisin* ["is *still* with you!"] to the abrupt MT in respect to the tithe in 3:8).

In a few cases, it may be possible to discern Hellenistic influences surfacing in the LXX's understanding of Malachi (e.g., the pious exhortations appended to 1:1; 3:5, 6, and the ambiguous[?] use of *ággélou* for the MT *mal'ākî* in 1:1 and 3:1; on angelology and Hellenism, see Russell [1976: 235–62] and cf. Hengel [1:206] who regards the name Malachi as an apocalyptic pseudonym).

Finally, the LXX's rendering of Malachi betrays certain theological motivations on the part of the translators, perhaps even suggesting principles of early Jewish exegetical practice (although Longenecker [p. 21] cautions against such use of the LXX, it seems exemplars of midrashic interests operative in the text of the LXX may be seen in the shift of the focus of activity from the priests to Yahweh in 1:13 and 2:13, the expansion on the divine curse in 2:2–3, the departure of the LXX from the MT in 3:6b, and the substitution of *epiphanē* for the MT *hannôrā'* in 3:23 [LXX 3:22]). (See the NOTES to the Translation for a more extensive discussion of the numerous variant readings of Malachi found in the LXX.)

Kruse-Blinkenberg (1967: 73) identified ninety-six divergences between the LXX and the MT in the book of Malachi. His catalog of variations between the two versions has been collated under nine distinct rubrics, including the inaccurate rendering of individual Hebrew words by the LXX (e.g., 1:3, 4, 8, 10, 11, 13, 14; 2:3, 5, 8, 9, 10, 15, 16, 17; 3:1, 5, 10, 13, 15, 16, 17, 19 [4:1], 22 [4:4], 23 [4:5], 24 [4:6]), translation of phrases and sentences by the LXX incongruent with the MT (e.g., 1:10, 12; 2:11, 12, 13, 15, 16; 3:7, 8, 9, 10, 11, 20), changes in word order and verse order in the LXX (e.g., 2:10; 3:22–24 [4:4–6]), inconsistent rendering of number in nouns by the LXX (e.g., 2:4; 3:24 [4:6]), variations in the LXX from the MT as to person (e.g., 1:4, 7, 9; 2:3; 3:16), the insertion of verbal forms in the LXX for substantives in the MT (e.g., 2:6), omission of specific words in the MT by the LXX (1:11; 2:9; 3:1, 21 [note some versions of the LXX omit this entire verse]), expansion of the MT by the LXX (e.g., 1:1, 2, 6, 7, 9; 2:2, 8, 13, 15; 3:2, 3, 5, 6, 19), and the LXX's interpretation of *mal'ākî* (1:1). Kruse-Blinkenberg's analysis of the Syro-Hexaplaris Ambrosianus (SHA, or the Syriac translation of the Hebrew Bible based upon the Greek Bible) and the LXX of the book of Malachi prompted the conclusion that the MT of Malachi demonstrates a corrupted text, at least in 1:3, 2:12, 2:15, and 2:16 (1967: 79).

Regrettably, the Greek Minor Prophets Scroll from Cave 8 at Qumran preserves no fragments of the text of Malachi (cf. E. Tov et al. *The Greek Minor Prophets Scroll from Nahal Hever* [*DJD* 8HevXIIgr]. Oxford: Clarendon Press, 1990).

3. Syriac Translations

The (Classical) Syriac translation informing this discussion is primarily that of *Vetus Testamentum Syriace* (III, 4) or *VTS*, (Leiden: Brill, 1980). This Syriac translation of the OT/HB known as the Peshitta (Syr) was based upon the Hebrew. The analysis of Kruse-Blinkenberg (1966) was based upon four editions of the Peshitta (SB, SC, SL, and SU; see pp. 95–96). Gelston's (1987) study compared the Basic Text of the *VTS* to six additional later manuscript families and groups of the Peshitta (see pp. 26–64).

The *BHS* has cited textual variants found in the Peshitta (Syr) for only seven verses of the book of Malachi (1:3, 12, 13 [2x]; 2:2, 17; 3:8, 16). The influence of the versions, especially the LXX, accounts for the alternative readings in all but two instances (1:3 where Syr understands the infinitive *něwôt* for *tannôt* and 1:13 where Syr omits the conjunction *waw*).

By way of general observation, the influence of the LXX on Syr has been noted in Mal 1:3, 4, 10, 13, 14; 2:2, 3, 4, 11, 13; and 3:6. Textual variants in T (see below Aramaic Targum) agree with those of Syr in 1:2, 13; 2:3 and 2:12. Verses containing additions to Syr not found in the MT include 1:4; 2:11; 3:6, 11, 19 [4:1], while deletions of the MT in Syr are noticed in 1:4, 9, 12, 14; 2:2, 16; and 3:11. Variations due to the translation process from Hebrew to Syr are numerous (e.g., 1:1, 2, 3, 4, 5, 6, 8, 9, 10, 11; 2:4, 12, 13, 16; 3:5, 6, 7, and 9). In two instances Syr reorders or rearranges the MT (1:2; 3:9). Finally, examples of specific grammatical changes in Syr from the MT may be documented, as in the substitution of a prefixing for an affixing form of the verb in 3:1, the use of the passive participle for the infinitive construct in 3:2, and the insertion of the infinitive construct for the participle in 3:3.

Kruse-Blinkenberg (1966 and 1967) identified more than one hundred divergences between the MT of Malachi and the Peshitta. The bulk of these concern the verbal system where the Syr renders the MT affixing (perfective) with prefixing (imperfective) forms, and Hebrew prefixing (imperfective) forms are rendered by participles in Syr (1966: 105). Only ten of these variant readings have been regarded as significant for the discussion of the text, interpretation, and theme of Malachi (1:13; 2:8, 11, 12, 13, 15, 16; 3:1, 6, 19 [4:1]). The single overlap between the critical apparatus of the *BHS* and this study of Kruse-Blinkenberg (1966) is Mal 1:13, and even there a different set of variants is discussed in the *BHS*. According to Kruse-Blinkenberg (1966: 97–105) Syr misunderstands the Hebrew of the MT in three of these ten significant divergences (2:8; 3:1, 19 [4:1]), paraphrases obscure passages in the MT to achieve a more intelligible reading in three others (2:12, 13, 15), reflects the influence of the LXX in another three cases (1:13; 2:11; 3:6), and once Syr changes the MT for the sake of harmonization with the OT/HB (2:16). None of these ten primary divergences was considered substantial for the reconstruction of the MT. (See the NOTES to the Translation for further discussion of the relationship of Syr to the MT.)

More recently, Gelston (p. 93) has compiled a catalog of thirty additional variants from the Twelve Prophets to be included in the First and Second Apparatus of the *VTS*. He considered these divergences superior to the readings of the Basic Text of the *VTS* and thus important for the reconstruction of the original Peshitta version. Gelston's study affects Malachi only in 1:4 where he would insert the variant *ḥaylthānā* in the Second Apparatus (thus reading the Syr equivalent of *YHWH ṣĕbā'ôt*; note that he rejects the same variant reading for Mal 3:13). Gelston (p. 156) has summarized well that the Peshitta is "an idiomatic and essentially faithful version of the Scriptures for reading in public worship"; yet, the variety of translation methods discernible in the version makes the reconstruction of the Hebrew *Vorlage* difficult and in every case places the burden of proof on the exegete claiming the superiority of Syr (p. 159).

Both Kruse-Blinkenberg (1966: 112) and Gelston (pp. 156, 159) have maintained the independent status of Syr in relationship to the LXX and T. In addition, both have acknowledged Syr constitutes a rather "free" translation of Malachi (Kruse-Blinkenberg 1966: 114; Gelston 1987: 159). Likewise, both admit that the LXX demonstrates only a sporadic influence upon Syr (Kruse-Blinkenberg [1966: 117]; Gelston [1987: 176–77]). However, whereas Kruse-Blinkenberg (1966: 116) has attributed the similarities between T and Syr to a common source, Gelston (p. 189–90) is reluctant to ascribe the interdependence between T and Syr to a common Hebrew *Vorlage* distinct from the MT, preferring instead to suggest a common exegetical tradition. Lastly, Kruse-Blinkenberg (1966: 113) and Gelston (pp. 129–30) concur that the MT is more original than

Syr, making it impossible to reconstruct or improve the MT by means of the Peshitta.

After his careful study of the Syro-Hexaplaris Ambrosianus (SHA), Kruse-Blinkenberg (1967: 79) has concluded that "it is quite impossible to reconstruct Malachi or part of this book by means of SHA." In fact, he regarded SHA as inferior to Syr and asserted that he found no evidence suggesting that SHA was based upon a Hebrew manuscript more original than the present MT (1967: 78, 80; cf. Gelston [pp. 101–4]). In accord with the conclusions of Kruse-Blinkenberg and Gelston, the significant readings of Syr at variance with the MT must be evaluated on the basis of individual merit because Syr does represent an important witness to the MT as a direct non-midrashic translation of the HB. However, references to Syr in the NOTES to the present Translation are treated more by way of information for demonstrating and understanding the early (Jewish or Jewish-Christian?) exegetical tradition represented by the Syriac Bible, rather than for wholesale or even modest reconstruction of the MT; as noted above, both Kruse-Blinkenberg (1966: 113) and Gelston (p. 130) have cautioned against the reconstruction of the MT on the basis of the Peshitta.

4. Aramaic Translations

Remarks pertaining to the Aramaic text of Malachi are founded upon the *Targum of Jonathan to the Prophets* (*TgNeb*) vol. 3 *The Bible in Aramaic*, ed. A. Sperber (Leiden: Brill, 1962). The English translations of the Targum of Malachi are those of Cathcart and Gordon.

The critical apparatus of the *BHS* identifies only four textual variants from the *TgNeb*, including the omission of the awkward *nybw* in 1:12 (understanding dittography as in Syr); reading a second-person form of the verb *bgd* for the MT *ybgd* in 2:15 (in agreement with the LXX and V); the addition of the third-person object suffix to the verbal root *yg'* in 2:17 (following the LXX, Syr, and V); and the substitution of the preposition *bêt* for the definite article in 3:8 (*hamma 'ăšer wě hattĕrûmâ*, cf. Syr and V [see Vulgate below]).

By way of general observation, T is characterized by a tendency towards midrashic paraphrase in terms of later Jewish piety (1:9, 10, 11; 2:3, 15; 3:6; cf. Verhoef 1987: 170). In addition, while T seems to understand the basic historical situation of Malachi (e.g., 2:11), the Aramaic text at times avoids difficulties in the MT by means of literalistic paraphrasing (e.g., 2:3) or obvious harmonization with an earlier tradition (e.g., the issue of divorce in 2:16). The Aramaic Bible seems to evidence patterns of agreement with the other versions in a number of variant readings (e.g., 1:4, 5, 8; 2:5, 10, 14; 3:16; etc.), although Kruse-Blinkenberg (1966: 112) has maintained that the number of singular divergences between T and Syr and the LXX is greater than the number of shared or common variants. Hence Kruse-Blinkenberg (1966: 113) and Gelston (pp. 180, 189) acknowledge the independent status of both T and Syr. Finally, T shows a propensity for plural forms over the singular noun of the MT (e.g., 1:4; 3:18), demonstrates preference for understanding the MT *wě* ("and") and *kî* ("for, because") in a conditional sense ("if," 1:2, 6, 13; 2:14, 16, 17; etc.), and on occasion T chooses to substitute a later idiom for a difficult or obscure phrase in the MT (e.g., 2:12; 3:10).

Kruse-Blinkenberg (1966: 110–12) has isolated six essential divergences between T and the MT of the book of Malachi that are peculiar to the Targum (including the pious expansion of 1:11; the free paraphrase of 2:11 [where T does understand the historical background of Malachi]; the interpretation of the MT *ûmaggîš minḥâ* as "priest" [*khyn*] in 2:12, thus assuming that 2:10–16 serves as a sequel to 2:1–9; the insertion of Abraham in the free paraphrase of 2:15; the harmonization of 2:16 with Deut 24:1–4, thus permitting, not prohibiting, divorce and the theological expansion upon Israel's covenant relationship with Yahweh in 3:6). These and other textual variants in the Targum illuminate the exegetical and interpretive tradition represented by T and the relationship of T (and Syr) to the LXX. However, Kruse-Blinkenberg (1966: 111) considered the Targum insufficient for the reconstruction of the MT.

In a separate study, Gelston (1987) has reached conclusions similar to those of Kruse-Blinkenberg (1966). Unlike the more generalized study of Kruse-Blinkenberg, Gelston observed certain stylistic features in the Targum of the Twelve Prophets, such as the introduction of prepositions and participles, the modification of verbal forms, the substitution of adjectives for suffixed nouns in the MT, and the insertion of certain words or idioms (e.g., the addition of *byt* before proper nouns). More specifically, Gelston (p. 181–83) has noted the tendency in T to interpret the MT *w'mrtm* in Mal 1:2, 6, 7, 13; 2:14, 17; 3:7, 8, 13 conditionally (*w'm tymrwn*, a feature of Syr as well), along with the Targum's modification and expansion of the MT by means of the "paraphrastic gloss" and the "explanatory gloss" (e.g., Mal 2:12, 16; 3:10). However, Gelston also expressed some reluctance about reconstructing the MT of the Twelve Prophets on the basis of the Aramaic Bible (see pp. 179–80). For Gelston (pp. 189–90) T and the similarities between T and Syr say more about dependence upon a common exegetical tradition in the related dialects than upon the Hebrew *Vorlage* of the MT (so Gordon [1994: 129]; see his discussion of the textual variants introduced by T in Mal 1:2, 6, 10, 13; 2:12, 16; 3:10).

5. Latin Translations

The Latin translation consulted is that of the *Biblia Sacra: Vulgatae* (Stuttgart: Württembergische Bibelanstalt, 1969), or *BSV*, as well as St. Jerome's commentary on the book of Malachi *Corpus Christianorum: Series Latina* LXXVI A (Turnhout: Brepols, 1970, pp. 901–42).

The textual apparatus of Malachi in the *BHS* edition of the MT appeals to the Latin Bible or Vulgate (V) only six times: 1:8 (some Latin MSS read *illud*, "it," copying the LXX *autò*; although the *BSV* reads *tuam*, "you," following the MT); 2:3 (where *brachium*, "forearm," agrees with the LXX *tòn ómon*, against the MT *zera'*); 2:9 (while MSS of both the LXX and V translate "peoples," according to J.M.P. Smith [1912: 41] the MT *lĕ kol-hā'ām*, "before all the people," is preferred because in context the priesthood is the recipient of the address); 2:15 (in what commentators concede is the most difficult verse in Malachi, many LXX and Latin witnesses read the second-person *tibgōd* for the MT third-person *yib-gōd*); 2:17 (the LXX, Syr, and V all supply the objective suffix for the MT *hôgāʿěnû* [i.e., *bammâ hôgāʿnuhû*, "how have we wearied *him?*"]; although Glazier-McDonald [1987a: 127] considers this superfluous since the object, Yahweh, is readily inferred from context); and finally 3:8 (where V and Syr assume the carryover of the preposition from the preceding clause [*bammeh*] and read *bammaʿăšēr wĕbattĕrûmâ* for the MT *hammaʿăšēr wĕhattĕrûmâ*; note here the LXX inserts the phrase *meth' hymōn eisin*, "tithes and offerings *are still with you*" [so R. L. Smith 1984: 320]).

Generally, the Vulgate represents a faithful witness to the MT, forwarding a dependable translation (e.g., 1:1, 2, 5, 6, 14; 2:5; 3:8, 18, etc.) and in some instances supporting the MT against the other ancient versions (e.g., 1:7, 12, 13, 14; 2:2, 4, 7, 11; 3:16, 20 [4:2]). On those occasions when the Vulgate deviates from the MT, the variants most often reflect the influence of the LXX (e.g., 1:9, 13; 2:3, 9, 12, 16; 3:2 [where the LXX *poià* and the Vulgate *herba* for the MT *bōrît* suggest alkaline plants as the origin of this soap, so J.M.P. Smith 1912: 68]; 3:16; and beginning a new chapter at 3:19) or constitute what J.M.P. Smith (1912: 43, 67) has observed as a "free translation" (e.g., 1:12; 2:17).

Minor additions (e.g., the conjunction *wě* in 1:11) or deletions (e.g., the negation *lōʾ* in 1:10) or interpretive alterations (e.g., the use of *nonne*, the interrogative adverb introducing a rhetorical question in 1:8 and 2:15; rendering *muqṭār* with the more general *sacrificatur* in 1:11; reading *proiciam* as a conflation of the MT *gōʿēr* and the LXX *aphorízō* [= Heb. *gōrēaʿ*] in 2:3; the translation *discipulum*, "scholar," for the difficult MT *ʿōneh* in 2:12; inserting the adversative *autem* in 2:16 for the LXX *kaì* [= MT *wě*]; understanding *penury* for *mě'ērâ* in 3:9; or even the reading *de armento*, "from the herd," for the MT *marbēq* in 3:20) make up the remainder of significant types of textual changes represented in the Vulgate.

6. Present Translation

The goal of Bible translation is ultimately "fidelity in meaning" between the original language(s) of Scripture and the target or receptor language (in this case English, cf. Fee and Stuart [1993: 34–37]). One's philosophy of translation determines in large measure the strategies employed for achieving this fidelity in meaning. This reading favors that segment of the continuum identified as "literal" or "formal correspondence" in translation theory (cf. Silva [1990: 135–39]).

I fully recognize that the task of Bible translation is interpretive. At times this means forsaking a more literal translation for one that represents a more idiomatic (or "dynamically equivalent") rendering of the text in question. At times it may mean emphasizing "emotional nuance" over "cognitive detail" (cf. Silva [1990: 134]). Deference for the rhetorical nature and disputational character of Malachi's speeches has consciously motivated the production of this translation. I have deliberately replicated emphatic constructions and at times have retained the emphatic word order of the MT (seeking to somehow convey that "incarnational" meaning of literature, cf. Ryken [1984: 13]). I must confess I was both surprised and pleased by the similarities at certain points between Petersen's (1995) translation of Malachi and my own; that despite the fact that the bulk of my work was completed prior to the publication of that Old Testament Library volume. Perhaps we are moving the discussion in the right direction.

Like Sasson (p. 13), I have followed closely the MT of Malachi, concurring with him that "commentators serve best when clarifying what lies before them instead of explaining what they imagine to have existed." Divergences from the MT in the ancient versions are duly cited and in some instances discussed fully in the NOTES. The wide range of solutions proposed for those few problem passages in Malachi are recorded as well. Brackets ([. . .]) denote the author's interpolation of perceived gapping in the oracles or alternately the amplification of a cryptic word or phrase (marking, in part, my inability to completely grasp the sense of the text).

The NOTES to the Translation for this reading of Malachi quote contemporary English versions for comparative purposes where appropriate, including *The New American Bible* (NAB) (New York: Oxford University Press, 1970); *The New English Bible* (NEB) (New York: Oxford University Press, 1970); *The New International Version* (NIV) (Grand Rapids: Zondervan, 1984); *Tanakh: The Holy Scriptures* (JPSV) (Philadelphia: Jewish Publication Society, 1985); *The New Jerusalem Bible* (NJB) (New York: Doubleday, 1985); and the *New Revised Standard Version* (NRSV) (Nashville: Thomas Nelson, 1989). The JPSV, NEB, NIV, and NJB are representative examples of the dynamic equivalence translation theory, while the NAB and the NRSV may be placed on a continuum moving away slightly from dynamic equivalence (or idiomatic translation) to a more literal translation establishing formal correspondence between the biblical text and the receptor language (see further Silva [1990: 129–39]; Fee and Stuart [1993: 28–44]).

In agreement with several of the recent commentators on the book of Malachi, the present translation adopts a minimalist approach to the reconstruction of the MT (e.g., R. L. Smith [1984]; Verhoef [1987]; and Glazier-McDonald [1987a]; cf. Malchow's indictment of Glazier-McDonald for her failure to adopt even a single emendation in the MT of Malachi. However, note Petersen (1995: 35) who "reformulates" the MT of Malachi in 1:1, 9, 11, 12; 2:2, 3, 11, 12, 13, 16, 17; 3:5, 13). I have included no alternative readings based upon conjectural emendations (as defined by Tov [1992: 351–69]). Suggested improvements of the MT of the book of Malachi are based solely upon manuscript evidence contained in the ancient versions of the OT/HB, primarily that of the Septuagint (LXX; cf. Tov [1992: 15] on those textual traditions whose relevance for the reconstruction of the MT has been proven). Here I have attempted to avoid the enthusiasm of some for reconstruction of the MT (e.g., McCarter [1986: 13–18]) and instead have opted for the more judicious approaches to textual emendation of R. W. Klein (1974: 74) and Tov (pp. 14–15). By way of procedure, I have essentially employed those standard principles or so-called rules of textual criticism outlined by R. W. Klein (1974: 74–75) and McCarter (1986: 72–75) for emending the MT (i.e., select the variant reading that best explains all others; the more difficult reading is preferable; the shorter reading is preferable; etc.), while remaining conscious of Tov's reminder that "to some extent textual criticism cannot be bound by fixed rules" (p. 309).

This reading of Malachi acknowledges the superscription (1:1) and the appendixes (3:22 [4:4] and 3:23–24 [4:5–6]) as secondary. In addition, I have "reformulated" portions of the MT of the book of Malachi in 2:4, 12, 15.

I. B. CANONICAL CONSIDERATIONS

Malachi is the last of the books constituting the collection known as the Twelve Prophets. This collection follows the Major Prophets in the Hebrew canon and is often labeled the "Minor Prophets." The Twelve are not of lesser importance than Isaiah, Jeremiah, and Ezekiel. Rather, as Augustine noted, they are "called minor from the brevity of their writings" (*CivDei* 18.29).

Both Jewish and Christian traditions have always positioned Malachi last among the Twelve Prophets. For the rabbis Malachi is the last among the later prophets (Haggai, Zechariah, and Malachi; cf. b. *Sanh* 11a and b. *Yoma* 9b). Talmudic legend places Malachi among the Jewish expatriates who returned to Jerusalem after the Babylonian Exile under the leadership of Joshua and Zerubbabel (b. *Zebaḥ* 62a) and dates his oracles to the second year of Darius I (520 B.C./E.; cf. b. *Meg* 15a). Because Haggai, Zechariah, and Malachi were deemed the only prophets belonging to the Second Temple period according to Jewish tradition, they were naturally placed at the end of the collection of the Twelve Prophets (cf. *EncJud* 11:50).

The early church regarded Malachi as an important theological bridge between the two dispensations, the Old and New Covenants (especially Mal 1:10–11 as an apologetic for a Gentile church, cf. Tertullian, *Marc* 4.8.1; Mal 3:1, 23–24 [4:5–6], as an apologetic for identifying John the Baptist as Malachi's "forerunner"; cf. Origen, *Comm in Jn* 2.17; 6.13; Mal 3:20 [4:2, "sun of righteousness"] as a divine epithet for Jesus Christ; cf. Cyprian, *Did* 4.35; and Mal 3:22 [4:4] as a defense of the "goodness" of Mosaic law as cited in *ConstAp* 6.4.19).

The grouping of the Twelve Prophets was recognized as early as Jesus Ben Sira (Sir 49:10) and was also familiar to Josephus (*AgAp* 1.8.3). The association of Malachi with the men of the Great Synagogue who purportedly edited the corpus of the Twelve Prophets placed the book above canonical dispute (b. *BBat* 15a). Moore's summary statement on the canonicity of Malachi remains valid, as "the canonical authority of Malachi has never been called in question. It is found in all the authoritative enumerations of the canonical books" (1974: 107; see further B. A. Jones [1995: 221–42]).

While the canonical authority of Malachi has never been in doubt, the independent status of the book continues to stir scholarly debate. Five decades ago

Bentzen (pp. 158, 161) popularized the notion that the oracles contained in Zechariah 9–11, 12–14, and Malachi 1–3 [MT] were related, largely because of the use of the term *maśśā'* in the superscriptions.[1] It is usually argued these three originally anonymous oracles were appended to Zechariah to round out the Twelve for the purpose of completing the sacred number (cf. Petersen [1995: 23–29]; B. A. Jones [1995: 20–21]).

Radday and Pollatschek concluded that the editor of the Twelve Prophets had a collection of materials remaining from the compilation of Hosea-Zechariah 1–8. They suggested this small library consisted of a few short but distinct manuscripts, which were attached to Zechariah 1–8 principally on the basis of size. The two longer oracles coalesced with Zechariah 1–8 to become Zechariah 9–11 and 12–14. Two shorter pieces, Malachi 1–2 and chapter 3, were then added to Zechariah with the superscription including *bĕyad mal'ākî* inserted for the purpose of framing a collection of prophetic books corresponding to the number of Israelite tribes. This clever editor turned a word found three times in the oracle, *mal'ākî*, into a name of a formerly unknown Hebrew prophet (cf. Nogalski [1993b: 188–89]).

However, I am inclined to agree with Childs (1979: 491–92) when he counters that the superscriptions in Zech 9:1; 12:1; and Mal 1:1 demonstrate only superficial similarities. For instance, he notes that *maśśā'* is used in its absolute form in Mal 1:1 as a distinct superscription. Further, Mal 1:1 reads *'el* ("to") rather than *'al* ("upon"), and in contrast to Zech 9:1 and 12:1 the superscription in Malachi includes the expression *bĕyad* ("by the hand of"). Lastly, the phrase *dĕbar YHWH* ("the word of Yahweh") stands with no accompanying verb.[2]

Consequently, Childs understands these expressions as demonstrating both the integrity and the consistency of the title of Malachi with like features of post-exilic literature. He then concludes that the oracles of Zechariah 9–11, Zechariah 12–14, and Malachi 1–3 [MT] had a literary history independent of one another. Thus, "the present independent status of Malachi did not arise from an arbitrary decision which separated it from the book of Zechariah. Rather its separate status is deeply rooted in the book's own tradition" (Childs [1979: 492]; cf. Redditt [1995: 100–11] on *maśśā'* in Zech 9:1).[3]

---

[1]A cursory survey of a concordance to the HB reveals the flawed nature of Bentzen's assumption, in that the title *maśśā'* is frequently employed by other prophetic books in the very same fashion as that of Zech 9:1 and 12:1 in oracles where authorship is beyond dispute (e.g., Isa 13:1; 15:1; 17:1; 19:1; 21:1; etc.; Nah 1:1; Hab 1:1).

[2]G. M. Tucker (pp. 56–70) identified *maśśā'* as a title forming part of certain prophetic superscriptions. These superscriptions were interpretations of collectors and editors of the prophetic tradition affirming the authority of the oracles as divine revelation. Tucker concluded, "while the superscriptions to the prophetic books do not represent a stage of canonization, they do reveal a decisive point when . . . the spoken prophetic word had become scripture" (p. 70).

[3]Childs's defense of the independent status of Malachi's oracle marks a sort of watershed in mainline (English) biblical scholarship. Conservative biblical scholars have traditionally upheld the integrity of Malachi's prophecy (e.g., Baldwin [1972a: 62–70, 77–81, 212]; Harrison [1969: 960]; Laetsch [1956: 508]; and Verhoef [1987: 155]).

Recent studies treating the book of Malachi have come full circle in that some main-

The date of Malachi's inclusion in the canonical prophetic collection is uncertain. Freedman (1963: 264; cf. 1991: 50–51) has offered the most plausible suggestion, understanding Malachi as part of the supplement to the prophetic collection compiled around 500 B.C./E. (with the final edition of the Book of the Twelve as late as Ezra-Nehemiah). This revision of the prophetic corpus may have been associated with the rebuilding of the Temple and the attempts to revive the Hebrew monarchy (ca. 520–500 B.C./E.). In addition, even though Joel, Jonah, and Zechariah 9–14 are more difficult to assess chronologically in the literary process shaping this prophetic supplement, Freedman proposed that they may have been part of the compilation as well.[4]

The date of canonization notwithstanding, Malachi's final position among the Twelve Prophets has been stable from at least the 3rd century B.C./E. (so Schneider [pp. 199–200]). Schneider (p. 149) has proposed the three postexilic prophets (the Haggai-Zechariah-Malachi corpus) were added to the nine preexilic (minor) prophets because their warning of divine judgment, call to repentance, and promise of future hope and restoration evidenced a continuity of authority with the earlier prophetic documents.

Both Schneider (pp. 144–45) and Pierce (1984a/b) argue for the unity of the Haggai-Zechariah-Malachi corpus, surmising the documents constitute a "spiritual history" of the Hebrew restoration community. However, Schneider (p. 149) interprets that history from the more positive perspective of worship renewal, while Pierce (1984b: 411) understands the record more negatively as one of covenant failure in postexilic Jerusalem. More specifically, Schneider (pp. 143–45) links Malachi to Haggai and Zechariah 1–8 given their shared interest in social justice, true penitence, and payment of the tithe. Eschatological themes and the indictment of corrupt leadership connect Malachi and Zechariah 9–14. Finally, Malachi functions as the literary and theological complement to Haggai and Zechariah in that he calls the restoration community to "complete" their worship

---

line biblical scholars, appealing to Childs, now assert the authenticity and integrity of Malachi's prophecy (e.g., Glazier-McDonald [1987a: 24–27] [but oblivious to Childs's work]; R. L. Smith [1984: 296–97]; and O'Brien [1990: 51–53]). This does not deny the importance of earlier voices espousing a similar viewpoint (e.g., Chary [1969: 223, 233]; cf. Eiselen [1907: 687–88]; and van Hoonacker [1908: 705]).

[4] D. N. Freedman (1963) reprinted (pp. 5–20) in *The Canon and Massorah of the Hebrew Bible: An Introductory Reader*. New York: KTAV, 1974; see also D. N. Freedman 1976: 130–36 and 1991: 60–61. Incidentally, Clements (1974: 54) has indirectly confirmed this approximate date for Malachi's insertion into the supplement of the prophetic corpus when he observed, "Their [i.e., Isaiah 56–66, Malachi, and Zechariah 9–14] preaching also was invested with the same eschatological reference which colored the preaching of the prophets of the Persian era [i.e., Haggai and Zechariah]." These eschatological themes (i.e., the salvation of Israel, divine judgment of the godless, and the restoration of covenant relationship with Yahweh) more naturally fit the religious and historical context of the early postexilic period. The Jewish accommodation of Persian political policies, the emphasis on Temple ritual, and the preoccupation with religious legalism characteristic of the later Ezra-Nehemiah period seem to confirm this assessment (cf. Hanson [1979: 286–87]). In a separate study, Schneider (pp. 147–52) has demonstrated the thematic and linguistic unity of the Haggai-Zechariah-Malachi corpus with the rest of the Twelve, but dates the inclusion of the collection to the time of Nehemiah.

to Yahweh, even as Haggai and Zechariah called the people to complete the Second Temple building project.[5]

I. C. LITERARY CONSIDERATIONS

I. C. 1. Authorship

The identification of the form *mal'ākî* remains problematic. Two defensible positions have emerged from scholarly debate. The first recognizes Malachi as the proper name of the writer of the oracles. The second understands Malachi as a title or appellative for the anonymous person responsible for the compiling of the book.[1]

[5]House has attempted to illustrate the unity of the Twelve by means of the "New Criticism" (cf. Barton [1984: 140–57]). His application of literary-dramatic categories to the corpus of the Minor Prophets yields a thematic unity in the pattern of Frye's "U-shaped" comic plot framework (pp. 123–24). Hosea and Joel represent the *problem*, while Amos, Obadiah, Jonah, and Micah introduce the *complication*. Nahum and Habakkuk constitute the apex of *crisis* in the plot. Finally, Zephaniah marks the *climax and falling action* of the comedic plot in the Twelve, capped by the *denouement* or *resolution* of the problem (Haggai, Zechariah, and Malachi).

To his credit, House's analysis of genre, structure, plot, characterization, and point of view within the Twelve Prophets does bring alternative perspectives to the questions associated with the redaction of the corpus. However, I concur with Mason (1991) who fairly evaluated the work and censured House's methodology as badly flawed and his conclusions so vague and general as to be true of the entire HB!

In addition to the salient points of Mason's critique, it must be noted that compressing the Twelve into the Procrustean mold of Aristotelian genre studies divorces the individual prophetic books from their original setting and historical context. This both mutes the vigor, vitality, and pathos of the prophetic word as oracular literature and by sheer reductionism introduces an artificial and simplistic thematic structure that reads the whole as *much less* than the sum of its parts. For example, the "comic-plot" schema discerns no shift in Hebrew prophecy from the preexilic to the postexilic periods, makes no distinction between the faithful remnant and the nation of Israel in respect to audience, and the U-shaped comedic paradigm collapses with but the slightest shift in theological emphasis. For instance, Obadiah could just as easily constitute *resolution* if one were to emphasize the sovereignty of God as a covenant-maker and keeper instead of divine judgment of the nations; likewise Malachi might be equally understood as *crisis* if the theme of judgment accompanying the day of the Lord is underscored (cf. Van Leeuwen [1993: 32] who remarks, "House employs categories from literary criticism . . . that in practice appear not always apt nor able to illuminate crucial data").

[1]On the redaction of Malachi, see Hanson (1979: 400; 1986: 281) who assigns Isaiah 55–66, Zechariah 10–11, and Malachi to a group of disenfranchised Levites; and Redditt (1994: 241; 1995: 155) who attributes the bulk of the book to an anonymous non-Zadokite Levite and the final product to a dissident Levitical redactor (cf. Nogalski [1993b: 185–87], Bosshard and Kratz [1990: 27], and Lescow [1990, 1993] who identify as many as three "redactional layers" in the book of Malachi).

Watts (1987a: 375) responds to this sort of speculation introducing extensive editorial activity in the disputations of Malachi by noting, "The literary structure of the book is

The supporting evidence adduced for regarding "Malachi" as a prophetic title includes the LXX translation "by the hand of his messenger" (*èn cheirì aggélou autoû*) for *mal'ākî* (most recently see Petersen [1995: 165–66]); the tradition of later Judaism (e.g., *TgNeb* [Sperber 3:500], and Rashi [1930: 108]) and church history (e.g., Jerome [*PL* 25: 1541–42], and Calvin [p. 459]) which identified *mal'ākî* as a title for Ezra the scribe; the similarities between the superscriptions of Mal 1:1 and the oracles of Second Zechariah (9:1 and 12:1), suggesting that these prophetic texts originally circulated as anonymous compositions (see I. B. Canonical Considerations above); the use of *mal'ākî* in 3:1, suggesting the insertion of *mal'ākî* in the superscription as a title for the anonymous prophecies; the fact that "Malachi" is a unique name in OT/HB literature; and the unlikelihood of Hebrew parents selecting such a name for any child (cf. J.M.P. Smith [1912: 19]).

As a proper noun "Malachi" may be translated "my messenger" or "my angel" (cf. Zech 1:9, 11), though context militates against the latter. Hence, despite the lack of attestation elsewhere, *mal'ākî* is similar to other OT/HB names ending in *î*, such as Beeri, "my well" (*bĕ'ērî*, Gen 26:34; Hos 1:1), Ethni, "my gift" ('*etnî*, 1 Chr 6:26 [41]), and Zichri, "my remembrance"[?] (*zikrî*, Exod 6:21; 1 Chr 8:19). Neither should this single occurrence of the name Malachi count as evidence against its use as a proper noun since both Habakkuk and Jonah are unique among the names of the Hebrew prophets. The notion that Hebrew parents would not entertain Malachi as a name for a child was countered long ago by von Orelli (p. 387) who suggested the prophet took on the name Malachi when he was called to his prophetic office (cf. G. L. Robinson [pp. 157–58] who regards the name of the prophet as his "stage name"). I would simply add here that the presumption of J.M.P. Smith (i.e., the "naming of the child" argument cited above) best be forgotten, especially given other Hebrew names like Jedidiah, Obadiah, and Abdiel.

The LXX has changed the first-person pronoun "my" (*emoû*) of the MT *mal'ākî* ("my messenger") to a third-person pronoun "his (*autoû*) messenger." Here Rudolph (1976: 247) has observed this shift occurred for stylistic reasons. But note the lack of supporting manuscript evidence which leads Baldwin (1972a: 212) to conclude that the alteration "made by the LXX translators, who took the word to be a common noun . . . only serves to reinforce the originality of the MT." Further, Childs (1979: 492) rightly points out that if the Greek text is original at this point, "the alleged connection of the superscription with [Mal] 3:1 is no longer so obvious."[2]

---

reasonably clear with little reason to think of earlier sources or much later redaction." J. J. Collins (p. 214) agrees, acknowledging that the brevity of the book and the tight weave of its message place the burden of proof on those scholars predisposed to some form of tradition-history approach to Malachi. On the supposed redaction of Malachi see further I. C. 2. Unity below.

[2] In addition, Childs (1979: 493) has well argued that attempts by a later editor to connect the author of the anonymous prophecies with the promised messenger of 3:1 by means of the secondary insertion of *mal'ākî* in the superscription misunderstands the theological

By contrast to the traditions acknowledging "Malachi" as a title for Ezra the scribe, there is also later Jewish tradition that recognized Malachi as the prophet's proper name (b. *Meg* 15a) and remembered him, along with Haggai and Zechariah, as men of the great synagogue (b. *BBat* 15a; cf. 2 Esdr 1:40 where Malachi is listed among the Twelve Prophets). Likewise, others among the church fathers (e.g., Pseudo-Epiphanius [*PG* 43:411–12], Dorotheous of Gaza [*PG* 88:1654–64], and Hesychius of Jerusalem [*PG* 93:1367–68]) not only recognized Malachi as a proper name but also went so far as to accept the first century A.D. Jewish lore collected in the *Lives of the Prophets* (cf. *ABD* 5:502). This tradition stated that Malachi was a Levite from the village of Sopha or Sophira of Zebulun. Even further, it claimed he was honored among the Jewish people for his piety and meekness and that he was given the name Malachi because he was "fair to look upon." However, the lateness of these traditions has prompted most modern scholars to dismiss the fanciful stories as valueless.

Several recent commentators have espoused the view that *mal'ākî* is indeed a proper name (e.g., in chronological order: Rudolph [1976]; Kaufmann [1977: 446 n. 1]; Childs [1979]; Kaiser [1984]; Alden [1985]; Glazier-McDonald [1987a]; Verhoef [1987]; Deissler [1988]; and O'Brien [1990]). For a catalog of scholars endorsing the view that *mal'ākî* is to be interpreted as a proper noun predating Rudolph's (1976) seminal work, see Verhoef 1972: 9–16. Some even suggest *mal'ākî* is a contracted form of the name *mal'āk(iy)yāh(û)* (e.g., Rudolph [1976: 247]; Childs [1979: 493]; Glazier-McDonald [1987a: 28]; and Verhoef [1987: 156]). The construction is possible philologically, after the pattern of theophoric names such as:

'ăbî (2 Kgs 18:2)→'ăbiyyāh(û) (= "Yah[u] is my [divine] father," 2 Chr 29:1), and 'ûrî (Exod 31:2)→'ûriyyāh(û) (= "Yah[u] is my firebrand," 1 Chr 11:41).

For biblical examples of Hebrew "Yah/Yahu" names that follow the similar pattern of contraction, see Laetsch (1956: 507–8); cf. Glazier-McDonald (1987a: 28), and Verhoef (1987: 156).

However, names like *zākēr* (1 Chr 8:31; cf. *zĕkāryāh(û)*, 1 Chr 9:37) suggest an alternative pattern since the form contains no first-person (singular) pronominal suffix (although here the meaning "Yah(u) remembers" or "Remember, O Yah(u)!" seems more appropriate). Therefore, while Rudolph's *mal'āk(iy)yāh(û)* is linguistically defensible, it is nonsensical as a Hebrew proper name (i.e., "Yah(u) is my messenger"). Thus, while I concur with the viewpoint of Childs (1979: 493), Glazier-McDonald (1987a: 29), and others who have affirmed Rudolph's (1976: 247) assertion that *mal'ākî* be construed as a construct-genitive relationship rather than a nominative-predicate relationship, it seems better to render the name *mal'āk(?)yāh(û)* or *mal'ākyāh(û)* after the example of *zĕkāryāh(û)* (since the problem of the connecting vowel remains). The name *mal'ākî*

---

hope of Second Isaiah and "wreaks havoc with the entire message of the book." See further the NOTES and COMMENTS below on 3:1.

may then be translated "angel" or "messenger of Yah(u)" in the sense that the prophet was sent as a divine agent from Yahweh (cf. WO'C § 9.5.1b, c on the *genitive of agency* and the *genitive of authorship*).

Malachi is almost an anonymous figure in that little else is known about the prophet. Like Obadiah, the superscription to his oracles traces no genealogical heritage, so any biographical information about the prophet must be gleaned from deductions based upon the contents of his writings. Malachi's prophecies do betray a strong interest in the Temple, priesthood, and the system of sacrificial worship (cf. 1:6–13; 2:1–4, 8–9; 3:3–4, 6–11). However, he speaks as one observing that system from the outside (cf. 1:6; 2:2). He also possessed a knowledge of both the Deuteronomic (1:8; cf. Deut 15:21) and Priestly (3:10; cf. Num 18:21) legal traditions.

Malachi was clearly a person of considerable personal piety, grasping the import of Yahweh's holiness and the seriousness of personal and community sin before God (cf. 2:17–3:4, 6–7, 13–19 [4:1]). His staunch convictions against idolatry (2:10–12), easy divorce (2:13–16), and social injustice (3:5) were a throwback to the days of the preexilic prophets. That Malachi was a person of integrity and courage is seen in his bold upbraiding of the influential priestly class and the social elite (cf. 1:1–14; 2:1–4; 3:2–4). Yet, he evidences great compassion for his people in the words of assurance and encouragement that open and close his message. So much so that Mason (1990: 256) proffered, "Malachi especially reminds us that the greatest service a preacher can render his congregations is not only to warn and rebuke them, but to direct their faith and hope towards God."

Finally, Malachi demonstrates considerable continuity with the covenantal message of earlier Hebrew prophets. He understood the primacy of the internal attitude and motives of the heart over the external form of ritualism (1:9–13; 2:2–3; 3:16–18; cf. Amos 5:12–15, 21–24; Mic 6:6–8). The prophet also recognized that the blessing and curse of God were rooted in personal and corporate obedience or disobedience to the stipulations of Israel's covenant charter (3:16–21 [4:3]). More important, he understood that the demands of covenant included a righteous ethic, a code of behavior consistent with the nature and character of God, the covenant maker (3:5–7; cf. Zech 7:8–12). Here Weiser's (1961: 277) observation is still cogent: "The book of Malachi breathes the spirit of an original, genuinely prophetic personality."

By way of an epithet, not only was Malachi a throwback to the prophetic tradition of monarchical Israel and Judah, but the *MidrRab* (Freedman and Simon 1939: 315) implies that this prophetic office ceased with Malachi when it asserts that the holy spirit departed Israel with the death of the last prophets, Haggai, Zechariah, and Malachi.

I. C. 2. Unity

The Bible invites three approaches: the historical, the theological, and the literary (see D. Robertson [1976: 547]). The historical approach is generally associated with the *historical-critical* method. As one dimension of the discipline of biblical criticism, the historical-critical method constitutes an interpretive tool aiding the exegetical process as applied to biblical texts. Historical-critical analysis emphasizes the literary form of the pericope in question, the historical situation prompting the writing of the pericope, the meaning of the given text for author and original audience, and the cultural background from which the text emerged (Krentz [1975: 2]; cf. Hayes [1979: 84–120]). More specifically, the historical approach is usually equated with historical criticism. Broadly understood, historical criticism investigates the local historical factors shaping the biblical text in order to reconstruct original moments in the life of ancient Israel. The goal of historical criticism is the writing of "the history of Israel," a chronologically ordered narrative objectively interpreting the nature and relationship of biblical events (Soulen [1981: 88]).

The theological approach to OT/HB interpretation dominated Jewish and Christian biblical scholarship until the enlightenment. A theological reading of the Bible assumes the Old Testament (and New Testament for the Christian church) are sacred texts, divinely inspired and thus a unique record of God's self-disclosure in human history. More than a literary anthology, the OT/HB constitutes a religious canon. Historically, the church has appealed to these ancient Hebrew documents (primarily Christologically) as revealed word of God (cf. Bruce [1984: 566]). This sacred tract recounting salvation history and the human response of faith informed Christian belief, as well as liturgical and ethical practice (cf. Bright [1975: 10]). The "fourfold sense" of Scripture remained the authoritative paradigm for Christian interpretation from the patristic period through the middle ages (i.e., the literal sense or surface meaning of the text; the moral sense — the text practically applied to ethical theory and practice; the allegorical sense — analysis of the text yielding the distillation of Christian doctrine; and the anagogical sense or typological meaning; cf. Grant [1984: 83–91]).

The literary approach to the Bible is the most recent and perhaps the most controversial of the approaches to biblical literature. Unlike the literary (or source) criticism stemming from the historical-critical methodology (which analyzes the literary character of the biblical documents for the purpose of answering historical questions), the literary approach to the Bible assumes only that the Bible is a literary object portraying the human predicament (cf. D. Robertson [1977: 2–7]). Above all, the Bible is considered "classic" literature to be read and understood as the voice of human experience speaking urgently to us (Alter [1992: 23]). By way of approach, the literary critic employs any method that "works" with other literature (explaining D. Robertson's [1976: 547] assessment that literary critics employ "very different and even incompatible methodologies").

Eissfeldt (p. 442) represents the majority of scholars applying a historical-critical method in the analysis of Malachi when he remarked that literary problems are barely discernible in the book — only Mal 2:11–12 (or 2:11b–13) and 3:22–24 [4:4–6] raise suspicion of nongenuineness. Random voices have raised doubts concerning the authenticity of other texts in Malachi, notably the superscription (1:1; e.g., Coggins [1987: 73]; Mason [1977: 139]; and Schneider [p. 149]), the phrase *kōh 'āmar YHWH* ("so said Yahweh"; e.g., Blenkinsopp [1983: 240]), 1:11–14 (deemed a "universalist" intrusion upon the "particularist" thought of Malachi; e.g., Horst [1954: 261, 265]; and Elliger [1950: 178]; cf. Utzschneider

[1989: 31] on the thematic role of Mal 1:11–14 in the second disputation), and all or parts of 3:1–4 (where the shift to third-person narrative is disruptive, so Mason [1977: 153]; cf. Malchow [1984]; Redditt [1995: 154]). Additionally, although Baldwin (1972a: 215) affirms the originality of 2:15–16, she has conceded that the two verses evidence signs of tampering at an early stage "to make their meaning more palatable." Finally, some scholars dispute the placement of 3:6–12 contextually, splicing it with 1:2–5 to more logically connect the threat of judgment with the call to repentance (e.g., Sellin [1930: 611] — but note Sellin and Fohrer [1968: 469–70] where Fohrer rejects Sellin's editing; cf. Weiser [1961: 276–77] who inserted 3:6–12 after 2:1–16 to fashion a lengthy sermon of repentance).[1]

Today the theological approach to the Bible continues under the rubric of *canonical criticism*. According to Sanders (1984: xv), canonical criticism has as its focus "the function of the Bible as canon in the believing communities which formed and shaped it and passed it on to their heirs of today." For Sanders, the key issues are canonical process and canonical hermeneutics. This means understanding both the stability of canonical authority in the community of faith and the adaptability of canonical authority to new historical contexts.

Like Sanders, Childs (1979: 82) seeks a hermeneutical approach that permits "the Bible to be read as sacred scripture." Even though Childs disparages the label *canonical criticism*, he shares Sanders's concern for the process and function of canon in the community of faith. Likewise, both advocate reading the Bible as a literary whole, emphasizing the intrinsic theological significance of the biblical documents for the contemporary community of faith. However, two striking differences surface when comparing the canonical approaches of Sanders and Childs. First, Sanders (1984: xvii) freely admits to a mystical working of

---

[1]The work of Lescow (1990, 1993) provides an example of a more radical assessment of the integrity of the disputations of Malachi. Even though he admits to a unified and coherent literary structure for the book, he posits the book took shape in three stages (cf. the three-stage redaction proposed by Bosshard and Kratz [1990: 27]). Originally, these anonymous oracles were prophetic didactic discourses arranged in a tripartite pattern of speech, objection or rebuttal, and Torah instruction. During stage two the prophetic discourses were transformed into disputations by an unknown editor as a response to the crisis in worship facing the restoration community in Jerusalem. These supplemental expansions and annotations included the interrogative elements of the book and largely account for the prosaic form of the text. The third phase of redaction witnessed the addition of extensive glosses of a theological and cultic nature rooted in the Torah-based reforms implemented in postexilic Yehud (see further Redditt's [1995: 152–55] discussion of the "composite" oracles of Malachi evidencing "extensive editorial shaping").

Lescow's thesis is less than compelling for a number of reasons. Primary among them are his failure to fully account for the simple and direct character of Malachi's oracles (indeed, forty-seven of the book's fifty-five verses are framed as first-person addresses of Yahweh to the Hebrew restoration community; cf. Kaiser [1984: 18]) and the artificial distinctions he makes between the prophetic speech-forms of discourse and disputation, considering that the didactic function of "Torah-instruction" occurs in both types of prophetic speech-forms (calling in question the necessary literary evolution from one form to the next, cf. Brueggemann [1978: 42] who argues that the prophetic consciousness was always devoted to the pathos and passion of "covenanting"). On the supposed redaction of Malachi, see further I. C. 1. Authorship above.

God's Holy Spirit during every stage of the canonical process, while Childs (1979: 76) speaks more reticently (and rationally) of "God's activity" in Israel's history. Second, and more significantly, Childs (1979: 75–77) insists upon the authority of the final canonical form of the OT/HB as a completed process and an end product—normative scripture historically conditioned. Sanders (1984: 32), however, argues for the "open-endedness" of the OT/HB canon because the interpretive process adapting canonical documents to new situations continues even after the stabilization of a canonical tradition.

As to what all this means for Malachi, the canonical approach of Sanders reads the entire book as canonical text and interpretation from the postexilic period of Israel's history and may be read wholly as "Word of God by living persons in communities of faith." By contrast, the canonical approach of Childs distinguishes canonical text and later interpretation since the final canonical form of the OT/HB text occurred at some specific point in time. Thus Childs (1979: 489–90) recognizes (and in the case of Malachi summarily dismisses) that secondary accretions may occur in the biblical documents (e.g., 1:11–14; 2:11–12) and in the case of the appendixes (3:22–24 [4:4–6]) posits a later redactor (by contrast Bosshard and Kratz acknowledge only Mal 1:2–13, 1:14b–2:9, 2:13–16, and 3:6–12 as original to the first layer of a three-stage redaction of the book of Malachi).[2]

Typically, the literary approach treats biblical texts as whole documents, reads the documents in the form in which they have been received, utilizes literary terminology to describe the linguistic, grammatical, and rhetorical phenomena within the document, appreciates the literary artistry of the document, and recognizes the human dimension of the biblical literature. Four recent examples of a literary approach to Malachi may be cited: Wendland (a literary/structural analysis), Clendenen (a structuralist approach emphasizing discourse typology [1987, 1993]), Glazier-McDonald (1987a, a literary/poetic analysis; cf. the review of Malchow [1989] criticizing her refusal to acknowledge additions and emendations in the text of Malachi), and O'Brien (source/form critical analysis). All admit no secondary additions to the text of Malachi and read the document as a unified whole, including the superscription (1:1) and the appendixes (3:22–24 [4:4–6]).

The three traditional approaches to the OT/HB are not mutually exclusive, but the assumptions undergirding each approach do give rise to tensions that militate against their complementarity and insulate them as discrete interpretive methods. For instance, even though the historical approach champions the importance of biblical event(s) in the space-time continuum, ironically the *historic-*

---

[2]The historical critical technique known as tradition history or (less accurately at times) redaction criticism may also be classified as a theological approach to the biblical documents to the degree that it emphasizes the final edition of a biblical text, acknowledges the structural and literary unity of that biblical text, and identifies those theological motivations guiding that final redaction (e.g., Polzin [1980]; Rendsburg; and D. N. Freedman [1991]; cf. the three-stage redaction of Malachi, all predicated upon the book's place as the conclusion of the Book of the Twelve, proposed by Bosshard and Kratz [pp. 45–46] and Nogalski [1993b: 211]).

ity and *reliability* of the Bible are the casualties of the method (cf. Krentz [1975: 1–5]; Hayes [1979: 106–20]). Soulen (p. 88) cogently probes the value of a method (i.e., historical-critical) that excludes God from the historical process (when that was the worldview of the biblical writers). How is it possible to understand *unique* events in history by analogy? Further still, whose standard of *objectivity* determines what objectively verifiable common experience controls this "reductionist history"? Such are the perils facing the historical critic!

By contrast, though the literary approach reads whole texts as artifacts rather than the atomistic fragments read piecemeal by historical criticism, the method slights the Bible as history (e.g., Alter's [1981: 23–46] reading the OT/HB as "prose fiction"), minimizes the Bible as "sacred text" (i.e., what makes the Bible as literature any more authoritative than LaPierre's, *The City of Joy?*), equates the role of reader with the role of author (cf. McKnight [1988: 263–67] on the role of the reader in *imagining* and *actualizing* the biblical text in the post-modern setting), and yields no interpretive consensus (cf. the critiques of D. Robertson [1976: 549] and Barton [1984: 140–57, 180–97]). Alas, pitfalls await the "new critic" too!

Likewise, although the theological approach rightly emphasizes the place of the Bible as a "road map" for faith and practice in the religious community, the method must first come to grips with the idea of biblical *truth* (cf. Robertson's [1977: 11–13] discussion of theological vs. literary truth) and determine that segment of the community for which the truth is normative (cf. Sanders [1984: 15–16]; D. N. Freedman [1991: 2–4]) — not to mention endure the polemic of biblical academicians seeking to marginalize the theological trajectory by demeaning its adherents as uncritical and anti-intellectual "conservatives" (e.g., Krentz's [p. 3] caricature [quoting Blank] "of unenlightened orthodox zealots"; cf. Hayes [1979: 167–73]).

Despite these liabilities, all three exegetical trajectories are crucial to the analysis of the Bible. A balanced reading of what the Bible *meant* and *means* depends upon a methodology integrating the historical, literary, and theological approaches.

So then, this study of Malachi attempts a synthetic analysis of the book, combining the best of all three approaches to the Bible: the historical, literary, and theological (on "synthesis" in commentary writing, cf. Alter [1992: 131–52]). By way of interpretive method then, I distinguish between the text's *univalency* as determined by the intent and worldview of the original writer/s (and/or editor/s)rooted in a particular historical context and the *multivalency* of a given text established by later interpreters (cf. Polzin [1980: 207–8]; Sanders [1984: 22–24]). I also choose to read the documents of the Bible as whole literary units (cf. Gibson [1993: 105] on "final form" criticism), practicing that type of rhetorical criticism that emphasizes both the literary architecture and artistry as well as the human drama of the biblical literature (cf. Boadt [pp. 87–88]; Alter [1992: 23–24, 209–10]).

Theologically, I share Bright's (1975: 10) concern that the Bible be studied as "sacred scripture" and that both the "Old and New Testaments be accorded their rightful place in the church as the ground and norm of her preaching, and her supreme rule of faith and practice." However, I reject Sanders's (1984: 37) "celebration of pluralism" in the biblical canon since he undermines biblical authority by relativizing what orthodoxy means by "word of God." According to Sanders's deconstructionist hermeneutic, the canon is authoritative only for the individual of faith as that reader actualizes the documents(s) in the existential moment.[3]

Rather, I prefer to understand the Bible as normative Scripture that "no longer functions for the community of faith as a free-floating metaphor, but as the divine imperative and promise to a historically conditioned people of God whose legacy the Christian church confesses to share" (Childs 1979: 77). Finally, I align myself with those who opt to read Malachi in a larger literary context, namely the Haggai-Zechariah-Malachi corpus (e.g., Pierce [1984a/b]; Redditt [1995: 189–91]) and the Twelve Prophets (e.g., Schneider; Watts [1987a: 379–80]; D. N. Freedman [1991]).

I. C. 3. Genre

Gunkel's (1928: 59–60) division of the OT/HB into two broad literary classifications has implications for the study of Malachi. He determined that prose and poetry were the primary literary types in the HB. Subdivisions of poetical literary types included the prophetic oracular saying and specifically the sub-types of vision, prophetic oracle, discourse, threat or promise, invective, and exhortation. Much of the subsequent German scholarship on Malachi has treated the book as poetry, believing the oracles were originally cast in a poetic form (e.g., Elliger [1950: 177–78]; Horst [1954: 264–74]; and Frey [1963: 140–80]; cf. Nowack [1922: 392] and Marti's [pp. 456–58] reaction to Torrey [1898]).

By contrast, most British and American biblical scholars have traditionally understood the oracles of Malachi as a prose composition. This includes the more disparaging appraisal of J.M.P. Smith (1912: 4–5) who adamantly classified Malachi as prose and noted that "the element of beauty is almost wholly lacking . . . neither in spirit, thought, nor form, has it the characteristics of poetry." R. H. Pfeiffer (p. 614) simply says "Malachi is of slight . . . literary importance," while S. R. Driver (1922: 358) regarded Malachi more prosaic than the rest of the prophets. Gottwald (1962: 829) bluntly observed that Malachi contained no poetic lines. Others such as G. L. Robinson (p. 160), Bewer (1933: 258), R. L. Smith (1984: 301), and Verhoef (1987: 166–67) laud Malachi's terse and vigorous style as fresh, lively, and even hinting of poetic rhythm.

Statistical studies tracing the occurrence of so-called prose particles in Mal-

---

[3] Here I would challenge Sanders's use of the phrase "communities of faith" because everyone in the community cannot actualize the text in the same way, nor can they share the identical experience within any given "existential moment." Thus Sanders's *fluid* and *pluralistic* biblical canon could never speak authoritatively to an entire community — only to isolated individuals within that community. His language of pluralism, however, nicely accommodates the assortment of diversifiers who would confuse biblical *authority* with socio-political *empowerment* (e.g., Chittister). Because Sanders's canonical criticism stems from a blend of both *reader-response* and *deconstructionist* literary theories, the pertinent critiques in Walhout and Ryken (pp. 124–48, 172–98) prove helpful.

achi corroborate the view that Malachi is indeed a prose composition (cf. Hill [1992: 479–80]). According to the prose-particle counting method of Andersen and Freedman (1980: 57–66), Hebrew prose is characterized by a relatively high density of these prose particles (i.e., the relative pronoun 'ăšer, the object marker 'ēt/'et-, and the sign of the definite article ha[·]). Typically, the frequency of these prose markers is 15 percent or more of the total words in a given text. By contrast, the frequency of these prose markers in Hebrew poetry is much lower (nearer 5 percent or less of the total words in a given text). Analyzed from this perspective, Malachi on the whole yields a prose-particle frequency of more than 16 percent.[1]

In a similar study, Hoftijer traced the frequency of 'et syntagmemes (i.e., the DDO 'ēt/'et- and the word or word group following it) through most of the OT/ HB. He concluded (pp. 76–77) that Malachi demonstrated an 'et syntagmeme density comparable to that of prose narrative elsewhere in the MT.[2]

Recently, Glazier-McDonald (1987a: 6) has attempted "to defend a poetic interpretation of [Malachi's] prophecy" (cf. Lescow [1990] who posits that Malachi's disputations represent sermonic expansions of originally poetic instructions). She has outlined the text in an elaborate and imaginative poetic-verse structure, especially noting parallelism and chiasm. This is possible in part because she subscribes "to a more flexible definition of poetry" (p. 4). Glazier-McDonald's analysis of each section of Malachi's prophecy highlights basic poetic devices like parallelism, repetition, and assonance (p. 4), nonparallelism and

---

[1] Malachi 1 = 11.4% (24 of 210 words), chapter 2 = 15.4% (37 of 241 words), and chapter 3 = 20.4% (67 of 328 words). The prose-particle counts for the rest of the postexilic prophets yield these data: Haggai 1 = 23.5%, chapter 2 = 21.8%; Zechariah 1 = 19.6%, chapter 2 = 16.3%, chapter 3 = 18.9%, chapter 4 = 18.5%, chapter 5 = 23.4%, chapter 6 = 17.9%, chapter 7 = 20.1%, chapter 8 = 34.1%, chapter 9 = 3.5%, chapter 10 = 16.1%, chapter 11 = 24.8%, chapter 12 = 22.1%, chapter 13 = 22.2%, and chapter 14 = 29.1%; see further Hill (1982: 107–8). Note here that Sasson's (p. 162) analysis of the prose-particle distribution in Jonah corroborates the generalization that these markers are typical of Hebrew prose and atypical of Hebrew poetry. His study shows a prose-particle count of 15.3% for the narrative in Jonah, while the count for the poem in chapter 2 is but 3.7%.

[2] Hoftijer (pp. 76–77) counts 18 'et syntagmemes in Haggai and concluded that the book is comparable to narrative material; he isolated 54 'et syntagmemes in Zechariah 1–8 and 45 in Zechariah 9–14 and concluded that the 'et syntagmeme density of Zechariah corresponds to that of narrative material — except in Zechariah 9 where it agreed with poetic material; and Hoftijer uncovered 35 'et syntagmemes in Malachi, again concluding Malachi agreed with densities noted in OT/HB narrative material.

Specifically, Hoftijer (p. 28) observed that the Type A syntagmeme (i.e., the DDO in conjunction with a *transitive* verb — loosely understood) exhibits a high frequency in narrative (or prose); while the density of the Type B syntagmeme (i.e., the DDO in conjunction with an *intransitive* verb — loosely understood) is considerably lower in narrative (or prose). Malachi 1 contains 6 Type A and 2 Type B syntagmemes, whereas chapters 2 and 3 contain only Type A syntagmemes, 6 and 5 respectively.

In addition, Hoftijer (p. 57) has discerned narrative (or prose) material tends to yield a high ratio of Type A syntagmemes to Type D syntagmemes (i.e., the DDO functions as an objectifying complement), while poetic material tends to reverse this phenomenon. Malachi 1 shows a ratio of Type A to Type D syntagmemes at 6 to 4, in chapter 2 it is 6 to 3, and in chapter 3 it is 5 to 2 — each representative of narrative (or prose) material in the OT/HB.

asymmetry (p. 31), tension of opposites (p. 47), repetition of key words (p. 48), alliteration (p. 84), and thematic parallelism (p. 207). Unfortunately, she offers no controls for discriminating the use of these amorphous literary categories in poetic texts apart from prophetic or prose narrative texts in the OT/HB. Even a cursory reading of Alter (1981), Kikawada and Quinn, Rendsburg, and Alter and Kermode reveals parallelism, alliteration, assonance, lexical repetition, etc., are common to Hebrew prose and poetry alike. According to Muilenburg (p. 18), the Hebrew poets and prophets tap a common source of conventional rhetorical practice.

What then actually distinguishes a biblical text as *poetic?* Is it the density of these types of literary features employed in a given text? Or is it the utilization of a wide variety of such literary features in combination within a given text? Here I echo the sentiments of O'Connor (p. 51) who demurred: "Parallelism cannot cover the field of Hebrew poetry unless it is not only left undefined, but allowed to cover so many phenomena that it is undefinable." Similarly, those literary features cited by Glazier-McDonald as primary poetic markers of the text of Malachi (e.g., assonance, alliteration, and ambiguity) are in reality only secondary and non-structural poetic elements. Citing Gottwald, O'Connor (p. 142) claims that such *ornamentation* possesses marginal status in creating poetic structure. Most significantly, the application of O'Connor's (pp. 423–24) precisely defined linguistic features that characterize Hebrew poetic discourse (i.e., gross structure [the *line* and its relationship to other lines], fine structure [syntactic patterns and *troping* devices connecting lines], and *figuration* and *ornamentation* [features of coherence]) fail to establish Malachi as a poetic text.

In a separate study, Wendland (p. 108) has identified ten literary features or figures of speech for the purpose of demonstrating that Malachi's "prophecy evinces a wide variety of . . . *poetic* forms." Specifically, he catalogs the use of parallelism (1:6), chiasm (1:2; 3:11), simile and metaphor (4:1), synecdoche and metonymy (2:11), rhetorical question (1:2, 13), antithesis (1:11), exclamatory utterances (1:12; 3:9), graphic diction (2:3), verbal shifts (3:9), and closure (1:6). Although I can agree with Wendland when he suggests that some biblical texts are more poetic or prosaic than others, I disagree with his designation of the above-mentioned speech characteristics as *literary-poetic forms.* Like Glazier-McDonald, Wendland only confuses the issue of genre classification in the prophets by labeling rhetorical style *poetic.* A better approach, following Muilenburg, is to regard these literary devices as *rhetorical* forms evidencing consummate literary skill on the part of the author/editor and useful for exhibiting structural patterns in a select composition.

What does all this mean for the oracles of Malachi? First, the book of Malachi is not representative of the genre of Hebrew poetry. Second, the author of Malachi "undeniably demonstrates considerable artistic proficiency, a fluency which reflects a definite rhetorical purpose" (so Wendland [1985: 112]). Third, as Wendland has noted, appreciation of Malachi's elevated literary style enhances both our understanding of the book's macro and microstructure and the prophet's message (see I. C. 4. Structure below). Fourth, in keeping with the earlier studies of genre classification in the Minor Prophets by Andersen and Freedman (1980: 57–66) and Meyers and Meyers (1987: lxiii–lxiv; 1993: 29–32), Malachi must be formally understood as *oracular prose* (i.e., the literary texture of Malachi is a combination of prosaic and rhetorical features approaching poetic discourse but distinctive of prophetic style).

I. C. 4. Structure

Whether one labels Malachi's oracles as discussion, dialogue, or disputation, there is widespread agreement as to the structure of the speech form: a prophetic declaration followed by the hypothetical audience rebuttal and concluding with the prophet's refutation (see I. C. 5. Form below). However, the same cannot be said for the structure of the book itself.

A majority of interpreters discern six oracles in Malachi's prophecy, following E. Pfeiffer's (p. 554) analysis: 1:2–5; 1:6–2:9; 2:10–16; 2:17–3:5; 3:6–12; 3:13–21 [4:3]).[1] However, there is little consensus as to the organization and structure of these pericopes. For instance, J.M.P. Smith (1912: 3) observed that the book was a "well planned . . . and harmonious whole"; whereas Baldwin (1972a: 214) affirmed the essential unity of the book but recognized no "particular literary structure" and the "haphazard" treatment of topics. Others mark specific organization or structure within literary units but make little or no comment as to the relationship of the individual oracles to each other (e.g., Mason [1977]; Glazier-McDonald [1987a]; and Alden). Still others view the six disputations as heavily redacted "composite speeches" contrived only as a "literary device" for didactic purposes (cf. Redditt [1994: 241; 1995: 152–55]) or fashioned merely as a "literary bookend" for the corpus of the Twelve Prophets (cf. Nogalski [1993b: 211]).

The earliest attempts at outlining structure in the book of Malachi are the paragraph markings found in the later manuscript traditions of the Hebrew Bible. The Masoretes carefully transmitted textual divisions or paragraph breaks by means of the Hebrew letters *sāmek* and *pēh*. The *sāmek* (ס) at the end of a verse (leaving an open space between verses within the line) denotes the separation of small literary units (*pārāšâ sĕtûmâ*); while the *pēh* (פ) marks larger pericopes (indicated by leaving an entire line blank between the textual divisions, *pārāšâ pĕtûḥâ*). Although these paragraph markings are extant in manuscripts dating to the Middle Ages, they may well reflect an ancient literary tradition since similar conventions are attested in the Qumran texts (*ABD* 6: 397; cf. Würthwein [1979: 20–21]; and Tov [1992: 50–54]).

The Leningrad Codex (L, upon which the *BHK* and the *BHS* editions of the HB are based) discerns minor paragraph breaks (*sāmek*) in the book of Malachi beginning at 1:14; 2:17; 3:13; and 3:19 (on the Leningrad Codex, see Tov [1992: 46–47]). Major textual units (*pēh*) are identified beginning at 2:10; 2:13; and 3:22. The Aleppo Codex (A) divides the text of Malachi at the same junctures (on the Aleppo Codex, see Tov [1992: 46–47]). The literary structure of Malachi perceived by the Masoretes may be outlined as follows:

[1] Some scholars mark seven disputations in Malachi: Verhoef (1987: 162) divides 1:6–2:16 into two pericopes: 1:6–14 and 2:1–9; Kaufmann (1977: 437) regards the Appendix (3:22–24 [4:5–6]) as an original literary unit. Others identify but five, for example, Kaiser (1984: 17) combines 2:1–9 with 2:10–16 and 2:17–3:6 with 3:6–12 into single pericopes.

Pericope I: 1:1–2:9
    Subunit A: 1:1–13
    Subunit B: 1:14–2:9
Pericope II: 2:10–12
Pericope III: 2:13–3:21
    Subunit A: 2:13–16
    Subunit B: 2:17–3:12
    Subunit C: 3:13–18
    Subunit D: 3:19–21 [4:1–3]
Pericope IV: 3:22–24 [4:4–6]

The MT paragraph divisions do prove helpful to the discussion of literary structure in Malachi on at least three accounts. First, the partition of the book into three large literary units underscores the centrality of the covenant theme to the message of Malachi. Note that Pericope I addresses the relationship of the priesthood to Yahweh's covenant, while Pericope III highlights the relationship of the people to Yahweh's covenant. The pivotal Pericope II draws attention exclusively to Judah's agnosticism and treachery with respect to the ancient covenant agreement between Yahweh and his people. Interestingly, Pericope II nearly occupies the midpoint of the book of Malachi, considering that Pericope I consists of 320+ words and Pericope III consists of 380+ words. Second, these MT textual divisions confirm the importance of the phrase YHWH *ṣĕbā'ôt* as a marker that concludes a distinct literary unit (cf. 1:13; 2:12; and 3:12). Third, the complete two-line blank space separating 3:22–24 from 3:21 [ס] is strong evidence the Masoretes regarded these last three verses as an appendix to the book of Malachi (and the entire prophetic corpus?).

However, the MT paragraphing fails to fully unravel the literary structure of Malachi. For example, the first disputation (1:2–5) directed to the general populace of postexilic Yehud must be included as part of a subunit directed against the Levitical priesthood in the Masoretic schema. Likewise, the MT textual divisions are inconsistent in recognizing the significance of the phrase YHWH *ṣĕbā'ôt* as a structural clue in framing the disputations of Malachi's oracles. In fact, the form of the disputation is largely ignored in the MT paragraphing. This suggests, perhaps, that the Masoretes were motivated by more than sheer literary concerns in their structuring of the text of Malachi (note that even the call to repentance [3:6–12] is incorporated into a much larger literary unity [2:17–3:12]). Thus, although the MT paragraphing informs the macrostructure of the book's literary organization, it is necessary to look elsewhere for insights that disclose the microstructure of the oracles.

A more recent method for divining organization in biblical literature is the structuralist approach which highlights key-word links that join sections within a pericope or join one pericope to another. The prominent example here is the study of McKenzie and Wallace (pp. 558–60) that documents covenant terminology, which connects the oracles of 1:6–3:12 with the idea of covenant relationship presumed in 1:2–5 (cf. Kaiser's [1984: 118–37] syntactical analysis of grammatical structure in Malachi). It should be noted that key-word links may hint at the relationship of smaller literary units but may not contribute to the delineation of literary structure within the whole of the corpus. For example, Mal 3:22–24 [4:4–6] may be a secondary addition to the text (so Mason [1977: 159–62]) or original to the prophecy (so Glazier-McDonald [1987a: 243–70]), depending upon the predilection of terms emphasized.

More common to discerning the larger structure of Malachi is the thematic approach which seeks to relate the content of the prophet's six oracles to overarching theological ideas. Several major themes dominate the discussions here, including theology proper (i.e., Malachi as a theology of Yahweh), covenant relationship, religious purity and social justice, and eschatology. Specific examples of such thematic approaches to the literary arrangement of Malachi are outlined below and in section I. C. 7. Message. While thematic approaches to the structure of Malachi enhance the interpreter's understanding of the tone and message of the book, they may not fully address structure as it relates to literary form and sequence (e.g., see below Achtemeier's random appeal to various portions of Malachi in order to create a courtroom setting and a lawsuit format).

Of special interest is Pierce's (1984a) understanding of the Haggai, Zechariah, and Malachi corpus as a "narrative profile" of postexilic Jerusalem — a somber, even recusant portrait of a community in need of confession, repentance, and covenant renewal. Here thematic analysis is extended to all three postexilic prophets for the purpose of demonstrating that these books form a coherent and meaningful literary unity within the Minor Prophets. Noting historical, literary, and theological links, Pierce understands Malachi as "anticlimactic" in his Haggai-Zechariah-Malachi thematic schema because Malachi ends where Haggai begins: with a religious community in disarray.

Building upon Longacre's work, Clendenen (1987) offers an insightful variation of thematic structure in Malachi rooted in rhetorical criticism. Broadly speaking, Malachi exemplifies a *hortatory* discourse type of persuasive speech characterized by the essential features of problem, command, motivation, and authority (of the speaker). Unlike the careful *notational* structure of narrative, hortatory structure possesses "no definite order . . . they [i.e., speeches] may be, as they are in Malachi, repetitive and recursive" (Clendenen [1987: 6]). Clendenen (p. 7) has observed the following hortatory structure in Malachi in three chiastic movements or embedded discourses:

First Movement: Priests Exhorted to Honor Yahweh	1:2–2:9
Motivation: Yahweh's Love	1:2–5
Problem: Failure to Honor Yahweh	1:6–9
Command: Stop Vain Offerings	1:10
Problem: Profaning Yahweh's Name	1:11–14
Motivation: Results of Disobedience	2:1–9
Second Movement: Judah Exhorted to Faithfulness	2:10–3:6
Motivation: Spiritual Unity	2:10ab
Problem: Faithlessness	2:10c–14
Command: Stop Acting Faithlessly	2:15–16
Problem: Complaints of Yahweh's Injustice	2:17

Motivation: Coming . . . Judgment	3:1–6
Third Movement: Judah Exhorted to Return to Yahweh	3:7–24 [4:6]
Command: Return to Yahweh with Tithes	3:7–10a
Motivation: Future Blessing	3:10b–12
Problem: Complacency in Serving God	3:13–15
Motivation: The Coming Day	3:16–21 [4:3]
Command: Remember the Law	3:22–24 [4:4–6]

Clendenen's rhetorical outline of Malachi does prove helpful in the analysis of literary structure in the book. Identifying the oracles as *hortatory* discourse clarifies the nature and purpose of the book's disputational format, since hortatory discourse represents a behavioral discourse style with a futuristic orientation. The division of the text into three movements also has the effect of heightening the chiastic arrangement of subject matter in Malachi's oracles (Lescow [1992: 238] parcels the book into three literary units but preserves the traditional paragraph divisions of the six oracles; cf. Bosshard and Kratz [1990: 27] on the three-stage redaction of Malachi as well). The issue of authority (of the speaker) in hortatory discourse contributes to an explanation of the repetition of [*kōh*] *'āmar YHWH šĕbā'ôt* ("so Yahweh of Hosts has said"). Lastly, subdividing the oracles into problem, command, and motivation increases our appreciation of the internal coherence of Malachi's message.

Clendenen's study, however, poses certain problems as well, especially in disrupting the natural relationship of the declaration, rebuttal, and refutation pattern of the catechetical disputations. Similarly, the outline forces the interpreter to ignore the standard division of the fourth disputation (2:17–3:5) for the sake of thematic movement and unity. (Interestingly, had Clendenen retained the normative division of the fourth disputation and excised the concluding appendixes, each of the movements then begin and end with the prophetic motivation.) Finally, Clendenen's preconvictions about the unity of Malachi's prophecy forces an unnatural understanding of the third movement in that it breaks the logical discourse pattern of the previous two movements, both ending with the motivation. Rather than underscoring the originality of Mal 3:22–24 [4:4–6], the placement of this "dangling" and "general" command (note all other commands are behavior specific) in Clendenen's rhetorical outline suggests just the opposite.

Several attempts at identifying a treaty or covenant structure in Malachi have been forwarded over the years, including Baldwin (1972a: 214, 216) who acknowledged "covenant" as a fundamental theme in Malachi and recognized a logical progression in subjects from election and privilege to judgment. Coggins (p. 77) also isolates a legal background for Malachi's oracles, noting the similarities of 1:6–2:9 with the *rîb* pattern, but asserting that "it would be impossible to reconstruct anything like a complete 'lawsuit' from Malachi." Verhoef (1987: 179–84) suggested that the book of Malachi loosely employed the suzerain treaty structure as a systematic principle for unifying the oracles (e.g., preamble = 1:1; historical prologue = 1:2–5; stipulations = 1:6–14, 2:1–9, 2:10–16, 3:6–12, 3:13–21 [4:3]; witnesses = Yahweh himself in 3:5; and blesings and curses = 2:17–3:5, 3:13–21 [4:3]).

Achtemeier (1986: 172) takes the covenant theme a step further, stating that "the Book of Malachi has been cast by its anonymous prophet in the form of a court case, tried before the priest in the temple, with the prophet playing the role of the priest in his imagination." She notes the book's theme of covenant relationship and the role reversal of the plaintiff (from Israel to Yahweh) in support of her thesis. Likewise, the legal setting conditions the question-and-answer format of the book. Achtemeier's sketchy understanding of Malachi's structure may be arranged [and in some cases reconstructed] in this order:

Malachi as a Legal Proceeding in a Court Setting
  I. Yahweh as Defendant
    A. Charges Filed by the Plaintiff Judah
      1. Yahweh has not loved Israel (1:2–5)
      2. Yahweh has neglected covenant promises (2:17–3:6)
  II. Role Reversal — Judah as Defendant
    A. Charges Filed by the Plaintiff Yahweh
      1. Judah has defiled the liturgy (1:6–14)
      2. Judah's priests are corrupt (2:1–9)
      3. Judah has profaned the marriage covenant (2:10–17)
      4. Judah has violated Yahweh's Covenant (3:5–7)
      5. Judah has robbed God of his tithe (3:8–15)
  III. Verdict of the Jury
    A. Yahweh Innocent (3:16)
    B. Affirmation of the Righteous (3:17–21 [4:3])
  IV. Final Remonstrance by Priest-Judge to Obey Mosaic Law (3:22 [4:4])
  V. Concluding Promise of Divine Mercy and Love (3:23–24 [4:5–6])

Although Achtemeier's understanding of Malachi as a "court case" addresses the macrostructure of the prophecy and establishes the "legal" tone of the book, one particular oracular covenant form has implications for the microstructure of Malachi. The *lawsuit* oracle is a stylized literary form used to depict a legal controversy between Yahweh and his covenant people Israel. Huffmon (pp. 285–86), summarizing the analysis of Gunkel and Begrich (pp. 329, 364–65), has outlined two basic lawsuit or *rîb* oracular formulas. The first includes

  I. A description of the scene of judgment
  II. The speech of the plaintiff
    A. Heaven and earth appointed judges
    B. Summons to the defendant (or judges)
    C. Address in the second person to the defendant
      1. Accusation in question form to defendant
      2. Refutation of the defendant's possible arguments
      3. Specific indictment

An alternative *rîb* pattern may be the following:

  I. A description of the scene of judgment

II. The speech by the judge
    A. Address to the defendant
        1. Reproach (based on the accusation)
        2. Statement (usually in the third person) that the accused has no
           defense
    B. Pronouncement of Guilt
    C. Sentence (in second or third person)

Huffmon (pp. 294–95) discerned two distinct forms or types of lawsuit oracles in the HB/OT. He described the first as *divine council lawsuits*, which "involve judicial proceedings between Yahweh and the various foreign nations and gods." The second, *covenant lawsuits*, specifically indict Israel for breach of covenant with Yahweh. According to Huffmon, these oracles often make appeal to the natural elements, the covenant witnesses, sometimes include a historical prologue, and are characterized by the distinctive introductory formula "Hear . . ."

Not long afterward, Harvey (1962: 181–88) identified parallels between the biblical prophetic lawsuit oracles and the prosecution of treaty violators in ANE sacral law. He offered a basic five-point outline of the *rîb* formula, which included an introduction (with an appeal to "hear" and an appeal to the natural elements), the interrogation, indictments (focusing on breach of covenant and recalling Yahweh's favor and Israel's ingratitude), declaration of guilt (reminding the accused of the futility of reparation through ritual), and the threat of total destruction.

Later Harvey (1967: 66) refined his understanding of the prophetic lawsuit structure and identified an incomplete *rîb* pattern in Mal 1:6–2:9 and outlined the text in the following fashion:

Question (1:6)
Indictment (1:7–9)
Cross-examination (1:10a)
Declaration of guilt (1:10b)
Threats and condemnation (2:1–9)

Harvey (1967: 53–55) regarded the prophet's (implicit) call for the Levitical priesthood to change their ways (2:2, 6–7) as a sort of ultimatum common to the close of Type B *rîb* oracles (i.e., the declaration of positive conditions necessary for the restoration of covenant relationship as opposed to the threat of destruction characteristic of the Type A *rîb* oracle). Also, Harvey's approach affirms the covenant theme of Malachi, and his connection of the indictment with the cross-examination also helps explain the question-answer format of the disputation speech (1967:67).

Most recently, O'Brien (1990: 63–64) employs Harvey's analysis of Mal 1:6–2:9 as a template for the entire book of Malachi. She compresses each of Malachi's oracles into the *rîb* structure of covenant lawsuit, acknowledging that the prophet "distinctively shaped this tradition" (1990: 79). The oracles are related only in that they represent a series of specific violations by Israel against

Yahweh and his covenant. This *rîb* form outline of Malachi is organized as follows:

I. Prologue (1:2–5)
II. Accusations
    A. First Accusation (1:6–2:9)
        1. Preliminaries   1:6a
        2. Interrogation   1:6b
        3. Indictment   1:7–10a
        4. Declaration of Guilt   1:10b–14
        5. Ultimatum/Punishment   2:1–9
    B. Second Accusation (2:10–16)
        1. Preliminaries   2:10a
        2. Interrogation   2:10b
        3. Indictment   2:11
        4. Declaration of Guilt   2:12
        5. Further Indictment   2:13–14
        6. Ultimatum/Warning   2:15–16
    C. Third Accusation (2:17–3:5)
        1. Indictment   2:17
        2. Ultimatum/Promise   3:1–5
    D. Fourth Accusation (3:6–12)
        1. Preliminaries   3:6
        2. Indictment   3:7a
        3. Ultimatum/Promise   3:7b
        4. Indictment   3:8–9
        5. Promise   3:10–12
    E. Fifth Accusation (3:13–21 [MT 4:3])
        1. Indictment   3:13–15
        2. Historical Account   3:16–18
        3. Ultimatum/Promise   3:19–21 [4:1–3]
III. Final Admonition (3:22 [4:4])
IV. Final Ultimatum (3:23–24 [4:5–6])

O'Brien's use of the lawsuit form as a literary grid for Malachi's prophecy does confirm the obvious — the covenant and legal context of the oracles. Concurring with Brueggemann (1968: 21), I would agree that the Hebrew prophets often applied covenant traditions to new circumstances. However, as McCarthy (1972: 78–79) has cautioned, the exact relationship of lawsuit to covenant remains ambiguous, and the basis for "the specifically *covenantal* character of the lawsuit is rather narrow."

Malachi does not contain the classic features of the *rîb* oracle (i.e., the call to "Hear!", the appeal to natural elements, etc.), nor does Malachi address the basic issue of the covenant lawsuit — namely idolatry. The superficial nature of O'Brien's *rîb* outline of Malachi is further evidenced by the lack of consistency in identifying lawsuit features (e.g., the accusation and interrogation of 1:2–5 are considered "historical prologue" to force an analogy to the treaty form parallel). Likewise, the series of "accusations" yield no coherence of form or continuity of legal procedure (due in part to O'Brien's indiscriminate application of Harvey's [1967: 44] complete *rîb* structure to a text identified by Harvey [1967: 66] as possessing an incomplete *rîb* pattern). Finally, the lawsuit outline blurs (if it does not ignore altogether!) the careful three-part structure of a recognized speech form dominant in the oracles — notably the disputation.[2]

By way of summary, I propose a "hybrid" structure for the book of Malachi derived from a synthesis of salient features gleaned from the outlines presented in the foregoing discussion. The outlines of Malachi offered above in conjunction with the translation of Malachi reflect these conclusions (see OUTLINES and TRANSLATION above).

First, Harvey, Achtemeier, O'Brien, and others are correct to accentuate the covenant context and legal tone and setting of Malachi's oracles. However important this covenant theme may be to the interpretation of the book, specific treaty and lawsuit forms within the prophecy are too ambiguous and ill-defined to be utilized as a paradigm for outlining literary structure in Malachi. (I suspect that the catechetical nature of Malachi's oracles means we should look for structural patterns analogous to late Hebrew wisdom tradition and didactic method in post-exilic Judaism — not formal treaty and lawsuit structures.)[3]

---

[2]The integrity of the covenant lawsuit form itself is suspect, as Boston (p. 199) noted, the variety in usage precludes its association with any specific form. Others like Horst (1954: 260–91) and Gemser (1955) have explained the form of the covenant lawsuit by appealing to ordinary legal procedures common to the prophetic milieu. Thus I side with McCarthy (1972: 79) who questioned the prophetic use of covenant traditions only in connection with treaty forms and asserted, "They [i.e., the OT prophets] apply the analogy of ordinary legal procedure in most of their contentions with a backsliding Israel."

[3]Cf. Whedbee who concluded that Hebrew wisdom tradition shapes the prophecies (especially indictment and judgment!) of Isaiah in a complementary fashion (earlier Boston [p. 202] noted in general "that the line between prophet and wise man must not be drawn too sharply"). What Whedbee (p. 148) has argued for the prophet Isaiah, one who was able to combine religious devotion, political perspective, and prophetic vision with "the wise man's empirical assessment," I contend was true for the Hebrew prophetic school in general. In this regard Van Leeuwen (1990: 297–98) admits nexus between the Hebrew prophets and the language, form, and idea of formal wisdom literature; yet he readily capitulates to those who deny that the prophets were sages in any technical sense, despite his contention that courtiers and counselors were expected to be wise (p. 306). How much wiser might the Hebrew prophets have been expected to be in order to establish credibility and gain a hearing as religious and political "outsiders"?

Gese (in Davies and Finkelstein [1984: 211]) has conjectured that Hebrew wisdom during the Persian period had "become a theological force which acquires a stronger and stronger connection with the Israelite traditions of revelation." It is only logical to assume that what Crenshaw (1969: 130) identified as the *paideia* of wisdom (i.e., its curriculum and pedagogy) also developed new strategies during the Persian period. The same "utter realism and healthy skepticism" Crenshaw attributed to Qoheleth has surfaced in Malachi (1985: 613). Brueggemann correctly isolates the rhetorical question (e.g., Job 28:12) as the literary and pedagogical bridge between the *disruption of prophecy* and the *discernment of wisdom* because such instruction is both dialogical and dialectical (1982b: 71–76; cf. Petersen [1995: 31–32] who suggests that the "diatribe-like" disputations of Malachi provide

Second, the integrity of the recognized speech form of the disputation must be preserved in the microstructure of Malachi's oracles (declaration, rebuttal, and refutation).

Third, stressing the interrogative nature of the prophetic assertion and hypothetical audience rebuttal demonstrates the recursive progression of Malachi's message and the book's place in the larger structure of the Haggai-Zechariah-Malachi corpus. Interestingly, Adamson (p. 805) traced the origin of the disputations in Malachi to a source deeper than the rhetorical method of the writer, suggesting that the form may have been rooted in "the protesting and questioning cries of the hecklers, when he first delivered his message on the streets."

Fourth, I affirm the traditional division of Malachi into six catechetical disputations. I view the initial disputation (1:2–5) as a prefatory speech establishing the context (covenant relationship with Yahweh), tone (judgment), and style (hortatory discourse) of the oracles. I regard the appendixes of Mal 3:22–24 [4:4–6] as secondary additions to the oracles.

Fifth, given the parallels observed by Clendenen in Malachi with the hortatory discourse type of persuasive speech, any attempt to outline the structure of Malachi must acknowledge the deliberate inversion or chiastic arrangement of subject matter and the importance of the speaker's authority for determining the boundaries of the disputations (i.e., specifically the repetition of [kōh] 'āmar YHWH ṣĕbā'ôt).

I. C. 5. Form

Broadly speaking, Malachi's oracles may be considered exemplars of Westermann's *judgment speech against the nation* category in that they accuse, indict, and announce judgment (1991: 169–76). More precisely, the form of Malachi's oracles may be linked to Westermann's *legal-procedure* and *disputation* prophetic speech formulations. Both are considered variant speech forms borrowed from the judicial-speech pattern (or trial speech; cf. March [1974: 168]). The legal-procedure prophetic speech form is a divine indictment, which includes threat of judgment without introduction by a messenger formula (cf. Mal 3:5). The disputation speech pits the prophet against an opponent and features the prophet's citation of the opponent's polemical response to the prophetic word of judgment and concludes with the prophet's refutation of that polemical response (e.g., Isa 28:14–19; Mic 2:6–11; Jer 8:8–9; Ezek 11:14–17; cf. Graffy's catalog of OT/HB disputations, pp. viii–ix). According to Patterson (p. 303), "The desired effect in both the covenant lawsuit and disputation speeches is to leave the opponent devoid of further argumentation and resigned to the divine decision."[1]

---

a clue to the social milieu of the prophet, because the diatribe was rooted in schools and pedagogical discourse in other cultural settings).

[1] Westermann (1969: 18) traced the origin of the disputation to the psalmic lament, which "had acquired the status of the vehicle best adapted to expressing the worshiping community's circumstances." The disputation emerged as the prophetic response to community complaint because "the disputations . . . look to the future and inveigh against the weariness and despair" of a community looking backwards. Interestingly, Carroll (1979: 168–

Originally, Gunkel identified the disputation (*Streitgesprach*) as a derived speech form of the prophetic invective resulting from conflicts in opinion between the prophet and his constituency (1963: 37). Gunkel maintained that the expression of divergent opinions between the prophet and his contemporaries was integral to understanding the prophet's message. He also stressed that this change in the oracular style of the writing prophets arose specifically out of the need to renounce those raising objection to the prophetic instruction. Over the years scholarly opinion has ranged from Hermisson's (pp. 665–68) denial of the disputation as a literary genre to the precise strictures imposed by Graffy (p. 105) upon the literary form of the disputation.[2] Murray (p. 99) has attempted to avoid the extremes by marking the disputation according to three constitutive elements: thesis, counterthesis, and dispute. Even though this outline may not be obvious in the rhetorical surface structure, Murray declares that the presence of these three elements in the logical deep structure of a text signals the literary form of *disputation*.

Following Gunkel's lead, E. Pfeiffer (1959: 554–56) understood the book of Malachi as a later development of the disputation speech-form. He proposed that Malachi contained six disputational speeches: 1:2–5; 1:6–2:9; 2:10–16; 2:17–3:5; 3:6–12; and 3:13–21 [4:3] (with 2:11–12 and 3:22–24 [4:4–6] regarded as secondary additions). Pfeiffer then outlined a three-part structure for the disputations in Malachi, consisting of an opening statement (*Behauptung*), an objection (*Einrede*), and an explanation (*Begrundung*; see further Graffy's [pp. 15–17] critique of Pfeiffer).

Variations of this form-critical understanding of Malachi's oracles are numerous, yet they generally acknowledge that disputation characterizes the style of the book. For example, Mason (1977: 136) described Malachi's distinct style as that of "questions and answers" or "prophetic dispute" and has suggested that the book reflects a typical example of Second Temple preaching (1982: 150; cf. Dentan and Sperry [1956: 1119] and Redditt [1995: 152] on the disputations as "literary device"). Ackroyd (1979: 327) has noted that the question-and-answer style is well suited to the exposition of earlier biblical materials applied to contemporary contexts. This question-and-answer formula has prompted Bennet (p. 379) to dub Malachi "the Hebrew Socrates." Others prefer to label Malachi's style as "cate-

---

72) argued that the shift in prophetic style after the exile was a result of the failure of prophecy in that the oracles promising national salvation never materialized. But Mason (1982: 142) has countered that the shift in the prophetic paradigm during the postexilic period was due to the successes of the earlier prophets in that the judgment of the exile confirmed their message and gave the community the hope of salvation in the future.

[2]Graffy restricts the identification "disputation speech" exclusively "to those texts where an opinion of the speakers is explicitly reported by the prophet and refuted by him" (p. 23). However, in summarizing the disputation speech form, Graffy falls victim to the same criticism he made of E. Pfeiffer in identifying the disputation speech by tone and purpose — not literary structure, when he concludes that the disputation is an encounter between the prophet and the people "in which the prophet meets the people where they stand . . . the disputation speech . . . confronts the inadequacies of man's opinions. The prophet's word comes to transform the hearts of the people . . ." (p. 129; cf. p. 16). This is precisely what occurs in the book of Malachi!

chetical" because the question-and-answer format of the oracles has a focused didactic purpose ("a mini-catechism of the covenant," so Boadt [1984: 464]; cf. Fischer; and Braun [1977]).

Still others, seeking to clarify the exact nature of Malachi's speech form, have opted for descriptors such as "discussion" or "dialogue." Here Boecker has supplanted the term "disputation speech" (*Disputationsworte*) with "discussion speech" (*Diskussionworte*), arguing that Malachi's oracles seek to persuade the audience to adopt a new position by engaging in dialogue — not to dispute their words (p. 79; cf. Adamson [p. 805] who traces the origin of Malachi's dialogues to the prophet's exchange with hecklers in the streets; here Mason [1990: 236] exaggerates Fischer's claims that Malachi represents stenographer-type reports of actual debates between the prophet and his audience).

This understanding of Malachi's speech form as discussion speech has been supported by Wallis (1967: 232) and refined by Graffy (p. 16) who argues that Malachi redefines the form of the classical disputation speech because the opening words "are of God or the prophet, not of the people." Rather than verbatim accounts of genuine debates, Rudolph (1976: 250) suggests that the disputations of Malachi represent the gist of a prophet's confrontation with his audience (cf. Petersen's [1995: 31] understanding of the oracles as "one-party diatribe"). By appealing to a later redactor who expanded the original didactic discourse of Malachi and stylized the prophecy into disputation speeches, Lescow (1990) has it both ways, identifying the disputation as *Streitreden* ("disputation-discourse") couched in a format like that of a dialogue or formal debate (thesis, demonstration of thesis, and affirmation of thesis; cf. Lescow's (1993) assessment of the speeches of Malachi as *kommunikativen Handlungspiels* ["communicative narrative"], sermonic expansions of originally poetic instructions).

Some, like G. L. Robinson (p. 161) and Freeman (1968: 348) have typified the form of Malachi as "didactic-dialectic," while Holtzmann (p. 3) identified the speech form as "casuistic-dialectic." Finally, Kodell (p. 95), Wolf (p. 59), Hendrix (pp. 468–70), Verhoef (1987: 162–63), and Petersen (1995: 34) agree in principle with Long's assessment of Malachi as "rhetorical dialogue" (1971: 135 n. 29).[3]

Glazier-McDonald (1987a: 21) is quite right to reject the identification of Malachi's speech form as "discussion" or "dialogue," as posed by Boecker and others, noting that discussion implies a deliberate recitation, debate, and analysis of alternative opinions (usually amicably). In addition, dialogue implies conversation between two or more parties. Neither is true for the oracles of Malachi. The prophet contests the stance of his audience toward Yahweh's covenant. More than persuade, Malachi disputes the position of the people by calling their arguments into question and challenging their conclusions. Finally, the oracles do

---

[3]On the identification and refinement of the disputation speech in OT/HB genre study, see the extensive discussion in Graffy (pp. 2–23). Graffy rejects the speeches of Malachi as representative of the genre of disputation speech as he defines the literary form. He contends that the purpose of the speeches in Malachi is to "convince the listeners of the initial stated point, not to reject the listeners' quoted opinion" (p. 22). Graffy offers no alternative label for the speech form as used in Malachi.

not represent examples of dialogue in the formal sense because the audience response is offered only hypothetically in the disputation framed by the prophet himself.[4]

E. Pfeiffer (p. 568) has correctly observed that Malachi represents a later development of the disputation speech form, in fact, the final expression of the form according to Westermann (1964: 125–26). Perhaps better suited to the study of Malachi is March's more generic understanding of the disputation as essentially "the answering of implied or expressed charges made against God by his people or against the prophet" (p. 168). The disputation speech more broadly defined properly focuses emphasis on the confrontational nature of prophetic ministry and the pathos of the prophetic message (as discerned by Heschel [2:1–11] and Brueggemann [1978: 44–61]).

Exactitude of definition notwithstanding, I concur with a majority of scholars who identify the literary form of Malachi as "disputation speech" (e.g., Baldwin [1972a: 213–14]; Blenkinsopp [1983: 240]; R. L. Smith [1984: 300]; Wendland [1985: 112]; Glazier-McDonald [1987a: 20–21]; Deissler [1988: 316]; Gottwald [1985: 510]; G. L. Klein [1987: 27]; Murray [1987: 111–12]; Redditt [1995: 152]). Further, I subscribe to the majority view that these disputation speeches were original to the prophet and not the product of clever reshaping contrived by one (or more) later redactors (e.g., Lescow [1993]; Redditt [1995: 152–55]), as there are no compelling reasons to jettison this traditional understanding of Malachi's composition (see 2. Unity above). Finally, I also agree with those scholars who regard the book as a catechism on covenant relationship with Yahweh. However, for the sake of simplicity, this study throughout will designate the prophetic speech form of Malachi only as "disputation."[5]

---

[4]Westermann (1964: 124–34) has refused to understand the disputation speech as a genre, given the heterogeneous nature the speech form demonstrates in the OT/HB. The expression "speech form" remains the most useful designation for this literary feature. Westermann (1964: 125) also attempted to distinguish between the *Disputationswort* (disputations reporting the exchange of both parties by means of direct speech) and *Bestreitung* (disputations in which the speech of the opposing party is reported by the speaker). Graffy (p. 9) prefers the terms "disputation" or "dialogue disputation" for these two types of disputations, ostensibly to trim the overgrowth of technical jargon utilized in genre study of the Bible. Admittedly, this distinction between the two types of disputations is useful, especially in comparative genre studies.

Despite the imprecision, however, I have opted to understand Malachi as "disputation" even though the prophet does not necessarily report the opposition speech by means of direct quotation. The translation "dialogue disputation" for *Bestreitung* both compromises the confrontational character of the disputation speech in prophetic ministry and confuses the issue of literary form by connoting that the oracles of Malachi are "dialogue" as Boecker has argued. This same criticism may be applied to Lescow's (1990, 1993) analysis of Malachi's speeches as well.

[5]I also agree with the assessments by Freeman, Holtzmann, G. L. Robinson, and Murray of Malachi's speech form as "dialectical" in that the prophet's oracles represent a logical and systematic progression of instruction on covenant relationship with Yahweh, beginning with Yahweh's love for all Israel, moving to the priority of genuine worship and the proper response of service (i.e., social justice), and concluding with Yahweh's covenant love for the believing remnant.

I. C. 6. Literary Features

Longman (pp. 67–68) has defined literature "as an act of communication between *author* and *reader* through a *text*." The analysis of literary features in a text serves "to describe not only what the text says, but also how it conveys the message" (Kikawada [1977: 67]). My understanding of the literary features present in Malachi's prophecy reflects the influence of the methodological approach of Muilenburg known as *rhetorical criticism*. In response to the inadequacies of form criticism, Muilenburg proposed the analysis of the formal literary features of a composition for the purpose of identifying structural patterns that ordered the work into a unified whole. He was also concerned with noting authorial integrity and creativity within the composition so as to recognize the unique and personal dimensions of the literature and better trace the development of the writer's argument (cf. Mack [1990: 9–17] for an overview of the rise of rhetorical criticism in biblical studies).

Below I have assembled a representative catalog of literary devices or rhetorical features observed in Malachi (by a variety of biblical scholars committed to a *rhetorical* reading of the book):

a) alliteration — Glazier-McDonald (1987a: 84) notes consonantal repetition in 2:10, 11, 12, 14;

b) anacoenosis (or common cause) — the appeal to others who have interests in common or share a common cause, cf. 1:6 ("If I am [your] father, where is my honor?");

c) anthropomorphism — examples of ascribing human characteristics to God, include: the "greatness" of God (1:14), God "sitting" (3:3), God as a "witness" (3:5), and God "opening" doors/windows (3:10);

d) chiasm — Wendland (p. 109) cites examples of inverted parallelism in 1:2; 3:11; cf. his more extensive chiastic structures for each of the disputations (pp. 116–19);

e) disputational style — combative dialogue structured in the form of a declaration, followed by a refutation, and a concluding rebuttal, cf. letter (i) below and especially 4. Structure above;

f) ellipsis — the deliberate omission of one or more words that are obviously understood but that must be supplied to make a construction grammatically complete, as in the case of the question "Why [doesn't he]?" posed in 2:14 (assuming the acceptance of offerings mentioned in 2:13);

g) encomium — Malachi uses this lyrical praise of an abstract quality or general character trait to indict the priests when he contrasts the "ideal" priest with those priests who are his contemporaries (cf. 2:4–9);

h) foil — the storyteller often makes use of a striking contrast to emphasize key elements or significant characters in the story, like Malachi's foil of Jacob/ Esau (1:2–5) and Yahweh/foreign gods (2:10–12);

i) hortatory style — denoted by terse sentences and direct speech (forty-seven of the book's fifty-five verses are first-person addresses by Yahweh) and including the notion of "recursiveness" (i.e., Malachi's oracles evidence congruency in that they refer to themselves; cf. Hendrix, and see 4. Structure above);

j) hyperbole — conscious exaggeration for effect, more to convey emotional truth than factual truth (cf. the extent of Yahweh's judgment according to the prophet in 3:19 [4:1], ". . . leave them neither a root nor a branch");

k) intertextual echo — e.g., Malachi's denunciation (and mockery?) of the priesthood by direct or veiled reference to the priestly blessing of Num 6:23–27 (see Alter and Kermode [1987: 229–30]);

l) irony — this expression of thought in a form naturally conveying the opposite intent nears sarcasm in 1:9, "And now, entreat the favor of the God, so that he may be gracious to us!";

m) metaphor — Wendland (p. 109) notes an example of this direct comparison in Mal 3:21 [4:3], ". . . indeed they will be ashes beneath the soles of your feet";

n) metonymy — this figure of speech substituting a word or phrase for a similar expression occurs in Mal 1:2, 3, where the ancestor's name (i.e., "Jacob, Esau") represents his posterity; or Mal 2:12, ". . . the daughter of a strange El" (= "idolatrous women");

o) panegyric appellation or the formal encomium, "God of Israel," in Mal 2:16;

p) personification — as in ascribing human capabilities to "the day of Yahweh," Mal 3:19 [4:1];

q) pseudo-dialogue — hypothetical construction of dialogue between parties (as one component of the disputational style), "'I have loved you,' Yahweh has said. But you have said, 'How have you loved us?'" (1:2);

r) rhetorical question — according to Wendland (pp. 109–10) the rhetorical question was among the stock literary devices of the Hebrew prophets, and Malachi often puts such questions in the mouth of Yahweh (e.g., 1:2, "Surely Esau was Jacob's brother?");

s) role reversal — Achtemeier (1986: 172) has called attention to role reversal of defendant and plaintiff in Malachi, as Yahweh puts Israel on the defensive with his counter accusations (e.g., 3:8–9);

t) satire — as a form of critical discourse satire exposes human folly or vice through ridicule (on satire in Mal 1:14, see Jemielity [1992: 184]);

u) simile — Wendland (p. 109) cites an example of this indirect comparison in Mal 3:19 [4:1], ". . . the day is coming, burning like an oven";

v) symbol — as visionary image in Mal 3:20 [4:2], "a sun of righteousness";

w) synecdoche — Wendland (p. 109) identifies this figure of speech as a part representing the whole, often indicating a point of increased emotive tension (e.g., "abomination" for "divorce" and "foreign religious influence" in 2:11);

x) syntactical variation — note the emphatic word order in 3:9, ". . . with the curse you are being cursed; yea, it is me you are robbing";

y) wisdom — quotation of a common proverb in 2:10, "Surely we all have one father?"

Although the survey is not a comprehensive index of the rhetorical features in the book of Malachi, it does demonstrate that Malachi's prophecy is a literary work of considerable artistic merit.[1] Although I cannot agree with Wendland's (pp. 120–21) assessment of the literature of Malachi as poetry, I can affirm all those benefits that he adduces emerge from a literary approach to the HB; namely, the heightened awareness of the artistic quality of Malachi (and hence a new appreciation for the oracles as literature), improvement in the quality of a translation from Hebrew to English, illumination of the text in respect to author and author's worldview, original audience, and enhancement of the message of the text for the contemporary reader.[2]

However, as helpful as the literary approaches to Malachi may be (e.g., Alter and Kermode, Wendland, and Hendrix), they primarily concentrate on form, structure, and technique in biblical texts.[3] To that end they fail as literary approaches because they have not dealt with the human experience that is the subject matter of literature. Literature *incarnates* human experience and constantly appeals to our *imagination* (so Ryken [1984: 13–14] and Alter [1992: xi]; or as Merton [1948: 200] chided, "the material of literature . . . is chiefly human acts — that is, free acts, moral acts").

Only those approaches that seek to convey the universal aspects of human activity and reality as it is experienced in the literature are truly literary in nature (cf. Alter [1992: 210], to read the Bible as literature means to encounter the "compelling immediacy" of the biblical text). The compelling immediacy of Malachi as literature is based on the aftermath of tragedy, in the universal responses of humanity to personal or national disaster (the Babylonian exile in this case), which leave scars of doubt, uncertainty, insecurity, and apathy.

Four essays on Malachi capture this "existential" quality of the biblical literature. The first grapples with the verity that human experience includes *disappointment* — sometimes hopes are dashed, promises go unkept, and expectations remain unfilled (see Braun [1977]; cf. Pierce [1984a, b] who reads the postexilic prophets as a *story* of covenant failure). The second (Hendrix) addresses our propensity as human beings to perceive and react in different ways to the same set of circumstances or a given situation. Malachi draws attention to the need all have for congruence in life and effectively models a pedagogical approach that "socratically coaxes" people to confront suppressed fears and emotions — even self-deception. Through the "recursiveness" of the indirect language of rhetorical

---

[1] For example, Wendland records the following additional rhetorical features in Malachi: antithesis (1:11), exclamatory utterance (1:9, 12), graphic diction (2:3), closure (1:6), idiomatic speech (1:8–9), exact (2:2) and synonymic repetition (3:16), inclusio (2:17–3:5), anaphora (2:10–16), and epiphora (1:12–14).

[2] On the importance of an author's worldview, see Alter (1992: xii); cf. Pilch (1991: 71–116) on the western value-preferences for *guilt-* and *ego-centered identity* in contrast to the Mediterranean value-preferences for *shame-* and *group-centered identity* and the NOTES & COMMENTS below.

[3] Or what Longman (pp. 70–71) isolates as the *aesthetic* and *entertainment* functions of biblical literature. He also identifies *didactic, doxological, theological,* and *historical* functions in biblical literature but omits the *incarnational.*

questions, Malachi's message trespasses the "private sector" of peoples' lives in a variety of ways so that "the prophet articulates what the people feel but ignore or deny" (Hendrix [1987: 467]). The third recognizes that God is a person to be loved and not an abstraction to be manipulated. This is an essential truth for people who crave ideologies combining faith with hope, thus infusing human existence with meaning (see R. W. Klein [1986]). The fourth is useful by way of negative example, because the antiliturgical bias of the writer serves nicely as a foil accentuating the most significant endeavor of all human experience — the worship of God (cf. S. W. Gray). Malachi reminds us that worship is basic to human life or, as St. Augustine discerned, there is a God-given instinct or desire inherent within humanity to praise God as Creator (*Conf* 1.1.1–4; cf. Isa 43:7). Malachi forcefully affirms that both form and spirit are integral to the worship of God. The holiness of God demands both a pure heart on the part of the wor-shiper and the vehicle of a formal liturgy that appropriately expresses the wor-shiper's adoration and devotion (see further Hill [1994: 11–29]).

I. C. 7. Message

The book of Malachi consists of six disputational oracles: 1:2–5; 1:6–2:9; 2:10–16; 2:17–3:5; 3:6–12; and 3:13–21 [4:3]. These disputations (or "diatribe-like discourses" according to Petersen [1995: 34]) are framed by the superscrip-tion (1:1) and two appendixes (3:22 [4:3]; 3:23–24 [4:5–6]). Three of the accusa-tions are directed against the people of Yehud generally (1:2–5; 2:10–16; 3:6–12), two against the skeptics within the community especially (2:17–3:5; 3:13–21 [4:3]), and one against the Levitical priesthood (1:6–2:9).

The three-group audience theory of Berquist (p. 125) injects the (contested) notion of social fragmentation from the later postexilic period into the early Per-sian period of Yehud's history. Attempts to rigidly assign the prophet's speeches to a distinct audience sub-group, whether the pious, the skeptics, or the evildoers, must be tempered by the covenant theme of the book and the dialogical charac-ter of the disputation format; both insinuate the corporate personality of the com-munity of Yehud as the recipients of his message (cf. Hanson's [1986: 278–82] and Redditt's [1994: 241] development of the two audience hypothesis). Granted the variety of sub-groups within Malachi's audience, the emphasis on "Jacob" (1:2; 2:12; 3:6), "Israel" (1:5; 2:11), and the word "one" in the third disputation (2:10, 15) all indicate that the prophet addresses the people of Yehud collectively as a restoration community, not as disparate and isolated socioreligious factions (even those scholars insisting upon the heavy redaction of Malachi's speeches ultimately identify the audience of the oracles as "the community of the redac-tor," e.g., Redditt [1995: 156]).

It is important to recognize that the oracles of Malachi fit the general stylistic pattern of preaching and teaching common to a "Second Temple tradition" ob-served by Mason (1990: 256–62). By way of hermeneutic, these Second Temple "rhetors" appealed authoritatively to other texts of Hebrew Scripture and exhib-ited a continuity with earlier prophetic tradition in their use of vocabulary. By way of literary form, this postexilic preaching and teaching tradition is marked by rhetorical devices, including word play and illustration, the appeal to past history, the rhetorical question, and the disputation speech form. Theologically, the focal points of the content of this Second Temple preaching were the person of God, his covenant relationship with Israel, and the urgency of a wholehearted personal response to the truth claims of the (prophetic) message.

The predominant theme of Malachi's prophecy is the covenant relationship between Yahweh and Israel (cf. Redditt [1995: 156] on the book's message of "family kinship between God and Israel"). In fact, the prophet specifically mentions the covenant of Levi (2:1–9), the covenant of the fathers and the covenant of marriage (2:10–16), and the messenger of the covenant (3:1). Malachi's use of identifiable covenant terminology like 'hb, 'rr, bgd, sĕgullâ, śn', šmr, etc., confirms this thematic understanding of the book (see McKenzie and Wallace for a discussion of these covenantal themes and terms).[1]

According to Fischer (p. 317) the literary form of Malachi outlines the essential teaching of the book. The prophet has shifted the locus of his message from the curse or blessing declarations to the introductory statements in which a divine declaration is made, countered by the hypothetical response of Israel in the form of a question and concluding with Yahweh's answer to the question posed.

Employing this approach in his analysis, Fischer summarizes the basic instruction of the disputations as follows: (1) Yahweh loves Jacob; (2) he is Israel's God and father and desires honest worship; (3) he is the father of all Israelites and expects true faithfulness; (4) God wants honesty, not words, because he is just; (5) God is faithful to his word and wants genuine worship; and (6) a repetition of God's desire for honesty (here Mason [1990: 256] notes that despite the strident posture of Malachi toward postexilic Jerusalem, he began his oracles with a message of encouragement and concluded with a similar word of encouragement).

Malachi's opening oracle is a restatement of Yahweh's love for Jacob obvious through the course of Israelite history (1:2–5). Amid growing skepticism because the "Zion visions" of Second Isaiah, Haggai, and Zechariah and the "Temple vision" of Ezekiel never materialized, the prophet sought to assure the restoration community in Jerusalem that God still maintained covenant love for them. By recalling the patriarchal covenants Malachi reminds the people that an important part of God's covenant love for Israel was the conditional nature of its conse-

---

[1] D. N. Freedman (1991: 61–63) understands the Latter Prophets (including the target of this study, Malachi) as an expansion of and supplement to the Primary History of the HB. He identifies the central concerns of the Primary History as the destruction of the nation (of Israel), the city (of Jerusalem), and the Temple (of Yahweh). The Latter Prophets provide an alternative perspective on the catastrophe of destruction and exile by portraying the aftermath of these events: the return, restoration, and renewal of Israel. The message of Malachi, one of covenant renewal with Yahweh, rehabilitation of the priesthood, and reform of societal ills, fits this paradigm. This prophet of the restoration was an important contributor to the creation of "a unique reality in the ancient Near East, a community almost literally brought back from the dead . . ." (D. N. Freedman [1991: 63]).

quent blessing for obedience to the treaty stipulations (Isa 51:1–8; Zech 6:15; cf. Leviticus 26 and Deuteronomy 28).[2]

Fischer (pp. 318–19) rightly observes that Malachi had to correct wrong thinking about the covenantal relationship with Yahweh. The vassal can place no demands on the suzerain. Loving God was not a cause for divine blessing but a condition, for God himself remains the only cause (cf. J. J. Collins [1984: 214–15]). This reminder of Israel's election as his special possession by the sovereign Lord also served to underscore the seriousness of the present situation (Deut 8:11–18; 14:2; Ps 135:4; cf. Rom 9:13). The prophet reinforces his argument by pointing to recent events in Edom (perhaps an invasion of Edom by Nabatean Arabs?), which served as a grim warning of impending divine judgment for those who despised the tokens of covenant like Esau (Gen 25:34; cf. Jer 49:7–22).[3]

Malachi's five remaining disputations contrast Israel's faithlessness with Yahweh's faithfulness through the recitation of specific violations of the covenant stipulations. These prophetic indictments against the restoration community for breach of covenant serve as a foil for the unchanging faithfulness of Yahweh to his word (3:6; cf. Deut 7:6–11; Zech 8:8). Because covenant maker Yahweh was Israel's father (Deut 32:6–12), he was deserving of conduct appropriate to the bond (Exod 20:12; Deut 30:1–10). Further, as covenant maker Yahweh was also a covenant keeper (Exod 6:6–8; 34:6–7; Pss 111:9; 121:3–4, 7–8; 136:23; Isa 46:8–13). He both expected and demanded no less from the Yehudites (2:10–12).

The second disputation consists of two sections: 1:6–14 and 2:1–9. Both censure the Levitical priesthood; the first for their insolence in discharging the duties associated with the cultus, and the second for the double standard in their teaching and their lack of moral leadership (cf. Num 20:12; Deut 18:1–8; 33:8–11). The apathetic priests were permitting impure sacrifices in the Temple liturgy in violation of the priestly code (Lev 22:20–22; Deut 15:21; 17:1). Malachi preferred the cessation of the Temple ritual to their religious indifference and even suggested that the gentiles offered more appropriate worship to God (1:10–11). No doubt the priests are indicted because their transgression of the holy covenant and disdain for the sacred office polluted the worship of the people (2:8–9). According to the curse formula in predictable fashion, the priesthood will experience the same contempt and abasement they have shown Yahweh (1:6; 2:9).

Lest the priests become scapegoats, the prophet rebukes the laity in the third oracle for their faithlessness to Yahweh (2:10–16). Even as the Levites had corrupted the priestly pact of Levi (2:4, 8), so the people of Yehud had transgressed the covenant of the fathers by marrying foreign women and divorcing their Hebrew wives (2:10–11, 14). Marriage is deemed a sacred covenant in the OT/HB,

---

[2] According to Mussner (p. 97), "the 'remembering' of God is an expression of his loyalty." It is this divine remembering that moves the history of Israel and makes the prayers of Israel meaningful and effective.

[3] Like Jeremiah, Malachi proves useful as an example of Brueggemann's (1978: 62) prophetic "criticizing" and "energizing" designed to awaken a spiritually numb people to "an alternative consciousness that can energize the community to fresh forms of faithfulness and vitality."

blessed by God and honorable among all people (Gen 2:24; Prov 5:18; 18:22; 19:14; 31:10; cf. Hugenberger). For Malachi the connections between covenant keeping with Yahweh and covenant loyalty with a mate are obviously based on the familial nature of covenant relationship described elsewhere in the Bible (cf. Isa 54:6; Jer 2:1–3; 31:32; Ezek 16:6 ff.; Hos 2:1–19; 11:1–4). The prophet not only condemns divorce generally among God's people, but also their remarriage to alien women because of the consequent contamination of Hebrew religion (cf. Num 25:1–9; 1 Kgs 11:1–4). God hates divorce (2:16), and these flagrant violations of covenant law will not go unpunished (2:11; cf. Exod 19:5–6; Deut 7:3–4; Josh 23:12; Ezra 9:1–2).

The fourth oracle (2:17–3:5) is a prophecy concerning the messenger of the covenant who prepares the day of God's visitation by judging Yehud's sin and purifying their worship through the cleansing of the priesthood (3:1–4; cf. Zeph 1:14–18; Zech 13:1). The faithlessness of the Jerusalem community extends even to false speech about Yahweh: they accused him of rewarding evil and being unjust (2:17; cf. Ps 73:12–13; Job 27:7–16; Mic 6:1–3; Hab 1:2–4, 13). This attitude toward God naturally spawned a variety of social abuses and moral ills in the restoration community (3:5). Ironically, it was the failure to authenticate the words of covenant relationship with behavior of like kind that led to Judah's exile into Babylonia a century prior (Deut 11:22; 12:1; 30:1–4; cf. Isa 1:12–17; 5:5–7, 26–30; Jer 7:1–7; Hos 4:1–10; Amos 2:6–8; Mic 3:1–4).

Contrary to the popular perception, Malachi contends in the fifth oracle that Yahweh has been just and ever consistent in his nature (3:6–12). The very fact that God has not consumed postexilic Jerusalem in his wrath for covenant transgression is testimony to his faithfulness and compassion (Pss 86:15; 111:4; Mic 7:18–20; Nah 1:1–3). The emphasis in this penultimate disputation is repentance, not tithing (3:6–7). The tithe was an important practice in Hebrew religion (cf. Lev 27:30; Num 18:26–28; Deut 12:18; 14:28–29); but given the list of covenant offenses already cited by the prophet, he can hardly be implying the mere reinstitution of the tithe would induce divinely bestowed prosperity. The stinginess of the people was but an outward manifestation of their spiritual bankruptcy. By calling for the "full" tithe the prophet invites genuine repentance, a return to Yahweh with the whole heart (3:10; cf. Isa 29:13; 44:22; 55:7; Joel 2:12–13, 18–19; Hag 2:17; Zech 1:3–4). Only this kind of honest personal and corporate worship will open the windows of heaven, to the point where Malachi dares the people to exhaust the bounty of God's covenantal blessing (3:10–12; cf. Deut 15:5–6, 10).

The seeming triumph of wickedness over righteousness and God's apparent slackness in judging sin are the key issues of Malachi's final disputation (3:13–21 [4:3]). In this indictment the prophet outlines the specific charges of injustice filed against Yahweh by the impudent complainers in Jerusalem (3:13–15). They contend that it has been futile to serve God because they have turned no profit (lit., "cut" or percentage due them, Hebrew *beṣaʿ*, 3:14) from their obedience to God's commandments. Neither did their personal piety, fasting, and repentance bring them advantage. In fact, their assessment of everyday reality showed that evildoers were the ones who actually tested God and escaped unscathed.

Continuing the careful distinction between the wicked and the righteous in his audience established at the outset of his oracles, Malachi then contrasts the words of the God-fearing believers (3:16–17). Unlike the mercenary approach of their compatriots, their response to God is genuine reverence and worship. The disputation concludes with the prophet's answer to the alleged inequity of Yahweh's treatment of the restoration community (3:18–21 [4:3]). The coming Day of Yahweh will indeed vindicate his justice, when the wicked are separated from the righteous by the fire of divine judgment (3:18). Although the righteous will escape the destructive wrath of God by virtue of their special covenantal relationship with him (Hebrew *sĕgullâ*), this divine fire will purify the faithful. Only then will they experience the blessings of messianic restoration (3:20 [4:2]; cf. Ps 107:20; Isa 63:1–6).

The closing verses of the book (3:22–24 [4:4–6]) are generally acknowledged to be editorial additions. The questions and answers are over, and the disputations have ceased. There is little to suggest that these verses are directly related to the previous section. However, they represent more than the simple legalistic correctives of a disenchanted scribal editor since they do preserve instruction complementary to the righteousness central to Malachi's message. The Deuteronomic connections of 3:22 [4:4] are numerous and well documented (e.g., J.M.P. Smith [1912: 81]; Mason [1977: 159–60]; Coggins [1987: 75–76]), and the verse may be an attempt to summarize the message of Malachi by reminding the people of Yehud that they remain under the authoritative tradition of Moses. The verse may also represent the work of the compiler of the Book of the Twelve (cf. Redditt [1995: 191–92]), who sought to link the Latter Prophets (Isaiah, Jeremiah, Ezekiel, and the Minor Prophets) with the Primary History (Genesis through Kings) of the HB by means of the postscript (see D. N. Freedman [1991: 36–41, 60–64]).

Elijah functions as a prophetic archetype in the second appendix (3:23–24 [4:5–6]), and the reference to him identifies the messenger of the covenant in 3:1. According to Childs (1979: 495–96), the effect of this second postscript is to balance the memory of the past with the anticipation of the future. While the verses seem an unduly harsh ending to Malachi and the Twelve, one must remember that the basic purpose of the prophetic ministry was to prepare the people of Yahweh for his day of visitation so that they might enter the rest of his salvation and escape the wrath of his judgment (cf. Isa 12:1–6; 33:2–6; 49:6–12; 52:7–12; Zeph 3:14–20; Zech 8:14–19).[4]

---

[4]On the message of Malachi, see further G. von Rad (1967: 254–55) who understood Malachi as a prophet concerned exclusively with covenant abuses and "blasé scepticism in religious matters" within the restoration community; K. Koch (1984: 179) who summarizes Malachi's purpose and message as that of coming "to terms, mentally, spiritually and ethically, with the non-appearance of the new eschatological beginning"; Newsome (p. 190) and Craigie (p. 226) who regard Malachi as a message of faith and hope aimed at a crisis of the spirit—doubt and indifference; Coggins (pp. 77–78) who views Malachi as a blend of condemnation with a treatise on the power of God; VanGemeren (pp. 204–8) who reads Malachi as a theology of Yahweh under the headings: Yahweh as Father and King, Yahweh's Righteous Love, Yahweh's Love for the Elect, and Yahweh as the Divine

I. C. 8. Theology

The postexilic date for the book, the marginal status of the Jerusalem restoration community within the Persian Empire, and the disputational format of the oracles should not lead us to disparage Malachi's theological significance. Although the literary grandeur of Isaiah and the profound personal intensity of Jeremiah are lacking, these comparisons are debatable anyway since each prophet was commissioned to fulfill a specific task in a particular historical and sociological context.[1] It remains more important to analyze how the prophet discharged that commission, examine the message through the lens of the broader prophetic movement in Israel, and seek to make appropriate contemporary application of the prophetic message. In this respect, Malachi proves a most fruitful and powerful theological study; in many instances the prophecy is a throwback to the classical prophets of the preexilic era.

Any attempt to discuss OT/HB theology is not without liability. The perils and pitfalls of OT/HB theology are so profusely documented that such appraisals of the discipline now provide sufficient scholarly excuse for avoiding the actual enterprise of "doing" theology (e.g., Hayes and Prussner or Ollenburger, Martens, and Hasel). Problems abound, like the riddle of *what* actually constitutes the theological center of the OT/HB. The question may be better posed adverbially, *where* and *when* — that is, does the theological center of the OT/HB reside in Occidental, Oriental, Hispanic, or African thought and of what century? Still other issues remain unsettled, like the problems associated with explaining the development of Israel's history and religion, the nature and extent of divine revelation, methodological approach, and the study of the Bible as canonical literature to name but a few (cf. Carroll [1990: 45] on the "hermeneutic maelstrom"). I have found the studies by Goldingay (1987) and Hasel to be the most helpful because they advance both descriptive and prescriptive treatments of the topic. The following paragraphs chart my own course through the precarious narrows known euphemistically as OT/HB theology.

By way of a theological center for the Bible, I align myself with Terrien and C. Barth who set forth the person and presence of God as the organizing tenet for OT/HB theology. Thus, covenant relationship, typological interpretation, or salvation history, etc., are but means by which the Bible manifests the person and presence of God. By way of methodology, I place myself in that camp so labeled by Hasel (p. 49) as "the new biblical theology" (and represented by Childs [1986] and C. Barth among others).

This methodological approach proves far superior to others, and I adduce

---

Warrior; and Watts (1987a: 380) who sees three primary themes binding the book of Malachi together: God's elective love for Israel, the reconciliation of "fathers" and "children," and the anticipation of the Day of Yahweh.

[1] Mason (1982: 142) calls for an appreciation of the postexilic prophets as products of their age and victims of the success of their predecessors. He explains that the derivative and exegetical nature of the prophetic ministry in the postexilic period was the result of increasing emphasis on written documents and the canonization process in later Israelite religion, which supplanted the "living" word.

these reasons: the new biblical theology attempts to take history and revelation seriously (thus preserving the paradox of Yahweh's transcendence and immanence and the mystery of faith), the approach presupposes a hermeneutic concerned both with what the text *meant* and what it *means*, and it affirms the essential unity of the Bible (in contrast to the atomizing tendencies characteristic of certain other approaches). This approach appreciates the relationship of the OT to NT and encourages what Clements (1978) describes as a dialectical understanding of the OT/HB foundational to both Judaism and Christianity. It fosters recognition of the tension between the OT/HB as literature and the OT/HB as canon; and finally, the approach affirms the ethical component of theology and the role Hebrew wisdom tradition plays in mediating the presence of God as disclosed in the Torah and Prophets (so Terrien [1978: 471–77]; Brueggemann [1982b: 67–90]).

I concur with those who view Malachi as primarily a theology of Yahweh (e.g., R. W. Klein [1986] and VanGemeren [1990]). The prophet's litany of divine attributes includes the nature and character of Yahweh as father of Israel (1:6; 2:5–7; 3:17), as well as master and king (1:6, 14). Lest the extremes of contemptuous familiarity or the diffidence of formality due to Yahweh's transcendence distort community perception, the prophet is careful to offer a balanced picture of the God of Israel. Malachi has little to say about the nations, yet it is clear he acknowledged God's sovereignty in human history (1:3–5, 11; on the nations as a literary foil for Israel's sinfulness in Mal 1:11, see Childs [1986: 105]).

Closely tied to Yahweh's sovereignty is his love for and election of Israel as a special people (1:2; 3:17; cf. Deut 7:6–11; Isa 41:8; cf. Redditt [1995: 156] [appealing to Bossman] on the family kinship theme in Malachi). While this choice on God's part and the subsequent covenant bond with Israel constitute the platform for the prophet's entire discourse, the message of Yahweh's love is not so much one of comfort as it is a warning (so Craigie [1985: 229]). Because Yahweh is so linked to Israel, he is faithful and unchanging, a covenant-keeper extending mercy to his own (3:6; Brueggemann [1991: 40] recalls that the only ground of hope for Israel is in the character of God as covenant-keeper). Yahweh is also just (2:17; cf. Isa 61:8), punishing those who trespass the covenant stipulations (3:5, 18, 21 [4:3]; cf. Zeph 1:12). As God of the covenant, Yahweh tests the faithful in order to purify them (3:1–4; cf. Isa 48:10); and as the giver of good gifts, he is not reluctant to bless and reward the obedience of his children (3:10–12; cf. Hanson [1979: 106–8] on the transformation of the judgment and salvation oracles in postexilic prophecy).[2]

Malachi's knowledge of and identification with the covenant tradition of his prophetic heritage place the book in the mainstream of OT/HB covenant theology (on Malachi's nexus with Deuteronomistic theology, see Coggins [1987: 75–76] and R. L. Smith [1987: 23–24]). For example, the prophet recognized Yahweh as both the maker and keeper of covenant with Israel (1:2; 2:10; cf. Exod 6:2–7; Jer 31:31–34), and he affirmed their status as "child" by virtue of this cove-

---

[2] Here Malachi provides a synopsis of the dual theme of the Latter Prophets identified by D. N. Freedman (1991: 69), the paradox of divine election, and divine judgment.

nant relationship (1:6; cf. Hos 1:10). Like his predecessors, Malachi understood the conditional nature of Israel's covenant relationship with Yahweh and the urgency of the community's obligation to remain faithful and obedient to the stipulations of the divine treaty (3:16–21 [4:3]; cf. Ezek 16:59–63). His agonizing over the seriousness of a breach of the covenant (2:1–8; cf. Jer 34:17–20) evinces a thorough acquaintance with the Deuteronomistic blessing and curse formulae (cf. Deut 28:1–57).

Similar to his preexilic counterparts, Malachi retains the divine prerogative of restoration for those who turn back to Yahweh in repentance (3:6–7; cf. Hos 6:1–3; Zeph 3:11–13). More important is the prophet's concern for justice for the socially disadvantaged among the covenant community (3:5; cf. Isa 1:16–17; Amos 5:14–15, 24). Malachi was keenly aware of the concept of individual and corporate responsibility within the covenant community and the attendant ethical duties incumbent upon those related to Yahweh and each other in this special relationship (2:7–9, 13–16; cf. Mic 6:8; Zech 8:16–17).

Those who contend that Malachi only appreciates the cultic and legalistic aspects of Israelite religion have failed to consider fully his instruction on the nature of personal faith (cf. J. J. Collins: 214–15 on the idea that "quality in a relationship" binds the themes of cultic service and universal vision). It is clear from the prophet's handling of the objection that it is vain to serve God (3:14), that he espoused no merit system. Those who are spared divine judgment earned no special favor, they simply "feared the Lord and honored his name" (3:16).

Malachi's insistence on true repentance for the renewal of genuine worship (3:2–4), personal piety that includes an agenda for social justice (3:5–7), and honesty in giving (3:8–12) indicates that the prophet prizes a vital and internal — not a hollow and external — religion (see Craigie's [pp. 242–44] thoughtful remarks on how Malachi's message shapes attitudes toward property, God, and others). Naturally the recognition of Yahweh's holiness and righteousness led to the conviction that service to God as a loyal vassal included rendering both liturgical and moral obedience to Yahweh (1:6–10; cf. Matt 23:23; Jas 1:27). Here Malachi penetrates the heart of OT/HB faith when he appeals for such a "walk" with the living God (2:6; cf. Gen 17:1; Deut 30:15–20; Brueggemann [1982a: 15–25]).

Malachi's concept of the priesthood as the repository of the knowledge of God for the people (2:5–7) may be a result of his association with Levitical circles, given the similarity of his oracles to the so-called Levitical sermons of Haggai and the Chronicler (so Mason [1977: 137]; cf. Mason's [1990: 257] later study dismissing the literary genre of "Levitical sermon"). The crucial role of the priests as guideposts of righteousness for the community is consistent with the teaching of both covenants regarding the responsibilities of those in leadership positions (Num 20:12; 1 Sam 15:22–23; Isa 1:23–26; Jer 5:5; cf. Luke 12:48; Acts 6:3; Rom 13:4; 1 Tim 3:1–3; Jas 3:1). Malachi's apprehension of the Levitical priesthood as servants of God, facilitators of worship, and ministers of covenant reconciliation aptly reflects the function of these cultic figures within the Israelite community (2:4–9; see C. Barth [1991: 152–65]).

The prophet's lofty doctrine on the institution of marriage as companionship with the spouse of one's youth (2:14) and the shared responsibility of child rearing (2:15) is reminiscent of Hebrew wisdom tradition (Prov 5:18; 10:1; 15:20; 31:26); while his censure of easy divorce anticipates the rigid instruction of Jesus and Paul in contrast to the Deuteronomist (2:16; cf. Matt 19:11; Mark 10:1–10; 1 Cor 7:1–16 vs. Deut 24:1–4). Both Jewish and Christian interpreters have observed that Malachi's prescriptive treatment of divorce reflects the "exclusivist" tendency of postexilic Judaism to reestablish ethnic purity in Israel (e.g., Carmody, et al. [1988: 258]; feminist interpreters note that time has effected little change in the patriarchy of postexilic Judaism, as the option of divorce is still the privilege of the husband, e.g., Laffey [1988: 159]).

Though influenced by Ezekiel's Temple vision, Malachi's eschatology shows no concern for a future Temple; rather, he is interested in the reform of abuses currently infecting the cult. The prophet does maintain clear distinctions between the fate of the wicked and the righteous in the restoration community, but pays scant attention to themes like the judgment of the nations or the universality of Yahweh's salvation, as in Zech 9–14 (12:1–19; 14:3, 9–21; cf. Koch [1984: 179] who admits that Malachi relativizes the salvation oracles previously announced by Haggai and Zechariah but likens the universalism of 1:11 to that of Trito-Isaiah). Malachi does not use the expression "day of Yahweh" (*yôm-YHWH*), but his understanding of "the day [that] is coming" (*hayyôm bā'*, 3:19 [4:1]) largely conforms to the conventional prophetic paradigm of threat and promise with attention given to the judgment of Israel's sin in violating Yahweh's covenant (3:5) and Yahweh's preservation and restoration of a righteous remnant (3:3–4, 16–17). Malachi's picture of final judgment has a focus different from that of Second Zechariah, yet the two do emphasize the refining or purification of the faithful by fire (3:2, 19 [4:1]; cf. Zech 12:6; 13:9; cf. 1 Cor 3:12–15; 2 Pet 3:10–12), and both recognize that God's ultimate purpose in judgment remains repentance (3:7; Zech 10:9–12; cf. Ezek 18:23, 30–32). Of special interest here is the striking contrast between the threatened "ban" or "curse" (*ḥērem*) at the end of Malachi 3:24 [4:6] and the repeal of the ban in Zech 14:11.[3]

Malachi does make original contributions to Hebrew eschatology with the introduction of the "book of remembrance" in which the names of the righteous are recorded (3:16). The concept is probably the result of Persian influence on postexilic Judaism (cf. Esth 6:1; Dan 7:10; 12:1) and points to the continued development of the Hebrew belief in afterlife. Malachi may have inspired the scattered references to such "books" of judgment, deeds, or life mentioned in the intertestamental literature (cf. Charlesworth [1983: 889; 1985: 171, 190, 226]), and the "book of remembrance" may have connections to the "book of life" used to separate the wicked from the righteous at the final judgment in the Apocalypse (Rev 20:11–15). The unique expression "the sun of righteousness" in 3:20 [MT 4:2] is reminiscent of the winged solar disc representing the sun god ubiquitous

---

[3]According to Petersen (1977: 42–43), Malachi approximates the "theological stream" of Joel 3–4 with respect to the day of Yahweh and provides an important link explaining the shift in OT/HB expectations from the return of prophecy in general to the arrival of an individual messenger who will function as an enforcer of Yahweh's covenant.

in Mesopotamian and Egyptian iconography and is likely another indication of Zoroastrian influence on the Hebrew understanding of the fiery consummation (so J. Gray [1974: 5]; cf. Keel [1978: 27–28] on this widespread symbol in the ancient world).

Finally, Malachi's obscure reference to the "forerunner" (mal'āk) who prepares the way for the arrival of Yahweh (3:1) has proven difficult to interpret. There is little consensus among scholars as to the identification of this messenger and the relationship of the messenger to the "messenger of the covenant" (mal'ak habbĕrît). It is unclear whether this messenger is the prophet Malachi, another prophet, an angel, or a manifestation of God himself. The combination of Moses and Elijah in the appendixes of Malachi personifies Hebrew legal and prophetic tradition, two of the basic building blocks of OT/HB thought. The references to Moses and Elijah, prominent figures in the Primary History, also suggest the Book of the Twelve (and the Latter Prophets) serve as a commentary on the Primary History — especially the Former Prophets (see D. N. Freedman [1991: 36–41, 60–64]). Thus, the book concludes with retrospect and prospect, reflections on the Law that ordered relationship with Yahweh and the Prophets who were the public conscience of that relationship with Yahweh (cf. Craigie [1985: 247–48]).

The second appendix (3:23–24 [4:5–6]) connects the messenger with Elijah reincarnate. Elijah's role as a herald proclaiming the appointed time of Yahweh's fury and the inauguration of the messianic age was an important part of later Jewish tradition associated with the prophet (cf. Sir 48:10; on messianism in Malachi, see Verhoef [1987: 345–46] and Keown [1987: 343–51]). The Christian reader of the OT has generally understood the Elijah prophecy to prefigure the ministry of John the Baptist (Matt 11:7–15) since the early church held the oracle to be fully realized in the relationship of John's mission with the initiation of the messianic kingdom of heaven by Jesus of Nazareth (Mark 1:2–8; Luke 1:16–17; cf. Matt 11:1–6 and see Newsome [1984: 194–95] and Goppelt [1982: 64] on typology). Although for Christians John played the role of Elijah the prophet, C. Barth (p. 352) charges that the implementation of the reconciliation of later generations continues as an ongoing task of the church's prophetic ministry (on the relationship between Jewish and Christian readings of the OT/HB in general, see further Levenson [1985: 187–217]).

By way of contemporary application, the book of Malachi suggests these representative topics or themes: God's love for his children (especially as an exhortation of reassurance to the jaded, cynical, confused, and disillusioned — so Braun [1977] and R. W. Klein [1986]), worship renewal (see S. W. Gray, Kuehner, Mallone, and Richardson, R. W. Bailey [1977: 27–36]), social justice (Brueggemann [1982a], Birch),[4] pedagogy and curriculum in religious education (Hendrix; note the parallels between Malachi's catechetical dialectic and Brueggemann's [1982b] canonical paradigm for education in Bible times), theodicy (Braun

---

[4] Malachi's cry for justice on behalf of the socially disadvantaged does not suggest a violent liberation theology, but a theology of pacifism and nonviolent resistance (cf. Merton [1968]) and a "social ministry" similar to that espoused by Hessel.

[1977], Scalise), stewardship (Craigie, Tilley, and R. W. Bailey [1977: 86–96]; cf. Ellul [1984: 43–55, 90–93] on the OT/HB ethic of wealth and money as a test), interpersonal relationships (Garland, Kaiser [1987], Locher, Rudolph [1981], R. W. Bailey [1977: 53–63]), contemporary preaching (Fasol, Gloer, Kaiser [1992], Wells, Yates, R. W. Bailey [1977: 37–52]; cf. Scott's [1953] classic on the relevance of the prophets), and ethical issues (Tillman).

I. D. HISTORICAL CONSIDERATIONS

The overwhelming majority of biblical scholars date the book of Malachi between 500 B.C./E. and the complementary ministries of Ezra-Nehemiah in Jerusalem (mid-fifth century B.C./E.). The historical context of Malachi's oracles, then, is the Persian empire era of ancient Near Eastern civilization. More specifically, Malachi is located at some point on the chronological continuum between the rule of King Darius I (522–486 B.C./E.) and the death of King Artaxerxes I (424 B.C./E.). Interestingly, Foerster (p. 14) noted, "Of the period 515 to about 460 B.C./E. we know just a little from the short book of Malachi." Foerster is correct to place Malachi in this historical period. I would even adjust the lower end of his chronological boundary to approximately 485 or 480 B.C./E. Hence, my discussion of the Persian background for the book of Malachi will be limited almost exclusively to the reign of Darius I.

For a more comprehensive treatment of the ancient Persian empire the reader is encouraged to consult the standard histories, including: *CAH* 4:1–25, 173–316; Olmstead, S. A. Cook, and R. N. Frye. Briant's (*ABD* 5:236–44) concise overview of the Persian empire provides an excellent orientation to the period. Yamauchi (1990) thoroughly documents the reigns of each of the Persian kings connected with postexilic biblical history (pp. 65–278) and provides extensive bibliography (pp. 525–47). In addition, Stolper, Hoglund, and Berquist (1995) prove helpful as a resource for Persian administrative policy in the postexilic Levant.

1. The Persian Period

A. Chronological Outline

Chart 1. The Kings of Persia from Cyrus to Darius III

Cyrus the Great	550–530 B.C./E.
Cambyses	530–522
Darius I	521–486
Xerxes	486–465
Artaxerxes I	464–424

Darius II Nothus   423–405
Artaxerxes II Mnemon   404–359
Artaxerxes III Ochus   359–338
Arses   337–336
Darius III Codomannus   335–330

Alexander the Great occupied Babylon and Susa, 331 B.C./E.; Persepolis and Ecbatana, 330 B.C./E.; death of Darius III 330 B.C./E.

B. REIGN OF DARIUS I

The English form of the name Darius is derived from the Greek *Dareîos* (cf. LXX, Hag 1:1). The Hebrew rendering, *dāryāweš*, closely approximates the Old Persian *Dārayāvaush* (from *Dāraya-Vahu-Manah*, meaning "he who sustains good thought"; cf. Yamauchi [1990: 129]). Three Persian kings were named Darius: Darius I or Darius the Great (522–486 B.C./E.), Darius II Nothus (423–405 B.C./E.), and Darius III Codomannus (335–330 B.C./E.). Darius I figures prominently in postexilic biblical history since it was during this Persian king's reign that a Second Temple was constructed in Jerusalem at the prompting of the prophets Haggai and Zechariah (Ezra 4–6; cf. Hag 1:1, 15; 2:10; Zech 1:1, 7; 7:1). It is likely Darius the Persian mentioned in Neh 12:22 was Darius II Nothus (so Yamauchi [1990: 130]; but Cross [1963: 121] has suggested Darius III Codomannus). There is no scholarly consensus as to the identification of Darius the Mede mentioned in the book of Daniel (5:31; cf. *ABD* 2:38–39).

Darius was not a descendant of Cyrus and Cambyses, but a member of a collateral Achaemenid family. Inscriptional evidence indicates that Darius and Cyrus had a common ancestor, so Darius had legitimate royal bloodlines (as a descendant of Teispes, the great, great, grandfather of Cyrus the Great, cf. *CAH* 4: 5). His father, Hystaspes (Vishtaspa), was the satrap of Parthia and still living when Darius ascended the throne in 522 B.C./E. According to Olmstead (p. 107), Darius was born about 550 B.C./E. and was nearly twenty-eight years old when he began to rule as king of Persia. Darius served among the "Immortals" (an elite force of ten thousand royal troops so-called by Herodotus, *Hist* 7.83) as a spearbearer under Cambyses in Egypt. Young (p. 37) speculates he may have been the commander of this special Persian military unit, and Darius's tomb inscription attests to his prowess as a soldier (Yamauchi [1990: 138]).

Although much of his energy was expended in military activity designed to stabilize regions under Persian control or expand the boundaries of the empire, Darius's legacy is also one of an able administrator and a shrewd bureaucrat. In addition to organizing the empire into satrapies, he improved the Persian legal system, initiated tax reform, standardized Persian weights and measures, established a uniform monetary policy, and created a postal network linking all the satrapies with the central government. He was also an accomplished builder evidenced by the royal road stretching from Susa to Sardis (some 1,500 miles), canals in Egypt and Mesopotamia, great palaces and public buildings in Babylon, Susa, and Ecbatana, and his new capital at Persepolis.

The circumstances under which Darius ascended the throne as king of Persia are documented in his royal apologia inscribed on the rock faced cliffs near Behistun (or Bisitun, see Fig. 7). According to the inscription, an imposter by the name of Gaumata usurped the throne and posed as Bardiya (called Smerdis by Herodotus), the son of Cambyses. Darius was party to a conspiracy of Persian nobles responsible for deposing and executing Gaumata, the false Bardiya. Herodotus claimed that Darius won the right to ascend the Persian throne from a group of nobles vying for kingship by means of hippomancy, or divination using horses (*Hist* 3.86–87). The veracity of Darius's account detailing the defeat of the usurper Gaumata is widely contested by historians. Skeptics contend that Darius murdered the real Bardiya and invented the Gaumata story, making him the real usurper and the Behistun inscription little more than royal propaganda officially legitimizing a hoax (see the discussion pro and con in Yamauchi [1990: 142–45]). What is certain is that Darius was not the logical heir to the Persian throne but a legitimate contender since he traced his ancestry to Teispes and that his consolidation of power as the new king was a protracted and bloody affair.

The Behistun inscription further records that Darius spent the first year of his reign quelling rebellions across the empire following his defeat of Gaumata the usurper:

> Says Darius the King: This is what I did by the favor of Ahuramazda in one and the same year after I became king. I fought nineteen battles; by the favor of Ahuramazda I defeated and took prisoner nine kings. One was Gaumata by name, a Magian; he lied; thus he said: 'I am Smerdis, the son of Cyrus'; he made Persia rebellious . . . I executed Gaumata the Magian who called himself Smerdis (Kent 1953: 131–32).

The controversy concerning the reliability of the state's "official" version of the new king's rise to power (accepted by Herodotus *Hist* 3.85–89) notwithstanding, Darius was busily engaged in suppressing revolts and initiating administrative reform during those early years after his ascension to the Persian throne. It has been suggested that Zerubbabel, then governor of Yehud, was deposed or even executed as a political liability during this purge by Darius due to his entanglement in a "messianic conspiracy" (including my previous assessment of Zerubbabel's place in the restoration community, cf. Hill [1981: 134]). However, Williamson (1988b: 1193–94) downplays such speculation and has concluded Zerubbabel avoided any inappropriate political involvement as governor of the province of Yehud (cf. Berquist [1995: 89]). Nevertheless, the sudden disappearance of Zerubbabel (a Davidic figure promoted by Yahweh's prophet Haggai, 2:20–23) from the documents recounting the life and history of the early restoration community in Jerusalem remains a conundrum for biblical commentators.

Upon the political stabilization of the core satrapies in Mesopotamia, Darius embarked on a campaign to reestablish Persian control in Egypt, one of the rebellious fringe provinces (519–518 B.C./E.). According to the Behistun inscription, Darius faced little opposition in Egypt due to his reverence for the Apis cult (following the precedent of his patronage of Yahweh of Jerusalem only a year or so earlier[?]; cf. Yamauchi [1990: 148]). In addition to the homage paid to the

Egyptian god, Darius commissioned the building of a temple to Amon at Hibis during a later visit to the region (497–496 B.C./E.) and granted monies from the royal treasury for the erection of a temple to Horus at Edfu. This imperialistic expansion shifted to the east along the Indus River valley in 516 or 515 B.C./E. and then to the northeast with the invasion of European Scythia (514 B.C./E.).

Darius's reign ended much as he began it, by waging military campaigns to crush rebellions among the fringe satrapies across the vast Persian empire. With the aid of the Athenians, the Ionian cities of Asia Minor and the island of Cyprus rejected Persian authority established by Cyrus the Great in 547 B.C./E. and revolted in 499 B.C./E. The Persian response was fierce, subduing the renegade vassals finally in 494 B.C./E. at the battle of Lade near Miletus. In retaliation against the Greeks for abetting the Ionian revolt (a violation of an earlier pact sealed in 507 B.C./E.), Darius commissioned an expedition against Athens in 492 B.C./E. Despite gains in Thrace and Macedonia, the campaign ended in failure when the Persian fleet was wrecked in a storm off Mt. Athos in the northern Aegean Sea. A second expedition unleashed against Athens met with a similar fate when the Persians were routed at the historic battle of Marathon in 490 B.C./E. Darius's plans for a third expedition were never realized, given his death in 486 B.C./E. at the age of sixty-four. The next chapter in the titanic struggle between East and West would be written by his son and successor, King Xerxes.

What significance does this historical backdrop, the reign of Darius I of Persia, have for the book of Malachi? Two assumptions undergird the discussion here. First, the validity of the typological analysis of the language of Malachi placing the date of the oracles near 500 B.C./E. is presumed. Second, the notion of *metahistory* Koch (1983: 73) attributes to the preexilic prophets is presupposed for their postexilic counterparts as well. History is the arena of Yahweh's purposeful activity moving irrevocably toward the *yôm YHWH*, the apocalyptic consummation of human experience (cf. Scott [1953: 146]). Although Petersen (1977: 1–16) has documented radical differences between the prophecy of the classical tradition and the deutero-prophetic tradition, this prophetic perspective regarding history remains a constant across the paradigms of early and late biblical prophecy. According to Petersen (1977: 16) not only is the deutero-prophetic literature dependent upon the early classical prophetic tradition (e.g., Yahweh's use of Nebuchadnezzar his "servant" in Jer 27:5–6 and Cyrus his "anointed one" in Isa 45:1 as instruments of his divine will), but it is also "held together by a general expectation of the future triumph of Yahweh." In fact, I would contend that this prophetic interpretation of history is probably heightened during the restoration period precisely because the Hebrew monarchy and classical prophecy had ceased. Malachi, and no doubt others awaiting Yahweh's "shaking of the nations" (cf. Hag 2:7, 21–22; Joel 3:9–12), observed current world events with keen interest. Fittingly, Malachi pronounces Yahweh's glory among the nations to those who should have readily recognized God's activity in human history on behalf of Israel — the priests (1:11, 14).

Specifically then, how might the reign of King Darius I of Persia contribute to our understanding of the book of Malachi? I offer these tentative suggestions in the form of questions in order to provoke further thought and discussion: (a) what is the relationship between the expansionist policies of Darius and the promulgation of his name as "King in this great earth far and wide" (cf. Kent [1953: 138]) and the so-called universalism of Mal 1:11, 14? (b) did the Levitical priesthood in Jerusalem rise to political prominence quite early in the history of the province of Yehud due to some act of intervention by Darius directed at Zerubbabel? and (c) how much of the general tone of religious apathy and despair characteristic of early restoration Yehud may be attributed to the people's recognition that what has been called Persian "religious tolerance" was little more than political pragmatism (clearly the Persians needed a Palestinian base of operations for the conquest and control of Egypt, cf. *ABD* 5:238–39)?

Finally, two particular events during the reign of Darius may have actually served as the occasion prompting the prophet Malachi to deliver his oracles to Yehud. Less likely is Darius's visit to Egypt in 497–496 B.C./E. at which time he commissioned the building of a temple to the god Amon at Hibis. No doubt the Persian king would have traveled through Palestine on his way to Egypt, perhaps even visiting the Jerusalem Temple built earlier under his auspices (note the possibilities in connecting such a royal visit with Malachi's announcement of the divine messenger appearing at Yahweh's Temple, 3:1–2). More likely is the defeat of the Persian army by the Greeks at Marathon in 490 B.C./E. Such an event might easily be interpreted prophetically as a signal that Yahweh was about to "shake the kingdoms of the earth" in accordance with Haggai's prior oracle (2:21–22). What better time to call the Hebrew restoration community to repentance?

C. Chronological Outline Relevant to Malachi

Chart 2: Exilic and Postexilic Israelite Chronology

NISAN YEAR			JULIAN YEAR	EVENT	REFERENCE
Year	Month	Day	Month/Day		
597			Apr	Jehoiachin exiled to Babylon	2 Kgs 24:15
593	V		July	Call vision of Ezekiel	Ezek 1:2
592	VI		Aug	Yahweh abandons Temple	Ezek 8:1
588	X	10	Jan 15	Siege of Jerusalem begins	2 Kgs 25:1
587	V	7	Aug 14	Fall of Jerusalem	2 Kgs 25:8
586?	VII		Oct	Assassination of Gedaliah	2 Kgs 25:25
582				Third Judahite deportation	Jer 52:30
561	XII	27	Mar 22	Amnesty granted Jehoiachin	2 Kgs 25:27

NISAN YEAR			JULIAN YEAR	EVENT	REFERENCE
Year	Month	Day	Month/Day		
559				Accession of Cyrus in Persia	
539	VII	16	Oct 12	Babylon falls	
	VIII	3	Oct 29	Cyrus enters Babylon	Dan 5:30–31
538 [to]	III	24	Mar 24 [to]	Cyrus's first year; edict of Cyrus	Ezra 1:1–4
537	III	11	Mar 11		
537?			Mar/Apr?	Return under Sheshbazzar	Ezra 1:11
	VII		Oct	Rebuilding of the altar	Ezra 3:1–3
536	II		Apr	Second Temple foundation set	Ezra 3:8
530			Aug	Accession of Cambyses	
522			Mar 11	Revolt of Gaumata	
			Mar 23?	Death of Cambyses	
			Sept 29	Accession of Darius I	
520	VI	1	Aug 29	Haggai's first oracle	Hag 1:1
			Aug/Sept?	Temple reconstruction resumed	Ezra 5:1–2
	VI	24	Sept 21	Haggai's second oracle	Hag 1:15
	VII	21	Oct 17	Haggai's third oracle	Hag 2:1
	IX	24	Dec 18	Haggai's fourth oracle	Hag 2:20
	VIII		Oct/Nov	Zechariah's first oracle	Zech 1:1
519	XI	24	Feb 15	Zechariah's visions	Zech 1:7
518	IX	4	Dec 7	Zechariah's second oracle	Zech 7:1
515	XII	3	Mar 12	Second Temple completed	Ezra 6:15

NISAN YEAR			JULIAN YEAR	EVENT	REFERENCE
Year	*Month*	*Day*	*Month/Day*		
490			Sept	Battle of Marathon; Malachi prophesies?	
458	I	1	Apr 8	Ezra departs Babylon	Ezra 7:7
	V	1	Aug 4	Ezra arrives Jerusalem	Ezra 7:8–9
	IX	20	Dec 19	Public assembly	Ezra 10:9
	X	1	Dec 29	Marriage review committee begins investigation	Ezra 10:16
445 [to] 444			Apr 13 [to] Apr 2	Twentieth year of King Artaxerxes I	Neh 1:1
445	I		Apr/May	Nehemiah approaches king	Neh 2:1
			Aug?	Arrives in Jerusalem	Neh 2:11
	VI	25	Oct 2	Completion of city wall	Neh 6:15
	VII	1	Oct 8 [to] Nov 5	Public assembly	Neh 8:2
	VII	15 [to] 22	Oct 22 [to] Oct 28	Feast of Booths	Neh 8:14
	VII	24	Oct 30	Fast	Neh 9:1
433 [to] 432			Apr 1 [to] Apr 19	Thirty-second year of Artaxerxes Nehemiah's recall and return	Neh 13:6

2. Persian Palestine

A. SATRAPY OF EBER-NAHARA

According to the OT/HB, Palestine was a part of the territory comprising the satrapy of Eber-Nahara, the land "across the river [Euphrates]" (Ezra 4:10; 8:36; Neh 2:7, 9). A *satrapy* was a region of the Persian empire with well-defined geographical boundaries under the administration of a satrap or governor. The satrap

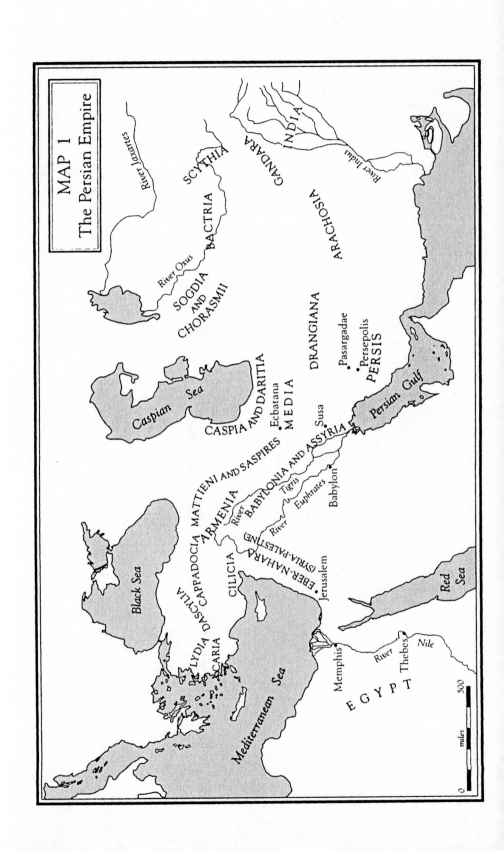

MAP 1
The Persian Empire

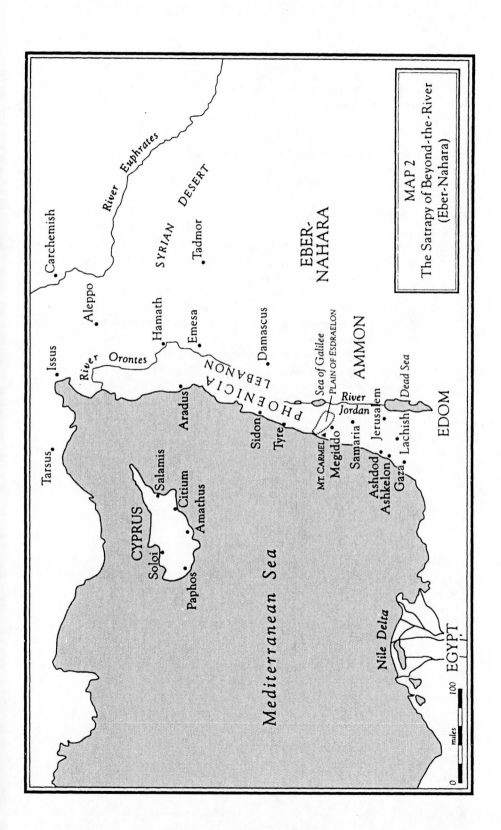

MAP 2
The Satrapy of Beyond-the-River
(Eber-Nahara)

was a royal appointee and as a protector of kingship, he was charged with expediting Persian political and bureaucratic policies in the province. The identification of this tract of land as the satrapy of the Eber-Nahara was simply a carryover from the Assyrian administration of King Esarhaddon (*ebir-nâri; ARAB* 2:229). J. Gray (1970: 143) has identified the Hebrew *kol-'ēber hannāhār* in 1 Kgs 5:4 [4:24] as a later designation for this same satrapy.

The Greek historian Herodotus credits Darius I with the reorganization of the Persian empire into twenty satrapies or protectorates (*Hist* 3.88–95). Stern (1984: 78) has attributed that satrapy list to a later time, perhaps the reign of Xerxes, since the sources contemporary with Darius I differ as to the enumeration of the satrapies. However, Cameron (p. 47) suggested that these Old Persian catalogs were not lists of satrapies but of people-groups representing the vastness and variety of nations under Persian dominion.

Originally, Palestine was part of a large satrapy known as "Babylon and Beyond the River" (Olmstead: 56), which later was divided into two subunits known as the protectorate of Babylonia (combined with Assyria as the ninth satrapy according to Herodotus, *Hist* 3.92; cf. Ezra 7:16) and the protectorate Beyond the River (cf. Ezra 7:21). It is unclear exactly when this administrative district, Eber-Nahara, became a separate satrapy; although Herodotus cited it as the fifth of the twenty satrapies established by Darius I (*Hist* 3.90). Both biblical and extrabiblical sources indicate a certain Tattenai was the governor of the trans-Euphrates region when construction on the Second Temple resumed under the impetus of Haggai and Zechariah in 520 B.C./E. (cf. *ABD* 6:336). Williamson (1985: 76) has deduced that the satrapy of Babylon and Beyond the River remained one administrative unit, since Tattenai is the Persian official presiding over Eber-Nahara only and thus subordinate to Ushtannu, the governor in charge of the entire satrapy. (See Map 1: The Persian Empire.)

Herodotus understood the Eber-Nahara satrapy to contain the southern portions of Syria, the whole of Phoenicia and Palestine, and the island of Cyprus (*Hist* 3.90). He marked the boundaries of the protectorate at Poseideion (al-Mina or Basit on the Orontes?) in the north and as far as Egypt in the south (near Lake Sirbonis, an ancient coastal lake situated between the River of Egypt on the east and Pelusium on the west, and Mt. Casius [one of the Mount Baal Zephon of Sinai, so named due to the influence of Canaanite religion in the region, see *ABD* 1:554–55], located on the narrow spit separating Lake Sirbonis from the Mediterranean Sea; *Hist* 3.5). Generally speaking then, the administrative district known as Eber-Nahara extended southward from the Upper Euphrates-Orontes River region through Syria, Lebanon, and Palestine and into the northern Sinai region. Excluded from the territory of the satrapy were those desert regions to the east and south of Sinai and the coastal plain from Gaza to Lenysus, all under Arab control (*Hist* 3.5, 91). However, Stern (1984: 79) cautions that continual adjustments in the geography and organization of the satrapies and their provinces probably took place, all having a bearing on the history of postexilic Yehud. (See Map 2: The Satrapy of Beyond-the-River [Eber-Nahara].)

B. PROVINCE OF YEHUD: ORGANIZATION AND STRUCTURE

Information concerning the provincial organization in Palestine during the Persian period proves scant, the OT/HB constituting the principal source. Aharoni (1979: 413) assumed the Persians tampered little with the internal structure they inherited from the Babylonians and Assyrians. Stern (1984: 80) essentially accepts Avi-Yonah's conclusions (pp. 12–13) that Persian Palestine consisted of four types of political entities: (1) national states, that is, districts whose borders coincided with the ethnic populations dwelling therein (e.g., Yehud, Samaria, Idumea, Ammon, Moab); (2) the Phoenician commercial cities along the Mediterranean coast (e.g., Dor and Ashkelon); (3) the Arab tribal districts (especially those regions south of Gaza and south and east of the Dead Sea); and (4) the Persian royal fortresses (e.g., Akko and Gaza).

The Persian satrapy was further subdivided into states or provinces (Hebrew *mĕdînâ*, Esth 1:1). Bright (1981: Plate XI) has carved out nineteen provinces in the Eber-Nahara satrapy, twenty counting Cyprus (dating to the time of Nehemiah, ca. 440 B.C./E.) These geopolitical units extend from the provinces of Hamath and Arvad in the north to Ashdod and Idumea in the south and include those Arab tribal districts stretching to the border of Egypt. Standard resources basically agree, marking ten or eleven provinces in Persian Palestine proper (cf. Avi-Yonah [1977: 30]; Meyers and Meyers [1987: xxxvi]; and Bright [1981: Plate XI]). These include two or three coastal districts and seven or eight interior provinces. Yehud was bordered by Samaria on the north, Ammon on the east, Idumea on the south, and Ashdod on the west. (See Map 2: The Satrapy of Beyond-the-River [Eber-Nahara].)

Given the current state of research, consensus as to geographical detail remains out of reach. For instance, Stern (1984: 81) contests Avi-Yonah's understanding (pp. 27–31) of political autonomy among the Phoenician coastal cities; while Avi-Yonah (p. 30) included Joppa in the province of Ashdod, whereas Meyers and Meyers (1987: xxxvi) locate that Sidonian city within the boundaries of Dor; and Bright (1981: Plate XI) placed Joppa in Samaria on a narrow tongue of land jutting to the coast (cf. Grollenberg [1956: 96], Map 23).

However, at least four certainties emerge from scholarly reconstructions of the provincial organization of the Eber-Nahara satrapy. First, the satrapy contained approximately twenty provinces or administrative units (quite probably more, considering that the territorial holdings of the Arab tribes are noted only generally). Second, the boundaries of these political districts established during earlier Assyrian and Babylonian rule remained largely intact. Third, the Phoenician coastal cities likely enjoyed some measure of commercial and political autonomy under the Persians. Fourth, continuing pressure from the Arab desert tribes no doubt resulted in some fluidity in the boundaries of the southern and eastern provinces of the satrapy.

The extent of territory under the jurisdiction of the Persian province of Yehud can be reconstructed only on the basis of biblical records. The northern boundary of Yehud included the cities of Gibeon, Mizpah, Bethel, and Beeroth (Neh 3:7, 15, 19; 7:32; Ezra 2:25, 29; Zech 7:2). The eastern boundary of the province was framed naturally by the Jordan River, while the southern boundary was aligned with the towns of Netophah, Tekoa, and Beth-zur (Ezra 2:22; Neh 3:5, 15, 27; 7:26). Avi-Yonah (p. 17) ascribed this considerable reduction in territorial holdings from that of the preexilic period to the Edomite occupation of southern Yehud (precipitated by the encroachment of the Arab tribes). The village of Keilah marked the southwestern corner of the province (Neh 3:17–18), with the western border delimited by the towns of Zanoah, Kiriath-jearim, and Chephirah (Ezra 2:25; Neh 3:13; Neh 7:29). The northwestern extremity of the province included the towns of Upper and Lower Beth-Horon, and from there the boundary jogged eastward toward Gibeon (cf. 1 Macc 3:24).[1]

The provincial administration of the satrapy was further localized in subunits known as districts (Hebrew *pelek*, Neh 3:9, 17; see also Map 4: The Province of Yehud). The province of Yehud was organized into six such districts, the district capital also providing the name for the entire political unit (Neh 3:9, 12, 14–18). Avi-Yonah (pp. 20–23) has proposed that these six districts were halved, creating twelve administrative subunits. Thus, each of the six districts possessed both a primary and a secondary political hub or capital. The six administrative districts of Yehud are listed in Chart 3 below:

Chart 3. Provincial Districts of Yehud

1) Jericho: primary capital, Jericho; secondary capital, Senaah
2) Mizpah: primary capital, Mizpah; secondary capital, Gibeon
3) Jerusalem: primary capital, Jerusalem; secondary capital, Netophah
4) Beth-zur: primary capital, Beth-Zur; secondary capital, Tekoa
5) Beth-Haccherem: primary capital, Beth-Haccherem; secondary capital, Zanoah
6) Keilah: primary capital, Keilah; secondary capital, Adullam[2]

Governance in the Eber-Nahara satrapy was modeled after the pattern found

---

[1] I am inclined to agree with Avi-Yonah (pp. 17–18) on the positioning of the cities of Lod, Hadid, and Ono outside the western boundary of Yehud (cf. Hayes and Miller: 734). Bright (1981: Plate XI), Stern (1984: 245–49), Meyers and Meyers (1987: xxxvi), and Yamauchi (1988: 598) err in placing these cities within the district of Yehud. Avi-Yonah offered as supporting evidence the proposed summit between Sanballat and Nehemiah in neutral territory in the plain of Ono (Neh 6:2) and Zechariah's lament that Yehud no longer inhabits "the plain" [of Ono] (Zech 7:7). To these arguments I would add that the loss of former Israelite territory in the south and west fits the tone of despair in Malachi and accounts for the Samaritan-Jewish hostilities in Ezra-Nehemiah (McEvenue [1981: 364]) and the later annexation of Lod (Lydda) from Samaria in 145 B.C./E. by the Hasmonean Jonathan, which suggests that Yehud had never wrested the western plain from Samaritan control during the early restoration period (1 Macc 11:34). See further the discussion in *ABD* 5:84.

[2] Note here that Aharoni (1979: 418) has modified Avi-Yonah's proposal by combining Jericho with Mizpah and enumerating but five administrative districts in Yehud. In addition, he assigns the city of Jericho to the Mizpah district as the secondary capital, the city of Gibeon to the Jerusalem district as secondary capital, and the city of Zanoah to the Keilah district as its secondary capital. He cites no secondary capital for Beth-Haccherem. See further the discussion in *ABD* 5:84.

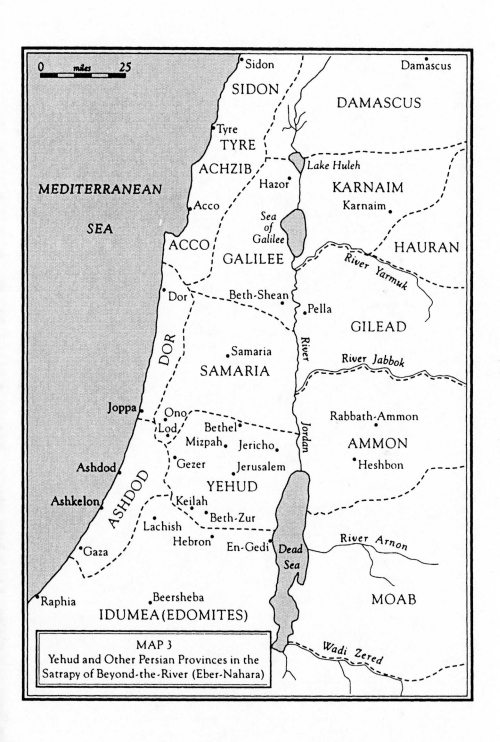

MAP 3
Yehud and Other Persian Provinces in the
Satrapy of Beyond-the-River (Eber-Nahara)

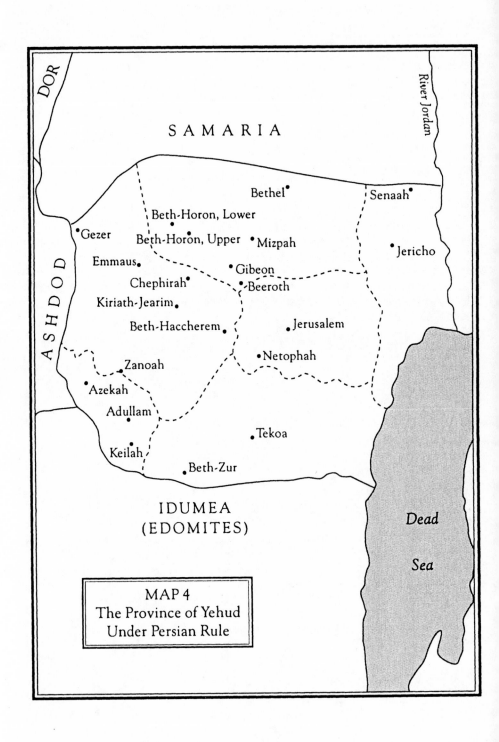

DOR

River Jordan

SAMARIA

Bethel

Senaah

Beth-Horon, Lower

Gezer

Beth-Horon, Upper   Mizpah

Jericho

ASHDOD

Emmaus

Gibeon

Chephirah

Beeroth

Kiriath-Jearim

Beth-Haccherem

Jerusalem

Netophah

Zanoah

Azekah

Adullam

Tekoa

Keilah

Beth-Zur

IDUMEA
(EDOMITES)

Dead

Sea

MAP 4
The Province of Yehud
Under Persian Rule

elsewhere in the Persian empire. The satrap or overseer in charge of the satrapy was a Persian royal appointee who ruled the Eber-Nahara provinces from a capital city (perhaps Damascus, but the location is disputed; cf. *ABD* 5:82). The provinces were supervised by autonomous dynastic governors (Hebrew *peḥâ*, Ezra 8:36; Neh 2:7; 12:26), usually natives of that province. If the records of Ezra and Nehemiah are any indication of provincial politics under Persian authority, the provinces enjoyed considerable latitude as they had opportunity to form leagues against a common enemy (Neh 4:8), bribe Persian officials (Ezra 4:4–5), sidestep the satrap in the provincial capital (or Babylon, if Eber-Nahara was still a subunit of the Babylonian satrapy), and appeal directly to the Persian king (Ezra 4:7).

Four other types of administrative personnel are mentioned in the biblical records, the officials (*śārîm*, Ezra 9:1), the leaders or prefects (*sĕgānîm*, Ezra 9:2; Neh 2:16), nobles (*ḥōrîm*, Neh 4:8 [15]), and the counselors (*yô'ăṣîm*, Ezra 4:5). The *ḥōrîm* and the *sĕgānîm* appear to be synonymous terms for administrative officials. They were not nobles in the sense of the landed aristocracy, but bureaucrats and men of influence. The *ḥōrîm* supervised the Jerusalem wall reconstruction (Neh 4:8 [14]), loaned capital to commoners (Neh 5:7), controlled the local economy (Neh 13:17), and wielded clout as a political body (Neh 6:17). The *sĕgānîm* were political officials distinct from, yet equated with, the *ḥōrîm*. Fensham (1982: 125) traces the term to the Akkadian *šaknu* and has suggested they formed a council of chiefs elected by the populace (see further North's analysis of Hebrew administrative titles in *ABD* 5:87–90; cf. J. L. McKenzie [1959] and McEvenue [1981: 358–64]). The counsellors (*yô'ăṣîm*) were likely lower level officials of the royal court bribed by the enemies of Yehud (Clines 1984: 76). In addition, the "heads of the families" (*ra'śê hā'ābôt*) are mentioned as leaders in the restoration community (Ezra 4:2). According to North (1992b: 87), they are to be equated with the community elders (Hebrew *zĕqēnîm*) who held positions of honor as consultants but possessed no real authority.

A number of inferences may be drawn from the geographical configuration and political structure of the Persian province of Yehud, which help illuminate the social setting of Malachi's oracles. The nearly 50,000 Hebrew expatriates emigrating to Palestine returned to a diminished province, occupying approximately less than half the former preexilic kingdom of Judah (*ABD* 5:84). Those Jews resettling in the province of Yehud encountered a resident alien population (Mal 3:5; Ezra 10:2; Neh 13:3, 23) and apparently established extensive settlements well beyond the political boundaries of the province (Avi-Yonah: 16, 19). Although Yehud's position near the border with Egypt may have proved strategic militarily for Persian designs on further conquests in the south, it yielded no payback commercially. The economic depression reported by Haggai (1:6) remained a dark cloud over Yehud well into the time of Ezra and Nehemiah (Neh 5:1–5). Together with drought and famine, a chief concern for the citizens of Yehud was the excessive satrapy tax levied by the Persian overlords (Neh 5:4) and the local tax imposed by the provincial governor (Neh 5:15).

C. Province of Yehud: Political and Religious History

The province of Yehud (the Aramaic designation "Yehud" is used following Meyers and Meyers [1987: xxxii]) was one of nearly two dozen political units in the Eber-Nahara satrapy. This section traces the development of the province of Yehud as an evolving state bureaucracy during the early Persian period.

1. Persian Custom

The Persians both inherited territories (and resident people groups) subjugated by their predecessors, Assyria and Babylonia, and expanded the boundaries of their empire through military conquest. However, unlike earlier ancient Near Eastern superpowers, the Persians adopted a more enlightened stance in the governance of vanquished nations. The patrimonial system of rule implemented by the Persian kings over the vast expanse of the empire permitted those people groups displaced by previous conquest and deportation to return to their native lands. According to Meyers and Meyers (1987: xxxii), Persian policy encouraged the people groups subject to their authority to retain local cultural and social patterns for the purpose of melding them into a cohesive and ordered political configuration.

Such policy held great significance for the Hebrews as one of many Persian vassal states since it meant that they might return to their homeland in Palestine, reestablish religious custom associated with the Temple of Yahweh, and develop local governance and judicial systems. However, Briant (p. 238) fails to discern any altruistic motives in Persian practice. He claims Persian royal policy was not so much a demonstration of cultural sensitivity and religious tolerance, as it was the expediency of political pragmatism — simply "an attempt to reconcile the central power with the local subjects" (Briant [1992: 239]). Such policy was designed to secure loyalty and establish stability in the Persian satrapies (here Williamson suggests that even the royal grants funding the Temple reconstruction project were likely "tax rebates"; *ABD* 5:85).

Significantly, C. Meyers (*ABD* 6:364) has observed that despite the presence of Yahweh's Temple, the province of Yehud still lacked political autonomy since there was no adjacent royal compound. Yes, the Persians would permit the Hebrews to repatriate Jerusalem and environs, rebuild the Temple of Yahweh, and reinstitute the Mosaic cultus; but the apocalyptic vision of a Davidic king uttered by Ezekiel (37:24–28) would remain just that under Persian domination.

2. Sheshbazzar

The restoration of postexilic Yehud commences in 538 or 537 B.C./E. with the Sheshbazzar's return to Palestine, leading an unknown number of Jewish emigrants out of Babylonia (Ezra 1:8, 11). This resettling of Yehud was made possible by the proclamation of Cyrus the Great permitting former Hebrew expatriates to repopulate Jerusalem and rebuild the Temple of Yahweh, the God of Israel (Ezra 1:1–4; 6:1–5). This policy of restoring local deities to their cities and supporting local religious customs has clear parallels in the Cyrus Cylinder issued after the Persian takeover of Babylon (cf. Rost [1961: 301–7]; Yamauchi [1990: 87–89]).

The enigmatic Sheshbazzar is called "the prince of Yehud" (*nāśî'*, Ezra 1:8) and was appointed "governor of Yehud" (*peḥâ*, Ezra 5:14) by King Cyrus. He was explicitly commissioned to return to Jerusalem and rebuild the Temple of Yahweh and restore the gold and silver Temple utensils confiscated earlier by Nebuchadnezzar to their rightful place (Ezra 1:2–7). Under his leadership, the first steps towards what Ackroyd (1979: 330) calls the "rehabilitation of national religious life" were taken, including the laying of a foundation for the Second Temple (Ezra 5:16) and reinstituting the Mosaic sacrificial system (Ezra 3:1–7; anachronistically attributed to Zerubbabel?, cf. Clines [1984: 65]). Little else is known about the identity of Sheshbazzar, his role as leader of the restoration movement in postexilic Jerusalem, or the extent of his activity as prince and governor of Yehud (see the discussion in *ABD* 5:1207–9).

Of particular interest are the titles ascribed to Sheshbazzar, *nāśî'* or "prince" and *peḥâ* or "governor." Satisfactory explanation of the epithet "prince of Yehud" (Ezra 1:8) is still wanting. The term *nāśî'* here may simply indicate that Sheshbazzar was a member of the Jewish nobility (Clines [1984: 41]), or it may connote both an administrative position vested with formal authority (Fensham [1982: 46]) and the legitimization of Sheshbazzar as a Davidic figure (Rost [1961: 301]). This unusual expression does have a parallel in 1 Chr 2:10 where Nashon is credited as the *něśî' běnê yěhûdâ*, or "prince of the descendants of Judah"; he was one of the staff officials charged by Moses and Aaron to assist in the tribal census and organization (Num 1:7; 2:3).

Albright (1921: 108–10) argued that Sheshbazzar and Shenazzar (1 Chr 3:18) were one and the same person, the fourth son of King Jehoiachin. If such is the case, the epithet *hannāśî' lîhûdâ* ("the prince of Yehud," Ezra 1:8) marked Sheshbazzar as a member of the House of David. Further, it may be argued that the Persians intended to establish a pliant political regime in Yehud by appointing a Davidic descendant as its first administrator. More recently however, Berger has contested such an identification upon careful linguistic analysis of the personal names. He concluded the names Shenazzar and Sheshbazzar signify two different individuals (cf. *ABD* 5:1203). Given the uncertainties associated with the transmission of names from one language to another in the ancient Near East, it seems best to adopt a minimalist approach and concede that Sheshbazzar was a prominent member of the tribe of Judah and probably a Davidic descendant (leaving open the question of his identification with Shenazzar) and that his jurisdiction as a Persian appointee was restricted to Jerusalem and environs (cf. Williamson [1985: 18]).

The title *peḥâ* (Ezra 5:14) proves more difficult to assess because the understanding of the word has ramifications for the exact nature of the post filled by Sheshbazzar and the provincial status of Yehud in the Eber-Nahara satrapy. Alt's essay remains the watershed for the study of the political history of Yehud during the Persian period. According to his thesis, Yehud did not gain full provincial status in the satrapy until the governorship of Nehemiah (445–433 B.C./E.). Central to his argument were the assumptions that the Persians merely retained the administrative system inherited from the Babylonians, which incorporated Yehud within the province of Samaria; and prior to Nehemiah the term *peḥâ* must be understood broadly as "officials" or "special commissioners" with duty-specific restrictions limiting their political authority. Rudolph (1949: 62; cf. Ackroyd [1979: 330]) championed Alt's thesis, and more recently it has been buttressed by the studies of Stern (1971 and 1984) and McEvenue treating recent archaeological evidence in the form of Persian period seals and bullae from Palestine (cf. Avigad).

However, Alt's theory has been rejected by M. Smith (pp. 193–201) and Widengren (pp. 509–11). More recently Meyers and Meyers (1987: 14–15) and Williamson (1988a: 59–82), in similar but independent studies of the pertinent archaeological data, have offered compelling reasons for abandoning Alt's hypothesis (see Hoglund's [pp. 69–86] recapitulation of the arguments; he too rejects the political reorganization hypothesis). They jettison Alt's reconstruction in favor of one that accords provincial status to the region of Yehud and understands the term peḥâ as a title for the Persian provincial governor. In deference to Stern (1984: 82) and McEvenue (p. 356), who qualify the title peḥâ (prior to Nehemiah) as little more than an official with ad hoc authority, the political environment of the early Persian period in Yehud intimates the possibility of expanding powers for the governor requisite with the continuing growth and stabilization of the provincial bureaucracy (Williamson [1988a: 77]; cf. Petersen [1995: 18]).

While I concur with Bright (1981: 363) that the political status of the restoration community remained ambiguous for many years, Eskenazi's (p. 1208) reconstruction of the history of Sheshbazzar serves nicely as a cautious and balanced summary statement. First, Sheshbazzar was appointed governor of the province of Yehud in the Eber-Nahara satrapy. Second, Yehud was established as a semi-independent province much like the other provinces of the satrapy. Although here I would add that Yehud was no doubt a developing provincial bureaucracy in transition from a provincial district supervised from Samaria to self-rule as a Persian province. Third, the extent of Sheshbazzar's administrative authority is unclear. The mandate by Cyrus to restore national religious life in Yehud suggests some political clout as well, given his reorganization of the former Babylonian territorial holdings (cf. CAH 4:14–15). Fourth, it is likely Sheshbazzar was a prominent member of the tribe of Judah. His Davidic ancestry is less certain and is best left an open question. Fifth, Sheshbazzar's failure to rebuild the Temple and restore sacrificial worship defies explanation, with financial difficulties and external pressures heading the list of suggestions (Ackroyd [1979: 330]). His ephemeral appearance in the OT/HB is probably due to just that, his failure to restore the Hebrew cultus!

3. Zerubbabel

The restoration of postexilic Jerusalem continued under the leadership of a Babylonian Jew named Zerubbabel (Ezra 2:2). Although his name is probably derived from the Akkadian zērbābili ("seed of Babylon"), he was the son of Shealtiel, Jehoiachin's eldest son, and thus traced his lineage to the family of David (Ezra 3:2, 8; 5:2). However, the Chronicler records Pedaiah, Jehoiachin's third son, as the father of Zerubbabel (see the discussion in ABD 6:1085).

Two other difficulties concerning the figure named Zerubbabel have been raised by biblical scholars. First, there is some confusion as to the exact identity of Zerubbabel because both he and Sheshbazzar perform similar functions as governor of Yehud (i.e., lay the foundation for the Second Temple, Ezra 3:8–10; 5:16; cf. Josephus *Ant* xi.i.3 [13–14] who equated Zerubbabel with Sheshbazzar). Williamson's (1988b: 1193) rationale for retaining the distinct identities of the two characters, Sheshbazzar and Zerubbabel, holds firm (cf. Myers [1968: 28] in response to Rudolph [1949: 30–31]).

Unlike Eskenazi (p. 1209), who understands the biblical accounts of the founding of the Second Temple as contradictory, I prefer the approach harmonizing the biblical data. Sheshbazzar set the Temple platform and/or initiated the laying of foundations for the superstructure (*yĕhab 'uššayyā'*, Ezra 5:16) in 537 B.C./E., while Zerubbabel laid the foundations upon which the Second Temple precincts were erected or completed (or expanded), the foundations set previously by Sheshbazzar (*yāsad*, Ezra 3:10; on the use of *ysd* as a technical term for building and construction, see *TDOT* 6:116). That both men receive credit for founding the Temple in biblical record is only natural, given the Chronicler's interest in the restoration of Jewish religious life (cf. Clines [1984: 88–89]).

According to Ezra 2:64–65, Zerubbabel led nearly 50,000 former Israelite captives back to Jerusalem from Babylonia. The second difficulty raised by Zerubbabel's activity is one of chronology. When did Zerubbabel's emigration occur? Either Ezra 2 must be read in context with Ezra 1 and the edict of Cyrus, placing Zerubbabel's journey near 538 B.C./E.; or Ezra 2 represents a summary statement of all those who returned to Jerusalem from Babylon, a composite emigration record covering those years from the edict of Cyrus to the completion of the Second Temple (cf. Williamson [1988b: 1193]). The latter is clearly more likely, and here I am attracted to Myers's (1968: 28) argument that Zerubbabel's return be placed near 522 B.C./E. (cf. Ezra 3:8). It may well be that the ascension of Darius I was the event prompting this mass emigration of Jews back to the land of covenant promise. This would explain the enthusiasm and vigor of the restoration community for the Temple construction project (Hag 1:12–15), as those more recent emigrants would not have been jaded by the previous two decades of failure to renew the Temple cult.

The term *peḥâ*, or governor, is applied to Zerubbabel only by the prophet Haggai (1:1, 14; 2:2, 21), although he is clearly the referent of the title "governor of the Jews" mentioned in Darius's letter to Tattenai, then governor of the Eber-Nahara satrapy (Ezra 6:7 and perhaps in 2:63?). Meyers and Meyers (1987: 13–16) have ably defended the view that Zerubbabel was the provincial governor of Yehud, which enjoyed limited autonomy in keeping with Persian administrative structure in the satrapies. His record as a civil administrator is limited exclusively to the successful resolution of political resistance on the part of the enemies of Yehud to the rebuilding of Yahweh's Temple (Ezra 4:1–5; 6:1–12). Zerubbabel exits the biblical narrative rather abruptly and his fate is uncertain. He may have been an elderly statesman at this time and simply died (cf. Myers [1968: 28]). Others have suggested that he may have been ousted by the Persian overlords as a political liability because he may have been suspected of planning a rebellion against Persian authority (cf. Yamauchi [1988: 639–40]; but Williamson [1988b:

1193–94] disagrees). It is more probable that our lack of information about Zerubbabel, other than his role in rebuilding the Temple, is but another example of deliberate omission on the part of the biblical writer given the theological purposes shaping the narrative (Japhet [1982: 82]; cf. Williamson's [1985: 45] caveat on using Ezra primarily for the purpose of historical reconstruction).

Zerubbabel's legacy as governor of the province of Yehud was the establishment of the Second Temple in Jerusalem and the reinstitution of the Mosaic sacrificial liturgy and the pilgrimage festivals (Ezra 6:13–22). He, along with the high priest Joshua, are heralded as the builders of the Second Temple (Ezra 3:8–11; 5:1–2). The work commenced in the sixth month of King Darius's second year of rule (520 B.C./E.), at the prompting of the prophet Haggai (1:1; Ezra 5:1–2). The Temple reconstruction project was completed in the twelfth month of Darius's sixth year, or March 12, 515 B.C./E. (Ezra 6:15).

Zerubbabel's most notable administrative achievement was the successful negotiation with King Darius I for complete Persian support of the Temple-rebuilding campaign in the face of opposition instigated by Tattenai, governor of the Eber-Nahara satrapy (Ezra 5:3–6:12). Despite these contributions to the restoration community, the prophets Haggai and Zechariah are accorded equal, if not greater, accolades for their roles in prompting and encouraging the people to complete the Temple reconstruction (Ezra 5:1; 6:15). Hindsight would indicate that Haggai's pronouncement of Zerubbabel as Yahweh's "signet ring" (2:23) had more significance for overturning the curse on the line of David (cf. Jer 22:24–30) and apocalyptic messianism (cf. Zech 12:7–13:1) than for legitimizing Zerubbabel and announcing a new Davidic era (note that Zechariah's eschatological projections focus on Joshua the high priest, 3:1–10; 6:9–15). This may help explain the response of bitter lamentation to Zerubbabel's Temple on the part of those who remembered the splendor of Solomon's edifice (Ezra 3:13) and the emphasis in the biblical narrative on the religious celebration associated with the restoration of Temple ritual instead of on the personage of Zerubbabel and his accomplishment (cf. Williamson [1985: 48]).

Beyer (ABD 6:1085) suggests that "Zerubbabel's connection with the line of David may have fueled messianic hopes in Judah" (cf. Hag 2:20–23). Meyers and Meyers (1987: 15) venture that Haggai's preference for the title *pehâ* for Zerubbabel was the result of his more active sponsorship of the Davidic line in contrast to Zechariah. However, attempts to construct a postexilic line of Davidic descendants prove more problematic and less useful than the reconstructions of the sequence of postexilic governors in Yehud. By the time of the prophet Malachi, the House of David is a nonfactor in the restoration community, politically and religiously.

Apart from Zerubbabel, the only other known Davidic descendant with any connection to the governorship in postexilic Yehud is Shelomith, the daughter of Zerubbabel (1 Chr 3:19). Testimony from a seal inscription does mention a *šlmyt* associated with Elnathan, the governor of Yehud (Avigad [1976: 13]), possibly the very same woman (Meyers and Meyers [1987: 12–13]; cf. Williamson [1988a: 70]). However, there is little uncontested evidence warranting the speculation that early postexilic Yehud was ruled by a dynasty of Davidic governors, or even for the so-called convergence between the governorship of Yehud and the Davidic family (Meyers and Meyers [1987: 13]; cf. Williamson [1988b: 1194], who surmises that even Zerubbabel kept himself clear of questionable political involvement as relates to the messianic hope in restoration Yehud).

Interestingly, the reconstruction of the Davidic line by Meyers and Meyers (1987: 14) does strengthen the argument for the 500 B.C./E. date for Malachi. The prophet makes no appeal to the family of David, implying they are no longer a factor in the restoration community (perhaps in correlation with the governorship of Elnathan, ca. 510–490 B.C./E.[?]; note that the "house of David" is relegated to an apocalyptic motif in Second Zechariah [12:8–13:1]). This demise of the Davidic family as political powerbrokers also helps explain the apathy and despair Malachi encountered. Hopes for a new Davidic era had been recently dashed. The key players in the provincial bureaucracy confronted by Malachi were clearly the priests (cf. Mal 1:6; 2:1; note as well the emphasis on the covenant with Levi — not David, Mal 2:4). Ackroyd's (1979: 331) observation is germane: "It may well have seemed the beginning of a new Davidic era to some; but the Chronicler, writing perhaps two centuries later, plays down the Davidic element." Malachi does too! We would best follow suit in our assessment of Malachi's oracles.

4. Early Provincial Governors of Yehud
The most obscure stage of postexilic Israelite history is that intervening period of early governors between Zerubbabel and Nehemiah. Based upon reconstructions from archaeological data forwarded by Avigad (see Chart 4), Meyers and Meyers (1987: xxxiv) enthusiastically aver, "We can now fill in the 'governor gap' for the period prior to Ezra and Nehemiah."

Chart 4. Persian Period Governors of Yehud

Dates	Governors	Davidic Line	High Priests
538	Sheshbazzar	Sheshbazzar	Jehozadak
520–510?	Zerubbabel	Zerubbabel	Joshua
510–490?	Elnathan	Shelomith	Joiakim
		Hananiah	
490–470?	Yeho'ezer	Shecaniah	Eliashib I
			Johanan I
470–	Ahzai	Hattush	Eliashib II
445–433	Nehemiah	'Elioenai	Joiada I

However, the reconstruction is predicated on contested archaeological data (cf. Stern [1984: 82–86]) and has no biblical corroboration. Moreover, the reconstruction proves flimsy at two key points: the catalog of governors' names is (most likely) incomplete and the terms of those officials cited cannot be dated with any precision. In fact, Williamson (1988a: 77 n. 56) dismisses the names of Yeho'ezer and Ahzai from the list of early governors of Yehud because the stamps attesting their tenure in office were found in a refuse dump at Ramat Rahel (Beth-

Haccherem?), raising serious question as to the date of the materials (Petersen [1995: 14] echoes similar concerns).

Here it seems prudent to certify the conclusions of Williamson (1988a: 77), who identified with certainty only three governors prior to Nehemiah (Sheshbazzar, Zerubbabel, and Elnathan) but still regarded that there was sufficient evidence to affirm the existence of a distinct province of Yehud within the Eber-Nahara satrapy. Further, Williamson has sided with M. Smith (p. 196) in interpreting Nehemiah's apologia (Neh 5:14–19) as a comparison of like with like; that is, governors of Yehud with governors of Yehud. However, this is not to suggest that the office of governor in Yehud was immune to administrative reform or historical development, as Williamson concedes.

5. Nehemiah

The exact date of Ezra's arrival in Jerusalem remains a topic of scholarly debate. Three options for the chronology of Ezra's ministry in the restoration community have emerged from the discussion.[3] Following the analysis of Cross (1975), I opt for the traditional view placing Ezra in Jerusalem during the seventh year of King Artaxerxes I, or 458 B.C./E. (cf. Ezra 7:8). There is general agreement that Nehemiah came to Jerusalem in 445 B.C./E., the twentieth year of King Artaxerxes I (cf. Neh 1:1; 2:1). This means that Ezra preceded Nehemiah by way of chronological order but suggests that they were contemporaries by way of religious and political activity in Jerusalem during the Persian period. Indeed, twice they appear together in the text, at the exposition of the Mosaic law (Neh 8:9) and the dedication of the wall of Jerusalem (Neh 12:26, 36; although some suggest that this association has been artificially introduced by a later redactor, e.g., Rudolph [1949: 148]).

Like their earlier compatriots, Haggai and Zechariah, Ezra and Nehemiah had complementary ministries in Jerusalem of both a spiritual and physical or material nature. Ezra, a Levitical priest and scribe trained in the law of Moses, is best remembered for his exposition of the Torah before the restoration community and the subsequent religious reform it inspired (cf. Neh 8:1–12). Nehemiah is celebrated for the organizational skills he demonstrated in supervising the reconstruction of large sections of the Jerusalem wall destroyed during the Babylonian siege in 587 B.C./E. (Neh 2:11–3:32; cf. Sir 49:13). Both men were members of

---

[3]The traditional view dates Ezra's arrival in Jerusalem to the seventh year of King Artaxerxes I, or 458 B.C./E. (cf. Ezra 7:8). A second view founded upon the assumption that the text of Ezra 7:8 has been corrupted through the course of manuscript transmission places Ezra's arrival in Jerusalem alternately in the "twenty-seventh" or "thirty-seventh" year of King Artaxerxes I (e.g., Bright [1981: 385–86]). A third approach, the late-Ezra view, completely disassociates Nehemiah and Ezra on the basis of the reference to the high priest Johanan (Neh 12:26). The Elphantine archives name Johanan as high priest in Jerusalem near the end of the fifth century B.C., thus Ezra's activity is better placed during the seventh year of King Artaxerxes II, or 398 B.C./E. (e.g., Eissfeldt [1965: 553–55]). For full discussions of the Ezra-Nehemiah chronological puzzle, see Ackroyd (1979: 328–42); Clines (1984: 14–24); and Williamson (1985: xxxix–xliv).

some standing in Persian royal circles, Ezra holding a position akin to counsel for Jewish affairs in the king's cabinet (Ezra 7:1–6; cf. Clines [1984: 99–100] and Fensham [1982: 99–100]) and Nehemiah serving King Artaxerxes I as a cup-bearer (Neh 1:11; 2:1–2; cf. Yamauchi [1990: 258–60]). Their combined efforts to revitalize the religious, social, and economic life of Persian period Jerusalem were rooted in nationalistic pride for the tradition of the Hebrew forefathers (Neh 2:3) and a genuine zeal for the reputation of the name of Yahweh in the midst of pagan opposition (Ezra 9:1–15; Neh 1:4–11).

The biblical record ascribes the title, governor (*peḥâ*) of Yehud, to Nehemiah (5:14; 10:1). For some, Nehemiah is the first true governor of an autonomous province of Yehud during the Persian period; his predecessors were understood to be little more than "controllers" or "special commissioners" (cf. Ackroyd [1979: 338]). As established in the foregoing discussion, it is now more accurate to regard Nehemiah as one of a series of several Persian appointed governors of the state of Yehud, which was granted provincial status in the Eber-Nahara satrapy by Cyrus the Great (cf. Williamson [1985: 242–44] and [1988a: 76–77]).

More recent scholars have touted Nehemiah as a parade example of organizational skill and administrative effectiveness (e.g., Bright [1981: 380–83]; cf. Rowley [1955]). During his twelve plus years in office he compiled a remarkable record of selfless governmental service (cf. Neh 5:14–19). Foremost among his achievements were his initiatives in repairing portions of the walls of Jerusalem (despite the opposition of a coalition of neighboring provincial governors, Neh 5:15–16; cf. 4:15–23), averting an economic crisis (Neh 5:1–13), and founding principled government policy with a view toward equity and social justice (Neh 5:10–11, 15; 11:1–2; cf. Yamauchi [1990: 258–78]).

In addition, Nehemiah used his platform as provincial governor to implement religious reforms, including the reinstitution of Temple ritual and Sabbath observance (Neh 8:13–18; 13:15–22), a Temple tax and rehabilitation of the priesthood (Neh 10:32–39), and the introduction of Mosaic law as the rule for community life (Neh 8:1–12). I disagree with North's (1992a: 1070–71) diatribe assessing Nehemiah as an amateur building contractor, vain and self-aggrandizing. No doubt Nehemiah was energetic and clever, but anyone who knows politics ancient or modern recognizes "things get done" in direct proportion to the "clout" carried by the leadership in office. North's discounting of the historical reliability of the memoir materials in Ezra-Nehemiah fails to negate the fact that archaeology and Jewish tradition attest that the Jerusalem wall was rebuilt (see Yamauchi [1990: 270–72]; ABD 3:757; cf. Sir 49:11). I suspect that Nehemiah's success in rebuilding the city wall and establishing the postexilic Jerusalem community politically and economically says more about his connections to the Persian king (Artaxerxes I, Neh 1:11–2:10) as the royal appointee to govern the province of Yehud than it does about Nehemiah's cleverness or the inability and ineffectiveness of previous provincial governors in restoring Jerusalem.[4]

---

[4]Hoglund (p. 244) suggests as much when he argues that the Ezra-Nehemiah missions were not "the result of the empire rewarding the Restoration community for loyalty in the

3. Implications for Malachi

What does this historical background, the early Persian period and the reign of Darius I, suggest for understanding the oracles of Malachi? The numerous implications for the tone, imagery, and message of the book have been sketched below under five distinct headings.

A. HISTORICAL

Malachi addressed a recently formed province in the Persian satrapy of Eber-Nahara during the reign of Darius I. Despite its provincial status and the presence of the Second Temple in Jerusalem, Persian Yehud struggled for political identity, an island amid a sea of hostile neighboring satrapy provinces. The office of provincial governor and the provincial bureaucracy were not only in an embryonic stage of development, but also faced the challenge of sharing political power with a potential rival in the Levitical priesthood and the institution of the Second Temple.

Because Egypt had been occupied and secured as yet another empire satrapy, Yehud and the other provinces of Palestine constituted little more than the political and cultural backwater of Persian interests. For their part, the Persians had set their sights on the conquest of the Greeks and control of the west. The series of colossal and historic contests between Susa and Athens sealed the fate of the Persian empire and shaped the relationship of Orient to Occident. It is quite possible that the Persian defeat at the hands of the Greeks in the battle of Marathon served as the occasion that prompted the oracles of Malachi.[5]

B. POLITICAL

If the example of Tattenai is representative of the satrapy governor's policy regarding the province of Yehud, then at best the Jewish restoration community has an unsympathetic (and hence unresponsive) political overlord. Despite Darius's commission providing for the rebuilding of Yahweh's Temple, there is little evidence to indicate that the Persian king demonstrated any more interest in the

---

face of regional revolts. Rather, their missions were an effort on the part of the Achaemenid empire to create a web of economic and social relationships that would tie the community more completely into the imperial system."

[5] Hoglund (pp. 51–69) dismisses the theories of Morgenstern and others proposing widespread political and social upheaval in the Levant during the first quarter of the fifth century B.C./E. While there may be little archaeological evidence attesting such unrest in Syro-Palestine, the fact remains that the Persians were defeated at Marathon in 490 B.C./E., and Darius's son Xerxes had to suppress revolts in Egypt (485 B.C./E.) and Babylon (484 and 482 B.C./E.) upon his succession to the Persian throne (cf. Yamauchi [1990: 193–94]). It seems highly unlikely that the Persian empire experienced no "ripple effect" from events of such magnitude, though the paucity of material evidence moves the discussion of any specifics associated with these sociopolitical disturbances into the realm of speculation. Further, it seems even more likely that such events may well have prompted the utterances of the prophet Malachi, especially with the echo of Haggai's oracle promising Yahweh's "overthrow of the nations" no doubt still reverberating through the early restoration community (Hag 2:21–22).

province of Yehud than the satrapy governor. Yehud and the Eber-Nahara satrapy were valuable to the Persians primarily as a land bridge for monitoring commerce between two continents and as a base for military operations directed against Egypt (cf. Petersen [1995: 19–20]).

The early demise of Haggai's prediction of a Davidic dynasty originating in Zerubbabel contributed to the political skepticism and cynicism encountered by Malachi. This loss of confidence in the ability of the Davidic family to orchestrate the restoration of Jerusalem envisioned by Ezekiel and Zechariah (implicit in the lampstand vision [4:1–14], though apparently postponed to an indefinite future time; cf. Meyers and Meyers [1987: 243]) polarized political power within the province as seen in the prominence of the Levitical priesthood in Malachi's message. In addition to the emergence of hierocracy in postexilic Yehud, the metamorphosis in the office of scribe from that of state bureaucrat to Mosaic lawyer also may have occurred in this early period, given the Persian practice of encouraging the development of local legal systems (Meyers and Meyers [1987: xxxii]).

C. SOCIAL
Contrary to the contentions of Glazier-McDonald (1987a: 85), the social ills confronted by Malachi were not so much the by-product of baalism, as sheer pragmatism on the part of the Jewish restoration community in response to the depressed local economy. Intermarriage with the resident alien population, neglect of the deprived and disadvantaged, and reneging on the tithe are but symptoms of the severe economic pressures faced by the province of Yehud (caused in part by a shortfall in the imperial budget and stingy satrapy treasurers; cf. Clines [1984: 207]; Petersen [1995: 20]).

Other factors, however, were responsible for the adverse conditions too, including natural disaster (Hag 1:6, 10), heavy taxation (Neh 5:15), and a local economy controlled by corrupt officials and nobles in league with the resident alien population (Neh 5:3, 7–8, 15). Given the selfishness of human nature, alms for the poor and Yahweh's tithe were necessarily forfeited to maximize personal financial interests; and what better way to obtain financial standing in the community than to marry into the "brokerages" of the resident aliens? Hardship and poverty precipitated by the sagging local economy apparently persisted well into the governorship of Nehemiah, and the direct ties between his religious and financial reforms tend to confirm that the motive for Jewish intermarriage was primarily economic, not religious (Neh 10:28–39 [29–40]; cf. Gottwald [1985: 432–34]; Nogalski [1993b: 198]).

D. RELIGIOUS
The religious apathy prompting the widespread abuse of the sacrificial system and neglect of the tithe condemned by Malachi (1:8; 3:8) was likely the result of both the diminished stature of the Second Temple and the unfulfilled predictions of the earlier prophets, Haggai and Zechariah. Apart from the debate as to the degree of inferiority of the Second Temple compared to Solomon's Temple (cf. *ABD* 5:354–64; see Figs. 11 and 12), the lament over the structure by those

who had seen Solomon's edifice (Ezra 3:12) was more for what it represented —
not its size and splendor. Solomon's Temple was the tangible symbol of Israel's
autonomy, the surety of the Davidic covenant, and the guarantee of Yahweh's
blessing and protection — all now nonexistent despite the presence of a Second
Temple!

No doubt the people perceived Haggai's prediction about the treasures of the
nations flowing in the Temple (2:7) and Zechariah's vision of peace and prosperity for Jerusalem (8:3–5) as failed prophecies and certain signs of Yahweh's disre-
gard for his elect (cf. Mal 1:2). Ezekiel's vision (chapters 40–48) of an Israelite
Temple-state centered in Jerusalem had quickly faded amidst the stark reality of
Persian domination and the problems of mere survival among the competing
provinces of the satrapy (cf. Berquist [1995: 100–2] on the emerging "pluralism"
during the Persian period and the problems it created for the worship of Yahweh
in Yehud).

E. THEOLOGICAL

Discernible theological developments in Malachi associated with the reign of
Darius I are more difficult to trace. Petersen (1977: 44) has noted that while
Malachi still affirms the triumph of Yahweh over the nations, expectation of a
coming Davidic figure with a political function (Hag 2:20–23) has given way to
that of a coming divine messenger with a prophetic function (Mal 3:1–2). Also,
Koch (1984: 178) has observed that Malachi senses a delay in the coming Day
of Yahweh and thus relativizes the salvation oracles proclaimed by Haggai and
Zechariah. It is possible that this modification of the prophet's eschatological
perceptions reflects some convergence with the Zoroastrian doctrine of successive world empires given the defeat of Darius at Marathon (cf. Reicke [1968:
32–33]; and Yamauchi [1990: 424] who claims that the strongest case for Zoroastrian influence among the Persian kings is during the reign of Darius).

The shift in prophetic emphasis from messages directed to specific political
and religious leaders (e.g., Hag 2:2, 20; Zech 3:1; 4:6), to the priesthood and
people generally (Mal 1:6; 3:8) may have been the result of Darius's political
purges across the empire and the recognition that human leadership is ephemeral. Given Malachi's affinity for vocabulary used by Jeremiah and Ezekiel, it is
even possible that the later prophet was profoundly affected by the notion of
individual responsibility before Yahweh as expressed in the "sour grapes" parable
(Jer 31:29–30; Ezek 18:1–4).

Finally, the "cultic" reform espoused by Malachi (1:6–14) in contrast to the
"spiritual" reform announced by Zechariah (7:8–12) may have stemmed from
the prophet's recognition that the stabilizing institution for the province during
the interim would indeed be Yahweh's Temple, not the Persian gubernatorial
appointee(s). This also helps account for the accent in Malachi on the role of
the Levitical priesthood as religious educators (2:7–8; cf. Ezek 7:26).

I. E. DATING THE ORACLES OF MALACHI

In his classic work on Malachi, von Bulmerincq (1926: 87–97) has outlined the range of possibilities for the dating of Malachi's disputations. Subsequent studies on this last book of the Twelve can be classified under the seven categories established by von Bulmerincq with only slight modification. His categories read as follows:

1) Malachi contemporary with or prior to Haggai and Zechariah 1–8,
2) Malachi before Ezra and Nehemiah,
3) Malachi during Nehemiah's first governorship,
4) Malachi between the first and second governorships of Nehemiah,
5) Malachi during Nehemiah's second governorship,
6) Malachi contemporary with Ezra and Nehemiah, and
7) Malachi during the late Persian or early Greek periods.

Recent scholarship and the significant works of past generations on the book of Malachi are catalogued according to von Bulmerincq's dating schema in Appendix A.

Traditionally the date of Malachi has been related to fixed postexilic historical events and hence to absolute chronological boundaries. These limits include a *terminus a quo* of 516/15 B.C./E. (the completion of the Second Temple), key events like the reform initiatives of Ezra and Nehemiah (ca. 458–432 B.C./E.), and a *terminus ad quem* of 180 B.C./E. (the citation in Sir 49:10 to the "Twelve Prophets"). Furthermore, these various viewpoints for the date of the book largely appeal to the same internal evidence — albeit interpreted somewhat differently in each case (e.g., analysis of the priesthood in Malachi led S. R. Driver [1922: 357] to conclude that Malachi was contemporary with Ezra and Nehemiah, cf. Petersen [1995: 5–6], whereas Spoer [1908: 185–86] understood Malachi's assessment of the priesthood to reflect the early Maccabean period). Typically, biblical scholars have focused on the thematic similarities, ritual practices, lexical parallels, and the contiguous descriptions of the religious, social, and political conditions within the Jewish restoration community in attempting to date the book. The essential arguments substantiating chronological claims for Malachi based upon this approach are summarized below.

1. Historical Factors

The book of Malachi makes little direct reference to historical events or personages contemporary with the prophet. A study of the internal evidence in Malachi yields three specific historical data traditionally discussed by biblical commentators: the destruction of Edom (1:2–5), the political oversight of Yehud by a "governor" (Heb. *peḥâ*, 1:8), and the presence of Yahweh's Temple in Jerusalem (1:10).

The history of Edom during the Babylonian and Persian eras concurrent with the exilic and postexilic periods of Hebrew history is so poorly documented that this reference to Edom in Malachi is of limited value. Edom did not oppose the Babylonian campaign against Judah in 587 B.C./E.; and according to Ps 137:7 and Obad 10–14, the Edomites were at least passive allies of the Babylonians (cf. ABD 2:292–93). This has led Lindsay to conclude that the kingdom of Edom probably escaped the ravages of Nebuchadnezzar's Palestinian campaigns. According to Bartlett (p. 293), the collapse of the Edomite kingdom may have been the result of a later series of campaigns by the Babylonian king Nabonidus in the southern transJordan sometime after 552 B.C./E.

The Greek historian and geographer Diodorus does report that Antigonus I (one of the *diadochus* or "successor" generals of Alexander the Great who carved out a kingdom in Macedonia and Thrace from Alexander's dismembered empire), attacked Nabatean Arabs then ruling Petra in 312 B.C./E. (*Bib hist* 19.95). He waged a series of campaigns against Cassander, Ptolemy, Seleucus, and Lysimachus in an attempt to reunify Alexander's kingdom. He was defeated and killed in battle at Ipsus in 301 B.C./E., with Lysimachus and Seleucus dividing the Antigonid kingdom. (Cf. *CAH* 6:462–504.)

All this would suggest that Malachi's reference to the destruction of Edom may be placed between 552 and 312 B.C./E. This assumes that Malachi acknowledges Edom in a literal and historical sense, not in a metaphorical sense, as a symbol of "wickedness" (so Ackroyd [1975: 224]; Mason [1977: 141]; and Coggins [1987: 75]).

Malachi's use of the term *peḥâ* does indicate kingship has ceased in Yehud. This rather vague title is used in the OT/HB to describe governmental officials during both the exilic and postexilic periods of Israelite history (cf. 2 Kgs 18:24; Jer 51:23; Ezek 23:6; Hag 1:1; Esth 8:9; Neh 3:7; etc.). Glazier-McDonald (1987a: 15) and Verhoef (1987: 157) assume that the expression denotes a Persian dignitary, while Mason (1977: 137) is less certain — noting the term alone cannot tell us if the book belongs to the Persian or Greek period. However, the word *peḥâ* was originally an Assyrian term and McEvenue (p. 362) has demonstrated that the preexilic biblical usage of *peḥâ* has military connotations. O'Brien (1990: 120) has commented that the lack of uniformity in meaning and the widespread utilization of the term precludes the assumption Malachi should be dated to the Persian period.[1]

The oracles of Malachi indicate that Temple service is fully operational, including animal sacrifice and a functioning priesthood (1:6–2:3). Thus, Malachi can be dated within but two historical time frames, the preexilic period of Israelite history prior to the fall of Jerusalem in 587 B.C./E. and the postexilic period after the reconstruction of the Second Temple (516–515 B.C./E.). Given the

---

[1]Those who dismiss the significance of Malachi's use of the term *peḥâ* as suggestive of a Persian date for composition strain in their emphasis on the extrabiblical usage of the word (e.g., O'Brien [1990: 118–20]). Preexilic contexts utilizing *peḥâ* in the MT have clear military connotations, while the postexilic contexts in which *peḥâ* is used have only political and bureaucratic connotations (cf. McEvenue [1981: 362–63]). The political and bureaucratic context of *peḥâ* in Malachi (1:8) fits the pattern of postexilic usage of the term.

weight of other related historical and linguistic factors, an overwhelming majority of biblical scholars have opted to date Malachi to the Second Temple period of Hebrew history. The lone exception here is O'Brien (1990: 147) who has dated the book to "anytime between 605 and 500" B.C./E. (with an apparent preference for a preexilic date[?]; cf. Redditt [1994: 241] who rightly observes that "it is difficult to avoid the conclusion that her *terminus ad quem* is really the *terminus a quo*").

2. Lexical and Literary Factors

Lexical data martialed as evidence for the dating of Malachi, apart from the references to a "governor" (*pehâ*) and the epithets applied to the priesthood, include the "book of remembrance" (*sēper zikkārôn*, 3:16) and the poignant image of restoration portrayed in the phrase "sun of righteousness" (*šemeš sĕdāqâ*, 3:20 [4:2]). Both expressions are considered "Persianisms" by some scholars, thus signifying a Persian date for the book of Malachi (e.g., Baldwin [1972a: 249]; J. Gray [1974: 5–6]; R. L. Smith [1984: 338]). In addition, certain commentators view the distinct disputational form of Malachi as a further indication of the book's postexilic origins (e.g., S. R. Driver [1922: 358]; Mason [1982: 142]; cf. Petersen [1995: 5–6, 31–33] on the influence of P in Mal 2:10–16 and the "diatribe-like" character of the disputations).

3. Intertextual Dependence

Malachi's knowledge of and/or appeal to the pentateuchal sources of D and P is often enlisted as evidence for a pre-Ezra and Nehemiah date for the book (e.g., Sellin and Fohrer [1968: 470]). This line of reasoning cites Malachi's apparent ignorance of Nehemiah's divorce legislation and his preference for Deuteronomistic terminology over that of the Priestly source. For instance, the prophet makes no distinction between priest and Levite (cf. Deut 18:1 and Num 3:9) and identifies the priests as sons of Levi — not Aaron (cf. Deut 31:9 and Lev 1:5). In regard to the Temple sacrifices and offerings, Malachi mentions only the male animal (1:4; cf. Lev 3:1, 6) and combines the wave offering with the tithe in the liturgy (3:8–10; cf. Deut 12:6 and Num 18:21–24 — but note that Malachi appa.ently refers to the Priestly tithe in Lev 27:30 rather than the Deuteronomistic legislation pertinent to the tithe in Deut 14:22–28!).[2]

---

[2] Those arguments based upon intertextual dependence assume the validity of distinct pentateuchal sources as unraveled by the documentary hypothesis — an assumption ever more suspect in light of ongoing linguistic and literary analysis of the Pentateuch and the entire OT/HB (e.g., Polzin [1976]; Alter [1981]; Kikawada and Quinn; Wenham [1977], [1985], and [1986]; Rendsburg; and Whybray). Although Mason (1977: 159) has cited additional examples of intertextual dependence, like Malachi's use of the Deuteronomic phrase "all Israel" (3:22 [4:4]; cf. Deut 1:1; 5:1; etc.) and the name Horeb for Mt. Sinai (common to the Elohist and Deuteronomy, 3:22 [4:4]; cf. Exod 3:1; 17:6; Deut 1:2, 6; etc.), he dismisses the argument for related reasons (p. 138). On the distribution of the so-called D and P sources in Malachi, see further von Bulmerincq (1926: 436–38); and E. M. Meyers (1986).

4. Religious, Sociological, and Political Factors

A majority of biblical commentators associate Malachi with the ministries of Ezra and Nehemiah, because he denounces the same abuses corrected by these postexilic reformers (see Drinkard's thorough discussion, pp. 388–89). Baldwin (1972a: 213) is representative of this position, noting that the prophet attacks mixed marriages and divorce (Mal 2:10–16; cf. Ezra 9:1–15; Neh 13:23–31), a lax and corrupt priesthood (Mal 1:6–2:9; cf. Neh 12:30, 44–47), liturgical decay, including neglect of the tithe (Mal 3:8–12; cf. Neh 13:4–22), and social injustice (Mal 3:5; cf. Neh 5:1–13).

The debate here is basically one of Malachi's preaching relative to the reforms of Ezra and Nehemiah. Did the prophet precede Ezra by some months or years (e.g., Eissfeldt [1965: 443])? Did Malachi follow Ezra but precede Nehemiah (e.g., Bright [1981: 378])? Did Malachi prophesy during Nehemiah's first (e.g., Pusey [2:461–62]) or second (e.g., Moore [1974: 103]) governorship? Or did Malachi upbraid Jerusalem during the interim between the governorships of Nehemiah (e.g., Verhoef [1987: 160])?

It should be noted that those scholars hypothesizing extensive redaction of the oracles of Malachi do so largely on the basis of sociological arguments. For instance, Nogalski (1993b: 199–200, 211) speculates that improving economic conditions in postexilic Yehud contributed to the "construction" of Malachi as a conclusion to the Book of the Twelve sometime after 400 B.C./E. Redditt (1994: 249–53) surmises that the oracles of Malachi address a postexilic Yehud polarized into clerical and laical factions, with the redactor (or composer?) of the book belonging to a peripheral Levitical group (cf. Wilson). Lastly, Utzschneider (1989: 86–87) understands Mal 1:6–2:9 as a *Schriftprophetie* ("writing prophecy") composed during the early Ptolemaic period (ca. 300 B.C./E.) as a result (in part) of the Hellenistic "internationalizing" of the Mediterranean world.

5. Theological Factors

Several scholars confidently locate Malachi in the Persian era of the postexilic period Hebrew history on the basis of theological theme. For example, Malachi's stance on divorce reflects the "exclusivist" tendencies of postexilic Judaism (so Newsome [1984: 193]), and his religious universalism echoes that of Trito-Isaiah (so Koch [1984: 179]). Malachi relativizes the earlier salvation oracles of Haggai and Zechariah, prompting Mason (1982: 142) to observe that the prophet fits the derivative and exegetical pattern of postexilic prophecy. Finally, both Petersen (1977: 44–43) and Clements (1974: 54) connect Malachi's eschatology with that outlined in other prophets of the Persian period (namely, Trito-Isaiah, Joel, and Second Zechariah).

6. A Date for Malachi

The foregoing survey of factors shaping the traditional understanding of the date for Malachi's oracles does yield a certain consensus, namely Malachi is a prophet of the postexilic era best associated with the reforms of Ezra and Nehemiah. However, date theories for the book of Malachi based on such approaches span four centuries from Haggai and Zechariah to the Maccabean period. Recognizing the acute limitations of dating Malachi's oracles on the basis of germane internal data, I proposed an alternative approach which assumes the validity of recent linguistic research in the typological categorization of biblical Hebrew (cf. Hill [1981]).

Rather than relating the book of Malachi to postexilic social conditions, religious practices, and historical events, which rely on an absolute chronology, this typological method developed by Polzin (1976) compares Malachi to preexilic, exilic, and postexilic biblical literature and therefore to a literary and relative chronological scale. The purely linguistic analysis utilized by this approach in dating the oracles of Malachi has the advantage of being far more objective than previous research, due to the statistical nature of the investigation.

The computer aided systematic application of Polzin's nineteen grammatical and syntactic categories to the Hebrew documents yields a typological continuum of BH demonstrating the relative chronological relationships of the target corpora to Polzin's and other selected corpora (for details, see Hill [1982] and [1983]). I have summarized essentials of the typological analysis of the postexilic prophets in APPENDIX B., including a description of Polzin's linguistic categories, a tabular display of the distribution of these linguistic features in the selected corpora, and a typological continuum demonstrating the relative chronological relationships of the target corpora to other select OT/HB corpora.

Broadly speaking, the prophetic control and target corpora fall on the continuum between the Classical Biblical Hebrew (CBH) of the Deuteronomic History corpus (Dtr) and the Late Biblical Hebrew (LBH) of the secondary additions to the Priestly corpus (Ps). The Priestly corpus (Pg) is usually dated to the early exilic period (ca. 550 B.C./E. according to West [1981: 65]); a round figure of 600–550 B.C./E. then seems plausible. If the Ps corpus dates to the activity of Ezra and Nehemiah in Jerusalem (cf. Schneider [1979: 148–49]), then the prophetic corpora may be placed in a time frame ranging roughly from about 600 to 450 B.C./E. Internal evidence (lexicography, date formulae, etc.) suggests that Jeremiah, Ezekiel, and the Pg corpus date to the first half of the sixth century B.C./E. Typological profiles indicate that Haggai, Zechariah 1–8 and 9–14, Malachi, Joel, and Jonah are to be dated within a common time period. On the basis of internal evidence (literary style and form, lexicography, date formulae, etc.), that general time frame for the postexilic prophets, Joel, and Jonah is the latter half of the sixth century B.C./E.

Despite the probable changes taking place in the language spoken in Jerusalem and environs due to the intermixing with the languages (or dialects) of the indigenous population groups, the written language of the postexilic prophets retains a high degree of typological continuity with the written language of the exilic period. This phenomenon is expected, even predictable, in that population groups isolated from their ethnic and linguistic roots tend to preserve the form of the language current at the time of separation from the larger language family. Quite naturally the Hebrews exiled in Babylonia perpetuated a "fossilized" form of the exilic Hebrew language they carried with them in the deportations from Judah (e.g., Jeffers and Lehiste [1979: 144] cite the failure of geographically remote Icelandic to develop the tonal opposition characteristic of the Baltic Sea language group despite its relationship to Norwegian as a sister-language). One can surmise that the postexilic prophets themselves were recently returned exiles and perhaps numbered among those who came to Jerusalem with Zerubbabel and Joshua (Ezra 2:1–2), hence the continuity with exilic language patterns.[3]

Based upon the evidence garnered from my earlier studies employing this typological analysis of the postexilic prophets, I dated Malachi (and Zech 9–14) to the period of pre-Ezran decline in Yehud (515–458 B.C./E.). Even though the Temple had been rebuilt and the sacrificial system restored, the vision of Ezekiel's "temple-state" quickly faded amid the stark reality of Persian domination

---

[3]O'Brien's (1990: 125–42) haphazard appropriation of data gleaned from the typological analysis of the postexilic prophets merits comment at this juncture. O'Brien (1990: 130–33) prefers to relate Malachi to preexilic and exilic corpora on the typological continuum, choosing to emphasize only the results of the typological analysis. She rejects external historical controls, including the date formulae of Haggai and Zechariah, in calling for a *purely* [emphasis mine] typological interpretation of the linguistic data (1990: 127).

O'Brien misunderstands the rudimentary elements of language theory and development in that by definition typological analysis of any language yields only relative data, which *must* [emphasis mine] be controlled by external linguistic, lexical, and historical factors (Polzin [1976: 15–19]; cf. W. P. Lehmann [1992: 51–62]). Taken to its logical conclusion, O'Brien's reasoning would place the book of Esther nearer the preexilic or exilic end of the biblical Hebrew language continuum; she admits no external controls by which "archaizing" or "fossilized" features of a language might be distinguished from the routine features associated with dynamic language change.

This failure to fully comprehend the significance of one of the foundational tenets of historical linguistics distorts the linguistic data and skews the typological analysis (i.e., the nature of language change given the particular variables of language contact, Hill [1981: 136–37]). Fishman (pp. 21–33) identifies this tendency for a minority cultural group to maintain and develop its particular heritage as "language maintenance phenomena." W. P. Lehmann (pp. 117–19, 130–31) understands this phenomenon as one tendency of a *relic area* with respect to "dialect geography" (i.e., the propensity for a minority culture [and dialect] separated from the *focal area* of its own language by a *transitional area* to both retain archaic features of its own heritage and introduce new local idioms of the majority culture). Malachi demonstrates typological correspondence to Jeremiah and Ezekiel because he was a part of the Hebrew community from Babylonia using an earlier form of LBH "frozen" in time — not because he was a contemporary of Jeremiah and Ezekiel!

Beyond this linguistic phenomenon, the lexical affinities between Malachi and Jeremiah and Ezekiel (see Hill [1981: 84–131]) may be attributable to both the cultic nature of their prophetic language (as all three have priestly connections) and the deliberate archaizing by the prophet rooted in the Jewish nationalism of the Persian period (see K. A. Mathews [p. 552]). Even further, Malachi's archaizing was necessarily theological because the prophet had to assure the people that despite the relativizing and delay of that earlier prophetic hope, the word of Yahweh still held continuity with the previous traditions promising divine restoration — now focused in a single person (cf. Petersen [1977: 42–43]; and Mason [1990: 261]). Finally, O'Brien's misapprehension of the disputation form of Malachi's oracles contributes to her erroneous assessment of the book's date; as Mason (1990: 235) has noted, the use of the rhetorical question and disputation form in Malachi are clearly stylistic features of postexilic preaching.

and the problems of mere survival in a city surrounded by hostile foreigners (cf. Hanson [1979: 280–86]). Given the typological profiles of the prophetic target and control corpora and continued analysis and reflection, a round figure of 500 B.C./E. still seems most reasonable for the date of the composition of Malachi. I grant that this analysis challenges the traditional dating theory for Malachi by only a half-dozen or so decades; yet, it effectively eliminates those positions dating Malachi after Nehemiah. Further, this analysis proves most helpful in supplementing previous attempts to trace the development of early postexilic Judaism and document the shift from CBH to LBH in Israelite history.[4]

It is likely that exilic Hebrew was largely preserved (at least as the written language) in the official and religious circles of the restoration community by the first-generation returnees from Babylon. This would account for the linguistic similarities of the postexilic prophets to one another, to the additional prophetic corpora, and to the Pg corpus examined by Polzin. Those original returnees probably influenced the restoration community for a maximum of fifty or sixty years; a *terminus ad quem* of ca. 475 B.C./E. for Malachi (and Zech 9–14) may be suggested. After 475 B.C./E. written works would and do reflect the language changes absorbed by the second-generation writers of the postexilic Hebrew community (e.g., the Ps corpus, likely associated with Ezra's ministry in Jerusalem).

Malachi's linguistic affinity to Haggai and Zechariah 1–8 and the hypothesis of language change between the first and second generations of returning exiles support a date of near 500 B.C./E. for the composition of Malachi. The typological profiles of Jeremiah and Ezekiel, the disputation format of Malachi's oracles, and the theological themes of the book may be adduced as further evidence locating Malachi early on in the period of pre-Ezran decline.[5] By way of compara-

---

[4]Given the contemporary example of continuing political ferment in the Commonwealth of Independent States, a decade (or even less) for this kind of despair and disillusionment among the general populace is not unthinkable. For example here, note the unrest and disaffection among citizens of the former U.S.S.R., especially in Russia where the aftermath of dashed political and economic aspirations continues to shape the landscape of Russian statecraft (cf. *US News* [1993] 114/1:38–44; [1994] 117/8:48; [1995] 118/8:56–57, 60; [1996] 120/22:41–45).

[5]Sasson (p. 27) has reasoned that the dating of a document to a specific time period should accomplish two reciprocal functions: "First, the intellectual positions of the period to which it [i.e., the document] is assigned ought to clarify the text; and second, the text should inform us about the period in which it [i.e., the document] is created." Dating Malachi very early in the period of pre-Ezran decline fulfills both of these criteria. The despair and doubt triggered in the restoration community by the apparent failure of the prophetic visions of Haggai and Zechariah soon characterized the "intellectual disposition" of the era — a disposition that pouted that Yahweh had indeed forgotten his covenant with Israel. By the same token, the text elucidates our understanding of the early postexilic period by highlighting the shift in the theological paradigm from the preexilic (and early exilic aftermath) prophetic indictments for idolatry and the promise of "full" restoration to the postexilic prophetic indictments for improper Temple ritual and the relativizing of earlier "salvation oracles."

Observe that O'Brien (1990: 132) must discount the issue of literary style as it relates to chronology because her *rîb* pattern for the book of Malachi fails to satisfy Sasson's reciprocal dating criteria. The Babylonian exile rendered the formal *rîb* pattern obsolete, if not irrelevant (the term *rîb* is not found in postexilic literature save the chronicler's commen-

tive study, the conclusions of von Bulmerincq (1926: 42–49), who dated the major portions of Malachi's oracle to ca. 480 B.C./E.; Koch (1984: 176), who placed Malachi's ministry around 500 B.C./E.; and the conclusions of D. N. Freedman (1963, 1974, and 1976; cf. *EncJud* 11:815), who has located the composition of the postexilic prophets and their incorporation into the canon of the OT/HB about 500 B.C./E., prove to be consonant with my analysis (cf. Welch [1935: 113] who revised his earlier opinion [1900] and regarded Malachi as a contemporary of Haggai and Zechariah).

I. F. THE STUDY OF MALACHI

I. F. 1. Malachi in the New Testament

The New Testament makes no mention of the prophet Malachi, but NT documents contain a number of quotations and allusions from the book of Malachi (cf. 2 Esdr 1:40 where Malachi is mentioned along with the rest of the Twelve Prophets as a leader of Israel). The more prominent, as recognized by *The Greek New Testament* (UBS4. K. Aland, et al., eds. New York: United Bible Societies, 1993), are cataloged below:

  1) Rom 9:13: *Jacob I have loved, but Esau I have hated.*
  *Mal 1:2–3: *Yet I loved Jacob, but Esau I hated.*

  The Apostle Paul quotes Mal 1:2–3 as a summary statement validating Yahweh's election of Israel through the patriarch Jacob in his treatise on God's election of Israel (beginning in Rom 3:1–4, interrupted by a lengthy excursus on righteousness through faith in 3:5–8:39, and concluding in Rom 9:1–13). Note that Paul utilized Mal 1:2–3 to make reference to the individuals (Jacob and Esau); whereas Malachi used the names to identify the two peoples proceeding from these eponymous ancestors. The quotation is essentially direct (i.e., MT = LXX = NT), with the exception of the inversion of the word order in the Jacob clause of Rom 9:13.

  2) Luke 6:46: *Why do you call me 'Lord, Lord,' and refuse to do what I say?*
  Mal 1:6: *. . . and if I am [your] master, where is my respect?*

  This citation is at best an allusion to Malachi, perhaps based upon the form and spirit of the rhetorical question posed by Jesus. The LXX translates the MT literally, but there is no lexical correspondence between LXX and NT.

---

tary on the reforms of King Jehoshaphat, 2 Chr 19:8–10), hence the shift to proto-apocalyptic vision, rhetorical question, and disputation oracle in the postexilic prophets (cf. Murray [1987: 115]).
* Listed in the Index of Quotations in UBS3, but omitted in UBS4.

3) 1 Cor 10:21: . . . *the table of the Lord* . . .
   Mal 1:7, 12: . . . *the table of the Lord* . . .

The allusion here is predicated upon the lexical correspondence of NT and LXX (*trapézēs kuríou // trápeza kuríou* [MT *šulḥan YHWH*]) and the context of ritual pollution (i.e., the sacrificial offering in the OT/HB and the Eucharist in the NT).

4) 2 Thess 1:12: *so that the name of our Lord Jesus Christ may be exalted in you* . . .
   Rev 15:4: . . . *Who will not fear, O Lord, and exalt your name?*
   Mal 1:11: *Indeed, from the rising of the sun to its setting, Great is my name among the nations!*

This allusion cited by UBS4 is based upon one word, the Greek rendering of MT *gādôl* with a form of *doxázō*, "to praise, glorify" (also utilized in both NT texts). (Note that in Mal 1:11b, LXX reads *méga tò ónomá* for the repeated phrase *gādôl šĕmî* in MT.) There is agreement between 2 Thess 1:12 and Mal 1:11 in the sense that both address the glorification of God's name within the context of a current historical situation (cf. *TDOT* 2:409–10, which suggests the divine epithet *gādôl* avers God's uniqueness as God of a people and its history); whereas in Rev 15:4 this glorification is eschatological.

5) Matt 23:3: *Absolutely, therefore, do whatever they teach you and obey it; but do not do as they do, for they do not practice what they teach.*
   Mal 2:7–8: *Surely from the lips of the priest they safeguard knowledge; and Torah they seek from his mouth; since he is the messenger of Yahweh of Hosts. But you yourselves have turned from the way. You have caused many to stumble over Torah. You have corrupted the covenant of Levi. Yahweh of Hosts has said.*

There is no lexical correspondence between NT and LXX here. The allusion is based solely upon the apparent thematic similarities between the (false) teaching and pretentious lifestyles of the corrupt priests of the postexilic period and the Pharisees of Jesus's day.

6) 1 Cor 8:6: *for us there is but one God, the Father,* . . .
   Mal 2:10: *Surely we all have one Father?*

Paul inverts Malachi's word order (*one God, the Father* vs. *one father* . . . *one God*) and uses "the Father" appositionally as part of the two parallel triplets equating God the Father and Jesus Christ. While "father" in Mal 2:10 may be a reference to Abraham as the patriarch of Israel (e.g., Baldwin [1972a: 237]), the use of the verb *bārā'* in the immediate context would suggest that the prophet intends God as Father since he is Creator of humanity (Gen 1:27) and Israel (Isa 43:1, 7, 15). Both Malachi and Paul understand God as Father in a more restrictive sense, that is, of the community of faith who recognize God as such. By way of general context, Malachi's teaching about God is framed within rhetorical questions (assuming an answer in the affirmative), while Paul makes a declarative statement.

7)   Matt 11:10: *See! I am sending my messenger ahead of you, who will prepare your way before you.*
     Mark 1:2: *See! I am sending my messenger ahead of you, who will prepare your way.*
     Luke 7:27: *See! I am sending my messenger ahead of you, who will prepare your way before you.*
     Mal 3:1: *See! I am sending my messenger, and he will clear a way before me.*

Matt 11:3 and Luke 7:19 are also allusions to the identity of Malachi's "messenger" posed in the form of a question to Jesus by agents representing John the Baptist. In response to a similar question regarding the perceived competition between the baptizing ministries of John the Baptist and Jesus, John denied that he was Messiah (= "the messenger of the covenant"?), but he affirmed he was indeed the "messenger" who prepares the way for the Messiah (John 3:28; cf. the pesher interpretation of the forerunner's function in Zechariah's Song, Luke 1:76).

Matt 11:10, Mark 1:2, and Luke 7:27 are nearly identical and constitute direct quotations of Mal 3:1. Both LXX and NT basically follow the word order of MT, including the literal rendering of MT idiom *lĕpānāy* (*prò prosópou mou*). The NT, however, reads the second-person (masculine singular) pronoun "you" (*sou*) for the first-person form ("me") of MT and LXX. In addition, LXX employs the unusual *epiblépsetai* ("survey, consider, give careful attention") for MT *pinnâ* ("clear, make ready, prepare," suggesting that LXX translators made no connections between Isaiah's use of *pinnâ* and that of Malachi, cf. Isa 40:3; 57:14; 62:10). Finally, LXX inserts the independent pronoun *egó* emphatically before *exapostéllō*.

Minor variations have been noted in NT quotations of Mal 3:1, including the use of *apostéllō* for LXX *exapostéllō* in all three gospels, reading *kataskeuásei* for LXX *epiblépsetai*. In each case, NT substitutes the second masculine singular pronoun *sou* ("before you") for the first-person pronoun ("before me") of MT. Lastly, note that while Mark omits the concluding phrase *émprosthén sou*, this gospel does associate the forerunner passage of Malachi with Isa 40:3 (cf. Archer and Chirichigno [1983: 165]; see also the commentary on the use of Mal 3:1 in NT in Hengstenberg 2:1238–58).

Keil (2:458) recognized a correlation between Mal 3:1 and Exod 23:20, noting that the divinely commissioned "messenger" (*mal'āk*) of each text has a similar prophetic function. Kaiser (1984: 83), R. L. Smith (1984: 329), and Glazier-McDonald (1987a: 130–31) are among the more recent exegetes offering expanded commentary on the relationship between the two passages. While much of the contemporary discussion is aimed at identifying two distinct eschatological figures in Mal 3:1 ("the messenger" [*mal'āk*] and the "messenger of the covenant" [*mal'ak habbĕrît*]), the nature of the preparatory ministries of these "forerunners" mentioned in Exod 23:20 and Mal 3:1 is equally important. Both are charged with the duties of providing (Torah) instruction for Israel and confronting covenant disobedience among the wayward people of God. However, Malachi's "messenger" is unique in that this figure alone is empowered for a ministry of reconciliation (cf. Mal 3:23–24 [4:5–6]); whereas the "messenger" (or "angel") of Exod 23:20 and the "messenger of the covenant" in Mal 3:1 purify Israel through judgment.

8)   Rev 6:17: . . . *the great day of their wrath has come . . .*
Mal 3:2: *But who is able to endure the day of his coming?*

Both texts make reference to the "day" of the Lord and the inability of mortals to "stand" in the face of divine judgment. While the ideas are certainly parallel, the Greek reads a form of *hupistēmi* instead of the expected *hístēmi* for MT *hā'ōmēd*, which is supplanted by *hístēmi* in NT. The strength of the allusion may rest upon the appeal of Rev 6:15–16 to OT/HB prophetic imagery.

9)   1 Pet 1:7: . . . *so that the genuineness of your faith . . . tested by fire . . .*
Mal 3:3: . . . *and he will purify the Levites, and refine them like gold and silver . . .*

Although NT shares no lexical parallels with LXX, the idea of the righteous being "refined by fire" is common to both texts.

10)   Jas 5:4: *Look here! The wages of the laborers who mowed your fields, which you have withheld by fraud . . .*
Mal 3:5: . . . *and against those extorting the wages of the laborer . . .*

This allusion is attributable to the lexical correspondence between NT and LXX on two counts (*misthòs* = "wages" and *áphustrépheō* = "defraud"). The context of social justice within the community of faith is common to both readings.

11)   Jas 4:8: *Draw near to God and he will draw near to you.*
Mal 3:7: *Return to me so that I may return to you.*

This is perhaps an allusion to Malachi's call to repentance. The LXX translates the Hebrew *šûb* conventionally with *epistréphō* ("return"), while NT uses a form of *eggízō* ("draw near, approach") and inserts the divine name God (*Theós*).

12)   Luke 1:78: . . . *by which the rising sun will come to us from heaven . . .*
Mal 3:20 [4:2]: *But . . . a sun of righteousness will arise for you . . .*

At best this is an allusion in the gospel to Malachi, based on the eschatological idea of the "dawn breaking" and revealing new developments in God's plans for the redemption of Israel. There are no lexical parallels between MT/LXX and NT.

13)   Matt 11:14: . . . *he is Elijah who is to come . . .*
Matt 17:10–12: . . . *Elijah has already come . . .*
Mark 9:11–13: . . . *Elijah has come . . .*

Mal 3:23 [4:5]/LXX 3:22: *See! I am sending Elijah the prophet to you before the coming day of Yahweh . . .*

Here according to the gospel writers, Jesus identified John the Baptist as the fulfillment of Malachi's Elijah "forerunner" prophecy. Black (pp. 9–11) identifies the pericopes of Mark 9:9–13 and Matt 17:9–13 as a didactic pesher on Mal 3:23–24 [4:5–6] and Isa 53:3.

14) Luke 1:17: *And he will go before him in the spirit and power of Elijah, to turn the hearts of the parents to the children, and the rebellious to the wisdom of the righteous . . .*

Mal 3:23–24 [LXX = 3:22–23 = 4:5–6]: *See! I am sending Elijah the prophet to you before the coming day of Yahweh — the great and the terrible [day]. And he will turn the heart of the forefathers to the[ir] descendants, and the heart of the descendants toward the[ir] forefathers . . .*

The gospel writer alludes to Mal 3:23 (LXX 3:22 = 4:5] with the appeal to Elijah. Luke quotes Mal 3:24a [LXX 3:23 = 4:6] verbatim in reference to John, the child of Zechariah and Elizabeth, because the ministry of the Elijah figure is one of reconciliation (clearly evident in John's preaching, cf. Luke 3:1–17). Here NT reads the plural of MT ['*ābôt* = *patérōn* and *bānîm* = *tékna*) and translates MT *šûb* with (the expected form of) *epistréphō*; whereas LXX reads the singular for "father" (*patròs*) and "son" (*huiòn*) and employs (the more uncommon) *apokathístēmi* for the Hebrew *šûb*.

The LXX diverges from the MT in 3:24b and reads "and the heart of a man to his neighbor" (*kaì kardían anthrṓpou pròs tòn plēsíon autoû*), perhaps due to the influence of Hellenistic ideals such as universal peace and the brotherhood of humanity (cf. Sir 48:10). The NT deviates from both MT and LXX in this second clause, inserting the clause "and the rebellious to the wisdom of the righteous" (*kaì apeitheîs en phronḗsei dikaiōn*).

More than the restoration of the parent-child relationship and cessation of familial discord, the variation in Luke captures the intent of Malachi in that the prophet, like his counterpart John the Baptist, was calling "the present rebellious generation into religious harmony with the righteous ones of former times . . . to reunite and consolidate Israel on the basis of the devotion of the forefathers" (Geldenhuys [1951: 66]).

I. F. 2. The Liturgical Use of Malachi

Given Malachi's concern for rejuvenating a calloused and jaded Levitical priesthood and his initiatives in restoring proper Second Temple worship, it seems only fitting to outline the liturgical use of the book of Malachi in Judaism and Christianity.

A. JUDAISM
The practice of reading selections from the HB as part of the synagogue liturgy is an ancient tradition. The annual cycle of readings begins on the Sabbath after

the festival of *Sukkot* (Booths or Tabernacles) and is completed on the last day of this festival (= *Simhat Torah*). The Torah or Pentateuch is subdivided into fifty-four *sědārîm* (סְדָרִים) or tractates, with two portions sometimes read on a single Sabbath to complete the reading cycle in a year. The corresponding pericope from the Prophets complementing the weekly Torah reading is known as the *haptārâ* (הַפְטָרָה), a term of obscure meaning. Some connect the word with the Latin *demissio* because in the Second Temple era the service ended with the *Haftarah* reading, while others posit the understanding "taking leave of" the *Shaharit* (שַׁחֲרִית, i.e., concluding the Scripture reading of the morning prayer service; cf. *EncJud* 16:1344).

According to Sasson (p. 28), the oldest witness to the custom of supplementing the Sabbath Law or Torah readings with extracts from the Prophets (or *Haftarot* readings) is a text in the book of Acts which states that Paul rose to give a speech after the reading of the Law and the Prophets in the synagogue at Pisidian Antioch (13:15). If the gospel account of Jesus reading from the prophet Isaiah as part of a Sabbath lesson is any indication (Luke 4:16–20), then the liturgical practice of reading complementary portions of the Law and Prophets in the synagogue service may well have been in place well before the destruction of the Second Temple (cf. *EncJud* 16:1343). Plummer (p. 120) has cautioned against reading any liturgical cycle of prophetic lessons into the Lucan account of Jesus's reading of Isaiah (61:1–2) in the synagogue. He acknowledged a reading from the Torah may well have preceded the reading from the Prophets, but remained skeptical of any fixed reading cycle in synagogue worship during the NT era. The current cycle of *Haftarah* readings does not include Isa 61:1–2; although the Sabbath reading for *Ki Tavo* (#50) pairs Deut 26:1–29:8 with Isa 60:1–22, and the Sabbath reading for *Nizzavim* (#51) matches Deut 29:9–30:20 with Isa 61:10–63:9.

Two selections from the book of Malachi are included in those readings from the Prophets to complement the Sabbath *Torah* readings: Mal 1:1–2:6 comprising the *Haftarat Toledot* read in conjunction with Gen 25:19–28:9; and Mal 3:4–24 comprising the *Haftarat Shabbat Haggadol* or the "great Sabbath" (preceding *Pesah* or Passover) read in conjunction with the regular weekly Torah portion assigned for that Sabbath. The literary connection in the *Haftarat Toledot* between Gen 25:19–28:9 and Mal 1:1–2:6 is based upon the patriarchal figures of Jacob and Esau (especially Mal 1:2–4).

Theologically, Hirsch (pp. 47–48) identified the relationship between the two texts as "the Esau-principle" (i.e., the worship of force as the means to conquer the world) in contrast to "the Jacob-principle" (i.e., the principle of life founded on the rule of Divine justice and love through the Torah). The reading of Mal 3:4–24 [4:6] on the Sabbath prior to Passover, especially the admonition of 3:23 [4:5] ("Remember the Law of Moses . . ."), recalls the revelation of the Torah to Moses at Sinai breathing national life into Israel and serves as "the most complete uniformity of the history of Israel directed by God from its earliest beginnings to its final goal in the distant future" (Hirsch [1966: 568]).

While there is no citation in the Passover or *Seder Haggadah* (i.e., the book-[let] containing or "telling" the order of the Seder service, including the prayers and blessings to be recited; so Donin [1972: 230]) of Malachi, the invitation extended to Elijah the prophet to join in the meal pronounced before the third *kiddush* or cup of wine (i.e., the sanctification of wine in proclamation of the festival; so Neusner [1993: 202]) is based on Mal 3:23 [4:5].

B. CHRISTIANITY

1. Roman Catholic tradition

The Daily Missal includes portions of Malachi in the two-year cycle of scriptural passages for the office of daily readings, specifically Mal 1:1–14 and 2:13–16 on Friday of week eighteen in year two and Mal 3:1–21 [4:3] on Saturday of week eighteen in year two. In addition, Mal 3:1–3, 23–24 [4:5–6] are read as part of the Mass for advent weekdays (Dec 23), and Mal 3:1–4 is read as part of the Candlemas liturgy (or Presentation of Our Lord Mass, Feb 2). *The New Roman Catholic Lectionary* (1969) retains the Mal 3:1–4 reading as part of the Presentation of Our Lord Mass, while Mal 1:14–2:2, 8–10, and 3:19–20 [4:1–2] are ordered respectively for the thirty-first Sunday of year one and the thirty-third Sunday of year three of the lectionary.

2. Protestant tradition

Among those more liturgical traditions of Protestantism, the book of Malachi is most commonly associated with Advent Cycle and the Nativity of St. John the Baptist (June 24). For example, the *Lutheran Service Book* prescribes Mal 3:19–24 [4:1–6] as the OT lesson for the second Sunday of Advent, Mal 3:16–18 for the St. John holy day (May 1), and Mal 3:22–24 [4:4–6] for the Nativity of St. John the Baptist (June 24). *The Book of Common Worship* (Presbyterian, USA) marks Mal 3:1–12 as the Palm Sunday reading in the first year of the lectionary. The second year of the lectionary orders Malachi chapters 1 and 3 on the twenty-fifth and twenty-sixth Sundays after Trinity Sunday respectively and Malachi chapter 4 on the next Sunday before Advent. By contrast, the *Book of Common Order* (Scottish Presbyterian) follows Roman Catholic tradition and reads Mal 3:1–5 as part of the February 2 Candlemas observance (i.e., commemorating the presentation of Jesus in the Temple). One final illustration, the Methodist *Book of Worship* reads Mal 1:11 as a part of the order of service for Epiphany, and Mal 3:1–3 comprises the Scripture Lesson for Christmas Sunday.

The Anglican and Episcopal *Book of Common Prayer* make the most extensive use of the book of Malachi, including Mal 1:6–11 (Wed); 2:1–10 (Thur); 3:1–15 (Fri); 3:16–3:24 [4:6] (Sat), as the daily readings for the week of the Third Sunday before Advent; Mal 3:1–6 and 3:22–24 [4:4–6] as the OT lesson for the First Sunday of Advent; and Mal 2:1–9 and 3:1–6 as part of the meditation for Amber Saturday (Third Sunday of Advent). In addition, OT readings from the book of Malachi are incorporated into the Daily Office on the Saturday after Epiphany (Mal 1:11), the seventeenth and twentieth Sundays after Trinity (Mal 2:1–10 and Mal 2:14), as well as the Nativity of St. John the Baptist (Mal 3:1–6, 19–24 [4:1–6]).

The book of Malachi fares less well in nonliturgical traditions, as *Orders and Prayers for Church Worship* (United Kingdom Baptists) takes note of the prophet only on the Sunday before Advent (after the twenty-second Trinity Sunday) in year two of the lectionary (Mal 1:1–6; 3:16–20 [4:2]); while the prayers and readings of the *Baptist Hymnal* (Southern Baptist Convention) omit Malachi altogether (see further Richardson). Likewise, Malachi is largely ignored by proponents of the diversity movement. Neither the *National Council of Churches Inclusive Language Lectionary* (1983) nor *Woman Word/Wisdom/Witness: A Feminist Lectionary & Psalter* (New York: Crossroad, 1990, 1991, 1993) include Malachi in the reading selections.

3. Orthodox tradition

The *Service Book of the Holy Orthodox-Catholic Apostolic Church* (I. F. Hapgood, ed. 6th Ed. Englewood [NJ]: Antiochian Orthodox Christian Archdiocese, 1983) includes no readings from the book of Malachi, nor does it contain any direct reference to the prophet or his book. However, the liturgies (including those of St. John Chrysostom and St. Basil the Great) are profuse with divine titles and prophetic epithets that are clear allusions to Mal 3:1, 23 [4:5] (i.e., the *messenger* who serves as the prophetic forerunner of the Day of the Lord) and Mal 3:20 [4:2] (i.e., the promise of the *sun of righteousness* who will arise in that day and offer healing to the faithful in Israel).

Repeatedly, the *Service Book* identifies John the Baptist as the NT fulfillment of the messenger of the covenant forecast by Malachi and gives him the title of "Forerunner" (pp. 32, 107, 122, 153, 162, 186, 187, 295, 324, 391, etc.). Additionally, the phrase "Sun of Righteousness" is a common epithet for Jesus Christ in the prayers and readings (e.g., pp. 26, 176, 198, 229, 268, 336, 427, etc.). One interesting variation of the title Forerunner occurs, "Forerunner of the Sun," conflating the ideas of Mal 3:1 and 3:20 [4:2].

Scattered references to the book of Malachi occur in certain of the other Orthodox liturgies, including the Liturgy of St. Mark, which quotes (all or part of) Mal 1:11 (LXX) as part of the Kiss of Peace, the Thanksgiving, and the Invocation (see Brightman and Hammond 1965: 123.33; 126.7–10; 134.27). A citation of Mal 1:11 (LXX) is also found in the Liturgy of the Coptic Jacobites in the Offering of Incense (see Brightman and Hammond [1965: 152.9]). Finally, the Prayers of the Syrian Rite make reference to Mal 2:5 (LXX; cf. Brightman and Hammond [1965: 12.15]).

BIBLIOGRAPHY

◆

This catalog of titles includes both works cited and select bibliography related to the book of Malachi. In addition, see the following annotated bibliographies on Malachi: B. R. Ellis (*SwJT* 38 [1987]: 48–51), G. Galeotti (*CTR* 2 [1987]: 141–44), H. D. Thompson (1995), and T. Longman, *Old Testament Commentary Survey* (Grand Rapids: Baker, 1995, pp. 168–69). For a comprehensive and chronologically ordered bibliography of pre-1925 scholarship on Malachi (arranged according to liturgical tradition), see von Bulmerincq 1926: 452–506 and 1932: 595–98.

ACHTEMEIER, E.
1986 *Nahum-Malachi*. Interpretation Series. Atlanta: John Knox.
1988 The Impossible Possibility: Evaluating the Feminist Approach to Bible and Theology. *Int* 42:45–57.
1992 *Nature, God & Pulpit*. Grand Rapids: Eerdmans.
1993 Why God Is Not Mother. *CToday* 37/9:16–23.
ACKROYD, P. R.
1970 *Israel Under Babylon and Persia*. Oxford: Oxford University.
1975 *Exile and Restoration*. 2d ed. Old Testament Library. Philadelphia: Westminster.
1979 The History of Israel in the Exilic and Post-Exilic Periods. In *Tradition and Interpretation*, 320–50. Oxford: Clarendon.
ADAMSON, J.T.H.
1970 Malachi. In *The New Bible Commentary*, 804–9. 3d ed. Grand Rapids: Eerdmans.
ADINOLFI, A.
1970 Il ripudio secondo Mal 2:14–16. *BeO* 12:246–56.
AHARONI, Y.
1962 *Ramat Rahel: Seasons 1959 and 1960*. Rome: Pontifical Biblical Institute.
1964 *Ramat Rahel: Seasons 1961 and 1962*. Rome: Pontifical Biblical Institute.
1979 *The Land of the Bible: A Historical Geography*. Rev. ed. Philadelphia: Westminster.

AHLSTRÖM, G. W.
1971   *Joel and the Temple Cult of Jerusalem.* Leiden: Brill.

ALBRIGHT, W. F.
1921   The Date and Personality of the Chronicler. *JBL* 40:104–24.

ALDEN, R. L.
1985   Malachi. In *The Expositor's Bible Commentary*, 701–25. Vol. 7. Grand Rapids: Zondervan.

ALLEN, L. C.
1976   *The Books of Joel, Obadiah, Jonah and Micah.* The New International Commentary on the Old Testament. Grand Rapids: Eerdmans.

1983   *Psalms 100–150.* Word Biblical Commentary 21. Dallas: Word.

1990   *Ezekiel 20–48.* Word Biblical Commentary 29. Dallas: Word.

ALLISON, D. C.
1984   Elijah Must Come First. *JBL* 103:256–58.

ALT, A.
1934   Die Rolle Samarias bei der Entstehung des Judentum. In *Festschrift Otto Procksch zum 60*, 5–28. Leipzig: Deichert-Hinrichs.

ALTER, R.
1981   *The Art of Biblical Narrative.* New York: Basic Books.

1992   *The World of Biblical Literature.* New York: Basic Books.

ALTER, R., AND F. KERMODE, EDS.
1987   *The Literary Guide to the Bible.* Cambridge, MA: Harvard University.

ALTHANN, R.
1977   Malachi 2:13–14 and UT 125:12–13. *Biblica* 58:418–21.

ANDERSEN, F. I., AND D. N. FREEDMAN
1980   *Hosea: A New Translation, with Introduction and Commentary.* Anchor Bible 24. New York: Doubleday.

1989   *Amos: A New Translation, with Introduction and Commentary.* Anchor Bible 24A. New York: Doubleday.

ANDERSON, A. A.
1972   *Psalms (1–72).* The New Century Bible Commentary. Grand Rapids: Eerdmans.

ANDERSON, B. W.
1983   *Out of the Depths: The Psalms Speak for Us Today.* Rev. ed. Philadelphia: Westminster.

ARCHER, G. L.
1974   *A Survey of Old Testament Introduction.* Rev. ed. Chicago: Moody.

ARCHER, G. L., AND G. C. CHIRICHIGNO
1983   *Old Testament Quotations in the New Testament: A Complete Survey.* Chicago: Moody.

AVIGAD, N.
1976   *Bullae and Seals from a Post-Exilic Judean Archive.* Qedem, vol. 4. Jerusalem: Hebrew University Institute of Archaeology.

AVI-YONAH, M.
   1977   *The Holy Land from the Persian to the Arab Conquest.* Rev. ed.
          Grand Rapids: Baker.
BAILEY, K. E.
   1976   *Poet and Peasant: A Literary Cultural Approach to the Parables in
          Luke.* Grand Rapids: Eerdmans.
BAILEY, R. W.
   1977   *God's Questions and Answers: Contemporary Studies in Malachi.*
          New York: Seabury.
BALDWIN, J. G.
   1972a *Haggai, Zechariah, Malachi.* Tyndale Old Testament Commentar-
          ies. London: Tyndale Press.
   1972b Malachi 1:11 and the Worship of the Nations in the OT. *TB*
          23:117–24.
BARR, J.
   1968   *Comparative Philology and the Text of the Old Testament.* Oxford:
          Clarendon.
BARTH, C.
   1991   *God with Us: A Theological Introduction to the Old Testament.*
          Grand Rapids: Eerdmans.
BARTLETT, J. R.
   1992   Edom. *ABD* 2:287–295.
BARTON, J.
   1984   *Reading the Old Testament: Method in Biblical Study.* Philadel-
          phia: Westminster.
BENNETT, T. M.
   1972   Malachi. In *The Broadman Bible Commentary,* 366–94. Vol. 7.
          Nashville: Broadman.
BENTZEN, A.
   1952   *Introduction to the Old Testament.* Vol. 2. 2d ed. Copenhagen:
          Gad.
BERGER, P.-R.
   1971   Zu den Namen *ššbṣr* und *šn'ṣr.* *ZAW* 83:98–100.
BERLIN, A.
   1994   *Zephaniah.* Anchor Bible 25A. New York: Doubleday.
BERQUIST, J. L.
   1989   The Social Setting of Malachi. *BTB* 19:121–26.
   1995   *Judaism in Persia's Shadow.* Minneapolis: Fortress.
BEWER, J. A.
   1933   *The Literature of the Old Testament.* Rev. ed. New York: Columbia
          University Press.
   1949   *The Book of the Twelve Prophets.* Harper Bible, vol. 2. New York:
          Harper and Brothers.
BICKERMAN, E.
   1984   The Babylonian Captivity. In *The Cambridge History of Judaism:*

Introduction, Persian Period, 342–58. Vol. 1. Cambridge: Cambridge University.

BIRCH, B. C.
1991 *Let Justice Roll Down: The Old Testament, Ethics, and Christian Life.* Louisville: W/JKP.

BLACK, M.
1986 The Theological Appropriation of the Old Testament by the New Testament. *Scot J Th* 39:1–17.

BLAKE, R. D.
1988 The Rhetoric of Malachi. Ph.D. diss., Union Theological Seminary.

BLENKINSOPP, J.
1977 *Prophecy and Canon: A Contribution to the Study of Jewish Origins.* Notre Dame, Ind.: University of Notre Dame.
1983 *A History of Prophecy in Israel.* Philadelphia: Westminster.

BLOCK, D. I.
1988 *The Gods of the Nations.* Evangelical Theological Society Monograph Series 2. Jackson, Miss.: ETS.

BLOMBERG, C. L.
1987 Elijah, Election, and the Use of Malachi in the New Testament. *CTR* 2:99–117.

BOADT, L.
1984 *Reading the Old Testament: An Introduction.* New York: Paulist.

BOECKER, H. J.
1966 Bemerkungen zu formgeschichtlichen Terminologie des Buches Maleachi. *ZAW* 78:78–80.

BOER, P. A. H. DE
1948 An Enquiry into the Meaning of the Term "massā'." *OTS* 5: 197–214.

BÖHME, W.
1887 Zu Maleachi und Haggai. *ZAW* 7:215–16.

BOLING, R. G., AND G. E. WRIGHT
1982 *Joshua: A New Translation with Notes and Commentary.* Anchor Bible 6. New York: Doubleday.

BONGERS, H. A.
1981 Some Remarks on the Biblical Particle *hălō'. OTS* 21:177–89.

BONNANDIÈRE, A. M.
1963 *Les douze petits prophètes.* Bibliotheque Augustiana. Paris: Etudes Augustiniennes.

BOSSHARD, E., AND R. G. KRATZ
1990 Maleachi im Zwölfprophetenbuch. *BN* 52:27–46.

BOSSMAN, D. M.
1989 Kingship and Religious System in the Prophet Malachi. In *Religious Writings and Religious Systems,* 127–41. Brown Studies Series 1. Atlanta: Scholars.

BOSTON, J. R.
1968   The Wisdom Influences upon the Song of Moses. *JBL* 87:166–78.
BOTTERWECK, G. J.
1960a   Jakob habe ich lieb — Esau hasse ich. *BibLeb* 1:28–38.
1960b   Ideal und Wirklichkeit der Jerusalemer Priester, Auslegung von Mal 1:6–10; 2:1–9. *BibLeb* 1:100–9.
1960c   Schelt-und Mahnrede gegen Mischehe und Ehescheidung, Auslegung von Mal 2:2, 10–16. *BibLeb* 1:179–85.
1960d   Die Sonne der Gerechtigkeit am Tage Jahwes, Auslegung von Mal 3:13–21. *BibLeb* 1:253–60.
BOMAN, T.
1960   *Hebrew Thought Compared with Greek.* Trans. J. L. Moreau. New York: Norton.
BRAUN, R. L.
1977   Malachi: A Catechism for Times of Disappointment. *CurTM* 4:297–303.
1986   *1 Chronicles.* Word Bible Commentary 14. Waco, Tex.: Word.
BRIANT, P.
1992   Persian Empire. Trans. S. Rosoff. *ABD* 5:236–44.
BRICHTO, H. C.
1963   *The Problem of "Curse" in the Hebrew Bible.* Journal of Biblical Literature Monograph Series 13. Philadelphia: Society of Biblical Literature.
BRIGHT, J.
1975   *The Authority of the Old Testament.* (1967) Reprint, Grand Rapids: Baker.
1981   *A History of Israel.* 3d ed. Philadelphia: Westminster.
BRIGHTMAN, F. E., AND C. E. HAMMOND
1965   *Liturgies Eastern and Western.* Vol. 1. (1896) Reprint, Oxford: Clarendon.
BROCKELMANN, C.
1956   *Hebräische Syntax.* Neukirchen: Kreis Moers.
BROOKS, J. A.
1987   The Influence of Malachi upon the New Testament. *SwJT* 38:28–31.
BROWN, M. L.
1987   "Is It Not?" or "indeed!": HL in Northwest Semitic. *Maarar* 4:210–19.
BRUCE, F. F.
1972   The Earliest Old Testament Interpretation. *OTS* 17:37–52.
1984   Interpretation of the Bible. In *The Evangelical Dictionary of Theology,* 565–68. Grand Rapids: Baker.
BRUEGGEMANN, W.
1968   *Hosea: Tradition for Crisis.* Atlanta: John Knox.
1978   *The Prophetic Imagination.* Philadelphia: Fortress.

1982a   *Living Toward A Vision: Biblical Reflections on Shalom*. Rev. ed. New York: United Church Press.

1982b   *The Creative Word: Canon as a Model for Biblical Education*. Philadelphia: Fortress.

1982c   *Genesis*. Interpretation. Atlanta: John Knox.

1991   *Jeremiah 26–52: To Build, To Plant*. International Theological Commentary. Grand Rapids: Eerdmans.

BUDDE, K.

1906   Zum Text der dreier letzen Propheten. ZAW 26:1–28.

BULLOCK, C. H.

1986   *An Introduction to the Old Testament Prophetic Books*. Chicago: Moody.

BULMERINCQ, A. VON

1926   *Einleitung in das Buch des Propheten Maleachi*. Dorpat: Mattiesen. (Band 1.)

1932   *Kommentar zum Buche des Propheten Maleachi*. Tartu: Krüger. (Band 2.)

CALKINS, R.

1947   *The Modern Message of the Minor Prophets*. New York: Harper & Brothers.

CALVIN, J.

1979   *Commentaries on the Twelve Minor Prophets*. Vol. 15. Trans. J. Owen. (1848) Reprint, Grand Rapids: Baker.

CAMERON, G.

1973   The Persian Satrapies and Related Matters. *JNES* 32:47–56.

CAPPELLUS, L.

1689   *Commentarii et Notae Criticae in Vetus Testamentum*. Amstelodami.

CAQUOT, A.

1969   Brève explication du livre de Malachie (I). *Positions Luthériennes* 17:187–201.

1970   Brève explication du livre de Malachie (II). *Positions Luthériennes* 18:4–16.

CARMIGNAC, J.

1963   Vestiges d'un Pesher de Malachie? [Malachie 1:14]. *RevQ* 4:97–100.

CARMODY, J., D. L. CARMODY, AND R. L. COHN

1988   *Exploring the Hebrew Bible*. Englewood Cliffs: Prentice Hall.

CARROLL, R. P.

1979   *When Prophecy Failed*. New York: Seabury.

1990   Whose Prophet? Whose History? Whose Social Reality? Troubling the Interpretative Community Again: Notes Towards a Response to T. W. Overholt's Critique. *JSOT* 48:33–49.

CASHDAN, E.

1948   *The Twelve Prophets: The Soncino Books of the Bible*. Ed. A. Cohen. Bournemouth: Soncino.

CATHCART, K. J., AND R. P. GORDON
   1989   *The Targum of the Minor Prophets*. Vol. 14. Wilmington, Del.: Michael Glazier.

CHARLESWORTH, J. H., ED.
   1983   *The Old Testament Pseudepigrapha: Apocalyptic Literature & Testaments*. Vol. 1. New York: Doubleday.
   1985   *The Old Testament Pseudepigrapha: Expansions*. Vol. 2. New York: Doubleday.

CHARY, T.
   1955   *Les prophètes et le culte à partir de l'exil*. Paris: Desclée & Cie.
   1969   *Aggée-Zacharie-Malachie*. Sources Bibliques. Paris: Gabalda.

CHEYNE, T.
   1894   Malachi and the Nabateans. ZAW 14:142.

CHILDS, B. S.
   1974   *Exodus*. Old Testament Library. Philadelphia: Westminster.
   1978   The Canonical Shape of Prophetic Literature. *Int* 32:51–52.
   1979   *Introduction to the Old Testament as Scripture*. Philadelphia: Fortress.
   1986   *Old Testament Theology in a Canonical Context*. Philadelphia: Fortress.

CHISHOLM, R. B.
   1990   *Interpreting the Minor Prophets*. Grand Rapids: Zondervan.

CHITTISTER, J.
   1990   *Job's Daughters: Women and Power*. New York: Paulist.

CLARK, D. G.
   1975   *Elijah as Eschatological High Priest: An Examination of the Elijah Tradition in Mal. 3:22–24*. Notre Dame, Ind.: University of Notre Dame.

CLEMENTS, R. E.
   1974   Patterns in the Prophetic Canon. In *Canon and Authority: Essays in Old Testament Religion and Theology*. 42–55. Philadelphia: Fortress.
   1975   *Prophecy and Tradition*. Growing Points in Theology. Atlanta: John Knox.
   1978   *Old Testament Theology*. Atlanta: John Knox.

CLENDENEN, E. R.
   1987   The Structure of Malachi: A Textlinguistic Study. *CTR* 2:3–17.
   1993   Old Testament Prophecy as Hortatory Text: Examples from Malachi. *JOTT* 4:336–353.

CLINES, D. J.
   1984   *Ezra, Nehemiah, Esther*. The New Century Bible Commentary. London: Marshall, Morgan & Scott.

COATS, G.
   1968   *Rebellion in the Wilderness*. Nashville: Abingdon.

CODY, A.
: 1969   A History of the Old Testament Priesthood. Analecta Biblical 35. Rome: Pontifical Biblical Institute.

COGGINS, R. J.
: 1987   Haggai, Zechariah, Malachi. Old Testament Guides. Sheffield: JSOT.

COHEN, A.
: 1948   The Twelve Prophets. Soncino Books of the Bible. London: Soncino.

COLLINS, C. J.
: 1994   The (Intelligible) Masoretic Text of Malachi 2:16. Presb 20: 36–40.

COLLINS, J. J.
: 1984   The Message of Malachi. TBT 22:209–15.

COOK, J. M.
: 1983   The Persian Empire. New York: Schocken.

COOK, S. A.
: 1978   The Inauguration of Judaism. In The Cambridge Ancient History, 167–99. Vol. 6. Cambridge: Cambridge University.

CRAIGIE, P. C.
: 1985   Twelve Prophets. The Daily Study Bible Series, vol. 2. Philadelphia: Westminster.

CRANFIELD, C.E.B.
: 1979   A Critical and Exegetical Commentary on the Epistle to the Romans. International Critical Commentary, vol. 2. Edinburgh: T. & T. Clark.

CRENSHAW, J. L.
: 1969   Method in Determining Wisdom Influence upon "Historical" Literature. JBL 88:129–42.
: 1985   Education in Ancient Israel. JBL 104:601–15.
: 1995   Joel: A New Translation with Introduction and Commentary. Anchor Bible 24C. New York: Doubleday.

CRESSON, B. C.
: 1972   The Condemnation of Edom in Post-Exilic Judaism. In The Use of the Old Testament in the New and Other Essays, 125–48. W. F. Stinespring Festschrift. Durham, N.C.: Duke University.

CROSS, F. M.
: 1963   The Discovery of the Samaria Papyri. BA 26:110–21.
: 1975   A Reconstruction of the Judean Restoration. JBL 94:4–18.

CROSS, F. M., AND D. N. FREEDMAN
: 1975   Studies in Ancient Yahwistic Poetry. Society of Biblical Literature Dissertation Series 21. Missoula, Mont.: Scholars.

DAHOOD, M.
: 1965   Psalms I: 1–50. Anchor Bible 16. New York: Doubleday.
: 1968   Psalms II: 51–100. Anchor Bible 17. New York: Doubleday.
: 1970   Psalms III: 101–150. Anchor Bible 17A. New York: Doubleday.

DAVIES, W. D., AND L. FINKELSTEIN, EDS.
1984 *Cambridge History of Judaism: Introduction, Persian Period.* Vol. 1. Cambridge: Cambridge University.

DEISSLER, A.
1988 *Zwölf Propheten III: Zefanja. Haggai. Sacharja. Maleachi.* Neue Echter Bibel 21. Wurzburg: Echter.

DEISSLER, A., AND M. DELCOR
1964 *Les petits prophètes.* La Sainte Bible, Pirot-Clamer 8, vol. 2. Paris: Letouzey & Ané.

DELAUGHTER, T. J.
1976 *Malachi: Messenger of Divine Love.* New Orleans: Insight.

DENTAN, R. C., AND W. L. SPERRY
1956 Malachi. In *The Interpreter's Bible,* 1117–44. Vol. 6. New York: Abingdon.

DODS, M.
1956 *The Post-Exilian Prophets.* Handbooks for Bible Classes and Private Students. (1879) Reprint, Edinburgh: T. & T. Clark.

DONIN, H. H.
1972 *To Be a Jew: A Guide to Jewish Observance in Contemporary Life.* New York: Basic Books.

DOSTOYEVSKY, F.
1956 *The Brothers Karamazov.* Trans. E. Fuller. New York: Dell.

DRINKARD, J. F.
1987 The Socio-Historical Setting of Malachi. *RevExp* 84:383–90.

DRIVER, G. R.
1938 Malachi. *JTS* 39:399–400 (in "Linguistic and Textual Problems: Minor Prophets III," pp. 393–405).
1956 Three Technical Terms in the Pentateuch. *JSS* 1:97–105.

DRIVER, S. R.
1901 *A Critical and Exegetical Commentary on Deuteronomy.* International Critical Commentary. Edinburgh: T. & T. Clark.
1906 *The Minor Prophets.* Century Bible, vol. 2. New York: Oxford.
1922 *An Introduction to the Literature of the Old Testament.* Rev. ed. New York: Scribner's Sons.

DUHM, B.
1911 Anmerkungen zu den zwölf Propheten. *ZAW* 31:81–110.

DUMBRELL, W. J.
1976 Malachi and the Ezra-Nehemiah Reforms. *RTR* 35:42–52.
1978 Kingship and Temple in the Post-Exilic Period. *RTR* 37:33–42.

DURHAM, J. I.
1987 *Exodus.* Word Biblical Commentary 3. Waco: Word.

EICHRODT, W.
1967 *Theology of the Old Testament.* 2 vols. Trans. J. A. Baker. Philadelphia: Westminster.

EISELEN, C. F.
1907 *The Minor Prophets.* New York: Eaton & Mains.

EISSFELDT, O.
   1965   *The Old Testament: An Introduction.* Trans. P. Ackroyd. New York: Harper & Row.
ELLIGER, K.
   1950   *Das Buch der Zwölf Kleinen Propheten II.* Das Alte Testament Deutsch. Göttingen: Vandenhoeck & Ruprecht.
   1963   Maleachi und die kirchliche Tradition. In *Tradition und Situation,* 43–48. A. Weiser Festschrift. Göttingen: Vandenhoeck und Ruprecht.
ELLUL, J.
   1984   *Money & Power.* Trans. L. Neff. Downers Grove, Ill: IVP.
   1986   *The Subversion of Christianity.* Trans. G. W. Bromiley. Grand Rapids: Eerdmans.
ERLANDSSON, S.
   1970   *The Burden of Babylon.* ConBOT 4. Lund: Gleerup.
ESKENAZI, T. C.
   1991   Sheshbazzar. *ABD* 5:1207–9.
EWALD, G.H.A.
   1881   *The Prophets of the Old Testament.* Vol. 5. Trans. J. F. Smith. London: Williams & Norgate.
EYBERS, I. H.
   1970   Malachi—The Messenger of the Lord. *TE* 3:12–20.
FASOL, A.
   1987   Preaching from Malachi. *SwJT* 38:32–34.
FEE, D. F., AND D. STUART
   1993   *How To Read the Bible For All Its Worth.* 2d ed. Grand Rapids: Zondervan.
FENSHAM, F. C.
   1962   Widow, Orphan and the Poor in Ancient Near Eastern Legal and Wisdom Literature. *JNES* 21:129–39.
   1982   *The Books of Ezra and Nehemiah.* New International Commentary on the Old Testament. Grand Rapids: Eerdmans.
FISCHER, J. A.
   1972   Notes on the Literary Form and Message of Malachi. *CBQ* 34:315–20.
FISHBANE, M.
   1983   Form and Reformation of the Biblical Priestly Blessing. *JAOS* 103:115–21.
   1985   *Biblical Interpretation in Ancient Israel.* Oxford: Clarendon.
FISHMAN, J. A.
   1966   *Language Loyalty in the United States.* The Hague: Mouton & Co.
FOERSTER, W.
   1964   *From the Exile to Christ.* Trans. G. E. Harris. Philadelphia: Fortress.

FOHRER, G.
1972   *History of Israelite Religion.* Trans. D. E. Green. New York: Abingdon.
FONTAINE, C. R.
1982   *Traditional Sayings in The Old Testament.* Bible and Literature Series, 5. Sheffield: Almond.
FOSTER, R. S.
1970   *The Restoration of Israel.* London: Darton, Longman & Todd.
FRANCE, R. T.
1982   *Jesus and the Old Testament.* (1971) Reprint, Grand Rapids: Baker.
FREEDMAN, D. B.
1979   An Unnoted Support for a Variant to the MT of Mal 3:5. *JBL* 98:405–6.
FREEDMAN, D. N.
1963   The Law and the Prophets. *VTSup* 9:250–65.
1974   The Law and the Prophets. Reprint. In *The Canon and Massorah of the Hebrew Bible: An Introductory Reader,* 5–20. New York: KTAV.
1976   Canon of the OT. *IDB Supp.* 130–36.
1980   *Poetry, Pottery, and Prophecy: Collected Essays on Hebrew Poetry.* Winona Lake, Ind.: Eisenbrauns.
1991   *The Unity of the Hebrew Bible.* Ann Arbor, Mich.: University of Michigan.
FREEDMAN, H., AND M. SIMON, EDS.
1939   *Midrash Rabbah.* London: Soncino.
FREEMAN, H. B.
1968   *An Introduction to the Old Testament Prophets.* Chicago: Moody.
FREY, H.
1963   *Das Buch der Kirche in der Weltwende: Die kleinen nachexilischen Propheten.* 5th ed. Die Botschaft des Alten Testaments 24. Stuttgart: Calwer.
FRYE, R. N.
1984   *The History of Ancient Iran.* Munich: C. H. Beckische.
FULLER, R.
1991   Text-Critical Problems in Malachi 2:10–16. *JBL* 110:47–57.
GAILEY, J. H.
1962   *Micah to Malachi.* Layman's Bible Commentaries. London: SCM.
GARLAND, D. E.
1987   A Biblical View of Divorce. *RevExp* 84:419–32.
GEHMAN, H. S.
1940   The "Burden" of the Prophets. *JQR* 31:107–21.
GELDENHUYS, N.
1951   *Commentary on the Gospel of Luke.* New International Commentary on the New Testament. Grand Rapids: Eerdmans.
GELIN, A.
1959   Message aux prêtres (Mal 2:1–9). *Bible et Vie Chrétienne* 30: 14–20.

GELSTON, A.
1987   *The Peshitta of the Twelve Prophets*. Oxford: Clarendon.
GEMSER, B.
1955   The RÎB -or Controversy-Pattern in Hebrew Mentality. *VTSup* 3:120–37.
GESENIUS, W.
1858   *Thesaurus philologius Criticus Linguae Hebraeae et Chaldaeae Veteris Testamenti*. Ed. E. Rödiger. Leipzig: Vogel.
GIBSON, J.C.L.
1993   Keeping Up with Recent Studies: Hebrew Language and Linguistics. *ExpTim* 104:105–9.
GLAZIER-MCDONALD, B.
1986   Malachi 2:12: 'ēr wě'ōneh — Another Look. *JBL* 105:295–98.
1987a *Malachi: The Divine Messenger*. SBL Dissertation Series 98. Atlanta: Scholars.
1987b mal'ak habběrît: The Messenger of the Covenant in Mal 3:1. *HAR* 11:93–104.
1987c Intermarriage, Divorce, and the bat- 'ēl nēkār: Insights into Mal 2:10–16. *JBL* 106:603–11.
1992   Malachi. In *The Women's Bible Commentary*. 232–34. Louisville: W/JKP.
GLOER, W. H.
1987   Preaching from Malachi. *RevExp* 84:453–64.
GOLDINGAY, J.
1987   *Theological Diversity and the Authority of the Old Testament*. Grand Rapids: Eerdmans.
1989   *Daniel*. Word Biblical Commentary 30. Dallas: Word.
GOPPELT, L.
1982   *TYPOS: The Typological Interpretation of the Old Testament in the New*. Trans. D. H. Madvig. Grand Rapids: Eerdmans.
GORDIS, R.
1976   *The Word and the Book. Studies in Biblical Language and Literature*. New York: KTAV.
GORDON, R. P.
1994   *Studies in the Targum of the Twelve Prophets*. Vetus Testamentum Supplement 51. Sheffield: JSOT.
GOTTWALD, N. K.
1962   Poetry. *IDB* 3:829–38.
1985   *The Hebrew Bible: A Socio-Literary Introduction*. Philadelphia: Fortress.
GOWAN, D. E.
1986   *Eschatology in the Old Testament*. Philadelphia: Fortress.
GRAESSER, C.
1975   The Seal of Elijah. *BASOR* 220:63–66.

GRAFFY, A.
1984 *The Prophet Confronts His People: The Disputation Speech in the Prophets.* Analecta Biblica 104. Rome: Pontifical Biblical Institute.

GRANT, R. M.
1984 *A Short History of the Interpretation of the Bible.* Rev. ed. Philadelphia: Fortress.

GRAY, G. B.
1926 The Foundation and Extension of the Persian Empire. In *The Cambridge Ancient History,* 1–25. Vol. IV. Cambridge: Cambridge University.

GRAY, G. B., AND M. CARY
1926 The Reign of Darius. In *The Cambridge Ancient History,* 173–228. Vol. IV. (See Cook, S. A. p. 102.) Cambridge: Cambridge University.

GRAY, J.
1957 *Legacy of Canaan: The Ras Shamra Texts and Their Relevance to the Old Testament.* Vetus Testamentum Supplement 5. Leiden: Brill.
1970 *1 & 2 Kings: A Commentary.* 2d. ed. Old Testament Library. Philadelphia: Westminster.
1974 The Day of Yahweh in Cultic Experience and Eschatological Prospect. *SEÅ* 39:5–37.

GRAY, S. W.
1987 Useless Fires: Worship in the Time of Malachi. *SwJT* 38:35–41.

GREENBERG, M.
1951 Hebrew Segullā: Akkadian Sikiltu. *JAOS* 71:172–74.
1983 *Ezekiel 1–20: A New Translation with Introduction and Commentary.* Anchor Bible 22. New York: Doubleday.

GREENE, J. T.
1989 *The Role of the Messenger and Message in the Ancient Near East.* Brown Judaic Studies 169. Missoula, Mont.: Scholars.

GROLLENBERG, L. H.
1956 *Atlas of the Bible.* Trans. J. M. H. Reid and H. H. Rowley. London: Nelson.

GUNKEL, H.
1928 *What Remains of the Old Testament?* Trans. A. K. Dallas. London: Allen & Unwin.
1963 *Die Israelitische Literatur.* (1925) Reprint. Darmstadt: Wissenschaftliche Buchgesellschaft.

GUNKEL, H., AND J. BEGRICH
1933 *Einleitung in die Psalmen: Die Gattungen der Religiosen Lyrik Israels.* Göttingen: Vandenhoeck & Ruprecht.

HALÉVY, J.
1909 Le prophète Malachie. *RevSem* 17:1–44.

HALS, R. M.
1989 *Ezekiel.* The Forms of the Old Testament Literature 19. Grand Rapids: Eerdmans.

HAMILTON, V. P.
    1990   *The Book of Genesis: Chapters 1–17*. New International Commentary on the Old Testament. Grand Rapids: Eerdmans.
HAMMERSHAIMB, E.
    1966   *Some Aspects of Old Testament Prophecy from Isaiah to Malachi*. Copenhagen: Rosenskilde & Bagger.
HAMMOND, P. C.
    1973   *The Nabataeans — Their History, Culture and Archaeology*. Studies in Mediterranean Archaeology 37. Gothenberg: Paul Astroms Forlag.
HANSON, P. D.
    1979   *The Dawn of Apocalyptic*. Revised. Philadelphia: Fortress.
    1986   *The People Called: The Growth of Community in the Bible*. San Francisco: Harper & Row.
HARBISON, E. H.
    1983   *The Christian Scholar in the Age of the Reformation*. (1956) Reprint, Grand Rapids: Eerdmans.
HARRISON, R. K.
    1969   *Introduction to the Old Testament*. Grand Rapids: Eerdmans.
HARTLEY, J. E.
    1992   *Leviticus*. Word Biblical Commentary 4. Waco, Tex.: Word.
HARVEY, J.
    1962   *Le rîb-pattern* réquistoire prohétique sur la rupture de l'alliance. *Bib* 43:172–96.
    1967   *Le plaidoyer prohétique contre Israël après la rupture de l'alliance. Etude d'une formule littéraire de l'Ancien Testament*. Paris: Desclée de Brouwer.
HASEL, G. F.
    1978   *Old Testament Theology: Basic Issues in the Current Debate*. Revised. Grand Rapids: Eerdmans.
HAYES, J. H.
    1979   *An Introduction to Old Testament Study*. Nashville: Abingdon.
HAYES, J. H., AND J. M. MILLER, EDS.
    1977   *Israelite and Judean History*. Old Testament Library. Philadelphia: Westminster.
HAYES, J. H., AND F. PRUSSNER
    1985   *Old Testament Theology: Its History & Development*. Atlanta: John Knox.
HEFLIN, J. N.
    1987   The Prophet Malachi, His World, and His Book. *SwJT* 38:5–11.
HENDERSON, E.
    1980   *The Twelve Minor Prophets*. (1858) Reprint. Grand Rapids: Baker.
HENDRIX, J. D.
    1987   "You Say": Confrontational Dialogue in Malachi. *RevExp* 84: 465–77.

HENGEL, M.
    1974   *Judaism and Hellenism.* 2d ed. 2 Vols. Trans. J. Bowden. Philadelphia: Fortress.
HENGSTENBERG, E. W.
    1956   *Christology of the Old Testament and a Commentary on the Messianic Predictions.* 2 Vols. (1854) Reprint, Grand Rapids: Kregel.
HERMISSON, H.-J.
    1971   Diskussionsworte bei Deuterojesaja." *EvT* 31:665–80.
HERTZBERG, W.
    1922   Die Entwicklung des Begriffes *mišpāṭ* im Alten Testament. *ZAW* 40:256–87.
HESCHEL, A. J.
    1962   *The Prophets.* 2 Vols. New York: Harper & Row.
HESSEL, D. T.
    1982   *Social Ministry.* Philadelphia: Westminster.
HILL, A. E.
    1981   The Book of Malachi: Its Place in Post-Exilic Chronology Linguistically Reconsidered. Ph.D. diss., University of Michigan.
    1982   Dating Second Zechariah: A Linguistic Reexamination. *HAR* 6:105–34.
    1983   Dating the Book of Malachi: A Linguistic Reexamination. In *The Word of the Lord Shall Go Forth. Essays in Honor of David Noel Freedman in Celebration of His Sixtieth Birthday,* 77–89. American Schools of Oriental Research, Special Volume Series 1. Winona Lake, Ind.: Eisenbrauns.
    1988   The Ebal Ceremony as Hebrew Land Grant? *JETS* 31:399–406.
    1989   Obadiah. In the *Evangelical Commentary on the Bible,* 638–43. Grand Rapids: Baker.
    1992   Malachi, The Book of. *ABD* 4:78–85.
    1994   *Enter His Courts with Praise! Old Testament Worship for the New Testament Church.* Nashville: Abbott-Martyn.
HIRSCH, M.
    1966   *The Haphtoroth.* Trans. I. Levy. London: Honig & Sons.
HOFTIJZER, J.
    1965   Remarks Concerning the Use of the Particle *'t* in Classical Hebrew. *OTS* 14:1–99.
HOGLUND, K.
    1992   *Achaemenid Imperial Administration in Syria-Palestine and the Missions of Ezra and Nehemiah.* SBL Dissertation Series 125. Atlanta: Scholars.
HOLLADAY, W. L.
    1958   *The Root ŠUBH in the Old Testament.* Leiden: Brill.
    1986   *Jeremiah 1: A Commentary on the Book of the Prophet Jeremiah Chapters 1–25.* Hermeneia. Philadelphia: Fortress.
    1989   *Jeremiah 2: A Commentary on the Book of the Prophet Jeremiah Chapters 26–52.* Hermeneia. Philadelphia: Fortress.

HOLTZMANN, O.
    1931   Der Prophet Maleachi und der Ursprung des Pharisaerbundes.
            ARW 19:1–21.
VAN HOONACKER, A.
    1908   *Les douze petits prophètes.* Paris: Gabalda & Cie.
HORNER, T. M.
    1960   Changing Concepts of the "Stranger" in the Old Testament. *ATR*
            42:49–53.
HORST, F.
    1954   *Die zwölf kleinen Propheten.* Handbuch zum Alten Testament
            1/14, vol. 2. 3rd Aufl. Tübingen: Mohr/Siebeck.
HOUSE, P. R.
    1990   *The Unity of the Twelve.* Journal for the Study of the Old Testament
            Supplement Series 97. Sheffield: Almond.
HUEY, F. B.
    1987   An Exposition of Malachi. *SwJT* 38:12–21.
HUFFMON, H.
    1959   The Covenant Lawsuit in the Prophets. *JBL* 78:285–95.
HUGENBERGER, G. P.
    1994   *Marriage as Covenant: A Study of Biblical Law and Ethics Govern-
            ing Marriage, Developed from the Perspective of Malachi.* Vetus Tes-
            tamentum Supplement Series 52. Leiden: Brill.
HVIDBERG, F. F.
    1962   *Weeping and Laughter in the Old Testament.* Leiden: Brill.
IBN EZRA, A.
    1951   *Miqra'ot Gedolot,* 166–69. Vol. 9. New York: Pardes. (Hebrew.)
ISAAKSSON, A.
    1965   *Marriage and Ministry in the New Temple.* Lund: Gleerup.
ISBELL, C. D.
    1980   *Malachi.* Grand Rapids: Zondervan.
JACOB, E.
    1958   *Theology of the Old Testament.* Trans. A. W. Heathcote and P. J.
            Allcock. New York: Harper and Row.
JAGERSMA, H.
    1981   The Tithes in the Old Testament. *OTS* 21:116–28.
JAPHET, S.
    1982   Sheshbazzar and Zerubbabel: Against the Background of the His-
            torical and Religious Tendencies of Ezra-Nehemiah. *ZAW* 94:
            66–69.
JEFFERS, R. J., AND I. LEHISTE
    1979   *Principles and Methods for Historical Linguistics.* Cambridge,
            Mass.: M.I.T.
JEMIELITY, T.
    1992   *Satire and the Hebrew Prophets.* Louisville: W/JKP.

JONES, B. A.
  1995   *The Formation of the Book of the Twelve: A Study in Text and Canon.* SBL Dissertation Series 149. Atlanta: Scholars.
JONES, D. C.
  1989   Malachi on Divorce. *Presb* 15:16–22.
  1990   A Note on the LXX of Malachi 2:16. *JBL* 109:683–85.
JONES, D. R.
  1962   *Haggai, Zechariah and Malachi.* Torch Bible Commentaries. London: SCM.
JONES, G. H.
  1984   *1 and 2 Kings.* New Century Bible Commentary, vol. 1. Grand Rapids: Eerdmans.
KAISER, W. C.
  1982   The Promise of the Arrival of Elijah in Malachi and the Gospels. *GTJ* 3:221–33.
  1984   *Malachi: God's Unchanging Love.* Grand Rapids: Baker.
  1987   Divorce in Malachi 2:10–16. *CTR* 73–84.
  1992   *Micah-Malachi.* The Communicator's Commentary, vol. 21. Waco, Tex.: Word.
KAUFMANN, Y.
  1977   *The History of the Religion of Israel: From the Babylonian Captivity to the End of Prophecy.* Vol. 4. New York: KTAV.
KEEL, O.
  1978   *The Symbolism of the Biblical World.* New York: Seabury.
KEIL, C. F.
  1975   *Commentary on the Twelve Prophets.* Vol. 10 (2 parts). Trans. J. Martin. (1873) Grand Rapids: Eerdmans.
KENT, R. G.
  1953   *Old Persian Texts and Grammar.* 2nd ed. New Haven, Conn.: American Oriental Society.
KEOWN, G. L.
  1987   Messianism in the Book of Malachi. *RevExp* 84:443–51.
KIKAWADA, I. M.
  1977   Some Proposals for the Definition of Rhetorical Criticism. *Semitics* 5:67–91.
KIKAWADA, I. M., AND A. QUINN
  1985   *Before Abraham Was.* Nashville: Abingdon.
KIMCHI, D.
  1951   *Miqra'ot Gedolot.* Vol. 9, 166–69. New York: Pardes. (Hebrew.)
KIRKPATRICK, A. F.
  1915   *The Doctrine of the Prophets.* London: Macmillan.
KLEIN, G. L.
  1987   An Introduction to Malachi. *CTR* 2:19–37.
KLEIN, R. W.
  1974   *Textual Criticism of the Old Testament: From the Septuagint to Qumran.* Guides to Biblical Scholarship. Philadelphia: Fortress.

1986   A Valentine for Those Who Fear Yahweh: The Book of Malachi. *CurTM* 13:143–52.

KNIGHT, G.A.F.

1985   *Isaiah 56–66: The New Israel.* International Theological Commentary. Grand Rapids: Eerdmans.

KOCH, K.

1983   *The Prophets: The Assyrian Period.* Trans. M. Kohl. Philadelphia: Fortress.

1984   *The Prophets: The Babylonian and Persian Periods.* Trans. M. Kohl. Philadelphia: Fortress.

KODELL, J.

1983   *Lamentations, Zechariah, Malachi, Obadiah, Joel, Second Zechariah, Baruch.* The Old Testament Message 14. Wilmington, Del.: Michael Glazier.

KÖHLER, L.

1957   *Old Testament Theology.* Trans. A. S. Todd. Philadelphia: Westminster.

KÖNIG, E.

1893   *Einleitung in das Alte Testament.* Bonn: Weber.

KRENTZ, E.

1975   *The Historical-Critical Method.* Guides to Biblical Scholarship. Philadelphia: Fortress.

KRUSE-BLINKENBERG, L.

1966   The Peshitta Book of Malachi. *ST* 20:95–119.

1967   The Book of Malachi according to Codex Syro-Hexaplaris Ambrosianus. *ST* 21:62–82.

KUEHNER, F. C.

1974   Emphases in Malachi and Modern Thought. In *The Law and the Prophets: Old Testament Studies Prepared in Honor of Oswald Thompson Allis,* 482–93. Phillipsburg, N.J.: Presbyterian & Reformed.

KUGLER, R. A.

1994   The Levi-Priestly Tradition: From Malachi to the Testament of Levi. Ph.D. diss., University of Notre Dame.

LABUSCHAGNE, C. J.

1966   *The Incomparability of Yahweh in the Old Testament.* Leiden: Brill.

LAETSCH, T.

1956   *The Minor Prophets.* St. Louis: Concordia.

LAFFEY, A. L.

1988   *An Introduction to the Old Testament: A Feminist Perspective.* Philadelphia: Fortress.

LAPIERRE, D.

1985   *The City of Joy.* Trans. K. Spink. Garden City, N.Y.: Doubleday.

LASOR, W. S.

1972   *The Dead Sea Scrolls and the New Testament.* Grand Rapids: Eerdmans.

LATTEY, C.
1935   *The Book of Malachi.* London: Longmans & Green.
LEHMANN, M. R.
1969   Biblical Oaths. *ZAW* 81:74–92.
LEHMANN, W. P.
1992   *Historical Linguistics: An Introduction.* 3rd ed. New York: Holt, Rinehart & Winston.
LESCOW, T.
1990   Dialogische Strukturen in den Streitreden des Buches Maleachi. *ZAW* 102:194–212.
1992   *Das Stufenschema: Untersuchungen zur Struktur alttestamentlicher Texte.* Beihefte zur Zeitschrift für die alttestamentliche Wissenschaft 211. Berlin: De Gruyter.
1993   *Das Buch Maleachi: Texttheorie — Auslegung — Kanontheorie. Mit einem Exkurs über Jeremia 8:8–9.* Arbeitzen zur Theologie 75. Stuttgart: Calwer.
LEVENSON, J. D.
1985   *Sinai & Zion: An Entry into the Jewish Bible.* New York: Harper.
1993   *The Hebrew Bible, The Old Testament, and Historical Criticism.* Louisville: Westminster/John Knox.
LEVINE, B. A.
1993   *Numbers 1–20: A New Translation, with Introduction and Commentary.* Anchor Bible 4. New York: Doubleday.
LEWIS, C. S.
1967   The Seeing Eye. In *Christian Reflections,* 167–76. Grand Rapids: Eerdmans.
LINDBLOM, J.
1962   *Prophecy in Ancient Israel.* Philadelphia: Fortress.
LINDHAGEN, C.
1950   *The Servant Motif in the Old Testament.* Uppsala: Lundequistka.
LINDSAY, J.
1976   The Babylonian Kings and Edom. *PEQ* 108:23–39.
LOCHER, C.
1981   Altes und Neues zu Maleachi 2:10–16. In *Mélanges Dominique Barthélmy: etudes bibliques offertes à l'occasion de son 60e anniversaire,* 241–71. Göttingen: Vandenhoeck & Ruprecht.
LONG, B. O.
1971   Two Question and Answer Schemata in the Prophets. *JBL* 90:129–39.
LONGACRE, R. E.
1983   *The Grammar of Discourse.* New York: Plenum.
LONGENECKER, R. N.
1975   *Biblical Exegesis in the Apostolic Period.* Grand Rapids: Eerdmans.
LONGMAN, T.
1987   *Literary Approaches to Biblical Interpretation.* Grand Rapids: Zondervan.

MCCARTER, K. P.
1980 *1 Samuel: A New Translation with Introduction and Commentary*. Anchor Bible 8. New York: Doubleday.
1986 *Textual Criticism: Recovering the Text of the Hebrew Bible*. Guides to Biblical Scholarship. Philadelphia: Fortress.

MCCARTHY, D. J.
1963 *Treaty and Covenant: A Study in Form in the Ancient Oriental Documents and in the Old Testament*. Analecta Biblica 21. Rome: Pontifical Biblical Institute.
1972 *Old Testament Covenant: A Survey of Current Opinions*. Richmond: John Knox.

MCEVENUE, S. E.
1981 The Political Structure in Judah from Cyrus to Nehemiah." *CBQ* 43:353–64.

MACINTOSH, A. A.
1969 A Consideration of Hebrew גער. *VT* 19:471–79.

MCKANE, W.
1970 *Proverbs*. Old Testament Library. Philadelphia: Westminster.
1980 משא in Jeremiah 23:33–40. In *Prophecy: Essays Presented to Georg Fohrer*, 35–54. Berlin: De Gruyter.
1986 *Jeremiah: A Critical and Exegetical Commentary*. International Critical Commentary, vol. 1, chaps. 1–25. Edinburgh: T. & T. Clark.

MCKENZIE, J. L.
1959 The Elders in the Old Testament. *Bib* 40:522–40.
1968 *Second Isaiah*. Anchor Bible 20. New York: Doubleday.

MCKENZIE, S. L., AND S. R. HAYNES, EDS.
1993 *To Each Its Own Meaning: An Introduction to Biblical Criticisms and Their Applications*. Louisville: Westminster/John Knox.

MCKENZIE, S. L., AND H. H. WALLACE
1983 Covenant Themes in Malachi. *CBQ* 45:549–63.

MCKNIGHT, E. V.
1988 *Post-Modern Use of the Bible*. Nashville: Abingdon.

MACK, B. L.
1990 *Rhetoric and the New Testament*. Minneapolis: Fortress.

MALCHOW, B. V.
1984 The Messenger of the Covenant in Mal 3:1. *JBL* 103:252–55.
1989 Review of *Malachi: The Divine Messenger*, by B. Glazier-McDonald. *JBL* 108:127–28.

MALLONE, G.
1981 *Furnace of Renewal: A Vision for the Church*. Downers Grove, Ill.: IVP.

MARCH, W. E.
1974 Prophecy. In *Old Testament Form Criticism*, 141–77. San Antonio, Tex.: Trinity University Press.

MARCUS, R.
1956   *Mebaqqer* and *Rabbim* in the Manual of Discipline 6:11–13. *JBL* 75:298–302.
MARSHALL, J. T.
1896   The Theology of Malachi. *ExpTim* 7:16–19, 73–75, 125–27.
MARTENS, E. A.
1994   *God's Design: A Focus on Old Testament Theology.* 2d ed. Grand Rapids: Baker.
MARTI, K.
1904   *Das Dodekapropheten erklärt.* Tübingen: Mohr.
MASON, R.
1977   *The Books of Haggai, Zechariah and Malachi.* Cambridge: Cambridge University.
1982   The Prophets of Restoration. In *Israel's Prophetic Tradition: Essays in Honour of Peter Ackroyd,* 137–54. Cambridge: Cambridge University.
1990   *Preaching the Tradition: Homily and Hermeneutics after the Exile.* Cambridge: Cambridge University.
1991   Review of *The Unity of the Twelve,* by P. R. House in *TS* 42:173–75.
MATHEWS, K. A.
1983   The Background of the Paleo-Hebrew Texts at Qumran. In *The Word of the Lord Shall Go Forth: Essays in Honor of David Noel Freedman,* 549–68. Winona Lake, Ind.: Eisenbrauns.
MATTHEW, V. H., AND J. C. MOYER
1991   Old Testament/Hebrew Bible Textbooks: Which Ones Are Best? *BA* 54:218–31.
MATTHEWS, I. G.
1935   *Haggai.* An American Commentary on the Old Testament. Philadelphia: American Baptist Publication Society.
MATTHEWS, J. G.
1931   Tammuz Worship in the Book of Malachi. *JPOS* 2:42–50.
MAYES, A.D.H.
1979   *Deuteronomy.* New Century Bible Commentary. London: Marshall, Morgan & Scott.
MAYS, J. L.
1976   *Micah: A Commentary.* Old Testament Library. Philadelphia: Westminster.
MENDENHALL, G. E.
1973   *The Tenth Generation: The Origins of the Biblical Tradition.* Baltimore: Johns Hopkins University.
MERRILL, E. H.
1994   *Haggai, Zechariah, Malachi: An Exegetical Commentary.* Chicago: Moody.
MERTON, T.
1948   *The Seven Storey Mountain.* New York: Harcourt, Brace, Jovanovich.

1968　*Faith and Violence: Christian Teaching and Christian Practice.*
　　　South Bend, Ind.: University of Notre Dame.

METTINGER, T.N.D.
1982　*The Dethronement of Sabaoth.* Coniectanea Biblica. OTS 18.
　　　Lund: Gleerup.

MEYERS, C. L.
1992　Temple, Jerusalem. *ABD* 6:350–69.

MEYERS, E. M.
1986　Priestly Language in the Book of Malachi. *HAR* 10:225–37.
1987　The Persian Period and the Judean Restoration: From Zerubbabel
　　　to Nehemiah. In *Ancient Israelite Religion: Essays in Honor of
　　　Frank Moore Cross,* 509–21. Philadelphia: Fortress.

MEYERS, E. M., AND C. L. MEYERS
1987　*Haggai, Zechariah 1–8: A New Translation, with Introduction and
　　　Commentary.* Anchor Bible 25B. New York: Doubleday.
1993　*Zechariah 9–14: A New Translation, with Introduction and Com-
　　　mentary.* Anchor Bible 25C. New York: Doubleday.

MICHEL, W. J.
1984　I Will Send You Elijah. *TBT* 22:217–22.

MILGROM, J.
1983　*Studies in Cultic Theology and Terminology.* Studies in Judaism and
　　　Late Antiquity 36. Leiden: Brill.
1991　*Leviticus 1–16: A New Translation with Introduction and Commen-
　　　tary.* Anchor Bible 3. New York: Doubleday.

MOORE, T. V.
1974　*A Commentary on Haggai and Malachi.* Geneva Series Commen-
　　　tary. London: Banner of Truth Trust. Reprint of *Prophets of the Res-
　　　toration,* 1856.

MORAN, W. L.
1963　The Ancient Near Eastern Background of the Love of God in Deu-
　　　teronomy. *CBQ* 25:77–87.

MORGENSTERN, J.
1963　Two Additional Notes to "The Suffering Servant" — A New Solu-
　　　tion. *VT* 13:321–32.

MUILENBURG, J.
1969　Form Criticism and Beyond. *JBL* 88:1–18.

MULLEN, E. T.
1980　*The Assembly of the Gods.* Harvard Semitic Monographs 24. Chico,
　　　Cal.: Scholars Press.

MÜLLER, D. H.
1896　Discours de Malachie sur les rites des sacrifices. *RB* 5:535–39.

MURRAY, D. F.
1987　The Rhetoric of Disputation: Re-Examination of a Prophetic
　　　Genre. *JSOT* 38:95–121.

MUSSNER, F.
    1984   *Tractate on the Jews: The Significance of Judaism for the Christian Faith.* Trans. L. Swidler. Philadelphia: Fortress.
MYERS, J. M.
    1968   *The World of the Restoration.* Englewood Cliffs: Prentice-Hall.
    1971   Edom and Judah in the Sixth-Fifth Centuries B.C. In *Near Eastern Studies in Honor of William Foxwell Albright,* 377–92. Baltimore: Johns Hopkins.
NEIL, W.
    1962   Malachi. In *The Interpreter's Dictionary of the Bible,* 228–32. Vol. 2. Nashville: Abingdon.
NEUSNER, J.
    1993   *The Way of Torah: An Introduction to Judaism.* 5th ed. Belmont, Cal.: Wadsworth.
NEWSOME, J. D.
    1984   *The Hebrew Prophets.* Atlanta: John Knox.
NIEBUHR, H. R.
    1951   *Christ and Culture.* New York: Harper & Row.
NOGALSKI, J. D.
    1993a   *Literary Precursors to the Book of Twelve.* Berlin: De Gruyter.
    1993b   *Redactional Process in the Book of Twelve.* Berlin: De Gruyter.
NOLL, M. A.
    1986   *Between Faith & Criticism.* New York: Harper & Row.
NORTH, R.
    1972   *Prophecy to Apocalyptic via Zechariah.* Vetus Testamentum Supplement 22. Leiden: Brill.
    1992a   Nehemiah. ABD 4:1068–71.
    1992b   Palestine, Administration of (Judean Officials). ABD 5:86–90.
NOWACK, W.
    1922   *Die kleinen Propheten.* 3d. ed. Handkommentar zum Alten Testament. Göttingen: Vandenhoeck & Ruprecht.
O'BRIEN, J. M.
    1990   *Priest and Levite in Malachi.* SBL Dissertation Series 121. Atlanta: Scholars Press.
    1995   Malachi. *CR:BS* 3:81–94.
    1996   Judah as Wife and Husband: Deconstructing Gender in Malachi. *JBL* 115:241–50.
O'CONNOR, M.
    1980   *Hebrew Verse Structure.* Winona Lake, Ind.: Eisenbrauns.
OESTERLEY, W.O.E., AND T. H. ROBINSON
    1955   *An Introduction to the Books of the Old Testament.* London: SPCK.
OGDEN, G. S.
    1988   The Use of Figurative Language in Mal 2:10–16. *BT* 39:223–30.
OGDEN, G. S., AND R. R. DEUTSCH
    1987   *Joel & Malachi: A Promise of Hope—A Call to Obedience.* International Theological Commentary. Grand Rapids: Eerdmans.

OLLENBURGER, B. C., E. A. MARTENS, AND G. F. HASEL, EDS.
1992   *The Flowering of Old Testament Theology: A Reader of Twentieth-Century Old Testament Theology, 1930–1990.* Winona Lake, Ind.: Eisenbrauns.

OLMSTEAD, A. T.
1948   *History of the Persian Empire.* Chicago: University of Chicago.

ORELLI, C. VON
1897   *The Twelve Minor Prophets.* Trans. J. S. Banks. Edinburgh: T. & T. Clark.

OSWALD, H. C., ED.
1975   *Luther's Works: Lectures on the Minor Prophets.* Vol. 18 (Hosea-Malachi). Trans. R. J. Dinda. St. Louis: Concordia.

PACKARD, J.
1902   The Book of Malachi. In *Lange's Commentary on the Minor Prophets,* 1–35. New York: Scribners.

PATTERSON, R. D.
1993   Old Testament Prophecy. In *A Complete Literary Guide to the Bible,* 296–309. Grand Rapids: Baker.

PAUL, S. M.
1991   *A Commentary on the Book of Amos.* Hermeneia. Minneapolis: Fortress.

PECKHAM, B.
1993   *History and Prophecy.* Anchor Bible Reference Library. New York: Doubleday.

PEDERSEN, J.
1954   *Israel: Its Life and Culture.* 4 vols. (1926) Reprint, London: Oxford University.

PEROWNE, T. T.
1901   *Haggai, Zechariah, and Malachi.* 2d. ed. Cambridge Bible for Schools and College. Cambridge: Cambridge University.

PETERSEN, D. L.
1974   Zerubbabel and Jerusalem Temple Reconstruction. *CBQ* 36: 366–72.
1977   *Late Israelite Prophecy: Studies in Deutero-Prophetic Literature and in Chronicles.* SBL Monograph Series 23. Missoula, Mont.: Scholars Press.
1984   *Haggai and Zechariah 1–8.* Old Testament Library. Philadelphia: Westminster.
1995   *Zechariah 9–14 and Malachi.* Old Testament Library. Louisville: Westminster.

PFEIFFER, E.
1959   Die Disputationsworte im Buche Maleachi (Ein Beitrag zur formgeschichtlichen Struktur). *EvT* 19:546–68.

PFEIFFER, R. H.
1941   *Introduction to the Old Testament.* New York: Harper.

PIERCE, R.
  1984a Literary Connectors and a Haggai/Zechariah/Malachi Corpus. *JETS* 27:277–89.
  1984b A Thematic Development of the Haggai/Zechariah/Malachi Corpus. *JETS* 27:401–12.

PILCH, J.
  1991 *Introducing the Cultural Context of the Old Testament.* New York: Paulist.

PILCH, J., AND B. J. MALINA, EDS.
  1993 *Biblical Social Values and Their Meaning: A Handbook.* Peabody, Mass.: Hendrickson.

PLUMMER, A.
  1926 *A Critical and Exegetical Commentary on the Gospel of St. Luke.* 5th ed. International Critical Commentary. Edinburgh: T. & T. Clark.

PÖLGER, O.
  1968 *Theocracy and Eschatology.* Trans. S. Rudman. Richmond: John Knox.

POLZIN, R.
  1976 *Late Biblical Hebrew: Toward an Historical Typology of Biblical Hebrew Prose.* Harvard Semitic Monograph 12. Missoula, Mont.: Scholars Press.
  1980 *Moses and the Deuteronomist.* New York: Seabury.

POPE, M. H.
  1977 *Song of Songs.* Anchor Bible 7C. New York: Doubleday.

PRESSEL, W.
  1870 *Commentar zu den Schriften der Propheten Haggai, Sacharja und Maleachi.* Gotha: Scholessmann.

PROCTOR, J.
  1993 Fire in God's House: Influence of Malachi 3 in the NT. *JETS* 36:9–14.

PROVAN, I. W.
  1991 *Lamentations.* New Century Bible Commentary. London: Marshall Pickering.

PUSEY, E. B.
  1977 *The Minor Prophets.* Vol. 2. (1860) Reprint, Grand Rapids: Baker.

RABIN, C.
  1955 Hebrew YĀD = Hand. *JJS* 6:111–15.

VON RAD, G.
  1961 *Genesis: A Commentary.* Old Testament Library. Trans. J. H. Marks. Philadelphia: Westminster.
  1962/65 *Old Testament Theology.* 2 vols. Trans. D.M.G. Stalker. New York: Harper & Row.
  1966 *Deuteronomy: A Commentary.* Old Testament Library. Trans. D. Barton. Philadelphia: Westminster.

1967   *The Message of the Prophets.* Trans. D.M.G. Stalker. New York: Harper & Row.

RADDAY, V. T.

1973   *An Analytical Linguistic Key-Word-in-Context Concordance to the Books of Haggai, Zechariah and Malachi.* The Computer Bible 4. Wooster: Biblical Research Associates.

RADDAY, V. T., AND M. A. POLLATSCHEK

1980   Vocabulary Richness in Post-Exilic Prophetic Books. ZAW 92: 333–46.

RADDAY, V. T., AND D. WICKMAN

1975   The Unity of Zechariah Examined in the Light of Statistical Linguistics. ZAW 87:30–55.

RAITT, T. M.

1971   The Prophetic Summons to Repentance. ZAW 83:30–49.

RASHI (SOLOMON BEN ISAAC)

1930   *Commentary on the Minor Prophets.* Vol. 1. Ed. I. Maarsen. Amsterdam: Hertzberger. Reprint. (Hebrew.)

REDDITT, P. L.

1994   The Book of Malachi in Its Social Setting. CBQ 56:240–55.

1995   *Haggai, Zechariah, Malachi.* New Century Bible Commentary. Grand Rapids: Eerdmans.

REHM, M.

1961   Das Opfer der Völker nach Mal 1:11. In *Lex tua Veritas,* 193–96. H. Junker Festschrift. Trier: Paulinus-Verlag.

REICKE, B.

1968   *The New Testament Era: The World of the Bible from 500 B.C. to A.D. 100.* Trans. D. E. Green. Philadelphia: Fortress.

RENDSBURG, G. A.

1986   *The Redaction of Genesis.* Winona Lake, Ind.: Eisenbrauns.

RENKER, A.

1979   *Die Tora bei Maleachi: Ein Beitrag zur Bedeutungsgeschichte von Tora im Alten Testament.* Freiburg: Herder.

REVENTLOW, H. G.

1993   *Die Propheten Haggai, Sacharja und Maleachi.* Das Alte Testament Deutsch 25/2 (9th ed.). Göttingen: Vandenhoeck & Ruprecht.

RICHARDSON, P. A.

1987   Worship Resources for Malachi. *RevExp* 84:479–86.

RINGGREN, H.

1966   *Israelite Religion.* Trans. D. E. Green. Philadelphia: Fortress.

ROBERTS, J.J.M.

1991   *Nahum, Habakkuk, and Zephaniah.* Old Testament Library. Louisville: Westminster/John Knox.

ROBERTSON, D.

1976   Literature, The Bible As. *IDB Supp* 547–51.

1977   *The Old Testament and the Literary Critic.* Philadelphia: Fortress.

ROBERTSON, O. P.
1990 *The Books of Nahum, Habakkuk, and Zephaniah.* New International Commentary on the Old Testament. Grand Rapids: Eerdmans.
ROBINSON, A.
1949 God the Refiner of Silver. *CBQ* 11:188–90.
ROBINSON, G. L.
1926 *The Twelve Minor Prophets.* New York: Doran.
ROBINSON, J.
1976 *The Second Book of Kings.* The Cambridge Bible Commentary. Cambridge: Cambridge University.
ROFÉ, A.
1988 The Onset of Sects in Postexilic Judaism: Neglected Evidence from the Septuagint, Trito-Isaiah, Ben Sira, and Malachi. In *The Social World of Formative Christianity and Judaism: Essays in Tribute to Howard Clark Kee.* Ed. J. Neusner et al., 39–49. Philadelphia: Fortress.
ROSS, J. F.
1962 The Prophet as Yahweh's Messenger. In *Israel's Prophetic Heritage: Essays in Honor of James Muilenburg,* 98–107. New York: Harper.
ROST, L.
1961 Erwägungen zum Kyroserlass. In *Verbannung und Heimkehr. Wilhelm Rudoldph zum 70. Geburtstage,* 301–7. Tübingen: Mohr.
ROWLEY, H. H.
1955 Nehemiah's Mission and Its Background. *BJRL* 37:528–61. Reprinted in *Men of God: Studies in Old Testament History and Prophecy,* 211–45. London: Nelson, 1963.
1961 *The Growth of the Old Testament.* London: Hutchinson.
1967 *Worship in Ancient Israel: Its Forms and Meanings.* London: SPCK.
RUDOLPH, W.
1949 *Esra und Nehemia.* Handbuch zum Alten Testament 20. Tübingen: Mohr.
1976 *Haggai-Sacharja-Maleachi.* Kommentar zum Alten Testament, Band 13, 4. Gütersloh: Mohn.
1981 Zu Mal 2:10–16. *ZAW* 93:85–90.
RUSSELL, D. S.
1976 *The Method and Message of Jewish Apocalyptic.* Old Testament Library. Philadelphia: Westminster.
RYKEN, L.
1984 *How To Read the Bible as Literature.* Grand Rapids: Zondervan.
RYKEN, L., AND T. LONGMAN, EDS.
1993 *A Complete Literary Guide to the Bible.* Grand Rapids: Zondervan.
SANDAY, W., AND A. C. HEADLAM
1902 *A Critical and Exegetical Commentary on the Epistle to the Romans.* International Critical Commentary. Edinburgh: T. & T. Clark.

SANDERS, J. A.
1972 *Torah and Canon.* Philadelphia: Fortress.
1984 *Canon and Community: A Guide to Canonical Criticism.* Philadelphia: Fortress.

SASSON, J. M.
1990 *Jonah.* Anchor Bible 24B. New York: Doubleday.

SCALISE, P. J.
1987 To Fear or Not to Fear: Questions of Reward and Punishment in Malachi 2:17–4:2. *RevExp* 84:409–18.

SCHNEIDER, D. A.
1979 The Unity of the Book of the Twelve. Ph.D. diss., Yale University.

SCHREINER, S.
1979 Mischehen-Ehebruch-Ehescheidung: Betrachtunges zu Malachi 2:10–16. ZAW 91:207–28.

SCHULLER, E. M.
1996 The Book of Malachi. In *The New Interpreter's Bible*, 841–877. Vol. 7. Nashville: Abingdon.

SCOTT, R.B.Y.
1948 The Meaning of Massā' as an Oracle Title. *JBL* 67:v–vi.
1953 *The Relevance of the Prophets.* New York: Macmillan.
1965 *Proverbs-Ecclesiastes.* Anchor Bible 18. New York: Doubleday.

SEBÖK, M.
1887 *Die syrische Uebersetzung der zwölf kleinen Propheten und ihr Verhaltniss zu dem massoretischen Text und zu den alteren Uebersetzungen namentlich den LXX und dem Targum.* Breslau: Preuss und Junger.

SEGAL, M. H.
1927 *A Grammar of Mishnaic Hebrew.* Oxford: Clarendon.

SELLIN, E.
1930 *Das Zwölfprophetenbuch übersetzt und erklärt.* Kommentar zum Alten Testament 12, vol. 2. Leipzig: Deichert.

SELLIN, E., AND G. FOHRER
1968 *Introduction to the Old Testament.* Trans. D. E. Green. Nashville: Abingdon.

SILVA, M.
1990 *God, Language, and Scripture: Reading the Bible in the Light of General Linguistics.* Grand Rapids: Zondervan.

SMIT, G.
1934 *De kleine profeten III: Habakuk, Haggai, Zacharia, Maleachi.* Texte und Untersuchungen. The Hague: Wolters.

SMITH, G. A.
1905 *The Book of the Twelve Prophets.* 2 vols. The Expositor's Bible. New York: Armstrong and Son.

SMITH, J.M.P.
1912 *A Critical and Exegetical Commentary on Haggai, Zechariah, Mal-*

achi and Jonah. International Critical Commentary, bk. 2, 1–88. Edinburgh: T. & T. Clark.

SMITH, M.
1971   *Palestinian Parties and Politics That Shaped the Old Testament.* New York: Columbia University.

SMITH, M. S.
1990   The Near Eastern Background of Solar Language for Yahweh. *JBL* 109:29–39.

SMITH, R. L.
1984   *Micah-Malachi.* Word Biblical Commentary 32. Waco, Tex.: Word.
1987   The Shape of Theology in the Book of Malachi. *SwJT* 38:22–27.

SNYMAN, S. D.
1984a   Chiasmes in Mal. 1:2–5. *Skrif en Kerk* 2:17–22. (Afrikaans.)
1984b   Haat Jahwe vir Esau? ('n Verkenning van Mal. 1:3a). *NGTT* 25:358–62.
1990   Antitheses in the Book of Malachi. *JNSL* 16:173–178.

SOULEN, R. N.
1981   *Handbook of Biblical Criticism.* 2nd ed. Atlanta: John Knox.

SPEISER, E. A.
1960   An Angelic "Curse": Exodus 14:20. *JAOS* 80:198–200.
1964   *Genesis: Introduction, Translation, and Notes.* Anchor Bible 1. New York: Doubleday.

SPERBER, A., ED.
1962   *The Bible in Aramaic: The Latter Prophets.* 3 Vols. Leiden: Brill.

SPOER, H. H.
1908   Some New Considerations towards Dating the Book of Malachi. *JQR* 20:167–86.

STARCKY, J.
1955   The Nabataeans: A Historical Sketch. *BA* 18:84–106.

STECK, O. H.
1991   *Der Abschluss der Prophetie im Alten Testament: ein Versuch zur Frage der Vorgeschichte des Kanons.* Biblisch-theologische Studien 17. Neukirchen-Vluyn: Neukirchener Verlag.

STENDEBACH, F. J.
1977   *Prophetie und Tempel: Haggai-Sacharja-Maleachi-Joel.* Stuttgart Kleinen Kommentar. Stuttgart: Katholisches Bibelwerk.

STERN, E.
1971   Seal-Impressions in the Achaemenid Style in the Province of Judah. *BASOR* 202:6–16.
1984   The Persian empire and the political and social history of Palestine in the Persian period. In *The Cambridge History of Judaism,* 70–87. Vol. 1. Cambridge: Cambridge University.
1989   What Happened to the Israelite Cult? Israelite Religion Purified after the Exile. *BAR* 15:4:22–29, 53–54.

STOLPER, M. W.
  1979 The Governor of Babylon and Across-the-River in 486 B.C. *JNES* 48:283–305.
SUTCLIFFE, E. F.
  1922 Malachy's Prophecy of the Eucharistic Sacrifice. *IER* 5:502–13.
SWETNAM, J.
  1969 Malachi 1:11: An Interpretation. *CBQ* 31:200–9.
TATE, M. E.
  1987 Questions for Priests and People in Mal 1:2–2:16. *RevExp* 84:391–407.
TAYLOR, J. G.
  1993 *Yahweh and the Sun: Biblical and Archaeological Evidence for Sun Worship in Ancient Israel.* Journal for the Study of the Old Testament Supplement Series 111. Sheffield: JSOT.
TEEPLE, H. M.
  1957 *The Mosaic Eschatological Prophet.* Society of Biblical Literature Monograph Series 10. Philadelphia: Society of Biblical Literature.
TERRIEN, S.
  1978 *The Elusive Presence.* New York: Harper & Row.
THOMAS, D. W.
  1949 The Root צנע in Hebrew, and the Meaning of קדרנית in Mal 3:14. *JJS* 1:182–88.
THOMPSON, H. D.
  1995 *Malachi: A Bibliography.* Delhi: ISPCK.
THOMPSON, J. A.
  1979 Israel's Haters. *VT* 29:200–5.
  1980 *The Book of Jeremiah.* New International Commentary on the Old Testament. Grand Rapids: Eerdmans.
TILLEY, W. C.
  1987 A Biblical Approach to Stewardship. *RevExp* 84:433–42.
TILLMAN, W. M.
  1987 Key Ethical Issues in Malachi. *SwJT* 38:42–47.
TORREY, C. C.
  1898 The Prophecy of Malachi. *JBL* 17:1–15.
  1905 'ēr wĕ'ōneh in Malachi ii.12. *JBL* 24:1–15.
TOSATO, A.
  1978 Il Ripudio: Delitto e Pena (Mal 2:10–16). *Biblica* 59:548–53.
TOV, E.
  1992 *Textual Criticism of the Hebrew Bible.* Minneapolis: Fortress.
TOZER, A. W.
  1978 *The Best of A. W. Tozer.* Comp. W. W. Wiersbe. Grand Rapids: Baker.
TUCKER, G. M.
  1977 Prophetic Superscriptions and the Growth of a Canon. In *Canon and Authority*, 56–70. Philadelphia: Fortress.

UTZSCHNEIDER, H.
1989   *Künder order Schreiber? Eine These zum Problem der "Schriftprophetie" auf Grund von Maleachi 1:6–2:9.* Beiträge zur Erforschung des Alten Testaments und des Antiken Judentums 19. Frankfort: Peter Lang.
1992   Die Schriftprophetie und die Frage nach dem End der Prophetie. Überlegungen anhand von Mal 1:6–2:16. *ZAW* 103:377–93.

VACCARI, A.
1963   Matrimonio e divorzio (Mal 2:15, 16). *CC* 114:357–58.

VANGEMEREN, W. A.
1990   *Interpreting the Prophetic Word.* Grand Rapids: Zondervan.

VAN LEEUWEN, R. C.
1990   The Sage in Prophetic Literature. In *The Sage in Israel and the Ancient Near East,* 295–306. Winona Lake, Ind.: Eisenbrauns.
1993   Scribal Wisdom and Theodicy in the Book of the Twelve. In *In Search of Wisdom: Essays in Memory of John G. Gammie,* 31–49. Louisville: W/JKP.

VAN SELMS, A.
1975   The Inner Cohesion of the Book of Malachi. In *Studies in Old Testament Prophecy,* 27–40. *OTWSA.* Potchefstroom: Pro Rege.

DE VAUX, R.
1965   *Ancient Israel: Its Life and Institutions.* 2 vols. New York: McGraw-Hill.

VERHOEF, P. A.
1966   Some Notes on Mal 1:11. *OTWSA:*163–72.
1972   *Maleachi.* Commentar op het Oude Testament. Kampen: Kok.
1987   *Haggai and Malachi.* New International Commentary on the Old Testament. Grand Rapids: Eerdmans.

VERMES, G.
1987   *The Dead Sea Scrolls in English.* 3rd ed. New York: Penguin.

VORSTER, W.
1989   Intertextuality and Redaktionsgeschichte. In *Intertextuality in Biblical Writings.* Ed. S. Draisma, 15–26. B. van Iersel Festschrift. Kampen: J. H. Kok.

VRIEZEN, T. C.
1970   *An Outline of Old Testament Theology.* 2nd ed. Newton, Mass.: C. T. Branford.
1975   How to Understand Malachi 1:11. In *Grace Upon Grace,* 128–31. L. J. Kuyper Festschrift. Grand Rapids: Eerdmans.

VUILLEUMIER, R.
1981   *Malachie.* Commentaire de l'Ancien Testament 9. Neuchatel: Delachaux & Niestlé.

WALDMAN, N. M.
1974   Some Notes on Malachi 3:6; 3:13; Psalm 42:11. *JBL* 93:543–49.

WALHOUT, C., AND L. RYKEN, EDS.
  1991   Contemporary Literary Theory: A Christian Appraisal. Grand Rapids: Eerdmans.
WALLIS, G.
  1967   Wesen und Struktur der Botschaft Maleachis. In Das Ferne und Nahe Wort, 229–37. L. Rost Festschrift. Berlin: Töpelmann.
WALTERS, P.
  1973   The Text of the Septuagint. Ed. D. W. Gooding. Cambridge: Cambridge University.
WALTKE, B. K. AND M. O'CONNOR
  1990   An Introduction to Biblical Hebrew Syntax. Winona Lake, Ind.: Eisenbrauns.
WATTS, J.D.W.
  1987a   Introduction to the Book of Malachi. RevExp 84:373–81.
  1987b   Isaiah 34–66. Word Biblical Commentary 25. Waco, Tex.: Word.
WEINER, A.
  1978   The Prophet Elijah in the Development of Judaism. London: Kegan Paul.
WEINFELD, M.
  1970   The Covenant of Grant in the Old Testament and the Ancient Near East. JAOS 90:184–203.
  1983   Social and Cultic Institutions in the Priestly Source against Their Ancient Near Eastern Backgrounds. In Eighth World Congress of Jewish Studies, Proceedings, 95–129. Jerusalem: World Union of Jewish Studies.
  1991   Deuteronomy 1–11: A New Translation with Introduction and Commentary. Anchor Bible 5. New York: Doubleday.
  1995   Social Justice in Ancient Israel and in the Ancient Near East. Minneapolis: Fortress.
WEISER, A.
  1961   The Old Testament: Its Formation and Development. Trans. D. M. Barton. New York: Association.
  1962   The Psalms. Old Testament Library. Trans. H. Hartwell. Philadelphia: Westminster.
WELCH, A.
  1900   Malachi, Book of. HBD 3:218–22.
  1935   Post-Exilic Judaism. London: Blackwood and Sons.
WELLHAUSEN, J.
  1963   Die Kleinen Propheten. 4th ed. Berlin: De Gruyter.
WELLS, C. R.
  1987   The Subtle Crisis of Secularism: Preaching the Burden of Israel. CTR 2:39–61.
WENDLAND, E.
  1985   Linear and Concentric Patterns in Malachi. BT 36:108–21.
WENHAM, G. J.
  1977   The Coherence of the Flood Narrative. VT 28:336–48.

1979   *The Book of Leviticus.* New International Commentary on the Old Testament. Grand Rapids: Eerdmans.

1985   The Date of Deuteronomy: Linch-Pin of Old Testament Criticism (Part One). *Them* 10:15–20.

1986   The Date of Deuteronomy: Linch-Pin of Old Testament Criticism (Part Two). *Them* 11:15–18.

1987   *Genesis 1–15.* Word Biblical Commentary 1. Waco, Tex.: Word.

WEST, J. K.

1981   *Introduction to the Old Testament.* 2nd Ed. New York: Macmillan.

WESTERMANN, C.

1964   Sprache und Struktur der Prophetie Deuterojesajas. In *Forschung am Alten Testament,* 92–170. Theologische Bucherei 24. Munich: Kaiser.

1969   *Isaiah 40–66.* Old Testament Library. Trans. D.M.G. Stalker. Philadelphia: Westminster.

1982   *Elements of Old Testament Theology.* Trans. D. W. Stott. Atlanta: John Knox.

1987   *Genesis: A Practical Commentary.* [Text and Interpretation.] Trans. D. E. Green. Grand Rapids: Eerdmans.

1991   *Basic Forms of Prophetic Speech.* Trans. H. C. White. (1967) Reprint, Louisville: W/JKP.

WEVERS, J. W.

1971   *Ezekiel.* The New Century Bible Commentary. London: Marshall, Morgan, & Scott.

WHEDBEE, J. W.

1971   *Isaiah & Wisdom.* Nashville: Abingdon.

WHYBRAY, R. N.

1987   *The Making of the Pentateuch: A Methodological Study.* Sheffield: JSOT.

WIDENGREN, G.

1977   The Persian Period. In *Israelite and Judean History,* 489–538. Philadelphia: Westminster.

WILLIAMS, D. T.

1993   The Windows of Heaven. *OTE* 5:402–13.

WILLIAMS, R. J.

1976   *Hebrew Syntax: An Outline.* 2nd ed. Toronto: University of Toronto.

WILLIAMSON, H.G.H.

1985   *Ezra, Nehemiah.* Word Bible Commentary 16. Waco, Tex.: Word.

1988a   The Governors of Judah under the Persians." *TB* 39:59–82.

1988b   Zerubbabel." *ISBE* 4:1193–94.

1992   Palestine, Administration of (Persian). *ABD* 5:81–86.

WILLIMON, W. H.

1985   *Sighing for Eden: Sin, Evil & the Christian Faith.* Nashville: Abingdon.

WILSON, R. R.
1980   *Prophecy and Society in Ancient Israel.* Philadelphia: Fortress.
WINCKLER, H.
1899   Maleachi. *AoF* II:531–39.
WOLD, D.
1979   The *Kareth* Penalty in P: Rationale and Cases. *SBLSP* 1:1–46.
WOLF, H.
1976   *Haggai and Malachi: Rededication and Renewal.* Chicago: Moody.
WOLFF, H. W.
1974   *Anthropology of the Old Testament.* Trans. M. Kohl. London: SCM.
1977   *Joel and Amos.* Hermeneia. Trans. W. Janzen, et al. Philadelphia: Fortress.
WOLMARANS, H. P.
1967   What Does Malachi Say about Divorce?" *HTS* 22:46–47. (Africaans.)
WOUDE, A. S. VAN DER
1982   *Haggai, Maleachi.* De Prediking van het Oude Testament. Nijkerk: Callenbach.
1986   Malachi's Struggle for a Pure Community. In *Tradition and Reinterpretation in Jewish and Early Christian Literature: Essays in Honor of Jurgen C. H. Lebram,* 65–71. Leiden: Brill.
WÜRTHWEIN, E.
1979   *The Text of the Old Testament.* 4th ed. Trans. E. F. Rhodes. Grand Rapids: Eerdmans.
WUTZ, F.
1933   *Die Transkriptionen von der Septuaginta bis zu Hieronymus.* Stuttgart: Kohlhammer.
YAMAUCHI, E. M.
1980a   The Archaeological Background of Ezra. *BSac* 137:195–211.
1980b   The Archaeological Background of Nehemiah. *BSac* 137:291–309.
1988   Ezra-Nehemiah. In *The Expositor's Bible Commentary,* 565–771. Vol. 4. Grand Rapids: Zondervan.
1990   *Persia and the Bible.* Grand Rapids: Baker.
YATES, K. M.
1942   *Preaching from the Prophets,* especially 213–20. Nashville: Broadman.
YOUNG, T. C.
1992   Darius. *ABD* 2:37–38.
ZIMMERLI, W.
1979   *Ezekiel 1: A Commentary on the Book of the Prophet Ezekiel, Chapters 1–24.* Trans. R. E. Clements. Hermeneia. Philadelphia: Fortress.
1982   *I Am Yahweh.* Trans. D. W. Stott. Atlanta: John Knox.

1983   *Ezekiel 2: A Commentary on the Book of the Prophet Ezekiel, Chapters 25–48*. Trans. J. D. Martin. Hermeneia. Philadelphia: Fortress.

ZVI, E. B., M. HANCOCK, AND R. BEINERT

1993   *Readings in Biblical Hebrew: An Intermediate Textbook*. New Haven, Conn.: Yale University.

TRANSLATION, NOTES, AND COMMENTS

◆

III. A. SUPERSCRIPTION (1:1)

1 ¹An oracle: the word of Yahweh to Israel through Malachi.

NOTES

1:1. *maśśā'*. The word is a verbal substantive (i.e., an infinitive construct after the Arabic *maqtal* pattern, cf. GKC § 45e; de Boer [p. 197]; and WO'C § 35.3.1 on the nominal uses of the infinitive) from the verbal root *nś'*, meaning "to lift, raise, bear, carry" (*CHAL*: 246–47). While the form of *maśśā'* is clearly understood, the syntactical relationship of the term to the following construct-genitive phrase is less certain. Biblical scholars of previous generations understood *maśśā' děbar-YHWH* as a construct chain and translated "the burden [or oracle] of the word of the Lord" (e.g., Calvin [1979: 461]; Luther [Oswald 1975: 391]; Henderson [1980: 445]; G. A. Smith [1905: 331]; J.M.P. Smith [1912: 18]; cf. Baldwin [1972a: 221]; Rudolph [1976: 253]; Glazier-McDonald [1987a: 24]), primarily on the basis of the Masoretic conjunctive accent of *maśśā'* (*mêrěkā*) and the tendency of the ancient versions to render the Hebrew *maśśā'* with an equivalent term in the genitive case (cf. LXX, T, V).

An alternative reading maintains an emphatic distinction between *maśśā'* and *děbar-YHWH*, "A burden! The word of Jehovah . . ." (e.g., Moore [1974: 94]) or "An Oracle. The word of Jehovah . . ." (e.g., Elliger [1950: 178]; Horst [1954: 264]; Chary [1969: 234]; cf. NAB, NEB, NIV, NRSV [NJB, "A message."] — all aptly censured by Meyers and Meyers [1993: 91] for their "disservice to the structure of intensification of prophetic authority").

More recently, biblical commentators have understood *děbar-YHWH* in an appositional relationship to *maśśā'* (e.g., R. L. Smith [1984: 301]; Verhoef [1987: 187]; Petersen [1995: 165]). Meyers and Meyers (1993: 90) have argued as much for the equivalent expression *maśśā' děbar-YHWH* in Zech 9:1 and 12:1, because "the relationship of 'oracle' to 'word of Yahweh' seems to be one of equivalence rather than possession." More precisely, the oracle formula *maśśā' děbar-YHWH* is a noun-noun appositional phrase of a *sortal* type, in that *děbar-YHWH* more narrowly defines the leadword *maśśā'* and indicates the (divine) quality or character of that leadword (WO'C § 12.3b, c; cf. Erlandsson [1970: 65] who regarded *maśśā'* and *dābār* as synonyms in Isaiah on the basis of usage in 2:1 [*ḥāzâ* + *dābār*] and 13:1 [*maśśā'* + *ḥāzâ*]).

dĕbar-YHWH. The use of *dābār* ("word") in a construct-genitive relationship with the divine name Yahweh occurs nineteen times in the Haggai-Zechariah-Malachi corpus. The phrase *dĕbar-YHWH* ("the word of Yahweh") appears in Malachi only in the superscription (1:1). The construction follows the pattern of the genitive of authorship, a particular form of agency involving speaking and writing (WO'C § 9.5.1c).

The phrase *maśśā' dĕbar-YHWH* is unique to Zech 9:1, 12:1, and Mal 1:1; although the expression *maśśā' YHWH* does occur in Jer 23:33, 34, 38. In those instances where *maśśā'* comprises part of a formula introducing a prophetic oracle, Malachi also conforms to the general pattern of omitting the definite article (Isa 13:1; 15:1; 17:1; 19:1; 21:1, 11, 13; 22:1; 23:1; 30:6; Nah 1:1; cf. the exceptional case in Hab 1:1). However, it should be noted that these examples are true construct-genitive relationships with a proper noun, unlike the noun-noun appositional construction of (Zech 9:1, 12:1, and Mal 1:1). I concur with the assessment of Meyers and Meyers (1993: 91) that this combination of *maśśā'* and *dĕbar-YHWH* is a distinctive feature of late biblical prophecy. See further the COMMENTS on 1:1 below.

'el-yiśrā'ēl. The preposition *'el* almost always appears with the connecting *maqqeph* in the MT, and such is the case here in Mal 1:1 (cf. WO'C § 11.2.2a). Here *'el* marks the simple dative "to" (Israel as the recipient of this divine message).

Both Syr and T read *'al* for the MT *'el.* The LXX translates *epí*, perhaps due to the influence of Zech 12:1 where the LXX reads *epí* for the MT *'al.* It is also possible the LXX interprets *maśśā'* in Zech 12:1 and Mal 1:1 more in the sense of "a burden against . . . ," rather than "an oracle to . . ." While the LXX shows a tendency to employ *prós* for the corresponding *'el* in the MT (e.g., Jer 50:1; Hag 1:1), one must guard against reading too much into the LXX's use of *epí* for *'el* in Mal 1:1; because elsewhere similar divine oracle formulae reading *'al* in the MT are variously rendered by the LXX with *prós* (e.g., 1 Kgs 16:1), *peri* (e.g., Jer 14:1), and *epí* (e.g., Jer 46:1 = LXX 32:1). Better said, the overlap demonstrated in the MT between the prepositions *'el* and *'al* is mirrored by a similar overlap in the prepositions *epí* and *prós* in the LXX (cf. WO'C § 11.4.3a). Clearly, the MT is the superior text (supported by the V, *ad*).

bĕyad mal'ākî. Literally, "by the hand of Malachi." The *circumstantial* use of the preposition *bêt* here with the preceding *genitive of authorship* (*dĕbar-YHWH*) demonstrates the agency of the prophet as the human instrument involved in speaking and/or writing the oracles, hence the translation "through" (cf. WO'C § 9.5.1c and 11.2.5d). Petersen (1995: 166) acknowledges the phrase *bĕyad*, "through," refers to prophetic intermediation and "places this discourse firmly within the ambit of prophetic authority." Steck (p. 133) suggests that the phrase establishes continuity with prophetic figures as early as Moses.

Glazier-McDonald (1987a: 27) has argued that the superscriptions most closely paralleling Mal 1:1 are found in Jer 50:1 and Hag 1:1; 2:1, 10:

*maśśā' děbar-*YHWH *'el-yiśrā'ēl běyad mal'ākî* (Mal 1:1);
haddābār 'ăšer dibber YHWH *'el-bābel 'el-'ereṣ kaśdîm běyad yirměyāhû han-nābî'* (Jer 50:1);
*hāyâ děbar-*YHWH *běyad ḥaggay hannābî'* [*'el-zěrubbābel*] (Hag 1:1; 2:1, 10).

She omits any discussion of the similarities in vocabulary (e.g., the use of the preposition *'el* in all three) and/or the differences in word order among the three (e.g., the shuffling of the three-part structure of oracle formula, audience, and agent in the three or the lack of a predicate in Mal 1:1). Nonetheless, she adduces the integrity of Malachi's superscription and forwards the comparison as further evidence supporting Child's (1979: 491–92) thesis that each of the three postexilic *maśśā'* oracles (Zech 9:1; 12:1; Mal 1:1) had a literary history independent of the others.

More compelling is Tucker's (pp. 66–68) observation that the prophetic superscriptions are markers of deliberate classification by scribal redactors for the purpose of cataloging these prophetic texts and their orators and/or authors. As such, they signify both the authoritative status of oracle as "canon" and suggest the longstanding recognition of each oracle as an independent composition in the larger prophetic corpus.

Interestingly, in those texts where the form *běyad* occurs as part of an oracular introduction indicating a genitive of authorship relationship, the noun in construct is always coupled with a proper name (e.g., Exod 9:35; 35:29; Lev 8:36; Num 9:23; 1 Kgs 16:12; 2 Chr 10:15; Isa 20:2; Jer 50:1; Hag 1:1, 3; 2:1, 10). Equally notable are those exceptional texts citing the earlier prophets collectively as agents of divine revelation (no doubt implied references to specific prophetic figures of Israel's past and possibly attesting their oracles as "canonical"; e.g., Neh 9:30; Zech 7:7, 12; cf. 2 Kgs 17:13).

The form *mal'ākî* is unique to the book of Malachi. This word may be a title or appellative for some anonymous person responsible for compiling the oracles in the book (inserted on the basis of 3:1; cf. Redditt [1995: 161–62]). Childs (1979: 494) has countered, however, that 3:1 is better understood as wordplay on the prophet's name in the superscription, because it preserves the message of the book, or the proper name of the orator (and writer?) of the prophecy.

I have summarized scholarly discussion pertaining to the form *mal'ākî*, and expressed my own view on the issue in the prolegomena sections of the commentary. A simple digest of that analysis includes these observations. First, *mal'ākî* is indeed a proper name for the prophet of God responsible for pronouncing and (presumably) writing (or dictating) the oracles bearing his name. Here I align myself with Rudolph (1976: 247), Childs (1979: 493), Verhoef (1987: 191), and Glazier-McDonald (1987a: 29) among others, who accept Masoretic tradition and read "Malachi" as a proper name.

The name *mal'ākî* is best construed as a construct-genitive relationship, perhaps after the pattern of *zěkaryāh(û)* in 1 Chr 9:37. Thus, *mal'ākî* may represent a shortened form of a theophoric name like *mal'akyāh(û)*. It is possible the name *mal'ākî* has preserved an archaic case ending, *î*, which served as a connecting vowel between the construct noun *mal'ak* and the absolute YHWH. This vowel *î* may have been a marker for the genitive case in older classical Hebrew, not the first-person pronominal suffix *î* ("my," producing the anomalous name "YHWH is my messenger"; on vestiges of the noun case system in the HB, see WO'C § 8.2, 9.2). The name *mal'ak(?)yāh(û)* may be rendered "the messenger/angel of Yahweh." See further I. C. 1. Authorship above.

The "expansionist" tendencies of the ancient versions in translating *mal'ākî* attest to both the philological difficulty of reading "Malachi" as a proper name and the paucity of additional biblical or historical data regarding any such prophet. Thus, for stylistic reasons the LXX renders the MT *bĕyad mal'ākî* with *èn cheirì aggélou autoû*, "by the hand of *his* messenger [angel]" (cf. Glazier-McDonald [1987 a: 27 n. 19]; note, however, that the Greek versions of Symmachus [σ] and Theodotion [θ] treat *mal'ākî* as a proper name). Both Syr and V render Mal 1:1 quite literally and understand Malachi as a proper name. The Targum agrees, although some versions translate "[by the hand of] my angel [messenger] whose name is called Ezra the scribe" (cf. Cathcart and Gordon [1989: 229]). This Targumic tradition is informative because it reflects an early opinion as to the identity of the last prophet in the corpus of the Twelve, and it may also suggest a *terminus ad quem* for the collection of the Twelve (or even the Latter Prophets?).

COMMENTS

The literary form of Mal 1:1 is technically that of *superscription*. By way of definition, a superscription is a statement of classification and/or identification prefixed to a literary work. The term serves both to mark the place of this statement, which precedes the body of the composition, and the nature of the statement as a scribal notation (Tucker [1977: 67–68]; or what Isbell [1980: 28] calls "editorial judgments"). The superscription serves to classify the oracle(s) or prophetic text and identify author, audience, date, and sometimes the occasion prompting the utterance. Not all the prophetic superscriptions contain each of these elements. In fact, while all the prophetic books of the OT/HB possess headings or introductions, four of these fifteen books have no such statement prefixed to them (Jonah, Ezekiel, Haggai, and Zechariah). Those that do include some type of superscription exhibit considerable variety in its structure and content (see Tucker's comparative analysis).

As a classifier of literature, the superscription is distinct from an introduction in that it stands outside the body of literature it prefaces (cf. Tucker [1977: 58]). Formally, the superscription serves to identify and catalog a particular piece of literature. In the case of the prophetic books, these superscriptions identify the works as "oracular" literature. The compound title of Malachi (i.e., *maśśā'* + *dĕbar-YHWH*) may be instructive as to the issue of the divine authority vested in the message. Whatever else the superscription or title may signify, it surely marked the disputation speeches of Malachi as revealed "word of God" and "received canon" for the Hebrew religious community (cf. Tucker [1977: 63, 68]).

Malachi is the only book of the Haggai-Zechariah-Malachi corpus prefixed by such a statement of classification and identification. However, the date formulae of Hag 1:1 and Zech 1:1 also include the identity of the prophet and the title "word of the Lord" (*děbar-YHWH*). Hence, they function practically, if not formally, as superscriptions to those books (similar to the pattern of date formula, author, and title in Ezek 1:1–3; cf. Tucker [1977: 59 n. 5]).

The superscription of Malachi identifies the author (Malachi) and the audience or recipients of his oracles (Israel) but registers no date formula and makes no mention of the occasion prompting the divine message. Tucker (p. 61) has offered the proposal that Malachi may actually contain two titles: *maśśā'* ("an oracle") and *děbar-YHWH* ("the word of Yahweh"), after the pattern of *maśśā'* ("an oracle") and *sēper ḥāzôn* ("the book of the vision . . .") in Nah 1:1. If so, the double title of this capstone book in the corpus of the Twelve externally connects Malachi theologically and canonically to the other prophetic books by the use of the title *maśśā'* (cf. Isa 13:1; 15:1; etc.; Jer 23:33–38; Nah 1:1; Hab 1:1) and internally links the Haggai-Zechariah-Malachi corpus by means of the title *děbar-YHWH* (cf. Hag 1:1; Zech 1:1).

I previously discussed the relationship of Malachi's oracles to Zechariah 9–11 and 12–14 given the similarities of the prophetic superscriptions of Zech 9:1, 12:1, and Mal 1:1 (see I. B. Canonical Considerations above). There I affirmed the independent literary status of Malachi, siding with Childs (1979: 491–92) who based his argument largely on the differences among the three superscriptions. Similarly, Glazier-McDonald (1987a: 27) has based much of her argument on the correspondence of Mal 1:1 to comparable prophetic superscriptions (especially Jer 50:1 and Hag 1:1; and to her credit she insists that the problem of the authorship of Malachi merits separate study and is not to be prejudged solely on the basis of alleged affinities to the superscriptions of Zech 9:1 and 12:1). Tucker's (1977: 68) form-critical study of prophetic superscriptions supports this conclusion, in that the scribal activity of cataloging and classifying literary works by means of the superscription by definition requires distinct and independent documents. This is especially true if Tucker's (p. 65) assessment of the importance of authorial identification for the purpose of validating divine revelation is accurate.[1]

The three superscriptions (Zech 9:1; 12:1; Mal 1:1) do serve to create three subunits in the Haggai-Zechariah-Malachi corpus (Zech 9–11, 12–14, and Mal 1–3 [4]). The inclusion of the title *děbar-YHWH* with the difficult *maśśā'* in the superscriptions effectively bridges this second half of the Haggai-Zechariah-Malachi corpus with the first half (Hag and Zech 1–8). Meyers and Meyers (1993: 90) have observed that the use of *běyad* in Mal 1:1 and Hag 1:1 forms an envelope construction joining the books of Haggai, Zechariah, and Malachi as a

---

[1] Pölger (pp. 23–25) has suggested that an apocalyptically oriented scribal school played an active role in collecting and editing the OT/HB prophetic corpus (including the superscriptions and colophons) around 200 B.C./E.

postexilic prophetic corpus (cf. Petersen [1995: 165], who suggests that the sequence of prepositions *bêt*, '*al*, and '*el* in the three *maś'ôt* oracles [Zech 9:1; 12:1; Mal 1:1] moves the discourse from invective against a foreign nation to affirmation of Israel).

The editorial joining of Zechariah 1–8 and 9–14 on the basis of theological theme and ethical imperative suggested by Childs (1979: 484) holds true for Malachi as well (note the instruction concerning the eschaton in Mal 3:1–4 connected with the moral imperatives in Mal 3:5–7; D. N. Freedman [1991: 60] has placed this editorial activity in the last quarter of the sixth century B.C./E. — a time frame consonant with my typological analysis of the language of the postexilic prophetic corpus [cf. Hill 1982 and 1983]).

The superscriptions also attest the three units as divine revelation (or "scripture" according to Tucker's [p. 70] definition). Perhaps they provide clues too as to canonical shape and arrangement of the concluding books of the Twelve Prophets as well (cf. Mason [1990: 238]). Finally, the superscriptions indicate that Zechariah 9–11, 12–14, and Malachi are indeed related but independent pericopes of prophetic literature. In addition, if Tucker's (p. 67) assessment of the importance of authorial identification for purposes of validating divine revelation is accurate, then the position understanding Zech 9–11 and 12–14 as anonymous oracles appended to a so-called First Zechariah is even more suspect (i.e., the superscriptions of Zech 9:1 and 12:1 mark the oracles as revealed "word of God" and their canonical arrangement with Zechariah 1–8 legitimately connect them with a divinely commissioned prophetic figure — Zechariah son of Berechiah).[2]

The indefinite form *maśśā'* proves as difficult to understand semantically as it is syntactically in relationship to *děbar-YHWH*.[3] The identification of *maśśā'* as a substantive from the verbal root *nś'* is uncontested. However, the words *maśśā'* meaning "burden" and *maśśā'* meaning "oracle, utterance" are cited as homonyms in the lexica derived from the same root word (cf. BDB: 672). Holladay (1986: 650) traces the explanation of the meaning "burden" to Jerome's understanding that a prophetic oracle is a "burden" when the message is one of menace, judgment, and doom (Latin *onus*; cf. *CChr* 76A:903). The commentaries of both Calvin (p. 461) and Luther (Oswald 1975: 391) perpetuate the view, later formalized in the comprehensive study of *maśśā'* by Gehman (heavily indebted to the use of the word in Jer 23:33–40). Glazier-McDonald (1987a: 25–26) repre-

---

[2] I would contend that the notion of "historicality" that Tucker (p. 68) attributed to the prophetic superscriptions with date formulae applies equally to all the prophetic superscriptions.

[3] The definite form *hammaśśā'* meaning "the oracle" is restricted to preexilic prophetic contexts. In each instance, the word refers to some form of catastrophic divine judgment (e.g., the exile of Judah, Jer 23:36; Ezek 12:10; Hab 1:1; the curse against Ahab's dynasty, 2 Kgs 9:25; and the destruction of Philistia, Isa 14:28). Two exceptional cases may be identified: first, in 2 Chr 24:27 the chronicler reports that many oracles were uttered against the Judean king Joash (the chronicler's use of *hammaśśā'* suggests dependence upon some preexilic source); and second, the words of Agur son of Jakeh are entitled "the oracle" (Prov 30:1, not only is the date of this wisdom pericope in dispute, but also the MT reading *hammaśśā'* is in question; an intonation of judgment may be perceived in the warning of Prov 30:6).

sents this interpretive tradition when she quotes the (now dated) study of Gehman in support of infusing the term *maśśā'* with connotations of "ominous import."

A second interpretive tradition translates "oracle," understanding *maśśā'* to be more directly related to *nāśā' qôl* ("lift the voice," traced to Michaelis by McKane [1980: 35, 38] who noted the term is used of oracles having little to do with threat and doom; cf. McKane [1986: 598–604]), or *nāśā' yād* ("lift a hand"; so Scott 1948: v–vi, who considered the expression an idiom for a solemn oath or a prophetic curse and read, "harsh oracle," in Isa 21:1–2).

Further variation has been introduced by Sellin (p. 547) and Rudolph (1976: 253) who have emphasized the (unnatural) tautological relationship of *maśśā'* and *děbar-YHWH* and translate (less technically) *ausspruch*, "declaration" or "utterance." Wilson (p. 249) has advanced the discussion by suggesting *maśśā'* represents a special type of (doom?) oracle associated with the Jerusalemite prophetic tradition. Although his arguments for competing Jerusalemite and Ephraimite prophetic traditions are less than compelling, Wilson is probably correct in identifying *maśśā'* as a distinct type of prophetic speech form.

Petersen (1977: 29) ventures that *maśśā'* meaning "oracle" is actually a defining characteristic of "deutero-prophetic" literature (i.e., later oracular material dependent upon the classical prophetic tradition — see his description [1977: 13]). Even though Petersen's assertion is compromised by his failure to distinguish carefully between the use of *maśśā'* as a title for a prophetic message and the content of that message so labeled, it does seem likely that some shift in the precise meaning of this technical term for a particular type of prophetic speech occurred in later prophetic tradition. The historical circumstance (theocracy vs. hierocracy), content, tone, and audience of the message were no doubt factors affecting this modification in the meaning of the term (cf. McKane [1986: 599] on the "proscriptive" nature of *maśśā'* given the theological implications of the prophetic message).

I concur with Holladay (1986: 650) who acknowledges *maśśā'* as a technical term for prophetic oracle in certain contexts (e.g., 2 Kgs 9:25) and "particularly as a title in some of the prophetic books (thus Isa 13:1)." The use of *maśśā'* in Mal 1:1 clearly fits that of the second case, the title of a prophetic book (both Syr and T translate *ptgm'*, "word"). Further, the content of Malachi's message has more to do with repentance, covenant renewal, encouragement, and hope than it does with threat and doom. The better reading here, demonstrated by the agreement in the English versions (NEB, NIV, NRSV; cf. JPSV, "pronouncement," and NJB, "message"), is "oracle" (so Holladay [1986: 650]; Verhoef [1987: 187]; Meyers and Meyers [1993: 88–90]; cf. McKane [1980: 37] who has noted that the use of *rēma* in the LXX for *maśśā'* in Zech 9:1; 12:1; Mal 1:1 "is connected with prophetic utterance").

Nevertheless, denoting *maśśā'* by "oracle" still begs the question of the connotation or significance of the term in Mal 1:1. Because the precise meaning of *maśśā'* still evades biblical scholarship, I am in sympathy with those who conflate the meanings "oracle" and "burden" in the term (e.g., R. L. Smith [1984: 301–2]; despite McKane's [1980: 39–40] contention that no nuance of "burden" should be attached to the homonym *maśśā'*, "oracle" or "utterance"). While I reject overt connotations of ominous threat and impending doom inherent in the rendering "burden" (in Malachi 1:1), I am inclined to agree with Baldwin (1972a: 221) and Verhoef (1987: 188) who suggest that Malachi's use of this technical prophetic term impregnates his message with a certain primacy and immediacy.

The phrase *děbar-YHWH* is part of a compound title in the superscription, linked with *maśśā'*. Tucker (pp. 58–59) defines "title" as "a word or concise phrase that constitutes the name of a particular literary work." As a literary classifier, *děbar-YHWH* identifies the book of Malachi as prophetic or oracular literature. Meyers and Meyers (1993: 91) have observed that the phrase *děbar-YHWH* occurs frequently in the Haggai-Zechariah-Malachi corpus, ostensibly for the purposes of demonstrating continuity with earlier Hebrew prophetic tradition, yet distinguishing this later biblical prophecy from its precursor.[4] I would add that this compound title peculiar to late biblical prophecy (cf. Zech 9:1; 12:1; Mal 1:1) tinges the message of Malachi with a sense of extreme urgency for the members of the restoration community. Unless they heed the prophet's message of repentance, his oracles do threaten swift and certain judgment.

In the oracular literature of the OT/HB, the phrase *děbar-YHWH* almost always "is a technical term for the prophetic word of revelation" (*TDOT* 3:111); or, as Isbell (p. 27) comments, *děbar-YHWH* refers "to the entire scope of the revelatory process." Thus this technical prophetic formula serves to both legitimize the recipient of the divine revelation (i.e., the prophet as speaker/author) and lend authority to the prophet's message as revealed "word of God."[5] Meyers

---

[4]The phrase *děbar-YHWH* occurs in the Haggai-Zechariah-Malachi corpus with *běyad* in Hag 1:1, 3; 2:1; with the preposition *'el* in Hag 2:10, 20; Zech 1:1, 7; 4:6, 8; 6:9; 7:1, 4, 8; and 8:18; with *maśśā'* in Zech 9:1; 12:1; Mal 1:1; and without any of the preceding complements in Zech 8:1 and 11:11. The phrase *děbar-YHWH* predominates in certain of the earlier prophets (e.g., the expression occurs more than one hundred times in Jeremiah and Ezekiel). The absence of this phrase, while perhaps related to the shift in the theological agenda of the postexilic prophets, is more likely attributed to the genre of disputation speech in Malachi, which evidences a predilection for *kōh 'āmar YHWH . . .* ("so Yahweh [has] said . . .").

Citing Mullen, Meyers and Meyers (1987: 7) trace this technical phrase for prophetic revelation (*děbar-YHWH*) to the language of the royal court in the ancient Near East where oral messages were delivered formulaically to verify the authenticity of the communication. Like the king sitting in council with advisors, Yahweh sits in divine council and issues his decrees. Based on this understanding, the "prophets are members of the divine council who act as couriers to deliver God's judgment to the people. The prophets utter the appropriate formulas to clarify the source of the message, the fact of its being transmitted, and the authority of its contents."

[5]Tucker (p. 70) contends that the compilers and editors of the prophetic tradition interpreted the literary form of the prophets' words as the "inscripturation" of divine revelation, authoritative for the Israelite religious community. Further, he discriminates between "scripture" (authoritative writings) and "canon" (a closed collection of authoritative writings). Thus, for Tucker (p. 70) "the superscriptions to the prophetic books do not represent a stage of canonization, [but] they do reveal the decisive turning point when — at least for certain circles in Israel — the spoken prophetic words had become scripture." What Tucker fails to appreciate is the fact that the historical distance between prophetic "words" and prophetic "scripture" may have been inconsequential (cf. the pentateuchal tradition

and Meyers (1993: 91) note that the combination of *maśśā'* and *dĕbar-YHWH* strengthens "the force and validity of the prophetic words at a time when such speech was rare."

While this may be the case, it seems more likely that the compound title in Mal 1:1 addresses the despair and disillusionment in the restoration community resulting from the apparent failure of the divine word pronounced by Malachi's earlier contemporaries, Haggai and Zechariah. Hence, the compound title serves to bolster the prophet's message as a hopeful and reliable word from God, given Malachi's "relativizing" of the (as yet unfulfilled) claims of Haggai and Zechariah regarding the restoration of Davidic rule. Finally, this prophetic formula, *dĕbar-YHWH*, both emphasizes the prophet's office as recognized servant of Yahweh (cf. Jer 18:18) and defines the prophet's duty as a mediator of Yahweh's covenantal word to Israel (on the "symbiotic" relationship of the *dĕbar-YHWH* formula in legal and prophetic literature, see *TDOT* 3:114–15).

Verhoef (1987: 190) errs in assuming that the accompanying verb *hāyâ* should be read with *'el-yiśrā'ēl* ("*came* to Israel"), a construction known as the "word-event" formula (i.e., *dĕbar-YHWH* as subject with verb *hāyâ*). He has failed to fully recognize the integrity of the constituent elements of the superscription as a literary form: author (speaker), audience, date, title, location, and occasion (prompting message). The verb *hāyâ* ("to be") does occur in several of the superscriptions to the prophetic books of the OT/HB (Verhoef cites Jer 1:2; Ezek 1:3; Hos 1:1; Joel 1:1; Mic 1:1; Zeph 1:1; and Zech 1:1). However, in every example, the phrase [*dĕbar YHWH*] *hāyâ 'el-*. . . is associated with the human agent of the divine message (as speaker/author), not the audience or recipient of the message (as would be the case in Malachi). Hence, Verhoef's presumption is unwarranted, especially if Tucker (p. 68) is correct in his assessment of the prophetic superscriptions that utilize certain terms and phrases with some precision as quasi-technical classifiers of oracular literature (on the so-called "word-event" formula see further *TDOT* 3:112–13). On the omission of *hāyâ* in Mal 1:1, see further the COMMENTS on *bĕyad* below.

The proper noun "Israel" designates the audience or recipient of these disputation speeches in accordance with the convention of the prophetic superscription, in the classification and identification of a literary work. This proper noun occurs in Malachi's oracles elsewhere only in 1:5; 2:11 and 2:16, and in the first appendix (3:22 [4:4]). Malachi also uses "Jacob" (1:2) or "descendants of Jacob" (3:6), "Yehud" (2:11), "Yehud and Jerusalem" (3:4), and simply "ancestors" to refer to the Hebrews (Yahweh's "special possession," cf. 3:16–17). "Israel" was the name given to Jacob, the second son of Isaac, after his encounter with the angel of Yahweh (Gen 32:28). Later, the name was applied to all tribes of Israel (cf. Exod 1:7; Deut 1:1), used subsequently as a geopolitical designation for those Hebrew tribes that made up the northern monarchy after the death of King Solomon (cf.

---

of the immediate "inscripturation" [and "canonization"?] of the Covenant Code, Exod 24:4; 25:16); the Deuteronomist's understanding of the "book of the law," Deut 31:9, 24; and perhaps more pertinent to prophetic literature, Jeremiah's dictation to his amanuensis Baruch, Jer 36:4).

1 Kgs 11:37–38); and finally "Israel" was applied to the whole remnant of the Hebrew nation both during the Babylonian captivity and upon their return to the province of Yehud under Persian supervision (cf. Ezek 3:1; Ezra 2:2).

Malachi uses Israel in 1:1 (and throughout) comprehensively in an ethnic and cultic sense, denoting the entire nation or people group known as the Hebrews. During the postexilic period "Israel" consisted primarily of the tribal associations of Benjamin, Judah, and Levi. The name, however, embraces all the Hebrew tribes, including those still living in the northern regions after the fall of Samaria and all those (even northerners) who returned to Palestine under the aegis of the Persian King Cyrus the Great (see the comprehensive discussion of the name "Israel" in *TDOT* 6:397–420). In a sense, Malachi addresses a "new Israel" constituted by the remnant of expatriates now settled in Jerusalem and environs, but representing the whole of the people of Yahweh disaffected and dispossessed by the Babylonians (on this "inclusive" use of Israel, see Meyers and Meyers [1987: 138]; and [1993: 309]).

This "new Israel" was founded on the rebuilt Temple, a reorganized Levitical priesthood, restored Temple ritual, and the oath of covenant renewal with Yahweh. Dumbrell (1976: 44–45) has observed that both Ezekiel and Ezra use the name "Israel" in a similar fashion. A comparative study of the Haggai-Zechariah-Malachi corpus reveals that the title "Israel" is absent from Haggai (cf. 1:12, 14) but occurs in Zech 1:19; 8:13; 9:1; 11:14; and 12:1 with essentially the same connotations present in Malachi (the lone exception is Zech 11:14 where "Yehud" and "Israel" are geopolitical terms specifying the divided preexilic Hebrew monarchies; cf. Meyers and Meyers [1993: 281] on the "kinship-based unity" of all the Hebrew tribes).

The complex-prepositional form *běyad* is a specialized use of the common noun *yād* ("hand"), signifying the agent through whom a specific word is sent or a particular action performed ("by the hand of," *TDOT* 5:410; cf. WO'C § 11.2.1b). This *instrumental* understanding is unambiguous, because the prophet Malachi is the human agent through whom God speaks to his people Israel. Implicit in this instrumentality is Yahweh as the source of the prophetic message, Malachi as Yahweh's divinely commissioned agent (and the legitimacy of the prophetic office), and the divine authority of the prophet's utterance(s) (cf. Andersen and Freedman [1980: 151] who have noted that "what Yahweh says does not lose its distinctiveness when it is repeated by human lips").

The use of *běyad* also says something about the nature and character of Malachi's prophetic message, in that it is not "visionary" (*ḥāzôn*, cf. Obad 1; Nah 1:1; Hab 1:1). Here the use of *běyad* may suggest something about the means of Malachi's prophetic revelation; at least it is not an ecstatic experience (cf. Isbell [1980: 30] who interprets *běyad* as an indication of the free expression of the prophet's personality in his message). Thus, while Malachi is "oracular speech" as *děbar-YHWH*, when coupled with the form *běyad* the oration is perhaps less accusatory and more dialogical in nature as a message of hope and encouragement (note the use of rhetorical questions in Jer 50:44–46; cf. 50:1). The use of *běyad* may also say something about prophetic responsibility as well, stressing the prophet's role as spokesman and watchman to Israel (cf. Ezek 3:4–11, 16–21).

Two syntactical categories describing the circumstance of the conjunction of *běyad* with an active verb have been identified by Meyers and Meyers (1987: 7; cf. *TDOT* 5:410): one denoting authority (often with the verb *ntn*, on this "*beth* of identity," cf. WO'C § 11.2.5e) and the other denoting instrumentality (frequently with the verb *dbr*, on this "*beth* of instrument," cf. WO'C § 11.2.5d). Budde (1906: 9–10) catalogued the form *běyad* among those expressions typical of LBH (cf. Childs [1979: 492]).

There are preexilic texts that state that Yahweh spoke (*dbr*) "through" (*běyad*) Ahijah the prophet (1 Kgs 12:15; 15:29) and Jehu the prophet (1 Kgs 16:7, 12; cf. Lindblom [1962: 58]). The Haggai-Zechariah-Malachi corpus differs from earlier prophetic literature not so much in its use of *běyad*, as it does in the utilization of *běyad* in combination with an active verb. The tendency in the Haggai-Zechariah-Malachi corpus (and later biblical Hebrew) is to couple *běyad* with the inactive verb *hāyâ* (e.g., Hag 1:1; 2:1, 10, 20; cf. Jer 50:1).

Malachi's superscription differs from those in the Haggai-Zechariah corpus because it omits any verb. Perhaps these variations in the oracle formulae of the later prophetic material were intended to draw attention away from the divine messenger and focus attention more directly on the divine message. However, despite this evolution of the oracle formula in the prophetic superscription, it is incorrect to assume that the postexilic prophets received the revelation of God differently than their preexilic counterparts. Andersen and Freedman (1980: 151) have reminded us that "through his call, the prophet finds himself immediately in the divine presence. The prophet never acquires the word; he merely reports what Yahweh has said in his hearing." This distinctive trait of the prophetic office characterized the postexilic prophets as well.

Meyers and Meyers (1987: 7) mention only the emphasis on the instrumentality of the prophet and the heightening of prophetic authority in respect to *běyad* (in Hag 1:1). Both comments are accurate, but it is possible that even this variance in the *děbar-YHWH* formula marks a deliberate shift in the postexilic prophets for theological reasons, so as not to confuse their message with the oracles of judgment and exile delivered by earlier prophetic voices. In this way, the postexilic prophets maintained continuity with the preexilic prophetic tradition and at the same time initiated a new phase of Israel's covenant relationship with Yahweh. Divine judgment for Israel's covenant violation(s) had been exacted in the Babyonian Exile; the issue now was covenant renewal with Yahweh — the time "to build and to plant" envisioned by Jeremiah (1:10). More than this, I suggest that the variations of the oracle formula in the postexilic prophets also says something about the tone (dialogical), content (instruction and encouragement coupled with judgment), and theological emphasis in the prophetic speeches of Malachi (the immanence of Yahweh instead of his transcendence given the shift in emphasis in the superscription from the messenger to the message; cf. Isa 66:1–2).

On the name *mal'ākî* ("Malachi") see the NOTES to 1:1 above and I. C. 1. Authorship. Additionally, Tucker's (1977) study of prophetic superscriptions has implications for the discussion of *mal'ākî* as the name of the prophet (and author of the oracles) versus *mal'ākî* as the title or epithet of an anonymous prophet.

According to Tucker (p. 68), "The fundamental intention of the superscriptions is to identify the prophetic books as the word of God." Tucker continues that this claim is qualified by the superscription in several ways, including the naming of the specific individual responsible for uttering (and/or writing) the prophetic message. If the purpose of the prophetic superscriptions is to "inscripturate" the prophetic books as authoritative writ for the Hebrew religious community, it seems little is gained in advancing the idea of authority by appealing to an ambiguous and unnamed prophet of Yahweh.

So by way of summary, what does the superscription (1:1) mean for the oracles of Malachi? First, the compound title identifying Malachi as both "oracle" (maśśā') and "word of Yahweh" (děbar-YHWH) marks the book absolutely as divine revelation and authoritative word of God to the Hebrew community of faith. The fact that the audience of the message has priority over the human speaker/author of the message in the order of the superscription may suggest that Israel was in desperate need of a word from God.

The superscription certainly legitimizes the prophet Malachi as Yahweh's agent, but the lack of a verb in the construction shifts attention away from the messenger to the message from God. Thus we know little about the prophet named Malachi who served as Yahweh's spokesman. The lack of a date formula in the superscription puts the issue of chronology in question as well. Lastly, the unique structure and content of Malachi's superscription portend the oracular form and content of the prophet's message. Malachi deals afresh with Yahweh's elect on the subject of covenant by means of a series of disputational speeches relying heavily on the use of rhetorical questions.

According to Tucker (p. 57), if the prophetic superscriptions are secondary texts, then they represent vestiges of an early Hebrew exegetical tradition. Whether or not the prophetic superscriptions are secondary additions (cf. Glazier-McDonald [1987a: 25–26] who argues for the originality of Mal 1:1), they do provide a link in the historical chain of Hebrew exegesis because they forward a system for classifying the prophetic literature and an understanding of that literature as sacred word of God.

The earliest versions of Malachi's superscription also betray ancient interpretive approaches to the book. For example, the LXX regards "Malachi" as a title for an unknown prophetic figure, perhaps associating the prophet with "the messenger/angel of Yahweh" mentioned in 3:1. Such a reading attests to the philological complexity of the form mal'ākî and has troubled interpreters from the very earliest stages of textual transmission. The addition of the phrase "whose name was Ezra the scribe" in some versions of the Targum indicates that some direct correspondence between Malachi's message of social justice and the reforms initiated in the restoration community by Ezra the scribe was also recognized by this ancient version (see I. A. Textual Considerations above).

This Jewish understanding of Malachi quite naturally shaped the early Christian interpretation of the book as well, as the church fathers also numbered Malachi among the Twelve prophets and regarded his message as a direct communication from God through the Holy Spirit (cf. Irenaeus Adv haer 4.17.5; Cyprian Did 9.22). In fact, the tradition of the Targum connecting the oracles of Malachi with Ezra persisted into the protestant reformation (cf. Calvin [1979: 459]). No doubt the influence of Hellenism contributed to the early Christian understanding of the prophet Malachi as an "angel" (e.g., Tertullian *AdvJud* 5). However, Calvin (p. 459) rejected this identification as "absurd" because God opted for the "ordinary ministry" of human beings, moving Christian interpretation closer to that of Jerome who acknowledged Malachi as an epithet of the (mortal) prophet (i.e., Ezra) serving God as a "divine messenger" (cf. *CChr* 56A:901, 903). Even the incorporation of portions of Malachi in the Jewish and Christian liturgy indicates that both later Judaism and early Christianity understood the message of Malachi quite literally (see I. F. 2. Liturgical Use of Malachi above).

One significant divergence between Judaism and Christianity surfaces in the liturgical use of the second appendix to the book (3:23–24 [4:5–6]). Judaism has maintained a more literal interpretation of the Elijah figure mentioned as the forerunner of the eschaton in Malachi (cf. m. ʿEduy 8.7), whereas Christian interpreters gravitated to a typological understanding of the Elijah figure on the basis of NT teaching concerning John the Baptist and the ministry of Jesus of Nazareth (Matt 11:7–15; cf. Irenaeus *Adv haer* 3.11.4; Justin Martyr *Dial* xlix).

III. B. First Oracle: Yahweh's Covenant Love for Israel (1:2–5)

1 ²"I have loved you," Yahweh has said. But you have said, "How have you loved us?" "Surely Esau was Jacob's brother?" Oracle of Yahweh. "Yet I loved Jacob; ³but Esau I hated. So I made his mountains a wasteland and his ancestral homeland a desert [haunt] for jackals." ⁴If Edom [should] say, "We have been demolished, but we will again build the ruins." Thus Yahweh of Hosts has said, "As for them, let them rebuild! But as for me, I will destroy. Then they will call them [the] 'Territory of Evil,' and the people whom Yahweh has cursed perpetually. ⁵And then your eyes will see, and [as for] you, you will say, 'May Yahweh be great over the territory of Israel!'"

The literary form of the first oracle is that of *prophetic disputation*, related to the *judicial* or *trial speech* pattern. The disputation speech pits the prophet against his audience in a type of "charge" versus "counter-charge" format featuring a *declaration* by the protagonist (the prophet Malachi), a *refutation* by the antagonist (the particular recipients of the oracle), and the emphatic *rebuttal* of the opponent's polemic by the protagonist (Yahweh's prophet). Here in the first disputation, "I have loved you" constitutes the prophet's declaration (v 2); the refutation from the audience is posed (hypothetically?) in the form of the question, "How have you loved us?" (v 2); and the prophetic rebuttal advanced in the proclamation "But Esau I hated" concludes the disputation pattern (v 3). Watts (1987a: 376) identifies 1:2a as *assertive* speech intended to assure the audience, and 1:2b–5 as *dialogical* speech designed to convince the audience of Yahweh's love for Israel. See further I. C. 5. Form above.

While the MT indicates no paragraph break between 1:5 and 1:6, the overwhelming majority of past and present interpreters has understood Mal 1:2–5 as a distinct literary unit largely on the basis of the disputation format. The first disputation demonstrates numerous literary features in addition to the hortatory style of the disputation, including chiasmus ([A] . . . "loved you"; [B] "Yahweh has said"; [B'] "But you have said"; [A'] . . . "loved us?", v 2; cf. Snyman 1984a), rhetorical question ("Surely Esau and Jacob were brothers?", v 2), foil or contrast ("I say/you say," v 2; "Jacob/Esau," vv 2–3), metonymy ("Jacob" for postexilic Yehud, v 2), and pseudo-dialogue ("but you say . . . ," v 3). See further I. C. 6. Literary Features above.

The integrity of the pericope has never been seriously challenged. The tone, theme, structure, and vocabulary of this first disputation have become the template by which scholars have gauged the authenticity of the rest of the book. The section poses no textual problems of consequence, save the phrase *nĕ'ūm YHWH* in 1:2 and the difficult *lĕtannôt* in 1:3.

The first disputation is directed to the restoration community in general and the basic message of this initial oracle is "Yahweh loves Jacob." The prophet's opening words function as the thesis disputation by introducing the combative tone (both admonition and exhortation), format (disputation), and theme (Yahweh's covenant with Israel; but strangely Nogalski [1993b: 194] regards Mal 1:2–5 as the conclusion of the Book of the Twelve; cf. Bosshard and Kratz). By identifying postexilic Yehud as "Jacob," the prophet reminds the people of Yahweh's election and love for the descendants of Abraham, Isaac, and Jacob, rooted in the promises of the patriarchal covenant(s).

Such reassurance was necessary amid growing skepticism due to the (apparent) failure of the "Zion visions" of Second Isaiah, Haggai, and First Zechariah. Malachi had to correct wrong thinking about the covenant relationship with Yahweh. As Yahweh's vassal, the restoration community was in no position to make demands on God as their suzerain. This thesis disputation challenges postexilic Yehud to consider the precedent of history, both in terms of God's faithfulness to Israel and his propensity to judge Israel for lapses of covenant obedience. Recent events in Edom only served to underscore the seriousness of the divine threat. Loving God was not a *cause* for blessing but a *condition*, for God himself remains the only *cause* (cf. J. J. Collins [1984: 214–15]). See further I. C. 7. Message above.

NOTES

1:2. *'āhabtî 'etkem.* The verb *'āhab* means "to like, love" (KBL 1:17–18) and depending on context may describe human sexual love, emotion and affection, familial relationships, norms for socioethical behavior, etc. (cf. *TDOT* 1:102–12 on the semantic range of *'āhab*). Theologically, when *'āhab* portrays the relationship between Yahweh and Israel, the term has covenant implications (cf. Eichrodt [1:250 ff.]; cf. Deut 7:8).

However, Eichrodt (1:256–57) has overstated the case in respect to the weakening of the covenant connotations of *'hb* in the postexilic period. Granted the word may be equated with *bhr* ("to choose, elect"; KBL 1:119–20). The verb *bhr* occurs in the Haggai-Zechariah-Malachi corpus only in Hag 2:23 (Yahweh's election of Zerubbabel) and Zech 1:17; 2:16 [12]; and 3:2 (Yahweh's choice of Jerusalem as his habitation); on the importance of Jerusalem as the "elect city" for the postexilic community, see Meyers and Meyers (1987: 124, 171, 187). The message of Malachi indicates that the other dimensions of covenant relationship are still operative in the term as well (e.g., *rhm, yš', hesed, yd', šwb*; cf. Verhoef [1987: 196–97]; *ABD* 2:434–41).

Given Malachi's concern for proper worship, the marriage covenant, and social justice, it seems the prophet understands the term *'hb* in much the same way as the Deuteronomist: "The . . . duty to reciprocate God's love . . . in the form of genuine obedience and pure devotion" (*TDOT* 1:115). The root *'hb* occurs in the Haggai-Zechariah-Malachi corpus only in Zech 8:17, 19; 13:6; Mal 1:2 [2x] and 2:11. In each case the Zechariah references including the root *'hb* fit Wallis's *socioethical behavior* usage, while in Mal 1:2 (and to a lesser degree Mal 2:11) the term *'hb* has clear covenantal connotations. Here the quasifientive (i.e., a verb describing both a state or quality and motion or change of state) form *'āhabtî* is a *durative stative perfective*, "indicating an ongoing emotional response" (WO'C § 30.5.3c). I have rendered the form with the present perfect "have loved" because Malachi speaks out of the prophetic tradition, which presupposes the whole of Israelite covenant history (but Van der Woude disagrees; cf. Verhoef [1987: 193 n. 1]). See the NOTES and COMMENTS on 2:11 below.

'āmar YHWH. The expression marks reported speech by Yahweh and occurs frequently in the Haggai-Zechariah-Malachi corpus (Hag 1:8; Mal 1:2, 13; 3:13; with *kōh* and amplified with divine epithets in Hag 1:2, 5; 2:6, 7, 9, 11; Zech 1:3 [2x], 4, 14, 16, 17; 2:12; 3:7; 4:6; 6:12; 7:9, 13; 8:2, 3, 4, 6, 7, 9, 14 [2x], 19, 20, 23; 11:4; Mal 1:2, 4, 6, 8, 9, 10, 11, 13, 14; 2:2, 4, 8, 16 [2x]; 3:1, 5, 7, 10, 11, 12, 13, 17, 19 [4:1], 21 [4:3]). The phrase *'āmar YHWH* is part of an ancient messenger formula authorizing the prophetic word as the word of God (Westermann [1991: 93]; i.e., a courier who delivers a letter simply repeating what the originator said; cf. Andersen and Freedman [1989: 229]; Mullen [1980: 209–10]).

The word *'āmar* "always expresses a personal relationship" and when denoting communication between persons (or entities regarded as personal), "the goal of *'āmar* is that another person (or persons might hear and understand and might reply, in the broadest sense of the word [reaction]"; *TDOT* 1:330–31). Theologically, the word *'āmar* is a term for divine revelation when God is the subject of an *'āmar*-event because the expression "Yahweh has said" implies "that God has been heard in the realm of nature and history, the arena of human experience and understanding" (*TDOT* 1:335).

wa 'āmartem. Here *'āmar* marks the reported speech of the people in response to the prophetic declaration of God's love for Israel. This speech pattern of declaration and reaction introduced by ʾāmar is characteristic of the disputations of Malachi. Although ʾāmar literally means "say," the connotation here is a "retort" indicating the continuity of a scene and participants but recognizing the shift in the direction (and tone?) of the exchange (the NEB, NIV, and NJB "ask" is weak; the reported audience refutation is every bit as rhetorical as the prophet's declaration). I understand the waw-relative in an adversative sense ("but"), because the two clauses are in contrast (so NAB, NIV, NJB, NRSV; cf. WO'C § 8.3b).

The adversative waw also has the effect of emphasizing the point-counterpoint construction of the disputations (T understands the waw conditionally, "if"; cf. Gordon [1994: 123]). Occasionally, the waw-relative suffix form after another suffix form functions as a simple copulative, maintaining the perfective aspect of the preceding verb, as is the case here (setting both reported speeches in past time, cf. WO'C § 32.1.1; note that the LXX, V, and Calvin [1979: 661] also understand a perfective aspect).

The refutation by the audience of Malachi's declaration in the disputations may be a hypothetical response concocted by the prophet for rhetorical purposes or it may represent reported speech heard by the prophet in his normal discourse with the restoration community. It is possible that Malachi anticipated the audience response in each of the disputations, but his oracles would have a more piercing impact on the Hebrew community if he were turning their own words against them. I have assumed the latter is the case for Malachi's disputations.

bammâ ʾăhabtānû. The interrogative pattern employing the inanimate pronoun *mâ* combined with the preposition *bêt* may be translated "in what?" (e.g., R. L. Smith [1984: 304]; Verhoef [1987: 193]) or "how?" (so NAB, NEB, NIV, NJB, NRSV; cf. WO'C § 18.3c). In the disputations of Malachi *bammâ* introduces an *exclamatory question,* here possessing intonations of surprise, doubt, and cynicism (cf. WO'C § 18.3f). The alternate form *bammeh* is actually more prevalent in Malachi, the *seghol* used even before letters that are not gutturals when not connected by *maqqeph* (cf. GKC § 37.e). The pointing *bammâ* before the ʾaleph is consistent with MT practice (cf. GKC § 102.k). The interrogative *bammâ* occurs in the Haggai-Zechariah-Malachi corpus only in Mal 1:2 and 2:17. See further the NOTES and COMMENTS on *bammâ* in 2:17, *bammeh* in Mal 1:6, 7; 3:7, 8; ʿal-mâ in 2:14; and *mâ* in 2:15; 3:13, 14.

The reported audience response "How have you loved us?" indicates that the restoration community understood the *durative* sense of ʾāhabtî. The skeptical retort *bammâ ʾăhabtānû* is prompted by the lack of any contemporary evidence justifying the prophet's declaration of God's covenant love for Israel. The emotional implications of the verb ʾhb are only unidirectional. The restoration community feels no compulsion to respond to Yahweh's love because they have perceived no tangible proof of Yahweh's covenant love (in the form of material blessing, cf. Mal 3:9–12).

hălôʾ-ʾāh. The interrogative *hē* with *lôʾ* is a type of double negative anticipating an affirmative answer. According to Waltke and O'Connor (§ 40.3), the form introduces *polar questions* (i.e., "yes-no" questions), and when used rhetorically they "require assent rather than reply." Such is the case for the use of *hălôʾ* in

Malachi (1:2; 2:10 [2x]). The Haggai-Zechariah-Malachi corpus shares this rhetorical feature with earlier Hebrew prophets, especially Isaiah, Jeremiah, and Ezekiel (cf. Hag 2:3; Zech 1:6; 3:2; 4:5, 13; 7:6; note the Haggai-Zechariah-Malachi corpus prefers exclusively the *scriptio plena* form of the interrogative). The interrogative is usually rendered "Was not?" (so NAB, NIV, NJB; cf. Glazier-McDonald [1987a: 31] and Verhoef [1987: 193]) or "Is not?" (so NEB, NRSV; cf. R. L. Smith [1984: 304]) in English. I prefer the translation "surely" or "indeed" because it heightens the force of the rhetorical question in the disputation speech form (cf. Bongers [1981: 178, 183] who reads "as you know" for *hălô'* in Deut 3:11 and "surely" or "indeed" for *hălô'* in Isa 8:19 and Amos 5:20; and Brown [1987: 202] who equates *hălô'* with the Ugaritic and Aramaic interjection *hălû'*, "surely").

'*āḥ*. This common noun appears only in Mal 1:2; 2:10 and elsewhere in the Haggai-Zechariah-Malachi corpus in Hag 2:22 and Zech 7:9, 10. The primary understanding of the word is "blood brother" in this context (cf. *TDOT* 1:189–90). Since the events associated with the Babylonian Exile were less than a century removed from Malachi's audience, it is likely the term '*āḥ* still held some (no doubt negative!) connotation of "kinship" between Israel and Edom for the restoration community (*TDOT* 1:190; cf. Obad 10, 12 and the psalmist's imprecation against Edom for their role as abettors in the destruction of Jerusalem, Ps 137:7–9).

'*ēśāw*. This proper name is found only in Mal 1:2, 3 and Obad 6, 8, 9, 18 [2x], 19, 21 among the Twelve. The reference is to the twin brothers, Jacob and Esau, born to Isaac and Rebekah (Gen 25:22–25). The names are intended to bring to mind the patriarchal traditions of Genesis regarding the rivalry of the two (Genesis 26, 27, 33). In Mal 1:3 Esau represents the Edomites, as the eponymous ancestor of that nation (Gen 36:1). Esau symbolized all those who in their arrogance and independence rejected the tokens of Yahweh's covenant and despised Israel as Yahweh's elect (cf. Gen 25:29–34; 26:34–35). Apparently the Edomites "inherited" such contempt for Israel, given their role as abettors in the Babylonian destruction of Jerusalem (cf. Obad 10–14). On the uncertain etymology of Esau, see *ABD* 2:574–75. See further verse 3 below.

lĕya 'ăqōb. Like Esau, Jacob refers both to the younger twin brother and son of Isaac and Rebekah in verse 2 and the eponymous ancestor of the Israelites in verse 3. According to Gen 49:1, 28 Jacob was the father of the twelve tribal heads of the Hebrew nation and one of three ancient biblical patriarchs (cf. *ISBE* 2:948–55). The name Jacob is commonly used in prophetic literature to identify the nation of Israel and is often combined with "Israel" in a word-pair (e.g., Micah 1:5; 3:1; cf. *ABD* 5:157).

Prior to the Babylonian Exile Jacob signified either the northern kingdom of Israel (e.g., Amos 3:13) or the southern kingdom of Judah (e.g., Obad 10) or both (e.g., Ezek 39:25). After the Babylonian exile the name Jacob was a synonym for all the Hebrews of the restoration community — apart from tribal affiliation. The name occurs in the Haggai-Zechariah-Malachi corpus only in Mal 1:2 [2x], 2:12; and 3:6 and designates the people of Israel except in this reference. The preposition *lamed* is an example of the *periphrastic genitive* with *lamed* showing possession with the indefinite 'āḥ in this verbless clause (i.e., "a brother of Jacob"; cf. WO'C § 9.7b).

nĕ'ūm-YHWH. Cited as a *nominal exclamation*, it is used independently of its grammatical context by Waltke and O'Connor (§ 40.2.3a) and translated "declaration[?] of YHWH." The word *nĕ'ūm* occurs frequently in the Haggai-Zechariah-Malachi corpus (32x), both as an opening and closing prophetic speech formula (Hag 1:9, 13; 2:4 [3x], 8, 9, 14, 17, 23 [3x]; Zech 1:3, 4, 16; 2:9 [5], 10 [6; 2x], 14 [10]; 3:9, 10; 5:4; 8:6, 11, 17; 10:12; 11:6; 12:1, 4; 13:2, 7, 8). The form *nĕ'ūm* occurs in Malachi only here, embedded in the first disputation. According to Westermann (1991: 188), the speech formula *nĕ'ūm-YHWH* (used in the middle and at the end of oracles) was original to the seer and adopted later by the prophetic movement (following Lindblom's [pp. 94, 104] somewhat artificial distinction between the *seer* who possessed the supernormal "faculty of knowing things that are concealed from ordinary men" and the *prophet* who functioned as "authoritative messengers from Yahweh").

The emphatic placement after the audience refutation and prior to the prophet's rebuttal in the introductory disputation (middle position) may mark the thesis statement of Malachi's oracles, "I have loved Jacob" (note the prefatory use of *nĕ'ūm* in Zech 1:3–4 in calling postexilic Yehud to repentance, the thesis statement of First Zechariah).

Again, the Haggai-Zechariah-Malachi corpus shares this *nĕ'ūm* oracle formula with prophets like Isaiah, Jeremiah, and Ezekiel but not the rest of the Twelve (*nĕ'ūm* is used nearly 300 times in Isaiah-Jeremiah-Ezekiel and only 37 times outside of the Haggai-Zechariah-Malachi corpus in the Twelve). The proposals of *BHK* and *BHS* to delete *nĕ'ūm-YHWH* (*metri causa* = "on account of meter") is unwarranted for two reasons: first, the proposition is based on the assumption that Malachi is poetry (in fact, as discussed in I. C. 4. Genre above, the book of Malachi represents a literary hybrid now classified as "oracular prose"; cf. J.M.P. Smith [1912: 23], "metrical considerations have no force in prose"); and second, the appeal to divine authority conforms stylistically to the oracles of Malachi (cf. J.M.P. Smith [1912: 23–24]). The LXX harmonizes *nĕ'ūm-YHWH* with the preceding *'āmar YHWH* and reads *légei kúrios*.

wā'ōhab 'et-ya'ăqōb. The *waw*-relative indicates a situation of logical consequence, permitting the translation, "yet" (cf. WO'C § 33.2.1d). On verbs exhibiting both stative ("I *love* Jacob") and fientive qualities ("I *loved* Jacob) see Waltke and O'Connor § 22.2.3b. While the non-progressive English translation is permissible, I have opted for the simple past tense, which implies an ongoing emotional response and reflects the historical consciousness of the prophetic office. Not coincidentally, the closest parallel to this phrase in Malachi is found in the first book of the Twelve (*kî na'ar yiśrā'ēl wā'ōhăbēhû*, Hos 11:1; cf. *'ōhăbem nĕdābâ*, Hos 14:5).

The covenant term '*hb* signifies the act of divine election, making Israel Yahweh's child (Andersen and Freedman [1980: 576]; on *'āhab* and *śānē'* as covenant vocabulary, see Moran). The sentiment expressed by this phrase accords with testimony elsewhere, especially Isa 41:8 ("Jacob, whom I have chosen") and

Amos 3:2 ("only you have I known among all the families of the earth"). No doubt Malachi also understood the reciprocal nature of *'hb* in covenant relationship with Yahweh (cf. Deut 7:9–10). The name "Jacob" denotes the blood brother of Esau and connotes the contemporary Hebrew community tracing its roots to this patriarch.

3. *'et-* *'ēśāw śānē'tî.* This phrase completes the chiastically ordered couplet, which cuts across the verse division, beginning with the last clause of verse 2: "I love Jacob, Esau I hate" (cf. Botterweck [1960a: 36–38]). The juxtaposition of "Jacob/Esau" recalls the narrative of fraternal rivalry and the prophecy Rebekah received concerning the "two nations" in her womb (Gen 25:21–27).

Esau, also called Hor (Num 21:4) and Seir (Ezek 35:15), is identified with the Edomites (see "Esau" above in v 2). The Edomites settled the region bordering the southeastern edge of the Dead Sea. According to Genesis a strong tribal organization existed in Edom from patriarchal times (36:1–30), and the nation had a form of monarchical government before the Israelites (36:31–43; although Bartlett discounts this information, *ABD* 2:288).

The book of Numbers indicates that Edom was entrenched territorially by the time of Israel's Exodus from Egypt (20:14–21), denying them passage to the east (cf. Levine [1993: 491–94]). Edom and Israel coexisted peacefully until the reign of King Saul (1 Sam 14:47), and later King David defeated the Edomites at the Valley of Salt (2 Sam 8:13–14). Judah controlled Edom as a satellite state until the time of Jehoram, when the Edomites successfully revolted and established autonomous rule (2 Kgs 8:20–22; cf. 1 Kgs 11:14–25; 22:47). Subsequent victories over Edom by the Judahite kings Amaziah (2 Kgs 14:7) and Uzziah (2 Kgs 14:22) were at best localized and temporary triumphs. It appears Nebuchadnezzar wrested control of the Negev from Judah as early as 597 B.C./E. (cf. 2 Kgs 24:8–17), with the Edomites moving into the area to fill the vacuum. In 587 B.C./E. Edom not only assisted Babylon in the sack of Jerusalem (Obad 10–14), but also occupied Judahite villages well into the Persian period (1 Esdr 4:50).

The exact date of Edom's collapse remains imprecise and the circumstances precipitating Edom's fall are uncertain. Though Nabonidus conducted several campaigns against Edom (from 552 B.C./E. on), Edom apparently remained largely independent until a coalition of Arab tribes overpowered and displaced the Edomites sometime during the fifth century B.C./E. (or a Nebaioth-Nabatean occupation, so Bartlett in *ABD* 2:293). By 312 B.C./E. inscriptional evidence indicates that the Nabateans had overrun the region of Edom, making Petra their capital city. The remaining Edomites either migrated to Idumea or were absorbed by the Nabatean Arabs through intermarriage.

An anti-Edomite polemic can be traced through the OT/HB from the mixed blessing granted Esau by Isaac (Gen 27:39–40), to the exilic imprecation of Edom for its part in the fall of Jerusalem (Ps 137:7), right through Malachi's avowal of Edom's obliteration (Mal 1:2–4). National oracles of judgment pronounced against Edom are prominent in the prophetic literature, including Isa 21:11–12; 34:5–17; Jer 49:7–22; Ezek 25:12–14; 35:1–15; Amos 1:11–12; and the book of Obadiah.

The verb *śānē'* ("to hate"; *CHAL*: 353) is the antonym of *'āhab* ("to love"), and they are used as a *polar* word-pair in legal and prophetic texts (e.g., Deut 7:10; 21:15–17; Ps 11:5; Hos 9:15; Amos 5:15; Mic 3:2). Normally *śānē'* has a person as its object and "in legal texts indicates a formal renunciation or severance of a relationship" (Andersen and Freedman [1989: 525]). R. L. Smith (1984: 305) and Petersen (1995: 168) correctly observe both *'āhab* and *śānē'* are best taken as "covenant language" in Mal 1:2–3.

Andersen and Freedman (1980: 545) have commented that the verb *śānē'* "describes the hostility of a broken covenant relationship" in Hos 9:15. That same emotion and hostility color this text as well, in that Esau (and consequently his descendants the Edomites) despised and rejected the tokens of covenant relationship with Yahweh (cf. Gen 25:34; 26:34–35). Myers (1968: 97) has urged a tempering of Malachi's language, preferring "reject" or "not-loved" as the semantic equivalent of *'āhab*, because the antithetical parallelism addresses election (note the combination of *'āzab* + *śānē'* in Isa 60:15; cf. Redditt [1995: 162], the contrast expresses "Judah's feelings").

Mason (1977: 141) has countered that God is free to elect and reject as he wills, and "he does not reject arbitrarily." God rejected Esau/Edom for good reason: they had created a realm of wickedness. The Edomites were guilty of false worship, violence, of rejecting God and hating his people Israel — all things Yahweh *hates* (Deut 16:22; Pss 5:6 [5]; 11:5; 129:5; etc.). Because Yahweh is a God who hates, he also judges and destroys in his wrath all those who oppose and hate him (cf. Exod 20:5; Deut 7:15; 30:7; 32:41).

If Yahweh is free to elect and reject as he wills, in part as expressed by *śānē'* (or his hate for wickedness and those who hate him), postexilic Yehud is in peril of the same judgment pronounced on Edom. This prompts Mason (1977: 141) to conclude that the "oracle may not be as comfortable [for restoration Yehud] as it has often been understood." The verb *śānē'* occurs elsewhere in the Haggai-Zechariah-Malachi corpus only in Zech 8:17 (the rendering "detest" by Meyers and Meyers [1987: 428] and NAB is weak, suggesting God's passive abhorrence — not the proactive and righteous judgment inherent in the term as it relates to Yahweh; cf. Ps 5:5–6 [4–5] and *ISBE* 2:631).

wā'āśîm. The basic meaning of the hollow verb *śym* is "to place, set," but in some contexts the word can mean "make" (BDB: 964). The verb *śym* governs two accusatives, *'et-hārāyw* and *'et-naḥălātô* in series (cf. WO'C § 10.3.1). The root *śym* occurs elsewhere in the Haggai-Zechariah-Malachi corpus in Hag 1:5, 7; 2:15 [2x], 18, 23; Zech 3:5; 6:11; 7:12, 14; 9:13; 10:3; 12:2, 3, 6; Mal 1:3 and 2:2 [2x], having the meaning "make" in Hag 2:23; Zech 7:12, 14; 9:13; 10:3; 12:3, 6; and Mal 1:3. The LXX is somewhat interpretive here, reading *tássō* ("appoint") for the expected *poiéō* ("make"; so Jer 6:8; Ezek 35:4; Zeph 2:13).

The *waw*-relative + prefixing conjugation after a suffixing verbal form (*śānē'tî*) "may take on the range of meanings associated with the perfective conjugation with the same time reference" (WO'C § 33.3.1b). The conjunctive-sequential *waw*-relative in this case may then indicate a nonprogressive stative aspect ("And so I make . . ." or "So I am making . . .") or a perfective aspect of time ("So I made . . . ," but not a "prophetic perfect" as Mason [1977: 141] suggests; see WO'C § 30.5.1e and § 39.2.2). The aorist *ētaxa* of the LXX supports this reading.

The context of possible rebuilding by the Edomites and further destruction by Yahweh suggests that Edom is the victim of (yet incomplete?) historical processes that will eventually obliterate them (v 4). The preterite translation used here assumes that some (destructive) event has occurred in Edom, which the restoration community might readily identify as a sovereign act of Yahweh, thus giving immediate credence to the prophet's contention that Israel's divine election remains secure (on human event as divine experience, see Heschel [1:170–72]). The divine judgment formula with *śym* + *šĕmāmâ* has parallels in the prophetic literature (e.g., Jer 6:8; Ezek 35:4; Zeph 2:13) and in the Haggai-Zechariah-Malachi corpus in Zech 7:14 (with *lĕšammâ*).

'et-hārāyw. Literally "his mountains" makes reference to the rugged highlands and inaccessible sandstone cliffs that were home to the Edomites (cf. Jer 49:10, 16; Obad 3–4). Their lofty and seeming impregnable habitations were not beyond the reach of Yahweh's wrath, swooping down upon them like the eagle after prey (Jer 49:22). Obadiah contrasts "Mount Zion" (v 17) with "Mount Esau" (v 19), but Malachi offers no such comparison. In fact, there is but one reference to the "mountain" of Yahweh in the entire Haggai-Zechariah-Malachi corpus (Zech 8:3), perhaps because the political autonomy associated with Mt. Zion had not yet been realized in the restoration community (cf. Obad 21).

The LXX *tá hória autóu* ("his borders") is a scribal error for the similar *tá oreiá autoú* ("his mountains"). Bartlett (*ABD* 2:293) has observed that Mal 1:2–5 "notes that Edom's hill country has been laid waste, but goes on to speak of the Edomites as contemplating rebuilding. Malachi does not see the land as empty (though he does see the Edomite effort as doomed to failure)." He equates Jer 49:7–22; Ezek 25:12–14; Obad 1, 7; and Mal 1:2–5 with the aftermath of Nabonidus's campaigns in Edom — a likely conjecture (cf. *ABD* 2:293).

šĕmāmâ. This vocabulary item occurs only here in Haggai-Zechariah-Malachi corpus and functions here as (substantive) *accusative of state* referring to the object of the verb (*'et-hārāyw*; cf. WO'C § 10.2.2d). The word is commonly translated "desolation" (so JPSV, NRSV; cf. R. L. Smith [1984: 304]) or "wasteland" (so NIV and Verhoef [1987: 194]; NAB, NEB, and Glazier-McDonald [1987a: 31] read "waste"). The term depicts a land conquered by an enemy, ruined, and left uninhabited (Jer 4:27; Ezek 6:14; 7:27; etc.) and is prominent in the oracles of the prophets Isaiah, Jeremiah, and Ezekiel (46 of the 55 times the word appears in the OT/HB).

The word *šĕmāmâ* is frequently part of a judgment formula introduced by *ntn* (e.g., Ezek 15:8; 33:28; 35:7) or *śym* (e.g., Jer 6:8) or even *'āśâ* (e.g., Ezek 35:14, 15). This threat of utter desolation is listed among the curses Yahweh may inflict upon Israel for covenant disobedience (Exod 23:29; Lev 26:33), usually by means of natural calamity or instrumentally through war waged by another nation (Joel 2:3; Zeph 1:14–16; cf. Holladay [1986: 167]). The divine punishment of Judah over which Edom gloated now comes full circle (Obad 12).

The sovereignty of God over the nations is readily seen in the numerous prophetic oracles pronouncing divine judgment on nations and cities of the biblical world (e.g., Judah, Jer 9:10 [11]; Babylon, Jer 50:13; Egypt, Ezek 29:12; Edom and Mt. Seir, Ezek 25:13–15; 35:7; and Nineveh, Zeph 2:13). Malachi's use of *šĕmāmâ* may be yet another example of dependence upon Joel, given the similar pronouncement that Edom would become a "desert wasteland" (*lĕmidbar šĕmāmâ*, 4:19 [3:19]; cf. Crenshaw [1995: 201]).

’*et-naḥălātô*. This noun, *naḥălâ* ("heritage, inheritance"; *CHAL*: 234) occurs only here in the Haggai-Zechariah-Malachi corpus. I have interpretively translated *naḥălâ* "ancestral homeland" because it is more expressive than "inheritance," which refers to a tract of land (so NEB; cf. JPSV, "his territory a home for beasts of the desert"). The combination of *hārāyw* + *naḥălātô* echoes the construct genitive *bĕhar naḥălātĕkā* denoting Mt. Sinai in Exod 15:17 ("in your hereditary mountain," D. N. Freedman [1980: 197]). The phrase has parallels in Ugaritic poetry where the expression refers to Sapon, the ancestral abode of Baal (*bḡr . nḥlty*, cf. Cross and Freedman [1975: 64]). As used in Mal 1:3, this distinctive combination must refer not only to the ancestral homeland of the Edomites, but also to the ancient abode of their god.

The territory of Edom was located on the southeastern rim of the Dead Sea and extended from the Brook Zered in the north to the Gulf of Aqaba in the south (cf. *ABD* 2:287–95). Egyptian records and archaeological evidence attest Edomite habitation of the area from ancient times (at least as early as the fifteenth century B.C./E.; cf. *ABD* 2:295–301). According to the book of Numbers, the Edomites were well established as a nation by the time of the Hebrew exodus from Egypt, when they denied Israel passage to the east and threatened them with a show of force (20:14–21; 21:4).

The word has clear covenant connotations for Israel, which certainly did not go unnoticed, calling to mind the allotment of the land of covenant promise to the Hebrew clans under Joshua (Josh 19:1ff.). No doubt the citation of *naḥălâ* also served to remind Israel of the converse, images of Yahweh and the land of Canaan as their "inheritance" painted in "word pictures" by earlier prophetic voices (e.g., Isa 19:25; 58:14; Jer 2:7; 3:19; Lam 5:2; Ezek 44:28; 47:14; 48:29; Joel 4:2 [3:2]).

While the prominence of the land of Canaan as the *naḥălâ* of Israel is touted by the Deuteronomist (4:21, 38; 19:10, 14; 21:23; etc.), it should be noted that Canaan was a secondary conquest of Yahweh. According to Exod 15:17, Yahweh's original homeland was the Sinai/Horeb region. Interestingly, when Yahweh comes to his Temple on the day of his visitation (Mal 3:1–2), he approaches from the east. This is the same compass point from which Yahweh and Israel first entered the land of Canaan after leaving the Sinai wilderness (Ezek 43:1–2).

lĕtannôt midbār. Noting the difficulty of the MT and citing the confusion in the ancient versions, Kruse-Blinkenberg (1967: 79) has included this phrase from Mal 1:3 among those passages in Malachi which do not represent the original text but a corrupted text. Admittedly, the MT "for jackals of the desert" is problematic, primarily because the feminine plural *tannôt* for the Hebrew *tan* ("jackal") is unattested (cf. the masculine plural *tannîm* in Isa 13:22; Mic 1:8; Lam 4:3). The jackal is both a wild and unclean animal according to priestly law and functions as a symbol of the desolation and defilement of Edom in a fashion similar to that of Isa 34:13, 14; 35:7.

Likewise, the readings of the ancient versions testify to the textual exigency from the earliest stages of manuscript transmission. For example, the LXX renders *eis dómata* ("to desert dwellings," an interpretation supported by Syr and SHA). The later Greek version of Aquila translates *eis seirēnas* ("to desert *sirens*"), while other Greek versions (σ and θ) read *eis anepíbata* ("into an inaccessible wilderness").

The Latin *dracones* of the V is the Hebrew equivalent *tannîn*, perhaps based on an alternate manuscript tradition (cf. Calvin [1979: 466–67], "serpents of the desert"). Since Cappellus the majority of biblical scholars, appealing to the LXX, have emended the MT *lĕtannôt* ("for the jackals") to *linôt* (or *linĕ'ôt*), a substantive meaning "pasturage" or "abode, habitation," from the root *nwh* (thus, "for wilderness pasturage" or "for desert dwellings"; so *BHK* and *BHS*).

Others have opted for more creative reconstructions of the MT, including Gesenius (p. 1511), who understood *tannôt* as a contacted form of the Aramaic *tanā'â* ("dwellings"; see the discussion in Keil [2:431]). Torrey (1898: 2) and van Hoonacker (p. 706) read *nĕwôt midbār* (following Nowack [p. 413] and assuming poetic parallelism with *šĕmāmâ*). Alternately, von Bulmerincq (1932: 27) read *lim'ôn tannîm* ("jackals' lair," on the basis of parallels in Jer 9:10; 10:22; 49:33). See the discussion in Glazier-McDonald (1987a: 32–34), who curiously rejects the emendation predicated upon poetic parallelism yet argues that Malachi is poetic largely on the grounds of *parallelism*.

However difficult, the MT *tannôt* is not unintelligible. Though irregular, Keil (2:431) understood *tannôt* as a feminine plural form of *tan* ("jackal"). Rudolph (1976: 254), Verhoef (1987: 203), Glazier-McDonald (1987a: 33), and Petersen (1995: 167) are among the more recent commentators who read the MT *tannôt* ("jackals") along with Keil. This reading of the MT *tannôt* is supported by several of the English versions (NAB, NIV, NRSV). Verhoef (1987: 203) has argued that the plural suffix *-ôt* originally marked no distinctive gender, but it seems more likely *tannôt* is one of those nouns that show both plurals as is more commonly the case in Mishnaic Hebrew (cf. Segal [1927: 132]). It is possible that *lĕtannôt* serves as a double-duty indirect object for both clauses (a type of reverse gapping), even as the verb *śym* does double-duty for the bicolon. Thus the two clauses are rendered: "I made his mountains a wasteland *for jackals*, and I *made* his ancestral homeland a desert *haunt* for jackals."

The combination of the verb *śym* + the preposition *lamed* indicates the indirect object of *goal* (WO'C § 11.2.10d). Verhoef (1987: 203) and Glazier-McDonald (1987a: 33) prefer the translation "turned into" for the construction *śym* + *lamed*, assuming that the preposition of *lĕtannôt* also governs *šĕmāmâ*. While plausible, both readings stretch the usage of *śym* + *lamed* of "turning something into something else" (so BDB: 964). It is possible to read the second object clause more simply, "(*and have given over*) his inheritance to the desert jackals" (Petersen [1995: 167]). That is, Yahweh has made Edom uninhabitable, the whole point of a *naḥălâ* being territory *inhabited* by people who have received or claimed the land as an inheritance.

4. *kî-tō'mar.* The emphatic adverb *kî* functions as a conjunction introducing a conditional clause of *situation* (i.e., condition [*kî*] + consequence [*kōh*], WO'C § 38.2a, d, 39.3.4e; cf. R. J. Williams § 446). The condition here is *irreal*, in that it (i.e., the restoration of Edom) is incapable of fulfillment (WO'C § 38.2.c). The English versions disagree, NEB understanding *kî* in a temporal sense ("when"), the NIV interpreting optatively ("may"), and the NAB, NJB, and NRSV reading the condition "if." Previously, von Bulmerincq (1932: 30) recognized the protasis + apodosis construction of *kî* + *kōh*, and the clause is best understood as an irreal condition (Rashi = *'im*, "if"; T = *'ry*, "if"; and V = *quod si* [adversative + conditional], "but if").

The LXX renders the MT *kî* with the causal *dióti* ("because") and inserts *ereî*, thus misconstruing *'ĕdôm russašnû* as part of the direct discourse ("because one will say, 'Edom has been overthrown' . . ."). The construction joining the adverb *kî* + the prefixing *tō'mar* expresses *contingency of future time*, involving the dependency of capability (i.e., "If Edom should say . . ."; cf. WO'C § 31.6.1 and 31.6.2).

The prefixing form *tō'mar* is ambiguous, permitting the reading "For you say, O Edom . . ." (second-person masculine singular) or "If Edom should say . . ." (third-person feminine singular). The context of verse 4 suggests that Edom should be understood in the third-person, as Edom is considered a feminine noun in Jer 49:17 and Ezek 27:16; 32:29 (so NAB, NEB, NIV, NJB, and NRSV).

'ĕdôm. See NOTES and COMMENTS on *'ēśāw* above in 1:2.

russašnû. The verb *ršš* is rare, occurring in the OT/HB only in Jer 5:17 (Polel imperfective, *yĕrōšēš*) and Mal 1:4 (Pual perfective). The root *ršš* means "to destroy, batter down, crush" (*CHAL:* 347, incorrectly identified as *rwš*, "be poor" in T and Syr; cf. LXX *katéstraptai* ["overturned"], V *destructi* ["destroyed"], and the Akkadian cognate *rašāšu* ["become angry," *AHW* 2:961]).

wĕnāšûb. The simple *waw* + prefixing conjugation after the suffixing conjugation is disjunctive since it introduces a contrast with the preceding clause (WO'C § 39.2.3). The verb *šwb* may be an independent verb in combination with *bnh* meaning "to return" in the physical sense of repatriation of the Edomite territory ("we will return and we will rebuild," R. L. Smith [1984: 304]). Or *šwb* may be an auxiliary verb used with adverbial *bnh* in the sense of "build again" or "rebuild" (cf. WO'C § 39.3.1b; JM § 177b). Given the parallel response of Yahweh using *bnh* ("let them rebuild"), it seems best to understand *šwb* as an auxiliary verb in this context (so NAB, NEB, NIV, NJB, and NRSV).

Elsewhere in Malachi (2:6; 3:7, 24 [4:6]), *šwb* possesses a theological connotation of "returning" to Yahweh, spiritually speaking, by means of repentance and covenant renewal (see the pertinent NOTES and COMMENTS). The implication of verse 4 is that tenacious Edom intends to restore its ancestral homeland and rebuild city and village from the rubble — a doomed enterprise. Ironically, Israel (and Yahweh) have returned (*šwb*) to the covenant homeland of the patriarchs and rebuilt the ruined cities (Zech 1:16; 8:3); but they too are doomed to a most meager existence unless they also return (*šwb*) to Yahweh (3:7, 9; cf. Zech 1:3–6).

wĕnibneh ḥŏrābôt. The coordinator *waw* is an example of the tendency of postexilic Hebrew to replace the sequential *wĕqtl* with the *wĕyqtl* construction

(WO'C § 33.4). The combination of *šwb* and *bnh* indicates that the activity of the verb *bnh* is actually "rebuilding" (cf. *TDOT* 2:168). Though not a *volitional form* in construction, the phrase *wĕnāšûb wĕnibneh* has the force of a purpose or result clause (cf. WO'C § 39.2.2; note the subjunctives *epistrépsōmen* ["let us return"] and *anoikodomēsōmen* ["so *that* we may rebuild"] in the LXX).

The denominative *ḥorbâ* means "desolate place, ruins" (KBL 1:350), used literally in this context of the rubble of the former Edomite strongholds (see the discussion of the root *ḥrb* in *TDOT* 5:150–54). This noun is unique to Mal 1:4 in the Haggai-Zechariah-Malachi corpus, but reflects the postexilic expectation that Yahweh would execute judgment upon the nations (cf. *TDOT* 5:154). It is likely that Malachi is dependent upon Jeremiah and Ezekiel, in that *ḥorbâ* appears in judgment oracles in the two books 24 times (more than half of all the OT/HB occurrences; see especially Jer 49:13 and the phrase *lĕḥorbôt 'ôlām* ["perpetual ruins"] applied to Edom).

kōh 'āmar YHWH ṣĕbā'ôt. The only instance in Malachi where the messenger formula *'āmar YHWH* (1:2, 13; 3:13), and the amplified *'āmar YHWH ṣĕbā'ôt* (1:6, 8, 9, 10, 11, 13, 14; 2:2, 4, 8, 16; 3:1, 5, 7, 10, 11, 12, 17, 19 [4:1], 21 [4:3]) is prefaced by the demonstrative adverb *kōh* (always initial in discourse, cf. WO'C § 39.3.4e). The adverb *kōh* introduces a section of discourse (vv 4–5) following the opening disputation (vv 2–3). As such, this statement concerning Edom constitutes a closing argument for the first disputation, proving convincingly that Yahweh indeed loves Israel. According to Andersen and Freedman (1989: 230), the function of the phrase *kōh 'āmar YHWH* is strictly prophetic, part of the messenger formula used as "the customary formal opening of an oracle."

Typically the divine name *YHWH ṣĕbā'ôt* is translated as a construct-genitive ("Yahweh/LORD of Hosts," e.g., NAB, NEB, JPSV, NRSV; but NIV, "LORD Almighty," NJB, "Yahweh Sabaoth"). The proper name *YHWH*, however, cannot be constructed in a genitive relationship to the following noun *ṣĕbā'ôt* and therefore stands in apposition ("Yahweh [the] Hosts," so JM § 131o). D. N. Freedman and O'Connor suggest that this divine epithet may have a verbal force in some instances, reflecting an archaic usage of the formula (*YHWH ṣĕbā'ôt* = "he creates armies"; *TDOT* 6:515).

According to Mettinger's (p. 12) analysis, the Haggai-Zechariah-Malachi corpus accounts for nearly a third of all OT/HB occurrences of the divine epithet *ṣĕbā'ôt* ("hosts," 91 of 284 times; see also the discussion of divine epithets in Meyers and Meyers [1993: 248–49]). Meyers and Meyers (1987: 18–19) admit that the recurrent usage of the formula marks a certain "archaizing" in the postexilic prophets (after the pattern of the preexilic prophets Isaiah and Jeremiah). They also advance an important insight when they acknowledge that *ṣĕbā'ôt* takes on a new meaning under the everted circumstances of the restoration period: "By referring to 'Yahweh of Hosts,' it asserts the fact of Yahweh's return to Zion and the reestablishment of his mighty power . . . 'Yahweh of Hosts' for Haggai and his colleagues reestablishes the preexilic conception of divine presence and expresses the ultimate authority of Yahweh, even over the Persian emperor or any other human ruler" (see their full discussion, especially p. 19).

The fact that Malachi employs some variation of the messenger formula *'āmar*

YHWH 24 times in 51 verses certainly emphasizes the divine origin of his message and connects his oracles with earlier prophetic tradition. Perhaps more significantly, however, it suggests a colossal crisis of authority in the restoration community given the despair over Persian domination (elsewhere in the Haggai-Zechariah-Malachi corpus: 6 times in Haggai [38 vv] and 23 times in Proto-Zechariah [121 vv], but only 11:4 in Second Zechariah). See further the discussion of 'āmar YHWH in verse 2 above.

hēmmâ yibnû wā'ănî 'ehĕrôs. The independent pronouns + finite verbs involve *logical structure*, setting up an *explicit antithesis* between Edom and Yahweh (cf. WO'C § 16.3.2d). The form *hēmmâ* is absent from Haggai and limited to this single occurrence in Malachi; but the independent pronouns *hēm* and *hēmmâ* appear in both First and Second Zechariah. The emphatic position of the personal pronouns in this antithetical structure permits rendering *hēmmâ* and *'anî* as object pronouns "*as for* them . . . but *as for* me . . .*"

yibnû. The free prefixing form of *bnh* here is ambiguous, representing a simple nonperfective or a volitional jussive. The English versions render the form variously as the expression of possibility (so NAB, NIV, NRSV, "They may rebuild") or conditionally (so NEB, "If they rebuild") and in a jussive mood (so NJB, "Let them build!"). Most recent commentators have understood *yibnû* as the *nonperfective of possibility*, noting the emphatic position of the independent pronoun, and translate "they may build" as well (e.g., R. L. Smith [1984: 304]; Verhoef [1987: 194]; and Glazier-McDonald [1987a: 31]; cf. WO'C § 31.4e). I prefer the jussive mood in this instance for two reasons: the rhetorical nature of the disputation commends this reading, and the discourse sets up a foil between a superior (Yahweh) and an inferior (Edom; cf. WO'C § 34.3a, b). The jussive force better emphasizes the authority and power of Yahweh as sovereign of the nations.

wā'ănî. The disjunctive *waw* is adversative, with the subject in initial position in each of the contrasting clauses (cf. WO'C § 8.3b). The oracles of Malachi use the form *'ănī* exclusively for the first-person independent pronoun (1:4, 6 [2x], 14; 2:9; 3:6, 17, 21), while the second appendix employs the variation *'ānōkî* (see the NOTES on 3:23 [4:5] below).

'ehĕrôs. The verb *hrs* ("to demolish, destroy"; KBL 1:256–57) occurs only here in the Haggai-Zechariah-Malachi corpus. The verb is used especially to describe the "tearing down" or the "destruction" of cities (2 Sam 11:25; Isa 14:17; Jer 31:40; etc.). This meaning is reinforced by those contexts in which *hrs* is paired with its antonym *bnh*, as is the case in Mal 1:4 (see especially Jer 1:10; cf. Ezek 36:36; Ps 28:5; Prov 14:1; Job 12:14). According to Münderlein those texts using *hrs* and/or *bnh* abstractly to describe the activity of Yahweh are relatively late and are probably dependent on the usage of the two verbs in the book of Jeremiah (*TDOT* 3:463).

wĕqārĕ'û lāhem. The *waw*-relative with the suffixing conjugation represents a situation of *simple consequence* with *wĕqārĕ'û* taking on the sense of the preceding nonperfective verb ("I myself will raze . . . and they will call them . . ."); cf. WO'C § 32.2.1d). The idiom *qr'* + *lamed* means "to name" or "give a name to" (BDB: 896). The preposition *lamed* functions here as an indirect object with *qr'* and marks the *lamed* of goal (i.e., altering the status of the nation of Edom,

WO'C § 11.2.10d; cf. GKC § 119t on the *lamed* of result after verbs of making, forming, changing, appointing, etc.).

gĕbûl riš'â. "A genitive that designates the 'territory' as the possession of persons or groups," used here as a derogatory epithet for the nation of Edom ("Territory of Evil," *TDOT* 2:365). This figurative use of *gĕbûl* is unique to Malachi in the OT/HB (cf. Isa 54:12, *wĕkol-gĕbûlēk lĕ'abnê-ḥēpeṣ* ["and all your border of *semi*-precious stones"]). The feminine noun *riš'â* is found also in Mal 3:15 and 19 [4:1]. The word may mean "guilt" (Deut 9:4–5; cf. Weinfeld [1991: 406]) or "wicked(ness), evil" (Ezek 5:6; 18:20; cf. Zimmerli [1979: 151]; Greenberg [1983: 111]). Specifically, *riš'â* refers to the evil or wickedness of idolatry (see the discussion of *riš'â* in Zech 5:6 in Meyers and Meyers [1987: 302–3]).

wĕhā'ām 'ăšer-zā'am YHWH. The noun *'ām* ("people") can refer generally to "people groups" larger than a clan or tribe (e.g., *mišpāḥâ* or *'elep*) and in some contexts may parallel the semantic range of *lĕ'ôm* (a substantial *ethnic* population, cf. *THAT* 2:299). When used of people groups, the word *'ām* implies populations bonded by some kind of unifying relationship, whether religious, political, cultural (and linguistic), or ethnic. The word *'ām* clarifies the earlier reference to *'ĕdôm*, the "people" or "nation" of Edom politically (and ethnically) speaking. The relative pronoun *'ăšer* is resumptive in the nominative function (WO'C § 19.3.b). Note also the heavy repetition of the consonants *'ayin* (4 times in six words) and *mem* (3 times in six words) in verses 4–5.

The verb *z'm* occurs in the Haggai-Zechariah-Malachi corpus only in Zech 1:12 and Mal 1:4, with YHWH the subject in each case. Wiklander (*TDOT* 4:107) cites the basic meaning of *z'm* as "threaten" or "injure," whether by words (= "curse, condemn"), by actions (= "punishment"), or in the sense of implicit emotional state or attitude (= "be angry"). Sometimes *z'm* is paired with *qbb* (a synonym of *'rr*, "to curse"), and in Num 23:7–8, *z'm* is matched with both *'rr* and *qbb* (with *z'm* positioned as the B-word of the pair in each case).

Wiklander concedes the difficulty in deciding whether or not the earlier meaning of "curse" for *z'm* continues into the postexilic period (*TDOT* 4:108; cf. Meyers and Meyers [1987: 116–17] who translate "be angry" for *z'm* in Zech 1:12). The English versions are in agreement, rendering *z'm* "wrath" or "anger" (NAB, NIV, NJB, NRSV) — except the NEB which reads "cursed eternally." I side with the minority understanding of the meaning of *z'm* in Mal 1:4, "cursed," because the context is one of a national judgment theophany (or even *doxology?*; cf. Ps 7:12 [11]) against Edom, and by definition one of the characteristics of the curse "is its unqualified and irrevocable execution" (Glazier-McDonald [1987a: 34]; cf. Petersen [1995: 167]). Such is guaranteed by the temporal modifier *'ad-'ôlām* ("perpetually"; cf. von Bulmerincq [1932: 37–38] and Rudolph [1976: 254 n. 4b]). Further, the book's deliberate archaizing tendencies widely recognized by commentators also suggest that Malachi intends this more harsh understanding of *z'm* (the LXX interprets with *paratássō* ["array against in battle"] as in Zech 1:6 for *zmm*; cf. *ápeileō* "to threaten" for *z'm* in Isa 66:14).

The primary reason for the curse of divine wrath and punishment is "human sin and enmity toward God, although ... whoever has fallen victim to God's wrath can appeal to God's mercy" (*TDOT* 4:110). However, the judgment theophanies of Isa 66:14 and Mal 1:4 seem to offer little hope for divine clemency (Mal 1:4 echoes the sentiments of Jer 49:13 regarding Edom; cf. Brichto [1963: 200–4]).

'ad-'ôlām. The word 'ôlām occurs here and in Mal 3:4 (without the preposition 'ad) and in the Haggai-Zechariah-Malachi corpus elsewhere only in Zech 1:5 (with the preposition lamed not 'ad). Marti (p. 462) deleted 'ad-'ôlām, but unnecessarily since the phrase commonly complements the curse formula and judgment oracles (cf. Deut 28:45–46; Jer 17:4–5). Most literally 'ad-'ôlām is rendered "forever" (so NAB, NEB, NJB, NRSV). But Boman (p. 151) has argued that our notion of eternity and forever is prejudiced "spatially" by western religious and philosophical ideology. The Hebrew understanding of "boundless time" in a temporal sense is better rendered "perpetually" (e.g., Zeph 2:9, KJV = "perpetual desolation" for ûšĕmāmâ 'ad-'ôlām; cf. NIV, Verhoef [1987: 205] "always"). According to McKane (1986: 388) the expression 'ad-'ôlām "conveys the sense of an awful finality." On the preposition 'ad, see the NOTES and COMMENTS on 1:11 and 3:10 below.

5. wĕ 'ênêkem. The first disputation ends as it began, with a prophetic declaration about Yahweh. The emphatic position of the noun in the opening clause calls attention to the experience of the restoration community. They complained that they had not witnessed Yahweh's love for them. Now they will witness it firsthand. The initial waw + non-verb are disjunctive, signaling a shift in action and participants and completing an episode (WO'C § 39.2.3). I understand the prophet to be making reference primarily to his previously stated thesis (i.e., the people will see that Yahweh loves Israel), not that they will see the continuing disintegration of the nation of Edom (i.e., "you will see (it)," so NAB, NEB, NIV, NJB, and NRSV; cf. R. L. Smith [1984: 304]; Glazier-McDonald [1987a: 31]). Granted, the omission of any object for the verb rā'â may be intentionally ambiguous, so that "Israel, by contrasting its condition with that of Edom, will be more deeply convinced that Jehovah's government of his people Israel was a gracious one" (Packard [1902: 8]).

tir'eynâ. The verb rā'â means "to see" in the sense of "perceiving" or "understanding" (CHAL: 327–28). Contemporary events in the land of Edom will confirm the prophet's thesis, that Yahweh loves Israel and hates Esau. Postexilic Yehud will recognize this as a demonstration of Yahweh's sovereignty and thus receive an answer to their earlier (cynical and arrogant) querry, "How have you loved us?" (v 2). The combination of 'ênêkem + rā'â here in 1:5 suggests that the fall of Edom had the same theological import as the Israelite Exodus from Egypt (cf. Deut 11:7).

wĕ'attem tō'mĕrû. The independent pronoun 'attem ("you," masculine plural) completes the triad of "I" ('ānî = Yahweh), "they" (hēmmâ = Edom), and "you" ('attem = Yehud) begun in verse 4 (note the order "I" [Yahweh], "you" [Yehud], and "they" [Edom] in vv 2–3). The emphatic use of the independent pronoun 'attem with the finite verb tō'mĕrû involves psychological focus; that is, the construction suggests a "'strong emotional heightening' and 'focused attention or deep self-consciousness'" (WO'C § 16.3.2e). The awareness or perception of Yahweh's love for Israel (attested by the events in Edom) prompts a reversal in the speech patterns of the restoration community, in that, instead of skeptical replies (*'āmar*, v 2), the people will respond with vows of praise. Following Ibn Ezra, Henderson (p. 448) incorrectly connects *wĕ'attem tō'mĕrû* with *mē'al ligbûl yiśrā'ēl* ("ye who dwell upon the land of Israel shall say from the locality you occupy . . . Jehovah be magnified").

yigdal YHWH. The expression is an epithet for Yahweh stemming from the so-called Zion tradition of the first Davidic corpus of the Psalter (*TDOT* 2:406–7; cf. Ps 48:1). The phrase *yigdal YHWH* occurs in Ps 35:27 and 40:17 [16] (= Ps 70:5 [4] except for the substitution of *'ĕlōhîm* for *YHWH*). This "greatness of God proclaimed on Zion includes in particular a universal kingship over the whole earth and over all gods" (*TDOT* 2:407; cf. Labuschagne).

The use of the imperfective finite verb (*gdl*, "be great"), instead of a predicate nominative construction with the adjective *gādôl* ("great," e.g., Pss 48:2 [1]; 96:4; 135:5), places emphasis on Yahweh showing himself to be great (*TDOT* 2:402). The imperfective may be construed as a declaration ("Yahweh is Great . . . ," so NAB, NEB, NIV, NJB, NRSV; cf. R. L. Smith [1984: 304]; Glazier-McDonald [1987a: 31]) or as jussive expressing volition (cf. WO'C § 34.3b). Understanding the phrase as a wish ("May Yahweh be great . . .") conforms to both the pattern of a jussive clause for a benediction (WO'C § 34.3c) and to the *oratio variata* (a jussive based on apostrophe, i.e., "direct address *to* a person, after a passage talking *about* that person, WO'C § 34.3d; so Calvin [1979: 661]; Henderson [1980: 448]). This statement stands in stark contrast to the "great mourning in Jerusalem" (elsewhere in the Haggai-Zechariah-Malachi corpus *yigdal* appears only in Zech 12:11).

mē'al. The complex construction joining *min* ("from") + *'al* ("upon") functions prepositionally with *lamed* (WO'C § 11.3.2). The form *mē'al* occurs elsewhere in the Haggai-Zechariah-Malachi corpus only in Zech 3:4; 4:12; and 11:13 (requiring the translation "from" or "by" in each case). Two distinct interpretive traditions compete here. One emphasizes the sovereignty of Yahweh in the destruction of Edom and the tendencies toward *universalism* in the later disputations (cf. Vriezen 1975: 130–31) and reads "*beyond* the borders of Israel." The implication is that Yahweh's domain is not restricted to Israel (Baldwin [1972b: 124]; cf. von Bulmerincq [1932: 41]; Rudolph [1976: 256]; R. L. Smith [1984: 306]; Wendland [1985: 120–21]; Glazier-McDonald [1987a: 31]; Redditt [1995: 163]; Petersen [1995: 167]; and Syr, T, NAB, NEB, NIV, NJB, NRSV).

The second appeals to the rendering of the construction *mē'al* + *lamed* elsewhere in the OT/HB (usually "above" or "over" as in GKC § 119c; cf. Ezek 1:25; Jonah 4:6; Eccl 5:7; Neh 3:28; 12:31, 37; etc.) and the immediate context of the first disputation (i.e., Yahweh's covenant relationship with Israel). This approach understands "Great is Yahweh *over* the territory of Israel" — in that Yahweh is rightfully acknowledged as Israel's suzerain (J.M.P. Smith [1912: 24]; Verhoef [1987: 206]; cf. the LXX *huperánō* and the V *super*). I concur with Verhoef (1987: 206) who concluded that "the greatness of the Lord is not so much seen in his judgment of Edom, but rather in the manifestation of his love for Israel" (cf.

Calvin's [p. 661] variation *"throughout* the border of Israel"). Besides, implicit in Malachi's allusion to the "Zion tradition" of the Psalter is the de facto rule over all the nations by Yahweh from his holy habitation in Jerusalem (*TDOT* 2:408). *ligbûl yiśrā'ēl.* Literally "boundary" or "border," *gĕbûl* may "also be defined by a genitive that designates the 'territory' as the possession of persons or groups" (*TDOT* 2:365). The translation "territory" is preferable to the rendering "border" (or the logical plural "borders") in the English versions, because the issue is the land circumscribed by the border(s) (e.g., NIV, NRSV; cf. NAB "land" and NEB "realm"; but JPSV and NJB "borders").

The word (*gĕbûl*) occurs in the Haggai-Zechariah-Malachi corpus only in Mal 1:4 and 5. Elsewhere, references including the phrase *gĕbûl yiśrā'ēl* attest to the sovereignty of Yahweh over the shape and extent of the boundaries circumscribing the territory of Israel (e.g., 1 Sam 7:13; 2 Kgs 10:32; Ezek 11:10–11). Ottosson has noted that "the frequent use of the expression *gĕbûl yiśrā'ēl,* 'the territory of Israel,' points to a conscious, most likely religious understanding of the boundary of the national territory whose Lord and God is Yahweh" (*TDOT* 2:366).

More than "religious," *gĕbûl yiśrā'ēl* is covenantal, as demonstrated by the Ebal "land-grant" ceremony within the treaty-renewal framework of Deuteronomy and Joshua (Hill [1988: 404]). Thus, the proper name *yiśrā'ēl* is used comprehensively to designate the territory and the people of postexilic Israel, both symbiotically united in covenant relationship with Yahweh (*TDOT* 6:403, 416–17). The proposed reading *gĕbûl* for *ligbûl* attributed to dittography in *BHK* and *BHS* rests on scanty textual evidence. In addition, deleting the *lamed* compromises the understanding of the idiom *mē'al + lamed* as a construction that transforms adverbs of place into prepositions (GKC § 119c).

COMMENTS

Malachi's first disputation is directed to all the people of the restoration community in postexilic Judah. This includes civil and religious leaders and the general populace, the pious, the pseudo-pious, and the impious (see R. W. Bailey [1977: 9]). Recognizing the religious diversity of the audience of this opening oracle helps mediate the range of scholarly opinion as to the tone of the prophet's first message.

No doubt there existed a minority population in Jerusalem that still "feared" Yahweh and "obeyed" his word (Hag 2:12). For this faithful remnant, the message of Yahweh's love for Israel probably proved a great source of inspiration and encouragement (so R. L. Smith [1984: 305]; Verhoef [1987: 195]). While for those jaundiced by apathy and despair as a result of "failed" salvation oracles pronounced previously by Haggai and Zechariah, Malachi's message served as a much-needed corrective to wrong thinking about covenant relationship with Yahweh (so Fischer [1972: 318–19]; Mallone [1981: 26–27]). Finally, for the jaded skeptics and irreverent cynics among Malachi's hearers, the message of Yahweh's love was a warning, a threat of divine judgment (so Boecker [1966: 77–80]; Craigie [1985: 229–30]).

The value of the disputational format of Malachi's oracles for effective prophetic ministry must not be discounted. The literary form of the dispute affords the prophet a confrontational stance with his audience in keeping with the legacy of his preexilic counterparts. Nevertheless, the disputation permits greater rapport with listeners (or readers) because the form is essentially didactic in nature (cf. Brueggemann [1982b: 71–76]). In addition, the rhetorical question characteristic of the disputational format proves advantageous in disarming the hearer or reader by anticipating audience response. As such, the purpose of disputation speeches "is to leave the opponent devoid of further argumentation and resigned to the divine decision" (Patterson [1993: 303]). For Malachi, this meant demonstrating that covenant relationship (and its attendant blessings/curses) was Yahweh's prerogative — not Israel's.

The gist of Malachi's opening disputation is "Yahweh loves Jacob." Further, the truth of God's love for Israel is obvious from lessons of history — past and present. Lastly, the demonstration of Yahweh's covenant love for his people necessitated their response of covenant loyalty and obedience.

2. Watts (1987a: 376) has analyzed Malachi's oracles as a series of "speech acts." He has noted that the phrase "I have loved you" (v 2a) is assertive and is intended to elicit a response of assurance from the Hebrew restoration community. The remainder of the oracle (vv 2b–5) is dialogical and is designed to convince the audience that the prophet's assertion is true. How could Israel doubt Yahweh's covenant love, and why would this first-person indicative statement of his relationship to Israel be received with such uncertainty and skepticism? Braun (1977: 293) attributed postexilic Yehud's apathy and despair to the seeming irrelevance of Yahwistic religion for their present distress. Prior to Babylonian Exile, "the besetting sins of the Jews were idolatry and superstition. Afterward they were prone to the other extremes of practical atheism and Epicureanism" (Moore [p. 104]).

Wells (pp. 41–42) has blamed Israel's *crisis of relevance* on the process of secularization that took place during the period of Babylonian Exile. The emphasis on Yahweh's inability to prevent the Babylonian onslaught created a spirit of apathy that verged on practical atheism. According to Wells (p. 47), it is this "loss of the experiential knowledge of the love of God" that resulted in Israel's "loss of identity as the people of God." For this reason, Yahweh's love for Israel constitutes the central argument of the opening disputation; the restoration community's *identity crisis* could be overcome only by the affirmation and experience of covenant relationship with the God of Abraham, Isaac, and Jacob. See further the comments below in verse 3 on "I loved Jacob" and the election of Israel.

The refutation of the prophet's declaration ("I have loved Jacob") by means of the rhetorical question ("How have you loved us?") measures the depth of despair, doubt and cynicism in the restoration community. Craigie (p. 227) claimed that the objection "rings with petulance and perversity . . . words . . . of self-centered persons who can no longer perceive the love of God in their lives." As Baldwin (1972a: 221) has aptly observed, "The atrophy of human love in the community (2:13–16) has undermined confidence in the divine love."

Like the audience of his earlier contemporary Haggai, Malachi's listeners were still "looking for much and finding little" — and blaming God for their situation (Hag 1:6, 9). A generation of religious indifference had distorted the people's reasoning, led them to false conclusions, and ultimately blinded them to the reality of God's love (cf. R. W. Bailey [1977: 5]; Craigie [1985: 228–39]). Gone was the steadfast conviction and unswerving faith of Habakkuk who rejoiced in Yahweh come feast or famine (Hab 3:17–19). This had been replaced by an attitude of despair akin to that encountered by the prophet Zephaniah because Judah had assumed God's impotence in addressing the problem of evil (Zeph 2:12).

Mason (1990: 239) has remarked that it is strange that Malachi should begin his accusations against the restoration community with this "nationalistic assurance of God's electing love of them in contrast to the Edomites." However, the issue in Mal 1:2–5 is not one of "nationalism." The postexilic Hebrew community needed a remedy for doubt and despair that was not contingent upon the state of Israel's current (or future) sociopolitical circumstances. Here Glazier-McDonald (1987a: 34) errs in understanding the references to "Jacob" and "Esau" only as symbols of nations and not as individuals. Indeed it is the individual characters of Jacob and Esau that infuse the symbols of Israel and Edom with explicit theological content. By identifying Esau as Jacob's "brother," Malachi juxtaposes "loyalty to self and clan" with "loyalty to God" within the context of national solidarity (cf. *TDOT* 1:192).

The story of Esau is one of selfishness and disdain for the tokens of Yahweh's covenant (Gen 25:34). Edom came to personify this kind of profane and self-centered existence. But the story of Jacob as Yahweh's choice to inherit the covenant of his fathers, despite his many faults and foibles, is one of great faith and obedience tempered by personal crisis (Gen 48:15; 49:18; cf. Ps 146:5; Heb 11:9, 20–22). The nation of Israel was supposed to personify this kind of "pilgrim" faith and zealous worship, but instead was now in jeopardy of despising the very tokens of Yahweh's covenant even as Edom had done. According to R. W. Bailey (p. 9), this classic example of oriental hyperbole contrasting Jacob and Esau was Malachi's most effective tool for communicating the concept of Israel's solidarity as the covenant people and demonstrating Yahweh's covenant love for Israel. The prophet's accusations in the remaining disputations and his challenge to priests and people alike to live out covenant fidelity with Yahweh issue from this demonstration of Israel's covenant solidarity and Yahweh's covenant love for Israel.

3. Malachi responds to the spiritual and ethnic identity crisis of postexilic Yehud with the chiastically ordered couplet "Yet I loved Jacob, but Esau I hated" (vv 2c–3a). Mallone (p. 28) has commented that faith in crisis often needs external evidence, "a sure footing outside our own individual experience, an objective signpost on which we can hang our mental convictions." Unfortunately, the people were eyeing the wrong "signpost." For Israel divine election was no longer a creed to believe in and live by, but "a collection of proofs which the people turn to their profit as a source of pride and glory" (Jacob [1958: 111]). Because

the people were not experiencing material blessing ("turning no profit," Mal 3:14), the creed of Yahweh's election was perceived to be invalid and untrue. Thus the prophet offers two pieces of evidence: Exhibit A, the word of divine revelation, and Exhibit B, a demonstration from recent history offered as proof of the veracity and reliability of Yahweh's communication to Israel. Indeed, God's word alone should have convinced Malachi's audience that Yahweh had not severed his covenant bond with Israel. However, the relativizing of earlier "salvation oracles" by the postexilic prophets necessitated the introduction of more tangible and dramatic supporting evidence (cf. Koch [1984: 178]). If they cannot accept God's word that he still loves Israel, then let them observe current events — the nation of Edom has been laid waste!

The word "love" ('*āhab*) when used of Yahweh's relationship to Israel can mean "choose" or "elect" (*TDOT* 1:112–13) and in that sense is equated with the verb *bḥr*, "to choose" (*TDOT* 2:82–86). The love of Yahweh is "an act of election which makes Israel Yahweh's child," both in the sense of privileged "heir" in a familial context and favored vassal of the suzerain in a political context (Andersen and Freedman [1980: 576–77]). Furthermore, the word signifies "complete love which demands all of one's energies" (*TDOT* 1:104). Yahweh's love for (and election of) Israel is the free and unconditional choice of the Sovereign of creation.

There was nothing about Israel that merited such favor (Deut 7:7–8; 9:4–5); God arbitrarily decided to "set his desire" on Abraham and his descendants to "love" ('*āhab*) them and "choose" (*bāḥar*) them out of all the people groups of the earth (Deut 10:15; cf. the discussion of Yahweh's election of Israel in Weinfeld [1991: 213–14, 367–68, 436–37]). Because Yahweh loved Israel with "eternal love," he extended his grace to them (Jer 31:2). The preeminent example of this extension of divine grace to Israel rooted in God's election was the Exodus from Egypt (Deut 4:37).

According to Malachi, this love was expressed almost as dramatically in the Israelite return from captivity in Babylonia (cf. Ps 89:31–35 [30–34]; Lam 3:22, 32). Seebass (citing Vriezen) has summarized, "In the OT the choice [i.e., divine election] is always the action of God, of his grace, and always contains a mission for man; and only out of this mission can man comprehend the choice of God" (*TDOT* 2:87).

Wallis suggests that the book of Deuteronomy was especially intended to educate Israel in "her duty to reciprocate God's love, not in the original sense of emotion, but in the form of genuine obedience and pure devotion" (*TDOT* 1:115). The prophet Malachi sought to perpetuate that pedagogical legacy by calling postexilic Yehud to "take seriously" her relationship with Yahweh (2:2; especially the priests who had perverted religious instruction) by offering "righteous worship" (3:3) and obeying God's commandments (3:14).

R. W. Bailey (p. 10) and Verhoef (1987: 201) correctly reject Calvin's (pp. 471–82) interpretation of Yahweh's "love" and "hate" as the "double predestination" of Israel and Edom. Neither is it appropriate to ascribe divine election only to the foreknowledge of the omniscient God (i.e., God rejected Esau *knowing* he would become an "immoral and godless" person, Heb 12:16–17). The old and new covenant pattern of divine testing and discipline of the elect indicates that human freedom is a reality—not an illusion (Gen 22:1; Deut 8:2, 16; Ps 11:5; Jer 9:7; Heb 12:5–11). Abraham was tested by God and proven faithful (Gen 22:12), and under Yahweh's discipline Jacob the knave became Israel, "a prince with God" (Gen 35:10); but the nation Israel failed the Lord's test in the settlement of Canaan (Judg 2:22; cf. 2:11).

All this implies that human (and national) destinies are not set in stone by divine council. God does relent and change his posture (as the prophet Jonah learned much to his annoyance, Jonah 4:2). Nor is it entirely correct to dismiss the doctrine of God's election of Israel as "divine consensus" after the fact (i.e., divine election was merely the result of "historical experience"; so R. W. Bailey [1977: 10]). If this were the case, the nation of Israel would never have developed a character justifying divine favor, given the penchant of the Hebrews for the "apostasy of the Canaanites" (Hos 11:2).

Patrick's humble concession is orthodox: "Belonging to Yahweh is a great gift which can only be explained by reference to his mysterious will" (ABD 2:436; cf. Terrien [1978: 265] on the "transcendence of God's freedom"). Jacob (p. 111) has exposed the fallacies inherent in attempts to rationally explain the mystery of divine election, insisting only that "God loves his people in order to achieve his aim with them" (cf. Sanday and Headlam [1902: 249] on the rabbinical teachings addressing divine election). This aim (or "mission" following Seebass above) remains twofold: first, to create a people for his name (Isa 43:7), a nation of priests who walk after God in holiness (Exod 19:6; Mic 4:5)—distinguishing the difference between the righteous and the wicked (Mal 3:18); and second, to establish his holy and righteous kingdom over the world (Ps 145:10–20; Isa 65:17–25; Zech 14:16–21).

The NT citation of Mal 1:2–3 by the apostle Paul in Rom 9:13 confirms this basic understanding of the mystery of Israel's election, in that divine adoption is the inscrutable choice of God, apart from human merit, and above any indictment of divine justice (Rom 9:14). Contextually, like Malachi, Paul addresses misappropriation of the doctrine of election by Jews who desire the benefits of God's love without the obligation of reciprocating in like manner with love, reverence, and obedience to divine law (cf. the discussion of divine election in Sanday and Headlam [1902: 248–51]). According to Cranfield (pp. 479–81), Paul's quotation of Mal 1:2–3 corroborates the birth narrative of Gen 25:23 (i.e., the elder Esau will serve the younger Jacob), thereby accomplishing God's purpose in the election of Israel—identifying the "true descendants" of Abraham (Rom 9:11; cf. 9:6–7). See further I. F. 1. Malachi in the New Testament above.

The term "hate" (śānēʼ) is a harsh word, especially when used of God's attitude toward and dealings with human beings whom he created. However, divine hate is the necessary corollary of divine love (TDOT 1:102). The prophet implies no "personal animosity" towards Esau (Baldwin 1972a: 223). Rather, "hate" coupled with "love" in the covenantal context of Israel's divine election here means "not loved" (i.e., "not chosen" or "rejected"; see Jacob [p. 109]; Myers [1968: 97]). Those commentators who detect overtones of bitterness and resentment in Malachi's words about Edom are probably near the truth (e.g., R. L. Smith [1984:

305]). The vindictive imprecation of Ps 137:7 attests Israel's craving for the divine vengeance upon this ally of Babylonia in the destruction of Jerusalem (cf. Petersen [1995: 169–70]; and Cresson [1972: 125] on the "damn-Edom" theology of the postexilic prophets).

Like Yahweh's love, Yahweh's "hate" is absolute and unconditional. It is not a question of degrees of love, "but of love or no love" (J.M.P. Smith [1912: 21]; cf. Elliger [1950: 180] and Laetsch [1956: 512] who interpret "hate" in the comparative sense of "love less" on the basis of a relative "love" and "hate" implied in Gen 25:28; 29:31; Deut 21:15–17). Both Yahweh's "love" (election) and "hate" (rejection) issue from his holiness, so much so that "the entire history of Israel is the work of [God's] holiness" (Jacob [1958: 90]).

Such an understanding is consistent with the portrayal of divine character elsewhere in the OT/HB, because Yahweh admits his "hate" for Israel and vows never to "love" them again on account of all their evil (Hos 9:15; cf. Andersen and Freedman [1980: 545] on "hate" describing the hostility of a broken covenant relationship). In fact, God hates evil and punishes evildoers, whether among the pagan nations (e.g., Pss 5:6 [5]; 31:7 [6]) or his own people Israel (e.g., Amos 5:15; Zech 8:17).

Understood from this perspective, Yahweh's "hatred" of Edom symbolized by Esau was justified because God "rejects those who create a domain for wickedness" (Mason [1977: 141]). In effect, by nursing a grudge against Israel, feuding with the Hebrew monarchies, and finally by gleefully joining in the pillaging and looting of the descendants of Jacob during their "day of calamity" (Obad 13), Edom brought divine judgment upon themselves (Baldwin [1972a: 223]). So it is with good reason that Craigie cautioned that "the lesson on love is a warning, and the example of Edom a threat" (p. 229; cf. Mason [1977: 141] who observed that this opening disputation "may not be as comfortable as it has often been understood to be"). God's covenant love is a two-edged sword. He is free to elect (love) and reject (hate) apart from any conditions or considerations (cf. Köhler [1957: 52]). Let postexilic Yehud (and all who are comfortable and secure in their knowledge as God's elect) beware!

Malachi regarded the destruction of the fortifications of Edom as visible evidence of God's love for Israel. More importantly, this evidence, demanded by the restoration community, both validated earlier prophetic discourses concerning the fall of Edom (e.g., Ezek 25:12–14) and lent credence to the import of Malachi's oracles. The task of the interpreter here is not so much the deciphering of who destroyed the nation of Edom and when it occurred on the continuum of ancient Near Eastern chronology (in a lengthy discussion, Glazier-McDonald [1987a: 35–41] finally admits, "Whether Mal 1:3 refers to Nabonidus' campaigns or to the results of the Nabataean incursions is unclear" [!]). Rather it is the affirmation that it did happen — a documented historical event (or process[?]; the date of Malachi better coincides with the chronology of the campaigns of Nabonidus, cf. *ABD* 2:293).

The thrust of Malachi's illustration of Edom's demise is theological — Yahweh's sovereignty. The prophet, however, develops no theological treatise on the sovereignty of God. Indeed, he simply asks his audience to consider the "historical experiences" of the two peoples (Craigie [1985: 227]). The doctrine of election is a paradox of theological "cause" and historical "result" (see R. W. Bailey [1977: 10]). No doubt the prophet apprehended a certain irony in the reversal of fortunes of the two nations given Israel's failure to recognize and appreciate the fact that the God who laid waste the highlands of Edom was the same Yahweh who had returned the Hebrew expatriates from Babylon and resettled them in their own covenant inheritance, the land promised to Abraham, Isaac, and Jacob.

Malachi's wordplay upon the "inheritance" (naḥălâ) of Edom is interesting in that Obadiah also envisioned a reversion of territory as "Mount Zion" dispossessed "Mount Esau" (vv 17–21). By framing his prediction of repatriation with Israel's possession of the Negev (vv 19a//20d), Obadiah indicates that the fall of Edom should be viewed as the trigger event setting in motion the fulfillment of Yahweh's covenant promises to Israel (see Hill [1989: 643]). Perhaps this text lies behind Malachi's use of Edom's recent history as an illustration of Yahweh's love for Israel?

4–5. The first disputation ends as it began, with a prophetic declaration about God and his relationship to Israel. The event of Edom's destruction orchestrated by the Sovereign Lord has two significant outcomes for postexilic Yehud. First, the overthrow and displacement of the nation of Edom signals the permanent demise of one of Israel's ancient rivals (cf. Gen 25:22–23; Ps 137:7). Second, this display of power by the Sovereign God of nations and history was a potential catalyst for spiritual awakening in postexilic Israel (i.e., the people will acknowledge "Great is Yahweh!").

According to Baldwin (1972a: 223), Yehud had best "take note and rejoice in her privileges, instead of bemoaning her lot." Malachi completely shatters any hopes that the Edomites may have had in returning to their traditional homeland and rebuilding their cities and fortifications (confirming the word of Ezekiel the prophet, 35:9). By contrast, Yahweh had permitted Israel to return to its ancestral homeland, establish a restoration community, and rebuild the temple of God. Yahweh's "love" for Israel was abundantly manifest in his temporary rejection of Jacob in the Babylonian Exile and gracious presence in restoring the Hebrews in the land of covenant promise (Zech 1:15–17). On the other hand, God's "hate" for Edom was made starkly evident in his perpetual rejection of Esau's heirs and the desolation of their native land (Jer 49:13).

Using Edom as a foil for Israel, the author exploits the literary device of antithesis to contrast the spiritual character of the two nations. On the basis of several OT/HB passages addressed to the Edomites, R. W. Bailey (pp. 9–10) has described that people as "irreligious . . . self-sufficient . . . profane, unrepentant, and without ideals or humility," traits and qualities implicit in their impudent call to rebuild the ruins, foolishly assuming that divine judgment might be canceled by sheer human initiative. On the contrary, Malachi implores postexilic Yehud to humbly recognize that only Yahweh can rebuild his nation. In effect, the prophet simply reminds the community of the theological insight of the psalmist, who acknowledged that it is Yahweh who must "build the house" and "guard the city" (Ps 127:1; cf. TDOT 2:173, "If God tears down, no one can rebuild without his help").

This marked difference between the "loved" and "hated" of Yahweh extended even to their proverbial epithets: Edom became the "Territory of Evil" and "The People Cursed by Yahweh Perpetually," while postexilic Yehud is called "The Holy Land" (Zech 2:12) and "The Holy Mountain" (Zech 8:3). Israel had experienced the covenant love of Yahweh but sadly did not recognize it in the fall of Edom nor appreciate it as the handiwork of God. The postexilic community had become like their ancestors who forgot the deeds of God (Ps 78:7–8). By calling the people to consider a comparison of the historical experiences of Edom and Israel, Malachi seeks to jog the community's memory and awaken their collective consciousness to the reality of Yahweh's unfailing love (Ps 77:8, 10–12; cf. Craigie [1985: 227]). Furthermore, the restoration community can have confidence in Malachi's prophetic word because God had demonstrated the utter reliability of his revelation in fulfilling the pronouncements of his servants Jeremiah (49:7–22) and Ezekiel (35:1–15).

According to Cresson (p. 148), impious Edom became a symbol of the hostile world and a token equated with the enemies of Israel and her God. Mason (1990: 240) incorrectly intuits that the issue in Mal 1:2–5 is not "some supposed historical event, such as the incursion of the Nabateans"; rather the thrust of the first disputation is a "general eschatological promise that God would overthrow all powers opposed to his rule."

While such violent eschatological forecasts are in keeping with the tenor of the postexilic prophets (e.g., Hag 2:22; Zech 9:1–8), Mason too hastily jettisons the historical for the symbolic. Given the context of Malachi's oracles (a recently founded restoration community characterized by disillusionment, despair, and apathy), yet another hollow and toothless prophecy about Yahweh's future judgment of the godless nations would do little to bolster morale or inspire covenant faith. No, it's the event of Edom's downfall (perhaps coupled with the "shaking of nations" when the Greeks and Persians battled at Marathon) recently witnessed but misinterpreted by postexilic Yehud that lends concrete reality to Malachi's message of Yahweh's love and a pressing urgency to his call to repent. The prophet's rebuttal to the people's refutation of Yahweh's love could be countered effectively only by "front page news" so to speak — EDOM HAS FALLEN!

If the first outcome of the prophetic declaration concluding that this thesis disputation is the destruction of Edom (the leitmotif of Ezekiel 35 according to Baldwin [1972a: 223]), then the second desired outcome of Malachi's declaration constitutes the leitmotif of the entire book: acknowledge Yahweh as the God of the covenant and behave accordingly by offering him right worship and by practicing social justice. The wordplay with *rā'â* in 1:5 ("then your eyes will see . . .") and 3:18 ("then once again you will see . . .") seems to be one of logical consequence. Yahweh has begun to separate the righteous from the wicked in his judgment of Edom. Now as the restoration community responds appropriately to God in covenant renewal and obedience to his law, they will truly experience the means by which Yahweh discriminates between the righteous and wicked in the long-awaited realization of abundant blessing associated with divine favor.

Interpreters disagree as to exactly what Yahweh's judgment of Edom will prompt the restoration community to say in response to this evidence of God's sovereignty. Either Yahweh will be proclaimed as "great *beyond* the territory of Israel," or he will be lauded as "great *over* the territory of Israel." Commentators opting for the understanding "beyond" do so on the basis of the universal character of Yahweh's rule as espoused in Mal 1:11, 14 (so Glazier-McDonald [1987a: 31]; Petersen [1995: 167]; cf. JPSV, NAB, NEB, NIV, NJB, NRSV—all read "beyond").

The usual meaning of *mē'al,* "above" or "over," is preferred here (cf. J.M.P. Smith [1912: 23]; von Bulmerincq [1932: 41–42]; and Verhoef [1987: 206]). Ottosson has rightly perceived the "religious" connotations associated with the phrase *gĕbûl yiśrā'ēl* ("territory of Israel," despite his incorrect assessment of Mal 1:5; TDOT 2:366). The boundaries of the national territory of Israel are defined and protected by covenant relationship with Yahweh. Since the identity and relationship of the deity and the people rest directly upon the fate of the land, postexilic Yehud feels little compulsion to affirm Yahweh as sovereign while they languish under the Persian yoke (cf. Deut 28:1 ff.; 30:1 ff.).

The context of the disputation, however, is Yahweh's "love" for Israel and his "hate" for Edom. Rudolph (1976: 254) has noted that this contrast between the two nations is a key factor against the reading "beyond" (though he fails to follow through on the logic of his conclusion). Yahweh can never be extolled as "great beyond the nations" until he is the sovereign of his own people Israel. In point of fact, it was this very relationship between the covenant-granting suzerain and the covenant-keeping vassal that bore witness to Yahweh's sovereignty over the nations (cf. Isa 26:15; 45:4–6). The events in Edom were intended to reassert the truth of numerous citations in Ezekiel to "God making himself known" to Israel and the nations (28:19, 22; 29:6, 9; etc.). Luther's adage (Oswald [1975: 391]) regarding the complainers of Israel in Malachi's first disputation remains apropos: "To be sure, among his own people God always appears weak, caring little for them." It is always the contemporary generation of Hebrews who must acknowledge God's greatness among themselves to maintain his covenant favor (cf. Deut 11:2). Malachi calls postexilic Yehud to make such a proclamation by the demonstration of loyalty to Yahweh and obedience to this covenant stipulations.

III. C. SECOND ORACLE: FAITHLESS PRIESTS REBUKED (1:6–2:9)

1 ⁶"A son honors [his] father, and a servant his master. If I am [your] father, where is my honor? If I am [your] master, where is my respect?" Yahweh of Hosts has said to you, "O priests — despisers of my name." But you say, "How have we despised your name?" ⁷[By] Offering, upon my altar, defiled food! But you say, "How have we defiled you?" When you say, "The table of Yahweh is despicable." ⁸"And when you present a blind [animal] for sacrifice, there is

no evil! Or when you present a crippled or diseased [animal], there is no evil! Bring it to your governor! Will he be pleased with you or grant you favor?" Yahweh of Hosts has said.

⁹"And now, [earnestly] entreat the favor of God, so that he may be gracious to us! From your hand this [thing] has come. Will he accept any of you?" Yahweh of Hosts has said. ¹⁰"Oh that one from among you might shut the doors, so that you would not kindle fire on my altar in vain! I take no delight in you," Yahweh of Hosts has said. "Indeed, I will not accept [any] offering from your hand. ¹¹Indeed, from the rising of the sun to its setting, 'Great' is my name among the nations. And everywhere incense is being offered to my name, even a pure offering. For 'Great' is my name among the nations," Yahweh of Hosts has said. ¹²But you are profaning it when you say, "The table of the Lord is defiled, and its fruit, its food, is despised." ¹³And you say, "What weariness!" "And you sniff at it," Yahweh of Hosts has said. "You bring stolen or crippled or diseased [animals] — and so you bring the offering. Shall I accept it from your hand?" Yahweh has said.

¹⁴"Accursed is the cheat who has a male in his flock, and he vows but sacrifices a blemished [animal] to the Lord. For I am a great king," Yahweh of Hosts has said, "and my name is revered among the nations."

2 ¹"And now, this charge to you, O priests! ²If you will not listen, and if you will not lay it to heart to give glory to my name," Yahweh of Hosts has said, "then, I will let loose the curse upon you, and I will curse your blessings. Indeed, I have already cursed it because you do not lay it to heart. ³See! I am rebuking your seed, and I will spread offal upon your faces — offal of your feasts. And so he will lift you up to it!"

⁴"Then you will know that I [myself] have delivered this charge to you, in order to revive my covenant with Levi," Yahweh of Hosts has said. ⁵"My covenant was with him, life [itself] and peace [itself]; and I gave them to him. [One of] reverence, and revered me; and he stood in awe before my name. ⁶True instruction was in his mouth, and no deceit was found on his lips. In peace and uprightness he walked with me, and he turned many from iniquity."

⁷"Surely from the lips of the priest they safeguard knowledge, and Torah they seek from his mouth, since he is the messenger of Yahweh of Hosts. ⁸But you yourselves have turned from the way. You have caused many to stumble over Torah. You have corrupted the covenant of Levi," Yahweh of Hosts has said. ⁹"So indeed, I myself will make you despised and abased before all the people. Inasmuch as you are not observing my ways, and [you are not] acting graciously in [matters of] Torah."

INTRODUCTION

The literary form of *prophetic disputation* persists throughout the book of Malachi (see the discussion of literary form in the introduction to III. B. First Oracle above). The second dispute is composed of two distinct speech-acts with Yahweh the subject of the first (1:6–14) and the Levitical priesthood the subject of the second (2:1–9). Variations in the standard three-part disputation pattern of declaration, refutation, and rebuttal may be observed, including the use of the conditional clause in announcing the declaration of the first and second speech-acts ("If I am [your] father . . . , 1:6; ". . . if you will not listen . . . ," 2:1), the curse to conclude the rebuttal of the first speech-act ("Accursed be the cheat," 1:14), and the substitution of the example of Levi for the refutation section of the second speech-act (2:4–7).

According to Watts (1987a: 376), two *dialogical/expressive* speech-acts comprise the second disputation (1:6–14 and 2:1–9). The first (1:6–14) is intended to persuade the audience that Yahweh is truly Lord. The second (2:1–9) both warns and threatens the priests of Yehud for their failure to honor Yahweh as Lord, functioning as the verdict passed on the offense(s) described in 1:6–14 (cf. Nogalski [1993b: 195]).

The paragraph divisions of the MT delineate three major literary units in the book of Malachi, differing somewhat from the sixfold disputation outline I have employed (identifying 1:6–2:9 as the second oracle). The initial pericope recognized by the MT highlights the relationship of the Levitical priesthood to Yahweh's covenant (1:2–2:9), with two subunits demarcated (1:1–13 and 1:14–2:9). This reading of Malachi follows the majority of commentators acknowledging 1:2–5 as a distinct literary unit and discerning further macrostructure in the pericope on the basis of the vocative, "O priests" (*hakkōhănîm*, 1:6; 2:1). In addition, microstructure is evidenced in the repetition of the emphatic adverb ʿattâ in 1:9 (with messenger formula concluding v 8) and the emphatic adverb kî (v 11, with the messenger formula concluding v 13). The curse pronounced in verse 14 stands as a sort of colophon concluding the first subunit of the disputation. Paragraphing in the second literary subunit (2:1–9) is less clear, but the *waw*-conversive of *wîdaʿtem* (2:4) and the disjunctive *waw* of *wěʾattem* (2:8) seem to mark new divisions in the text.

Recent studies have demonstrated the literary cohesion of the second disputation, emphasizing the intertextuality of the pericope, whether composed by the prophet himself (cf. Rudolph [1976: 262]; Redditt [1994: 244]) or redacted by some clever "prophetic writer" well versed in these earlier oracular traditions (so Utzschneider [1989: 17]; cf. Nogalski [1993b: 195–96]; Petersen [1995: 176–77]). For example, Utzschneider (1989: 97–102), in an attempt to establish the prophetic phenomenon of *Schriftprophetie* (the prophetic interpretation of earlier written traditions by later writers/editors), isolates numerous "catchwords" in Mal 1:6–2:9 from various OT/HB "source texts." More striking (and convincing!) is Fishbane's (1983; 1985: 332–34) analysis of Mal 1:6–2:9 as a postexilic example of *haggadic* exegesis of Num 6:23–27. Fishbane (1985: 334) catalogs the key terms shared in the two texts and then notes that the prophet has taken the contents of the priestly blessing and ironically contraposed them, "transforming the sacerdotal blessing into a curse . . . an anti-blessing, a veritable contrapuntal inversion of the sound and sense of the official Priestly Blessing simultaneously performed in the shrine."

The integrity of portions of the second disputation has been challenged, notably 1:11–14; the unusual theme of the universal worship of Yahweh is considered intrusive, given the immediate context of the prophet's message (e.g., Horst [1954: 261, 265]; Sellin [1930: 594]; van der Woude [1986: 66]; Utzschneider [1989: 84–87]; although Elliger [1950: 189] questioned the originality of 2:2, 7 in addition to 1:11–14). Those upholding the authenticity of the passage consider the section an eschatological projection (e.g., Baldwin [1972b: 117–24]; Mason [1977: 144–45]; Rudolph [1976: 262]; Glazier-McDonald 1987a: 60–61; cf. Nogalski [1993b: 194–95 n. 46]; Petersen [1995: 183–85]). Redditt (1994: 244) mediates the debate by suggesting that originally three separate sayings of the prophet (1:6–10; 1:11–14; 2:1–9) were united around the theme of "the name of Yahweh" to form the second disputation. The repetition of key lexical items unifying the two literary subunits of the second dispute (Mason [1977: 144–45]; Glazier-McDonald [1987a: 47]; cf. Petersen [1995: 185 n. 35] who suggests that the deliberate repetition serves to show that the prophet's dialogue with his audience is not moving in a productive direction) and the recursive nature of Malachi's disputations argue forcefully for the integrity of the pericope (cf. Wendland, Hendrix; Peckham [1993: 794–95]). Minor textual problems noted in both the *BHK* and *BHS* are addressed separately in the NOTES below.

Like the other oracles of Malachi, the second disputation features pseudodialogue ("but you say . . . ," 1:6) and a rhetorical question (e.g., "Shall I accept it from your hand?" 1:13) as part of the "banter" between the prophet and the Levitical priesthood. The incorporation of exclamatory words such as *hinnēh* ("See!" 2:3) and *ʿattâ* ("Now . . . ," 1:9; 2:1) and the utilization of the vocative (*hakkōhănîm* ["O priests"], 1:6; 2:1) contribute to the hortatory style of the two speech-acts. In addition, the foil created between Yahweh and the priests by means of first-person and second-person suffixed pronouns intensifies the confrontational tone of dispute (e.g., 1:6, *lākem* ["to you *priests*"] and *šĕmî* ["my name *Yahweh*"]). Finally, literary devices abound in the dispute, among them, anacoenosis (i.e., an appeal to others based on a shared common cause, 1:6), taunting irony bordering on sarcasm (1:9), satire (1:14, cf. Jemielity [1992: 184]), and the encomium of the "ideal" priest Levi (2:4–7).

Both speech-acts of the second dispute are addressed to the "priests" of Yehud (1:6; 2:1). Mason (1977: 148; 1990: 244), among others (cf. Hanson [1979: 265–69]; [1986: 283]), contends that Malachi differentiates between "priest" and "Levite." According to this analysis, the prophet rebukes the Zadokite/Aaronite priesthood in 2:8–9, not the Levitical pedagogues. O'Brien (1990: 143–44), however, has demonstrated convincingly that Malachi uses the terms "priest" and "Levite" synonymously and that "the book demonstrates no evidences of acrimony between the groups described by these terms" (cf. *ABD* 1:4–5; 4:305–9). The privileged position of this audience explains both the lengthy speeches of the dispute (18 vv, the longest of the book's six disputations) and the biting tone and harsh language of the prophet's rebuke. The Levitical Priests had failed in discharging the duties of their sacred trust — teaching Israel the law of Yahweh (cf. Deut 33:10). By default, the people of Yahweh were led astray for lack of the knowledge of God (cf. Hos 4:6).

NOTES

1:6. *bēn yĕkabbēd 'āb.* The verb *kbd* means "honor" in the Piel stem (*CHAL:* 150). The simple prefix conjugation is a *progressive nonperfective,* indicating an ongoing situation (WO'C § 31.3a, b). The combination of *bēn* ("son") and *'āb* ("father") depict a familial relationship in which the expression of the social value of "ascribed honor" is standard protocol (see Pilch [1991: 49–70] on "honor" and "shame" in the biblical world).

Glazier-McDonald (1987a: 49) notes the alliteration with *'alep* and the assonance with *hiriq-yôd* in verse 6bc, suggesting it functions as an "intensifier" in forcing the issue to the forefront of the audience's consciousness (*w'm-'b 'ny 'yh kbdy w'm-'dwnym 'ny 'yh mwr'y*). The entire expression is an example of *anacoenosis,* or an appeal to others based upon a common interest or cause. Interestingly, the Book of the Twelve opens and closes with Israel portrayed as an "ungrateful son" (Hos 11:1; Mal 1:6; cf. Baldwin [1972a: 225]; Watts [1987a: 379]).

wĕ'ebed 'ădōnāyw. The conjunctive *waw* ("and," WO'C § 39.2.5) joins the parallel lines of the couplet (v 6a + b = ABC//A'C').

The masculine noun *'ebed* is used here in the sense of a "subordinate" or a "servant in a dependent position of trust," not as a "slave in bondage" (*CHAL:* 262). The first appendix (3:22 [4:4]) parades Moses as the supreme example of a true "servant" of Yahweh (see the discussion of *'abdî* in the NOTES).

The word *'ādôn* means "lord, master" and in context suggests a "superior, suzerain" or even a "sovereign" (cf. KBL 1:12–13; see the discussion of *'ădōnîm* below). The third-person suffixed pronoun ("*his* master/lord") personalizes the dependent relationship (and perhaps should be understood with *'āb* ["*his* father," so Arabic, Syr, and Ethiopic] as a type of backward or inverted gapping; cf. WO'C § 11.4.3).

The gapping (or ellipsis) of the verb *yĕkabbēd* (or *yîrā'* ["fears"] following the LXXS [*phobēthēsetai*], and Jerome [*CChr* 76A:906, *timebit*]; cf. S. R. Driver [1906: 302]; Rudolph [1976: 251]) in the second clause ("and a servant respects/fears his master") is a poetic feature in the OT/HB (O'Connor [1980: 122–27]; note the gapping of the verb *kabbēd* in Prov 3:9). Unlike Glazier-McDonald (1987a: 49–50), who assumes the poetic nature of the entire disputation on the basis of isolated features like verb gapping, it seems better to recognize verse 6ab as the citation of a common folk saying or proverb (perhaps even a priestly saying based on the decalogue, Exod 20:12; Deut 5:16; cf. *ABD* 2:822–23; Ogden and Deutsch [1987: 82]). This would explain the poetic structure of the isolated synonymous couplet in verse 6ab embedded in the "oracular prose" of Malachi (see I. C. 3. Genre above). By appealing to a popular traditional saying (the truth of which cannot be challenged, cf. Mason [1977: 143]), the prophet artfully broaches the topic of the dispute — deference for the "greater" by the "lesser" (and what a stroke of irony if Malachi indicts the priests with their own teaching!). See further the discussion of *kābēd* in TDOT 7:13–22.

wĕ'im-'āb 'ānî. The coordinating *waw* is understood variously as a conjunctive *waw* ("and," NJB), a conjunctive-sequential *waw* ("then," NAB, NRSV), or more appropriately as an epexegetical *waw* ("now," JPSV; cf. WO'C § 39.2.4).

The hypothetical particle *'im* ("if") introduces a (verbless) *real* conditional clause (WO'C § 38.2).

The two words *'āb* ("father") and *'ānî* ("I") form a verbless clause of identification (WO'C § 8.4.1a). The masculine noun *'āb* ("father") serves as a title for God as the ideological and spiritual progenitor of Israel (KBL 1:2). Here "father" is indefinite as a generic noun of class (WO'C § 13.8b). The independent pronoun *'ānî* functions as the predicate of the verbless clause and conveys a "selective-exclusive" sense emphasizing the subject (Yahweh as divine father, WO'C § 16.3.3b; cf. *TDOT* 1:17–18). The literal but awkward "If [your] father *am* I" is rephrased inverting the Hebrew word order in the English versions ("If I *am* [your] father"). The insertion of the personal pronoun "your" compensates for the (omitted but) implied audience "Israel" addressed by the prophet. See further the discussion of *'āb* ("father") in the NOTES for 2:10; 3:7, 24 [4:6] below.

'ayyēh kĕbôdî. The interrogative *'ayyēh* introduces a question of circumstance serving as the apodosis of the preceding conditional clause ("if I am [your] father, where *then* . . . ?"; cf. WO'C § 18.1a, 18.4). The question is ironical, much like those of Zech 1:5, where the prophet demands the attention of the listener by raising an issue rhetorically (cf. Meyers and Meyers [1987: 95]). See further the discussion of the locative interrogative *'ayyēh* in the NOTES for 2:17 below.

The masculine noun *kābôd* may mean "distinction, respect, honor" ascribed to an authority figure (e.g., a "father") in nontheological contexts (*CHAL*: 151; *TDOT* 7:27). In theological contexts like that of Mal 1:6, *kābôd* has the connotation of giving honor to Yahweh (cf. *TDOT* 7:27–28). The citation was no doubt intended as an allusion to the decalogue (*kabbēd 'et-'ābîkā wĕ'et-'immekā*, ["Honor your father and mother . . ."], Exod 20:12). The word occurs elsewhere in the Haggai-Zechariah-Malachi corpus in Hag 2:3, 7, 9; Zech 2:9 [5], 12 [8]; Mal 2:2 with the meaning "splendor" or "glory" (cf. Meyers and Meyers [1987: 50, 54]). The first-person suffix pronoun "*my* honor" continues the contrast established between Yahweh and Yehud with the pronouns "I" and "you" (cf. Ps 4:3, *'ad-meh kĕbôdî likĕlimmâ*, ["How long will my honor be shamed?"]). See further *kābôd* in 2:2 below.

'ădōnîm. The masculine noun *'ādôn* may refer to an earthly "lord" or "master," a royal figure like a "king," or even to "God" himself (*CHAL*: 4; cf. *TDOT* 1:59–72). The plural *'ădōnîm* only rarely refers to a single individual (cf. 2 Kgs 22:17; 2 Chr 18:16; Isa 19:4). The synonymous parallelism with *'āb* ("father") requires the singular meaning "lord, master" (cf. the curious plural *bĕ'ālāyw* in the similar proverb of Isa 1:3). The form is usually understood as an intensive or majestic plural, with God the implied subject of the prophet's comparison (e.g., Verhoef [1987: 208 n. 2]; cf. WO'C § 7.4.3). See further the discussion of *hā'ādôn* in the NOTES for 3:1 below.

môrā'î. The *maqtal* noun *môrā'* occurs in Mal 1:6 and 2:5 and elsewhere in the MT only in Gen 9:2; Deut 4:34; 11:25; 26:8; 34:12; Pss 9:21 [20]; 76:12 [11]; Isa 8:12, 13; and Jer 32:21 (cf. *TDOT* 6:293). The word may mean "fear, terror" or "awe" depending upon context (KBL 2:560; cf. Ogden and Deutsch [1987: 83] on "fear" of Yahweh as both "respect" and "dread"). Fuhs explains *môrā'* as "terror instilled by God" (distinguished from terror evoked by God's presence) with expectations for "obedience to the revealed will of God" (*TDOT* 6:303, 313; 7:31). Because the context presupposes Israel's covenant relationship with Yahweh, the English renderings "fear" (NEB), "reverence" (JPSV, NAB), and "awe" (NJB) are preferred to the weaker "respect" (NIV, NRSV; cf. Ps 76:12 [11]; Isa 8:13).

'āmar YHWH ṣĕbā'ôt lākem. According to Holladay (1986: 82), the perfect tense ("has said") is preferable in rendering *'āmar.* The picture is that of the prophet repeating a message heard while standing in the divine assembly (as opposed to an utterance of the moment prompted by the sudden possession of God's spirit). The messenger formula (*'āmar YHWH* [*ṣĕbā'ôt*]) is repeated eleven times in the second disputation (1:6, 8, 9, 10, 11, 13 [2x], 14; 2:2, 4, 8), ironically emphasizing the divine authority vested in this word to the priests (who should have recognized it immediately!). See also discussion of *'āmar YHWH* in the NOTES for 1:2 and 1:13.

The *datival* preposition *lamed* marks the indirect object of the verb of speaking (*'āmar,* cf. WO'C § 11.2.10d). The construction of the messenger formula with *lākem* is unique to v 6 in the disputes of Malachi, perhaps emphasizing the culpability of the priesthood for the plight of Yehud.

hakkōhănîm bôzê šĕmî. The *hē'* affixed to *kōhănîm* ("priests") marks a definite addressee (in the vocative, "O priests"). The MT understands the construction as the definite article (cf. WO'C § 13.5.2c; JM § 137g); but given the context, it is possible that the particle *ha[-]* represents a distinct vocative marker like the Ugaritic *la* and the Arabic *yâ* (cf. *UT* § 12.6; Dahood [1965: 21]).

The "priests" (*kōhănîm*) are the target audience of Malachi's second disputation. This (plural) noun occurs in Malachi only in the prophet's second oracle (1:6; 2:1, 7). O'Brien (1990: 146–47) has demonstrated that Malachi uses the term *kōhēn* ("priest") in an inclusive sense, making no distinction between priest and Levite in rank or function (i.e., the dual roles of proper sacrifice and proper teaching; see Meyers and Meyers [1987: 384–85] on "the enhanced status and enlarged responsibilities of the priesthood . . . in the postmonarchic world of the restoration"). Like his earlier contemporaries Haggai and Zechariah, Malachi understood the priests collectively as the "national leaders" of Yehud and the logical complement to the citizenry of the province (Meyers and Meyers [1987: 387]; note the similar inclusive understanding of the term "priest" [*kōhēn*] in Hag 2:11, 12, 13; Zech 7:3, 5). See also *kōhēn, TDOT* 7:60–75.

The verb *bzh* means "to despise" (KBL 1:117) and occurs in the Haggai-Zechariah-Malachi corpus only in Mal 1:6 [2x], 7, 12; 2:9. The word connotes "breach of covenant" and "disloyalty" in a "sacral-legal" relationship, much as it does in Ezek 16:59 (*TDOT* 2:62–63; cf. Ezek 17:16, 18–19). Given the juxtaposition of Jacob and Esau in the opening disputation (1:2–5), the prophet no doubt alludes to the episode recorded in the traditions of the Hebrew patriarchs when Esau "despised" (*bzh*) his birthright and sold it to Jacob for a meal (Gen 25:34). The priests of Yehud, like Esau, have despised their "birthright" (the covenant with Levi, 2:4) and are in danger of forfeiting their position of privilege and ministry (2:3). Even more, they jeopardize the standing of the entire community before Yahweh because of their misteaching (2:8). On the structure of the audience's speech (*wa'ămartem bammeh bāzînû 'et-šĕmekā* ["but you say, 'How have we despised your name'?"]), see the discussion of *wa'ămartem bammâ 'ăhabtānû* in the NOTES for 1:2 above.

The "name" (*šēm*) of Yahweh is a key theme in the second dispute, occurring eight times in the oracle (elsewhere in the book only in Mal 3:16, 20 [4:2]). The word "name" is a "distinguishing mark" for establishing one's identity in the biblical world (*ABD* 4:1002). Here the term *šēm* ("name") represents the essence of God's being, especially his sovereignty, love, and faithfulness to Israel as revealed in his covenant name "Yahweh" (and perhaps equated with the "Temple presence" of Yahweh; cf. Ogden and Deutsch [1987: 83] on the development of God's immanence and transcendence in Israelite theology). The priests have shunned the very person of Yahweh by despising his name. The expression "despisers of my name" (*bôzê šĕmî*) stands in contrast to the phrases "those contemplating his name" (*ûlĕḥōšĕbê šĕmô*, 3:16) and "the fearers of my name" (*yir'ê šĕmî*, 3:20 [4:2]). The first-person suffixed pronoun ("*my* name") accents the unfolding contrast between Yahweh and the residents of Yehud and further establishes the confrontational tone of the disputational form of the oracles. See further the discussion of *šĕmô* in the NOTES for 3:16 below.

7. *maggîšîm 'al-mizbĕḥî*. The opening clause of v 7 answers, in specific terms, the reported question posed by the priests in v 6 ("How have we despised your name?"). The priesthood of Yehud has demonstrated its disdain for Yahweh in the discharging of their duties associated with the Temple sacrifices. The gapping of the subject "priests" (assumed from v 6) adds to the force of the prophet's indictment (cf. GKC § 116s; the English versions invariably supply the subject "you" [JPSV, NEB, NIV] or the instrumental preposition "by" [NAB, NJB, NRSV]). The participle describes an ongoing state of affairs involving habitual or repeated action (WO'C § 37.6d). The verse introduces "the scandalous conditions in which the priests offer sacrifice" (Glazier-McDonald [1987a: 50]). On the Hiphil participle *maggîšîm* see the NOTES for 2:12 (*ûmaggîš*) and 3:3 (*maggîšê*) below.

The preposition *'al* denotes a simple locational sense, "upon" (WO'C 11.2.13b). The word "altar" (*mizbēaḥ*) occurs in Mal 1:7, 10; 2:13 and elsewhere in the Haggai-Zechariah-Malachi corpus only in Zech 9:15; 14:20. Like the citation in Zech 14:20, this reference to Yahweh's altar has no modifier and may refer to the bronze altar of sacrifice or the altar of incense (cf. Meyers and Meyers [1993: 483]). Because sacrificial animals are specifically mentioned in the larger context of the second disputation (vv 8, 14), it seems likely that the prophet intends the bronze altar of sacrifice located in the east courtyard anterior to the sanctuary. The suffixed personal pronoun ("*my* altar") is a *genitive of inalienable possession*, signifying that the bronze altar of sacrifice belongs intrinsically to Yahweh — not to the priests who serve there (WO'C § 9.5.1h, 16.4d). See further the discussion of *mizbaḥ YHWH* in the NOTES for 2:13 below.

leḥem mĕgō'āl. The noun *leḥem* may refer literally to "bread" (*CHAL*: 175) but more likely represents any "foodstuffs" offered as a sacrifice to God as a synecdoche of species (Cashdan [1948: 339]; cf. Num 28:2). The context of Malachi indicates that this "food" is primarily that of animal sacrifices (v 8). The only other occurrence of *leḥem* in the Haggai-Zechariah-Malachi corpus is the reference to sacrificial meat in Hag 2:12. Meyers and Meyers (1987: 55–56) identify the sacrifices in questions as the *šĕlāmîm* (peace) offerings, freewill votives intended "to secure Yahweh's blessing upon the produce of the land, the flocks, and herds, and the people" (cf. Lev 7:15–16). Malachi may be referring to the *šĕlāmîm* offerings as well, because Yehud still languishes under an agricultural blight (3:11–12).

The Pual participle *mĕgō'āl* occurs only in Mal 1:6, 12 in the MT. The verb *g'l* (II) is primarily a LBH term and means "to be ritually defiled" in the Pual stem (KBL 1:169–70). The word may refer to the "soiling" of the hands or clothing with blood as a result of committing a violent crime (e.g., Isa 59:3; 63:3; Lam 4:14; Zeph 3:1; cf. Roberts [1991: 212]). The verb also signifies a ritual defilement, pollution, contamination that disqualifies or renders a person religiously unfit (e.g., priests without the proper genealogical pedigree, Ezra 2:62; Neh 7:64; cf. Petersen's [1995: 178–79] discussion of *g'l*), or an object (e.g., food offerings, Mal 1:6, 12) for the Temple cultus (cf. Redditt [1995: 164], "unacceptable, unfit"). As in Lam 4:13–14, Malachi implies that the entire community has become defiled as a result of priestly impropriety in the offering of Temple sacrifices (cf. Provan [1991: 118]). Here the participle is used adjectivally (cf. WO'C § 37.4).

gē'alnûkā. The priests' reported response is one of surprise and (feigned?) resentment, "How have we defiled you?" The verb *g'l* (II) in the Piel stem means "to pollute, desecrate" (KBL 1:170). The suffixing form conveys the sense of simple past time or the *recent perfective* (employing the auxiliary "has/have"; WO'C § 30.5.1b).

The *BHS* proposes emending the MT *gē'alnûkā* to *gē'alnûhû* on the basis of the LXX (*ēlisgēsamen autoús*, e.g., J.M.P. Smith [1912: 27]; NRSV). The argument that the shift in person better agrees with the antecedent of the verb ("the altar of Yahweh") is compromised by the LXX *autoús* (the third-person masculine plural form suggests Hebrew -*hem* not -*hû*). The emendation is unnecessary as Glazier-McDonald (1987a: 50–51), Verhoef (1987: 216), and Petersen (1995: 176 n. b, 179) have noted; the reported speech of the priests (in the form of a question, v 7) is recursive, harking back to the prophet's charge against the priests for "despising" Yahweh's name (v 6).

be'ĕmorkem šulḥan YHWH. The Qal infinitive construct + the preposition *bêt* denote the temporal proximity of events ("*when* you say . . . ," WO'C § 36.2.2b). On the verb *'āmar* see the discussion of *wa'ămartem* in the NOTES on verse 2 above.

The construct-genitive phrase *šulḥan YHWH*/['*ădōnāy*] ("the table of Yahweh/the Lord") is unique to Mal 1:7, 12 in the MT. Given the reference to bloody sacrifices (v 8), the expression is not a reference to the "Table for the Bread of Presence" (an important piece of the sanctuary furniture, Exod 25:30). Rather, the phrase stands in synonymous parallelism with "my altar" (*mizbĕḥî*, cf. Ezek 44:16; so Rudolph [1976: 261]). The "altar" is likely the altar of burnt offering located in the east courtyard between the gate and the sanctuary proper (although J.M.P. Smith [1912: 27] suggests that the general expression "the table of Yahweh" refers to both the "show-bread" table and the altar of burnt offering, Baldwin [1972a: 226] equates the phrase with slaughtering tables provided at the gates of the inner court).

nibzeh hû'. The occurrence of the Niphal participle *nibzeh* three times in the dispute (1:6, 12; 2:9) and the repetition of the verb *bzh* in the second oracle (1:6 [2x]) mark the word as one of several key vocabulary items establishing tone and theme. The Niphal stem has a passive sense in that "the subject is in the *state* of being acted upon" (WO'C § 23.2.2), while the participial predicate emphasizes a "durative circumstance" (WO'C § 37.6b). The form *nibzeh* means "despised, despicable," but note the array of (sometimes interpretive) renderings in the English versions (KJV, NIV, "is contemptible"; NEB, NRSV, "may be despised"; JPSV, "can be treated with scorn"; NJB, "deserves no respect"; NAB, "may be slighted").

The third-person (masculine singular) independent pronoun *hû'* ("he/*it*") has a nominative function (as a surrogate for *šulḥan YHWH* ["table of Yahweh"], cf. WO'C § 16.3.1a) in the participial clause of identification (WO'C § 8.4.1). The subject pronoun completes the alternating pattern of subjects constructed in verses 6–7 ("my name" [Yahweh]//"altar"//"you" [Yahweh]//"table" [= altar]).

8. *wĕkî-taggišûn*. The conjunctive *waw* coordinates the general indictment (v 7) with specific illustrations of the charge (v 8), but is usually left untranslated (cf. WO'C § 39.2.5). The clausal adverb *kî* has a temporal sense ("when," so JPSV, NAB, NIV, NJB, NRSV; but NEB [following LXX] = conditional, "if") and introduces a concrete example of how the priests (continue to) despise Yahweh's altar. See *CHAL*: 155 on the overlap between the temporal and conditional understanding of *kî*.

The Hiphil prefixing conjugation *taggišûn* is a *nonperfective of capability* (or a real modal), denoting the subject's capacity for performing the action expressed by the verbal root (WO'C § 31.4c). According to Waltke and O'Connor (§ 31.7.1), the paragogic *nun* marks "contrastivity" (i.e., exception to normal practice). This being the case, the prophet uses the form to punctuate the fact that the priests discern no malpractice in this particular deviation from normal expectation (i.e., offering blemished sacrificial animals in lieu of healthy ones). On the verb *ngš*, see the *maggîšîm* in verse 7 above, *ûmaggîš* and *maggîšê* in 2:12 and 3:3 below.

'iwwēr lizbōaḥ. The legislation of Deuteronomy (15:21; cf. 17:1) expressly forbids the offering of blind animals as a sacrifice to Yahweh (*'iwwēr*, "blind in one or both eyes"; *CHAL*: 268). The purpose of the suppliant in so doing is obvious, seeking personal advantage (or "profit," cf. Mal 3:14) by offering an animal of impaired economic value (von Rad [1966: 108]; cf. Petersen [1995: 180] on Malachi's dependence upon Deuteronomy here).

The preposition *lamed* marks the indirect-object, here a dative of goal or objective (WO'C § 11.2.10d). The construction implies that the prophet is referring to animal sacrifice generally and not specifically to the "firstling" offering of Deut 15:21. The Qal infinitive construct *zēbōaḥ* is used as a cultic term for "sacrifice," not "profane slaughter" (cf. Mayes [1979: 225, 227–28, 253–54]). See further the discussion of the verb *zbḥ* in the NOTES on verse 14 below.

'*ên rāʿ*. The blunt phrase, unique to Mal 1:8 in the MT, is ambiguous. Helpful parallel constructions include, *wĕʾēn lēb* ("without heart [sense]," Jer 5:21; Hos 7:11) and [*wĕ*]'*ên dābār* ("there is nothing," Num 20:19; 1 Sam 20:21; McCarter [1980: 338]).

The ancient versions (LXX, V, Syr, Arabic), along with many English versions, interpret the construction as an interrogative (e.g., NAB, "is it not evil?"; NIV, NJB, NRSV, "is that/this not wrong?"). See WO'C § 39.3.3b on the negative adverb '*ên*.

Alternately, and more appropriately, the expression may be understood as a sarcastic declaration by the prophet, "there is no evil!" (JPSV, "it doesn't matter!"; NEB, "there is nothing wrong"; cf. Cashdan [1948: 339], "*it is no evil*. In your eyes; in your view of your duties to God"). Given the general attitude of the priests and people of Yehud, Malachi's cryptic words should be understood as a caustic rebuke. The priests have been deliberate in their infringement of the laws governing sacrifice, assuming "the main thing is to perform the sacrificial duties . . . the ritual itself is working *ex opere operato*" (Verhoef [1987: 218]; cf. Rudolph [1976: 257], "*macht das nichts aus!*"; Glazier-McDonald [1987a: 44], "*declaring it* not bad!"; Petersen [1995: 174], "and think there is nothing wrong").

The deliberate echo of Deut 17:1 (*kōl dābār rāʿ*, "any evil thing" [i.e., any serious defect]) in the use of the adjective *rāʿ* ("evil") here reminds the priesthood of the covenantal implications of such sacrifices, as they are an abomination (*tô ʿēbâ*) to Yahweh. See further the discussion of *rāʿ* in the NOTES on 2:17 below.

pissēaḥ wĕḥōleh. The "lame" (*pissēaḥ*, CHAL: 294) and the "weak" or "sick" (*ḥōleh*, KBL 1:316–17) are additional animal categories outlawed for ritual sacrifice by the pentateuchal ordinances. The Qal participle from the verbal root *ḥlh* (I) may be understood substantively (WO'C § 37.2) and is used figuratively to depict the people of Israel as weak or ill animals poorly tended by their shepherds (i.e., their leaders) in Ezek 34:4, 16. The terms identifying the types of animals prohibited for sacrifice ('*iwwēr, pissēaḥ, ḥōleh*) are all unique to Malachi in the Haggai-Zechariah-Malachi corpus (Klein [1986: 145] comments that "such carcasses were not even proper for human consumption"). The *phrasal waw* after a negative particle has an alternative force ("or," WO'C § 39.2.1b).

haqrîbēhû nāʾ lĕpeḥātekā. The verb *qrb* in the Hiphil stem means "bring, offer, present" (CHAL: 324). The imperative form is used sarcastically (WO'C § 34.4b). The volitional expression stands as a challenge to the priests of Yehud. They may invalidate the prophetic indictment of "despising Yahweh" by simply making a gift of these blemished sacrificial animals to their earthly governor. Obviously the proposal remains untested, because the priests cannot even entertain the thought of presenting these unfit animals to the governor of Yehud! The suffixed object pronoun (*-hû*, "he/it") refers generally to any one of the three categories of defective sacrificial animals cited by the prophet. According to Waltke and O'Connor (§ 34.7), the particle *nāʾ* is a *logical* rather than a *precative* particle and is better left untranslated. On the verb *qrb*, see further the NOTES on *wĕqā-rabtî* for 3:5 below.

The preposition *lamed* marks the indirect object, a dative of goal or objective ("*to* your governor," WO'C § 11.2.10d). The suffixed possessive pronoun (*-kā*, "*your* governor") establishes a contradistinction between the domains of Yahweh ("*my* altar," v 7) and the people of Yehud ("*your* governor," v 8), insinuating a confusion of loyalties on the part of the Levitical priesthood.

hăyirṣĕkā 'ô hăyiśśā' panêkā. The interrogative *hē'* introduces a *polar question*, and in each case an exclamatory "No!" is the rhetorical answer (WO'C § 40.3b; cf. J.M.P. Smith [1912: 28], "It is most easily understood as a rhetorical question, the answer to which is patent to all"). The verb *rṣh* means "be pleased with, well-disposed toward, favorable to" (*CHAL*: 345) and occurs in Mal 1:8, 10, 13 in the context of accepting (or rejecting!) a sacrifice or gift in the ritual sphere (cf. Petersen [1995: 181], "One ironic speech deserves another").

The prophet Haggai commissioned Zerubbabel and Joshua to rebuild Yahweh's Temple so that he might "be pleased" (*rṣh*) with it (or better, "accept this action," Petersen [1984: 51]; Hag 1:8). Ironically, the Book of the Twelve begins (Hos 8:13) and ends (Mal 1:8, 10, 13) with Yahweh's "displeasure" (*rṣh*) with his people. The LXXS, A, Q (*ei prosdéxetai autó*), and V (*illud*) understand *hăyirṣĕhû* ("will he be pleased with *it*?"; cf. J.M.P. Smith [1912: 28]; NJB). Glazier-McDonald (1987a: 51) correctly recognizes that such an emendation is unnecessary since the inferior quality of the offering has already been established: "Rather, it is a question of how the governor will react to emissaries bearing such gifts" (cf. Petersen [1995: 176 n. c]).

The coordinator *'ô* separates alternatives in the main clauses (WO'C § 39.2.6b). The construction *hăyiśśā' pānêkā* (lit. "will he lift your face") is an idiom for "accepting someone kindly, be favorably disposed toward" (*CHAL*: 246). Verhoef (1987: 219) understands the figure of speech in the sense, "grant a cordial reception to" in Mal 1:8, 9; but the context of formal entreaty of a dignitary suggests that the phrase has a more technical meaning like "grant a favor" (*nāśā'tî pānêkā*, Gen 19:21; note that the purpose of the offerings to Yahweh is basically to secure a blessing upon agricultural production, 3:10). The expression has a pejorative connotation in Mal 2:9, showing partiality or favoritism (cf. Lev 19:15, *lō'-tiśśā' pĕnê-dāl* ["you shall not favor the poor"]).

9. *wĕ 'attâ*. The conjunctive *waw* joins two related clauses (WO'C § 39.2.5). The temporal adverb *'attâ* has a logical force ("you offer [v 8] . . . and *now* [v 9] . . . ," in reference to the sequence of priestly duties in offering the *šĕlāmîm* sacrifice and invoking Yahweh's blessing on the suppliant; WO'C § 39.3.1h). The repetition *wĕ 'attâ* (1:9; 2:1) marks new paragraphs or distinct sections of the prophet's argumentation in the second disputation (cf. WO'C § 39.3.4f).

hallû-nā' pĕnê-'ēl. The Piel imperative *hallû* means to "appease, flatter" (*CHAL*: 316–17; JPSV, NAB, NIV, NRSV, "implore"; NEB, "placate"; NJB, "try pleading"). The combination of the verb *ḥlh* (I) + the noun *pānîm* is an idiom belonging to "the religious language of the laity," designating "a gesture of respect, of worship, and of submission, performed with the purpose of seeking favor" (*TDOT* 4:409). Yahweh is always the object of the *ḥlh* (I) + *pānîm* idiom, but the exact relationship of the derived meaning ("entreat the favor of," [BDB: 318]) and the literal meaning associated with *ḥlh* (I) "be weak, sick" ("mollify the face," Meyers and Meyers [1987: 384]) remains uncertain (cf. *TDOT* 4:407–9).

Elsewhere in the Haggai-Zechariah-Malachi corpus, the expression *lĕḥallôt* *'et-pānîm* occurs in Zech 7:2, 8:21, 22. Theologically, the idiom conveys the important idea that "an official human entreaty can persuade God to respond to the petitioner in some way" (Meyers and Meyers [1987: 384]). Petersen (1995: 181) understands the construction ("seek God's favor") as a sort of laic "call to worship," an activity that may or may not involve sacrificial ritual. The formula occurs 16x in the MT (Exod 32:11; 1 Sam 13:12; 1 Kgs 13:6 [2x]; 2 Kgs 13:4; 2 Chr 33:12; Job 11:19; Pss 45:13 [12]; 119:58; Prov 19:6; Jer 26:19; Dan 9:13; Zech 7:2; 8:21, 22; Mal 1:9), but the closest parallel to Mal 1:9 (perhaps not coincidentally?) is 1 Kgs 13:6 (*ḥal-nā' 'et-pĕnê-YHWH 'ĕlōhêkā*, "entreat the favor of Yahweh your God" [an ominous commission for the priesthood given the outcome of the episode for the "man of God" from Judah]).

There is a certain irony in the wordplay of *ḥallû* (v 9) with *ḥōleh* (v 8), in that the priests attempt to "placate" Yahweh with "sick" animals (all of which sickens Yahweh, v 11)! The construct-genitive *pĕnê-'ēl* ("the face of God") calls to mind the patriarchal tradition of Jacob's wrestling match prompting a divine blessing at Peniel (*pĕnî'ēl*, Gen 32:31 [30]), because Yehud seeks a similar divine blessing. On the *logical* particle *nā'* see the discussion of *haqrîbēhû nā'* in verse 8 above (cf. Verhoef [1987: 220], the particle *nā'* strengthens the imperative "in the sense of ridicule").

wîḥānēnû. The second clause in the sequence *imperative* + *waw* + *prefix conjugation* expresses purpose or result ("so that," WO'C § 34.6; cf. 39.2.2 on the conjunctive-sequential *waw*). The Qal stem *ḥnn* means "to favor, be gracious" (*CHAL*: 334), and the verb is unique to Mal 1:9 in the Haggai-Zechariah-Malachi corpus. The prefix conjugation is used in a modal sense, denoting the *nonperfective of possibility* (WO'C § 31.4e). The command to entreat the favor of Yahweh echoes the priestly benediction (Num 6:25–26) and the petition of the psalmist (Ps 67:2 [1]). "The verb expresses another of the fundamental attributes of Yahweh, revealed in the creedal proclamation originating in the ancient formula found in Exod 34:6–7 ('*ēl raḥûm wĕḥannûn*, 'a God merciful and gracious')" (Andersen and Freedman [1989: 508]).

The prophet's charge to the priests to implore Yahweh to treat Yehud kindly is not so much a call to repentance (so Ibn Ezra and Kimchi; cf. Cashdan [1948: 340]) as it is a sarcastic jibe at their intercessory function. The allusion to the Aaronic benediction (Num 6:24–26) is significant because the priestly ministry of cultic mediation was supposed to yield divine blessing upon Israel, not the curse of drought and want that the community of Yehud experienced (cf. 3:11). The two small inscribed silver plaques found at Keteph Hinnom (dating to the 7th–5th centuries B.C./E.) suggest that this priestly blessing was known and in popular use at the time of Malachi (see Levine [1993: 238]).

The prophet personalizes his message by including himself in that community by using the first-person plural object pronoun (-*nû*, "us"; that Malachi intends the people of Yehud as the object of Yahweh's favor is clear from the following clause, although Glazier-McDonald [1987a: 53–54] suggests that the object pronoun "us" refers both to the priests and the people in an "ironic twist"). The tone of verse 9ab is one of challenge, even taunt; for what good can come from improper sacrifice?

miyyedkem hāyĕtā zō't. The preposition *min* is causal (WO'C § 11.2.11d; cf. Verhoef [1987: 200], "*on account of you*"; Glazier-McDonald [1987a: 44], "*since all this was your doing*"). The clause places blame for improper sacrifice with the priesthood ("the fault is yours," NRSV; cf. Syr, "for this disaster has been brought by your means"). The emphatic position of the indirect object ("from your hand") and the suffixed pronoun (-*kem*, "your") underscore "the immense responsibility of the priests to be the mediators between God and his people" (Verhoef [1987: 220]; cf. LXX, *en chersìn humôn gégonen taûta*, "by your hands these things have been done"). Attempts to render the construction in a partitive sense fail to establish the culpability of the Levitical priesthood for Yehud's plight, clearly the intent of the prophet's condemnation (e.g., NIV, "with such offerings from your hands"; cf. the conditional clause of the NEB, ["*if* you do this"], misunderstanding the temporal sense of *kî* in v 8).

The Qal suffixing conjugation *hāyĕtā* (*hyh*, "to be") is an *indefinite perfective*, representing a past situation without specificity (WO'C § 30.5.1b). The feminine demonstrative *zō't* ("this") has a nominative function, referring primarily to the "inadequate interior disposition [of the priesthood] which reveals itself in cultic inadequacies" (Glazier-McDonald [1987a: 54]). Indirectly, the prophet may be alluding to the lack of divine blessing in Yehud, tragically manifest in the drought and blight affecting agricultural production (cf. 3:10–12). A similar construction in Isa 50:11 (*miyyādî hāyĕtâ-zō't lākem*, "from my hand this *thing* has come to you") offers intriguing possibilities as an intertextual echo creating a foil between what Yahweh has received from the priests of Yehud and what those who "walk in darkness" receive from Yahweh.

10. *mî gam-bākem.* The animate interrogative pronoun *mî* ("who?") functions nominatively and may express a desiderative sense (see WO'C § 31.4 on the optative mood) in exclamatory questions with a nonperfective verb ("*Oh that someone* would shut the doors," WO'C § 18.2f; cf. the more literal rendering of the partitive construction in the KJV, "who *is there* even among you").

The emphatic adverb *gam* may be used to introduce intensive clauses (GKC § 153; cf. Glazier-McDonald [1987a: 54–55]). The "word of addition" rivets attention upon the priesthood, who were divinely ordained to strictly maintain the prescriptions for ritual sacrifice outlined in the Mosaic law (cf. WO'C § 39.3.4cd). Those authority figures who should have halted cultic sacrifice due to impropriety were the very ones sanctioning impure offerings!

The preposition *bêt* is a partitive marker used almost rhetorically to impugn the entire priestly corps, because none of them was willing to terminate the cultic abuses by (temporarily?) discontinuing Temple operations (WO'C § 11.2.5f, 18.2b; cf. the comparative or estimative understanding of the NEB, "far better . . ."). It may be possible to detect some dependence upon Haggai (2:3, *mî bākem hanniš'ār,* "who among you remains . . . ?") in Mal 1:10, considering that the glory of Yahweh is at issue in both contexts (cf. Meyers and Meyers [1987: 49–50]).

The difficulty of Malachi's idiomatic language here is attested in the divergences of the ancient versions (e.g., the LXX *dióti* [= Heb. *kî*] is causal and the Qal stem *yisgōr* is read as a Niphal passive, "because even among you the doors shall be shut"; V omits *gam*; Syr paraphrases, "who is there among you who would guard my doors . . . ?").

wĕyisgōr dĕlātayim. The coordinating *waw* (+ imperfective) constitute an unmarked connector, here used epexegetically or emphatically (WO'C § 33.4b, § 39.2.4; "yea, let him shut the doors"). The verb *sgr* means to "shut, close" (*CHAL:* 253) and is unique to Mal 1:10 in the Haggai-Zechariah-Malachi corpus. The Qal prefixing conjugation signifies the *nonperfective of desire,* denoting a desire or wish of the subject (WO'C § 31.4h). This desire of Yahweh to "bar" (*sgr*) ritual sacrifices by locking out the Levitical priests stands in stark contrast to Yahweh's desire to "open" (*ptḥ*) the windows of heaven and bless those who return to him (3:10).

The noun *delet* ("door," KBL 1:223–24) is dual in form, used literally in reference either to the double doors of the Temple entrance from the court of the priests (so Mason [1977: 144]) or the entrance(s) to the court of the priests where the tables for sacrifice were located (so Baldwin [1972a: 227]; cf. 1 Kgs 6:31–32; Ezek 41:23–24). Petersen (1995: 182–83) agrees with Baldwin, identifying "the doors" only in a general sense as those of the gates to the courtyards. In either case, the closing of the Temple doors at the wrong time "denotes the interruption of sacrificial worship" (*TDOT* 3:232; cf. 2 Chr 28:24; 29:3). According to Petersen (1995: 183), Yahweh's response is radical because the order halts the "calendrical . . . system of sacrifices."

The Temple gatekeepers were descendants of Levi through Kohath and Korah, and according to the Chronicler they were organized into a sacred guild during the Second Temple era (1 Chr 9:17–27; 26:1–19). Here T embellishes "doors" (*dĕlātayim*) with the phrase "doors of the house of my holiness" (cf. Gordon 1994: 67). The Qumran community appealed to the language of Mal 1:10 in its condemnation of the priestly establishment associated with the Jerusalem Temple (Vermes [1987: 87]; cf. Baldwin [1972a: 227]; Dumbrell [1976: 45 n. 12]; R. L. Smith [1984: 312]).

wĕlō'-tā'îrû mizbĕḥî ḥinnām. The coordinating *waw* has a consequential force with the imperfective form ("so that," WO'C § 33.4b) and sustains the modal *nonperfective of desire* ("you would not *continue to* kindle fire," WO'C 31.4h). The construction implies a present time frame, indicating habitual or ongoing activity (WO'C § 31.3be). On the negative adverb *lō'* + the prefixing conjugation, see further the discussion of *wĕlō' tibgōdû* in the NOTES for 2:15 below.

The Hiphil stem *'wr* means to "set light to, kindle" (KBL 1:24; cf. Ps 18:29 [28]; Isa 27:11). The verb is unique to Mal 1:10 in the Haggai-Zechariah-Malachi corpus, but the occurrence of the Hiphil stem *'wr* in Num 6:25 further strengthens Fishbane's argument that Malachi's second disputation is a carefully crafted exposition of the priestly benediction of Num 6:23–27 (1985: 332–34; cf.

E. M. Meyers [1986]). Until the priests are "illumined" (*'wr*) by Yahweh, they waste their time kindling the altar fires in his Temple (cf. Ps 18:29 [28]). Both the LXX and V change the MT masculine plural *tā'îrû* to a singular form (see Gordon [1994: 119, 128] on the weakening of the MT *'wr* with the more general *qrb* + *'al* ["offer upon"] in T and Syr).

The adverb *ḥinnām* may mean "without compensation, in vain, without cause" (KBL 1:334). The word is unique to Mal 1:10 in the Haggai-Zechariah-Malachi corpus and functions here as an adverb of manner describing the *results* of an action ("vainly," WO'C § 39.3.1j). The term implies motivation for advantage or profit, as in the case of Jacob's labor contract with Laban (Gen 29:15). The defiled sacrifices were meaningless and worthless for two reasons: they were unacceptable as offerings of worship to Yahweh, and they yielded no benefit (by way of divine blessing or "profit," 3:10–11, 14) to the worshiper (cf. JPSV, "to *no purpose*"; NIV, "*useless* fires"; NJB, "*pointless* fires"). Rabbinic interpretation understands *ḥinnām* in the sense "for nothing, gratis" and assumes that the prophet calls the priesthood to abandon "price-gouging," because fees were demanded for Temple services like closing doors and kindling fires (cf. Cashdan [1948: 340]).

'ên-lî ḥēpeṣ bākem. On the clausal adverb *'ên* as the predicator of nonexistence in verbless clauses, see WO'C § 37.5e, 39.3.3b.

The terms *ḥēpeṣ* and *rāṣâ* sometimes occur together in the anticultic speeches of the prophets and are important to the understanding of the theology of ritual sacrifice in Israel. Yahweh takes no "pleasure" (*ḥēpeṣ*, v 10) in the Levitical priests because he cannot "accept" (*rāṣâ*, vv 10, 13) the offerings they present to him (*TDOT* 5:101; cf. von Bulmerincq [1932: 103–4]), indicating a direct relationship between the offering and the suppliant (cf. Jacob [1958: 295]). The offering of inferior sacrifices to Yahweh issues from stubborn and evil hearts far from God (Isa 29:13; Jer 7:21–23). Such irreverence must be rejected by Yahweh and repudiated by his prophet. Here preexilic and postexilic theologies converge, in that Yahweh still "delights" (*ḥēpeṣ*) in obedience more than self-serving ritual (1 Sam 15:22; cf. Isa 58:3). See further the discussion of *'ereṣ ḥēpeṣ* in the NOTES for 3:12 below.

The preposition of specification (*bêt*, "in, with" [*bākem*]) "qualifies the realm with regard to which the verbal action obtains" (WO'C § 11.2.5e). Given the disputational nature of the oracle, the more forceful "I take/have no pleasure/ delight in you" (JPSV, NAB, NEB, NRSV) is preferred over the less pointed "I am not pleased with you" (NIV, NJB). The real issue is the malpractice of the Levitical priesthood, not the blemished sacrifices (cf. Andersen and Freedman [1989: 527]).

ûminḥâ lō'-'erṣeh miyyedkem. The clausal *waw* is usually understood either as a conjunctive ("and," so JPSV, NRSV; cf. R. L. Smith [1984: 308]) or as a coordinator with alternative force ("neither," so NAB; cf. Glazier-McDonald [1987a: 44], "nor"). Given the disputational format and vitriolic tone of the oracle, the coordinator may be considered an emphatic *waw* ("yea, indeed," WO'C § 39.2.4b). The emphatic position of the indefinite and generic noun *minḥâ* ("offering") lends support to this supposition and suggests that Yahweh no longer accepts *any* sacrificial offerings from the priests of Yehud (not just the defiled *šĕlāmîm* offerings). On *minḥâ*, see further the NOTES on 2:12, 13; 3:3, 4.

The (negated) Qal prefixing conjugation of *rṣh* represents a specific future-time situation contingent upon some other (expressed) situation (i.e., the offering of defiled sacrificial animals, vv 7–8; WO'C § 31.6.2b). The shift from third-person to first-person in the verbal forms of v 10 is not only characteristic of "high style" (Andersen and Freedman [1980: 510]), but also reminds the Levitical guild that the Temple cultus exists solely for the sake of honoring Yahweh (v 11). The argument from the lesser ("governor," v 8) to the greater ("Yahweh of Hosts," v 10) serves to underscore the degree to which God has rejected the priests of Yehud and their ministry (cf. Zimmerli [1979: 417] on *rṣh* as a technical priestly term). Malachi's dependence upon both the Priestly and Deuteronomic traditions is evident, in that Yahweh can "accept" (*rṣh*) the priests (Ezek 43:27) and "accept" (*rṣh*) the work of their hands (Deut 33:11) only when they obey his word and keep his covenant (Deut 33:9) and present pure offerings to him (Ezek 43:22, 23, 25). On the verb *rṣh*, see further the NOTES on verse 8 above.

The repetition and inverted clausal position of *miyyedkem* ("from your hand") in verses 9c and 10e create a partial envelope construction, emphasizing the malfeasance of the Levitical priesthood, who are personally responsible for the cultic misdeeds as Yahweh's covenant mediators (cf. *TDOT* 5:408–9).

11. *kî mimmizraḥ-šemeš wĕ'ad-mĕbô'ô*. The particle *kî* is understood alternately as a logical conjunction ("for," e.g., JPSV, NAB, NRSV; cf. WO'C § 39.3.1d), an adversative conjunction ("but," e.g., NJB, R. L. Smith [1984: 308]), a causal conjunction ("because," e.g., Deissler [p. 322]), or as an emphatic adverb ("verily," e.g., Calvin [1979: 662]; Verhoef [1987: 209]). Petersen (1995: 176 n. f) discounts Malachi's consistent use of the particle *kî* as a clausal marker (e.g., 1:4, 8; 2:7, 11; etc.) and reads *kĕmimmizraḥ* (*"Just as* the rising and setting sun") for the MT *kî mimmizraḥ* (thus creating a "cosmic analogy" expressing the significance of Yahweh's name). The disputational tone and style of the speech suggest that *kî* is better understood as an emphatic adverb ("indeed"), but this may be another case in which the logical sense of the conjunction and the emphatic sense of the adverb should not be too strictly separated (cf. WO'C 39.3.4e).

Likewise, the second clausal *kî* (*-gādôl šĕmî baggôyîm*) is rendered variously as a logical conjunction ("for," e.g., JPSV, NAB, NRSV), a causal conjunction ("because," e.g., NIV), or a resultative conjunction ("since," e.g., NJB). Although contested, the integrity of verse 11 is assured by the repetition of language (e.g., *šĕmî* ["my name"]; cf. Rudolph [1976: 262–63]) and theme (e.g., the "universal" worship of Yahweh; cf. Mason [1977: 145]).

The phrase ("from the rising of the sun *even* [understanding the conjunctive *waw* emphatically] to its setting") is a *merismus*, "indicating totality of place" (Glazier-McDonald [1987a: 55]). This literary figure of "distribution" specifies the territorial extent of the nations paying homage to Yahweh: everyplace from the east to the west (NEB, "from furthest east to furthest west"; cf. Verhoef [1987: 223]). The expression has parallels in Pss 50:1; 113:3; Isa 45:6; 59:19. The context of Ps 50:1 is especially significant in relation to Malachi's disputation, because in recalling Israel's covenant with Yahweh (v 5), the psalmist denounces animal sacrifice (vv 12–15) and implores the people of God to bring the sacrifices of "thanksgiving" and "right living" (v 23; cf. Mason [1977: 144]). If the Battle of Marathon (490 B.C./E.) is indeed the event prompting the disputations of Malachi, then the reference to "east" and "west" may have special connotations for the prophet's audience (see further I. D. 1. Historical Considerations: The Persian Period above).

gādôl šĕmî baggôyîm. The adjective *gādôl* ("great") functions as the predicate in the verbless clause and when used in connection with the name of God, the term *gādôl* "forms the nucleus of the statement" (*TDOT* 2:398; cf. WO'C § 14.3.2). The repetition of the expression is emphatic, designed to remind the people of Yehud of a truth they somehow had forgotten — "Great is Yahweh" (cf. Baldwin [1972a: 228]). The epithet echoes the sentiments of Jer 10:6 (*gādôl 'attâ wĕgādôl šimkā*, "you are great, and your name is great") and may constitute a liturgical refrain of sorts (cf. Ps 76:2, *bĕyiśrā'ēl gādôl šĕmî* ["in Israel Great is my name"]; on the phrase as a vestige of theophany in ancient Israel, see Weiser [1962: 42]).

Despite Baldwin's (1972a: 228, 230) protest to the contrary, the tense of the assumed verb "to be" in the nominal clause is present or durative ("great *is* my name" or "my name *continues to be* great"; cf. WO'C § 14.3.2). The goal of creation is to praise God; and by virtue of his role as creator, Yahweh is "great" universally in his creation — including the nations of humanity (cf. Westermann [1982: 90–102]).

The repetition of the key words "great" (*gādôl*) and "name" (*šēm*) in the second dispute suggests a carefully crafted structure for the first half of the oracle (1:6–14). The form *šĕmî* is found at the end of verses 6 and 14, while the refrain *gādôl šĕmî* ("great is my name") marks verse 11 as a transitional link bridging the literary panels of 1:6–10 and 1:12–14. In addition, the word "great" connects 1:6–14 with 1:5, and the word "name" joins 1:6–14 and 2:1–9 (cf. 2:2, 5). See further the discussion of *gādôl YHWH* in the NOTES for 1:5, and *šĕmî* in the NOTES on v 6 above.

The preposition *bêt* (*baggôyîm*) has the spatial meaning, "*amid* a domain" ("among the nations," WO'C § 11.2.5b; cf. Petersen [1995: 174]). Given the reference to Yahweh as "king" (*melek*) in v 14, the noun *gôy* ("nation") should be understood in a political and territorial sense, since the nations were "destined to become a part of Yahweh's inheritance" (*TDOT* 2:432). Ironically, Yahweh's dealings with his people Israel were orchestrated so that the "nations" might know that he is truly God (Ezek 37:28; 38:16; 39:7, 23), because the tribes of Jacob were ordained to be the light of Yahweh's salvation to all "nations" (Isa 49:6, 22). Tragically, the nations now instruct postexilic Yehud in the "greatness" of God. See further the discussion of *haggôyîm* in the NOTES for 3:12 below.

ûbĕkol-māqôm muqṭār muggāš lišmî. The conjunctive *waw* joins two overlapping situations, the rising of the sun and the burning of an incense offering (WO'C § 39.2.5).

The *spatial* sense of the preposition *bêt* marks location ("in," WO'C § 11.2.5b), while the general quantifier *kōl* is a *genitive of measure* and has a universal distributive meaning ("every," WO'C § 9.5.3f, 15.6c). The common noun *māqôm* designates an unspecified "place" or "location" (*CHAL:* 212) and in combination with *bĕkol-* is an idiom for "everywhere" or "anyplace" (Exod 20:24; Num 18:31; Josh 1:3; Prov 15:3; etc.; cf. BDB: 880). Like his earlier contemporaries Haggai (2:7) and Zechariah (8:22), Malachi calls upon his audience to recognize that the worship of Yahweh extends universally to the nations. How much more should the "elect" of God, Israel, offer Yahweh true worship?

The sequence of two Hophal participles, *muqṭār* and *muggāš*, is both awkward and rare. The construction has prompted a remarkable array of emendations by biblical commentators over the years, including reading *muqṭār* as a verb ("smoke is made to rise") and omitting *muggāš* as the work of a glossator (so Wellhausen [1963: 205]; J.M.P. Smith [1912: 43]), deleting *muqṭār* as extraneous to the context (so von Bulmerincq [1932: 118]), inserting a conjunctive *waw* between the participles and rendering the forms as verbs ("incense is burned *and* . . . is offered," so Keil [2:438]; Müller [1896: 536]), repointing *muqṭār* as a noun (*miqṭār*, "incense"; so Chary [1969: 241]), changing the word order of the MT (*muqṭār lišmî ûmuggāš* . . . , "incense burned *to my name and* . . . "; so Sellin [1930: 596]), or simply excising the entire verse as an intrusion from a later source (so Elliger [1950: 187–88]; Horst [1954: 265–67]).

The MT may be read as it stands if *muqṭār* is understood as a substantive ("incense"), even as the Hophal participle *mošḥāt* functions as a noun in v 14 ("a blemished animal"; cf. WO'C § 37.2). Rehm's (p. 194 n. 6) example of a similar combination of participles forming a subject-predicate relationship is compromised by the definiteness of the construction (*habbōgēd bōgēd wĕhaššôdēd šôdēd*, Isa 21:2; but cited as supporting evidence for the MT of Mal 1:11 by Glazier-McDonald [1987a: 57]). More instructive is the LXX *thumiáma proságetai* ("incense is offered"), suggesting the interpolation of *muqṭār* as a noun (cf. Calvin [1979: 662]). This analysis has the endorsement of a majority of the English versions (JPSV, NIV, NJB, NRSV) and several recent treatises on Malachi (e.g., Baldwin [1972a: 228–29]; Rudolph [1976: 259]; R. L. Smith [1984: 309] "oblation"; Verhoef [1987: 225]; Glazier-McDonald [1987a: 44], "burnt sacrifice"; Petersen [1995: 174]; cf. NAB, "sacrifice"; NEB, "fragrant sacrifice").

The unique Hophal participle *muggāš* is an intransitive passive of *ngš* ("is being offered"; cf. WO'C § 28.2). The form should be retained as original to the MT, because the prophet uses the verb *ngš* six times as a synopsis of the priestly ministry, "offering" sacrifices to Yahweh (1:7, 8 [2x], 11, 2:12; 3:3). The striking juxtaposition of the Hophal participles *muqṭār* and *muggāš* at the very midpoint of verse 11 dramatically heightens the contrast between "the nations" (where Yahweh "is" or "will be" great) and the province of Yehud (where Yahweh's own priests "despise" his name, v 6). There is some debate as to whether the participle refers to present time (so Mason [1977: 144]) or imminent (eschatological) future time ("is *about* to be offered," so Baldwin [1972a: 230]; cf. WO'C § 37.6). Despite the difficulties theologically, the participle is best understood as a reference to the present situation (or even a durative circumstance[?], cf. WO'C § 37.6b, d). Understanding the participle in the future tense not only diminishes the ironic force of Malachi's rebuke in the disputational format, but also indicates "immanency," when the prophet uses the so-called *futurum instans* participle with *hinnēh* (3:1, 19 [4:1]; cf. WO'C § 37.6f).

The preposition *lamed* ("*to* my name") is *datival*, marking the indirect object of the verb of "giving" (WO'C § 11.2.10d). According to Cashdan (p. 339), "The name and the personality were so closely associated in Hebrew thought as to be almost identical" (cf. Isa 42:8, *'ănî YHWH hû' šěmî*, "I am Yahweh, that is my name"). According to an ancient pentateuchal tradition, Yahweh expected worship from Israel "everyplace" he caused "his name to be remembered" (through theophany, Exod 20:24; cf. Durham [1987: 320]). Because Yahweh is Creator, it is only natural that all creation should extol his universal glory (cf. Ps 148:5, 11–12).

ûminḥâ ṭěhôrâ. The attributive adjective *ṭāhôr* means "pure" or "clean" in a cultic sense (*CHAL*: 121–22; cf. WO'C § 14.3.1). Elsewhere in the Haggai-Zechariah-Malachi corpus, the word occurs only in Zech 3:5, in the description of the high priest Joshua's turban "where ritual purity and not hygienic cleanliness is involved" (Meyers and Meyers [1987: 191]). The Levitical priests of Malachi's day were guilty of the same indiscretion censured by Ezekiel, the failure to discern between the spheres of the holy and profane, the clean and the unclean (22:23–31). The Temple vision of Ezekiel forecasts a coming age when the priests will no longer manipulate the purity laws arbitrarily for their own benefit, but "these distinctions will be set up fresh and guaranteed" (Zimmerli [1979: 468]). The "pure offering" Malachi envisions anticipates this cultic rejuvenation and stands in stark contrast to the defiled and unacceptable sacrifices offered by the priests of postexilic Yehud (vv 7–8), although Ringgren rightly observes that "here there are echoes of the notion of proper intention" as well (*TDOT* 5:293; cf. Rehm [1961: 195–96]). See further the discussion of the verb *ṭhr* in the Notes on 3:3 below.

12. *wě'attem měhallělîm 'ôtô*. The interclausal *waw* is disjunctive ("but"), introducing a shift in participants (the nations vs. the priests of Yehud) and a contrast in action (a pure offering vs. a polluted offering, WO'C § 39.2.2). The independent personal pronoun *'attem* ("you," masculine plural) is a simple surrogate for the "priests" of Yehud (*hakkōhănîm*, v 6) and functions as the subject of the participial clause (WO'C § 16.3.1a). The use of the independent pronoun *'attem* further heightens the contradistinction between Yahweh (*'ānî*, v 6) and the priests and continues the foil established between Yahweh and Yehud in the opening disputation (cf. 1:2).

The Piel participle *měhallělîm* means "profane, desecrated" (*ḥll* [I], KBL 1:319) and emphasizes a durative circumstance or an ongoing state of affairs ("but you *are* desecrating it," WO'C § 37.6b). The profanation of Yahweh's Temple has come full circle, in that previously Yahweh gave up his own sanctuary to desecration by the Babylonians as punishment for Israel's apostasy (*měhallēl 'et-miqdāšî*, Ezek 24:21; cf. Isa 47:6), and now the very guardians of Israel's covenant relationship with Yahweh habitually desecrate his Temple with impure sacrifices (cf. 2:7).

The suffixed marker of the definite direct object (*'ôtô*) refers to the name of

Yahweh mentioned in verse 11 (cf. WO'C § 10.3.1). The BHS ignores the conjectural emendation of 'ôtî ("me") in the BHK, although the meaning of clause is unaffected because the name of God is God Himself (Cashdan [1948: 341]). be'ĕmorkem šulḥan 'ădōnāy mĕgō'āl hû'. The Pual participle mĕgō'āl ("become impure, be defiled") functions substantivally as the predicate of the verbless clause (WO'C § 37.2). The independent pronoun hû' ("he," or "it" in reference to Yahweh's table) has the role of copula in the classifying (verbless) clause (WO'C § 16.3.3d). See further leḥem mĕgō'āl in the NOTES for verse 7 above.

On the clause be'ĕmorkem šulḥan 'ădōnāy, see be'ĕmorkem šulḥan YHWH in the NOTES for verse 7 above. The substitution of the divine name 'ădōnāy ("Lord of all," cf. TDOT 1:68) for the covenant name YHWH in verse 12 may be instructive. If the conjecture by Eissfeldt has any merit (i.e., that in later periods of Hebrew history the divine name 'ădōnāy became more prominent, given the increasing distinction between the sacral and secular spheres; TDOT 1:72), then the prophet may infer that Yahweh is "Lord of all" tables of sacrifice (whether in Yehud or among the nations, v 11) since Yahweh is "Lord of all" creation (cf. Ps 50:10–11). The verse parallels 1:6e and 7c, and the repetition of key words (e.g., šĕmî) and phrases (be'ĕmorkem šulḥan . . .) links the first two paragraphs (vv 6–10 and vv 12–14) of the second disputation. Thematically, the second paragraph continues the indictment of the Levitical priesthood for liturgical malpractice.

wĕnîbô nibzeh 'oklô. The MT is problematic, attested by the divergences in the ancient versions in an attempt to mediate the difficulties (e.g., LXX, kaì tà epitithémena exoudénôntai brōmáta autoû, "and his foodstuffs placed thereon are despised"; cf. NJB, "the food offered on it deserves no respect"). The noun nîb is rare, used figuratively concerning speech (Q: nîb śĕpātāyim [K: nwb śptym], "fruit of the lips") elsewhere only in Isa 57:19[18]. Hence, the word nîbô is often deleted as an error of dittography with nibzeh, given that the word is omitted in T, Syr, and some Hebrew manuscripts (e.g., NEB, NRSV; cf. S. R. Driver [1906: 308]; J.M.P. Smith [1912: 43]; Rudolph [1976: 251]; Petersen [1995: 176 n. g]).

If nîbô is retained as original to the MT, then 'oklô is redundant and excised by some commentators as an explanatory gloss (e.g., R. L. Smith [1984: 308]). Calvin (p. 662) understood the Niphal participle nibzeh adjectivally modifying 'oklô ("its provision is his contemptible food"). Finally, Sellin (p. 597) includes the independent pronoun hû' as part of the final clause ("it, and its fruit are despised"; cf. Keil [2:436]; R. L. Smith [1984: 308]) and assumes that 'oklô represents a corruption of kullô ("all of it"). My analysis preserves the MT on the basis of the principle of the lectio difficilior (agreeing with Glazier-McDonald [1987a: 62] [the need for emendation is obviated by "the fact that no major translation difficulties are posed by the line"] and Verhoef [1987: 232] [who argues that "both the 'produce' and the 'food' of the altar are the offering itself"; cf. JPSV, "the meat, the food, can be treated with scorn").

Baldwin (1972a: 230), along with some English versions (e.g., JPSV, NAB, NEB, NRSV), render the Niphal participle nibzeh modally as an expression of capability ("can be despised") or possibility ("may be despised"), assuming the statement records "the Lord's assessment of their intentions." The confrontational nature of the disputational speech form, the forceful language of the prophet in the pericope, and the very fact that the priests were already "despising" Yahweh's name in their malpractice of the Temple sacrifice all argue for a more direct translation of the clause. On the verb _bzh_, see the discussion of _bôzê_ and _bāzînû_ in the NOTES for verse 6 and _nibzeh_ in the NOTES for verse 7 above.

13. _wa'ămartem hinnēh mattĕlā'â wĕhippaḥtem 'ôtô._ The _waw_ + suffixing conjugation (_wa'ămartem_) after a predicate participle represents an explanatory, imperfective situation (WO'C § 32.2.5b).

The presentative word _hinnēh_ introduces an exclamation of immediacy (JPSV, "Oh, what a bother!") and is sometimes left untranslated for the sake of vividness (NAB, NIV, "What a burden!"; cf. WO'C § 40.2.1a, b).

The feminine noun _tĕlā'â_ is rare, occurring only in Exod 18:8; Num 20:14; Lam 3:5; and Mal 1:13. The word is derived from the verb _l'h_ and is usually translated "hardship, trouble" (_CHAL_: 390) but literally refers to "the effects of exhaustion, weariness" (Levine [1993: 491]). The interrogative _mâ_ ("what?") is exclamatory (WO'C § 18.3f), and the _dagesh forte_ in the _taw_ (ת) is usually explained as an example of assimilation of an originally audible ה in _mâ_ (תְּלָאָה + מָה = מַתְּלָאָה; cf. GKC § 37b). Some English versions render the interrogative _mâ_ adverbially "how" (e.g., NEB, "How irksome!"; NJB, "How tiresome it all is!"; cf. Petersen [1995: 174], "What a nuisance!"; see KBL 2:512, 551). The Syr ("from our toil") and T ("from our misery") support the vocalization of the preposition _min_ + _tĕ'ālâ_ (cf. von Bulmerincq [1932: 143]; see Gordon [1994: 128] and Gelston [1987: 181] on the addition of the pronoun suffix ["our"] in T and Syr).

The Hiphil suffixing conjugation _nph_ occurs only in Job 31:39 and Mal 1:13. The Qal stem _nph_ means to "blow, gasp" (_CHAL_: 241), and the Hiphil stem is usually rendered "sniff at [in contempt]" in Mal 1:13 (BDB:656; cf. Pope [1977: 225] on Job 31:39, "snuffed out the life"). The modern English versions are in agreement that the expression signifies a gesture of insolence and derision (NEB, "you sniff at it"; NIV, "and you sniff at it contemptuously"; NJB, "you sniff disdainfully at me"; NRSV, "you sniff at me"); the ancient versions modify the MT second-person form to a first-person form, making Yahweh the subject and softening the indictment against the Levitical priesthood ("_I_ blew it away" [_kaì exephýsēsa autà_ = a harmonization with Hag 1:9?], LXX; "and _I_ have sniffed at it," Syr cf. Kruse-Blinkenberg [1966: 98]). Malachi's use of the verb _nph_ may represent ironic wordplay with the Qal stem _wĕnāpaḥtî bô_ in Hag 1:9. Yahweh "blew away" (_nph_) the agricultural yield of the land of Yehud because his Temple still lay in ruins (cf. Meyers and Meyers [1987: 3]). Despite the fact that the Temple had been rebuilt by the time of Malachi, the people of Yehud still languished on underproductive soil (3:9–11) because the priests "sniff at" (or "snort," so Redditt [1995: 166]) their sacrificial duties (cf. von Bulmerincq [1932: 144–47]).

Some ancient versions (Syriac, Arabic, Aramaic, Ethiopic) and Jerome (_CChr_ 76A:911–12) read _'ôtî_ ("_at me_," so NRSV) for the MT _'ôtô_ ("_at it_"). The textual variant represents a classic example of "scribal corrections" (_Tiqqun Sopherim_) intended "to remove objectional expressions referring to God" (Würthwein [1979: 18]).

wahăbē'tem gāzûl we'et-happissēaḥ we'et-haḥōleh. The copulative waw (wa-

hăbē'tem) represents two situations as coordinate with one another and continues the imperfective aspect established by the previous syntactical construction ("and you say . . . and you sniff . . . and you bring"; cf. WO'C § 32.3a, b). The Hiphil suffixing conjugation *hăbē'tem* has an imperfective aspect and is used "as a fixed term in cult terminology . . . to denote the bringing of sacrifices," whether by people in general or by the priests, as is the case here (*TDOT* 2:25). On the verb *bw'*, see further the discussion of *hăbî'û* in the NOTES on 3:10 below.

The Qal passive participle *gāzûl* is unique to Mal 1:13 in the Twelve. The verb *gzl* means to "rob, seize violently, loot" (KBL 1:186); and with respect to the sacrificial animal, the word may describe that which has been "stolen" (JPSV, NJB; so Petersen [1995: 174]), "seized" (NAB), or "taken by violence" (NRSV). Glazier-McDonald (1987a: 63) sides with the interpretations of the NEB ("mutilated") and the NIV ("injured"), arguing that "a priest would be unable to recognize a pilfered animal." According to Schupphaus (*TDOT* 2:457), the term *gzl* "denotes a powerful, unlawful snatching away or stealing." In Malachi this "unlawful snatching" may even include trespassing and the poaching of animals for use as sacrificial offerings. There is an ironic twist to Malachi's use of *gāzûl*, in that Deuteronomic warnings for covenant disobedience include Israel's victimization as one alone and "robbed" (*gzl*) continually (Deut 28:29).

The emendation of *gāzûl* to *hā'iwwēr* ("the blind," cf. v 8) by Wellhausen (p. 205), Nowack (p. 416), and Marti (p. 465) is unnecessary. The gapping of the definite direct object marker and the definite article (['*et-hag*] *gāzûl*) may serve an emphatic purpose.

The *phrasal waw* (*wĕhappissēah*) connects items in a series and may be understood in a consecutive sense ("and," e.g., JPSV, Glazier-McDonald [1987a: 45]) or better, in an alternative sense ("or," e.g., NAB, NIV, NJB, NRSV; WO'C § 39.2.1b).

The adjective *pissēah* designates a "lame" person or animal, from the verb *psh* (II) ("to limp"; *CHAL*: 204). The word is used as a substantive with an accusative function (cf. WO'C § 14.3.3). The legislation of the Pentateuch prohibits offering animals with such defects as sacrifices to Yahweh (Deut 15:21). The definiteness of the form may represent an example of the *anaphoric* use of the definite article (WO'C § 13.5.1d; cf. the series of indefinite items in v 8). See further the discussion of *pissēah wĕhōleh* in the NOTES for v 8 above (note that R. L. Smith [1984: 308] interrupts the series of phrasal *waws* by connecting *wĕ'et-hahôleh* with the following *wahăbē'tem*, "and the sick you bring as an offering").

wahăbē'tem 'et-hamminhâ. The clause is rendered in a variety of ways in the English versions due to its terseness and its ambiguous relationship to the preceding clause (or left untranslated as in the NEB). The triad of copulative *waws* (*wĕhippahtem . . . wahăbē'tem . . . wahăbē'tem*) suggests a conjunctive and sequential series of events ("you sniff . . . you bring . . . you offer," so NIV, Verhoef [1987: 209–10]). The context of the second disputation (especially 2:2) permits understanding the clause as a sarcastic summary statement condemning the ennui of the priests as they mechanically perform the ritual sacrifice ("thus you dutifully bring an offering"; cf. KJV, JPSV, NRSV; Glazier-McDonald [1987a: 45]). It is even possible to read the clause as an emphatic statement of prophetic outrage at such sacrilege in Yahweh's Temple (e.g., NAB, "yes, you bring it as a sacrifice"; NJB, "you bring that as an offering!"; cf. Calvin [1979: 662]).

Likewise, the ancient versions yield little by way of interpretive consensus (e.g., LXX interprets the clause conditionally [*kaì eàn phérēte tēn thusían*, "if you should bring an offering"; and Syr takes *wahăbē'tem . . . wahăbē'tem* as hendiadys, "you bring offerings"). So while I appreciate the nuances of the prophet's grammatical construction, it seems logical to retain the integrity of the copulative *waw* sequence emphasizing the heartless protocol of the priests in offering the ritual sacrifices.

ha'erṣeh 'ôtāh miyyedkem. The clause echoes Yahweh's rejection of blemished sacrifices in v 10 (*ûminḥâ lô'-'erṣeh miyyedkem*) and forms an envelope construction marking vv 10–13 as a literary unit (cf. Petersen [1995: 185] who discerns two related dialogic interchanges [vv 6–11 and 12–14]). The interrogative *hē'* (*ha'erṣeh*, "shall I accept . . . ?*) introduces both a rhetorical and an exclamatory polar question ("Indeed, I shall not accept . . . !"; cf. WO'C § 18.1c, 40.3b). Tragically, and ironically, Zerubbabel's Temple was erected so that Yahweh "might be pleased with it" (*wě'erṣeh-bô*, Hag 1:8). By the time of Malachi, Yahweh can take no pleasure in his Temple because the ritual sacrifices offered to him by the corrupt priesthood are unacceptable (*lō'-'erṣeh*, v 10).

'āmar YHWH. Despite the limited textual support in the ancient versions (LXX, Syr[w]), the *BHS* suggests the insertion of *ṣĕbā'ôt* ("hosts") in the messenger formula (presumably because this reflects the pattern of the second disputation, cf. 1:6, 8, 9, 10, 11). The same structure holds true for the messenger formula when used at the conclusion of the other MT paragraph breaks as well (cf. 2:12, 16; 3:12, 21 [4:3]). The MT is probably superior, the principle of *lectio brevier* (or "shorter reading") operative in this instance. The variation not only breaks the monotony in a repetitive series of messenger formulas, but also may serve to highlight the curse pronouncement (v 14) concluding the first speech-act of the disputation (vv 6–14).

14. *wě'ārûr nôkēl.* The coordinating *waw* has a conjunctive function but is best left untranslated given the emphatic nature of the clause (cf. WO'C § 39.2.5). The verb *'rr* means to "curse, bind with a curse" (KBL 1:90–91); and the (Qal passive) participial formula "is the most powerful 'decree' expressed by an authority, and by means of it a man or a group that has committed a serious transgression against the community or against a legitimate authority (God, parents) is delivered over to misfortune" (*TDOT* 1:411). Malachi is the only prophet of the Twelve resorting to the "curse" (*'rr*), but much after the pattern of Deuteronomy chapters 27:15–26 and especially Jer 48:10 (*'ārûr 'ōṣeh mĕle'ket YHWH rĕmîyâ*, "accursed be the one who is negligent in doing the work of Yahweh"). Petersen (1995: 186–87) concurs, relating the curse to the violation of a vow (specifically the substitution of a blemished sacrificial animal for a healthy one). The "covenant-based curse" thus affects "not only the one who pledged the animal but also the ritual officiant — decision maker" (Petersen [1995: 187]).

The Hebrew root *'rr* is related etymologically to the Akkadian *arāru*, "to ban, block off" (cf. *CAD* 1/2:234–36). Operationally, to inflict a curse is to impose a "ban or barrier, a paralysis on movement or other capabilities" (Brichto [1963:

216–17]). Further, according to Brichto (p. 82), "Since YHWH is speaking, the *'ārûr* [curse] should be taken as a pronouncement of doom rather than as a wish." On the verb *'rr*, see further the NOTES on 2:2 and 3:9 below (cf. Speiser [1964: 24 n. 14] who links the basic meaning of *'rr* to banishment or ostracism from an established socioreligious group).

The verb *nkl* is a rare word in the OT/HB, occurring only in Gen 37:18; Num 25:18; Ps 105:25; and Mal 1:14. The Qal participle is unique to Mal 1:14 in the MT and means "act cleverly, cunningly, deceitfully" (*CHAL:* 238). The relative participle is anarthrous, implying an "indefiniteness of class" (i.e., "accursed be *anyone* who cheats" cf. WO'C § 13.2b, 37.5). The connotation here is not cleverness but deceit: in context the word describes a "conniver" (Brichto [1963: 82]) or a "cheat" (JPSV, NEB, NIV, NRSV) who has reneged on a vow to Yahweh by substituting an inferior animal for a sound one in ritual sacrifice (cf. NJB, "rogue" = "a dishonest person"). The curse actually extends culpability for malpractice in Temple sacrifice beyond the priesthood to the suppliant who disobeys the divine prescriptions for animal sacrifice and attempts to deceive Yahweh (and the priests?) through the formality of liturgy.

wĕyeš bĕ'edrô zākār. The existential particle *yēš* signifies ownership in this context ("*there is* in his flock" or "*has* in his flock," JPSV; cf. WO'C § 10.3.2b, 37.5f).

The preposition *bêt* has a spatial sense, marking location within an area ("*in* his flock," WO'C § 11.2.5b). The word *'ēder* (I) means "flock" or "herd" (*CHAL:* 266) and is used elsewhere in the Haggai-Zechariah-Malachi corpus in Zech 10:3 as a pastoral figure for the people of Judah (cf. Meyers and Meyers [1993: 98]).

The noun *zākār* denotes the male gender of a species of both humankind and animals (*TDOT* 4:82). The context here indicates a male animal from the flock, probably a ram. The priestly legislation prescribing votive or freewill offerings (see *wĕnōdēr* below) requires that a male animal be sacrificed (Lev 22:19; cf. *TDOT* 4:84). The *BHS* proposes *zākeh* ("pure") for the MT *zākār*, while Rudolph (1976: 260) inserts *zākeh* as a modifier omitted through homeoarcton (but this presupposes an original reading of *zākeh zākār*, which seems unlikely). Glazier-McDonald (1987a: 64) is correct to dismiss the emendation because the "wholeness" of the sacrificial animal is implicit given pentateuchal law and the antithetical parallelism of *zākār* with *mošhāt* ("polluted, blemished" [animal]).

wĕnōdēr wĕzōbēah mošhāt la'dōnāy. The conjunctive *waw* joins two clauses describing related situations (WO'C § 39.2.5). The verb *ndr* means "make a vow" (*CHAL:* 229), and the Qal participle calls attention to a future event (with conditionality, cf. WO'C § 37.6f). Once a vow is made to Yahweh, it must be kept, or the party swearing the vow incurs guilt (Deut 21:21–23). No doubt Malachi wishes that the people and priests of Yehud would heed the command of the psalmist (*nidărû wĕšallĕmû laYHWH* ["make vows and fulfill *them* to Yahweh"], Ps 76:12 [11]; cf. Dahood [1968: 221]) or learn the lesson of Jonah (*'ăšer nādartî 'ăšallēmâ* ["what I have vowed, let me fulfill"], 2:10 [9]; cf. Sasson [1990: 200–1]). Baldwin (1972a: 231) correctly identifies the particular example of animal sacrifice as the votive or freewill offering, often "vowed under stress as a thanksgiving if God will grant deliverance" (e.g., Gen 28:20–22; Num 30:2). Such freewill offerings might be made by anyone, priest, people, or alien (Lev 22:17–20), but the vow must be fulfilled with the sacrifice of an unblemished male animal (Lev 22:21–25; cf. Deut 12:11, 17).

The coordinating *waw* (*wĕzōbēaḥ*) suggests a conjunctive-sequential relationship with *wĕnōdēr* ("and vows, and *then* sacrifices . . . , e.g., NIV; cf. WO'C § 39.2.2) or even a disjunctive relationship ("*but* sacrifices," e.g., NAB; cf. WO'C § 39.2.3). Here the verb *zbḥ* refers to the ritual slaughter of an animal (cf. *TDOT* 4:11; on *zbḥ*, see further the NOTES for v 8 above). The participial clauses *wĕnōdēr wĕzōbēaḥ* function as predicates of *nôkēl* ("the cheat who . . . vows, but sacrifices . . .").

The Hophal participle *mošḥāt* occurs only in Prov 25:26 and Mal 1:14 in the MT and is used substantively as the object of *zōbēaḥ* in Malachi. The verb *šḥt* means to "become corrupt, be spoiled" (*CHAL*: 366–67), and *mošḥāt* is usually rendered "blemished *animal*" (so JPSV, NIV, NJB, NRSV; cf. NEB, "damaged victim"; NAB, "gelding," assuming a direct relationship between Mal 1:14 and Lev 22:24).

The datival *lamed* of interest marks Yahweh as the deity for whom the action of sacrifice is directed (cf. WO'C § 11.2.10d). Despite the proposal of the *BHS* (*laYHWH*), the MT *la'dōnāy* is to be retained because the repetition of this divine name (see v 6 above) bolsters the structural integrity of 1:6–14 as a literary subunit of the second disputation and answers the theological question raised in v 6 ("if I am Lord . . . ?") — Yahweh is Lord indeed!

kî melek gādôl 'ānî. The conjunction *kî* ("for") functions as a logical marker introducing a subordinate clause (WO'C § 39.3.4e).

The phrase "a great king" (*melek gādôl*) may be an allusion to the hymnic creedal affirmation "Yahweh is . . . a great king over all the earth" (*melek gādôl 'al-kol-hā'āreṣ*, Ps 47:3 [2]) or "Yahweh . . . is a great king above all gods" (*ûmelek gādôl 'al-kol-'ĕlōhîm*, Ps 95:3; cf. Meyers and Meyers [1993: 467] on the use of "king" in the cultic language of ancient Israel). According to Dahood (1965: 284), the expression is another term for "suzerain" or "overlord." Yahweh is given the title of "King" elsewhere in the Twelve only in Zeph 3:15 and Zech 14:16 (cf. Isa 41:21; 44:6).

Berlin's (p. 143) insight that "when the Lord is recognized as king, pridefulness and disobedience are gone" applies to the circumstances addressed by Malachi as well. If the Levitical priesthood had acknowledged properly Yahweh's sovereignty, then they would not have been under prophetic indictment for malpractice with respect to the Temple sacrifices. According to Meyers and Meyers (1993: 467), the epithet "King Yahweh of Hosts" (Zech 14:16) is an "unparalleled expression of Yahweh's universal power and rule," pregnant with both theological and eschatological significance for postexilic Yehud. Malachi seems to use the royal appellative in much the same way as Second Zechariah, but implies that the eschatological dimension of Yahweh's rule of the nations is already in the initial stage of implementation (cf. 3:1, 19 [4:1]).

The independent pronoun *'ānî* serves as the subject of the identifying verbless clause (WO'C § 8.4b; 16.3.3). This variation of the self-introduction formula reveals Yahweh as the ultimate sovereign over Yehud and the nations and answers the rhetorical questions posed in v 6 concerning the honor due him (cf. Zimmerli [1982: 1–28]).

ûšĕmî nôrāʾ baggôyîm. The conjunctive *waw* continues the self-introduction formula (cf. WO'C 39.2.5). The emphatic position of the messenger formula (*ʾāmar YHWH ṣĕbāʾôt*) both reinforces the authority and veracity of the divine declaration and enhances the unity of verses 10–14 as a literary subunit of the second disputation by creating a partial chiastic structure in the inversion of *šĕmî baggôyîm//ʾāmar YHWH ṣĕbāʾôt* in verses 11 and 14. On *ûšĕmî . . . baggôyîm,* see further the NOTES for verse 11 above.

The Niphal participle *nôrāʾ* means "be feared, reverenced, held in honor" (CHAL: 142), and when used in combination with *gādôl,* the term refers to the numinous nature of God—"terrible . . . identical with his holiness" (TDOT 6:300). This "terribleness" is both an attribute of Yahweh (e.g., Exod 15:11) and his name (e.g., Deut 28:58; Ps 99:3). The parallelism of *melek gādôl* and *ûšĕmî nôrāʾ* in v 14 suggests dependence on Ps 47:3 [2] (*kî-YHWH ʾelyôn nôrāʾ melek gādôl . . . ,* "because Yahweh Most High is terrible, a great king . . ."). See further the discussion of *wĕhannôrāʾ* in the NOTES for 3:23 [4:5] below.

Biblical commentators are quick to recognize the climactic structure of the triad of divine announcements in 1:5, 11, and 14 (with *gādôl* the common element of all three, e.g., Glazier-McDonald [1987a: 64]). More significant and less widely appreciated, however, is the complementary relationship between the rhetorical questions of v 6 and the divine pronouncements of verses 11 and 14. The first, "where is my honor (*kĕbôdî*)?" (v 6c), finds its rejoinder in the declaration "great (*gādôl*) is my name among the nations!" (v 11b). The second, "where is my reverence (*môrāʾî*)?" (v 6d), has its reply in "for I am a Great (*gādôl*) King . . . and my name is Terrible (*nora*) among the nations!" (v 14d). The arrangement neatly connects v 6 with vv 11 and 14, creating a well-crafted and thematically unified literary panel within the second disputation (cf. Petersen [1995: 185]).

2:1. *wĕʿattâ ʾălêkem.* The temporal adverb *ʿattâ* blends the logical and emphatic functions as it introduces a shift or transition "in argumentative tack with a continuity in subject and reference" (WO'C § 39.3.4f; cf. Petersen [1995: 187]). The conjunctive *waw* is typical of the construction that sometimes prefaces separate stages of development in the discussion of a single topic (e.g., 1:9–14 [*wĕʿattâ,* 1:9]; 2:1–3 [*wĕʿattâ,* 2:1]; cf. Isa 5:1–5). The preposition *ʾel* marks an ethical dative of interest or advantage ("for," WO'C § 11.2.2). The emphatic position of the predicate (*ʾălêkem*) in the verbless (or nominal) identifying clause further accents the Levitical priesthood as the *addressee* of the prophet's message (cf. WO'C § 8.4).

hammiṣwâ hazzōʾt. The definiteness of the construction calls attention to the *identity* of the referent, not the *class* to which the referent belongs (WO'C § 13.2b). The feminine noun *miṣwâ* means "command [single], commandment [sum of all]" (CHAL: 210). According to Petersen (1995: 187), the phrase summarizes the stipulations of Deuteronomy (Deut 7:11) and is "something that is readily doable (Deut 30:11)." The Deuteronomic term occurs elsewhere in the Twelve only in Mal 2:4 (see 2:4 below).

Following von Bulmerincq (1932: 173), Glazier-McDonald (1987a: 64–65) understands *miṣwâ* as a synonym for *mišpāṭ* ("judgment, verdict"), assuming that Malachi's speech of punishment directed against the priests commences at 2:1 (cf. NIV, "this admonition"). It seems better, however, to side with D. R. Jones (p. 189) and others (e.g., Verhoef [1987: 237–38]; Petersen [1995: 187]), in identifying "this commandment" with the contents and maintenance of the covenant of Levi mentioned in 2:4 (where the parallel expression *hammiṣwâ hazzō't* serves as a cataphoric reference to [*bĕrîtî*]'*et-lēwî* ["my covenant with Levi"]). In this sense, the prophet's "decree" (NEB) or "charge" (JPSV) does not stand as a separate verdict of judgment. Rather, the reference is to the command of the priestly office as a divinely ordained institution (cf. the *miṣwâ* of the king, 1 Sam 13:13; and the *miṣwâ* of the prophet, 2 Kgs 13:2). The essence of "this commandment" is summarized in "observing" the word of Yahweh, "keeping" his covenant, "teaching" Jacob God's law, and "offering" sacrifices upon Yahweh's altar (Deut 33:9–10). It is this standard by which Malachi indicts and judges the priests.

The feminine demonstrative pronoun *zō't* ("this") serves as an attributive adjective and marks the forward *direction of reference* [cataphora] (i.e., *hammiṣwâ hazzō't*, 2:4; WO'C § 17.3d, 17.4.2e).

hakkōhănîm. The *hē'* affixed to *kōhănîm* ("priests") marks a definite addressee (in the vocative, "O priests"). The MT understands the construction as the definite article (cf. WO'C § 13.5.2c; JM § 137g); but given context, it is possible the particle *ha[-]* represents a distinct vocative marker like the Ugaritic *la* and the Arabic *yâ* (cf. UT § 12.6; Dahood [1965: 21]). The Levitical priesthood constitutes the prophet's target audience for the entire second disputation. See also *hakkōhănîm* in the NOTES for 1:6.

2. *'im-lō' tišmĕ'û.* The protasis of a *real conditional* clause [i.e., a condition fulfilled in the past or still capable of being fulfilled] is introduced, in the negative, by *'im-lō'* ("if not," WO'C § 38.2d; on the particle of contingency *'im*, see WO'C § 31.6.1). The Qal prefixing conjugation form of the verb *šm'* indicates the condition still has the potential for fulfillment (pending repentance on the part of the priests, cf. 3:7). Here the verb *šm'* means "listen, hear" in the sense of "heed, obey" (JPSV; cf. Deut 28:15). Ogden and Deutsch (p. 90) connect the idiom with the Shema (Deut 6:4–9). On the verb *šm'*, see further the discussion of *wayyišma'* in the NOTES on 3:16 below.

wĕ'im-lō' tāśîmû 'al-lēb. The conjunctive *waw* expands the protasis (*wĕ'im-lō'*), conjoining the two conditional clauses (cf. WO'C § 39.2.5).

The idiom *śym* + [*'el/ 'al*] + *lēb* [*āb*] occurs 28 times in the MT, 6 times in the Haggai-Zechariah-Malachi corpus (Hag 1:5, 7; 2:15, 18 [2x]; Mal 2:2 [2x]). The expression means "take to heart, pay attention to" (CHAL: 351). The majority of English versions render the phrase quite literally ("lay it to heart," JPSV, NAB, NRSV; "set your heart," NIV; but NJB, "sincerely resolve"; cf. Holladay [1986: 388]).

Unlike Haggai who calls postexilic Yehud to "reflect upon" (see Meyers and

Meyers [1987: 24]) or "consider" (so NRSV) their ways, Malachi employs the idiom more forcefully. The construction of the idiom in Mal 2:2 (*śym* + *ʿal* + *lēb* [*āb*]) follows the pattern of Jeremiah (12:11) and Second Isaiah (42:25; 57:1, 11) and reflects the same prophetic passion in the "wooing of a disobedient people" back to covenant relationship with Yahweh (cf. Westermann [1969: 325]). It is possible that the prophet intends the phrase to evoke thoughts of covenant responsibility in his audience (cf. Deut 11:18; see Weinfeld [1991: 340] on the *śym* + *lēb* idiom in political loyalty oaths in the ancient Near East). The priests are to "publicize" the truth that all glory belongs to Yahweh, in their sacrificial duties, prayers, and songs. The priests must "lay to heart" this "popularizing" of the truth that Yahweh possesses all the glory, not just the truth itself.

lātēt kābôd lišmî. The preposition *lamed* + the Qal infinitive construct *lātēt* from the verb *ntn* form a purpose clause ("*in order* to give . . . ," WO'C § 36.2.3d). The expression *lātēt kābôd* may be translated "give glory" (e.g., NAB) or "show honor" (e.g., JPSV). Theologically, the former is more appropriate, given that elsewhere proper sacrifice (even that offered by pagan Philistines!) "gives glory" (*ûnĕtattem . . . kābôd*) to Yahweh (1 Sam 6:5; cf. Ps 115:1, "to your name give glory" [*lĕšimka tēn kābôd*]; Jer 13:16, "give glory to Yahweh . . ." [*tĕnû laYHWH . . . kābôd*]). The sacrifices of the priests of Yahweh were intended to give glory to his name, and the priests served in the sanctuary sanctified by his "glory" (*kābôd*, Exod 29:43).

The repetition of *kābôd* ("glory, honor") connects 2:1–3 with the first rhetorical question of 1:6c above ("where is my honor?" [*kĕbôdî*]), even as the word *môrāʾ* ("fear, reverence) in 2:5 links 2:4–9 with the second rhetorical question of 1:6d ("where is my homage?" [*môrāʾî*]). Thus, both halves of the second oracle are structured as responses to the hypothetical questions posed at the onset of the disputation (see the NOTES for 1:14 above). Likewise, the repetition of the word "name" (*šēm*) is one of the lexical hinges joining the two halves of the second dispute (cf. 1:6, 11, 14; 2:2, 5).

wĕsillaḥtî bākem ʾet-hammĕʾērâ. The relative *waw* + suffixing conjugation express a consequential nonperfective aspect and begin the apodosis of the conditional clauses ("*then* I will send . . . ," WO'C § 32.2.1c).

The Piel suffixing conjugation from the verb *šlḥ* means to "send" (CHAL: 372; see the discussion of the verb *šlḥ* in 2:16; 3:1, 23 [4:5] below). The Piel stem suggests the more forceful "let loose" (CHAL: 371; cf. Petersen [1995: 175]). The first-person form of the root is commonly used formulaically in the Prophets of afflictions "unleashed" by Yahweh upon individual, cities, or nations as punishment for gross misconduct (or in the case of Israel, covenant violations; cf. Jer 9:15 [16]; 24:10; 49:37; Ezek 5:17; 7:3; 14:21; 28:23; 39:6; Hos 8:14; Amos 1:4, 7, 10, 12; 2:2, 5). This judgment formula in the Prophets may trace its roots to the refrain of Amos, "I will send fire" (*wĕsillaḥtî ʾēš*, 1:4, etc.; cf. Paul [1991: 48–50]).

The (datival) suffixed preposition *bākem* ("upon you") has a spatial sense, "on" a surface or individual (WO'C § 11.2.5b).

The definite direct object *hammĕʾērâ* is an infrequent vocabulary item in the MT, occurring only in Deut 28:20; Prov 3:33; 28:27; and Mal 2:2; 3:9. The word is usually understood as a "curse" or "malediction" (CHAL: 181). The definiteness of the term used in combination with the verb *šlḥ* suggests that the prophet has "the curse" of the warnings of Deuteronomic law in mind (*yĕšallaḥ YHWH bĕkā 'et-hammĕ'ērâ* ["Yahweh will send the curse upon you"], Deut 28:20). See further the discussion of *hammĕ'ērâ* in the NOTES for 3:9 below.

wĕ'ārôtî 'et-birkôtêkem. The relative *waw* + suffixing conjugation express a consequential nonperfective aspect and expand the apodosis of the conditional clauses ("*and then* I will curse . . . ," WO'C § 32.2.1c). The definite direct object *birkôtêkem* is plural ("your blessings"), but some English versions harmonize the form with the subsequent *'ārôtîhâ* ("I have cursed *it*") and render the accusative in the singular (following the LXX, *tēn eulogían humōn*; cf. NAB, NJB). Conversely, the JPSV, NIV, and NRSV retain the MT "blessings" but emend the suffixed object pronoun of the following verb (*'ārôtîhâ*) to harmonize the plural form with the number of *birkôtêkem* ("I have cursed *them*"; cf. Petersen [1995: 175]).

The MT is the superior reading whether one interprets the divine curse against the priestly "blessings" as a malediction aimed at the Levitical function of blessing the congregation of Israel (so Keil [2:442–43]) or whether one regards the "blessings" as meaning the material benefits that the priests and Levites received as compensation for their service in the cultus (so S. R. Driver [1906: 308]; cf. Petersen [1995: 189], "Yahweh is simply allowing the priests to receive their portion of second-rate sacrifices"). The former includes the priestly pronouncements assuring fecundity accompanying the votive offerings intended to secure agricultural fertility (apparently failed blessings according to Mal 3:11; so Glazier-McDonald [1987a: 65–66]). The latter also includes the blessing of special rank and privilege (so von Bulmerincq [1932: 179–80]; Rudolph [1976: 265]). In any case, the "blessings" of the priests are understood in a comprehensive manner referring to status or function (or both), thus justifying the use of the singular suffixed object pronoun in the form *'ārôtîhâ* ("I have cursed *it* [categorically]"). Petersen (1995: 189) regards the prophet's statement as "a radically innovative claim" in that he has combined the "conditionality" of the Sinaitic treaty with the covenant of grant in order to explore the covenant relationship between Yahweh and the Levitical priesthood.

wĕgam 'ārôtîhâ. The clausal adverb *gam* has an emphatic force ("indeed," WO'C 39.3.4d). The Qal suffixing form *'ārôtîhâ* represents a situation that occurred in the recent past, requiring the auxiliary "have" (WO'C § 30.5.1b; but note that the NEB and NJB read an imperfective, "*I will* lay a curse"). Several of the English versions insert the adverb "already" in an effort to convey the idea of the *recent perfective* (e.g., NAB, NIV, NRSV).

The feminine singular suffixed pronoun *-hā* ("her/it") is awkward in combination with the plural *birkôtêkem* ("your blessings") and must be emended (e.g., Calvin [1979: 514], see *birkôtêkem* above) or understood in some collective or categorical sense (Verhoef [1987: 239]) or even given a distributive meaning ("*each* blessing"; cf. Henderson [1980: 451]; Keil [2:443]). In either case, "the priests' failure to honor Yahweh's name will result in curses appropriate to their office" (R. W. Klein [1986: 146]). On the verb *'rr* ("to curse") see the discussion of *wĕ'ārûr* in the NOTES on 1:14 above and *nĕ'ārîm* on 3:9 below.

kî 'ĕnĕkem śamîm 'al-lēb. The adverb *kî* introducing the subordinate clause has a causal force ("because"), explaining the reason why Yahweh has already invoked a curse upon the Levitical priesthood (cf. WO'C § 39.3.4).

The suffixed clausal adverb *'ĕnĕkem* (a predicator of nonexistence, "you do not") both negates the participle and functions as the subject of the participle (WO'C § 37.5e, 37.6a).

The Qal participle *śamîm* (*śym*, "to place, set") serves as the predicate of the verbless clause and emphasizes a *durative circumstance* (i.e., the priests have not and even now are not conscientiously ascribing glory of Yahweh, cf. WO'C § 37.6b).

3. *hinĕnî gō'ēr lākem 'et-hazzera'.* The presentative exclamation *hinĕnî* ("See! I . . ."; see WO'C § 16.3.5b, 40.1.2b) with the participial clause (*gō'ēr . . .*) may describe immediate circumstances ("I am rebuking . . ." [so R. L. Smith 1984: 309]; cf. WO'C § 37.6de) or future circumstances with immanency — the so-called *futurum instans* participle (See! "I am *going* to rebuke . . ." [so NJB]; cf. WO'C § 37.6f). The construction is best understood as the *futurum instans* and a continuation of the apodosis of v 2 given the preceding participle *śamîm.*

The Qal participle *gō'ēr* ("rebuke," KBL 1:199–200) is often emended on the basis of the LXX *aphorízō* ("separate, take away"). For example, J.M.P. Smith (p. 36) reads *gōdēa'* ("cut off," KBL 1:180) and translates "I am going to hew off the arm for you" (cf. NEB, NJB, "I will cut off your arm" [= defrock or render unfit for priestly ministry]). Petersen (1995: 176 n. i) asserts the LXX *aphorízō* presupposes the Hebrew *gōrēa'* ("I am *removing* your progeny"; see *gr'* [I] in KBL 1:203–4). The MT *gō'ēr,* however, fits the prophetic idiom of the Second Temple era (e.g., Isa 50:2; 51:20; 54:9; 66:15; Zech 3:2), and is in keeping with the vocabulary of Malachi (cf. 3:11). In fact, reading *gō'ēr lākem* in 2:3 creates an effective parallel with *wĕgā'artî lākem* in 3:11, as Yahweh turns his rebuke away from the priests and toward "the devourer" should the restoration community repent (3:7). Also, the double entendre of the Hebrew ("I will rebuke your seed") has much to commend it (cf. Glazier-McDonald [1987a: 67–68]), given the context of crop failure in postexilic Yehud (Syr = "Behold, I will rebuke the seed of the ground"; cf. Baldwin [1972a: 233]).

The preposition *lamed* (*lākem,* "to you") denotes the *dativus incommodi* (or *lamed* of disadvantage), marking the person(s) *against* whom an action is directed ("your seed," JPSV; "your offspring," NRSV; cf. WO'C § 11.2.10d). The emphatic arrangement of the suffixed prepositions (*'ălêkem,* v 1; *bākem,* v 2; *lākem,* v 3; and *'ălêkem,* v 4) introduces a certain polarity between Yahweh and the priests and heightens the confrontational nature of the disputation format. The translation is an attempt to preserve the intentional ambiguity of the MT ("See! I am rebuking — *against* you — the seed.").

The definite direct object *hazzera'* ("the seed") may be repointed *hazzĕrōa'* ("the [fore]arm"). The LXX *ōmos* ("shoulder") and the V *brachium* ("forearm") support this reading (NEB, NJB, "arm"; NAB, "shoulder"; cf. J.M.P. Smith [1912: 45]; Rudolph [1976: 265]). The MT *zera'* ("seed") has the advantage of wide distribution in the Haggai-Zechariah-Malachi corpus (Hag 2:19; Zech 8:12; Mal 2:3, 15). Retention of the MT *zera'* also creates a certain dramatic irony between the second and third disputes, in that the "godly offspring" (*zera*ʿ *ʾĕ-lōhîm*, 2:15) sought by Yahweh could only be developed by means of sound priestly instruction (2:8) — yet the priests own "offspring" are rebuked!

wĕzērîtî pereš ʿal-pĕnêkem. The relative *waw* + suffixing conjugation (*wĕzērîtî*) after a participle describes a nonperfective consequential situation ("and I will spread," WO'C § 32.2.5a).

The Piel stem *zrh* means to "scatter, spread" ("strew," JPSV, NAB) or, more interpretively, to "smear" (Glazier-McDonald [1987a: 45]) or to "throw" (NJB). The verb *zrh* occurs elsewhere in the Haggai-Zechariah-Malachi corpus only in Zech 2:2 [1:19], 4 [2x]; [1:21] in reference to the "scattering" or exile of Judah among the nations (cf. Meyers and Meyers [1987: 137]). A similar act of desecration by Yahweh intended to render the high places of Judah unfit for cultic use is recorded in Ezek 6:5 (*wĕzērîtî ʾet-ʿaṣmôtêkem sĕbîbôt mizbĕḥôtêkem*, "and I will scatter your bones around your altars"; cf. Wevers [1971: 60]). Baldwin (1972a: 233) notes that T "dispenses with the metaphor and translated 'I will make visible on your faces the shame of your crimes'" (cf. Cathcart and Gordon [1989: 232]).

The definite direct object marker *ʾet-* is gapped from the preceding clause (*ʾet-hazzeraʿ*) for emphasis. The preposition *ʿal* has a simple locational sense, "upon," the most common of the spatial senses (WO'C § 11.2.13b).

pereš haggêkem. The masculine noun *pereš* occurs only 7 times in the OT/HB, always in the context of ritual animal sacrifice (Exod 29:14; Lev 4:11; 8:17; 16:27; Num 19:5; Mal 2:3 [2x]). The word is usually translated "dung" or "excrement" (Milgrom [1991: 239]), but more technically the term denotes the "undigested contents of the stomach not normally burned on the altar from considerations of delicacy" (Levine [1993: 462]; cf. NIV, NJB, "offal" = the waste parts of a butchered animal). According to Levitical law (Lev 4:11–12; 8:17; 16:27), *pereš*, along with the animal's head, legs, and entrails, are to be disposed by burning on the ash heap outside the camp (cf. the LXX *ėnystron* ["fourth stomach of ruminating animals"] for *pereš*).

The word *hag* may mean "procession, round dance, festival" (KBL 1:289–90) and occurs in the Haggai-Zechariah-Malachi corpus elsewhere only in Zech 14:16, 18, 19. Malachi refers to religious "feasts" in general (so NAB), perhaps as a metonymy for the "sacrifices" offered at the festivals (cf. JPSV, "festal sacrifices"; NJB, "solemn sacrifices"; but NEB, "pilgrim-feasts"). There's a certain irony in the prophet's condemnation, in that the priests have shown decorous sensitivity in the handling of offal from the animal sacrifices but have failed to accord equal respect to Yahweh himself (cf. Levine [1993: 462]). This punishment threatened by Yahweh is an act designed both to degrade and humiliate the priests (so Glazier-McDonald [1987a: 68]; cf. Nah 3:6) and render them unfit to perform their priestly duties because they would be ritually unclean (so Verhoef [1987: 242]; cf. Ezek 4:12–15). What Glazier-McDonald and Verhoef miss is that the portent of smearing dung upon the priests' faces is merely a symbolic action representing spiritual deficiencies that already disqualify them from priestly service. Malachi's denunciation of the priests calls to mind Yahweh's harsh disavowal of both the sacrifice and the people who offer the sacrifices in Amos 5:21 (cf. Andersen and Freedman [1989: 527]).

wĕnāśā' 'etkem 'ēlāyw. The MT is problematic, given the abrupt shift to the third-person in the Qal stem verb *nś'* ("lift, raise, carry [away], bear," CHAL: 246–47; lit. "and he will lift you up unto it") and the ambiguity of the suffixed preposition (*'ēlāyw*, "to it"). The integrity of this last clause has been challenged by some (e.g., Eiselen [1907: 717]; Dentan and Sperry [p. 1131]; both the *BHK* and *BHS* conjecture that the clause is secondary), while J.M.P. Smith (1912: 46) contends that the MT suffers from a "wrong distribution of letters, dittography, haplography, and confusion between א and ע" (emending to *nāśā'tîkem mē'ālay*; cf. Petersen [1995: 176 n. j], *wĕniśśā'tem mē'ālay*).

The relative *waw* + suffixing conjugation (*wĕnāśā'*) conclude the nonperfective consequential situation described by the combination of the participle (*gō'ēr*) + the *waw*-relative *wĕzērîtî* ("And so, [I] will lift you . . ."; cf. WO'C § 32.2.5a).

The LXX and Syr emend to *wĕnāśā'tî* ("and I will lift/carry"), in keeping with the first-person subject (Yahweh) of vv 2–3 (understanding the Qal infinitive absolute *nāśō'*, so NEB, NRSV). Alternately, the verb *nāśā'* is understood in an indefinite or impersonal transitive sense and rendered by the passive "and you shall be carried to it" (Laetsch [1956: 521]; Verhoef [1987: 243]; so JPSV, NAB, NIV). Glazier-McDonald (1987a: 68) concurs, citing examples (all third-person plural forms!) from GKC § 144fg, documenting indefinite subject verbs translated as passives.

Assuming *nāśā'* is a Qal suffixing form; one solution is to acknowledge the indefinite subject of *nāśā'* ("*one* will lift/carry"; cf. GKC § 144d) and retain the transitive sense (and active voice) of the form ("one will carry *you*"; cf. NJB, "and sweep you away with it"; Petersen [1995: 175], "you will be carried away from me"). The abrupt shift from first-person to third-person in the verbal forms is probably due to the prophet's reluctance to ascribe the menial (and ritually defiling) duty of transporting the priests (likened to the "sacrificial offal") to the ash heap directly to Yahweh (cf. Andersen and Freedman [1980: 510]).

If the ancient versions are correct in identifying Yahweh as the subject of the clause, a better solution may be to understand the verb *nś'* as the infinitive absolute (*nāśō'*). Yahweh, as the subject of the clause, may be inferred from *hinĕnî* ("See! I am . . .") and *wĕzērîtî* ("and I will spread"). This reading of the MT retains both the continuity and the force of Yahweh's actions against the Levitical priesthood. By analogy, Yahweh will dispose of the priests even as they dispose waste materials of the animal sacrifices ("And so *I* will lift you up to it!"; cf. LXX, Syr).

The verb *nāśā'* + the datival preposition *'el* mark direction, "lift or carry *to/unto*" (WO'C § 11.2.2; cf. BDB: 670). The translation "lift up" for *nāśā'* is awkward in context, prompting many commentators to emend the MT *'el* ("to") to the compound preposition *mē'āl* ("from beside" = "away from," e.g., J.M.P. Smith [1912: 46]; Petersen [1995: 175]; so NEB, NRSV), assuming an incorrect word division in the MT. See BDB: 671 on the idiom *nāśā'* + *'al* ("to carry away").

The subject of the masculine singular suffixed pronoun (*'ēlāyw*, "to him, *it*") is ambiguous. The divergences in the ancient versions (cf. LXX, *eis tò autó* ["to the same"], Syr "with *it*" [= *bô*], and T "from *it*" [*mnyh*]) attest the difficulty of the form. Interpreters commonly read *'ēlay* ("to me"), deleting the *waw* as an error of dittography with the following *waw* of *wîda'tem* in 2:4 (e.g., Petersen [1995: 176 n. j]); but Rudolph [1976: 260] suggests *'ālâ* ["one will take up *a curse* against you"]).

If the MT *'ēlāyw* is correct, the logical referent of the suffixed preposition (however uncouth) is "the offal of your feasts" (*pereš haggêkem*). Such an interpretation prompts Baldwin (1972a: 233) to conclude: "The imagery was boldly uncomplimentary to those whose birth and training had set them apart for sacred duties . . . the invective of the eighth-century prophets against the cultus . . . was polite by comparison." The prophet's crude upbraiding of the priests confirms that the promise made to the High Priest Joshua (as recorded in Zech 3:7) was fully conditional and could be annulled by misconduct on the part of the Levitical priesthood (cf. Mason [1977: 146]; Meyers and Meyers [1987: 194]).

If the final *waw* of *'lyw* is a dittograph with the initial *waw* of the first word in 2:4 (*wyd'tm*), then the referent of the first-person suffixed pronoun is Yahweh himself ("*I* will lift you up to *me*"). Such a rendering contradicts the disgrace and humiliation of the Levitical priesthood anticipated in context as the logical consequence of the violation of the "covenant of Levi" (2:4), unless *nāśā'* + *'el* may mean "to carry *away from*," in LBH ("And so I will carry you away from me"). The prepositions *'el* and *'al* appear to be interchangeable with *nāśā'* in the expression "lift up *to*" (cf. Ezek 18:6, 15 with Ezek 27:32). The reverse, however, is not the case with *'el* and *'al* in the expression "carry away *from*." It seems in this instance that the exact meaning of the MT as it stands, or in some emended form, still eludes the interpreter.

4. *wîda'tem*. The *waw*-relative + suffixing conjugation may be understood as a simple consequential (future time) situation ("then you shall know . . . ," e.g., NJB; cf. WO'C § 32.2.3a, c) or ascribed volitional force ("Know, then, that I . . . ," e.g., NRSV; cf. WO'C § 32.2.3d; so Petersen [1995: 176 n. k]).

The form *wîda'tem* constitutes a type of recognition formula in (the nonvisionary sections of) prophetic literature (cf. Meyers and Meyers [1987: 167]). Here the issue is not so much the recognition of divine authority invested in the prophet as it is that "a recognition will be awakened in Israel . . . recognition rooted in the proceedings by which a fact is ascertained through specific things or events ('signs')" (Zimmerli [1979: 133]). More precisely, this recognition awakened in Yehud pertains to the person of Yahweh and the divine initiation of the ancient covenant with Levi.

kî šillaḥtî 'ălêkem. The clausal adverb *kî* has a logical sense ("that," WO'C § 39.3.4e). The LXX inserts the independent pronoun *égō* (= Heb. *'ānî* ["I"]) in the clause (*dióti égō éxapéstalka*). The reading may well be original, the omission of the pronoun *'ānî* explained as the result of homeoteleuton (the scribe's eye skipping from the *yôd* in *ky* to the *yôd* in *šlḥty*, thereby eliminating the word *'ny* from the clause *ky 'ny šlḥty 'lykm*). The emphatic construction complements the confrontational nature of the disputational format and has its parallel in 2:8 below (*'attem sartem*). This balancing of independent pronouns has been observed already as a feature of Malachi (e.g., 1:4–5 [*w'ny 'hrws//w'ttm t'mrw*]).

The Piel suffixing conjugation *šillaḥtî* ("I sent . . . *this commandment*") stands in contrast to *wĕšillaḥtî* in v 2 ("I will send . . . *the curse*"). The suffixing form is rendered alternately as a *constative perfect* ("sent," e.g., NAB, NJB [assuming that the definite direct object "this commandment" hearkens back to the Levitical covenant of antiquity, cf. Deut 33:8–11]; cf. WO'C § 30.1d) or as a *recent perfective* ("have sent," e.g., JPSV, NRSV [perhaps assuming that the definite direct object "this commandment" refers to Zechariah's charge to the high priest Joshua, cf. Zech 3:7]; cf. WO'C § 30.5.1b). The expression *šillaḥtî . . . 'ēt hammiṣwâ hazzō't* is unusual and may have liturgical associations (cf. *haššōlēaḥ 'imrātô*, Ps 147:15; *yišlaḥ dĕbārāw*, Ps 147:18.

The preposition *'el* marks a simple dative ("*to* you"), that is the Levitical priesthood as the recipients of Yahweh's commandment (WO'C § 11.2.2). The masculine plural suffixed pronoun further accents the exchange between Yahweh ("*I* [*myself*] sent") and the priests of Yehud ("*you* will know . . . to *you*").

'ēt hammiṣwâ hazzō't. See the discussion of *hammiṣwâ hazzō't* ("this commandment" or "this charge" in the NOTES for 2:1 above.

lĕhayyôt bĕrîtî 'et-lēwî. The MT understands *lhywt* as a Qal infinitive construct (*lihyôt*). The preposition *lamed* (see WO'C § 36.2.3d) may be rendered as a purpose clause ("*in order to be* my covenant with Levi," so NAB; Verhoef [1987: 244]) or as a result clause ("*so that* my covenant with Levi *may be*" [i.e., continue, endure, hold], so JPSV, NIV, NJB, NRSV; cf. LXX, Syr). The essential idea of the clause thus becomes one of Yahweh's maintenance of his covenant with Levi (so Glazier-McDonald [1987a: 68–69]).

The difficulty of the clause is attested by the numerous proposed emendations of the MT *lhywt*. For example, Horst (p. 266) and Chary (1969: 167) read *mihyôt bĕrîtî* ("*from being* my covenant") and understand 2:4 as the abrogation of Yahweh's covenant relationship with the Levitical priesthood. Sellin (p. 599) went further, suggesting that the text originally read *lĕhātēt* (*ḥtt* = "broken, shattered") but was deliberately revised because a broken Levitical covenant was unthinkable for later generations.

The proposed emendation of the BHS (*lĕhayyôt*) has much to commend it because the harsh words of the prophet in 2:2–3 are not intended to annul the Levitical covenant; nor are they designed to simply maintain the status quo. Rather, Malachi seeks the rehabilitation of the Levitical priesthood. His words call for the restoration or reinstatement of the covenant with Levi as it was in the former days (cf. Petersen [1995: 190]). Hence, the verb *hyh* here has the sense of "revive, be actualized" (KBL 1:309; cf. Petersen [1995: 175], "to enforce my covenant with Levi").

The greater questions puzzling commentators are the relationship between "this commandment" and the reference to "my covenant" and exactly what the Levitical priests are supposed to learn from Yahweh's charge. One approach equates "this commandment" (*hammiṣwâ hazzō't*) with "my covenant" (*bĕrîtî*) in an absolute sense as both the condition by which the priests serve Yahweh and the standard by which they are judged and punished (see R. W. Klein [1986: 146] on the "two-sided" covenant of Levi; cf. Ezek 44:13, priests who cause Israel to "stumble" in iniquity forfeit their cultic privileges). This view takes seriously the conditionality attached to priestly service by the prophet Zechariah (3:7; cf. NEB, "my covenant with Levi falls to the ground" [i.e., God is revoking the special privileges of the priests "because of their faithlessness"; Mason [1977: 147]). See further the discussion of _lēwî_ ("Levi") in _TDOT_ 7:483–503.

A second interpretation distinguishes between "this commandment" (_hammiṣwâ hazzō't_) as the condition by which the priests serve Yahweh and the means by which they are led to repentance (2:1–3; cf. Baldwin [1972a: 233–34]) and the perpetual covenant (_bĕrîtî_) established by Yahweh with Levi as the priestly ancestor of the Israelite nation (cf. Glazier-McDonald [1987a: 69]). The latter view is more in keeping with the context of the prophet's message. Malachi "expresses the hope that the covenant between Yahweh and Levi may be salvaged" (Petersen [1995: 190]). The basic sense of the preposition _'et-[lēwî]_ is comitative ("_with_ Levi," WO'C § 11.2.4). On _bĕrîtî_ ("my covenant") see the NOTES on v 5 below.

5. _bĕrîtî_. The original meaning of the Hebrew _bĕrît_ suggests "imposition" or "obligation," and when used to signify a formal agreement between two parties, the word denotes "oath and commitment" (cf. _TDOT_ 2:255–56). There are two basic types of covenants found in the OT/HB and the ANE: the obligatory type (suzerain-vassal treaty) and the promissory type (covenant of grant; see Weinfeld [1970]). Both covenant types create some kind of relationship, usually between a "superior" (deity or royalty) and an "inferior" (suppliant or subject). The (renewable) suzerain-vassal treaty binds the recipient to an authority figure (whether God or king) by means of claims and demands and includes the threat of sanctions and punishment for violation of the treaty terms (e.g., Yahweh's covenant with Israel at Sinai, Exodus 19–24; cf. _ABD_ 1:1183–88). The covenant of grant in the Bible is a unilateral and irrevocable commitment on the part of God to an individual, family, or nation (e.g., Yahweh's covenant with Abram, Genesis 15; cf. _TDOT_ 2:270–72).

Reciprocity in the relationship between Yahweh and Israel exists only as the ideals of these two covenant types intersect. Both are "one-way" covenants: technically only Yahweh is bound in the promissory type and only Israel is bound in the obligatory type. Both are distinct in literary form, Israelite historical context, and theological implication (cf. _TDOT_ 2:266–72, 275–76). Malachi alludes to Yahweh's covenant of grant with Abram (Genesis 15) in the clause "I loved you" in the opening disputation (1:2–5). The prophet makes direct reference to the suzerainty type Sinaitic covenant in the use of terms like "commandment" (_mišmeret_, 3:14) and "law" or "instruction" (_tôrâ_, 2:6, 8, 9). The language of Mal 2:4–8 suggests that the covenant of Levi is a promissory type grant, because the curses are directed against the priests for violating the "religious" rights of the people of Yahweh (cf. Weinfeld [1970: 185]).

It is only on the basis of this interface of the two separate covenant traditions between Yahweh and Israel that Glazier-McDonald (1987a: 70) can speak of the "mutual commitments" of the covenant of Levi (including Yahweh's obligation to bestow life and peace upon the priests, provided the priests reciprocated with reverent conduct honoring Yahweh; cf. Petersen [1995: 190] on the value of this covenant relationship for the entire community of Yehud).

The suffixed possessive pronoun ("_my_ covenant") reminds the priests and all

Yehud that Yahweh alone initiates covenant relationship. The Bible nowhere records the establishment of this compact between Yahweh and Levi, the eponymous ancestor of the Levitical priesthood. The OT/HB preserves several allusions to such a covenant, including Exod 32:26–29 (in response to the purge by the sons of Levi after the golden calf episode; cf. Baldwin [1972a: 234]); Num 25:11–13 (in response to the heroic deed of Phinehas; cf. E. M. Meyers [1986: 232]; Glazier-McDonald [1987a: 79–80]); Deut 33:8–11 (the poetic blessing of the tribe of Levi; cf. Blenkinsopp [1983: 242]; Verhoef [1987: 245]); Jer 33:20–21 (harking back to a covenant with the Levites; cf. *ABD* 4:294–95, 297–310). Although not explicitly identified as a covenant, the language of Malachi has affinities with the blessing of Moses on the tribe of Levi (Deut 33:8–11). On *bĕrît* ("covenant") in Malachi, see further the NOTES on 2:10, 14; 3:1.

hāyĕtâ 'ittô. The Qal perfective *hāyĕtâ* suggests a sense of past time (*definite preterite*), because verse 2 indicates that Yahweh has already begun to curse the Levitical priesthood ("was," NEB, NJB, NRSV [but JPSV, "had"]; cf. WO'C § 30.5.1b). The preposition *'ēt* has a comitative sense ("with"), marking both accompaniment and interest (WO'C § 11.2.4a). The masculine singular suffixed pronoun ("him") identifies Levi (and presumably his descendants, v 4; cf. Henderson [1980: 452] who restricts the reference not to Levi personally, but to Phinehas on the basis of Num 25:12–13) as the object of the covenant relationship. The combination of *bĕrît* + *hyh* is inverted in verse 4 [MT] (*lihyôt bĕrîtî*) and verse 5 (*bĕrîtî hāyĕtâ*).

haḥayyîm wĕhaššālôm. The blessings of covenant relationship for Levi (and the Levitical priesthood) included "life" and "peace." The two nouns, "life" (*ḥayyîm*) and "peace" (*šālôm*), are joined by the phrasal *waw*-copulative elsewhere only in Prov 3:2 (. . . *ḥayyîm wĕšālôm* . . .). Appropriately, the wisdom of obeying the commandments of Yahweh forms the context in Proverbs. The two terms of the expression modify each other and possess almost an unlimited combination of nuances that include wholesome and prosperous activity, vivifying peace, robust health, length of days, and vibrant well-being (cf. *TDOT* 4:333–35). The prophet leaves the various connective possibilities of the expression to his audience (cf. Petersen [1995: 190]).

The ambiguity of the clausal relationship between *bĕrîtî* ("my covenant") and *haḥayyîm wĕhaššālôm* ("life and peace") has prompted alternate interpretations, including understanding *haḥayyîm wĕhaššālôm* in a genitive relationship with *bĕrîtî* ("my covenant with him was *a covenant of* life and peace," so JPSV, NAB, NJB, NRSV; cf. LXX, V), equating "life and peace" with the covenant of Levi ("my covenant was with him — life and peace — and I gave them to him"; cf. Keil [2:444]; Laetsch [1956: 520]), and reading the phrase "life and peace" in clausal relationship with the following verb *wā'ettĕnem* ("and I gave him life and peace," so NEB; R. L. Smith [1984: 309]; cf. Syr). According to J.M.P. Smith (p. 38), both the syntax and MT accentuation favor reading the phrase "life and peace" as an appositive with "my covenant" (Packard [1902: 13]; Petersen [1995: 175]; cf. WO'C § 12.2). The definiteness of *haḥayyîm wĕhaššālôm* is thus anaphoric (cf. WO'C § 13.5.1d). Mason (1977: 147) connects the promise of blessing to

Joshua the high priest (Zech 3:7) with the covenant benefits of life and peace in Mal 2:5, but this association is not certain.

wā'ettĕnem-lô. The *waw*-relative + the Qal prefixing form of *ntn* continue the definite preterite value of *hāyĕtâ* ("and I gave *them*" [the suffixed object pronoun representing the aforementioned benefits, "life and peace"]) and testify to the fact that Yahweh has always fulfilled his covenant obligations (cf. WO'C § 33.3.1). The preposition *lamed* marks a benefactive dative ("to him" [i.e., Levi, v 4]; WO'C § 11.2.10d).

môrā' wayyirā'ēnî. The masculine noun *môrā'* means "fear" in the sense of "awe, reverence" (*CHAL:* 187) and provides a partial answer to the question addressing reverence (*môrā'*) for God in 1:6 (see NOTES above). Syntactically, the form is variously rendered as an accusative (the compound direct object of *wā'ettĕnem* ["and I gave him life and peace . . . *and fear*], e.g., Calvin [p. 663]; J.M.P. Smith [1912: 38]; Glazier-McDonald [1987a: 45]; NAB, "fear I put in him"; cf. NEB, "I laid on him the duty of reverence") or adverbially ("reverently he feared me," cf. LXX; or "I gave them to him in fear," so R. L. Smith [1984: 309]) or in a genitive relationship with *bĕrîtî* ("a covenant of respect," NJB; "and of reverence," JPSV). Others simply delete the form (e.g., Petersen [1995: 175], "These I allocated to him and he feared me").

The word *môrā'* ("reverence") is best understood in association with *bĕrîtî* ("my covenant"), either as a genitive or an appositive along with *hahayyîm wĕhaš-šālôm* ("life and peace"; so Redditt [1995: 168]). Baldwin (1972a: 235) has well summarized, "This reaction of *awe* at God's *name* was far removed from the insolence of those who offered that which cost them nothing (1:8, 13), were bored with worship (1:13) and yet had utmost confidence in themselves (1:6c)."

The *waw*-relative + Qal prefixing form of *yr'* ("to fear") signifies an event of logical consequence and continues the definite preterite value of the previous two clauses ("and so he feared me"; cf. WO'C § 33.3.1d). The verb *yr'* in this context encompasses the notions of reverence of the numinous nature of God and loyalty to the God of the covenant demonstrated by obedience to the divine ordinances (cf. *TDOT* 6:300, 306–8, 313). The referent of the suffixed object pronoun ("and he feared *me*") is Yahweh, further underscoring the reciprocity of fulfilled obligations in the covenant between Yahweh and Levi (cf. Verhoef [1987: 247]). On the verb *yr'* in Malachi, see further the NOTES on 1:14 above and 3:5, 23 [4:5] below.

ûmippĕnê šĕmî niḥat hû'. The combination of the preposition *min* ("from") + the plural construct form of the masculine noun *pānîm* ("face") is used idiomatically in a locational sense ("before, in the presence of," BDB: 818; cf. Judg 5:5, *mippĕnê YHWH* ["before Yahweh"] in Boling and Wright [1982: 101]). In context, the construct genitive phrase *ûmippĕnê šĕmî* ("and before my name") refers primarily to the priestly duties connected with the sacrificial liturgy — discharged "in the presence of" Yahweh (cf. Lev 10:2; 22:3). The emphatic position of the phrase serves to heighten the covenant obligation of the priests to revere and honor Yahweh. The word "name" (*šĕmî*, "my name") occurs eight times in the second dispute (1:6 [2x], 11 [3x], 14; 2:2, 5), emphasizing the focal point of priestly service—the name of Yahweh. On *šĕmî* as a synonymous term for Yahweh himself, see the NOTES on 1:6 above.

The Niphal suffixing conjugation *niḥat* is unique to Malachi in the MT, and the verbal root *ḥtt* occurs only here in the Haggai-Zechariah-Malachi corpus (cf. Rudolph [1976: 260 n. 5]; Glazier-McDonald [1987a: 70]; Petersen [1995: 176 n. m]). The verb *ḥtt* in the Niphal stem means "be broken to pieces, dismayed, terrified" (KBL 1:365) and in the context of Mal 2:5 "be put in awe" (BDB: 369). The verbs *yr'* and *ḥtt* are frequently found in synonymous parallelism, but only in Mal 2:5 is this word pair used for the fear of God (cf. *TDOT* 5:280). The independent pronoun (*hû'*, "he") is emphatic in the sense that it involves *logical contrast* or evinces *explicit antithesis* between Levi and the priests of Yehud (cf. WO'C § 16.3.2d).

6. *tôrat 'ĕmet hāyĕtâ bĕpîhû*. The construct-genitive (*tôrat 'ĕmet*) is an adjectival genitive phrase, one specifying features of the other in attribution ("true instruction"; cf. WO'C § 9.5.3a). The feminine noun *'ĕmet* ("trustworthiness, constancy, faithfulness, truth," KBL 1:68–69) occurs only here in Malachi, although according to Zechariah, *'ĕmet* will characterize Yahweh's restoration of Jerusalem (7:9; 8:3, 8, 16, 19). Unlike the audience addressed by Hosea, people unacquainted with "faithfulness" (*'ĕmet*, 4:1), Levi was a paragon of constancy before God.

The phrase is unique to Mal 2:6 in the MT (cf. *bĕtôrat YHWH* ["in the law of Yahweh"], Ps. 119:1. The psalm probably dates to the same time period as the book of Malachi, further evidence of the interest in and devotion for Torah during the postexilic period [cf. Allen 1983: 140–41]). It refers not to the "law of Moses" (see the discussion of *tôrat mōšeh* in the NOTES for 3:22 [4:4] below), but to juridical and pedagogical functions of the Levitical priesthood predicated upon the Mosaic legal tradition (cf. Petersen [1995: 190]). The expression does not require that such priestly instruction be restricted to oral tradition only, as this teaching may well have been rooted in written documents (Glazier-McDonald [1987a: 71]; cf. Andersen and Freedman [1980: 509]). This "true instruction" of Levi serves as a foil for the "instruction" (*battôrâ*) of Malachi's Levitical contemporaries, teaching that caused many to stumble (v 8).

The construction *bĕpîhû* ("in his mouth") is an idiom for one's speech (BDB: 805; cf. Holladay [1986: 377]). The genuineness of Levi may be contrasted with the wicked person who has no truth "in his mouth" (*bĕpîhû*, Ps 5:5). Normally, one's speech is a reflection of the inner self, one's person and character. The Hebrew prophets, however, recognized that at times Israel's hypocrisy was such that speech was not always an accurate barometer of the heart condition (cf. Jer 12:2; Ezek 33:31).

wĕ'awlâ lō'-nimṣā' biśpātāyw. The coordinating *waw* is conjunctive, joining verse 6a and verse 6b in an unusual type of synonymous (ABC) parallelism, employing the contrast of a positive and a negative statement (cf. WO'C § 39.2.5).

The feminine noun *'awlâ* ("perversity, wickedness," *CHAL*: 267) is unique to Mal 2:6 in the Haggai-Zechariah-Malachi corpus. Traditionally *'awlâ* is rendered "iniquity" (e.g., KJV, NRSV; cf. JPSV, "perverse"; NAB, "dishonesty"; NJB, "guilt"). The word describes "wickedness" generally (Job 6:29, 30; Ps 37:1), and depending upon context may refer to "violence" (Micah 3:10; Hab 2:12) or "injustice" (Hos 10:13). In Mal '*awlâ* specifies sins of speech, especially deceitfulness — the antithesis of '*ĕmet* (Job 13:7; 27:4; Isa 59:3; cf. Petersen [1995: 191] on "perversity as an appropriate antonym for 'true Torah'" with respect to improper behavior).

The negative adverb *lō*' + the Niphal suffixing form *nimṣā*' affirm by negative statement the legacy of trustworthy teaching and sound speech ascribed to Levi. Here the verb *māṣā*' means "[was not] found" in the sense that sins of speech were beyond detection in Levi because '*awlâ* was not intrinsically a part of his character (cf. BDB: 594). Apparently Levi (and those priests faithful to his example) understood that the "fruit" of true worship "was found" (*nimṣā*') in Yahweh (Hos 14:9 [8]; cf. Andersen and Freedman [1980: 647]). Baldwin (1972a: 235) reminds us "that words are an index of character as a theme of the Scriptures," and truthful words were vital to the twofold priestly ministry of mediation and instruction (cf. Mason [1977: 147]).

bĕšālôm ûbĕmîšôr hālak '*ittî*. The preposition *bêt* is used spatially to mark location "in, within" an area or domain (i.e., "in" the domain of "peace," WO'C § 11.2.5b). In this context, *šālôm* means "peace with God" in the sense of fellowship and right relationship (BDB: 1023; see also the discussion of *šālôm* in v 5 above).

The *phrasal waw* is conjunctive (WO'C § 39.2.1b). The masculine noun *mîšôr* most often identifies literally "a plain" or "level ground" (Deut 3:10), but metaphorically the word denotes "fairness, righteousness" (Pss 45:7 [6]; 67:5 [4]; cf. CHAL: 193). The word is rare in the Twelve Prophets, occurring only in Zech 4:7 and Mal 2:6. Elsewhere in the Latter Prophets *mîšôr* ("fairness") is used in synonymous parallelism with *ṣedeq* ("righteousness") in reference to the rule of the "shoot" from the stump of Jesse (Isa 11:4; cf. Weinfeld [1995: 33]).

The Qal suffixing conjugation *hālak* means "walk" in the theological sense of covenant obedience and a worshipful lifestyle, "setting God as the center of human life" (TDOT 3:395; cf. Baldwin [1972a: 235], "an expression denoting close communion with God, but used sparingly"). The *definite preterite* aspect of the perfective is maintained throughout the recollection of Levi's faithfulness (cf. WO'C § 33.3.1d).

The comitative use of the preposition '*ēt* ("with") signifies accompaniment in the form of companionship or fellowship (WO'C § 11.2.4). The juxtaposition of *bĕrîtî hāyĕtâ* '*ittô* in verse 5 ("my covenant was *with him*") and *hālak* '*ittî* in verse 6 ("he walked *with me*") admirably portrays the ideal of mutuality in covenant relationship (cf. Glazier-McDonald [1987a: 71]).

wĕrabbîm hēšîb·*mē*'*āwōn*. The coordinating *waw* is conjunctive in a logical or sequential sense, in that many were turned from iniquity *as a result* of the priests' (i.e., Levi and his descendants) sound instruction and blameless walk with Yahweh (cf. WO'C § 39.3.3, 39.2.5).

The attributive adjective *rabbîm* ("many") stands alone as a substantive in the accusative position (cf. WO'C § 14.3). It is possible the word *rabbîm* already possesses connotations similar to those associated with the later Qumran documents in which *rabbîm* is a technical term for the "lay members" of the religious community (i.e., "and he [the priest] turned many [lay members of the community] away from sin"; cf. Marcus [1956: 301–2] and Morgenstern [1963: 331–32] on *rabbîm* as a "sectarian" term at Qumran). There's an ironic force in the emphatic position of *wĕrabbîm* because now the priesthood has caused "many" (*rabbîm*) to stumble in Yehud (v 8), and the priests themselves are in need of "turning back" (*šwb*) to Yahweh (cf. 3:7).

The Hiphil perfective *hēšîb* continues the *definite preterite* value of the suffixing conjugation initiated in v 5 (WO'C § 33.3.1d). Both by word and example the priests of an earlier era induced the people of Israel to desist from sinning and to return to God in repentance (cf. Verhoef [1987: 249]). On the verb *šwb* ("turn, return," *CHAL:* 362–63) see further the discussion of the form in the NOTES for 1:4 above and 3:7, 18, 24 [4:6] below.

The preposition *min* has an ablative sense, designating movement "away from" a specified beginning point (here from "evil"; cf. WO'C 6 11.2.11b). The word *'āwōn* ("offense, sin, iniquity," *CHAL:* 268) emphasizes the subjective side of transgression, both human volition and consequent guilt (cf. Wolff [1974: 81]). The term is used profusely in Jeremiah and Ezekiel to describe Judah's sin but occurs in the Haggai-Zechariah-Malachi corpus only here and in Zech 3:4, 9 (where *'āwōn* is not so much a description of personal sinfulness as it is an abstraction of iniquity and guilt, cf. Meyers and Meyers [1987: 189]).

7. *kî-śiptê kōhēn yišmĕrû-da'at.* The particle *kî* may be understood as a conjunction introducing a subordinate clause ("for," so NAB, NIV, NRSV) or as a clausal adverb used logically ("because," so R. L. Smith [1984: 309]) or emphatically ("Verily," so Verhoef [1987: 236]; "Indeed," so Petersen [1995: 175]). Reading *kî* as a clausal adverb (used emphatically) is clearly preferable, although this may be an instance where the logical and emphatic senses "should not be too strictly separated" (WO'C § 39.3.4e). J.M.P. Smith (pp. 41–42) ably repudiates those who question the integrity of segments or all of verse 7 (e.g., Marti [1904: 467–68]; Nowack [1922: 418–19]; BHK; cf. Verhoef [1987: 249]).

The word *śāpâ* ("lip") is a type of metonymy in which the "lips" as a physical organ represent the function of speech (BDB: 974–75; cf. *biśpātāyw* in v 6). The construct genitive *śiptê kōhēn* ("lips of a priest") refers specifically to the pedagogical duties of the priest, preaching and teaching the "law" (*tôrâ*) of Yahweh to Jacob (cf. Deut 33:10; see Mason [1990: 244–45] on the preaching tradition of the Second Temple).

The indefinite singular *kōhēn* ("a priest") represents a generic noun of class (WO'C § 13.8b). The priests as a cadre of mentors "were to mediate God's instructions concerning ethics and morals and ritual when persons came to them for Torah, teaching out of a knowledge of God gained in intimate prophetic-like communion with him" (Achtemeier [1986: 178]). Dentan and Sperry's (pp. 1132–33) summary of Malachi's assessment of the loftiness of the Levitical office and the primacy of the priestly teaching ministry remains apropos: "This verse contains both the noblest statement of the function of priesthood to be found in the Old Testament and the highest estimate of its dignity."

The Qal prefixing conjugation *yišmĕrû* ("they safeguard") is unambiguous. The ancient versions and modern English versions assume that *śiptê kōhēn* serves as the subject of the verb *yišměrû* in the clause (e.g., LXX, "For the priest's lips should keep knowledge"; JPSV, "For the lips of a priest guard knowledge"). Recent commentators are in agreement (e.g., Glazier-McDonald [1987a: 45]; Petersen [1995: 175]), usually ascribing a modal or optative sense to *yišměrû* (the *nonperfective of deliberation*, "denoting the speaker's or subject's deliberation as to whether a situation *should* take place," WO'C § 31.4f; cf. NJB, "the priest's lips *ought* to safeguard knowledge"). This reading is problematic, however, in that the construction violates basic rules of grammar related to the agreement in gender of subject and verb (cf. Ps 31:19 [18], *tē'ālamnâ śiptê šāqer* ["let lying lips be silenced"]; but Prov 10:21, *śiptê ṣaddîq yir'û* ["the lips of the righteous sustain many"]). The preference for masculine over feminine forms, especially in LBH, is well attested and that may be the case here (Polzin [1976: 52–54]; cf. GKC § 132d, 145pt; WO'C § 6.5.3).

Recognizing 2:6d and 2:7ab as a related tricolon, with *rabbîm* serving as the subject of the last two clauses, has much to commend it:

wěrabbîm hēšîb mē'āwōn
kî-śiptê kōhēn yišměrû-da'at
wětôrâ yěbaqšû mippîhû;
"and many [lay members] he turned from iniquity.
Surely, [from] the lips of the priest they safeguard knowledge,"
"and Torah they seek from his mouth."

First, *rabbîm* (masculine "many") serves as a logical complement to the masculine plural verbs *yišměrû* ("they safeguard") and *yěbaqšû* ("they seek"). Second, the bicolon of verse 7ab is arranged in a chiastic structure (A B C / C' B' A'), with the backward or inverted gapping of the preposition *min* ("from") understood in v 7a (see the NOTES on 1:6, 7 above for other examples of backward gapping in the disputations). Third, there is discernible symmetry in the MT accentuation of the three clauses (3 + 3 + 3). It is possible the prophet quotes here a popular adage or liturgical ode in praise of the Levitical priesthood, thus accounting for the almost poetic rhythm of the construction.

The verb *šmr* means "guard, keep" in the sense that the priests are to "preserve" the knowledge of God as an agent of his covenant by carefully maintaining and accurately transmitting the received theological traditions about Israel's God, Yahweh (BDB: 1037; cf. Redditt [1995: 169], "the translation 'guard' catches both nuances of obeying and preserving"). On the verb *šmr* see further the NOTES for 2:9, 15, 16; 3:7, 14 below.

The word *da'at* ("knowledge") is "the knowledge of God in the torah for which the priest is responsible" (Andersen and Freedman [1980: 352]). Citing Wolff, Botterweck elaborates that this aspect of the Levitical ministry consisted chiefly of "the priestly task of preserving and handing on a specific body of knowledge concerning God, which can be learned but also forgotten" (*TDOT* 5:478; cf. Ogden and Deutsch [1987: 92] for specific examples of this educational function). The term occurs primarily in judgment oracles in the Prophets, and its usage in Mal 2:7 fits this pattern (cf. *TDOT*: 476). The noun *da'at* occurs only in Hos 4:1, 6; 6:6; and Mal 2:7 in the Twelve, suggesting Malachi's dependence upon the indictment of the priests in Hos 4:4–6 for his rebuke of the priests of Yehud. The theme of the "knowledge of God" thus forms an envelope for the collection of the Twelve Prophets, making the nexus seem more than coincidental.

wĕtôrâ yĕbaqšû mippîhû. The coordinating waw is conjunctive, linking interrelated clauses (WO'C § 39.2.5). The emphatic position of the word tôrâ highlights the logical relationship of the word pair da'at ("knowledge") and tôrâ ("instruction"). Here the term tôrâ refers to both the priestly function of giving instruction and to the deposit of theological knowledge entrusted to the priests (see the discussion of Hos 4:6 in Wolff [1974: 79]; cf. J.M.P. Smith [1912: 40]). On the meaning of tôrâ as "instruction" see the NOTES for v 6 above. The alternate reading of the JPSV ("For the lips of a priest are observed; knowledge and ruling are sought from his mouth") stands alone.

The Piel prefixing conjugation yĕbaqšû is usually understood to describe a modal or optative situation, the nonperfective of deliberation ("denoting the speaker's or subject's deliberation as to whether a situation should take place," WO'C § 31.4f; cf. NRSV, "people should seek"). The word bqš functions theologically in context, expressing the idea of "seeking God" through instruction in his law (cf. TDOT 2:236). In this case, the word connotes "desire" as much as "obligation."

If, however, rabbîm (v 6d) actually serves as the subject of the clause, then the third-person masculine plural form is not indefinite (an example of the pseudopassive use of the Qal stem ["his mouth is where the law should be sought"], NJB; cf. WO'C § 22.7a). Rather, the verb yĕbaqšû represents a customary nonperfective ("they [lay members] seek") or even a nonperfective of obligation ("they [lay members] must seek") given the role of priest as teacher of Torah (cf. WO'C § 31.3b, 31.4g). On the verb bqš, see further the discussion of mĕbaqqēš in the NOTES for 2:15 and mĕbaqšîm in the NOTES on 3:1 below.

The spatial preposition min has a locational sense, describing the place where a thing or person originated ("from his mouth," WO'C § 11.2.11b). On the construction of preposition min + the noun peh ("mouth") as the organ of speech, see BDB: 805. The suffixed pronoun (-hû', "his" [i.e., kōhēn or "priest"]) marks a genitive of agency (cf. WO'C § 16.4d). Note the inversion of peh ("mouth") and śāpâ ("lips") in vv 6–7.

kî mal'ak YHWH-ṣĕbā'ôt hû'. The clausal adverb kî has a logical or causal force ("since, because," NAB, NEB, NIV, NJB; cf. WO'C § 39.3.4e).

The construct-genitive phrase mal'ak YHWH-ṣĕbā'ôt is unique to Mal 2:7 in the MT and marks the only place where the term mal'āk ("angel, messenger") is applied to the priestly office (see the discussion of mal'āk in the NOTES for 1:1 above and 3:1 below). The title "messenger" is reserved for the prophets of Yahweh, and the word is a technical expression for one who has been in God's presence and is thereby commissioned to bring a message from him (cf. Hag 1:13, "messenger of Yahweh" [mal'ak YHWH]; see Meyers and Meyers [1987: 34]).

Malachi's sanctioning of the Levitical priesthood as mediators of the divine will should not be interpreted as the abrogation of such mediation by angelic

Figure 1. King Darius I, Audience Scene from the Treasury Relief. King Darius I depicted on the southern wall of the royal storehouse at Persepolis receiving a foreign dignitary. The king sits behind two incense burners, while pairs of attendants stand at each end of the canopy. The crown prince (Xerxes) stands behind the seated Darius. The scene calls to mind Malachi's charge to Yehud to fill Yahweh's "storehouse" (3:10). *Courtesy of the Oriental Institute of the University of Chicago*

Figure 2. King Darius I. King Darius I ruled ancient Persia from 521 to 486 B.C./E. Darius' legacy is one of an ambitious general, energetic builder, able administrator, and shrewd bureaucrat. The defeat of the Persians by the Greeks at the Battle of Marathon (490 B.C./E.) may have prompted Malachi's oracles, the prophet interpreting that event in light of Haggai's forecast of a "shaking of the nations" (Hag 2:21–22). *Courtesy of the Oriental Institute of the University of Chicago*

Figure 3. Eastern Stairway of the Apadana. The Apadana was a great audience hall, begun by Darius I and completed by Xerxes. It is estimated that the structure could accommodate a crowd of nearly 10,000 people. The stairway reliefs of the Apadana depict delegations from nearly two dozen ethnic groups from across the Persian Empire bringing tribute to King Darius (see Yamauchi 1990:346–56). Three times Malachi reminds his audience of Yahweh's exalted position "among the nations" (1:11, 14). *Courtesy of the Oriental Institute of the University of Chicago*

Figure 4.
Processional of Servants, Palace
of Darius I. "Bring it to your governor!
Will he be pleased with you . . . ?"
(Mal 1:8). Close-up of the southern stairway,
west flight (south side, north face) of the Palace of Darius I.
The relief shows royal servants bringing offerings of agricultural produce
and livestock to the king. The scene calls to mind Malachi's satirical command to the priests concerning blemished and diseased animals being offered as sacrifices to Yahweh. *Courtesy of the Oriental Institute of the University of Chicago*

Figure 5. Cylinder Seal of Darius I, with Impression. "'For I am a great king,' Yahweh of Hosts has said" (Mal 1:14). The agate cylinder seal was found at Thebes, Egypt, and dates to 500 B.C./E. The cuneiform inscription names Darius and his title, "The Great King," in three languages: Elamite, Babylonian, and Old Persian. *Copyright British Museum*

Figure 6. Palace of Darius I. The Palace of Darius I at Persepolis (general view of the southern stairway from the south). This royal residence was completed by Xerxes. The floor plan of Darius' palace inspired the standard features found in later Persian residential buildings. *Courtesy of the Oriental Institute of the University of Chicago*

Figure 7. Behistun Relief. The Behistun Relief depicts King Darius I (life-size scale) standing atop the insurgent Gaumata and facing defeated rebel kings of the Persian provinces (at two-thirds life-size scale). The winged solar-disc image (see Figure 13) hovers over the bound prisoners. The relief and inscription were carved around 518 B.C./E. on the sheer rock-face cliff some 79 m (228 ft.) above the plain of Kermanshah. The site (modern Bisitun) is located 20 km (12.4 mi.) east of Kermanshah in Iran on the old caravan road from Ecbatana to Babylon. *Courtesy of the Oriental Institute of the University of Chicago*

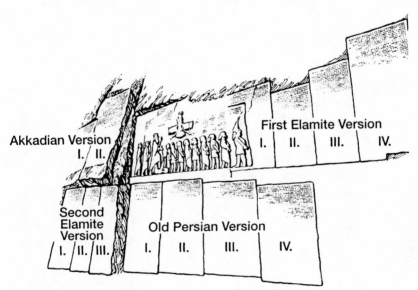

Figure 8. Behistun Inscription. The Behistun Inscription is the Mesopotamian counterpart of the Egyptian Rosetta Stone. The rock-face panels of the inscription are arranged around the relief centerpiece of Darius I (see Figure 7) and cover an area 7 m (23 ft.) high and 18 m (59 ft.) wide. The trilingual inscription recording the circumstances of Darius' rise to power is carved with cuneiform characters in Akkadian, Elamite, and Old Persian and proved to be instrumental in the decipherment of the cuneiform languages. *Adapted from Trüpplemann in Yamauchi 1990:132–33*

Figure 9. Winged Bull, Gate of Xerxes (Gate of All Nations). "Indeed . . . Great is my name among the nations" (Mal 1:11). The massive Gate of all Nations was located above the grand stairway leading up to the terraced royal complex at Persepolis (see the reconstruction in Yamauchi 1990:344). The elaborate gatehouse afforded foreign dignitaries access to the Apadana, or great audience hall. Malachi reminds postexilic Yehud that Yahweh is both the God of Israel (1:5) and God of the nations (1:11, 14). *Courtesy of the Oriental Institute of the University of Chicago*

Figure 10. Fire Altar, Central Facade of the Tomb of Darius I. "Oh . . . that you would not kindle fire on my altar in vain" (Mal 1:10). Fire was venerated in Zoroastrian religion, and considered a symbol of the god Ahuramazda. The Persian magi and even the Persian kings are depicted attending fire altars in service to Ahuramazda. Malachi employs this religious image common to the ancient world to describe both the worship of Yahweh and the character of Yahweh's judgment on the day of his visitation (3:2, 19[4:1]). *Courtesy of the Oriental Institute of the University of Chicago*

Figure 11. Solomon's Temple
(ca. 960–587 B.C./E.)
King Solomon achieved fame as the builder of Yahweh's Temple in Jerusalem. The elaborate building project took seven years to finish. The shrine symbolized God's presence in Israel and was dedicated as a "house of prayer" (1 Kgs 8:27–32). The permanence of the Temple structure testified to God's covenant faithfulness (1 Kgs 8:15). The Temple retained the same general floor plan as the Mosaic Tabernacle, but the sanctuary was redesigned vertically — emphasizing Yahweh's transcendence (1 Kgs 8:27–30).

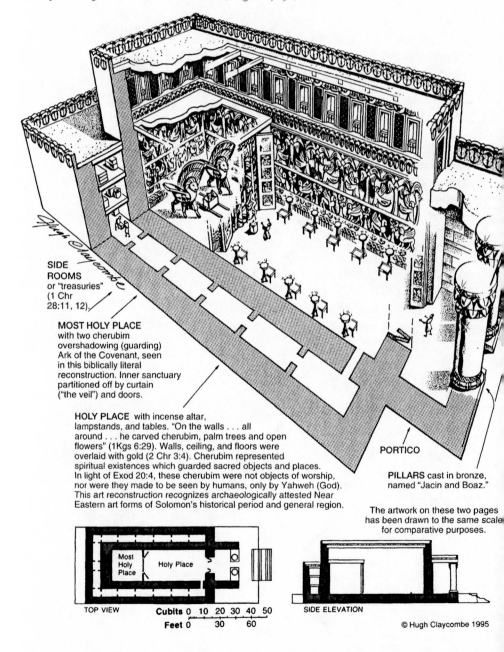

SIDE ROOMS
or "treasuries"
(1 Chr 28:11, 12).

MOST HOLY PLACE
with two cherubim overshadowing (guarding) Ark of the Covenant, seen in this biblically literal reconstruction. Inner sanctuary partitioned off by curtain ("the veil") and doors.

HOLY PLACE with incense altar, lampstands, and tables. "On the walls . . . all around . . . he carved cherubim, palm trees and open flowers" (1Kgs 6:29). Walls, ceiling, and floors were overlaid with gold (2 Chr 3:4). Cherubim represented spiritual existences which guarded sacred objects and places. In light of Exod 20:4, these cherubim were not objects of worship, nor were they made to be seen by humans, only by Yahweh (God). This art reconstruction recognizes archaeologically attested Near Eastern art forms of Solomon's historical period and general region.

PORTICO

PILLARS cast in bronze, named "Jacin and Boaz."

The artwork on these two pages has been drawn to the same scale for comparative purposes.

Most Holy Place   Holy Place

TOP VIEW   Cubits 0 10 20 30 40 50
                  Feet 0   30   60

SIDE ELEVATION

© Hugh Claycombe 1995

Figure 12. Zerubbabel's Temple
(ca. 515–20 B.C./E.)
The foundation of Zerubbabel's Temple was laid in the second year after the Israelites returned from the Babylonian captivity (ca. 538 B.C./E., Ezra 3:3). Construction was halted due to opposition by adversaries of Yehud (Ezra 4:4), and was resumed later at the instigation of the prophets Haggai and Zechariah (520 B.C./E., Ezra 5:1; 6:14; Hag 1:1; Zech 1:1). Malachi laments the "useless" fires kindled in the edifice, and actually calls for the closure of the building given the negligence of the priests and the apathy of the people (3:10).

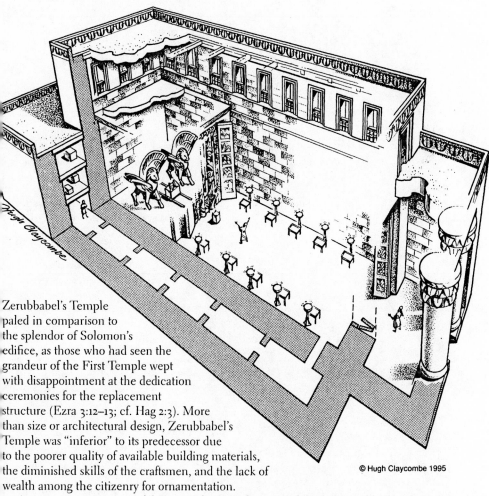

Zerubbabel's Temple paled in comparison to the splendor of Solomon's edifice, as those who had seen the grandeur of the First Temple wept with disappointment at the dedication ceremonies for the replacement structure (Ezra 3:12–13; cf. Hag 2:3). More than size or architectural design, Zerubbabel's Temple was "inferior" to its predecessor due to the poorer quality of available building materials, the diminished skills of the craftsmen, and the lack of wealth among the citizenry for ornamentation.

© Hugh Claycombe 1995

Artistic representations of the postexilic Temple vary widely. It is possible that the side-room "treasuries" and the portico with pillars were modified or even excluded from the design of Zerubbabel's Temple. Although it is represented in this model, there is uncertainty as to the placement of a (replica?) of the Ark of the Covenant in the Most Holy Place. The presence of the ten tables and lampstands, part of the furnishings in the Solomonic period (1 Kgs 7:27, 49), is in doubt as well (cf. 1 Macc 4:49; 10:3). The intent here is to capture visually a sense of the diminished state of the Temple as one factor contributing to the depression and apathy of the restoration community in the early postexilic period.

Figure 13. Ahuramazda Symbol, Persepolis Council Hall. "But a sun of righteousness will arise for you" (Mal 3:20[4:2]). The winged sun disk was originally a motif associated with the Egyptian deity Horus. The icon was later borrowed by the Assyrians, Israelites, and Persians. The image depicting (falcon or eagle) wings against a full sun represented the guardianship of the deity, an emblem of divine effulgence as well as protection and blessing for those overshadowed by the "wings" of the deity. King Darius I first used this figure on the Behistun inscription. *Courtesy of the Oriental Institute of the University of Chicago*

Figure 14. Foundation Documents of Xerxes (Harem Text). "A book of remembrance was recorded in his presence, [enrolling] the fearers of Yahweh" (Mal 3:16). Official Persian documents were written on scrolls of leather or papyrus, as well as inscribed on tablets of clay or stone. Malachi's "book of remembrance" is considered a "Persianism" and has a parallel in "the book of records" mentioned in Esth 6:1. Even as the Persian kings memorialize the names of loyal subjects in their records of past events, so Yahweh logs the names of his faithful both to remember and to reward the loyalty of the righteous. *Courtesy of the Oriental Institute of the University of Chicago*

(or even prophetic) messengers (e.g., J.M.P. Smith [1912: 40]). Rather, Malachi affirms the complementary role of human and angelic agents in the mediation of Yahweh's word and will. Even as Zechariah's "Interpreting Angel" (*hammal'āk haddōbēr bî*, 1:9) initiates a new development in the function of angelic mediators, it is possible that Malachi ascribes a similar duty to the priests as "interpreters" of the divine will (so Henderson [1980: 452]; cf. Meyers and Meyers [1987: 114]). Baldwin (1972a: 236) suggests that the prophet's own name could have inspired this description of the priest as "the messenger of Yahweh of Hosts." One wonders whether this wordplay on *mal'āk* ("messenger") constitutes a veiled reference by the prophet to his own membership in the Levitical priesthood. He was clearly familiar with priestly concerns and Temple practices. This would help explain the length of the second disputation (directed to the guild of priests) and the affinities between the language of Malachi and the books of Jeremiah and Ezekiel (prophets identified as belonging to the priestly class, Jer 1:1; Ezek 1:3).

J.M.P. Smith (p. 40) and others (e.g., Glazier-McDonald [1987a: 72]) suggest that the "priestly torah" renders the "prophetic torah" superfluous and the prophetic office obsolete. Baldwin (1972a: 236) rightly notes that Zechariah's fourth vision depicts the high priest Joshua with access to Yahweh's presence and thus equipped to be a messenger. This was always the case, however, because the priests were ordained to serve perpetually in Yahweh's presence (Exod 29:44; cf. Lev 10:11). Malachi does not signal the transition of messenger status from prophet to priest, but the clarification of the ideal of priest as teacher of Yahweh's law (see R. L. Smith [1984: 318] on the priesthood as "guardians" and "instructors" of the knowledge of God; cf. Jer 18:18, the "instruction" [*tôrâ*] of the priest . . . the "word" [*dābār*] of the prophet"). Verhoef (1987: 250–51) aptly recognizes that Malachi vouches for both the continuity between prophet and priest as messenger of Yahweh and the contrast between the "proclamation" (*dābār*) of the prophet and the "instruction" (*tôrâ*) of the priest (cf. Ezek 7:26; Mic 3:11).

The independent pronoun *hû'* ("he") is the subject of the verbless clause of classification (in which the predicate [*mal'ak YHWH-ṣĕbā'ôt*] refers to a general class of which the subject [*kōhēn*] is a member, WO'C § 8.4.2, 16.3.3d).

8. *wĕ'attem sartem min-hadderek*. The coordinating *waw* before a non-verb constituent has a disjunctive force, here involving a shift in scene and participants (WO'C § 39.2.3).

The emphatic use of the independent pronoun (*'attem*, "you") with the finite verb involves *psychological focus*, drawing attention to the culpability of the priests ("but you *yourselves* have turned aside . . ."; cf. Glazier-McDonald [1987a: 72], the pronoun heightens the contrast between the "ideal" [v 6] and the "actual" [v 7]). The form *wĕ'attem* has its counterpart in 1:12, the repetition connecting the two halves of the dispute and underlining the prophetic indictment against the priests (profaning the table of Yahweh, 1:12; turning aside from the way of Yahweh and abetting the same in others by their misteaching and negative example, 2:8).

The verb *swr* means to "turn aside, fall away, desert" (*CHAL*: 254) and occurs in Mal 3:7 as well as in this review of Hebrew history (*sartem mēḥuqqay*, equating *ḥuqqay*, "my statutes," with *hadderek*, "the way"). The Qal suffixing conjugation represents the *persistent perfective*, pointing to a single situation that started in the past but continues into the present (WO'C § 30.5.1c).

The preposition *min* has an ablative sense, designating movement "away from" a specified beginning point (WO'C § 11.2.11b). The common noun *derek* ("way, path") with the definite article identifies a unique *theological* referent (WO'C § 13.5.1b). Malachi's reference to "the way" is the divine way of Yahweh's covenant made known to Israel through the teaching of his statutes and ordinances (Exod 18:20; cf. Pss 25:8–10; 77:14 [13]; 119:14, 30, 32, 33). Adherence to "the way of Yahweh" by means of obedience to his statutes and ordinances guarantees "the functioning of the sphere of act and condition within the movement of human life. Yet, the preeminence of the *derek* of Yahweh . . . does not bring about a mechanical functioning of this sphere but makes possible the return (*šwb*) from a false *derek* and thus allows the evildoer to avoid stumbling" (*TDOT* 3:289).

The language of the entire clause seems to echo the account of the post-Exodus golden calf apostasy led by Aaron (*šarû mahēr min-hadderek*, Exod 32:8; cf. Deut 9:12, 16; Judg 2:17), as well as the Deuteronomic warning against apostasy upon entry into the land of Canaan (*wĕsartem min-hadderek*, Deut 11:28; 31:29).

hikšaltem rabbîm battôrâ. The gapping of the clausal coordinator (and probably the independent pronoun '*attem*, "you") in v 8b and 8c further magnifies the malfeasance of the priests by accentuating the cause and effect relationship of their misdeeds: "but *you yourselves* have turned aside from the way . . . *you* [*yourselves*] have caused many to stumble . . . *you* [*yourselves*] have violated the covenant of the Levites."

The verb *kšl* occurs only in Zech 12:8 and Mal 2:8 in the Haggai-Zechariah-Malachi corpus, and the plain sense of the word is to "stumble, totter, fall down" (*CHAL*: 166; cf. NAB, "falter"). Figuratively, *kšl* means to stumble morally, fall into iniquity (BDB: 506; cf. Hos 14:2, *kî kāšaltā baʿăwōnekā* ["because you have stumbled in your iniquity"]).

Here the word does not refer to Yahweh's punishment of an offense (e.g., Hos 4:5; cf. Wolff [1974: 77]; Andersen and Freedman [1980: 351]), but to the consequences or results of that offense (i.e., deviation from the "covenant way" of Yahweh). The Hiphil stem identifies the priests of Yehud as the agents responsible for the spiritual and moral collapse of the people (cf. WO'C § 27.1b, the Hiphil stem signifies "to [actively] *cause* an event"). Like those priests condemned by Hosea (4:4–6), the priests addressed by Malachi were guilty of depriving the people of the knowledge of God and instruction in covenant keeping with Yahweh (Andersen and Freedman [1980: 352–53]; cf. Ezek 44:12 for a similar indictment of the Levitical priesthood, *wĕhāyû lĕbêt-yiśrāʾēl lĕmikšôl ʿāwōn* ["and they became to the house of Israel a stumbling-block of iniquity"]). Ultimately, "God was misrepresented . . . by their [i.e., the priests'] unworthy lives and then by their erroneous teaching" (Baldwin [1972a: 236]).

The attributive adjective *rabbîm* ("many") stands alone as a substantive in the accusative position (cf. WO'C § 14.3). Deplorably, the priests of Yehud effected the complete reversal of the Levitical ideal: instruction that turned "many" (*rabbîm*) away from evil (v 6). The repetition of the word *rabbîm* in v 8 supports the idea that this may be a technical term of sorts for the laity of Yehud and that the *rabbîm* ("*the* many") are indeed the subject of v 7 (according to WO'C § 14.3.1c, the attributive adjective *rabbîm* is definite in itself and may dispense with the article).

The ambiguity of the datival prepositional phrase *battôrâ* has prompted nuanced readings of the prophet's intent: first, understanding the preposition *bêt* as a circumstance of agent ("by," WO'C § 11.2.5d) and regarding *tôrâ* as priestly "instruction" ("by your teaching," NIV, NJB, and T; "by your instruction," NAB, NRSV; cf. S. R. Driver [1906: 311]; Rudolph [1976: 259]; Glazier-McDonald [1987a: 45]), and second, assigning the force of an adversative circumstance to the preposition *bêt* ("against, from," WO'C § 11.2.5d) and interpreting *tôrâ* as the law of Yahweh ("to fail *following* in the law," LXX; cf. Henderson [1980: 452]; Calvin [p. 528]; "at the law," Syr; Eiselen [p. 719]; Packard [1902: 10, 14]; Petersen [1995: 175]; cf. Kruse-Blinkenberg [1966: 98–99]).

The plain sense of the idiom *kšl* + preposition *bêt* is to "stumble at, over, something" (BDB: 505). The people of Yehud stumbled over, or violated, the covenant law of Yahweh. They did not "stumble over" the instruction of the priests, rather they violated the Law of Moses because of the misinterpretation of the law by the Levites. The definiteness of the form *battôrâ* ("in *the* law/instruction"; cf. WO'C § 13.5.1c on the use of the article to designate *a well-known thing* or *person*), coupled with the lack of any suffixed possessive pronoun attached to the noun *tôrâ*, supports the notion that the ultimate issue for Malachi was the violation of Yahweh's covenant law (the standard by which divine judgment was always meted out; cf. Hos 4:6; 8:1; Amos 2:4; and the admonition of Mal 4:4, "Remember the law of my servant Moses").

šiḥattem bĕrît hallēwî. The verb *šḥt* in the Piel stem means "spoil, ruin, corrupt" (CHAL: 366–67). This is the only place in the OT/HB where *šḥt* is directly applied to a covenant (*bĕrît*; cf. Exod 32:7, *kî šiḥēt ʿammĕkā*, "because your people have become defiled"; Hos 9:9, *hēʿmîqû-šiḥētû*, "they have deeply defiled themselves" [see Andersen and Freedman 1980: 534]). In view of the fact that Malachi forecasts purification of the Levitical priesthood (3:3–4), *šḥt* in this context is better understood as the corruption (e.g., JPSV, NRSV) or violation (e.g., NIV; cf. Baldwin [1972a: 236]; Petersen [1995: 175]) of the covenant of Levi, not its voiding (e.g., NAB, NEB) or annulment (cf. Verhoef [1987: 252–53]). Yahweh will punish and shame the priests as judgment for this breach of covenant, but they may be purified through repentance and restored to office (cf. J.M.P. Smith [1912: 41], "they may have been false to their vows"). Given Malachi's dependence upon Deut 31:29 in verse 8a, even this choice of vocabulary may have been influenced by similar Deuteronomic concerns (there *kî-hašḥēt tašḥitûn* precedes *wĕsartem min-hadderek*). See further the discussion of the verb *šḥt* in the NOTES for 1:14 above and 3:11 below.

The construct-genitive phrase "the covenant of Levi" (*bĕrît hallēwî*) is unique to Mal 2:8 in MT. The intrinsically definite name "Levi" is construed with the definite article (*hallēwî*), perhaps elevating Levi (or the Levites?) to a position of uniqueness (cf. WO'C § 13.6a) or used collectively for the "Levites" as a class (see Eiselen [1907: 720]; S. R. Driver [1901: 121]; cf. JPSV, "the covenant of the Levites"). The latter understanding eliminates the need to identify specifically the ambiguous covenant made with Levi (see further the discussion of *bĕrît* in the NOTES for vv 4, 5 above). Rather, "the covenant of the Levites" is taken generally as a reference to the distinctive responsibilities of the Levitical priesthood, especially their commission to minister before the Lord (Deut 10:8–9) and teach the law of Yahweh to Israel (Deut 33:8–11). The proper noun Levi is mentioned elsewhere in the Twelve only in Zech 12:13 (*bêt-lēwî*; see further the discussion of *lēwî* in *TDOT* 7:483–503).

9. *wĕgam-'ănî nātattî 'etkem.* The clausal *waw* represents a conjunctive-sequential situation ("and so," NEB, NIV, NRSV; cf. WO'C § 39.2.2). The coordinating adverb *gam* has an emphatic force with the following independent pronoun ("indeed," WO'C § 39.3.4d; cf. the logical force of the JPSV, NJB, "in [my] turn"). The LXX omits the word (cf. Kruse-Blinkenberg [1967: 73]).

The personal pronoun (*'ānî*) used in combination with the finite verb (*nātattî*) involves *psychological focus*, indicating "strong emotional heightening" ("I myself . . . ," WO'C § 16.3.2e). Here the Qal stem form of *ntn* ("to give, put, set") has the sense "make, constitute" (cf. BDB: 681). The suffixing conjugation is an *instantaneous perfective*, representing a situation occurring at the very moment the statement is uttered ("and so I *make* you," NRSV; cf. WO'C § 30.5.1d).

Mason (1977: 147; 1990: 244) distinguishes between the (Zadokite/Aaronite) "priests" (*hakkōhănîm*, 1:6; 2:1) and the "Levites" (2:4–9) in the second disputation, suggesting that the "you" of the suffixed definite direct object marker (*'etkem*) rebuked by the prophet is the Zadokite/Aaronite priesthood only. The reference to the "covenant of Levi" (v 8) thus serves as an *apologia* (or testimonial) of sorts, legitimizing (and even a promotion from?) the secondary cultic role to which the Levites were demoted after the return from Babylonian Exile. O'Brien (1990: 111–12), however, has argued cogently that the terms "priest" and "Levite" are equivalents in the book of Malachi.

nibzîm ûšĕpālîm. The repetition of the verb *bzh* in 1:6 and 2:9 contributes to a type of envelope construction emphasizing the reversal of fortunes (the priests had "despised" Yahweh, v 6 — now Yahweh will make the priests "despised," v 9). The pronouncement overturns the divine blessing granted the Levites in Deut 33:10–11, and the divine retribution is meted out on the principle of "measure for measure" (cf. Cashdan [p. 344]). On the Niphal participle *nibzîm*, see the discussion of *nibzeh* in the NOTES for 1:7, 12 above.

The adjective *šĕpālîm* may mean "deep (below the surface), low (in height), humble" given the specific context (*CHAL*: 381), and the word is unique to the Haggai-Zechariah-Malachi corpus. Here *šĕpālîm* is joined in synonymous parallelism with *nibzîm*, necessitating the translation "humble" in a pejorative sense (JPSV, NJB, "vile"; NAB, "base"; NRSV, "abased"; NEB, "mean"; NIV, "humiliated"). The adjective is used as a substantive and serves as an accusative of specification (cf. WO'C § 10.2.2e, 14.3.3c).

lĕkol-hā'ām. The datival or indirect object *lamed* has a spatial sense and marks the *goal* of the verb *ntn* ("*before* all of the people," WO'C § 11.2.10b, d). The general quantifier *kōl*, a universal distributive, is used in a genitive of measure (cf. WO'C § 9.5.3f, 15.6c). On *kōl*, see further the discussion of *lĕkullānû* in 2:10 and *kullô* in 3:9.

The noun *'ām* is definite and probably refers to "the people" serviced by the priesthood, the inhabitants of Yehud (i.e., synonymous with *rabbîm* as a term for "the laity" of the community; cf. WO'C § 13.5.1b). The ancient versions inappropriately read a plural form (*'ammîm*, "peoples"), thus setting the prophet's address to Yehud among "the nations" (*tà ĕthnē* [some manuscripts of LXX; so T, V, Arabic]; cf. Henderson [p. 453]; J.M.P. Smith [1912: 41]).

kĕpî 'ăšer 'ênĕkem šōmĕrîm 'et-dĕrākay. The construction *kĕpî 'ăšer* ("inasmuch as, because"; cf. BDB: 805; CHAL: 289) is unique to Mal 2:9 in the MT (prompting the BHS to suggest deleting the word *'ăšer*). The integrity of the MT should be upheld, because "special conjunctions in various combinations are used to introduce causal clauses" (GKC § 158a). All the more so here, given the fact that this causal clause concludes the argumentation of the second dispute.

The suffixed pronouns complete the foil contrasting the priests (*'ênĕkem*, "*you* are not") with Yahweh (*dĕrākay*, "*my* ways"). The repetition of *'ênĕkem* links verse 2 and v 9 in a cause ("you do not lay it to heart") and effect ("you have not kept my ways") relationship explaining the priests' corruption of the covenant of Levi. See further the discussion of *'ênĕkem* in the NOTES for 2:2 above.

The combination of the verb *šmr* with the noun *derek* (an accusative of thing) occurs 15 times in the MT and means to "observe, keep a way" in the sense of obeying a command, fulfilling an obligation, or adhering to the conditions of an agreement (cf. CHAL: 377). Those who "observe the ways" of Yahweh are blessed (*wĕ'ašrê dĕrākay yišmōrû*, Prov 8:32). Conversely, the priests of Yehud are cursed because they have strayed from Yahweh's covenant (v 2). The "way" (*derek*) of Yahweh is justice and righteousness (TDOT 3:284). The plural *dĕrākay* ("my ways") refers to the statutes, precepts, and ordinances that constitute the law (*tôrâ*) of Yahweh, the guide posts marking out the divine way (especially in the Torah-Psalms [1, 19, 119]; cf. TDOT 3:286–88). See further the discussion of *šmr* in the NOTES for v 7 and *derek* in the NOTES for v 8.

wĕnōśĕ'îm pānîm battôrâ. The interclausal *waw* is disjunctive, specifying a contemporary circumstance as an example of priestly deviation from "the ways of Yahweh" ("but," NAB, NIV, NRSV [so LXX, *allà*]; cf. WO'C § 39.2.3b).

The idiom "show favor" (*nś'* + *pānîm*) is usually understood to have a negative connotation in this context ("show partiality, favoritism [toward]," CHAL: 246; cf. Verhoef [1987: 253]; Redditt [1995: 169]; Petersen [1995: 192–93]). The charges of corruption against the priests remain unspecified, apart from their misinterpretation and misteaching of the covenant legislation of Yahweh (cf. JPSV, "show partiality in your rulings"; NJB, "being partial in applying the law"). Assuming, however, that *'ênĕkem* is the gapped subject of the participle *nōśĕ'îm* in verse 9d (possessing no clear subject), then the meaning of verse 9c and verse 9d must be parallel in the sense that both are negated clauses. A literal rendering would read "and *you are not* lifting up faces [of the people] in Torah" (cf. Petersen [1995: 176 n. o]). Not only have the Levitical priests failed to keep the ways of Yahweh's Torah, but also they have been derelict in "raising faces in the Torah"; that is, they have neglected to demonstrate the grace of kindness (and fairness?) in their administration of the rules of Torah — their sworn duty as representatives of Yahweh to the people of Israel (cf. Deut 33:8–11). The construction *nś'* + *pānîm* ("raise the face/s") may form an envelope of sorts for the second disputation (cf. 1:8, *hăyiśśā' pānêkā*). Ironically, the prophet begins the oracle with the question "Will he [i.e., God] lift up your face?" (1:8). He concludes the second disputation by answering that question with the assertion "You are not lifting up the faces of the people in the Torah" (2:9). How ludicrous to suppose the priesthood might expect God to grant them favor when they could not reciprocate in like kind to the very people they were commissioned to serve! The Qal participle *nōśē'îm* approximates the prefix conjugation and emphasizes a durative circumstance (WO'C § 37.6b). On the construction *nś'* + *pānîm*, see further the NOTES on 1:8, 9; 2:3 above.

On *battôrâ* as priestly teaching or instruction, see the discussion of *tôrat 'ĕmet* in the NOTES for verse 6 and *battôrâ* in the NOTES for v 7 above.

COMMENTS

1:6–8. At issue in this section of Malachi's second disputation are the Mediterranean core cultural values of *honor* and *shame*. Honor may be *ascribed* (i.e., the social status or position into which one is born) or *acquired* (i.e., the social status or position earned or achieved through challenge and response, "a social game that goes on in the culture all the time," Pilch [1991: 53]). Likewise, *shame* may be understood negatively as "shamelessness, without a sense of shame" (i.e., disgrace, reproach, ignominy) or positively as "having a sense of shame, avoidance of shame" (i.e., dignity, pride, self-respect; cf. K. E. Bailey [1976: 131–32]).

The prophet emphasizes the *ascribed honor* of Yahweh as Creator and Redeemer of Israel, attempting to *shame* the priests of Yehud into offering Yahweh proper worship. Interestingly, the second dispute reverses the argumentation of the first in which Malachi acknowledges Israel's *ascribed honor* by virtue of Yahweh's election (1:2–5). The proposition that Yahweh deserves "honor" (1:6) is pressed home by comparative degree in the analogy between the ascribed honor due a human governor and that due Yahweh (1:8). If this were not enough, the prophet proceeds to further *shame* the Levitical priesthood by reminding them of their *acquired status* achieved through the covenant with Levi initiated by Yahweh (2:4–5). Sadly, the disparaging circumstances of the early postexilic era of Israelite history apparently had numbed the priests to the point where they were unresponsive to their own core social values. On the Mediterranean values of *honor* and *shame* in the NT, see further the parable of The Friend at Midnight (Lk 11:5–13; cf. K. E. Bailey [1976: 119–33]).

1:9–14. The prophet's avowal of the worship of Yahweh among the nations in verse 11 remains a *crux interpretum* for the book of Malachi. The various interpretive options are succinctly summarized by R. L. Smith (1984: 313; cf. Gordon

[1994: 56]): (a) a prediction of the mass according to the early Roman Catholic view; (b) a reference to the worship of the Jewish Diaspora (so Justin Martyr *Dial Trypho* xli; cf. Ogden and Deutsch [1987: 86]); (c) the syncretistic understanding that Malachi refers to the worship of the high God in all religions (e.g., G. A. Smith [2:358]; see the discussion in Verhoef [1987: 224–32]); (d) the metaphorical view that suggests that some pagan worship supersedes the adulterated worship of postexilic Yehud (e.g., Mason [1977: 144–45]; cf. Tate [1987: 398–99]); (e) the eschatological approach that anticipates the imminent conversion of the nations and the worldwide worship of Yahweh (e.g., Baldwin [1972a: 230]; cf. Glazier-McDonald [1987a: 60–61]). Achtemeier (1986: 177) is probably correct in her assessment that verse 11 and verse 14 do not refer to the worship of the heathen or Diaspora Jews or even Jewish proselytes, but to "the future establishment of the kingship of God over all the earth . . . , the purpose that underlies every prophetic book." Contextually, this imminent future idea fits the eschatological emphasis of the book of Malachi as whole (cf. Tate [1987: 399]). See further Redditt's (1995: 165–66) summary of the alternate views.

Biblical commentators are quick to recognize the climactic structure of the triad of divine declarations proclaiming Yahweh's greatness among the nations in Mal 1:5, 11, 14 (e.g., Glazier-McDonald [1987a: 64]; Petersen [1995: 187]). There is less agreement, however, on the meaning and relationship of the three verses. Mason (1977: 145) has correctly observed that verse 14 completes the lesson of verse 11, structurally dividing the oracle into two segments (1:6–11, 12–14), each containing similar charges raised against the priests and climaxing in the "universal" worship of Yahweh. Moreover, the universal worship of Yahweh is the central theme of the second dispute (cf. Verhoef [1987: 222]). Although this theological trajectory receives less attention than the theme of Yahweh's judgment of the nations in exilic and postexilic biblical literature, it by no means represents "an extreme or isolated point of view"; rather, "it . . . bursts the bounds of a religious ideology that tries to transform God into an easily manageable possession" (Ogden and Deutsch [1987: 87]). Finally, not only does Malachi affirm Yahweh's merciful intentions to cause the light of his salvation to shine upon all nations (Isa 42:4, 6; 49:6; 51:4), but also, in his reference to the nations, the prophet verifies the pronouncements made by his earlier contemporaries Haggai and Zechariah (Hag 2:7, 22; Zech 2:11; 8:22–23; cf. Joel 2:12–14).

2:1–3. The people of Yehud indict God in Malachi's first disputation (1:2–5). Now the roles are reversed as God indicts the priests because they are directly responsible for the moral and spiritual condition of the people of Yehud. In view of "the most stringent verdict of punishment" pronounced by God as both prosecutor and judge, Achtemeier (1986: 180) rightly raises the question: "Is that an exercise of a God of love?" She responds emphatically in the affirmative because "it is only when God leaves us alone that he no longer loves us" (Achtemeier [1986: 180]). Heschel (1:194) concurs, noting God's judgment is conditional not absolute: "A change in man's conduct brings about a change in God's judgment. No word is God's final word." It seems the postexilic prophets Haggai, Zechariah, Malachi, and Joel all assume that God, along with his many other attributes (cf.

Exod 34:6–7), will relent of planned judgment in the face of repentance — an essential part of the lesson the prophet Jonah learned so painfully (4:2).

2:4–6. Wells (pp. 49–51) aptly points out Malachi's remarkable use of irony in exposing the dual and recursive crises of commitment (1:6–9; 2:1–5) and responsibility (1:10–14; 2:6–9) in the second disputation. Both concepts, commitment (promise) and responsibility (stipulation), lie at the heart of covenant relationship — the unifying theme of the book of Malachi (cf. ABD 1:1180–83). The first is subjective and voluntary in nature, the personal dimension of a relationship. The second is objective and compulsory in nature, the interpersonal dimension of a relationship. The synergistic interplay of both is absolutely essential to establishing and maintaining any meaningful relationship.

Malachi explodes the fallacy that the perfunctory discharging of responsibilities by the Levitical priesthood, without the corresponding commitment to the covenant stipulations, is sufficient to maintain a relationship with Yahweh (1:13). The prophet drastically proposes the closure of the Temple (1:10), first by contrasting the worship of Yehud with that of the nations (1:11–12), and then through the comparison of Levitical ideal with the current realities of priestly function (2:7–8). Wells (p. 44) roots the twin crises of commitment and responsibility in Yehud's accommodation to secularism, specifically the spirit of skepticism. The priests of Yehud might have responded to the despair and doubt of the people of Yehud with courage, hope, and faith — instead of compromise, neglect, and ennui (cf. Wells [1987: 50]). R. W. Bailey (p. 28), appealing to Tennessee Williams's *Cat on a Hot Tin Roof*, describes the priestly charade as *mendacity*, a system of "living lies." Much like Jeremiah's audience, the priests of Yehud have forgotten Yahweh and trusted in lies (Jer 13:25) — especially the lie that one can appease Yahweh by accepting obligatory *responsibility* apart from demonstrating heartfelt *commitment*.

2:7–9. Malachi insists that the internal substance and external form of the worship of Yahweh are equally important. Like his preexilic predecessors, Malachi's prophetic ideal was not the abandonment of cultic worship, but the renewal of Israel's worship by a return to the proper observance of the prescribed forms of ritual (Mal 1:8) and a return to a personal piety characterized by righteousness and justice (Mal 3:5; cf. Jer 33:18; Mic 6:6–8). Craigie (p. 232) recalls that "worship, properly conducted, is an expression of lives lived in the knowledge of God and in relationship with God. Worship is ordered into particular forms so that this knowledge of God may be given full and rich expression in the lives of the people." True sacrifice to Yahweh is not merely a dutiful "payment" to God, but rather the "symbolic offering" of the worshiper's very life to the One God who established covenant relationship with Israel (cf. R. W. Bailey [1977: 33]).

Ultimately, the purpose of covenant in biblical thought is "to create new relationships in accordance with stipulations given in advance" (Mendenhall [1973: 200]). This means that although Yahweh's covenant with Levi was "ideological" in nature, it was essentially "behavioral" in function. The covenant stipulations, "the laws of God," were intended to regulate this relationship between God and his people (cf. Wells [1987: 61]). As covenant-keepers themselves, the Levitical priesthood was charged to model covenant keeping for the rest of Israel through the teaching of the Mosaic law and the service of worship leadership in the cultus (Deut 33:8–11). Right behavior on the part of the people of Israel in covenant relationship with Yahweh was dependent upon sound priestly instruction of the Mosaic law and virtuous priestly example in the ministry of worship (cf. Hos 4:4–6). Sadly, the priests of Yehud upbraided by Malachi failed on both counts, "first by their unworthy lives and then by their erroneous teaching" (Baldwin [1972a: 236]). What hope for "sheep" without a "shepherd?" (Jer 50:6; Zech 10:2; cf. Baldwin [1972a: 236] on the omnitemporal sense of Malachi's message concerning leadership in biblical thought).

III. D. THIRD ORACLE: FAITHLESS PEOPLE REBUKED (2:10–16)

2 [10]Surely we all have one father? Surely one God has created us? Why then do we break faith with each other, thereby profaning the covenant of our forefathers. [11]Yehud has broken faith, and an abomination has been committed in Israel and Jerusalem; for Yehud has profaned the holiness of Yahweh, because he loved and married the daughter of a strange El. [12]May Yahweh cut off any man who does this — witness or respondent — from the tents of Jacob; even the one who brings an offering to Yahweh of Hosts!

[13]And this second [thing] you do: tears cover the altar of Yahweh — weeping and wailing; because there is no longer a turning to the offering nor receiving a favor from your hand. [14]But you say, "Why?" Because Yahweh, he serves as a witness between you and the wife of your youth; with whom you [even you] have broken faith, though she is your marriage partner and the wife of your covenant. [15]Surely [The] One made [everything]? Even a residue of spirit belongs to him. And what does The One seek? A seed of God. So guard yourselves in your own spirit! Stop breaking faith with the wife of your youth!

[16]"Indeed, [The One] hates divorce!" Yahweh, the God of Israel, has said. "For he covers his clothing with violence," Yahweh of Hosts has said. So guard yourselves in your own spirit! You shall not break faith!

The literary form of *prophetic disputation* persists throughout the six oracles of Malachi (see the discussion of literary form in the introduction to III. B. First Oracle above). The prophet modifies the disputational format slightly by prefacing the initial declaration (2:11) with a series of three rhetorical questions (2:10). The proclamation "Yehud has broken faith" (2:11a) is accented by an oath formula threatening malediction: "May Yahweh cut off . . ." (2:12). The prophet then resumes his declaration in verse 13, "tears cover the altar of Yahweh . . ." Finally, Malachi again resorts to the interrogative as a prelude to his rebuttal of the audience refutation (2:15–16). Watts (1987a: 376) has identified Malachi's third oracle as a combination of a *dialogical/expressive* speech-act intended to persuade the audience ("Why do you break covenant?"; 2:10–12) and an *assertive* speech-act intended to assure the audience ("I hate divorce and violence," 2:13–16).

Schreiner (p. 218) is dubious of attempts to uncover the original setting of Malachi's third dispute. Others, however, are more assertive. For example, Ahlström's (p. 49) fixation with religious syncretism in ancient Israel leads him to regard the reference to "weeping" in verse 13 as the vestige of some fertility rite still performed in postexilic Yehud. Verhoef (1987: 263) is no doubt much closer to the truth when he suggests that the oracle was prompted by a feast of penance due to crop failure in Yehud (Mal 3:10–12; cf. Zech 7:5; 9:19).

The MT marks major paragraph breaks (*pārāša pĕtûḥâ* [פ]) in 2:9 and 2:12 and a minor paragraph stop (*pārāšâ sĕtûmâ* [ס]) in 2:16. Thus, 2:10–12 constitutes Pericope II, while 2:13–16 forms subunit A of Pericope III in the *BHS*. An overwhelming majority of biblical commentators recognizes a direct connection between the literary units of 2:10–12 and 2:13–16 and amalgamate the two into the third of Malachi's disputations (especially the phrase, *wĕzō't šēnît ta'ăśû* ["And this second *thing* you do"] in 2:13a). The key lexical items, *'eḥād* ("one") and *bgd* ("break faith"), link the two halves of the disputation (2:10–12 and vv 13–16). The force of the emphatic *kî* ("Indeed") permits ascribing paragraph status to the prophet's concluding admonition (v 16, cf. NIV).

Scholars are unanimous in their assessment of 2:10–16 as a "notoriously difficult" passage to interpret (cf. G. A. Smith [2:365]; J.M.P. Smith [1912: 47]; Welch [1935: 120]; Baldwin [1972a: 240]; Craigie [1985: 236–37]). Both textual corruption and grammatical anomaly combine to make this section the most problematic of Malachi's oracles (especially v 15, one of the most obscure verses in MT according to Dentan and Sperry [p. 1136]). Mason (1990: 245) proffers sound advice when he tenders that Vuilleumier's plea for caution be extended to the entire pericope. Here the orality attributed to the disputational format and the troublesome topic of divorce only compound the several complex factors making the MT "virtually unintelligible" (so Mason [1990: 245]). Nevertheless, "the very bad state of the text bears its own witness to the probability that it did originally condemn divorce outright" (Mason [1977: 150]; cf. Baldwin [1972a: 240]). A full discussion of the assorted textual problems ensues in the NOTES below.

Malachi's third oracle contains one of the two passages in the book upon which Eissfeldt (p. 442) casts "a suspicion of non-genuineness," 2:11–12 (e.g., Craigie [1985: 237]) or 2:11b–12 (so Mason [1990: 245]) or 2:11b–13a (e.g., Sellin and Fohrer [1968: 470]; Eissfeldt also). This conjecture has been widely supported by biblical scholars of previous generations (in addition to Verhoef's [1987: 263 n. 6] catalog of names, cf. von Bulmerincq [1932: 368–73]). Among the primary reasons for adducing the secondary status of these verses (thought to represent the more parochial interests of Ezra and Nehemiah) are the shift from first-person discourse to third-person narrative (so Mason [1977: 149]), the separation of the charge of faithlessness in verse 10 from the application of that message in verses 13–16 (so Craigie [1985: 237]), the contradictory teaching of 1:11 and 2:11 with respect to "the nations" (e.g., Marti [1904: 469–70]), and the duality of the prophet's message in 2:10–16 (i.e., the malpractices of mixed marriage and divorce, e.g., Sellin [1930: 602]).

Ogden and Deutsch (p. 94) are representative of a trend in more recent scholarship devoted to Malachi in their assertion that "from another point of view" the prophet's censure of mixed marriages does not necessarily stand in opposition to the universalism promoted in 1:11. These "alternative perspectives" tend to highlight the literary structure and form of the disputation speech and the web of rhetorical features unifying verses 10–12 with verses 13–16 in upholding the integrity of the pericope 2:10–16 (or in some cases with the exception of isolated words or phrases; e.g., Rudolph [1976: 268–69]; Deissler [1988: 327–28]). For example, Baldwin (1972a: 238) has noted that the argument of Malachi progresses from the general to the particular in the third oracle, certainly in keeping with the dialectical nature of the disputation. Further, Verhoef (1987: 264) demonstrates the structural coherence of the passage, emphasizing the foil of "one" and "foreign" with respect to covenant relationship. Finally, Glazier-McDonald (1987a: 83–84) documents numerous examples of lexical repetition and recurring rhetorical features serving to unify the literary unit (many of these advanced earlier by von Bulmerincq [1932: 371–72]). This analysis sides with those exegetes affirming the integrity of Mal 2:10–16, agreeing with J. J. Collins's (p. 214) appraisal of redactional activity in the disputations of Malachi as "inconclusive" given the brevity of the book (cf. Petersen [1995: 195]; Redditt [1995: 153–54] on 2:10–16 as a "composite").

The third disputation is aimed at the greater restoration community, leaders, priests, and people, making up the "one" people of Yahweh. The basic thrust of the oracle is two-pronged: the concatenous crimes of mixed-marriage and divorce. Both are supercilious and reprehensible misdeeds before Yahweh, an affront to the essence of covenant relationship socially and religiously — faithfulness and loyalty. These transgressions defiled the people of Yehud, polluted their worship of God, and made a sacrilege of Yahweh himself. Those who read Mal 2:10–16 figuratively as a series of metaphors for the priesthood fail to appreciate the hortatory nature and confrontational posture of the disputation-speech form (e.g., Ogden [1988: 272]). The priests may have been guilty of sanctioning such marriage and divorce; in fact, Ogden and Deutsch (p. 94) are probably correct in linking the misteaching of the priests (2:1–9) with the practice of intermarriage and divorce in postexilic Yehud (2:10–16). The emphasis on "one" in the disputation indicates that the entire community stood under the prophet's condemnation and the threat of divine judgment.

The third disputation (faithlessness in marriage, 2:10–16) and the fifth disputation (faithlessness to God, 3:6–12) mirror images of disloyalty and betrayal in Yehud as correlative literary panels; and both are set upon the hinge of divine judgment threatened in the fourth disputation (2:17–3:5). The purpose of the third speech is didactic (corrective instruction on the topics of marriage and divorce countering the spurious tutelage of the Levitical priests, 2:1–9) and admonitory (a timely warning for circumspect self-examination as a prelude to the prophet's formal indictment of Yehud in 2:17–3:5 and as preparation for the prophet's call to repentance in 3:7).

NOTES

2:10. *hălô' 'āb 'eḥād lĕkullānû.* The interrogative *hē'* identifies a rhetorical question, intended "to give information with passion" (i.e., indeed, the Hebrews have "one father," WO'C § 18.1c, 2g). These two opening rhetorical questions mark the third dispute as unique among the prophet's disputations; all the others commence with a declarative statement. Ogden and Deutsch (p. 94) note that the intensity and urgency of the plea for unity is heightened because the prophet includes his own person ("we") as he speaks directly to his audience. The significant changes in the form and style of this disputation call attention to the central theme of Malachi's message, loyalty to God and to one another through the ancient covenant still binds them together as Yahweh's elect. The rhetorical questions anticipate an answer in the affirmative, and the interrogative may be translated emphatically with "surely" (cf. WO'C § 40.3 n. 48).

The parallelism of the two interrogative clauses (v 10ab) suggests that Malachi is equating "father" with "God" (so Mason [1977: 149]) not one of the patriarchal ancestors of Israel like Abraham or Jacob as is more commonly assumed (so Baldwin [1972a: 237]; cf. Jerome [*CChr* 76A:921] and Calvin [1979: 539]). The prophet has already described God metaphorically as "father" (*'āb*, see the NOTES for 1:6 above). The motif of comparing God with a human father (using *'āb*) is unique to Malachi in the Twelve but no doubt echoes texts like Deut 32:6 (*hălô'-hû' 'ābîkā qāneḵā,* "surely he is your father who created you?") and Jer 31:9 (*kî-hāyîtî lĕyiśrā'ēl lĕ'āb,* "because I have become a father to Israel"). According to Ringgren, "The real point of this figure is that Yahweh cares for the people and is responsible for their existence" (*TDOT* 1:17).

The numeral *'eḥād* ("one") serves as an attributive adjective modifying the noun "father" (WO'C § 14.3). In this case the numeral also marks "specific indefiniteness" (WO'C 13.8a). Israel owes its existence and identity to a single source, Yahweh and his covenant (cf. Glazier-McDonald [1987a: 83], "the paternity of Yahweh . . . is incontrovertible"). The prophet calls for unity in postexilic Yehud because the community springs from a single cause; Israel's corporate identity or personality is rooted in Yahweh alone.

The construction of the preposition *lamed* + the general quantifier *kōl* + the object pronoun *-nû* forms the predicate of the verbless clause. The preposition *lamed* has a quasi-locational function expressing possession (WO'C § 11.2.10d). There is a sense in which the *lamed* of indirect object also connotes the *lamed* of interest or advantage (WO'C § 11.2.10d): three of the four clauses in the two parallel lines (v 10ab) utilize the suffixing pronoun *-nû* ("us/our") to designate the prophet's intended audience — all the people of Yehud.

The substantive *kōl* ("all, every," *CHAL*: 156–57) is a genitive of measure in construct relationship with the first-person (plural) object pronoun "us" (*-nû*, literally "to all of us"; cf. WO'C § 9.5.3f). The general quantifier *kōl* indicates that the prophet understands his audience to be the entire community of Yehud. More important, he personalizes his message by including himself in that community by utilizing the first-person plural suffixing pronoun.

hălô' 'ēl 'eḥād bĕrā'ānû. On the interrogative particle *hē'* introducing a rhetorical question, see the discussion of *hălô'* above.

The phrase *'ēl 'eḥād* ("one God") is unique to Mal 2:10 in the MT and is best understood in synonymous parallelism with "one father" of verse 10a. Given the balanced poetic structure of the two lines (v 10ab, 4 + 4), it is possible that the prophet is quoting (an ancient or more recent?) a confessional statement about Yahweh (perhaps an allusion to the famous creedal statement of Deut 6:4–5; cf. Fontaine [1982: 242–51] on "proverb performance in prophetic books"). Yahweh is both Father and Creator of Israel. More than a monotheistic credo, however, the prophet's statement underscores the distinctiveness and uniqueness of Yahweh as Creator and his exclusiveness as Israel's Father (cf. *TDOT* 1:196–97). Like Zech 14:9 (*YHWH 'eḥād*), the expression *'ēl 'eḥād* probably draws on diverse traditions (e.g., Job 31:15, "surely one fashioned us in the womb?" [assuming the gapping of *hălô'* and that *'eḥād* stands alone as the subject of the clause, not an adjective modifying *reḥem*]; cf. Meyers and Meyers [1993: 439–40] on "the oneness" of God and Israel's obligation of covenant loyalty).

The cardinal number "one" (*'eḥād*) is repeated 4 times in the third disputation, perhaps establishing a deliberate contrast between "the *faithful* One" and "*faithless* Israel" (*bgd*; cf. Mason [1990: 246]).

The verb *bārā'* ("to create") is unique to Mal 2:10 in the Haggai-Zechariah-Malachi corpus and occurs elsewhere in the Twelve only in Amos 4:13 (see the discussion in Andersen and Freedman [1989: 453–54] of the line "Creator of the wind" in this cosmic hymn). The word *bārā'* denotes exclusively divine creation (see *TDOT* 2:246). The term attests the majesty of God as Creator and the incomparability of his creation (Isa 40:26, 28), the primacy of humanity as the pinnacle of God's creation (Deut 4:32; Isa 42:5; 45:12, 18), and the nation of Israel as God's special creation (Isa 43:1, 7, 15). The verb *bārā'* takes on "soteriological characteristics" in Second Isaiah, connoting Yahweh's activity not in the distant past but "in the immediately imminent future" (*TDOT* 2:247). This theological perspective seems to color Malachi's message as well. The fact of "God's oneness determines the unity and hence the continuity of the history between God and his people" (Westermann [1982: 32]).

It is significant that the prophet makes two strong allusions to the New Covenant of Jeremiah (chapters 31–33) in verse 10ab, God as "Father" (Jer 31:9) and God as "Creator" (Jer 31:22). The disputes of Malachi, in part, are based on the assumption by the restoration community that Yahweh's "new" covenant is not yet operative in Yehud and that the word of the Lord by the prophets has failed. The intertextual echoes to that initiative seem to counter this prejudgment made by Malachi's audience.

The LXX unnecessarily substitutes "you" (*humōn/humās* for the MT "we" in v 10ab). There is no reason, theological or otherwise, to exclude the prophet from the community he addresses.

The LXX (A,B,Y), OL, and Arabic, among other ancient versions and commentators, transpose the lines of verse 10a and 10b. J.M.P. Smith (p. 58) suggests that this was due to a desire to accord God first place in the ordering, because the word "father" was interpreted as a reference to Abraham or another human being. Sellin (p. 602) and Elliger (1950:190–91) are among those scholars who question (unnecessarily) the authenticity of verse 10.

maddûaʿ nibgad ʾîš bĕʾāḥîw. The interrogative *maddûaʿ* (a compound of the interrogative *mâ* + the Qal passive participle of *ydʿ* ("to know," literally "what being known"; cf. BDB: 396) introduces a question of circumstance and occurs only in Mal 2:10 in the Twelve (cf. WO'C § 18.1 and p. 324, n. 17, 40.3a). The use of *maddûaʿ* in Malachi reflects the style of Jeremiah (e.g., 2:31; 8:5, 22; etc.).

The Qal suffixing conjugation form *nibgad* means "to deal treacherously with" (KBL 1:108; cf. Petersen [1995: 194], "act faithlessly"). The verb *bgd* is repeated 5 times in Malachi's third disputation (2:10, 11, 14, 15, 16), isolating "faithlessness" as the central thesis of the oracle (so Ogden [1988: 265]). The verb is found in the Twelve elsewhere only in Hos 5:7; 6:7; Hab 1:13 and 2:5. The denominative verb *bgd* "expresses the unstable relationship of a man to an existing established regulation" (*TDOT* 1:470; cf. the Arabic "outwit" [KBL 1:108] and "*garmenting*" = "cheat, defraud" [Isbell 1980: 50]).

The verb *bgd* signifies faithlessness or treacherous behavior in marriage (e.g., Exod 21:8), covenant relationship with Yahweh (e.g., Jer 3:8, 11, 20, 21, using the figure of marriage; Hos 5:7; 6:7), with respect to the created order (equated with the "wicked" [*rĕšāʿîm*], Prov 2:22; Isa 24:16) and in human agreements (i.e., breach of covenant or treaty, e.g., Judg 9:23; cf. *TDOT* 1:470–73). The word *bgd* in this third disputation is used specifically in reference to faithlessness in marriage, the betrayal or violation of a promise to one's legal spouse (*TDOT* 1:470). Although such traitorous behavior may be committed against either partner in the marriage, verse 14 suggests that the wife was the primary victim of this treachery in Yehud (cf. Exod 21:8).

The context of Malachi's oracle indicates that this faithlessness is not deceptive or secretive disloyalty as in Hos 5:7 (cf. Andersen and Freedman [1980: 395]). Rather, the faithlessness Malachi indicts is public and legal in the form of divorce of a marriage partner (vv 14–16; cf. Garland [1987: 419–21] on "legal" divorce in biblical times). The prophet understands this as an act of betrayal against the marriage partner, probably because the divorce(s) granted were not in accordance with the stipulations of the divorce laws of the Mosaic covenant (Exod 20:14; Deut 5:18; 24:1–4; cf. *ABD* 2:217–19). Treachery of this sort is tantamount to adultery, which explains the prophet's strong language in this regard, because such faithlessness is an affront to Yahweh and his covenant (see NOTES on *ḥll* below).

Malachi accuses the people of hypocrisy and breach of contract in regard to the marriage covenant. The same depravity that made "repentance impossible" and that led to "complacent religiosity" in Hosea's audience manifests striking parallels in Malachi's audience (see Andersen and Freedman [1980: 395]). The prophet's censure of divorce in Yehud permits the further denunciation of faith-less behavior in the community (3:5) and sets the tone for the theme of divine judgment introduced in the fourth disputation (3:2–3).

The phrase 'îš bĕ'āhîw (literally "a man to his brother") is an idiom expressing reciprocity (in this case faithless behavior toward "each other"; cf. KBL 1:44). The preposition bêt frequently accompanies the verb bgd, meaning "with" or even "against" in an adversarial sense (cf. KBL 1:108). A similar expression of reciprocity (of speech) occurs in 3:16 below, 'îš 'et-rē'ēhû (literally "a man to his neighbor").

lĕhallēl bĕrît 'ăbōtênû. The preposition lamed + ḥll mark an infinitive clause of result expressing the consequence or outcome of the preceding verb (bgd, WO'C § 36.2.3d).

The verb ḥll (I) means "to profane, desecrate" in the Piel stem (here a Piel infinitive construct, cf. TDOT 4:410). The word occurs elsewhere in the Haggai-Zechariah-Malachi corpus in Mal 2:11 and in the Twelve in Hos 8:10; Amos 2:7; Jonah 3:4; and Zeph 3:4. According to Andersen and Freedman (1989: 319), ḥll may refer to pollution through violation of any covenant rule. Malachi's audi-ence has "profaned" or "failed to acknowledge as holy" the covenant of Yahweh in their transgression of the stipulations concerning divorce. There is a sense in which the community has committed sacrilege with respect to Yahweh's name as well, because Yahweh seals his covenant word with his own name (Isa 45:23; cf. TDOT 4:410–12). The parallel construction of bgd with bryt + ḥll indicates behavior that violates or invalidates Yahweh's covenant, a breach of contract mer-iting divine punishment (note the combination of bāgĕdû + 'ābĕrû bĕrît in Hos 6:7; cf. Andersen and Freedman [1980: 439]).

The expression "covenant of our ancestors" (bĕrît 'ăbōtênû) is unique to Mal-achi among the Prophets. The only parallel to the expression is found in Deut 4:31 (bĕrît 'ăbōtekā, "the covenant of your ancestors"). It is possible the prophet implies that postexilic Yehud should not attribute the same lapse of memory they have demonstrated in response to Yahweh's covenant to Yahweh himself—who will not forget his covenant.

According to Glazier-McDonald (1987a: 86), the phrase should be understood restrictively as a reference to the people of Israel, not universally as a reference to all humanity (cf. Achtemeier 1986: 181). There is disagreement, however, as to the identity of the covenant Malachi has in mind. J.M.P. Smith (p. 48) repre-sents those who interpret the covenant as a figure "denoting the general obliga-tion of loyalty to one another." Others understand "the covenant of our ances-tors" more specifically as the Abrahamic covenant (e.g., Baldwin [1972a: 237]), the covenant at Sinai (Redditt 1995: 170), or in context, the covenant of Levi (so Mason [1977: 149]; cf. 2:4).

This essay is aligned with those of commentators who recognize "the covenant of our fathers" as an allusion to Israel's covenant experience at Sinai given the echo of Deuteronomic language and the explicit social obligations of Mosaic law (e.g., D. R. Jones [1962: 194]; Henderson [1980: 453]; Glazier-McDonald [1987a: 87–88]; Verhoef [1987: 267]). The ambiguous translation "forefathers" has been retained, permitting the allusion to the covenants of the patriarchs (so

NEB) but understanding the inclusive meaning "ancestors," whose referent is the nation of Israel (see the NOTES for 3:7 below; cf. NJB, NRSV, "ancestors").

11. *bāgĕdâ yĕhûdâ.* The Qal suffixing form of *bgd* conveys a perfective sense, a situation that occurred in the recent past (hence the auxiliary verb "has," WO'C § 30.5.1b). The verb pair *bgd* + *ḥll* are ordered in synonymous parallelism in verse 10cd and verse 11ac. On the meaning and distribution of the verbs *bgd* and *ḥll* see the NOTES for verse 10 on *nibgad* and *lĕḥallēl* above. Similar charges of faithlessness against Israel/Judah occur in Jer 3:8, 11, 20; 5:11; Hos 5:7; 6:7. Petersen (1995: 194) claims that *bāgĕdâ* constitutes a "dittographic expansion" and reads *bāgad*.

The subject "Yehud" (*yĕhûdâ*) is construed here as a feminine noun in verse 11a, while in verse 11c the same subject "Yehud" (*yĕhûdâ*) is understood as a masculine noun. Glazier-McDonald (1987a: 89) considers the shift in gender an indicator of "totality," stressing "the enormity of the people's offense by enunciating that betrayal is practiced everywhere in the country." Elsewhere, however, Judah (*yĕhûdâ*) is construed as a feminine noun simply for the sake of assonance in the rhyme-scheme (cf. Lam 1:3). Such may be the case here (but see O'Brien [1996: 247–50] who believes this gender shifting "feminizes" God in Malachi). See further the discussion of "Yehud" (*yĕhûdâ*) in the NOTES for 3:4 below.

wĕtô'ēbâ ne'ĕśtâ. The conjunctive *waw* joins two related clauses (WO'C § 39.2.5). The emphatic placement of the subject "abomination" (*tô'ēbâ*) underscores the severity of the prophetic indictment.

The feminine noun *tô'ēbâ* occurs only here in the Twelve, but is found more than 60 times in Deuteronomy, Jeremiah, and Ezekiel (books upon which the vocabulary of Malachi tends to exhibit dependence). The word denotes "something abominable, detestable, offensive" (*CHAL:* 388; cf. Holladay [1986: 88], "loathsome" in Jer 2:7). J.M.P. Smith (p. 49) cites the singular number of *tô'ēbâ* as evidence against interpreting the text primarily as a reference to literal marriages. It is possible, however, to understand the detestable offenses in a collective sense, as is the case in Jer 6:15; 8:12; Ezek 16:50. The singular form also permits the retention of assonance with *yĕhûdâ.*

Three interpretive options have emerged from the scholarly discussion of this text. The literal approach, attested as early as Jerome (*CChr* 76A:923), understands Malachi's indictment as the "abomination" of intermarriage with non-Hebrews by citizens of postexilic Yehud (e.g., Chary [1969: 256–57]; Baldwin [1972a: 238]; Achtemeier [1986: 181]; Verhoef [1987: 269–70]; Ogden and Deutsch [1987: 94]). The figurative approach perceives the prophet's statement either as a metaphor for unholy alliances made by Yehud with foreign nations (so J.M.P. Smith [1912: 49]) or as a typological allusion to the practice of idolatry (as a result of intermarriage) in postexilic Yehud that has profaned Yahweh and his Temple cultus (so S. R. Driver [1906: 313]; Hvidberg [1962: 120]; Petersen [1995: 198–200]; cf. O'Brien [1996: 247–50]).

Those who interpret the clause metaphorically, restricting the connotation of the term *tô'ēbâ* to idolatry only, overstate the case (see Torrey 1898). According to Weinfeld (1991: 376–77), the common denominator of the laws and dicta to which the word *tô'ēbâ* is appended is "hypocritical attitude and false pretension."

Such hypocrisy may manifest itself in the social sphere (dealing perversely with others, Deut 24:4; 25:15) or in the cultic sphere (dealing perversely with Yahweh, Deut 17:1; 18:9–11; 23:19; cf. Holladay [1986: 88] on the use of *tô'ēbâ* in reference to both sexual sins and idolatry).

This writer agrees with the majority of recent commentators choosing to interpret "abomination" (*tô'ēbâ*) explicitly as a citation of the (ongoing?) practice of divorce for the purpose of ethnic intermarriage in postexilic Yehud (e.g., Verhoef [1987: 269–70]; Redditt [1995: 171]; cf. the extensive discussion in Glazier-McDonald [1987a: 89–91]). There is no doubt that the "abomination" of intermarriage with non-Hebrews has implications of religious compromise with the idolatrous cults of these aliens (cf. S. R. Driver [1906: 313]). The offense condemned by the prophet, though, is essentially that of violation of the stipulations for Hebrew marriage outlined in pentateuchal legislation (Exod 34:15–16; Lev 20:2–5; Deut 7:3); specifically targeting Canaanites and by implication all such exogamy (i.e., marriages outside the family, so Verhoef [1987: 270]).

Malachi regards such intermarriage as a profanation of Yahweh's holiness and a desecration of his Temple as the embodiment of that holiness (cf. Ezra 9:1, 11, 14). Apparently, Yahweh's intransigence with respect to his covenant relationship with Israel extends even to abuses associated with the marriage covenant (cf. Mason [1990: 245]).

The verb *'śh* means "to do" in the sense of "act" or "commit" (*CHAL:* 285; see also the NOTES for 2:12, 13, 15, 17; 3:15, 17, 19 [4:1], and 21 [4:3] below). The Niphal stem is passive, indicating an "agent-oriented" and loathsome "state" of affairs (cf. WO'C § 23.2.2). The suffixing conjugation continues the perfective sense of (recent) past events in Yehud expressed by the preceding verb *bāgĕdâ* (cf. WO'C § 35.5.1b).

bĕyiśrā'ēl ûbîrûšālāyim. The preposition *bêt* attached to the place names "Israel" and "Jerusalem" conveys a locative or spatial sense in the two words ("in" or "within" an area, WO'C § 11.2.5b). The simple conjunctive *waw* joins "Israel" and "Jerusalem" in a type of hendiadys for the territory of postexilic Yehud (WO'C § 32.3b).

The wordpair "Yehud-Jerusalem" identified the state and capital of the Jewish community during the postexilic period. The substitution of the name "Israel" (*yiśrā'ēl*) for "Yehud" (*yĕhûdâ*) in verse 11 may represent an "inclusive insertion," accounting for those northerners who lived in Judah after the fall of Samaria and northerners who immigrated to Palestine under Persian rule (cf. Meyers and Meyers [1987: 138]). In this way, the name "Israel" not only demarcates a geographical region, but also unifies the people within that region by addressing them as *all* "Israel" (similar to the superscription, 1:1; cf. D. R. Jones [1962: 195] on "Israel" as "the true people of God" and Baldwin [1972a: 238] on the names "Judah" and "Israel" as recognition that the repatriates in Yehud are "the contemporary inheritors of the ancient promises"). A partial chiastic structure is formed in the arrangement of "Judah . . . Israel" and "Jerusalem . . . Judah."

The construction of Malachi preserves the unusual triad of names found in Zech 2:2 [1:19], "Judah, Israel, and Jerusalem." According to Glazier-McDonald (1987a: 89), the appellative "Israel" specifically identifies the "cultic congregation" of the Jerusalem Temple. If this is the case, the name "Israel" also constitutes a lexical bridge of sorts linking the second (1:6–2:9) and fourth (2:17–3:5) disputations with the third. Although the prophet has broadened the scope of his audience to now include the entire postexilic community, he continues to recognize the centrality of the priesthood for the spiritual life of the nation. See further the discussion of *yĕhûdâ wîrûšālāyim* in the NOTES for 3:4 below.

kî hillēl yĕhûdâ. The adverb *kî* is alternately understood as a subordinating conjunction in a logical sense ("for," so JPSV, NJB, NRSV) or in a causal sense ("because," R. L. Smith [1984: 319]; WO'C § 39.3.4e). Reading *kî* as the subordinating conjunction "for" agrees with the majority opinion and seems more correct in that the clause explains almost epexegetically the nature of the abomination; but this may be yet another example where the logical and causal senses of *kî* should not be too strictly separated (note the LXX *dióti* and the V *quia*; and Rudolph [1976: 268] [ambiguously], *denn* = "for, because").

The Piel suffixing form of *hll* continues the recent past-time reference of the perfective (WO'C § 30.5.1b; and see the discussion of *lĕhallēl* in v 10 above). The repetition of the subject "Yehud" (*yĕhûdâ*) emphasizes the accountability of the present generation of Israelites to Yahweh for the covenant stipulations. The prophet's redundant language is both "inclusive" (addressing the entire community) and "exclusive" (restricting the onus of responsibility to the contemporary citizens—preventing the denial of the charges or the displacing of the blame).

qōdeš YHWH. The construct genitive phrase *qōdeš YHWH* means literally "the holiness of Yahweh" (cf. WO'C § 9.5.3b on the attributive genitive). The only parallel construction is found in Lev 19:8 (*kî-'et-qōdeš YHWH*, "that holy to Yahweh") in reference to ritual sacrifice. The noun *qōdeš* ("holiness," CHAL: 314) occurs elsewhere in the Haggai-Zechariah-Malachi corpus in Hag 2:12; Zech 2:16 [12], 17 [13]; 8:3; 14:20, 21 (see the discussion of *'admat haqqōdeš* and *qodšô* in Meyers and Meyers [1987: 170–72]).

The noun *qōdeš* may refer to the sanctuary or Temple of Yahweh, perhaps as a symbol of Yahweh's holiness in postexilic Yehud (so Luther [Oswald 1975: 403]; J.M.P. Smith [1912: 48]; von Bulmerincq [1932: 254]; Rudolph [1976: 268]; R. L. Smith [1984: 319]; Verhoef [1987: 268]; Glazier-McDonald [1987a: 82]; Redditt [1995: 171]; NAB; NIV; NJB; NRSV; cf. Pss 20:3 [2]; 93:5). The word may also connote more ambiguously *something* "holy to Yahweh" like his covenant (so Pusey [2:482]), his people Israel (so Keil [2:449]; Henderson [1980: 453]; Laetsch [1956: 525]; Achtemeier [1986: 182]), or even the covenant of marriage (so Kimchi; cf. Cashdan [1948: 345]; JPSV, "what is holy to Yahweh"; cf. LXX *tà hágia kuríou*). Finally, the expression *qōdeš YHWH* may denote the very character of Yahweh, "holiness" as the supreme essence of his being (so Calvin [1979: 664]; Schreiner [1979: 210]; NEB).

The word "holiness" (*qōdeš*) is used in antithetical parallelism with "profane" (*hll* or *hōl*) elsewhere in Lev 10:10; 19:8; 22:15; Num 18:32; Ezek 22:26; 42:20; 44:23; and Zeph 3:4 (perhaps indicating Malachi's dependence upon other sources for the construction).

If the relative pronoun *'ăšer* functions as a true relative in verse 11b, then the majority interpretation of "the holiness of Yahweh" as the Second Temple has currency (e.g., Syr, NAB, NIV, NRSV, cf. 1:10; 2:12; 3:1). If *'ăšer* functions as a conjunction in context, as seems likely, then the expression *qōdeš YHWH* is best taken as a reference to the character of YHWH. The more ambiguous translation, "the holiness of Yahweh," is retained in an attempt to acknowledge the possibility of a dual understanding of the phrase (cf. Mason [1977: 149]).

'ăšer 'āhēb. The relative pronoun *'ăšer* has the force of a conjunction in this context, introducing a causal dependent clause ("*because* he loved and married," see BDB: 83; cf. NEB, "by loving and marrying"). This means that verse 11b is a continuous and declarative statement, with "Yehud" (*yĕhûdâ*) serving as the subject of verse 11b. The disjunctive accent (*zāqēp qāṭōn*) over *'āhēb* may be explained as an attempt by the Masoretes to prevent the misunderstanding of YHWH as the subject of *bā'al* (cf. the exegetical tradition represented in the early expansion of Mal 2:11 in T, "*. . . for the people of the house of* Judah *have* profaned *their soul which was holy before* the Lord *. . . ;*" see Cathcart and Gordon [1989: 233]; cf. Packard [1902: 15]).

Petersen (1995: 198–200) revives the "cultic" interpretation by emending *'ăšer 'āhēb* to *'ăšērâ 'āhēb* ("he loves Asherah"), restoring the *hē'* as a supposed error of haplography. Quite apart from the lack of any supporting textual evidence for this reconstruction, we have argued previously that there is little evidence for wholesale idolatry among the Israelites during the early Persian period (see I. D. 2. Persian Palestine above; cf. Stern [1989] on the purification of Israelite religion in Second Temple Yehud). Also, the sociological context of postexilic Yehud suggests that this intermarriage was motivated by economic, not religious, concerns (as Myers [1968: 98] cogently observes; see I. D. 3c. Social Considerations above). A logical consequence of Hebrew marriage into the local (and alien) "cartels" (already solidly established by the time of Hebrew repatriation from Babylonia) was the adoption of local policies concerning "business as usual" — rife with injustice (cf. Mal 3:5).

The Qal suffixing conjugation *'āhēb* is rendered as a definite preterite ("he [i.e., Yehud] loved," but NEB, "loving"), the prophet understanding that the marriage has already occurred (WO'C § 30.5.1b; on the verb *'hb* ["to love"], see the NOTES discussing *'āhabtî* and *'ăhabtānû* in 1:2 above). The use of the verb *'hb* may allude to the covenant "love" of Yahweh for Israel cited in the first disputation (1:2–5). If so, the subordinate causal clause may constitute a subtle foil with the declaration "Yahweh has loved Jacob" (1:2). The fact that Yahweh has loved Jacob but Yehud has loved and married an alien god thus explains the warning at the close of the third disputation (2:16) and the necessity for the judgment of postexilic Yehud forecast in the fourth dispute (3:1–2). The proposed emendation of the *BHS* (reading the resumptive pronoun due to haplography with the *waw* of the following word *ûbā'al*, *'āhēbô*, "which he loves *it*") is unwarranted (see Mason [1977: 149–50]).

ûbā'al bat-'ēl nēkār. The coordinating *waw* is rendered variously as a simple conjunctive ("and," e.g., NAB, NRSV), a causal conjunctive ("because," e.g.,

Rudolph [1976: 268]), or an epexegetical *waw* ("by," e.g., NEB, NIV, Verhoef [1987: 262]). Because the verbs *'āhēb* and *bā'al* are logical complements, the conjunctive *waw* is preferred (cf. WO'C § 39.2.5).

The verb *bā'al* may mean "to rule over" or "to marry" (KBL 1:142), but context indicates the latter meaning ("to marry") is intended in Mal 2:11. The verbal root *b'l* is unique to Malachi among the Twelve. The LXX, OL, and Syr have all mistaken *bā'al* ("marry") as an addiction to idol-worship (so Kruse-Blinkenberg [1966: 99]; cf. Verhoef [1987: 269]).

Theologically, Malachi's use of *bā'al* echoes the language of the restoration visions of Second Isaiah (especially 54:5; 62:4). According to Watts (1987b: 237), the imagery of marriage is appropriate to Yahweh's reestablishment of his people in their own land. The marriage motif intimates that Yahweh has "turned" back to Jerusalem and the Israelite community after the abandonment and desolation of Babylonian Exile (so Westermann [1969: 376]). Nonetheless, as Israel's "maker" and "husband" (Isa 54:5), Yahweh can nurture his people only as they respond to him in obedience as "owner" or "master" (such "ownership" is implicit in the OT/HB understanding of marriage, cf. KBL 1:142).

By marrying into the clans of the surrounding "alien" people groups, postexilic Yehud "broke faith" with Yahweh, violating the stipulations of the covenant agreement and jeopardizing their compact with him. The gravity of the situation is compounded by the prophet's recognition that in intermarriage of this sort one weds both an "alien" and an "alien deity" (cf. Glazier-McDonald [1987a: 91]). The disastrous outcome of the religious syncretism embraced by the Israelites during the preexilic period probably accounts for Malachi's unusual choice of words here, insinuating that the "adultery" of divorce and remarriage to "aliens" was tantamount to "idolatry" (cf. 2:14–16). The dangers of such liaisons should have been self-evident, attested by the prophet's pointed rhetorical question in verse 14!

The construct-genitive phrase "daughter of a foreign god" (*bat-'ēl nēkār*) is unique to Mal 2:11 in the Twelve. The combination *'ēl nēkār* ("foreign god") occurs elsewhere in Deut 32:12 and Ps 81:10, and the plural *'ĕlōhê [han] nēkār* ("foreign gods") is found in Gen 35:2, 4; Deut 31:16; Josh 24:20, 23; Judg 10:16; 1 Sam 7:3; 2 Chr 33:15.

The word "daughter" (*bat*) may be understood in a literal sense ("female child, young woman," TDOT 2:333–34) or in a figurative sense (e.g., "city," TDOT 2:336). Commentators are divided in their interpretation of the phrase "daughter of foreign god," whether literally as a reference to "foreign women" (so J.M.P. Smith [1912: 50]; von Bulmerincq [1932: 257–60]; Chary [1969: 257]; Glazier-McDonald [1987a: 92–93]; Ogden and Deutsch [1987: 94]; Redditt [1995: 171]) or as a metaphor for a "foreign goddess" (i.e., an alien deity, so Torrey [1898: 9–11]; Hvidberg [1962: 121–22]; Petersen [1995: 199–200]).

Chary (1969: 257) has convincingly countered the arguments that an ordinary woman is not addressed as a "daughter of god" by noting that the Moabites are designated as "sons" (*bānāyw*) and "daughters" (*běnōtāyw*) of Chemosh (Num 21:29). Likewise, the "sons" (*bānāyw*) and "daughters" (*běnōtāyw*) of Yahweh are not gods and goddesses, but the people of Israel (Deut 32:19). The expression is

used in the collective sense of "foreign women" who have married into the Hebrew clans of Yehud, much like the biblical figure designating the collective inhabitants of a place by means of personification (e.g., *bat-bābēl*, Zech 2:11 [7];
bat-ṣiyyôn, Zech 2:14 [10]; cf. Meyers and Meyers [1987: 164]). The prophet's
phraseology in protest of the practice of intermarriage with non-Hebrews in postexilic Yehud serves as both reminder and warning that "foreign cults penetrate
into Israel through the daughters of foreign nations" (*TDOT* 2:337; cf. Glazier-
McDonald [1987a: 92–93]).

Among the ancient versions, both V and T support the reading of the MT,
while the LXX "and has pursued other gods" (*kai epetēdeusen eis theoùs
allotrious*) is probably an accommodation to the practice of "mixed marriages"
in Hellenistic Judaism (cf. Verhoef [1987: 269]). The OL and Syr are dependent
on the LXX.

The noun *nēkār* ("that which is foreign," BDB: 648–49) functions as an attributive adjective (WO'C § 14.3.1). The *disunity* of community represented by the
phrase "daughter of a foreign god" (*bat-'ēl nēkār*) stands in contrast to the *unity*
of Yehud in Yahweh affirmed in verse 10 (*'āb 'eḥād . . . 'ēl 'eḥād*; cf. Glazier-
McDonald [1987a: 92–93]). One wonders if Malachi's unusual language is a
veiled reference to the blessing pronounced on the "foreigner" (*ben-hannēkār*)
who maintains Yahweh's covenant (Isa 56:3, 6). Perhaps the prophet's audience
has appealed to this tradition as justification for the practice of intermarriage (but
note that the direction of the union there is "foreigner" *to* "Yahweh's covenant,"
not "Hebrew" *to* "foreigner" as was apparently the case in postexilic Yehud). The
entire clause specifies the nature of the abomination committed by the Yehud:
the profaning of Yahweh's holiness by intermarrying with foreign women in violation of covenant stipulations.

12. *yakrēt YHWH*. The verb *krt* means "to cut off" (*CHAL*: 165). The word
occurs elsewhere in the Haggai-Zechariah-Malachi corpus in Hag 2:5; Zech 9:6,
10 [2x]; 11:10; 13:2, 8; 14:2. Though harsh, the traditional understanding of *kārat*
("cut off" in the sense of blotting out or destroying the evildoer and his descendants, so Calvin [1979: 548]; Keil [2:450–51]; Eiselen [1907: 723]; J.M.P. Smith
[1912: 50]; cf. JPSV, "leave no descendants") is preferred over the milder "ban-
ish" or "excommunicate" (so Achtemeier [1986: 182], NEB; cf. Pss 101:8;
109:13; Jer 44:7; see the discussion of *krt* in Meyers and Meyers [1993: 367–68]).
The Hiphil jussive form *yakrēt* expresses malediction (WO'C § 34.3c). On the
"interpretive" and "sensational" *exolethreúsei* of the LXX, cf. Andersen and
Freedman 1989: 252–53.

The English versions universally read *yakrēt* as a jussive ("*may* the Lord . . .";
cf. WO'C § 34.2.1b), but some ancient versions render the form as a simple
Hiphil prefixing conjugation signifying a future or nonperfective tense ("Yahweh
will . . . "; e.g., LXX [cf. Walters 1973: 237], Syr). The combination of the verb
krt ("cut [off]") + the preposition *min* occurs frequently in the OT/HB, often as
the expression of a wish or desire with Yahweh acting as the agent (e.g., Deut
12:29; 19:1; Isa 9:13 [14]; Ezek 14:8; 21:8 [3], 9 [4]; Amos 1:5, 8; etc.). The
verb *krt* is especially prominent in the Pentateuch as a divine penalty for certain
violations of the Mosaic law (e.g., Lev 7:20, 21, 25, 27; 17:4, 9; etc.; see the dis-

cussion of *kārēt* in Milgrom [1991: 457–60]). According to Meyers and Meyers (1993: 367), "such technical, cultic language . . . is used . . . for the removal of persons or elements that are disruptive of the covenant between Yahweh and Israel" (cf. *TDOT* 7:345). Given the covenant theme of Malachi's disputations, even some kind of wordplay here with the covenant formula *krt bĕrît* ("cut/make a covenant") cannot be ruled out (cf. Zech 11:10). What powerful irony in the "cutting off" of those "cut into" Yahweh's covenant!

On the divine name *YHWH* see the notes for the Superscription (1:1) and 1:2 above.

lā'îš 'ăšer ya'ăšennâ. The preposition *lamed* ("to, for") has an accusative function, governing the direct object "the man . . ." (WO'C § 11.4.1b; a "solecism of the later period" according to GKC § 117n).

The common noun *'îš* denotes a "man" or even a "husband" (KBL 1:43) and occurs elsewhere in Mal 2:10; 3:16, 17. The word "man" is understood in a gender-specific manner given the divorce laws in patriarchal societies of this time period (contra NRSV, "*anyone* who . . ."). The construction *lā'îš* is definite, in reference to those who have (already) married foreign women (v 11; cf. WO'C § 13.5.1d on the *anaphoric* use of the definite article). The relative pronoun *'ăšer* has a nominative function in the dependent relative clause (without resumption, WO'C § 19.3a; cf. *kĕ'îš 'ăšer-yē'ôr*, Zech 4:1).

The Qal stem prefixing form of *'śh* may be understood as a persistent perfective (present tense) or a habitual nonperfective (a repeated situation still occurring in present time, cf. WO'C § 31.3a, e). The feminine singular object suffix ("the one who does *it* [*this*, NRSV]") refers to the act of marrying a non-Hebrew mentioned in verse 11. On the verb *'śh*, see the NOTES for 2:17; 3:15, 17; 19 [4:1], 21 [4:3] below.

'ēr wĕ'ōneh. This enigmatic combination of Qal participles joined by conjunctive *waw* is unique to Mal 2:12 in the MT. Literally, the verb *'wr* in the Qal stem means "be awake, astir, lively" (*CHAL:* 268; although the form is usually emended to *'ēd* [עֵד] "witness" from *'ēr* [עֵר] "answerer, arouser" [so BHS], but LXX *héōs* = Hebrew *'ad*, "until"). The verbal root *'ānâ* (I) means "to answer" (*CHAL:* 277). The translation of S. R. Driver (1906: 314) represents the traditional understanding of this pair of words ("him that waketh and him that answereth" [i.e., everyone]; cf. von Orelli [p. 394] "he that calls and he that makes reply" [i.e., all in the house]). Neither the root *'wr* nor *'nh* (I) occurs elsewhere in Malachi.

The ancient versions render the two verbal nouns variously (LXX, "*until he is cast down* from the tents of Jacob"; Syr and T, "son and grandson" [so Chary 1969: 256, 258; and Baldwin 1972a: 239]; V, "master and disciple" [so Luther]), as do the modern English versions (NAB and NJB, "[both] witness and advocate"; NEB, "nomads or settlers" [based on the Arabic]; NIV, "whoever he may be" [so Verhoef 1987: 270–71]; NRSV and Redditt [1995: 171], "any to witness or answer"; cf. Fuller [1991: 51] on the proposed term *'d* in 4QXII).

Biblical commentators, whether by emendation or interpretation of the MT, provide little help in forging any consensus as to the meaning of the expression (e.g., Calvin [1979: 664]: "the prompter and the respondent"; D. R. Jones [1962: 195], "Er and Onan" [as *types* of children born from such a union, cf. Gen 38:2–4, 7, 10]; Barr [1968: 165, 243, 250, 333], "gad about, stay at home"; Rudolph [1976: 268–69], "guardian and confidant"; and Glazier-McDonald [1987a: 95–98] who strains to infuse the construction with sexual connotations, "the aroused one and the lover"; cf. Petersen [1995: 194–95], "involving nakedness and improper cohabitation"). See J.M.P. Smith (pp. 50–51) for a review of the earlier history of alternative readings.

The distillation of scholarly opinion does yield three premises. First, it seems likely that the two nouns (*'ēr wĕ'ōneh*) constitute a type of idiom or technical phrase associated with some aspect of community life; for example, "camp life" in the rousing of families in the morning (so J.M.P. Smith [1912: 50]; cf. the Arabic proverb, "there is not in the city a caller, nor is there a responder" [i.e., the city is desolate]) or even religious life as a prohibition against any representative bringing an offering for an excommunicated person (Redditt [1995: 171]; cf. Wellhausen [1963: 207]; Fuller [1991: 51]). Second, this emphatic insertion is intended to suggest merismus, representing a "totality" of some sort (Mason [1977: 150]). Third, the meaning of the phrase is best connected with the verb *krt*, either as a qualification of the degree to which the offender is "cut off" from the community (e.g., socially and/or religiously, cf. Ogden and Deutsch [1987: 94]) or as an extension of the malediction pronounced against those practicing such divorce (e.g., Jerome *CChr* 76A:921–22; Keil [2:451]). The latter view makes good sense, understanding the construction as an extension of the malediction to include the aiders and abettors of those in Yehud practicing intermarriage with non-Hebrews. The disputational style and judicial nature of the oracle justify the emendation of the MT *'ēr* ("the one awake") to *'ēd* ("witness"). Thus the idiom probably has legal connotations, perhaps related to the juridical procedure requiring two witnesses (a "witness" and an "answerer" [i.e., a corroborating witness], cf. Deut 17:6; 19:15). In series then, the prophet's imprecation extends to those who were a party to such marriages, whether in a legal or cultic sense. This interpretive approach also has the advantage of retaining the involvement of the wider audience in the prophet's message, since culpability extends beyond those who have divorced their Hebrew wives and remarried non-Hebrews.

mē'āhŏlê ya'ăqōb. The preposition *min* conveys a partitive sense, describing the separation of the offenders "from" the rest of the Israelite community (WO'C § 11.2.11e). The construct-genitive, "tents of Jacob," occurs only in Num 24:5; Jer 30:18 and Mal 2:12. The phrase is an equivalent expression for the community of Yehud, since a tent and its inhabitants constitute a social unit (cf. *TDOT* 1:121; Glazier-McDonald [1987a: 93] associates the plural *'āhŏlê* ["tents"] with the Jerusalem Temple and unnecessarily restricts the scope of the idiom to the "cultic community"). The word "tent" is not to be taken as an archaic allusion to Israelite pastoral nomadism; rather, "the term . . . functions as an alternate word designating a habitation or home" (see the discussion of "tents of Yehud" [*'āhŏlê yĕhûdâ*, Zech 12:7] in Meyers and Meyers [1993: 328]). The prepositional phrase, "from the tents of Jacob," is the indirect object of the verb *yakrēt* ("he will cut off"). On the name, "Jacob," see further the NOTES for 1:2 above and 3:6 below.

ûmaggîš minḥâ. The coordinating *waw* may be understood as a conjunctive *waw* connecting elements of a series ("and," so LXX, Syr, JPSV; with alternative force, "or," NRSV) or an emphatic *waw* ("even," so NEB, NIV; cf. WO'C § 39.2.1b). The emphatic *waw* is more appropriate given the disputational format of the oracle and the egregious nature of the offense. The prophet's malediction extends even to citizens "aiding and abetting" those practicing divorce (cf. the expansion of T, Cathcart and Gordon [1989: 233–34]).

The Hiphil participle of *ngš* ("approach, draw near") identifies the one who "brings" or "presents" an offering to the Lord (*CHAL:* 228). Broadly speaking this includes anyone guilty of compromising Yahweh's covenant by intermarriage to a non-Hebrew but still attempts to appease him by offering ritual sacrifice at the Temple (cf. Glazier-McDonald [1987a: 99]). More narrowly understood, the participial clause refers technically to the priest as the ordained custodian of the Temple offerings (e.g., von Orelli [1897: 394–95]). It seems best to concur with J.M.P. Smith (p. 51) and recognize the expression as a comprehensive summary statement censuring anyone party to such intermarriage — in any way. Jerome interprets here "and whoever is willing to offer a gift upon the altar for men of this description" (cf. Keil [2:451], "May God not only cut off every descendant of such a sinner out of the houses of Israel, but anyone who might offer a sacrifice for him in expiation of his sin"). The expression has its parallel in the plural, "presenters of an offering" (*maggîšê minḥâ*), in 3:3 below.

The noun *minḥâ* pertains to "offering" or "sacrifice" in cultic contexts, whether meat or cereal offerings (*CHAL:* 202). See the NOTES for 1:10 above and 3:3 below.

laYHWH ṣĕbā'ôt. The preposition *lamed* imparts an allative or terminative sense ("to, toward") with the verb of motion (*ngš*, WO'C 11.2.10bc). According to Watts (1987b: 237), the later use of the divine title "Yahweh of Hosts" hearkens back to older Israelite theology, especially worship around the Ark of the Covenant, the Exodus, the wilderness trek, and the settlement of Canaan. This is in keeping with the covenant theme emphasized in Malachi. On "Yahweh of Hosts," see further the NOTES for 1:4 above.

13. *wĕzō't šēnît ta'ăśû.* The conjunctive *waw* joins two interrelated situations (intermarriage and divorce; cf. WO'C § 39.2.5). The Masoretes apparently understood the *waw* as a disjunctive marker, given the insertion of the *pārāšâ pĕtûḥâ* (פ) after the messenger formula of 2:12 (see I. C. 4. Structure above).

The feminine singular demonstrative pronoun *zō't* ("this") has both an emphatic force (indicating divorce is a weighty matter for Yahweh, v 16; cf. WO'C § 17.4.3d) and a relative force (*cataphora*, i.e., referring to following nouns; cf. WO'C § 17.4.2e). Syntactically, the demonstrative *zō't* functions like a predicate adjective with *šēnît* ("this *is* a second thing . . ."; cf. WO'C 17.4.1).

The feminine singular ordinal *šēnît* ("second") extends the indictment of verse 11 ("for Yehud has profaned . . ."). The numbering adjective *šēnît* occurs elsewhere in the Twelve in Jonah 3:1; Hag 2:20; and Zech 4:12. The English versions render the ordinal šēnît ("second") with more dynamically equivalent phrases such as "and this you do as well" (NAB, NRSV) or "another thing you do" (NIV; cf. Glazier-McDonald [1987a: 99]) or "and here is something else you do" (NJB) or even "this also you do" (Petersen [1995: 194]). There is no need to excise šēnît as a later editorial insertion (e.g., Sellin [1930: 603]; cf. *BHS*). The first offense, profaning Yahweh's sanctuary (outlined in vv 10–12), was the result of foreign marriage among the Hebrews. The "second" offense, a natural consequence of the first, was the desecration of Yahweh's altar with hypocritical laments (decrying Yahweh's intransigence over the divorcement of legitimate Hebrew wives due to this intermarriage (vv 13–16). The LXX mistakes šēnît ("second") for śānēʾtî ("I hate"; cf. śānēʾ in 2:16).

The Qal prefix conjugation form of the verb ʿśh ("to do, make") is a progressive nonperfective, indicating an "ongoing" situation ("you are doing" or "you continue to do," WO'C § 31.3b). The juxtaposition of the prefix conjugation taʿăśû with the suffix conjugation hillēl (v 11 above) helps establish the consequential relationship between intermarriage and divorce in postexilic Yehud. See further the NOTES for ʿśh in 2:11, 12 above and 2:15; 3:21 [4:3] below.

kassôt dimʿâ ʾet-mizbaḥ YHWH. The Piel infinitive construct kassôt proves difficult. The LXX, Syr, and V all read a second-person masculine plural prefix conjugation of ksh, as do the English versions (cf. *BHS* tĕkassû = LXX ekalýptete; so Petersen [1995: 195 n. e]). The verb ksh (I) means "to cover" in the Piel stem (BDB: 491) and is attested in the Haggai-Zechariah-Malachi corpus only in Mal 2:13, 16 (on ksh, see TDOT 7:259–64). The word is used figuratively of tears "flooding" (NIV) or "drowning" (NEB) the sacrificial altar. Reading the infinitive construct kassôt is preferable here because it underscores the ongoing activity implied by the nonperfective taʿăśû (so LXX; Calvin [1979: 664]; Keil [1:451]; Henderson [1980: 454]; Packard [1902: 15]). In addition, the form has its complement in Qal infinitive construct pĕnôt also in verse 13 and is in keeping with the style of graphic diction employed in the third oracle (see the introductory comments above on the variations in the disputational format observed in this pericope).

The feminine singular collective noun dimʿâ is usually translated "tears" (KBL 1:227). The word may be construed as the subject of the verb ksh (so T) or, more commonly, as the indirect object of ksh (with preposition bêt ["with"] supplied) in series with "weeping" (bĕkî) and "wailing" (ʾănāqâ, so most English versions). Either way, the language expresses the intensity and zeal with which the worshipers of Yehud sought Yahweh. The cultic understanding of "tears" as a reference to the weeping of women for Tammuz or Adonis is fittingly dismissed as "a curiosity of interpretation" by J.M.P. Smith (p. 52). Likewise, R. L. Smith (1984: 323) rules out the approach inferring that the divorced Hebrew women of Yehud were the ones weeping before Yahweh (see Jerome [CChr 76 A:924]; cf. T). Rabbi Eliezer lamented that the very altar of the Temple sheds tears when a man divorces his wife (b. Giṭṭ 90b, b. Sanh 22a), perhaps an attempt to dramatize Yahweh's response to the tragedy of divorce.

The construct-genitive "the altar of Yahweh" or "Yahweh's altar" (mizbaḥ YHWH) is unique to Mal 2:13 in the Prophets (see the discussion of mizbĕḥî in the NOTES for 1:7, 10 above). The phrase is prominent in Priestly (Lev 17:6; 2 Chr 6:12; 8:12; 15:8; etc.) and Deuteronomic (Deut 12:27; 16:21; 26:4; 27:6; 1 Kgs 8:22; etc.) materials and reveals the exclusivity of Hebrew worship of Yahweh, the appropriateness of liturgy and ritual, and the loyalty of the worshiper. The sanctity of Yahweh's altar is attested by the theophany that occurs there as a part of the Sinai charter (Exod 9:23–24) and the ability of the altar to transform the clean into the holy through contact (Exod 29:37).

More significantly, according to Milgrom (1991: 251), "the altar . . . is the earthly terminus of a divine funnel for man's communion with God . . . Israel's altar may not bring God to earth but it enables man, through his worship, to reach heaven." The laments of the worshipers in postexilic Yehud reveal the profound recognition that their communion with Yahweh has been severed. The site-specific reference to Yahweh's altar lends credence to understanding "holiness" (qōdeš) in verse 11 as a parallel expression for Yahweh's Temple or sanctuary in Jerusalem.

běkî wa'ănāqâ. The masculine noun běkî ("weeping," KBL 1:130) occurs elsewhere in the Twelve only in Joel 2:12 ("return unto me with all of your heart, with fasting, with weeping [běkî] . . ."). According to Hamp (TDOT 2:119–20), this word for "weeping" has numerous religious connotations, including public acts of repentance (e.g., Ezra 10:1; Joel 2:12) and in connection with popular laments expressing public distress (so Mal 2:13). J.M.P. Smith (1912: 51), among others, considers the phrase "weeping and groaning" as an expansion of the original text since it adds nothing essential and its placement is awkward syntactically. However, there is a clear pattern of epexegetical apposition in the oracles of Malachi (e.g., 2:11, 12, 3:19 [4:1]). Moreover, such constructions are entirely in keeping with the recursive nature of the disputational literary form (cf. Clendenen [1987: 6]).

The phrasal waw conjoins nouns in a series, in this case only attached to the last item of the list (WO'C § 39.2.1b; the NIV breaks the series, ". . . tears. You weep and wail . . ."). This combination of "weeping" (běkî) and "sighing" ('ănāqâ) is unique to Mal 2:13 in the MT. The feminine noun 'ănāqâ ("sighing," KBL 1:72) is peculiar to Hebrew poetry, registered elsewhere only in Pss 12:6 [5]; 79:11; 102:21 [20]. Given the context of the affliction in each of the psalmic references, the rendering "groaning" (so NAB, NRSV), "moaning" (JPSV, NEB), or "wailing" (NIV, NJB) seems more appropriate (cf. Dahood [1965: 74]).

mē'ên 'ôd pěnôt 'el-hamminḥâ. The compound negative (preposition min + negative adverb 'ên) serves double duty, negating the infinitive construct pěnôt (see WO'C § 36.2.2g) and (though gapped) negating the following infinitive construct lāqaḥat. The preposition min ("from") can denote cause or effect (CHAL: 200; cf. WO'C § 11.2.11d). The clause is best understood in a causal sense ("because," so J.M.P. Smith [1912: 59]; von Bulmerincq [1932: 278]; R. L. Smith [1984: 320]; cf. NAB, NIV, NRSV) rather than as a result clause ("thus, so that," so Glazier-McDonald [1987a: 82]; cf. NEB). When juxtaposed with the negative adverb 'ên (the negative characteristically employed in LBH with the infinitive construct), the temporal adverb ʿôd means "no longer" (WO'C § 36 n. 22; cf. Petersen [1995: 194]).

Several of the English versions (JPSV, NEB, NJB; cf. *BHK* and *BHS*) read the proposed emendation *mēʾên* (Piel perfective of *mʾn*, "to refuse"; see the discussion in J.M.P. Smith [1912: 59] and von Bulmerincq [1932: 278–79]). The LXX translates *ek kópōn* ("because of troubles," = Heb. *mēʾāwen*; cf. 4QXIIa in Fuller [1991: 52]) and reads the form as part of the noun phrase *bĕkî waʾănāqâ* ("... weeping and groaning because of troubles ...").

The Qal infinitive construct *pĕnôt* is unique to Mal 2:13 in the Twelve. The verbal root *pnh* ("turn, turn aside or around") occurs elsewhere in the Haggai-Zechariah-Malachi corpus in Hag 1:9 (*pānōh*) and Mal 3:1 (see the discussion of *pinnâ* in the NOTES for 3:1 below). The combination of the Qal stem verb *pnh* + the preposition *ʾel* means literally "to turn toward" and is usually understood figuratively in the sense of "consider" (NJB; cf. NIV, "pay attention to"), "regard" (JPSV, NAB, NRSV; cf. BDB: 815), or "accept" (Petersen [1995: 194], who also notes that the Hebrew formulation is impersonal ["there is no more accepting the offering"]). The implied subject ("he," in the English versions) of the infinitive *pĕnôt* is Yahweh (an insertion proposed by the *BHS*). The language echoes Ezek 36:9 (*ûpānîtî ʾălêkem*, "I will turn to you") and Ps 102:18 [17] (*pānâ ʾel-tĕpillat ...*, "he turns to the prayer ..."). Yahweh can only "turn" (*pnh*) to the worship of Yehud after it has been purified by the "return" (*šwb*, 3:7) of the people to Yahweh.

The preposition *ʾel* marks movement "toward" a direction (the altar of sacrifice) and has a sense of specification ("concerning") as well (cf. WO'C § 11.2.2a). The noun *minḥâ* ("offering, sacrifice," *CHAL*: 202) is definite, as in 1:13. Here the generic article marks a class of things, the various offerings and sacrifices the Hebrew worshiper may offer at the Temple (cf. WO'C § 13.5.1f). On *minḥâ*, see further the discussion in the NOTES for 1:10, 11, 13 and 2:12 above, and 3:3, 4 below.

wĕlāqaḥat rāṣôn miyyedkem. After a negative (*mēʾên*), the phrasal *waw* has an alternative force ("nor," WO'C § 39.2.1b). The verb *lqḥ* means "take, receive" (*CHAL*: 178–79) and occurs only here in Malachi (but elsewhere in the Haggai-Zechariah-Malachi corpus in Hag 2:23; Zech 6:10, 11; 11:7, 10, 13, 15; 14:21). The Qal stem infinitive construct *lāqaḥat* completes a triad of infinitives in verse 13. Although unusual, this cluster of forms in verse 13 appears to mark the midpoint of Malachi's oracles (Mal 1:2–2:12 = 364 words; Mal 2:14–3:21 [4:3] = 366 words; at least according to Radday and Wickman's [1973:B] somewhat imprecise definition of a "word" in BH [i.e., "a group of characters separated from another group by a blank space or by the punctuation mark (:)"]). Theologically, verse 13 calls attention to sincere (Temple) worship, actuated by love of Yahweh and obedience to his covenant, as the key to unlocking the message of Malachi.

The masculine noun *rāṣôn* means "favor, acceptance, goodwill" (*CHAL*: 345–46) and occurs only in Mal 2:13 among the Twelve. The construction of *rāṣôn* with the verb *lqḥ* is unique in the MT. Rudolph (1976: 269), following von Bulmerincq (1932: 280), understands *rāṣôn* as an "accusative of condition" describing the manner in which the offering is received (so NAB, NIV, NRSV; cf. R. L. Smith [1984: 319]; Verhoef [1987: 273]; Petersen [1995: 194]). The clause is better understood as a parallel construction (infinitive construct + direct object, with inverted gapping of mē'ên [cf. Petersen 1995: 194] and miyyedkem), with rāṣôn and minḥâ in synonymous relationship (so NEB; cf. Calvin: [p. 664]; J.M.P. Smith [1912: 51]; Keil [2:451]; Glazier-McDonald [1987a: 82]). It seems that Malachi employs the word "favor" (rāṣôn) somewhat sarcastically (cf. LXX, ". . . or receive anything from your hands as a favor"). The offerings of Yehud contrast to those presented by obedient worshipers in Second Isaiah (56:7) and call to mind Jeremiah's rejection of Judah's sacrificial worship (6:20).

The preposition min ("from") is locational, describing the place where the offering originated (WO'C § 11.2.11b). The common noun "hand" (yād) is singular, although some English versions and commentators render the form as a plural ("hands," e.g., NIV; cf. Verhoef [1987: 262]). The idiom expresses ownership or control (TDOT 5:409; cf. NEB and NJB, "from you"). In Malachi the construction miyyedkem seems to constitute a technical expression associated with the practice of liturgical sacrifice (cf. 1:9, 10, 13). The second-person masculine plural possessive suffix "your" (. . . kem) resumes the prophet's contact with his audience established at the onset of verse 13 by the verb ta'ăśû. The pronominal suffix also foreshadows the responsibility placed on Malachi's audience by means of the heavy emphasis of the second-person possessive pronouns in verses 13–16.

14. wa'ămartem 'al-mâ. On the verb 'āmar marking the reported speech of the audience in response to the prophetic declaration, see the discussion of wa'ămartem in the NOTES for 1:2 above. The waw-relative conveys an adversative sense ("but," JPSV; cf. Glazier-McDonald [1987a: 82], "yet"), according to the disputation pattern (declaration, v 13; refutation, v 14a; and rebuttal, v 14b–d).

In combination with the preposition 'al ("on, upon"), the interrogative mâ ("what") has the sense "on what basis, why?" (WO'C § 18.3d; cf. Jer 8:14; 9:11; Ezek 21:12). The reported audience response seems to be one of genuine disbelief that their acts of piety have laid no claim on God (so Verhoef [1987: 273–74]) not an act of defiance (so Ogden and Deutsch [1987: 96]). The prophet had already provided one answer in explanation of Yahweh's rejection of the worship offered by the people of Yehud, that of intermarriage with non-Hebrews (vv 10–12).

'al kî-YHWH hē'îd. In combination with the preposition 'al ("upon"), the coordinating particle kî means "because" (similar to the more frequent 'al 'ăšer, BDB: 758). The construction is that of a clausal adverb introducing a causal clause (WO'C § 38.4, 39.3.1). Malachi now begins his diatribe against divorce in Yehud, enunciating a second reason for Yahweh's repudiation of sacrificial worship.

The Hiphil suffixing conjugation hē'îd can mean "warn, admonish" (Gen 43:3), "assure" (Deut 8:19), or "call/serve as a witness" (Job 29:11; Isa 8:2; cf. CHAL: 266–67). The covenant context of Malachi's third disputation demands the translation "serve as a witness" (after the manner of 'wd in Deut 4:26; 30:19; 31:28; 32:46). The verb 'wd occurs in the Haggai-Zechariah-Malachi corpus only in Zech 3:6 ("charged," Meyers and Meyers [1987: 194]) and Mal 2:14. The verb is usually translated as a *persistent perfective* (i.e., a situation that started in the past but continues into the present, WO'C § 30.5.1c; e.g., NJB, "stands as a witness . . .").

Given the covenantal language of Mal 2:10–16 (e.g., *běrît* [v 10], *bāgĕdâ* [v 11], *tôʿĕbâ* [v 11], etc.), the term has solemn legal connotations (Achtemeier [1986: 182]). The emphatic placement of the covenant name YHWH adds to the judicial tone of clause (cf. Verhoef [1987: 274], "God's being a witness also implies that he eventually would be witness for the crown and prosecutor!"). The use of the verbal root *ʿwd* in verse 14 may strengthen the argument for emending the MT *ʿēr* ("watcher") to *ʿēd* ("witness") in verse 12.

bênĕkā ûbên ʾēšet nĕʿûrekā. The preposition *bên* expresses an *exclusive* sense when used in paired phrases (*bên* X *ûbên* Y, cf. WO'C § 11.2.6c). Ogden and Deutsch (p. 96) are probably correct in noting that the shift in style to the singular (i.e., the second-person masculine pronominal suffix *-kā*) makes "this particular charge more personal and direct." The combination of *hēʿîd* + *bên . . . ûbên* is found elsewhere in the MT only in the covenant sealed between Laban and Jacob (Gen 31:44, with the terms in reverse order). More striking is the parallel between Malachi's language (*bên . . . ûbên* + *ʾiššâ*) and that of the curse pronounced upon the serpent in Gen 3:15 (. . . *bênĕkā ûbên hāʾiššâ . . .*).

The construct-genitive phrase *ʾēšet nĕʿûrekā* ("wife of your youth") occurs only 4 times in the OT/HB (Prov 5:18; Isa 54:6; Mal 2:14, 15). The noun *ʾiššâ* means "wife" here, understood as a merism with *ʾîš*, "husband" (*TDOT* 1:225). The plural noun *nĕʿûrîm* means "youth, early life" (BDB: 655). According to J. L. McKenzie (1968: 139), the phrase "wife of your youth" signifies "the first of the wives, the one who had the privileged position, and whom one married when one was still possessed of the passions of the young." The broken marriage leaves the woman in a state of forsakenness, loneliness, and shame (Westermann [1969: 273]) and is similar to the cruel separation of the widow bereft of the "husband of her youth" (Joel 1:8; cf. Wolff [1977: 31]). Baldwin (1972a: 240–41), Craigie (1985: 236–37), and Achtemeier (1986: 182–83) all comment on the high view of marriage espoused (at least implicitly) in Malachi's disputation treating divorce in Yehud: a partnership of mutual companionship, faithfulness, and loyalty.

ʾăšer ʾattâ bāgadtâ bāh. The relative pronoun *ʾăšer* introduces a dependent relative clause with resumption in the accusative function ("with whom . . . "; cf. WO'C § 19.3.b). The relative clause is omitted in 4QXIIa, see Fuller 1991: 52.

The Qal suffix conjugation *bāgadtâ* is a second-person masculine singular form (an *indefinite perfective*, WO'C § 30.5.1b), continuing the more personal and direct speech of the prophet. The emphatic independent pronoun *ʾattâ* ("you *yourself* have broken faith"; but cf. Petersen [1995: 194], "you have acted faithlessly") involves *psychological focus*, strengthening the force of the indictment (cf. WO'C § 16.3.2e).

This third occurrence of the verb *bgd* in the dispute connects the paragraph addressing intermarriage (vv 10–12) with the divorce section (vv 13–16) and indicates that the prophet treats both intermarriage with non-Hebrews and divorce as equally serious covenant violations. The real issue is faithless behavior in Yehud, of which intermarriage and divorce are merely symptoms. Verhoef (1987: 275) is correct to connect the two practices; that is, the desertion and divorce of the Israelite wife as a result of a later marriage to a non-Hebrew. It is likely that economics motivated this reprehensible conduct, because intermarriage was probably a requisite for entering the well-established mercantile guilds of postexilic Palestine (see ABD 4:564; cf. Myers [1968: 98] who suggests that Hebrews were marrying Samaritan women in order to reclaim land lost during the Exile). The implications of Mal 2:14 for the issue of polygamy versus monogamy are unclear (cf. ABD 4:565–67).

The verb *bgd* often marks the accusative with the preposition *bêt* ("deal treacherously" or "break faith *with*"), a circumstance of specification (KBL 1:108; cf. WO'C § 11.2.5d). The feminine singular suffixed pronoun (*bāh*, "with her") is resumptive, stressing the plight of the "wife of your youth" (*'ēšet nĕ'ûrekā*). See further the discussion of *nibgad* in the NOTES for verse 10 above.

wĕhî' ḥăbertĕkā wĕ'ēšet bĕrîtekā. The independent pronoun *hî'* ("she") is the subject of the dependent verbless clause (cf. WO'C § 16.3.3 on the *identifying* verbless clause). The pronoun *hî'* ("she") stands as a foil to *'attâ* ("you"), emphasizing the two central characters of the debate. The coordinating *waw* is epexegetical, specifying the sense of the preceding clause (i.e., identifying the pronoun "her," WO'C § 39.2.4). The sequence of suffixed pronouns and independent pronouns in the final three clauses of verse 14 both accents the reciprocal nature of the marriage relationship and solemnizes the sanctity of such unions:

"between *you* . . ."
"wife of *your* youth . . ."
"*you yourself* have dealt treacherously . . ."
"with *her* . . ."
"though *she* . . ."
"*your* marriage partner . . ."
"wife of *your* covenant . . ."

The feminine noun *ḥăberet* ("marriage companion," KBL 1:289) is unique to Mal 2:14 in the MT (LXX = *koinōnós*, "joint-partner, sharer"; cf. Petersen [1995: 194], "spouse"). The word is related to the verbal root *ḥbr* (I) (Qal, "to ally oneself"; KBL 1:287–88). In the Piel stem the verb is used in architectural contexts to signify a "seam" or "joint" in building and construction (e.g., Exod 26:6, 9, 11; cf. TDOT 4:195–96). The connotation of the word seems to be one of "permanent bonding" (cf. Paul's use of *kolláomai* [literally "to glue, cement"] in his commentary on the biblical concept of "one flesh," 1 Cor 6:16–17). Garland (p. 420) argues that the expression suggests that the wife is not property to be discarded at will but an "equal . . . as a covenant partner," because the word "is normally used of men to designate their equality with one another" (on this idea of "partner," see further the postexilic portrait of the idealized wife in Prov 31:10–31; cf. Sellin and Fohrer [1968: 322–23]). The English versions read alternately "partner" (so JPSV, NEB, NIV, NJB) or "companion" (so NIV, NRSV).

The phrasal *waw* is conjunctive, linking "marriage partner" (*ḥăberet*) and "the wife of your covenant" (*'ēšet bĕrîtekā*) in a sort of hendiadys construction explaining the construct-genitive "the wife of your youth" (*'ēšet nĕ'ûrekā*, cf. WO'C § 39.2.1b). Like the word *ḥāberet*, the phrase *'ēšet bĕrîtekā* is unique to Mal 2:14 in the MT. No doubt these singular expressions were intended to heighten the sense of importance attached to the issues of intermarriage and divorce in Yehud. The phrases "wife of your youth" and "wife of your covenant" are complementary, depicting a spousal loyalty based on the idealism of youthful passion and the reality of societal and legal mores (Verhoef [1987: 274]; cf. Petersen [1995: 194], "your covenantal wife"). In fact, Glazier-McDonald (1987a: 101) has noted that the threefold description of the wife as "wife of your youth," "marriage partner," and "wife of your covenant" further "serves to emphasize the closeness, the intimateness of the relationship between the marriage partners and to make the treacherous behavior of the spouse even more odious."

Biblical commentators are divided on the question of identifying the "covenant" (*bĕrît*) to which the prophet makes reference. Among others, Eiselen (1907: 724), Torrey (1905: 9), Isaaksson (1965: 31), and Glazier-McDonald (1987a: 101) equate the "covenant" of verse 14 with the "covenant of the fathers," verse 10. This covenant is associated with the Mosaic covenant of the Sinai tradition, and the issue for interpreters is the marriage contract preserving endogamy or marriage within one's clan (see Deut 7:3; cf. S. R. Driver [1906: 315], and see the discussion in *ABD* 4:563–65). By contrast, scholars such as Calvin (1979: 554), Keil (1:452), Baldwin (1972a: 39), Mason (1977: 150), and especially Hugenberger construe the Hebrew marriage contract as a solemn covenant to which Yahweh is witness (cf. Gen 31:50; Prov 2:17). Here the issue for the exegete is the relationship of law and covenant in Hebrew social and religious practice (*TDOT* 2:264–66; cf. Garland [pp. 419–22]).

Arguments addressing the status of marriage in postexilic Yehud, whether legal contract or sacral covenant, are inconclusive (as demonstrated by Glazier-McDonald [1987a: 101–3]; cf. *ABD* 2:217–19). The deliberate ambiguity of the language in Malachi permits enough latitude for the accommodation of both views, making rigid distinctions between Hebrew marriage as "covenant" or "contract" unnecessary — even undesirable (cf. the English versions: "your covenanted spouse," JPSV; "your betrothed wife," NAB; "your wife by solemn covenant," NEB; "wife of your marriage covenant," NIV). Even as Yahweh serves as a witness to both the pledge of marriage and the betrayal of divorce, so under his sovereign purview the institution of marriage retains both legal and sacred dimensions for Israelite society. More important to the message of Malachi are the implications of faithless behavior in the social sphere for the religious life of the restoration community in ancient Yehud. See further Hugenberger's extensive treatment of the topic (he forcefully concludes marriage is a "covenant" in the OT/HB and that sexual union consummating the marriage ritual constitutes a "covenant ratifying act" (pp. 278–79, 342–43).

15. *wĕlō'-'eḥād 'āśâ*. Biblical commentators are quick to repeat the sentiments of J.M.P. Smith (p. 54, "this verse . . . is hopelessly obscure"), Welch (1935: 120, ". . . the verses [2:10–16] cannot form the basis of any sure conclusion"), and Baldwin (1972a: 240, "it is impossible to make sense of the Hebrew

as it stands . . . each translation, including the early versions, contains an element of interpretation") in their analysis of verse 15. Almost any translation is defensible, although Baldwin's interjection that any interpretation of verse 15 must be in agreement with the context of the pericope (i.e., the admonition for husbands to remain faithful to their wives) is still appropriate. This analysis assumes that verses 15–16 are original to the prophet's message (cf. Redditt [1995: 173–74]), not the work of some "unknown epigone" applying the exposé of Asherah worship (vv 13–15a) to the "individual Yahwist" in verses 15–16 (Petersen [1995: 205–6]).

The coordinating *waw* + the negative adverb *lōʾ* are usually regarded an interrogative construction (e.g., JPSV, NAB, NEB, NIV, NJB, NRSV). J.M.P. Smith (p. 54), however, challenges this rendering of *wĕlōʾ-ʾeḥād* *ʿāśâ* ("*and* [*is it*] *not* one he made?"). The *item*-type negation (here *ʾeḥād*) is rare in BH (cf. WO'C § 39.3.2a on clausal vs. item negative adverbs) and represents an emphatic construction (cf. GKC § 152e). Given this unusual grammatical structure and the disputational format of Malachi's oracles, it may be helpful to understand *wĕlōʾ* rhetorically (akin to *hălôʾ*, "surely, one, he made").

The cardinal numeral *ʾeḥād* ("one") is grammatically ambiguous, standing either as subject of the verb *ʿāśâ* (so JPSV, NEB, NRSV) or the object (so NAB, NIV, NJB; cf. WO'C § 11.4.3 on grammatical ambiguity and 15.2.1 on the cardinal numerals). As subject of the clause, "one" may refer to God (echoing the divine epithets of verse 10, so R. L. Smith [1984: 321]), or to the party initiating divorce in Yehud (so Glazier-McDonald [1987a: 106]). As object of the verb *ʿāśâ* ("he [i.e., God] made *one*"), it is unlikely that the numeral "one" refers to the "wife" (*ʾēšet*, v 14) since *ʾeḥād* is masculine (cf. NEB, NRSV). It is possible that the word refers to the bonding of male and female as "one flesh" in the covenant of marriage (JPSV) or to the idea of the organic unity of humanity created male and female in the image of God (NAB, NIV, NJB; cf. Packard [1902: 32], "But did he not make one [pair]").

The repetition of the words "one" (*ʾeḥād*) and "faithlessness" (*bgd*) was probably intended to elicit multiple images associated with Israel's covenant history. By way of creed, Israel professed Yahweh as "One" (Deut 6:4). By way of cosmology, Israel affirmed the organic unity of humanity created male and female (Gen 1:27; 2:23). By way of theological anthropology, Israel inherited a tradition of marriage bonding male and female as "one flesh" (Gen 2:24). By way of historical precedent, the annals of Israel attest the unswerving loyalty and faithfulness of Yahweh to his elect people (Deut 32:4; cf. Ps 78:57). Whatever the exact meaning of verse 15, the treachery and faithlessness of divorce as practiced in postexilic Yehud stand diametrically opposite the legacy of covenantal "oneness" and "faithfulness" Israel received from Yahweh (cf. Jer 32:39; Ezek 37:17). The people are not "one" with each other; how can they then hope to be "one" with Yahweh and inherit the blessings of covenant relationship incorporated into his charter with them (cf. R. L. Smith [1984: 321])?

Admittedly, the masculine noun *ʾeḥād* may serve double-duty as both subject and object. Such a construction would be in keeping with the orality of the prophetic ministry and the elliptical nature of the disputational format of Malachi's oracles. Such a construction certainly heightens the contrast between Yahweh's faithfulness and Yehud's faithlessness and the loyalty of marriage and the betrayal of divorce. Most Jewish commentators recognize the word "one" as a reference to Abraham and his relationship to Hagar (cf. Cashdan [1948: 347]; cf. Keil [2:453]; S. R. Driver [1906: 316]; D. R. Jones [1962: 193–94]; Baldwin [1972a: 237]; Garland [1987: 429 n. 9]).

The English versions agree in identifying the Qal suffixing conjugation *'āśâ* as the verb of the initial clause (*wĕlō'-'eḥād* *'āśâ*). The translation of the MT *'āśâ* ("make" vs. "do," see CHAL: 284–85) is contingent upon whether the interpreter reads *'eḥād* ("one") as the divine subject of the clause ("Did not the one God *make* her," NEB and NRSV; or ". . . *make* all," JPSV; or ". . . *make* one being," NAB; or ". . . *create* a single being," NJB) or a human subject of the clause (e.g., "and not one *does* it [i.e., divorces his wife]," Glazier-McDonald [1987a: 82]; Redditt [1995: 173]; or ". . . *did so*," Keil [2:451]; or "No one . . . would *act* that way," Verhoef [1987: 162]). In keeping with Baldwin's (1972a: 240) guideline for interpreting verse 15 contextually, it seems best to acknowledge that *'āśâ* describes the work of God or Yahweh (v 14, if this divine name is the antecedent of the verb), whether this "work" is the creation of "woman" (so NRSV; Redditt [1995: 173]), "everything" or "all humanity" (so JPSV; cf. Petersen [1995: 194], "Has not [the] One made [us]?"), or even the creation of man and woman as a single being — ideally and functionally "one" as ordained in the marriage relationship (NAB; NIV, NJB).

ûšě'ār rûaḥ lô. The *waw* is probably best understood in an epexegetical sense, clarifying the preceding clause ("*even* a residue of spirit belongs to him," cf. WO'C § 39.2.4). The construct-genitive phrase *šě'ār rûaḥ* ("remainder/remnant of spirit") is unique in the MT and is usually emended to *šě'ēr* ("flesh, body, self," CHAL: 357) making the word pair "body"/"spirit" (e.g., Chary [1969: 260–61]; Baldwin [1972a: 204]; Rudolph [1976: 270]; so NAB, NEB, NIV, NJB, NRSV). Like Calvin (1979: 556), Petersen (1995: 194) understands *šě'ār* literally as "remnant" (although later Calvin [p. 664] opted for the rabbinic interpretation, "exuberance of spirit").

The word *rûaḥ* in this context refers to the "life force" or "life principle" animating all living things (BDB: 925; cf. Glazier-McDonald [1987a: 107] and Redditt [1995: 173] who associate the phrase with "sexual capacity"). The preposition *lamed* is quasi-locational, functioning as an indirect object marker and indicating possession ("*belonging* to him," WO'C § 11.2.10d). The ancient versions (LXX, V, Syr) and most earlier commentators (e.g., Henderson [1980: 454]; Keil [2:451]; Eiselen [1907: 724]) render the phrase quite literally (cf. Petersen [1995: 194], "his *vigorous* remnant").

Assuming the idea of "oneness" bridges verses 14 and 15, the prophet apparently makes an analogy between the "bonding" of husband and wife in marriage and the "bonding" of God with his creation (commentators connecting Mal 2:15 with the creation of humankind in Genesis 1 and 2 include Glazier-McDonald [1987a: 107]; Ogden and Deutsch [1987: 96]). God is so intimately knitted to the created order that he possesses even the residue of life principle in his creation (especially human creatures). The cryptic line ("Surely One has made [all things], even a residue of spirit belongs to him") may be a (partial) quotation from a contemporary proverb, song, or even funeral dirge. It is possible that the saying reflects postexilic attitudes (or theological teaching) regarding the female as the "residue" of the spirit of the male, from the creation account in which woman was made from man (Gen 2:20–24). Clearly verse 14 gives prominence to the "wife" in the marriage relationship. Perhaps the prophet seeks to elevate the status of the woman in Israelite society by appealing to a tradition that gives equal standing to male and female as creatures of God (cf. Ogden and Deutsch [1987: 96] on "easy" divorce in the ANE and Malachi's "new and much stricter approach").

ûmâ hā'eḥād mĕbaqqēš. The coordinating waw is almost universally understood as a conjunctive ("and") joining two clauses describing an interrelated situation (i.e., Yahweh's faithfulness to his creation and his search for faithfulness of like kind among his people, cf. WO'C § 39.2.5a). The interrogative mâ represents an accusative of specification (as in 3:14, ûmah-beṣaʿ ["what profit . . ."]; WO'C § 18.3b and n. 16). The inanimate interrogative pronoun mâ ("what thing . . .") directs attention to the outcome of covenant faith, godliness, and faithfulness in personal ethics or behavior.

The cardinal numeral "one" (ʾeḥād) is definite, thereby determining or specifying an aforementioned substantive (cf. GKC § 126d). The immediate antecedent "one" (wĕlōʾ-ʾeḥād . . .), is ambiguous (either subject or object of ʿāśâ). Biblical commentators are divided as to whether the prophet uses the word "one" as divine subject ("One" = God [or better "Yahweh" gapped from v 14]; so LXX [reading állos for MT ʾeḥād], JPSV, NEB, NIV, NRSV; S. R. Driver [1906: 316]; Rudolph [1976: 270]; R. L. Smith [1984: 319]) or as human subject ("one" = a man created by God, so Syr, NAB, NJB, Cashdan [p. 347], Verhoef [1987: 262], Glazier-McDonald [1987a: 106]).

The analysis of S. R. Driver (1906: 316) is most compelling here, recognizing "The One" as divine subject of the participle. Thus the numeral connects verse 15 with the divine titles "One Father" (ʾāb ʾeḥād) and "One God" (ʾēl ʾeḥād) in verse 10; cf. Petersen [1995: 203] on this "transition" from the fatherhood of God to divine offspring. This repetition or echo of ʾeḥād also serves to link the section 2:10–12 with 2:13–15 in the third dispute. Finally, S. R. Driver (1906: 316 n. 4) suggests that such a translation ("And what does the One seek? A seed of God.") provides a solid rationale for Malachi's stance against divorce: "we are all members of God's family, and should treat one another accordingly." Further, the prophet's allusions to the creation of male and female (Gen 1:27) and the divine prescription for human marriage as "one flesh" (lĕbāśār ʾeḥād, Gen 2:24) intimate that the "godly offspring" Yahweh seeks are those who faithfully maintain this divine ideal for marriage.

The Piel participle (mĕbaqqēš) functions as the predicate of the clause and emphasizes a durative circumstance ("and what does the One continually seek," WO'C § 37.6b). The verb bqš ("seek [to find], search for," BDB: 134–35) occurs in disputes two, three, and four in a sequence that calls attention to the reciprocal nature of covenant relationship with Yahweh (2:7, the people should "seek" instruction from the priests; 2:15, God "seeks" a godly offspring; and 3:1, the people "seek" the epiphany of Yahweh). Whereas Zechariah envisioned the nations "seeking Yahweh of Hosts in Jerusalem" (8:21; cf. Meyers and Meyers [1987: 438–39] on the progression of "seeking Yahweh" in postexilic Yehud), Malachi depicts a turnabout with Yahweh seeking out righteous Israelites in Jerusalem! *zera' 'ĕlōhîm*. The prophet answers his own question. The "One," Yahweh, seeks godly "offspring" (so NAB, NIV, NRSV) or "children" (so NEB; cf. JPSV, "godly folk"; Petersen [1995: 194], "godly progeny"). The masculine noun *zera'* ("seed," a *conventional collective* according to WO'C § 7.2.1c) is used figuratively to signify "descendants, offspring, children" (KBL 1:282–83). The construct-genitive (*zera' 'ĕlōhîm*, "the seed of God") is peculiar to Mal 2:15 in the MT and is usually understood in the sense of an attributive adjective modifying *zera'* ("*godly* descendants, so JPSV, NAB, NEB, NIV, NRSV; cf. WO'C § 14.3.1; Petersen [1995: 195 n. h]). Malachi is alone among the Twelve in this figurative use of the word "seed" (*zera'*; see the NOTES for 2:3 above as well). The LXX perceives the divine name *'ĕlōhîm* as the subject of the participle *mĕbaqqēš* ("And what does God seek?").

The divine name *'ĕlōhîm* can also be used in the superlative sense that the thing or person originated with God or belonged to him (WO'C § 14.5b; cf. von Bulmerincq [1932: 300]; Cashdan [1948: 347], "a seed given of God"; and NJB, "God-given offspring"). This reading offers much to commend it. Indeed, such an understanding permits one to recognize that God is ultimately the source of human procreativity (Glazier-McDonald [1987a: 108]; cf. S. R. Driver [1906: 316], "seed of God" = children as the gift of God). Cashdan (p. 347) presses this emphasis and concludes that those in Yehud who intermarried with non-Hebrews were stricken with barrenness, deprived of "the very expression of their union — children" (Glazier-McDonald [1987a: 109]; cf. Syr, ". . . a man seeks one offspring from God").

This approach, however, is misguided in that it fails to interpret the phrase "the seed of God" (*zera' 'ĕlōhîm*) in conjunction with the theme of the third disputation (Yehud's *faithlessness*) and the message of the entire book (the antithesis of Yahweh's *faithfulness* and Israel's *faithlessness*). Similarly, Ogden and Deutsch (pp. 96–97) err in supposing that Malachi, like Ezra (cf. *zera' haqqōdeš* in Ezra 9:2), is primarily concerned with Hebrew ethnic purity (it seems more likely Ezra 9:2 has adapted the phrase *zera' 'ĕlōhîm* from Mal 2:15 for polemical purposes related to "Jewishness" in the later postexilic period). The core issue is not human procreation, nor is it ethnic purity. Rather, the prophet's thrust is the treachery and betrayal manifest in the practice of intermarriage and divorce in Yehud and the theological ramifications that such behavior has for Israel's covenant relationship with Yahweh (here Ogden and Deutsch [1987: 97] move closer to a correct assessment of Malachi's instruction).

For this reason, the superlative expression "the seed of God" is better understood as "what is free from all vice and blemish . . . for what is excellent is often called God in Hebrew" (Calvin [1979: 558] [putting aside his invective against polygamy]; cf. Rudolph [1976: 270], "descendants *according to the will* of God"). Yahweh seeks "the seed of God," descendants of Abraham, Isaac, and Jacob who love him, obey him, and hold fast to him (Deut 30:19–20) and those who love justice, hate wrongdoing, and act faithfully (Isa 61:8–9). If the idea of the superlative sense of the divine name "God" (*'ĕlōhîm*) is that which belongs to God (WO'C § 14.5b), then Israel will be "the seed of God" only when they imitate his holiness through covenant obedience (Baldwin [1972a: 241] aptly notes that the family was "to be the school in which God's way of life was practiced and learned"). It is no coincidence that the next disputation (2:17–3:5) targets the people of Yehud for Yahweh's purifying judgment, yielding righteous worship (3:4) and abolishing social injustice (3:5). The more literal translation, "the seed of God" (the phrase is definite by virtue of the fact that the divine name *'ĕlōhîm* is an intrinsically definite noun, WO'C § 13.4b) is preferable here because it is in keeping with the cryptic and ambiguous structure and language of the entire verse (cf. Calvin [1979: 558]; Glazier-McDonald [1987a: 82]).

wĕnišmartem bĕrûḥăkem. The conjunctive-sequential *waw* represents the entreaty form (WO'C § 32.2.3d; "so . . . ," JPSV, NIV, NRSV [V = *ergo*]), indicating that self-assessment is the logical response to question what Yahweh seeks in Yehud (cf. WO'C § 39.2.2). J.M.P. Smith (p. 55) quips, "This is an admonition growing out of verse 15a, whatever that passage may mean."

The Niphal suffixing conjugation *nišmartem* is reflexive (i.e., "to guard oneself," WO'C § 23.4b). The reversion to the masculine plural verb form shifts the prophet's focus back to the audience at large (note the plethora of singular pronouns sandwiched between *wa'ămartem* [v 14] and *nišmartem* [v 15]). According to Waltke and O'Connor (§ 23.4b), the Niphal reflexive in the plural tends to be distributive (i.e., "and you [*each one*] take care to yourselves" [i.e., *to each other*]). The construction is also *benefactive*, in that the subject acts in its own interest (WO'C § 23.4d, perhaps connoting a certain volitional force as well [?]; cf. WO'C 32.2.1d). See further the NOTES on the verb *šmr* in 2:7, 9 above and 2:16; 3:7, 14 below.

The construction *bĕrûḥăkem* is unique to Mal 2:15, 16 in the MT. The preposition *bêt* is spatial ("in" [the domain] of your spirit," R. L. Smith [1984: 319]; NIV; cf. WO'C § 11.2.5b). The feminine noun *rûaḥ* ("spirit") should be understood in the sense of "mind, disposition, temperament, moral character" as in Eccl 7:9; Isa 59:21; and Hag 1:14 (cf. BDB: 925; CHAL: 334). The word "spirit" ("life," JPSV, NAB, NJB) should be retained in the translation (e.g., ". . . take heed to your spirit," J.M.P. Smith [1912: 55] [= Glazier-McDonald 1987a: 82]; "preserve your vitality," Petersen [1995: 194]; NEB, "Keep watch on your spirit"); there is probably wordplay of some sort intended with *rûaḥ* ("spirit") in verse 15a (contra Verhoef [1987: 263], "so take heed to yourselves"; NRSV, "So look to yourselves"). The array of renderings in the English versions attest to the difficulty in translating the phrase given the obscure context of verse 15 (JPSV, "So be careful of your life-breath"; NAB, "you must then safeguard life that is your own"; NJB, "Have respect for your own life then").

ûbĕ'ēšet nĕ'ûrekā 'al-yibgod. The conjunctive *waw* joins related clauses and continues the force of the preceding entreaty form (*wĕnišmartem*; cf. WO'C § 39.2.5). The vetitive (negative *'al* + prefixing conjugation) is an urgent (but less emphatic than the *lô'* + prefixing conjugation) prohibition, insisting that activity already in progress be stopped (R. L. Smith [1984: 320], and see the discussion of the vetitive in WO'C § 34 n. 6; GKC § 107o, 152f distinguishes the vetitive ["a simple warning"] from the prohibition ["a more emphatic form"]).

The repetition of the phrase "wife of your youth" (*[bĕ]'ēšet nĕ'ûrekā*) at the beginning of verse 14 and the end of verse 15 encases a literary subunit in the third disputation. See the NOTES for verse 14 above.

The negative particle *'al* + the second-person jussive constitute the negative imperative (WO'C 34.2.1b, 34.4a; on the negative imperative in the Haggai-Zechariah-Malachi corpus, see further Meyers and Meyers [1987: 52, etc.]). Emending the MT *yibgōd* to *tibgōd* (so LXX, θ, V) may be justifiable given the confrontational nature of the disputation and the preceding second-person verb form *wĕnišmartem* (so NEB, NIV, NJB).

Alternately, the MT *yibgōd* is intelligible and is deemed superior by many interpreters (e.g., Packard [1902: 17], Keil [2:453–54], Verhoef [1987: 263], Glazier-McDonald [1987a: 109]), because the shift in person is acceptable when there is no change in subject (cf. Isa 1:29), and the indefinite warning ("let *him* not break faith") anticipates the declaration of verse 16 (so JPSV, NRSV; cf. Petersen [1995: 194], "let no one act faithlessly"). The summons to "cease and desist" seems the more forceful option since the prophet apparently combats an entrenched practice — not the potentiality of a hypothetical situation. On the verb *bgd*, see verses 10, 11, and 14 above.

16. *kî-śānē' šallaḥ*. Certain of the ancient versions render the clausal *kî* conditionally ("if"; cf. WO'C § 38.2d) in an attempt to soften the harshness of Malachi's prohibitive command and bring the prophet's teaching more in line with the legal prescriptions for divorce in Deut 24:1–4 (LXX, Syr, T [according to Kruse-Blinkenberg (1966: 104), these ancient versions were "corrected in order to avoid inconsistency with Deuteronomy"]; so NEB; Luther (Oswald [1975: 406–7]; Chary [1969: 260–61], Schreiner [1979: 217]; Deissler [1988: 329]; C. J. Collins [1994: 40]). The English versions largely agree, understanding *kî* as a causal coordinator introducing a purpose clause ("for, because," JPSV, NAB, NJB, NRSV; cf. R. L. Smith [1984: 319]; Rudolph [1976: 261]; Glazier-McDonald [1987a: 82]). Given volitional force of preceding admonition and in keeping with the disputational format, the clausal *kî* is better understood in an emphatic sense ("indeed, surely," WO'C § 39.3.4e; cf. Petersen [1995: 195 n. j], *kî* is asseverative).

The verb *śn'* means "hate" in the Qal stem (*CHAL*: 353). The third-person masculine singular form proves awkward if Yahweh [through his prophet] is the speaker (as the messenger formula implies). For this reason, the MT perfective *śānē'* is sometimes emended to the first-person perfective form *śānē'tî* found in 1:3 ("I hate . . . ," R. L. Smith [1984: 320]; so *BHK/BHS* and most English versions). However, 4QXIIa furnishes a variant reading with a second-person verb form (*ky 'm śnth šlḥ*, "but if you hate [her], send [her] away"; cf. Fuller [1991: 54–56]). Rudolph (1976: 270) identifies *śānē'* as a verbal adjective used participially, with the subject Yahweh inferred from context ("because I hate . . ."). He further theorizes that the independent pronoun *'ănî* ("I") fell out of the text due to haplography given the similarity of the words אני and צנא.

Glazier-McDonald (1987a: 110–11), following van Hoonacker (1908: 728), repoints the MT *śānē'* as a Qal participle (*śōnē'*) and then construes the infinitive *śallaḥ* as a Piel perfective (*śillēaḥ*). Earlier, Ewald (5:81–82) repointed *śānē'* as a Qal participle *śōnē'* and the Piel infinitive construct *śallaḥ* as a Piel infinitive absolute *śallēaḥ* (cf. Petersen [1995: 194–95 n. j], "Divorce is hateful" [understanding the infinitive absolute *śallēaḥ* as original to the MT]). This construction represents a *casus pendens* or nominative absolute, with the participle *śōnē'* serving as the subject for the verbs *šlḥ* and *ksh* ("for one who divorces because of aversion"; cf. WO'C § 37.5a).

Recently D. C. Jones (1990: 683) has offered support for Glazier-McDonald's analysis by attempting to clarify the meaning of the LXX translation of Mal 2:16. He claims that *'allà eàn misēsas exaposteilēs* has been misconstrued as a subjunctive followed by an imperative ("If you hate, divorce!"; e.g., Kruse-Blinkenberg [1966: 103–4]). Rather, the construction is one of a participle and a subjunctive ("If hating you divorce" or "If you divorce out of hatred") with following apodosis (cf. C. J. Collins [1994: 38–40] who appeals to the argument of D. C. Jones [1990] for reading the MT *śallaḥ* as a rare *a*-class Piel perfect[ive], "if having hated you should divorce").

Nevertheless, the MT *śānē'* makes excellent sense if one presumes that the subject, *hā'eḥād* ["The One," i.e., Yahweh], of the verb has been gapped from verse 15 ("Indeed, *The One* hates divorce . . ."). This reading preserves the integrity of the MT, rendering "cosmetic surgery" of the text unnecessary (the ancient versions clearly represent "interpretive corrections" of a harsh prohibition). Further, this reading reveals still another example of the prophet's literary artistry in the juxtaposition of "The One" (Yahweh) and "sending away" (i.e., the dissolution of "one" through divorce).

The verb *śn'* describes Yahweh's hostility in response to a broken covenant relationship in 1:3 (i.e., Esau's rejection of Yahweh's covenant tokens; cf. Andersen and Freedman [1980: 545] on Hos 9:15). Likewise this text is tinged with the same hue of emotion and hostility as Yahweh reacts to the dissolution of the marriage covenant in Yehud. The *persistent (present) perfective* translation, "hates," represents a situation that started in the past but continues to the present time (WO'C § 30.5.1bc). The NIV gaps the verb *śn'*, fashioning a type of synonymous parallelism between the two clauses ("I hate divorce . . . and I hate a man's covering himself . . ."; cf. Henderson [1980: 455]). See the discussion of *śānē'tî* in the NOTES for 1:3 above.

The Piel infinitive *śallaḥ* means "to send, stretch out" or even "send away," connoting expulsion or divorce in marital contexts (BDB: 1018–19; cf. Deut 22:19, 29; 24:1, 3, 4; Isa 50:1). The infinitive construct functions nominally in the accusative frame (cf. WO'C § 36.2.1d). The assumption here is that Malachi addresses injustices deriving from legal divorce in Yehud (i.e., formalized with the "proper" documents of divorce) not expulsion of a spouse (cf. Mayes [1979: 322–23]). The prophet's codicil on divorce seems to allude to both the ideal of heterosexual monogamous marriage ordained in Genesis 1 and 2 (so Rudolph [1981]) and the divorce statutes of the Mosaic Law (Deut 24:1–4, so Schreiner). The occurrence of the verbs *śn'* and *šlḥ* in Deut 24:3 gives rise to the interpretation that "hating" or "aversion" was the motivation for divorce (cf. LXX, b. Giṭṭ 90b; so Glazier-McDonald [1987a: 82]). Craigie (2:237) admits that Malachi is not a legislator, but a prophet expressing Yahweh's displeasure over the social cancer of divorce routinely practiced in Yehud. There is, however, a sense in which the prophet brings a new and more rigorous understanding to the postexilic Hebrew community, in an attempt to correct abuses resulting from liberties taken in the application of the Mosaic divorce laws (Deut 24:1–4; cf. Ogden and Deutsch [1987: 98]). See further the discussion of the verb *šlḥ* in the NOTES for 2:2, 4 above and 3:1, 23 [4:5] below.

'*āmar YHWH* '*ĕlōhê yiśrā'ēl.* The messenger formula ('*āmar YHWH*) + the divine epithet "the God of Israel" ('*ĕlōhê yiśrā'ēl*) occur in combination in the Twelve only in Zeph 2:9 and Mal 2:16. The construction is profuse in Jeremiah (occurring 46x), suggesting that Malachi has intentionally connected his disputation with the (oath-like) tone and (forboding) messages of Josiah's prophet (cf. Jer 7:21–26; 9:15–16; etc.). According to Roberts (p. 200), the title ("God of Israel") stems from the "Zion theology" asserting God's hegemony over all Israel; it depicts Yahweh's election of Israel and his unique covenant relationship with the Hebrew nation (cf. *TDOT* 1:277–78). J.M.P. Smith (1912: 55–56), among others, omits the phrase as a gloss (because it separates the protasis from the apodosis, constitutes the sole occurrence of the title in Malachi, and is superfluous in view of the following messenger formula). On the messenger formula, see further the NOTES for 1:2 above.

wĕkissâ ḥāmās 'al-lĕbûšô. The coordinating *waw* may be understood as a simple conjunctive joining parallel clauses ("and," so NAB, NIV, NRSV; cf. WO'C § 39.2.5) or consequentially as the apodosis of a conditional clause ("*then*," implied in the NEB; cf. Glazier-McDonald [1987a: 110–13]; see WO'C 39.2.2) or even as a causal *waw* assigning the reason for a declaration ("for," so Calvin [1979: 665], Eiselen [1907: 726]; cf. GKC § 158a). Given the legislative tone of verse 16, it seems best to regard the *waw* epexegetically as a clarification of the preceding declaration about divorce ("for," cf. WO'C § 39.2.4).

The verb *ksh* occurs only in Mal 2:13 and 2:16 in the Haggai-Zechariah-Malachi corpus and in the Piel stem means "to cover, conceal" (*CHAL*: 161; cf. *TDOT* 7:259–64). The form is awkward and has prompted numerous emendations of the MT Piel suffixing conjugation *kissâ*, most notably reading the Piel infinitive absolute *wĕkasseh* as the compound object of *śānē'* ("and *the* covering" [that is, God hates both acts: divorcing and covering up the injustice], e.g., Nowack [p. 423] and Marti [p. 472], following Wellhausen [p. 208], so also *BHS*). Petersen (1995: 195 n. 1) follows Sellin's (p. 601) reconstruction, *kĕkasseh* ("like a garment that covers"). The ancient versions only confuse the issue (e.g., Syr = *lō' yĕkasseh*, "let him not conceal"; cf. 4QXIIa, *yksw*; T = "*you*" [masculine singular] shall not cover . . ."; the LXX translates the MT *wĕkissâ* with the future indicative *kaì kalýpsei asébeia*, "*then* ungodliness will cover . . .").

The MT *kissâ* is intelligible (and defensible, especially given the third-person masculine singular pronominal suffix attached to *lĕbûš*, cf. Verhoef [1987: 279]): "for violence covers his garment" (see Glazier-McDonald [1987a: 110–13]; cf. Packard [p. 17]; Verhoef [1987: 279–80] on *wĕkissâ* . . . as a clause of emphatic apposition indicating the degree to which God hates divorce [note here JPSV, "and covering oneself with lawlessness as with a garment"]). See further the discussion of *kassôt* in the NOTES for verse 13 above.

The masculine noun *ḥāmās* occurs only here in the Haggai-Zechariah-Malachi corpus but surfaces more than two dozen times in other prophetic writings (especially Ezek [7:11, 23; 8:17; 12:19; 28:16; 45:9] and Hab [1:2, 3, 9; 2:8, 17]). The word means "violence, wrong" (KBL 1:329; cf. JPSV, "lawlessness"; NAB, "injustice") and implies "brutality" of some sort — whether words or deeds (Holladay [1986: 208]; cf. Petersen [1995: 194] who prefers "wrongdoing" because the English word "violence" inappropriately suggests physical abuse). The syntactical position of *ḥāmās* is ambiguous, understood either as the indirect object of *ksh* (so T, Syr, and English versions) or better as the subject of the verb (*ksh*), which accords with the confrontational tone of the prophet's disputational style (so LXX and V).

The context of Malachi indicates that this "violence" or "wrongdoing" is a social crime, an "unscrupulous infringement of the personal rights of others" probably motivated by greed rather than hate in this case (*TDOT* 4:482; cf. p. 485). The "social crime" of divorce may have included the injustice of false accusation (cf. *TDOT* 4:483). No doubt such estrangement was considered "violence" because divorce both fractured the "social glue" of the divinely ordained marriage covenant and deprived the divorced woman of the dignity and protection concomitant with the spousal agreement (Craigie [1985: 237–38]; cf. Pilch and Malina [1993: 67–70] on the biblical value of "Faithfulness").

The expression "for violence covers his clothing" (*kissâ ḥāmās 'al-lĕbûšô*) is unique to Mal 2:16 in the MT (cf. Ezek 24:7, *lĕkassôt 'ālāyw 'āpār* ["to cover it with dust"]). The sequence of the verb *ksh* + preposition *'al* is an idiom for "covering over, conceal" (GKC § 119bb; cf. BDB: 492 on *'al* + the accusative of object [covering]). The meaning of the clause is disputed and the culling of interpretive stances among biblical commentators yields no consensus (as attested by the diverse translations in the English versions).

The difficulty lies in the meaning of *lĕbûšô*, "his *garment*" or "clothing" according to lexical entries for *lĕbûš* (e.g., KBL 1:516; cf. *TDOT* 7:457–68). Some have recognized "his garment" as a metaphor for "his wife" on the basis of Arabic usage (e.g., Henderson [1980: 455]; cf. NEB, ". . . his spouse, he overwhelms her with cruelty"). While it is plausible that the term is merely a colloquialism for treating a spouse unjustly (so Glazier-McDonald [1987a: 111]), the Hebrew word *lĕbûš* nowhere in the OT/HB has such a meaning (cf. Eiselen [1907: 726]; Verhoef [1987: 279]). The LXX translates *lĕbûšô* ("his garment") with *ènthymḗmatá sou* ("your thoughts" or "imaginations").

A second approach comprehends *ksh* + *lĕbûš* ("covering a garment") as a figure of speech based on the technical phraseology of spreading one's garment as symbolic action for taking a wife, according to ancient custom (cf. Deut 22:30; Ruth 3:9; and Ezek 16:8; and J.M.P. Smith [1912: 55–56]). According to Glazier-McDonald (1987a: 111–12), the covering of the garment with violence "suggests that the protection [of marriage] is taken away in view of the marital problems faced." The NJB ("and people concealing their cruelty under a cloak") offers an intriguing alternative reading here, given the emphatic position of the object ḥāmās ("violence, wrongdoing"; cf. Calvin [1979: 561]). In effect, the prophet engages in wordplay by declaring that one conceals the social crime [of divorce] "with his garment," that is, by the act of marriage symbolized in "covering with a garment" (cf. Schreiner [1979: 226–28]; *TDOT* 7:467).

The cultic interpretation of Verhoef (1987: 280) associates the "covering [*ksh*] of the garment with violence" (v 16) with the "covering [*ksh*] of the altar with tears" (v 13) and emphasizes "the aggravated circumstance of sinning [i.e., intermarriage and divorce] combined with religious activity" (i.e., the desecration of Yahweh's sanctuary with impure sacrifices — including violence committed against the votive animals!). No doubt there is a connection between the sin of divorce and the practice of sacrificial worship in Yehud, but Verhoef slights the ignoble social connotations attached to Malachi's use of "violence" (ḥāmās). The "dirty linen" proposal of Glazier-McDonald (1987a: 112), following van Hoonacker (1908: 729), rather tritely treats the "violence" of divorce as little more than the public blazoning of private "family feuds." Surely the severe language and forceful construction of verses 15–16 disclose that the prophet decried the practice of divorce in Yehud for more than the mere grist it supplied for the community gossip mill!

The most reasonable option is that of Keil (2:454) and others, who simply equate the reference to "his garment" (*lĕbûšô*) with the man initiating the divorce proceedings (cf. NIV, ". . . a man's covering himself with violence, as well as with his garment"). One's dress may serve as a figurative expression for one's person and inward character (cf. Zech 3:4; Isa 64:5). The man who, motivated by greed, divorces his Hebrew wife and marries a non-Hebrew perpetrates gross injustice, just as if his clothing were stained with the blood of a murder victim (cf. Baldwin [1972a: 241]; Rudolph [1976: 275], "flecked with blood traces"). According to Laetsch (p. 530), the "violence"] of divorce is an irremoveable stain on the man's cloak — "his reputation, stigmatizing him as guilty . . . of outrageous criminality."

'āmar YHWH ṣĕbā'ôt. The messenger formula sometimes concludes the disputation in Malachi (e.g., 2:17–3:5; 3:6–12; 3:13–21 [4:3]). For this reason, some commentators (e.g., J.M.P. Smith [1912: 56]) and *BHS* consider that the two clauses following are secondary additions to the MT. There is a distinct pattern in the use of the clause, however, in that the messenger formula closes each of the last three disputations but occurs prior to the conclusion of the first three disputations (cf. 1:4c; 2:8d; and 2:16bd).

The repetition of the messenger formula in verse 16b and 16d is vital to the third disputation because not only has Malachi introduced a new and more stringent approach to divorce (cf. Ogden and Deutsch [1987: 96]), but also the prophet equates the practice of divorce in Yehud with "violence" (ḥāmās; cf. Baldwin [1972a: 241]). The word is used synonymously for the most heinous of covenant violations (cf. *TDOT* 4:480) and often occurs in the most severe of prophetic indictments against Israel (e.g., Isa 59:6; Jer 6:7; 20:8; Ezek 7:11, 23; 8:17; 12:19; Amos 3:10; Hab 1:2–3). Such instruction needs divine authorization (cf. Mason

[1977: 150] on "the probability that it [Mal 2:13–16] did originally condemn divorce outright"). On the messenger formula, see further the NOTES for 1:2 above.

wĕnišmartem bĕrûḥăkem. The admonition should be retained as original to the disputation since the repetition of the clause forms a type of envelope construction with its counterpart in verse 15c. The echo of this clause in verse 16 also serves to emphasize the prophet's warning to the restoration community. Even more, it heightens individual accountability in the aftermath of the disputation upbraiding of the priests (1:6–2:9) and prepares the audience for specific charges of social injustice filed in the subsequent disputation (2:17–3:5). The NJB "Have respect for your own life then, and do not break faith" adduces both the personal and the corporate implications of Malachi's message, because "it is in the best interests of the individual as well as the community that families should not be broken by divorce" (Baldwin [1972a: 241]). See further the NOTES discussing *wĕnišmartem bĕrûḥăkem* in verse 15 above.

wĕlō' tibgōdû. The English versions understand a simple conjunctive *waw* ("and") connecting clauses describing related situations (WO'C § 39.2.5). The preceding *waw* + suffixing conjugation verbal form (*wĕnišmartem*) is reflexive and conveys a degree of volitional force, permitting the conjunctive-sequential rendering "so that . . ." (so Eiselen [1907: 726]; Henderson [1980: 455]; Packard [1902: 15]; cf. WO'C § 33.4b, 39.2.2).

The negative adverb *lō'* + the Qal prefixing form *tibgōdû* represent the nonperfective of prohibition expressing a negative command or instruction "you shall not break faith . . ." (cf. WO'C § 31.5d). This construction is the most emphatic form of the prohibition and denotes the "strongest expectation of obedience" (GKC § 107o). The nonperfective of prohibition is common in legislative contexts, and it is possible that Malachi understands this negative instruction as a new legal precedent (a codicil of sorts appended to the Mosaic law making explicit what had been assumed implicitly?). Milgrom (1991: 229) notes that the violation of prohibitive commandments involves an act, setting up "reverberations that upset the divine ecology." The prophet recognizes that deeds in violation of prohibitive commandments generate impurity, "which can be lethal to the community of Israel unless it is purified" (Milgrom [1991: 230]).

The Qal prefixing conjugation form of *bgd*, like the preceding verb *nišmartem*, reverts back to the more inclusive plural number. Whether one identifies the *waw* as a conjunctive or a conjunctive-sequential coordinator, the two clauses are related in that the two behaviors (i.e., guarding one's spirit and abstaining from divorce) exhibit a cause and effect relationship. The third disputation concludes with a forceful combination of literary features, including a (vetitive) warning ("stop breaking faith," v 15d), a divine declaration ("I hate divorce," v 16a) + messenger formula ("Yawheh, the God of Israel, has said," v 16b), an expansion of the divine declaration ("for he covers his clothing with violence," v 16c) + messenger formula ("Yahweh of Hosts has said," v 16d), and a prohibitive commandment ("you shall not break faith," v 16e).

Even as the literary structure of the book of Malachi hinges on the third dispute, so also the message of Malachi pivots on the issue of faithfulness vs. faithlessness as mirrored in the marriage and divorce customs of Yehud.

COMMENTS

2:10–13. The change of style from an adversarial second-person indictment (2:8–9) to an inclusive first-person plea (2:10) is striking. The prophet now speaks to his audience as a fellow citizen of Yehud, a compatriot (cf. Ogden and Deutsch [1987: 94]). The intentional disjunction in form signifies that this dispute addressing intermarriage and divorce is crucial to the prophet's message (cf. Rudolph [1976: 272 n. 4]; the fact that v 13 constitutes the statistical midpoint of Malachi's disputations substantiates this analysis). Tate's (p. 402) understanding of the rhetorical questions in verse 10 as "ironic lament" has some merit then, because the "citizen" Malachi expresses the questions the priests and the people should have been raising. Given this perspective, the abrupt shift to a third-person report in verses 11–12 is not so much an intrusion, as it is a resumption of the prophet's role as "messenger."

Whether one interprets "one father" (v 10) as God (so Verhoef [1987: 265]) or as an ambiguous reference to the Hebrew patriarchs (e.g., Abraham [D. R. Jones 1962: 193–94] or Jacob [so Ibn Ezra] or even Adam [see Keil 2:448]); it is clear that the prophet intends the corporate personality of "national" Israel — not the universal "community" of humanity (so G. L. Robinson [1926: 167]; cf. Baldwin [1972a: 237]). The twin theological concepts of God's creation and God's fatherhood of Israel are paired only rarely in the OT/HB, heightening the importance Malachi places on issues of marriage and divorce for the social and religious life of Yehud (e.g., Deut 32:6; Isa 63:16; 64:7 [8]; cf. Westermann [1969: 393] on Israel's reluctance to designate God as "father").

The multiplication of proper names used as descriptors of Yehud only serves to magnify this reality (cf. Baldwin [1972a: 238] on the names "Yehud" and "Israel" [and "Jerusalem"] as titles legitimizing the repatriates of Yehud as the community of God and heirs of the ancient covenant promises). The point is that Yahweh holds claim over Israel as Creator and Father (Achtemeier [1986: 181]), and the covenant relationship between the "One" God and his "one" elect people is characterized by faithfulness (cf. Craigie [1985: 237]). The practice of intermarriage with non-Hebrews and the divorce of legitimate wives jeopardize this "organic unity" of Yehud as Yahweh's elect because the two related customs stand in diabolical antithesis to this principle of faithfulness (cf. Cashdan [1948: 345] on Yahweh's expectations for behavior in Israel).

The clause "and *he* loved and married the daughter of a strange El" (*'āhēb ûbā'al bat-'ēl nēkār*) remains a *crux interpretum*. Torrey's (1898: 4) contention that Malachi's rebuke in the third disputation is "directed against the encroachment of some foreign cult in Israel" has been championed of late by Hvidberg (1962: 120–22), Isaaksson (1965: 31–32), Ahlström (1971: 26–27, 49), Glazier-McDonald (1987a: 89–93), and Petersen (1995: 198–200).

R. L. Smith (1984: 323–24), Verhoef (1987: 267–70), and Redditt (1995: 172–74) are among those biblical commentators who have recently defended the traditional or literal view that Mal 2:10–16 is primarily concerned with mixed marriages and divorce. In support of the literal approach, it is hard to fault Har-

rison's (p. 70) logic that "perhaps the strongest argument in favor of the . . . position is the existence of this abuse [i.e., intermarriage and divorce] in the [later]
post-exilic community" (see Ezra 9–10; cf. Mason [1977: 151] who aptly notes
that elsewhere in the OT/HB Yahweh is always the husband when the marriage
metaphor is applied to covenant relationship [contra O'Brien 1996: 248–49]).
The preponderance of evidence, as well as the vast majority of biblical exegetes,
points to the correctness of the traditional or literal interpretation. Nevertheless,
Tate's (p. 402) discretion is laudable: "It is doubtful that there is any reason to
separate sharply between the two interpretations. Intermarriage with foreign
women would have gone hand in hand with the worship of foreign gods."

Malachi understands marriage as a fundamental social bond (so Craigie
[1985: 236]). In fact, biblical commentators are quick to applaud what Achtem-
cier (1986: 182) cites as "one of the most sublime understandings of the marital
relation" in the OT/HB (see Verhoef [1987: 280]; Wells [1987: 52–55]). (Not
surprisingly, this is often ignored in feminist studies on Malachi. Cf. Laffey's [p.
156] derisive locution on the prophet's exhortation to marital faithfulness).
Glazier-McDonald (1992: 233) correctly observes that "the prime pitfall of intermarriage is not the loss of ethnic purity" (cf. Rofé [p. 42] who views Mal 2:10–16
as an extension of the Mosaic interdict that forbade intermarriage with seven
Canaanite people groups [Exod 34:16; Deut 7:1–3; cf. Deut 23:3] to the neighboring peoples of Yehud); but neither is the scourge of intermarriage, at least for
Malachi, "the resultant incorporation into the Yahweh cult of the rites of other
gods" (Glazier-McDonald [1992: 233]; although to her credit she does recognize
that the issue in postexilic Yehud is not one of polygyny vs. monogyny, cf. 1987a:
14–15; contra Schreiner [1979: 226–28]). Rather, Malachi's condemnation of
exogamy in Yehud targets sedition, the betrayal of legitimate and lifelong marital
relationships with insidious social and religious consequences (cf. Jer 5:11; Hos
14:5 [4]). Here the message of Malachi "shows an acute awareness that the terms
of the covenant bound them in loyalty to each other as well as to God" (Mason
[1977: 149]).

The harsh language of the imprecation (v 12) appended to the indictment
charging treachery in the restoration community (v 11) prompts many interpreters to regard the two verses as an interpolation (e.g., Mason [1977: 149–50]). This
approach, however, exchanges the secondary issue of nationalism (based upon
later socioreligious ideology in Yehud) for the primary issue of Malachi's disputation: covenant faithfulness in Yehud. By way of classification, Malachi's curse is
of the retributive type focused on the theme of humanity (related more specifically to the theme of fertility by some, e.g., Cashdan [1948: 346]) and invoking
divine agency (cf. Brichto [1963: 10–12]).

Elsewhere in the Haggai-Zechariah-Malachi corpus the jussive of exhortation
is employed in Zech 8:9 (cf. Meyers and Meyers [1987: 419]), while the impreca-
tory jussive appears in Zech 11:17 (cf. Meyers and Meyers [1993: 291]). Malachi's malediction stands in contrast to the promise in Zech 14:2 that half of the
city of Jerusalem shall not be "cut off" (krt) in the Day of Yahweh (here krt signifies banishment or exile, cf. Meyers and Meyers [1993: 417]). Apart from the
exact meaning of "cut off" (krt) in the context of the curse, two things are certain:

the imprecation sounds an alarm as to the dire nature of the offense, and it was deemed necessary by the prophet because apparently some in his audience were oblivious to the exigency of the current situation (so Ogden and Deutsch [1987: 94]).

Three interpretive options have emerged from the scholarly debate over the meaning of "cut off" (*krt*) in Malachi's malediction (2:12): cultic excommunication (e.g., Glazier-McDonald [1987a: 93]), banishment or ostracism (legal, social, religious, and otherwise, e.g., Ogden and Deutsch [1987: 94]; this approach does imbue the divine retribution with a certain irony considering that intermarriage was motivated largely by desires for social status and economic advancement), and "destruction" by way of (premature) death and/or extirpation of descendants (e.g., J.M.P. Smith [1912: 50]). Such analysis is in keeping with the semantic range set by Milgrom (1991: 457–60) for *krt* as a divine penalty, including childlessness and premature death, death before age sixty, death before the age of fifty-two, extirpation of descendants (Milgrom places Mal 2:12 in this category), and the death of the soul upon physical death.

The personalized form of the prophet's malediction demonstrates the individualistic nature of the sin of intermarriage (so J.M.P. Smith [1912: 50]). The remedy for such impurity in Yehud is similar to that of Levitical law: removing the transgressor from the community (e.g., "purging" evil, Deut 13:5; 17:7, 12; 19:13; etc.; cf. *TDOT* 2:203–4). The word *krt* ("cut off") may be used as a legal term for the penalty attached to certain forms of sexual and religious misconduct (e.g., 7:21, 27; 17:4, 9; 18:29; 19:8; 20:17–18; 22:3; cf. Wold [1979]). Malachi's curse (2:12) fits this pattern in that the context has both moral and cultic implications, and the tone of the disputation is clearly legal.

The combination of *krt* ("cut off") and *tôʿēbâ* ("abomination") occurs elsewhere in Lev 18:29 and Ezek 14:6–8. Zimmerli (1979: 303–5) and Hartley (1992: 100) concur that in these two cases the word *krt* ("cut off") is part of a legal formula signifying that Yahweh will punish the guilty party. The human role in the act of punishment consists "in excluding the sinner from the community and thus precluding him from the possibility of reconciliation and of reentry into the sphere of 'life'" (Zimmerli [1979: 303–4]). The gist of Malachi's imprecation should probably be understood in this same manner, the "banishment" of the guilty party in the form of social and religious excommunication — until such time as Yahweh chooses to deliver a sudden divine blow of judgment (perhaps including the extirpation of descendants). The modification of verse 12 from curse to conditional clause in the earliest of ancient versions attests to both the severity and the originality of Malachi's malediction.

2:13–16. Like the pericope addressing intermarriage (2:10–12), this paragraph treating divorce has been the subject of no less debate (cf. the four interpretive views on v 15 outlined in S. R. Driver [1906: 315]). Does Malachi ground his instruction on the topic in the creation of humanity as "one" and the ideal of marriage as portrayed in Genesis 1–2 (so Rudolph [1981: 85–86])? Or does the prophet base his teaching about divorce on the Deuteronomic tradition (Deut 24:1–4, so Schreiner [1979: 211, 217, 227–28] who contends that the issue is not so much one of divorce as remarriage)? Further, does verse 16 refer to divorce (so Achtemeier [1986: 181–82]) or perhaps to the neglect, separation, and even the abuse of a spouse due to bigamy or polygamous marriage (so Van der Woude [1986: 68–69])?

All these questions are of paramount importance for the overall understanding of Malachi's message and, to a greater or lesser degree, have been broached in the analysis of Mal 2:10–16 in the NOTES above. Garland (p. 421), however, raises an issue of equal salience: the refashioning of Malachi's rigorous stance against divorce by the earliest of the ancient versions so that divorce was not condemned, merely controlled by "due process." Tragically, the prophet's message apparently had little impact on the marital customs of the restoration community. While traces of faithfulness remained, faithlessness won out, as evidenced by reforms of Ezra and Nehemiah as they confronted these same abuses some five decades later (Neh 13:23–27).

The admonition to remain loyal to the spouse of one's youth (2:14–15) went unheeded because the biblical ideal of lifelong companionship and partnership in marriage is all too easily jettisoned for a relationship of convenience (true for ancient and modern society alike, cf. Wells [1987: 52–53]). Achtemeier's (1986: 182–83) forceful essay decrying the "violence" of divorce merits careful reading, lest we also mute the siren of the prophet's alarm. Nevertheless, Garland's (pp. 419, 427–28) advocacy for restraint and sensitivity on the divorce issue is commendable on two scores: first, the divorce epidemic has affected a large percentage of people in contemporary (secular and religious) society; and second, the biblical texts pertaining to divorce are notoriously difficult to interpret.

Whether one identifies the creation story (Genesis 1–2) or the Mosaic law (Deut 24:1–4) as the ligature for Malachi's treatise on divorce, there is a consensus among biblical commentators that the prophet advances an enlightened view of the marriage relationship (e.g., Craigie [1985: 236–37]; Achtemeier [1986: 182]; Verhoef [1987: 280]). Such concern for righteousness in human relationships is in keeping with the message of social justice and reconciliation embedded in Malachi's oracles (e.g., 1:2–3; 2:5; 3:5, 20 [4:2] and especially the second appendix, 3:23–24 [4:5–6]).

The polemic against divorce had a sociological function then, serving to augment the ongoing stabilization of traditional Hebrew society in postexilic Yehud (cf. Wells [1987: 51–52] on the role marriage plays in socializing the members of a culture). However, Malachi's diatribe against the treachery of divorce is more than simply an exhortation to fidelity in marriage. Rather, the prophet seeks to "ensure the continuity of traditional religious practice" in Yehud — the maintenance of covenant relationship with Yahweh (Ogden and Deutsch [1987: 97]). The divorce customs of Yehud contributed both to the dehumanization of women in Hebrew society (cf. Wells [1987: 51]) and the depersonalization and desacralization of covenant relationship with Yahweh because he is loving Father of all Israel (Mal 1:2–3; 2:10, 15). Yahweh hates divorce "because it violates the covenant relationship both with God and with the wife, because it is a cruel act of violence, and because it negatively affects the rearing of godly offspring" (Garland [1987: 421]; cf. Hugenberger [1994: 166–67]). How can Yahweh "return" to his people (cf. Mal 3:7) when they cannot even "return" to each other as husband and wife bonded together in covenant relationship? How can the community of Yehud "return" to Yahweh (cf. Mal 3:6) when crimes of marital faithlessness only compound the charges of social injustice against restoration Israel?

III. E. FOURTH ORACLE: JUDGMENT AND PURIFICATION (2:17–3:5)

2 [17]You have wearied Yahweh with your talk. Yet you say, "How have we wearied [him]?" When you say, "Everyone practicing evil is good in Yahweh's eyes, and in them he takes pleasure." Or "Where is the God of judgment?"
3 [1]"See! I am sending my messenger, and he will clear a way before me. Then suddenly he will enter his temple — the Lord, whom you seek; and the angel of the covenant, whom you desire. See! [He] is coming," Yahweh of Hosts has said. •
[2]But who is able to endure the day of his coming? And who can survive at his appearance? Because he is like the smelter's fire and like the launderers' soda powder. [3]He will remain a refiner and purifier of silver, and he will purify the Levites and refine them like gold and silver — until they belong to Yahweh, bearers of an offering in righteousness. [4]Then the offering of Yehud and Jerusalem will be pleasing to Yahweh, as in days of old — like the former years.
[5]"Yes, I will draw near to you for judgment; then I will be a ready witness against the sorcerers, against the adulterers, against those swearing falsely, against those withholding the wage of the laborer — the widow and the orphan, and those who turn away the sojourner — that is, [all] who do not revere me," Yahweh of Hosts has said.

The literary form of *prophetic disputation* persists throughout the book of Malachi (see the discussion of literary form in the introduction to the First Oracle above). This oracle reflects the standard three-part disputation pattern of declaration ("You have wearied Yahweh with your talk," 2:17a), refutation ("How have we wearied [him]?", 2:17b), and rebuttal ("See! I am sending my messenger . . . ," 3:1). Watts (1987a: 376) has identified Malachi's fourth oracle as both an *assertive* speech act intended to assure the audience (2:17–3:1) and an *expressive* speech act framed as a threat to the hearer or reader (3:2–5).

The paragraph divisions of the MT delineate three major literary units in the book of Malachi, differing somewhat from the six-disputation outline I have employed (identifying 2:10–16 as the third oracle). The fourth and fifth oracles (2:17–3:5 and 3:6–12) make up the second subunit of the third pericope in the MT paragraphing (2:13–3:21), a treatise on the relationship of the people to the covenant of Yahweh (see I. C. 4. Structure above).

Most commentators discern further microstructure in this literary unit on the basis of the emphatic adverb *kî* in 3:6 and the messenger formula concluding

3:5. The exclamation *hinnēh* and the messenger formula in 3:1, the interrogative *mî* in 3:2, and the *waw*-relative in 3:5 suggest paragraphing within the oracle unit itself (2:17–3:5). Some recensions of the LXX and certain biblical scholars propose an alternative textual division, reconfiguring the fourth disputation (by including v 6 and in some cases v 7 with 2:17–3:5; cf. Keil [2:461–62]; Packard [1902: 21]; J.M.P. Smith [1912: 66–67]; and Kaiser [1984: 88]). See further the introductory remarks to the Fifth Oracle and the discussion of *kî* in 3:6 below.

The grammatical difficulty and theological importance of the fourth oracle are attested by the numerous divergences in the ancient versions, including the inaccurate rendering of individual words in the MT by the LXX (e.g., 2:17; 3:1, 5), the expansion of the MT by the LXX (3:2, 3, 5), and grammatical substitutions observed in Syr and T (e.g., 2:17; 3:1, 2, 3). See the pertinent discussions in the NOTES below.

The integrity of the fourth disputation has been widely challenged, with all or parts of Mal 3:1b–4 considered secondary to the book given the shift from first-person to third-person speech and the topic of the Levitical priesthood (e.g., Mason [1977: 152]; Malchow [1984]; Redditt [1995: 176]; Petersen [1995: 211–12]; cf. Verhoef [1987: 283] for a catalog of scholars endorsing the authenticity of the passage and those disputing it). However, the eschatological scope of the fourth oracle marks this disputation as a distinct literary unit quite apart from the contemporary emphasis of the third (2:10–16) and fifth (3:6–12) oracles. Further, the chiastic patterns embedded in the structure of Mal 2:17 and 3:1 (see Verhoef [1987: 176–77]) and the rhetorical style characteristic of the disputation (see especially Wendland, Clendenen [1987, 1993], and Watts [1987a]) support the literary unity of the fourth oracle.

Like the other oracles of Malachi, the fourth disputation includes a rhetorical question (e.g., "who can endure the day of his coming?", 3:2) and pseudo-dialogue (e.g., "Yet you say," 2:17). The repetition of the exclamation *hinnēh* in 3:1 contributes to the hortatory style of the oracle, while the nostalgic appeal to the "former days" of Israelite history personalizes the disputation (3:4). In addition, the oracle is marked by a vivid simile (3:2–3) and the use of anthropomorphism in the characterization of the Lord (as one who sits [3:3] and one who acts as a witness [3:5]).

The fourth oracle is addressed to the "pious skeptics" in the restoration community at large, including the priests (3:3). That Malachi addresses the righteous (or self-righteous?) within the community is evident from both the emphasis placed on the order of purification (vv 3–4) before judgment (v 5) and the reference to those who reverence Yahweh in 3:16. Here the prophet confronts all who have construed God's apparent noninvolvement in the present distress as the failure of divine justice. Like Job and his theological tutors, postexilic Yehud must learn that external acts of religious piety press no claim upon God (cf. Job 21:7; 41:11).

This disputation forecasts the arrival of "the angel of the covenant" who prepares the people for the day of God's visitation by judging their sins and purifying their worship through the cleansing of the Levitical priesthood (3:1–4). The faithlessness of postexilic Yehud extends even to false speech about Yahweh, for they accused him of rewarding evildoers and being unjust (2:17). Naturally, this attitude toward God spawned a variety of social abuses and moral ills in the restoration community (3:5). According to VanGemeren (p. 204), the third disputation (faithlessness in marriage, 2:10–16) and the fifth disputation (faithlessness to God, 3:6–12) both pivot on the fulcrum of divine judgment threatened in the fourth oracle (2:17–3:5).

NOTES

2:17. *hôga'tem.* The Hiphil form of *yg'* occurs only in Isa 43:23, 24, and Mal 2:17. The basic meaning of the verb is "grow tired, become weary" (*CHAL:* 127). The passage in Second Isaiah features wordplay constructed on the word *yg'*. Israel has *wearied* of (serving) Yahweh (Qal stem *yg'*, 43:22), but Yahweh has not *wearied* Israel with burdensome cultic demands (v 23). By contrast, Israel has *wearied* Yahweh with her penchant for sin and iniquity (v 24). J. L. McKenzie (1968: 60–61) is probably correct in understanding this sin as insincere prayer and mechanical worship.

Malachi's indictment is similar. The postexilic community has wearied God with "religious" words and cultic activity devoid of any loyalty, conviction, or devotion (cf. Calvin [1979: 563], "saddened his spirit" based on Ps 106:33). That dutiful but heartless religiosity is the real issue is confirmed by the later reported speech of the prophet lamenting that service to God had yielded no profit for the community (3:14). The suffix conjugation indicates a past-perfect sense ("have wearied"). However, the perfective form of *yg'* may also suggest a present-perfect or habitual significance in this context, hence the use of the participle (*paroxý-nantes*) in the LXX for the MT *hôga'tem* (cf. WO'C § 30.4b).

YHWH. The divine name serves as the direct object of the verb *yg'* (cf. WO'C § 10.2.1c). The absolute and freestanding form of the covenant name of God occurs five times in the fourth disputation (2:17 [2x]; 3:1, 3, 4), perhaps emphasizing Yahweh's covenant relationship with Israel and the personal side of his divine character (see the comprehensive discussion of the divine name *YHWH* in *TDOT* 5:500–21).

bĕdibrêkem. The preposition *bêt* marks a circumstance of instrument (WO'C § 11.2.5d). The plural form of *dābār* + possessive pronoun means literally "your words." The phrase denotes speech or talk, perhaps connoting behavior as well. Glazier-McDonald (1987a: 127) errs in translating "prattle" (i.e., childish or foolish babble). Given the context of religious ritual, these "words" are to be construed generally as hypocritical speech pertaining to Yahweh and the Temple liturgy. Specifically, Malachi condemns the accusation that God is unjust because of the misperception that he approves the behavior of evildoers (2:17bc). That the questions are legitimate and posed in all seriousness is evidenced in the care taken by the prophets and other orthodox defenders of the faith to refute the complaints, even though they rejected them as false charges.

wa'ămartem bammâ. On the reported speech formula introducing the audience refutation of the prophet's words, see the discussion of *wa'ămartem bammâ 'ăhabtānû* in 1:2 above. The *waw*-relative possesses an adversative sense ("but"), contrasting the two clauses (cf. WO'C § 8.3b; both T and Syr understand this clause conditionally, "if"). The variation *bammeh* occurs in the reported speech formulae of 1:6, 7; and 3:7, 8. A more literal rendering of *bammâ* illuminates the verb *yg'*, in that Malachi's audience protests the prophet's charge of any wrongdoing by repudiating the notion that somehow they (i.e., the "religious" element of postexilic community) had wearied God. Given the context of proper ritual (3:3–4), the question posed by Malachi's audience ("in what *thing* [or *way*] have we wearied Yahweh?") anticipates the remonstrance of innocence in 3:7. Why should the people repent when they have dutifully participated in the sacrificial ritual?

hôgā'ĕnû. This Hiphil affixing form is usually emended to read *hôga'nuhû.* The object "him" (i.e., Yahweh in the first clause) is implicit and is supplied in the ancient versions (LXX, Syr, T, and V; cf. Petersen [1995: 206]). The NAB, NEB, NIV, NJB, and NRSV all concur. Keil (2:455) and Glazier-McDonald (1987a: 127) are among the dissenting minority adhering to the MT, understanding the omission of the direct object as deliberate gapping in the second clause (note the gapping of *be'ĕmorkem* in the next line as well). I have supplied the implicit object pronoun "him" in italics even though it is not a part of the MT reading (after JPSV). The LXX interprets the MT *yg'* ("weary, tire of") with *parōxýnamen* ("provoke, irritate") in each instance.

be'ĕmorkem. The infinitive construct with preposition *bêt* "denotes in general the temporal proximity of one event to another" (WO'C § 36.2.2b). The infinitive construct governs two reported speeches coupled by the coordinating conjunction *'ô.*

kol-'ōśēh rā'. The general quantifier *kōl* ("all, every") is a genitive of measure (WO'C § 9.5.3f). Such exaggeration is typical of those genuinely distressed by the problem of theodicy (e.g., Elijah the prophet, 1 Kgs 19:1–10, or the poet, Psalm 73) or those disillusioned by the realities of life (likely the case with Malachi's audience since their hopes for restoration as promised by God had not yet materialized, cf. 2 Pet 3:4). The prophet Isaiah dealt with those who "called evil good" (*hā'ōmĕrîm lāra' ṭôb,* 5:20). It seems Malachi's audience is perilously close to the same sort of insolence.

The Qal participle *'ōśēh* (*'śh,* "to do, make") functions as the predicate of the clause (governing the phrase *ṭôb bĕ'ênê YHWH*) and describes an ongoing state of affairs (cf. WO'C § 37.6bd).

The substantive *rā'* ("evil, wrong") is used elsewhere in Malachi to categorize those who offer improper sacrifices to God (1:8). Again, there is a haunting sense of irony in the prophet's reported speech. Those who have been offering "evil" sacrifices are complaining about the lack of divine justice against "evildoers!" Glazier-McDonald (1987a: 127) has commented that "men consider the upheaval in their lives to be the result of a reversal in the divine sphere."

This phrase *'ōśēh rā'* depicting evildoers is similar to the description of evildoers in the sixth disputation (*'ōśê riš'â,* 3:15; and *'ōśēh riš'â,* Mal 3:19 [4:1]).

Elsewhere in Malachi the evildoers are described as "the arrogant" (*zēdîm*, 3:15, 19) and "the wicked" (*rĕšāʿîm*, 3:21 [4:3]). The Qal participle *ʿōśēh* also occurs in Mal 3:17 and 3:21 [4:3], where the "doings" of God are contrasted with the "doings" of the wicked.

ṭôb bĕʿênê YHWH ûbāhem hûʾ ḥāpēṣ. Malachi has apparently combined elements of two formulaic expressions from Deuteronomy in casting the reported speech of his audience concerning God's injustice. The phrase incorporating *ʿśh* + *rāʿ* + *bĕʿênê* + *YHWH* ("do evil in the sight of Yahweh") occurs in Deut 4:25; 9:18; 17:2; and 31:29. The contrasting phrase combining *ʿśh* + *ṭôb* + *bĕʿênê* + *YHWH* ("do good in the sight of Yahweh") is found in Deut 6:18; 12:25, 28; 13:19 [18]; and 21:9 (a stock phrase in Deuteronomic literature for the approval of behavior, cf. Weinfeld [1991: 347]). In each case, context underscores the behavioral obligations of Israel established by their covenant relationship with Yahweh. By appealing to the Deuteronomic tradition, the prophet Malachi not only identifies himself with the teachings of the Mosaic tradition, but in so doing he also accuses his audience of espousing the antithesis of Deuteronomic covenant instruction. The wisdom of Prov 17:15 is pertinent in this context:

The one who pronounces the righteous a wrongdoer,
and the one who pronounces the wrongdoer righteous;
surely the two of them are *the abomination of Yahweh* (*tôʿăbat YHWH*).

The clausal *waw* is a simple conjunction ordering the two clauses, but it also functions as a copulative *waw* with the suffixing conjugation (*ḥpṣ*) marking hendiadys or complementary aspects of a complex situation (WO'C § 32.3b, § 39.2.1c). The juxtaposition of *ṭôb* and *ḥāpēṣ* in a partial chiastic structure in the two clauses emphasizes the contrast between Yahweh's standard of "good" proclaimed by the prophet and the postexilic community's practical observations of "good" as tempered in the crucible of human experience.

The adjective *ṭôb* ("good, pleasing, desirable," etc., CHAL: 122–23) occurs in the Haggai-Zechariah-Malachi corpus only in Zech 1:13, 17; 8:19; 11:12; and Mal 2:17. Again in Deuteronomy, those described as "good" (*ṭôb*) are those who obey the statutes of Yahweh's covenant (6:18, 24; 10:13; 12:28; 30:15). This is no doubt an undercurrent in Malachi's invective as well.

The verb *ḥpṣ* is unique to Mal 2:17 in the Haggai-Zechariah-Malachi corpus. However, Malachi does use the participle or adjective *ḥāpēṣîm* in 3:1 and the verbal abstract noun *ḥēpeṣ* in 1:10 and 3:12. The meaning of the root *ḥpṣ* ranges between "desire, pleasure" and "transaction, intention" (TDOT 5:93). Interestingly, the reported speech of the audience in the fourth disputation reverses the message of the prophet in the second disputation, where Yahweh takes *no delight* in those who offer improper sacrifices (1:10; cf. TDOT 5:101). Such misperception and distortion of divine truth are common among those confronted by a historical reality that contradicts their preconceived (and sometimes faulty) theological paradigm. This is clearly the case with Malachi's audience (3:14; cf. TDOT 5:103–4).

ʾô ʾayyēh. Malachi employs the rare clausal coordinating conjunction *ʾô* ("or") in interrogative statements in 1:8 and 2:17. In each case, the coordinator 'ô "works by reducing identical material associated with two conjoined clauses, leaving only what is different" (WO'C § 39.2.6b). The LXX substitutes the copulative conjunction *kai* ("and") for the expected '*ê* ("or"; also Syr and Sellin [1930: 606] among other commentators).

The adverbial interrogative '*ayyēh* ("where?") occurs in the Haggai-Zechariah-Malachi corpus only in Zech 1:5; Mal 1:6 [2x]; and 2:17. Characteristically, the form controls verbless clauses (cf. WO'C § 18.4c). Malachi employs the locative particle '*ayyēh* in the reported speech of the people, "Where is the God of judgment?" Ironically, the interrogative was applied to God in Mal 1:6 as well: "Where is my honor?" and "Where is my respect?" Had the people shown Yahweh the honor and respect due him as the God of the covenant promises, perhaps they would have recognized the judgment of God acted out in their very midst. The prophet could have answered the question about God's judgment by appealing to Zechariah 1:5, "Where are your ancestors?" The God of justice had visited Israel in a most dramatic way not long before — in the Babylonian Exile!

The tone and intent of the question raised by Malachi's audience has its preexilic parallel in the story of Elisha's succession of Elijah the prophet (2 Kgs 2:14). Upon retrieving Elijah's mantle, Elisha struck the waters of the Jordan in order to part the river and cross to the other side. According to the LXX, nothing happened when Elisha struck the waters of the Jordan the first time (cf. J. Robinson [1976: 26]), prompting the prophet to say, "Where is Yahweh, the God of Elijah?" He then struck the waters of the river a second time with the mantle and the river parted, and Elisha crossed to the other side. The incident "made plain to him and the watching prophets that the power in him was the same in character and purpose as had been in Elijah" (J. Robinson [1976: 27]). Postexilic Yehud was still waiting for a similar sign of divine confirmation.

'*ĕlōhê hammišpāṭ*. The epithet "God of the judgment" is unique to Mal 2:17 in the Haggai-Zechariah-Malachi corpus. This divine title is also found in Isa 30:18, "Yahweh is the God of judgment" (*kî-'ĕlōhê mišpāṭ YHWH*). The context of Isaiah's declaration serves as the answer to the question posed by the restoration community: Yahweh waits to be gracious to Israel, and blessed are those who wait for him. The Syr reads the construct-genitive phrase, "the God *who renders righteous* judgments" (cf. T, "Where *is it that* God does justice?").

The English versions (NEB, NIV, NRSV) and most commentators render *mišpāṭ* with the abstraction "justice" (e.g., Glazier-McDonald [1987a: 122]). The issue, however, is more than the question of God's character as a "just God" (cf. NAB). Malachi's audience is calling for a just God to "do justice," to fulfill his role as divine Judge and enact retributive judgment against evildoers (note the KJV, ". . . the God of judgment; cf. NJB, ". . . God of fair judgment"). The definite article is attached to *mišpāṭ* ("judgment"), suggesting that Malachi has in mind "the judgment" of the eschaton — the Day of Yahweh.

Malachi employs the construct-genitive form ('*ĕlōhê*, "God of") of the divine name '*ĕlōhîm* here and in 2:16, where the prophet uses the epithet "the God of Israel" ('*ĕlōhê yiśrā'ēl*). Generally speaking, the contexts in which Malachi utilizes the appellative 'ĕlōhîm make reference to God in the abstract, the idea of deity, the universal God, and Creator of the world (e.g., 2:10, 15; 3:8; cf. TDOT 1:273–84). However, the epithet "God of Israel" designates this universal God as the covenant God of the Hebrews (cf. TDOT 1:278; see further the discussion in 2:16 above). There is also a sense in which Malachi uses 'ĕlōhîm as a synonym for YHWH (e.g., 1:9; cf. TDOT 1:284). In fact, this is often the case with the names YHWH and 'ĕlōhîm in the MT. While 'ĕlōhîm is a more generic divine name, the more personal YHWH and 'ĕlōhîm are used interchangeably in the OT/HB. See the discussion of 'ēl in the NOTES for 1:9 and 2:10 above, and the discussion of 'ĕlōhîm in the NOTES for 2:15 above.

The noun mišpāṭ ("legal decision, justice," etc., CHAL: 221) occurs in the Haggai-Zechariah-Malachi corpus in Zech 7:9; 8:16; Mal 2:17; 3:5; and 3:22 [4:4]. Zechariah emphasizes the importance of executing justice within the Hebrew judicial system in order to achieve social harmony in imitation of divine justice (see Meyers and Meyers [1987: 399, 427]). Note that the use of the word mišpāṭ in Mal 2:17 and 3:5 forms a type of partial envelope construction framing the disputation. Malachi's audience asks, "Where is the God of judgment?" The God of justice replies, "Surely, I will draw near to you for judgment!"

3:1. hinĕnî šōlēaḥ. The exclamation hinnēh + participle is a type of messenger formula that anticipates a pronouncement or speech of some kind (cf. Westermann [1991: 100–16]). The prophet's message is one of judgment accompanying the divine visitation for the purpose of purification (vv 2–3). Waltke and O'Connor (§ 40.2.1b) have identified this construction (particle hinnēh + participle) as a presentative exclamation of immediacy, connoting an ominous imminency. The subject of the verbless clause expressed in the suffixed pronoun î ("I") is Yahweh, identified in the messenger formula at the end of verse 1. See further the NOTES on hinĕnî in 2:3 above and hinnēh 'ānōkî šōlēaḥ in 3:23 [4:5] below.

mal'ākî. The noun mal'āk ("messenger, angel") + the first-person pronominal suffix functions as the indirect object of the predicate participle in the verbless clause (cf. WO'C § 10.2.1i, § 37.6) and "serves as a wordplay on the prophet's name in the superscription" (Childs [1979: 494]). See further the discussion of the name mal'ākî in NOTES and COMMENTS for the book's superscription (1:1) above.

This phrase hinĕnî šōlēaḥ mal'ākî ûpinnâ-derek lĕpānay is probably a reworking of the passage describing the activity of "the angel" sent as a forerunner before Israel at the time of the Exodus from Egypt (hinnēh 'ānōkî šōlēaḥ mal'āk lĕpānekā lišmorkā baddārek, Exod 23:20; and wĕšālaḥtî lĕpānekā mal'āk, Exod 33:2). Glazier-McDonald (1987a: 130–32) correctly rejects Petersen's (1977: 42–45) equation of "my messenger" (mal'ākî) with the "messenger/angel of the covenant" (mal'ak habbĕrît) as Yahweh's "covenant enforcer." Both the context and the construction of Mal 3:1 indicate that the two central characters of the verse, the angel of the covenant and the Lord, are not to be identified with the forerunner messenger. Rather, the relationship of these two characters ("the angel/messenger of the covenant" and "The Lord") is the question.

ûpinnâ-derek lĕpānay. The waw-relative + suffixing conjugation represent a situation of *simple consequence* and continue the immediate future aspect of the preceding exclamation of immediacy (WO'C § 32.2.1cd). The Piel stem of the verb *pnh* may mean to "turn away" or "repel" (i.e., an enemy, Zeph 3:15), "clear out" (i.e., the ground for planting, Ps 80:10 [9]), "prepare, make ready" (i.e., a tent for guests or a stable for animals, Gen 24:31), or even "clear the way" with the object *derek* (CHAL: 293).

The Piel stem *pnh* is unique to Mal 3:1 in the Haggai-Zechariah-Malachi corpus, but the Qal stem *pnh* ("turn") occurs in Hag 1:9 and Mal 2:13. See the NOTES on *pĕnôt* in 2:13 above. The LXX employs forms of *epiblépein* ("survey") to render the MT *pnh* in Mal 2:13 and 3:1, instead of the expected *hetoimádzein* ("prepare"; cf. Gen 24:31; LXX) — seemingly suggesting a less active role for the forerunner(?). The Christological hermeneutic of the reformers is evident in Luther's rendering "provide a reputation" (Oswald [1975: 408]).

The combination of (Piel imperative) *pnh* + *derek* occurs three times in Second Isaiah (40:3; 57:14; and 62:10), and in each case the context of the phrase is an oracle of salvation and restoration addressed to Israel. In Isa 40:3 "prepare the way of YHWH" (*pannû derek YHWH*) includes straightening out curves in the roadway and grading the road to achieve a smooth surface. The image is similar in Isa 57:14 (*pannû-derek*) and 62:10 (*pannû derek hā'ām*) in that "clearing the way" means removing obstacles and obstructions in the roadway to permit easy passage. The phrase is indefinite in Mal 3:1, "clear *a* way . . ." (so NEB, NJB). The background of this "highway construction" imagery of Second Isaiah and Malachi is the practice of clearing roads for passage of the king in ancient oriental monarchies (cf. J. L. McKenzie [1968: 16]). Westermann (1969: 38–39) reads the language of Second Isaiah against the backdrop of the great processional highway of Babylon used for cultic parades and enthronement festivals (Glazier-McDonald [1987a: 138–39] assumes this for Mal 3:1 as well).

While the coming of Yahweh to judge, purify, and restore postexilic Yehud possesses the imagery of theophany (cf. J. L. McKenzie [1968: 11]), it seems less clear that this motif in Mal 3:1 emphasizes the "power" and "glory" of Yahweh (so Glazier-McDonald [1987a: 137]; cf. Westermann [1969: 39]). Nor should Malachi's reference to the "processional way" of Yahweh be understood primarily as a "new" or "second" exodus — a parallel to the Hebrew Exodus from Egypt. Rather, the processional motif of Mal 3:1 should be read against the theme of the prophet's disputations, the theme of covenant relationship with Yahweh. Note that the "way of Yahweh" does not enter Jerusalem from the directions of the Diaspora, but from the wilderness of the Arabah to the southeast (cf. Watts [1987b: 80]). Earlier Ezekiel had depicted Yahweh's abandonment of the Jerusalem Temple prior to its destruction by the Babylonians (chapters 9–11). Now Yahweh returns to Zion from the south, evoking the covenant traditions associated with Mt. Sinai (Isa 40:3; cf. 63:1–3, 7–9).

Malachi employs the processional motif of Second Isaiah as a metaphor assuring the restoration community of Yahweh's eventual covenant presence in Jerusalem (cf. Isa 40:11; on the "procession" as a literary motif, see ABD 5:469–73). Granted, his appearance meant judgment for the purpose of purification, but the goal of this divine chastisement was the abiding presence of God with his people symbolized in the rehabilitation of the Levitical priesthood and the Temple liturgy. The divine presence reestablished in Jerusalem as envisioned by Haggai (1:13) and Zechariah (1:16; 2:5; 8:3) would soon be a reality according to Malachi. Yahweh only dwells with those of contrite heart and humble spirit (Isa 57:15).

Clearing the way before Yahweh's epiphany means removing the "obstacles" of self-interest, spiritual lethargy, and evil behavior embedded in the people of God. This was the task of Yahweh's messenger, preparing the "processional way" by turning Israel away from their own wicked and covetous ways (Isa 57:17) so that the people of God might be called a "holy people" and Zion might be known as a "city not abandoned" (Isa 62:10–12).

lĕpānay. The combination of the substantive *pānîm* ("face") + the preposition *lamed* is an idiom meaning "before" (not considered a compound preposition, cf. GKC § 199c). The preposition *lamed* conveys both a spatial sense with motion as well as *interest* or *advantage* for Yahweh, the beneficiary of this preparatory activity (cf. WO'C § 11.2.1b,d). The suffixed object pronoun "me" (*-ay*) continues the emphasis upon the activity of Yahweh prior to his epiphany. See the NOTES on *pānîm* in 1:9 above, *lĕpānāyw* in 3:16, and *lipnê* in 3:23 [4:5] below.

ûpit'ōm. The interclausal *waw* before a non-verb is disjunctive, signaling the completion of one episode and the beginning of another (in this case distinguishing the activity of the messenger from that of Yahweh and the messenger of the covenant, cf. WO'C § 39.2.3). The adverb *pit'ōm* means "suddenly" or "surprisingly" and is unique to Mal 3:1 in the Twelve Prophets. Elsewhere in prophetic literature the adverb *pit'ōm* possesses an ominous quality, because it is used to describe the "sudden" visitation of Yahweh for judgment against Jerusalem (Isa 29:5; 30:13; cf. Jer 6:26). Second Isaiah and Jeremiah utilize the word in forecasting the "sudden" collapse of Babylon (Isa 47:11; Jer 51:8). The emphatic position of *pit'ōm* is instructive. The skeptics within the restoration community have assumed Yahweh's disinterest and noninvolvement in the spiritual climate of postexilic Jerusalem. They are mistaken. Those who discerned God's ways throughout Israelite history recognized a pattern of "divine pronouncement" followed by Yahweh's "sudden activity" (*pit'ōm 'āśîtî*, Isa 48:3). Malachi's audience will experience a similar scenario.

yābô' 'el-hêkālô. In combination with the *futurum instans* participle (*hinĕnî šōlēaḥ*) the prefixing form of *bô'* should be understood as an *incipient present nonperfective* (i.e., the beginning of a situation, WO'C § 31.3d). The preposition *'el* marks the termination of movement (WO'C § 11.2.2a). The combination of *bô'* + *'el* here means "come into" or "enter" (so NJB). Zechariah predicted that Yahweh's presence would again grace the Jerusalem Temple (Zech 2:14; 8:3; cf. Meyers and Meyers [1987: 168, 413]). Malachi's critics protest that God has in effect abandoned his city and his people when they ask, "Where is the God of judgment?" The divine presence will once again adorn the Jerusalem Temple. However, the people had best beware because "Yahweh's coming is never something harmless" (*TDOT* 2:44). His arrival heralds the judgment of purification, beginning with the Temple and the Levitical priesthood (*TDOT* 2:37). On the verb *bô*', see further the pertinent NOTES in 1:13 above and 3:2, 10, 19 [4:1], 23 [4:5], and 24 [4:6] below.

The noun *hêkāl* ("temple," see *TDOT* 3:382–88) occurs in the Haggai-Zechariah-Malachi corpus in Hag 2:15, 18; Zech 6:12, 13, 14, 15; 8:9; and Mal 3:1 in reference to Zerubbabel's Temple (see the discussion of *bĕbêtî* in 3:10 below). The use of the suffixed pronoun in connection with the Jerusalem Temple (*hêkālô*, "his temple," 3:1; *bĕbêtî*, "my house," 3:10; and *mizbĕḥî*, "my altar," 1:7, 10) emphasizes Yahweh's supremacy as "owner" and "occupant" of the edifice and serves to heighten the priests' irreverent and contemptuous service of Yahweh (1:13; 2:2; see further Pilch and Malina [1993: 160–61] on the biblical social value of "Service").

hā'ādôn. The Haggai-Zechariah-Malachi corpus uses *'ādôn* ("lord, master") in Zech 1:9; 4:4, 5, 13; and 6:4 (a title of respect for Yahweh's angelic messenger); and in Mal 1:6 (in reference to the status of an *earthly* master or slave owner). The noun *'ādôn* ("Lord") as an epithet for Yahweh is found in Zech 4:14; 6:5; and Mal 3:1. Elsewhere in the OT/HB, *'ādôn* with the definite article is always paired with *YHWH* indicating that this is whom Malachi has in mind as well (cf. Exod 23:17; 34:23; Isa 1:24; 3:1; 10:16, 33; 19:4). The term *'ādôn* emphasizes Yahweh's role as sovereign over all the world and further enhances Malachi's description of the eschatological day of Yahweh (cf. *TDOT* 1:61–62). This word also serves double duty, functioning as the subject for the preceding verb *yābô*' and marking the direct object of the the following participle *mĕbaqšîm*. The insertion of *hā'ādôn* between the two related clauses may constitute wordplay with *'ădônîm* in the rhetorical question of the second disputation ("If I am lord, where . . . ?", 1:6), for there will be no question that Yahweh is Lord when he comes!

'ăšer-'attem mĕbaqšîm. The relative pronoun *'ăšer* has an accusative function in this dependent clause without resumption (cf. WO'C § 19.3a). The independent pronoun *'attem* ("you," masculine plural) identifies Malachi's audience as the subject of the clause and continues the dialogical force and tone of the rhetorical questions introducing the disputation in 2:17.

The Piel participle *mĕbaqšîm* functions as the predicate of the dependent relative clause (cf. WO'C § 37.6). The verb *bqš* ("discover, find, search for"; KBL 1:152) occurs in the Haggai-Zechariah-Malachi corpus in Zech 6:7; 8:21, 22; 11:16; 12:9; Mal 2:7, 15; and 3:1. The only other occurrence of the Piel participle in the corpus of the postexilic prophets is *mĕbaqqēš* in Mal 2:15. The two passages create a foil yielding a certain irony in that Yahweh "seeks" a righteous or godly offspring (2:15); and in their "desire" for the Day of Yahweh (3:1), the restoration community hastens the very judgment that will purge the sin preventing them from becoming the "godly seed" of Yahweh.

Glazier-McDonald (1987a: 141–42) assumes that the combination of *bw*' + *bqš* in Mal 3:1 depicts a grand and reciprocal "pervasive sense of movement" on the part of Yahweh and the Yehudites toward some great "cultic" gathering. Indeed, Zechariah envisioned such a meeting between God and his people (8:21, 22). However, the cultic activity of "seeking" (*bqš*) and "entreating" (*ḥll*) Yahweh described by Zechariah presupposed recognition of his authority and obedience to his covenant stipulations (cf. Meyers and Meyers [1987: 438–39]). Such is not the case in Mal 3:1. The despairing pious Jews of the Yehud seek divine judgment on evildoers, not a cultic meeting with God (as indicated by the distorted dogma of 2:17, i.e., Yahweh has reckoned evildoers good).

Like the audience of the prophet Amos, the Yehudites fail to fully comprehend their request. Their desire for the Day of Yahweh will speed its coming and "they will get what they asked for, but it will not be what they wanted" (Andersen and Freedman [1989: 521]). Elsewhere, the use of *bqš* in the Psalter implies the purification specified in the entrance psalm requisite for meeting with Yahweh (Ps 24:6), as well as the response of joy captured in the proclamation "Let Yahweh be Great!" (Pss 40:17 [16]; 70:5 [4]; 105:3; cf. *yigdal YHWH*, Mal 1:5).

ûmal'ak habbĕrît. The *waw* may serve epexegetically, specifying the identity of "The Lord" (*hā'ādôn*) who is coming, by restating the previous clause (WO'C § 39.2.4). Often the epexegetical *waw* is rendered in English with "that is," but in this context the emphatic meaning of "yea" or "even" seems preferable (". . . The Lord, *even* the angel of the covenant . . ."; cf. WO'C § 39.2.4b). If Malachi intends *ûmal'ak habbĕrît* as a third eschatological figure, which seems likely, then the *waw* functions as a simple conjunction ("and"; cf. WO'C § 39.2.5).

The construct-genitive phrase *mal'ak habbĕrît* has no OT/HB parallel. However, the phrases *mal'ak 'ĕlōhîm* ("the angel/messenger of God," Gen 21:17; Exod 14:19) and *mal'ak YHWH* ("the angel of YHWH," Zech 1:11, or "the messenger of YHWH," Hag 1:13) are commonly found in the OT/HB. The word *mal'āk* means "messenger," whether a divine being (an "angel") or human being (*CHAL*: 196). For this reason, the identity of the *mal'ak habbĕrît* in Mal 3:1 is disputed. Laetsch (1956: 409), Chary (1969: 264), Rudolph (1976: 278), and Verhoef (1987: 289) side with the LXX *ággelón* and read "the angel of the covenant," understanding the *mal'āk* as a heavenly being and the angelic guardian of Israel (so NJB; cf. Petersen [1995: 211], "a minor deity").

Other biblical commentators (presumably) identify the *mal'ak habbĕrît* as a human figure and translate "the messenger of the covenant" (e.g., Achtemeier [1986: 184]; Glazier-McDonald [1987a: 122]; Mason [1991: 250]; so also NAB, NEB, NIV, NRSV). The reading "the angel of the covenant" is preferred. The implied audience or reader, the Jews of postexilic Yehud, would have understood "angel" on the basis of the parallel with "the angel of Yahweh" in Exod 23:20–23. Recent commentators on Malachi have shown little sympathy for Malchow's hypothesis that Mal 3:1b–4 is a later interpolation identifying "the angel of the covenant" with the Hellenistic era high priest Onias III (as part of an elaborate apologetic by later Judaism for a "priestly messiah").

The definiteness of the phrase *mal'ak habbĕrît* also proves difficult, because the specific covenant the prophet has in mind is ambiguous. The immediate antecedents of "the covenant" are the covenant of marriage (2:14) and the covenant of Levi (2:5). The context of the fourth dispute suggests the long-standing covenant between Yahweh and Israel, especially the blessings and curses associated with the Mosaic covenant tradition (Deuteronomy 28). However, the assertion by Malachi's critics in 2:17 (i.e., that Yahweh delights in the evildoers) provides a clue as to the covenant to which the prophet makes reference.

At first blush, the contention of the Yehudites appears to be little more than "sour grapes." After reflecting upon the historical circumstances and theological perspective of the restoration community, I am now convinced that that was exactly the case, "sour grapes." That is, Jeremiah and Ezekiel had forecast a day when the "sour grapes" parable would be invalidated and made obsolete (Jer 31:29; Ezek 18:3). The gist of the "sour grapes" parable was divine punishment of one generation for the sins of a preceding generation given the concept of Israel's corporate personality as established by the terms of the Mosaic covenant (cf. Exod 19:6). Under the terms of the new covenant the community would no longer be held hostage to the covenant "misbehavior" of an earlier constituency. Rather, individuals were now to be held accountable for their own sins.

It may well be that the issue of corporate responsibility vs. individual responsibility for Yahweh's covenant stipulations lies at the heart of Malachi's reported speech in 2:17. Malachi's audience presumed that this "new covenant" was now operative because a restoration community had been established and the Temple had been rebuilt. That postexilic Yehud still languished spiritually and economically could mean but one of two things: either the "new covenant" had not yet been implemented, or this "new covenant" was a hoax because it was ineffective. Malachi's audience calls for an explanation (i.e., "What has happened to individual responsibility before God?") and for action (i.e., "Where is the God of judgment?" may be paraphrased, "Where is this *new covenant?*").

'ăšer-'attem hăpēṣîm. On 'ăšer-'attem, see 'ăšer-'attem mĕbaqšîm above. The adjective hăpēṣîm serves as the predicate of the relative clause and makes "an assertion about the subject of the clause" (WO'C § 14.3.2a). The self-righteous skeptics of the community accused God of "taking delight" (ḥpṣ) in the evildoers (2:17; cf. TDOT 5:103–4). The prophet turns the table on his audience in the use of ḥāpēṣ by drawing attention to their faulty logic in analyzing the current situation. On the one hand, they indict God for sanctioning evil in the province of Yehud; but on the other hand, they assume the Day of Yahweh will result in the judgment of the wicked. According to Malachi, both suppositions are incorrect. God neither overlooks the evil perpetrated by his people, nor is the judgment associated with the Day of Yahweh restricted only to evildoers — "who is able to endure his coming?" See further the NOTES on verse 2 below.

It is also possible to read these parallel clauses of the prophet's digression in complementary fashion. The construction of 'ăšer-'attem mĕbaqšîm mirrors that of 'ăšer-'attem hăpēṣîm. The relative pronoun has an accusative function in relationship to the participles in both cases. The pair of relative clauses indicate a type of hendiadys, representing two aspects of a complex situation (". . . the Lord, and the messenger of the covenant whom you eagerly await"; cf. WO'C 32.3b). Malachi's audience is "seeking" or "desiring" Yahweh's appearance "purposefully" or "eagerly." This is precisely what (certain) parties within Yehud have craved, the coming of Yahweh as Divine Judge. There will indeed be a sudden and unexpected epiphany at the Temple of Yahweh (whether one divine figure or two), but the consequences of this event eagerly awaited by the postexilic religious community will yield a startling reversal of human calculations. Their zeal for the appearance of Yahweh at his Temple ought to have been tempered by the reality that divine judgment will begin with them, not their enemies — as Malachi is not loath to observe. As is often the case, popular expectation for the outcome of the Day of Yahweh is tragically mismatched with the reality of the event (cf. Amos 5:18, "Woe to those who crave the day of Yahweh"; and see the discussion in Andersen and Freedman [1989: 520–22]).

hinnēh-bā'. The particle *hinnēh* introduces a presentative *exclamation of immediacy* (WO'C § 37.6f, § 40.2.1b; cf. GKC § 116p, "it is intended to announce an event as imminent, or at least near at hand [and sure to happen]"). The predicate *bā'* is derived from the middle weak verb *bw'* ("to come") and is ambiguous in that it may be a Qal suffixing conjugation form or a Qal participle. Those identifying *bā'* as a suffixing conjugation form must understand the verb as a perfective of present time ("he comes," so Verhoef [1987: 282]; cf. WO'C § 30.4b). The majority of commentators read *bā'* as a Qal participle because another participle precedes the ambiguous form (*mĕbaqšîm*), and the ambiguous form is combined with the exclamatory particle *hinnēh* (cf. WO'C § 37.6def). Reading *bā'* as a participle also completes the symmetry of *hinnēh* + participle ("See! I am sending") at the beginning and at the end of the verse ("See! [He] is coming"). The participle functions as the predicate of the clause, and the tacit referent of the subject, "he," is "the angel of the covenant" cited in the previous clause. See further the discussion of *hinnēh* in the NOTES for 1:13 above and 3:23 [4:5] below, and on the *futurum instans* construction of *hinnēh* + participle, see the NOTES for *hinnēh 'ānōkî šōlēaḥ* in 3:23 [4:5] below.

'āmar YHWH ṣĕbā'ôt. See the discussion of the messenger formula in the NOTES for 1:4 above. Here the phrase marks a paragraph break in the fourth disputation.

2. *ûmî*. The interclausal *waw* has a disjunctive role, introducing a contrast or change of action with *continuity of setting* (WO'C § 39.2.3b). The personal interrogative pronoun *mî* ("who") has a nominative function and introduces a rhetorical question having connotations for both self-abasement (directed to the "righteous") and insult (directed to the "wicked"; cf. WO'C § 18.2g). The indefinite interrogative ("who") finds its antecedent in those "eager" for Yahweh's coming (*'attem mĕbaqšîm*, 3:1) — the same crowd of people impugning God's justice in 2:17. The rhetorical question anticipates the reply, "no one." However, the prophet does answer the rhetorical question in the final disputation, noting that those who revere Yahweh will be spared in the day of his coming (3:16–17).

The first two clauses of verse 2 are rhetorical questions and stand in synonymous parallelism in an ABC schema (interrogative pronoun + participle + object). The contents of verses 2–3 actually constitute the prophet's answer to the charge by the people that Yahweh sanctions evildoers (2:17). Indeed, Yahweh intends to purge the evil within the restoration community and the outcome will be the purification of Israel's worship (v 4). The combination of the two rhetorical questions emphasizes the fact that it is no small thing to desire the Day of Yahweh. His imminent coming will be more than a surprise, it will be inimical.

mĕkalkēl. This Pilpel participle is unique to Malachi 3:2 in the MT. The root *kwl* means "to hold in, contain" (*CHAL*: 152–53) or even "support, nourish" (see Meyers and Meyers [1993: 287–88]). The Pilpel form of *kwl* is well attested in the OT/HB (e.g., Gen 45:11; 50:21; 1 Kgs 8:27; Neh 9:21; Jer 20:9; etc.) but occurs elsewhere in the Haggai-Zechariah-Malachi corpus only in Zech 11:16 (*hanniṣṣābâ lô' yĕkalkēl*, "the exhausted ones [?] he will not sustain"). Based on the parallelism with *hā'ōmēd* in the following line, *mĕkalkēl* is usually rendered "endure" (so NAB, NEB, NIV, NRSV; but NJB "resist" and JPSV "hold out").

'*et-yôm bô'ô*. The particle '*ēt* marks a direct object (WO'C § 10.2.1c) comprising the construct-genitive *yôm* + the Qal infinitive construct *bô'* (see WO'C § 36.2.1d). This construct-genitive phrase with *bw'* is pregnant with eschatological implications associated with the Day of Yahweh (cf. *TDOT* 2:34–44). Similar phrases denoting the presence of Yahweh in Jerusalem in the Haggai-Zechariah-Malachi corpus include *hinĕnî-bā'* ("See! I am coming . . . ," Zech 2:14 [10]; cf. Meyers and Meyers [1987: 167–68]) and *hinnēh malkēk yābô'* ("Look! Your king comes . . . ," Zech 9:9; cf. Meyers and Meyers [1993: 123]). See further the discussion of *hayyôm bā'* in 3:19 [4:1] and the discussion of *yôm* in 3:21 [4:3] and 3:23 [4:5].

ûmî hā'ōmēd. See the discussion of *ûmî* ("and who") above. The Qal active participle from '*md* ("to stand") occurs frequently in the Haggai-Zechariah-Malachi corpus (Hag 2:5; Zech 1:8, 10, 11; 3:1 [2x], 3, 4, 5, 7; 4:14; 14:12; Mal 3:2). In this context, the meaning "stay alive" (Exod 21:21) or "be preserved" (Jer 32:14) is most appropriate, hence the translation "survive" (cf. *CHAL*: 275). According to Baldwin (1972a: 243), the word '*md* has military connotations, meaning "who will stand his ground?" (cf. 2 Kgs 10:4; Amos 2:15). The harshness of this imagery is justified given the fact that several of the crimes for which the prophet indicts Yehud are capital offenses (see v 5 below). Luther's (Oswald [1975: 409]) interpretive understanding of '*md* ("who will *regulate* or *control* the day of the Lord?") has some merit if the restoration community has assumed that perfunctory participation in prescribed ritual may manipulate God.

Interestingly, the prophet Haggai indicated that Yahweh already "stood" ('*ōme-det*, 2:5) among his people. Yahweh's presence in the postexilic community was expressed or exemplified in the form of his "spirit" (*rûḥî*), hence the Qal feminine participle used in agreement with the feminine subject "my spirit" (i.e., Yahweh's spirit). That was then; but now or in the near future when the day of Yahweh arrives, "no one will be able to . . . uphold and assert himself . . . when he appears" (Verhoef [1987: 290]). Yahweh himself will be present in the restoration community.

The repetition of the participial form in verse 2 underscores the imminency and the urgency of the ongoing process of divine intervention in the restoration community initiated in 3:1 (*hinĕnî šōlēaḥ*, "Look! I am *about to* send . . ."; cf. WO'C § 37.1f, 6f). The article attached to the relative participle as a predicate identifies the subject *mî* ("who?"; WO'C § 37.5d).

bĕhērā'ôtô. The Niphal infinitive construct of *r'h* means "to appear, become visible, make one's appearance" (*CHAL*: 328). The infinitive construct with the preposition *bêt* denotes the temporal proximity of related events (WO'C § 36.2.2b) and is usually translated "at" or "when" (so NAB, NEB, NIV, NJB, NRSV). The form is used elsewhere to describe the appearance of Yahweh to Israel, in Judg 13:21 and 1 Sam 3:21 (*lĕhērā'ōh*). Malachi's announcement of

Yahweh's appearance signals a type of reversal, in that Israel was commanded "to appear" before Yahweh (*lērā'ôt*, Exod 34:24; Deut 31:11) so that they might learn to fear him (cf. Deut 31:12–13). Now Yahweh will appear before Israel, and they will indeed learn to fear him.

The combination of *bô'ô* + *běhērā'ôtô* clearly indicates that the backdrop of this fourth disputation is the Day of Yahweh, the day of his epiphany when he appears in his glory over Israel (Isa 60:2; Ps 102:17 [16]; Zech 9:14). Meyers and Meyers (1993: 149) have noted that the use of the Niphal form of *r'h* + *'al* draws on the language of theophany. It is possible that Malachi represents a further development of this language of theophany by expanding upon the motif of Yahweh's "encampment" at his Temple introduced in Second Zechariah (9:8).

kî-hû'. The particle *kî* is a subordinating conjunction introducing a *logical* noun clause ("for, because"; WO'C § 38.7–8, § 39.3.4e). The independent personal pronoun *hû'* ("he") is a simple surrogate for the noun phrase *ûmal'ak habběrît* ("the messenger of the covenant") in 3:1 (cf. WO'C § 16.3.1b). The emphatic position of the personal pronoun in the verbless *identifying clause* calls attention to the work of purification performed by this "messenger" figure (cf. WO'C § 16.3.3b). The LXX amplifies the immediacy of Yahweh's intervention by inserting the present indicative *eisporeúetai* after *kî-hû'* ("because he enters . . .").

kě'ēš měsārēp. The preposition *kaph* may be ascribed to the category of *agreement in manner or norm* because the point of the comparison is correspondence or identity (WO'C § 11.2.9). The noun *'ēš* ("fire"; KBL 1:92) occurs in the Haggai-Zechariah-Malachi corpus in Zech 2:9 [5]; 3:2; 9:4; 11:1; 12:6; 13:9. Fire as a symbol of theophany and the idea of divine judgment likened to a devouring fire are common motifs in the OT/HB, where Yahweh himself is a "consuming fire" (Deut 4:24; cf. *TDOT* 1:425–28).

The Piel participle *měsārēp* is derived from the root *srp*, "to smelt, refine, test" (*CHAL*: 311), and is unique to Mal 3:2, 3 in the MT. Malachi borrows the imagery of God refining his people Israel by "smelting" away the dross of their wickedness from the prophets Isaiah (1:25), Jeremiah (6:29; 9:6 [7]), and Ezekiel (22:17–22). This motif occurs elsewhere in the Haggai-Zechariah-Malachi corpus in Zech 13:9. Meyers and Meyers (1993: 394–95) have detected a shift in the prophetic use of the smelting imagery from the preexilic to the postexilic periods. Neither Second Zechariah nor Malachi emphasizes the corruption of Israel (due to idolatry), nor do they focus on the destructive aspects of divine judgment. Rather, the postexilic prophets chose to stress purification (*ṭhr*, Mal 3:3; cf. Zech 13:1) and covenant renewal as the outcome of Yahweh's testing (note the covenant expressions "he [Israel] will say, 'Yahweh is my God'" in Zech 13:9 [*wěhû' yô'mar YHWH 'ělōhāy*] and "presenters of a righteous offering" in Mal 3:3 [*maggîšê minḥāt biṣdāqâ*]).

The conjoined construct-genitive phrases function as compound objects in the verbless clause. The prophet appeals to the imagery of two common trades in the ancient world (i.e., the smelter and the fuller) to demonstrate the pattern of divine judgment—testing and cleansing (cf. Ps 66:10; Dan 11:35; 12:10). According to Second Isaiah, the smelting furnace of Yahweh is adversity (48:10).

Such trial and testing are designed to distinguish the righteous in Israel from the wicked (cf. Mal 3:16–18). This time the divine "refining" will not be in vain (cf. Jer 6:29–30).

ûkĕbōrît mĕkabbĕsîm. The simple conjunctive or copulative *waw* joins two related clauses (WO'C § 39.2.5). On the preposition *kaph*, see under *kĕ'ēš* above. The noun *bōrît* occurs only in Jer 2:22 and Mal 3:2. The word describes an alkaline salt or soap (soda powder) derived from the iceplant (*Mesembrianthemum cristallinum*, so KBL 1:159) or the "soda" plant (*Salsola kali*, so Holladay [1986: 99]), used as a laundry detergent. The noun is derived from the root *brr*, "to purge, sift, purify" (KBL 1:163). The LXX *póa* ("grass, herb, lye") and the Latin *herba* ("plant, grass, herb") support the suggestion that alkaline plants are the source of this lye or "soap." Deliberate wordplay with *bryt* ("covenant" in 3:1) may explain the choice of the unusual *bryt* ("alkali soda") in this context.

The verbal root *kbs* means "to full, clean" or "wash by treading, kneading, and beating" (KBL 2:459). The word may refer literally to bathing (e.g., Lev 14:8) or the washing of clothes (e.g., Lev 14:9; 15:8) or metaphorically to the spiritual cleansing of personal sin and guilt (Ps 51:4 [2], 9 [7]; Jer 2:22; 4:14). The Piel participle *mĕkabbĕsîm* is unique to Mal in the MT (cf. WO'C § 37.5).

Malachi probably alludes to Jeremiah's call for Israel to "cleanse" their hearts of wickedness so that they may be saved (4:4). Glazier-McDonald (1987a: 147–48) has sided with von Bulmerincq (1932: 358) in interpreting the phrase *ûkĕbōrît mĕkabbĕsîm* against the backdrop of smelting metals, because lye or potash may be used as a reagent in separating the dross from the precious metal (so Petersen [1995: 207 n. b]). Such an understanding seems unlikely given the usage of *bōrît* in Jer 2:22, combined with the fact that the root *kbs* is never employed in contexts associated with metals or metallurgy. This approach also fails to recognize the two-stage process of Israel's restoration to Yahweh: testing (symbolized in the smelting process) and cleansing (symbolized in the washing process, cf. Redditt [1995: 177] on the *two* symbols of God's justice).

3. *wĕyāšab*. The *waw*-relative + suffixing conjugation indicate a nonperfective viewpoint (in this case a future aspect) and signifies a grammatical construction of logical succession (cf. WO'C § 32.1.3, § 32.2). The verb *yšb* occurs only in this verse in Malachi, although the root has a much wider distribution in the Haggai-Zechariah-Malachi corpus (Hag 1:4; Zech 1:11; 2:8 [4], 11 [7]; 3:8; 5:7; 6:13; 7:7 [2x]; 8:4, 20, 21; 9:5, 6; 10:6; 11:6; 12:5, 6, 7, 8, 10; 13:1; 14:10, 11 [2x]). The word *yšb* basically means "to sit, sit down, crouch, dwell, live" (*CHAL*: 146). According to Verhoef (1987: 290), the smiths of ancient times "sat" bending forward over their small smelting furnaces to assay the purity of the metal by its color (cf. the LXX *kathíeitai* ("sit, sit down"). This view enjoys wide support among commentators.

However, alternate readings are possible and perhaps preferable. Meyers and Meyers (1993: 395) render *yāšab* "gets set" ("As he *sets* to refine . . .") in the sense of commencing the smelting process. The verb *yāšab* can also mean "to stay" (Gen 24:55) or "remain" (e.g., 1 Kgs 11:16; cf. Calvin [1979: 574], *yšb*, "to sit, is intimated continuance"). This understanding of *yāšab* better accounts for the emphasis on the arrival of the messenger of the covenant and his ministry of purging postexilic Yehud in 3:1–2. It also facilitates the reading of the subsequent participles (*měṣārēp* + *měṭahēr*) without an intruding word of comparison ("*as* a refiner . . ."; e.g., NIV, NRSV). Lastly, such an interpretation clearly indicates that this will be a temporary "smelting" of Israel, not an endless purge of God's people. They will be purified and offer sacrifices of righteousness (v 4).

Elliger (1950: 194–97), Chary (1969: 263–65), and Rudolph (1976: 279–80) are among those scholars who regard Mal 3:3 as secondary, perhaps an insertion based upon the prophet's indictment of the priests in 1:6–2:9. Each has argued that the shift in focus from the community to the Levites interrupts the theme of the oracle. See the counterarguments in Verhoef (1987: 283–84), Glazier-McDonald (1987a: 149), and Redditt (1995: 177, who suggests that the transition "is not unlikely for an author").

měṣārēp ûměṭahēr kesep. See the discussion of *měṣārēp* in verse 2 above. The conjunctive or copulative *waw* joins two overlapping clauses (WO'C § 39.2.5). The Piel participle *měṭahēr* is unique to Lev 14:11 (*hakkōhēn haměṭahēr*, "the cleansing priest") and Mal 3:3 in the MT. The word connotes purifying or cleansing in respect "to what is ethically and religiously good" (*TDOT* 5:294; see further the discussion of *wěṭihar* below). The participles describe "an ongoing state of affairs" (WO'C § 37.6d). The noun *kesep* ("silver") occurs in Malachi only in 3:3 (2x). Although J.M.P. Smith (1912: 64), Elliger (1950: 609), and the NEB omit "silver" (*kesep*) as a gloss due to dittography; the phrase *měṭahēr kesep* hints at Malachi's interdependence with Zech 13:9 and should be retained as original (cf. Meyers and Meyers [1993: 394–95]). See also the discussion of *kaz-zāhāb wěkakkāsep* below.

Most translators supply a word of comparison ("as, like") to connect the verb *yāšab* ("to sit") with the following compound participial phrase *měṣārēp ûměṭahēr kesep* (so JPSV, NIV, NJB, NRSV; cf. JM § 129a [n. 5] on the phrase as a whole referring to a single entity). Alternately, the expression may be translated as it reads by understanding *yāšab* to mean "remain" or "stay," given the emphasis upon the *arrival* of the messenger of the covenant. That is, "he will *remain* a refiner and purifier of silver . . . *until* they become bearers of a righteous offering" (cf. NAB, "he will sit refining and purifying [silver]"; NEB, "he will take his seat, refining and purifying"; and Meyers and Meyers [1993: 395], "As he sets to refine and purify silver"). The LXX *chōneúein* ("melt") for the MT *ṣrp* somewhat blurs the imagery of purification since the term connotes casting molten metal, not separating the dross from the molten material.

wěṭihar. The consequential *waw*-relative + the suffixing conjugation continue the nonperfective sense of the preceding *waw* + suffixing form (cf. WO'C § 32.2.1d). The Piel form of *ṭhr* means "sweep clean, scour, purify" depending upon context (*CHAL:* 122; cf. KBL 2:369–70), and the verb is unique to Mal 3:3 in the Haggai-Zechariah-Malachi corpus. The majority of OT/HB occurrences of *ṭhr* refer to ritual or cultic purity (*TDOT* 5:291). The word as used in Malachi speaks figuratively of the forgiveness of sins in general, cleansing and purification as the result of contrition, confession, and repentance (Ps 51:9 [7]; cf. *TDOT* 5:294–95). Malachi shares this interest in ritual purity with the prophet Ezekiel (36:25, 33; 37:23); only those who are ceremonially "clean" or "pure" may participate in the formal worship of Yahweh (cf. *TDOT* 5:292). See the discussion of *ûminḥâ ṭĕhôrâ* ("pure offering") in 1:11 above.

'et-bĕnê-lēwî. The sign of the definite direct object characteristic of prose narrative in the OT/HB identifies the result or effect of the transitive verb's action (WO'C § 10.2.1f). The expression "the sons of Levi" is unique to Mal 3:3 in the Haggai-Zechariah-Malachi corpus. The phrase signifies the Levitical priesthood; and because only Hebrew males were eligible to serve as priests in this patriarchal society, the literal translation "sons" is justified (cf. Exod 29:8–9). O'Brien (1990: 47) has demonstrated that the terms "priest" and "Levite" are used interchangeably in Malachi. The emphasis here seems to be one of legitimacy; that is, the divine authorization of the Levitical priesthood to function in this role of "bearers" of the sacrifices to Yahweh (see further the discussion of "Levi" (*lēwî*) in 2:4, 8 above; cf. *TDOT* 7:483–503). Von Bulmerincq's (1932: 366) suggestion to read the ancient versions and equate the Levites with the offering presented to Yahweh (" and Yahweh will bring *them* [i.e., the Levites] for an offering in righteousness") is untenable.

The process of "smelting and purifying" the restoration community is aimed explicitly at the Levitical priesthood. Malachi rebuked the Levites in the second disputation for failing in their duties as ministers of the sacrificial ritual and as teachers of Mosaic law (especially 1:8, 10, 13; 2:6–8). Given their role as mediators of Yahweh's covenant and as representatives of Israel as the people of God, the purification of postexilic Yehud must begin with the Levites (see Verhoef [1987: 291]). Yahweh's "refining" of the priesthood should be connected with the "abasement" (*špl*) of the Levites (2:9). Spiritual cleansing is possible only after humiliation leading to contrition and repentance. The central role given to the Levitical priesthood in the purification of the entire restoration community furthers the suggestion that Malachi's generation witnessed the continuing political development of postexilic Yehud into a Levitical hierocracy.

wĕziqqaq. The root *zqq* means "to purify, filter" (KBL 1:279) and is used in conjunction with the smelting of precious metals in five of seven MT occurrences: 1 Chr 28:18; 29:4; Job 28:1; Ps 12:7 [6]; and Mal 3:3. The lone use of the Piel (perfective) form of *zqq* in the OT/HB here should be understood synonymously with *ṭhr* ("refine, purify"). The verb *zqq* is unique to Mal 3:3 in the Twelve Prophets and occurs in prophetic literature elsewhere only in Isa 25:6 (in reference to "strained" or "filtered" wine, *šĕmārîm mĕzuqqāqîm*; cf. Oswald [1975: 464]). See the discussion of *wĕṭihar* above on the *waw*-relative + suffixing conjugation.

'ōtām. The pronominal accusative marks the definite direct object of the transitive verb *zqq* (cf. WO'C § 10.3.1). The "descendants of Levi" in the preceding clause serve as the antecedent of the pronoun ("them"). As Yahweh's representatives of the restoration community, the priests must be purified before the people of Jerusalem and Judah (v 4) can present righteous offerings to God (cf. Mal 2:7–8).

kazzāhāb wĕkakkāsep. The preposition *kaph* marks a comparison of *agreement of manner or norm*, denoting correspondence or identity (WO'C § 11.2.9). Although Malachi 3:2–3 employs more detailed metallurgical imagery than that of

Zech 13:9, the similarities in vocabulary and syntactical structure suggest some interdependence between the two texts. The figurative use of "gold" (*zāhāb*) and "silver" (*kesep*) in the Haggai-Zechariah-Malachi corpus is restricted to these two texts. The logical outcome of this comparison, which establishes correspondence between the Levites. and precious metals, is purity: ethical and religious purity like that of refined gold and silver. The definiteness of *kazzāhāb wĕkakkāsep* is puzzling but probably represents an instance of the generic definite article often found with materials or in comparisons (cf. WO'C § 13.5.1f, g).

Meyers and Meyers (1993: 394–95) have noted that the reverse order of the two metals in Zech 14:14 and Mal 3:3 ("gold and silver") reflects the "economics of availability" of the two precious metals (perhaps due to new sources of silver discovered during the Persian period?). The sequence of elements in the "process" of divine judgment in the two texts may also be instructive:

Zech 13:9 — fire (*'ēš*), refining (*ṣrp*), testing (*bḥn*), resulting in restored covenant relationship with Yahweh;
Mal 3:2–3 — fire (*'ēš*) + alkali soda (*bōrît*), refining (*ṣrp*) + purifying (*ṭhr*), resulting in a pure sacrificial ritual.

The process of divine testing is more extensive in Malachi and is focused solely on purification. Likewise the expected yield is more specific with respect to the cultic ritual. This may indicate that the Levitical hierocracy was more firmly entrenched in the restoration community during Malachi's prophetic ministry than it was when Second Zechariah was written (?).

wĕhāyû. The consequential *waw*-relative + the suffixing conjugation *hyh* continue the nonperfective sense of the preceding *waw* + suffixing forms ("*then* they will be . . ." [NIV], "*until* they are . . ." [NRSV], or "*that* they may be . . ." [NAB]).

laYHWH. The preposition *lamed* marks an indirect object of goal or purpose (cf. WO'C § 11.2.10d). The combination of *hyh* + *lamed* is an idiom expressing ownership or possession ("they will *belong to* Yahweh . . . ," cf. KBL 1:244). The disjunctive accent (*zāqēp*) over the *waw* in YHWH (ליהוה) indicates the Masoretes connected the prepositional phrase *laYHWH* with the verb *wĕhāyû*. The outcome of the divine "refining" of the Levites is a priesthood rightfully "owned" or "possessed" by Yahweh. When purified and sanctified, the Levites will belong to Yahweh in a very special sense. Then they will "lay to heart" the sacrificial ministry and then "true instruction will be upon their lips" (cf. 2:2, 6).

maggîšê minḥâ. The Hiphil participle from *ngš* ("to draw near, approach"; KBL 2:670–71) may be translated "those who bring near, offerers," or "presenters." In cultic contexts the verb *ngš* connotes the formal presentation of offerings and sacrifices before Yahweh in Temple worship (see the discussion of *ngš* in 2:12 above). The phrase *maggîšê minḥâ* is an *epexegetical* construct-genitive in apposition with the subject of the verb, the Levites as the ministers of the ritual sacrifice in Yahweh's Temple (cf. WO'C § 9.5.3c). The Levites were the officially sanctioned "bearers" of the sacred offerings in Tabernacle and (later) Temple worship (Exod 29:44). See further the discussion of *minḥâ* in Mal 1:10, 11; and 2:12 above.

biṣdāqâ. The circumstantial use of the preposition *bêt* is one of specification (WO'C § 11.2.5e). The feminine substantive *ṣĕdāqâ* occurs in the Haggai-Zechariah-Malachi corpus in Zech 8:8; and Mal 3:3, 20 [4:2]. The word may mean "godliness" in respect to religious attitude, "honesty, justice," or even "blameless behavior" (*CHAL:* 303). Renderings suggesting honesty and blameless behavior best fit the context (cf. Glazier-McDonald [1987a: 154], "right order"). The phrase functions as an adverbial accusative of manner with *maggîšê minḥâ* calling attention to the way in which the action of sacrifice is performed, not the offering itself (i.e., "bearers of an offering *righteously*"; cf. WO'C § 10.2.2e). The outcome of Yahweh's purification of the priesthood results in a reversal in the posture of Levitical ministry from disdain, contempt, and carelessness to honesty and integrity (cf. 1:6, 13; 2:2). The false dichotomy between the proper spirit and manner of worship introduced by Verhoef (1987: 291) only distorts Malachi's instruction. The two are inseparable as the second disputation clearly demonstrates (cf. 1:8, 13; 2:2).

The phrase *biṣdāqâ* also has an important technical meaning in this context, affirming the legitimacy of the status and role of the Levites as cultic functionaries (cf. the rites of priestly ordination, Leviticus chapters 8 and 9). Ultimately, the entire nation of Israel will be established "in righteousness" (*biṣdāqâ*, Isa 54:14).

4. *wĕʾārĕbâ*. The *waw*-relative + suffixing conjugation continue the nonperfective sense of the preceding verse (*wĕyāšab* + *wĕṭihar* + *wĕhāyû*). The form *wĕʾārĕbâ* completes a logical sequence of events, hence the translation of the consequential-*waw* "then" (cf. WO'C § 32.2.1). The verb *ʿrb* (III) ("be pleasing"; KBL 2:877) is unique to Mal 3:4 in the Haggai-Zechariah-Malachi corpus, occurring elsewhere in the Twelve Prophets only in Hos 9:4 (there identified with the Ugaritic *ʿrb*, "to bring," by Andersen and Freedman [1980: 526]). The goal of the messenger of the covenant is the ritual cleansing of the Levitical priesthood and Temple cultus (3:3). Until the divine messenger completes the work of purification within the community, the sacrifices of the expatriates will remain distasteful to Yahweh like those denounced by Jeremiah (*lōʾ-ʿārĕbû*, 6:20). Given this understanding of the sacrificial ritual, the prophet's use of the root *ʿrb* may be instructive. The basic meaning of *ʿrb* (I) is to "stand surety for" or "give security on behalf of" (KBL 2:876–77). Only when the priesthood is cleansed will the Temple liturgy "stand surety" for Yehud's sins.

laYHWH. The preposition *lamed* marks an indirect object of goal with the stative verb *ʿrb* (WO'C § 11.2.10d; cf. § 20.2k, l). See the discussion of YHWH above in 2:17 and *laYHWH* in 3:3 above. The emphatic position of the object *laYHWH* (also 3:3c) calls attention to the true purpose of the sacrificial ritual, honoring Yahweh. The construction also highlights the contrast between what the priests have been and what they will become as Yahweh's servants (cf. Glazier-McDonald [1987a: 153]).

minḥat yĕhûdâ wîrûšālāyim. This construct-genitive phrase is unique to Malachi in the OT/HB. Only Malachi mentions the *minḥâ* ("offering") in the Haggai-Zechariah-Malachi corpus (see further the discussion of *minḥâ* in 1:10,

11, 13; 2:12, 13; and 3:3 above). Given the previous references to "sons of Levi" (3:3), the phrase illustrates the representative nature of the Levitical priesthood earlier. It also exposes the core issue of the disputation, improper sacrificial ritual tendered by the Levitical priesthood (cf. 1:7, 10, 13; 2:2, 8) — burdensome to Yahweh (2:17) and a mockery of his covenant (1:6–8).

The word pair *yĕhûdâ wîrûšālayim* identify the state and capital of Israel during the postexilic period. The geopolitical terms represent the whole of the covenant people Israel in contrast to the nations (1:11), Yehud viewed as an extension of Jerusalem. The same combination occurs in Zech 14:14 and is reversed in 14:21. Meyers and Meyers (1993: 486) have noted that the pairing of Yehud and Jerusalem is the result of Jerusalem's "sacral and political centrality." The phrase designated the southern Hebrew kingdom in preexilic prophetic literature (e.g., Isa 1:1; 2:1; Jer 19:7) and as the recipient of Yahweh's blessing of restoration was infused with eschatological significance by Joel (4:1 [3:1]). During the later postexilic period *yĕhûdâ wîrûšālayim* is especially associated with Davidic kingship, evoking connotations of the promises associated with the Davidic covenant (e.g., 2 Chr 2:6; 24:9; 29:8; 32:9; 34:3; Ezra 10:7; etc.). See further the discussion of *yĕhûdâ . . . yiśrā'ēl ûbîrûšālayim* in 2:11 above.

kîmê 'ôlām. The combination of the preposition *kaph* + the noun *yôm* ("day") + the noun *'ôlām* ("long time, dim past, eternity") is a Hebrew idiom for a bygone era, ancient days. The expression occurs elsewhere in the Twelve in Amos 9:11 and Micah 7:14, 15. In each case the context is one of restoration, whether the settlement in Canaan after the Exodus from Egypt (Micah) or the reestablishment of the Davidic monarchy (Amos). According to Paul (pp. 290–91), the phrase *kîmê 'ôlām* signifies "a nostalgic reflection upon the ideal period of the Davidic empire." However, given Malachi's reference to the patriarchs in the first disputation, the expression should not be restricted exclusively to any one time period. See further the discussion of *'ôlām* in 1:4 above.

ûkĕšānîm qadmōniyyôt. The adjective *qadmōnî* ("eastern, formerly"; CHAL: 313) occurs elsewhere in the Haggai-Zechariah-Malachi corpus only in Zech 14:8 (in reference to the Dead Sea as in Joel 2:20; cf. Meyers and Meyers [1993: 437]). Similar expressions occur in the allusion to the Hebrew exodus from Egypt in Isa 43:18 (*qadmōniyyôt*, "former *things*") and the days of the preexilic prophets cited in Ezek 38:17 (*bĕyāmîm qadmōnîm*, "former days"). Taken together, the two expressions allude generally to those several times in Hebrew history when the Israelites faithfully served Yahweh.

5. *wĕqārabtî 'ălêkem lammišpāṭ*. The NIV ("so") and NRSV ("then") understand the conjunctive *waw* in a consequential sense (so R. L. Smith [1984: 326]; cf. Henderson [1980: 458] who reads the adversative "but"). However, verse 5 constitutes Yahweh's answer to the second question posed by the skeptics in 2:17, "Where is the God of judgment?" This being the case, the *waw* introduces a statement of exclamation and certitude ("I *shall* draw near to you for judgment . . ."; cf. JPSV, "I will step forward . . .") and may even be understood emphatically ("yes, surely"; cf. WO'C § 39.2.1b). Wordplay employing *mišpāṭ* ("judgment" in 2:17 and 3:5) frames the disputation.

The verb *qrb* is unique to Hag 2:14 and Mal 3:5 in the Haggai-Zechariah-

Malachi corpus. The combination *qrb* + *'el* means to "come near" or "draw near" in the sense of approach or visit (so NJB, "I am coming to put you on trial . . ."). The *waw*-relative + suffixing conjugation assume the nonperfective value of the preceding *waw*-relative + suffixing verb form (see the discussion of *wĕ'ārĕbâ* in v 4 above). Intonations of a covenant lawsuit abound in the vocabulary of verse 5 (*qrb*, "draw near"; *mišpāṭ*, "judgment"; *'ēd*, "witness"; etc.), suggesting a courtroom drama (cf. NEB, "I will appear before you in court"; JPSV, "I will step forward to contend against you").

The preposition *'el* ("to, unto") marks the direction of movement inherent in the verb *qrb* (WO'C § 11.2.2a). The suffixed personal pronoun (= *kem* = "you" masculine plural) serves as the direct object of the independent verbal clause (WO'C § 10.2.1c, § 16.4f).

The preposition *lamed* indicates the indirect object of purpose (WO'C § 11.2.10d). The construction *lammišpāṭ* is definite ("the judgment"), probably a reference to the judgment described earlier in 3:2–3 associated with the day of Yahweh's coming (3:1; cf. WO'C § 13.3f). On *mišpāṭ*, see further the pertinent discussion in the NOTES for 2:17 above and 3:22 [4:4] below.

wĕhāyîtî. The *waw*-relative continues the nonperfective sense of the preceding *waw* + suffixing conjugation form (see *wĕqārabtî*). The construction also signifies a simple consequential situation, the verb *hāyâ* both advancing the situation of the previous clause and emphasizing the future time of that event ("*then* I will be . . ."; cf. WO'C § 32.2.3, § 32.2.6).

'ēd mĕmahēr. The noun *'ēd* is unique to Mal 3:5 in the Haggai-Zechariah-Malachi corpus and means "witness" in the sense of providing personal testimony (KBL 2:788–89). The word suggests a legal proceeding and calls to mind the *legal procedure* variation of the prophetic judgment-speech form found in the oracles of Jeremiah (29:23) and Micah (1:2; cf. Westermann [1991: 199]). As a "witness" in the trial against the restoration community in Yehud, Yahweh acts as both an accuser and as a provider of evidence (cf. Mays 1976: 40). Yahweh has this legal prerogative by virtue of his role as "witness" to the divine covenants with Israel (cf. Holladay [1989: 139]). He will accuse and indict because he knows firsthand that the people are guilty of violating his covenant stipulations. Interestingly, when Israel is fully restored to covenant relationship with Yahweh, they will be his "counter-witnesses" against the testimony of the nations (Isa 43:9–10).

The Piel participle of the verb *mhr* ("hasten"; KBL 2:553–54) functions as an attributive adjective modifying "witness" (*'ēd*; WO'C § 37.4). The phrase *'ēd mĕmahēr* is unique to Mal 3:5 in the OT/HB and is usually translated "swift to bear witness" (so NAB, NRSV) or "quick to testify" (so NIV; cf. the NJB "ready witness" and the NEB "prompt to testify"). If the participle *mĕmahēr* indeed serves as an attributive adjective, then the translation "swift witness" (Calvin [1979: 665]; Glazier-McDonald [1987a: 122]; R. L. Smith [1984: 326]; Petersen [1995: 206]), "ready witness" (NJB), or "relentless witness" (JPSV) is preferable. Yahweh will be both "quick" and "purposeful" in his role as witness against the evildoers in postexilic Yehud (cf. Baldwin [1972a: 244], "expert witness").

A similar use of *mhr* is found in Ps 45:2 [1] in the phrase *sôpēr māhîr* ("ready scribe" [NRSV] or "nimble scribe" [NAB]) and Ezra 7:6 *sôpēr māhîr* ("skilled scribe" [NRSV]. It is possible that the phrase signifies a "learned scribe" (so A. A. Anderson [1972: 347]) or an "expert scribe" (so NEB). However, the literal reading, "swift scribe," may also be appropriate because ancient scribes were probably evaluated according to both speed and accuracy (much like their modern counterparts). In any case, these texts indicate that the qualifier *māhîr* was applied to different classes of specialists or members of guilds.

bamĕkaššĕpîm. The preposition *bêt* (of animate instrument) is understood as an adversative ("against," cf. WO'C § 11.2.5d; on the variant form of the definite article, see § 13.3d). The Piel participle is usually understood as "one who practices sorcery" (i.e., black magic and witchcraft, ABD 4:468; cf. WO'C § 5.3b on the participial designation of professions). The word is unique to Mal 3:5 in the Haggai-Zechariah-Malachi corpus and identifies those "concerned primarily with influencing people or events for personal gain or that of their clients" (Redditt [1995: 177]). Despite the prohibition of such activity in Deuteronomic law (Deut 18:10) and the attendant penalty of banishment (or premature death at the hand of God [?], Lev 20:6; cf. G. J. Wenham [1979: 242]), the practice of sorcery plagued both preexilic and postexilic Yehud (cf. Mic 5:11 [12]; Isa 47:9, 12). Note that the LXX renders the masculine participles *mĕkaššĕpîm* and *mĕnā'ăpîm* with feminine forms, perhaps as collectives (cf. Walters [p. 95]).

ûbamnā'ăpîm. The *waw* is a simple conjunctive joining related object clauses; on the adversative preposition *bêt* and the variant form of the definite article, see *bamĕkaššĕpîm* above). The word *nā'ap* means "commit adultery" and usually describes the adulterous act of a man with a woman (cf. Andersen and Freedman [1980: 160]). The verb *n'p* is unique to Mal 3:5 in the Haggai-Zechariah-Malachi corpus. The biblical prohibition against adultery is found in the Ten Commandments (Exod 20:14; Deut 5:17 [18]), and such an offense carried the death penalty for both parties (Lev 20:10). Apparently the plight in Yehud had not changed much from that faced by Jeremiah the prophet, "the land is full of adulterers" (*mĕnā'ăpîm mālĕ'â hā'āreṣ*, 23:10). This rampant immorality was caused (in part) or compounded by an ungodly priesthood (Jer 23:11; Mal 2:8).

ûbannišbā'îm laššāqer. On the conjunctive *waw* and the adversative preposition *bêt*, see the discussion of *ûbamnā'ăpîm* above. The Niphal participle of *šb'* is found in the Haggai-Zechariah-Malachi corpus in Zech 5:3, 4 and Mal 3:5. The participle denotes a "continuing state of affairs" (WO'C § 37.5, 37.6e). The noun *šeqer* may mean "lie, falsehood, deception" depending upon context (CHAL: 383) and occurs in the Haggai-Zechariah-Malachi corpus in Zech 5:4; 8:17; 10:2; 13:3; and Mal 3:5 (the *'atnāḥ*; a major disjunctive accent and principal verse divider in the MT explains the lengthened vowel in the pausal form *laššāqer* [for *laššeqer*]).

The preposition *lamed* is definite and conveys the quasi-locational sense of *manner* (i.e., *in regard to*) usually rendered adverbially (WO'C § 11.2.10d). The parallel phrase *hannišbā' bišmî laššāqer* ("the one who swears falsely by my name," Zech 5:4) probably explains the insertion of *tō onómatí mou* in Mal 3:5 in some LXX manuscripts (see D. B. Freedman [1979]; cf. Petersen [1995: 207 n.] c). Holladay (1986: 245) understands "swearing falsely" to "swear an oath insincerely or dishonestly" and attributes the phrase (Niphal *šb'* + *laššeqer*) to

282 TRANSLATION, NOTES, AND COMMENTS

priestly rhetoric (cf. Jer 5:2; 7:9). Meyers and Meyers (1987: 284, 286) further clarify by specifying "swearing falsely" as lying under oath or perjury in contested lawsuits requiring sworn testimony before Yahweh (cf. Exod 20:7, 16; Lev 5:24 [6:5]; 19:12). Glazier-McDonald's (1987a: 164) attempts to equate *šbʿ* + *šqr* with idolatry in connection with Jer 5:2, 7 fit neither the literary context of Malachi's dispute nor the historical context of Yehud during the early Persian period.

ûbĕʿōšĕqê šĕkar-śākîr. On the conjunctive *waw* and the adversative preposition *bêt* see the discussion of *ûbamnāʾăpîm* above. The verb *ʿšq* occurs in the Haggai-Zechariah-Malachi corpus only in Zech 7:10 and Mal 3:5 and may mean "oppress, exploit," or "extort" given the specific context (cf. KBL 2:897). On the relative use of this Qal participle denoting continuous or ongoing activity, see Waltke and O'Connor § 37.5, 6e.

The construct-genitive phrase *šĕkar-śākîr* ("wages of the laborer") has proven difficult for biblical commentators, some deleting *šĕkar* as an error of dittography (e.g., J.M.P. Smith [1912: 68]; Petersen [1995: 207] n. d; cf. *BHS* and NEB) and others emending the text on the basis of pentateuchal legislation forbidding the Israelites from defrauding the wages of their fellows (Lev 19:13; Deut 24:14–15; e.g., von Bulmerincq [1932: 383]; Deissler [1988: 332]). The construction is awkward but not unintelligible. I concur with the readings of the JPSV, NAB, NIV, NRSV, and the majority of modern commentators who understand the phrase as a construct-genitive (e.g., Chary [1969: 266–67]; Rudolph [1976: 276]; Glazier-McDonald [1987a: 165]).

In a prophetic context, the root *ʿšq* suggests the stronger members of the community are taking advantage of those who are weaker (e.g., Hos 12:8 [7]; Amos 3:9; 4:1; Jer 7:6; 22:3; etc.). Mosaic Law prohibited the "withholding" (*ʿšq*) of wages from laborers (Lev 19:13; Deut 24:14). Either the translation "defraud" the wages of the laborer (so NAB, NIV) or "extort" the wages of the laborer (note Zimmerli's [1979: 372, 469] understanding of *ʿšq* in Ezek 18:18 and 22:29 and that of Meyers and Meyers [1987: 399–400] in Zech 7:10) for *ʿšq* seems appropriate given the context of Mal 3:5. Since intimidation and oppression in such economic concerns may be dishonest as well as cruel (cf. Andersen and Freedman [1980: 616]).

ʾalmānâ wĕyātôm. The noun *ʾalmānâ* is usually rendered "widow, wife whose husband is dead" (KBL 1:58). The use of the term in Mal 3:5 suggests a woman divested of her male protector and provider; (cf. *TDOT* 1:288). The "widow" and the "orphan" (*yātôm*, [children] without a father; cf. *TDOT* 6:479) are frequently paired in contexts emphasizing social justice (e.g., Deut 10:18).

Both Zech (7:10) and Mal (3:5) reverse the more common word order of "orphan and widow" found in pentateuchal and prophetic language (e.g., Deut 10:18; 26:12; Isa 9:16 [17]; Jer 7:6; 22:3; Ezek 22:7; etc.), preferring instead the word order of the prohibition against exploiting the "widow and orphan" in Exod 22:21. Meyers and Meyers (1987: 400) cite this reversal of word order in Zech (7:10) as an example of an innovative oracular style that reshapes familiar material (perhaps imitated in Malachi?).

The widow and orphan represent two of the socially disadvantaged elements of ancient societies, people easily susceptible to economic exploitation. As protector of the socially disadvantaged, God made provision for defending and helping the widow and orphan by placing Israelite society under obligation to them through covenant relationship (Ps 68:6 [5]; cf. *TDOT* 1:291). Mosaic law guaranteed protection of the widow and orphan from mistreatment (Deut 10:18; 24:17; 27:19) and offered them certain privileges in the form of a type of social security (Deut 14:29; 16:11, 14; 24:19–21; 26:12–13).

The appeal for demonstrating attitudes and actions consistent with the social justice concerns of Yahweh's covenant is a common theme in the Prophets (*TDOT* 2:481; see Birch [1991: 242–79]). In fact, Mason (1990: 251) has concluded that the list of evildoers and their unjust deeds in Zech 7:8–10; 8:16–17; and Mal 3:5 represent "catechetical-like summaries of the ethical teaching of the preexilic prophets and the 'stock-in-trade' of the preachers." The indictment in Mal 3:5 suggests that the restoration community failed to heed Zechariah's admonition against oppressing the widow and orphan (Zech 7:10). The adversative preposition *bêt* and the Qal participle from *ʿšq* are implied from the preceding clause (note the LXX insertions *toùs katadynasteúontas chḗran*, "those oppressing the widow," and *toùs kondylízontas òrphanoùs*, "those mistreating orphans"; cf. Andersen and Freedman [1989: 315] on the liberty of the LXX to remedy difficulties in the MT with a paraphrase).

ûmaṭṭê-gēr. The conjunctive *waw* continues the series of related clauses addressing covenant violations rampant in postexilic Yehud. The Hiphil participle from *nṭh* may be translated "turn away" or "turn aside" (so NAB; cf. NEB and NRSV, "thrust aside"; JPSV, "subvert [the cause of]"). The construct-genitive form proves awkward to translate (literally "thrusters aside of *the* alien"); but the emphasis in verse 5 is on divine judgment *against those* perpetrating evil deeds, so the construction fits the pattern (Petersen [1995: 207 n. e] reconstructs *ûbĕmaṭṭê gēr*). It appears that widows, orphans, and sojourners within the restoration community were denied the help they were entitled to under the provisions of Mosaic Law (i.e., "their needs were spurned").

According to Andersen and Freedman (1989: 316), the use of *nṭh* in Amos 2:7; 5:12; Job 24:4; Isa 10:2; and 29:21 indicates the unfortunate of society were not only denied justice but deliberately and maliciously treated with physical abuse and bodily injury — literally "pushed aside" from the street and the gate. Malachi's list of miscreants insinuates little has changed from preexilic times with respect to the treatment of the socially disadvantaged.

The noun *gēr* occurs in the Twelve only in Zech 7:10 and Mal 3:5. The word is derived from the root *gwr* (I) meaning "to dwell as an alien and dependant" (KBL 1:184). The term signifies one who has separated himself or herself from clan and homeland for any one of a number of reasons (e.g., famine, Ruth 1:1). Legally speaking, the *gēr* or sojourner "occupies an intermediate position between a native (*ʾezrāḥ*) and a foreigner (*nokrî*)" (*TDOT* 2:443). In Zech 7:10 the sojourner (or legal immigrant, *gēr*) is paired with the "poor" (*ʿānî*; see the discussion in Meyers and Meyers [1987: 400–1]). In Mal 3:5 the resident alien or sojourner is classified along with the widow and the orphan as a socially disadvantaged inhabitant of Israel protected by Hebrew law (see further *TDOT* 2:442–48). This law was rooted in God's love for the alien or sojourner and in the precedent of Israelite history because once they were "aliens" in Egypt (Deut 10:18–19).

The verb *nṭh* often takes *mišpāṭ* ("justice") as its object in legal contexts pertaining to the socially disadvantaged (i.e., the widow, orphan, and alien). For example:

> *lō' taṭṭeh mišpāṭ*..., "you shall not pervert justice...," Exod 23:6; cf. Deut 16:19,
>
> *lō'taṭṭeh mišpaṭ gēr yātôm*..., "you shall not thrust aside *the* justice of an alien or orphan...," Deut 24:17,
>
> *'ārûr maṭṭeh mišpaṭ gēr-yātôm*..., "cursed be anyone who perverts justice *for* alien or orphan," Deut 27:19.

This may account for the variation in the LXX *ékklinontas krísin prosēlýtou* ("those thrusting aside *justice for* the sojourner") in Mal 3:5 (read by von Bulmerincq [1932: 386] and the NIV, "deprive aliens of justice"; cf. the NJB, "rob the settler of his rights"). Given the legal context of these OT/HB parallels, it may well be that Malachi has employed an abbreviated form of the combination *nṭh* + *mišpāṭ* + *gēr* to decry the perversion of justice in postexilic Jerusalem (cf. Glazier-McDonald [1987a: 167]). The context of Malachi's disputations suggests that the prophet rebuked economic oppression, not the miscarriage of justice (note the preceding clause combining *'šq* + *śkr*, terms having economic connotations). Either way, the social classes of widow, orphan, and sojourner were doubly helpless: prey to unscrupulous merchants and bureaucrats and victims of jaundiced and corrupt judges (cf. Andersen and Freedman [1989: 502]).

wĕlō' yĕrē'ûnî. The conjunctive *waw* joins this clause to the list of evildoers charged in the prophet's sweeping indictment. The *waw* also functions epexegetically, summarizing or restating the basic sense of this catalog of covenant violators ("that is," see WO'C § 39.2.4).

The negative adverb *lō'* negates independent verbal clauses (WO'C § 39.3.3a) and serves to further emphasize this last element of the list by intimating a connection between *doing* evil and *not fearing* Yahweh. The phrase also provides a general description of the wicked by categorizing the behavior of the evildoers on the basis of a single common denominator, the failure to revere God (cf. Baldwin [1972a: 244], "all who ride roughshod over other people reveal that they *do not fear* the Lord of hosts . . .").

The perfective form of *yr'* is a *durative stative perfective* peculiar to quasi-fientive verbs and indicating an ongoing psychological or emotional response (WO'C § 30.5.3c; on the quasi-fientive verb, see § 22.2.3). Ironically, the Haggai-Zechariah-Malachi corpus begins with the restoration community responding to Haggai's message by "fearing Yahweh" (*wayyîr'û hā'ām mippĕnê YHWH*, 1:12), but ends with the accusation that most of postexilic Yehud no longer "fears Yahweh" (cf. *yir'ê YHWH*, "reverers of Yahweh" in 3:16). On the verb *yr'*, see further the pertinent NOTES in Mal 1:14; 2:5; 3:23 [4:5].

'āmar YHWH ṣĕbā'ôt. The messenger formula marks the end of the pericope,

as is the case in the fifth and sixth disputations as well (cf. 3:12, 21). See the discussion of this messenger formula in 1:4 above.

COMMENTS

2:17. Mason (1991: 250) has observed that Malachi stands in the tradition of his precursors, Haggai and Zechariah, preaching a message of assurance in regard to future hope and exhorting the religious community to a life of covenant faithfulness during the interim.

The prophet's fourth oracle forecasts a time when covenant loyalty will be a defining trait of postexilic Yehud (a theme throughout the book). This eschatological day will also mark the community as true worshipers of Yahweh. As such, this disputation serves as a foil bridging the third (2:10–16) and fifth (3:6–12) oracles indicting the restoration community for faithlessness to God and each other and offers a solution for that offense in the form of divine judgment resulting in the ritual purification of the people. Wells (p. 45) is justified in isolating the crisis in Malachi to the meaning and value of covenant relationship with Yahweh for postexilic Jerusalem.

The real substance of the fourth disputation is that of disparity (real or perceived) between divine justice and human justice, between the ideal and the reality of the retribution principle as it is played out in covenant relationship with Yahweh. Verhoef (1987: 287) is not completely correct in his assessment that the unrest in postexilic Yehud stems from the perception that the law of retribution was inoperative. On the contrary, the righteous within the restoration community resented the fact that they languished under the "corporate curse" of the law of retribution due to the covenant disobedience of other (even previous?) community members. It seems that the "pious skeptics" of Yehud clamored for the "new" covenant paradigm of Jer (31:29–30) and Ezek (18:3–4), divine justice executed upon an individual rather than a corporate (or generational) basis.

Theologically speaking, the problem of theodicy led to false conclusions about God's application of the retribution principle in postexilic Yehud. Malachi's audience assumed that the blessings and curses clause of the Mosaic covenant had been revoked because as yet they (the "righteous") had not experienced God's blessing, while the wicked appeared to be thriving. In turn, these same people (and the priests from whom they had learned the retribution principle, Mal 2:8) presumed that they had earned an "exemption" from divine judgment by virtue of their formal piety attested by participation in the Temple cult.

According to Luther (Oswald [1975: 407]), human reason "has a false idea about God." Not surprisingly, the faulty logic of the restoration community resulted in a practical atheism (Baldwin [1972a: 242]). By charging God with injustice, the people actually endorsed a theology of doubt that impeached the divinity of the Godhead and challenged the very existence of God (cf. Calvin [1979: 566]).

However, as Wells (p. 55) has noted, the issue was not so much a crisis of belief as it was a crisis of lifestyle. The crux of the matter was not God's judgment as meted out in the retribution principle of covenant relationship, but Israel's purity as Yahweh's vassal. God is never localized in human circumstances (cf. Lewis [1967: 167]). Likewise, divine justice is always linked with the outworking of God's ethical demands within the realm of human social justice (Mal 3:5). This means that God's judgment will first be directed to those who ask for it, the "righteous" who have been entrusted with the oracles of God—including the covenant stipulations concerning "right behavior" (cf. Deut 16:20). Hence the NT imprecation, "let judgment begin with the household of God" (1 Pet 4:17).

The (self?)-righteous skeptics of Malachi's audience challenged God on two accounts: first, they accused him of injustice in responding to sin within the community; and second, they questioned his concern for and presence in the affairs of community life (2:17). The gravity of the contention is attested by the inclusive nature of the prophet's response, addressing not just the "pious skeptics" but the entire restoration community. These challenges impugning divine justice raise the question of propriety in approaching the Almighty, a subject important to everyone in the religious community (whether they know it or not).

There is small debate as to whether Malachi's reported speech represents an expression of honest doubt by a "righteous remnant" as in the case of Job (e.g., 6:30; 10:2; etc.) and Habakkuk (1:2–3; 2:1) or the cynical social commentary of a jaded populace interested only in displacing blame. The fifth disputation offers some perspective on approaching God in times of distress and perplexity, teaching that human beings may test or challenge the Lord from a posture of faith (Mal 3:10)—not a posture of unbelief and disobedience (cf. Mal 3:15). This commentary, coupled with the sarcastic retort of the prophet (3:1), indicates that Malachi dismissed the genuineness of his audience's query. Their complaint had the formal semblance of the honest doubt that characterizes the psalmist's laments (e.g., Pss 13:1–3; 60:12 [10]; 74:1), but it lacked the personal conviction and spiritual character evidenced in psalms of "desperate trust" in Yahweh (cf. B. W. Anderson [1983: 77]).

In turn, the issue of motive in one's approach to God encourages reflection aimed at fostering spiritual renewal. R. W. Bailey (p. 72) applies a Hegelian-like dialectic to the religious development of postexilic Yehud, suggesting that they were in an aesthetic or ritualistic stage marked by "intellectual arrest" and "incipient moral decay." Such spiritual decline may be reversed by a renewal movement based on moral reform, exactly the remedy prescribed by Malachi in the call for social justice (3:5).

3:1. The ambiguities of this verse continue to perplex biblical scholars (cf. Petersen [1995: 209]). The text refers to three distinct figures: "my messenger," "The Lord," and "the angel of the covenant." The question is one of determining how many different persons are enumerated and with whom each is to be identified. Numerous proposals have been forwarded in an attempt to unravel this skein of enigmatic figures. These proposals may be sorted under three interpretive categories: the three-character approach, the two-character approach, and the single-character approach.

The three-character approach identifies three distinct persons or figures in

Mal 3:1: a messenger, the angel of Yahweh, and the Lord himself. Most often, these three figures are understood in some combination of human and divine characters (although some Jewish interpreters have recognized three separate angelic or divine beings, e.g., Rashi [the messenger = angel of death, the angel of Lord = the angel of the covenant, and the Lord God]). The messenger figure is regarded variously as a human character (a prophet or even Elijah, so Kimchi [1951]; cf. Cashdan [1948: 349]), a (heavenly?) messianic forerunner in Jewish interpretation (so Ibn Ezra), or an angelic being (so Rashi). Most Christian interpreters connect the messenger figure to the Hebrew prophetic tradition generally or to Malachi specifically (although Duhm [1911: 182]; Horst [1954: 271]; Dentan and Sperry [1956: 1137]; Lindblom [1962: 421]; and Petersen [1995: 211] equate the messenger figure with some sort of angelic being; see further the discussion of the two-character approach below).

There is almost universal agreement among both Jewish and Christian interpreters that the reference to the Lord (*hā'ādôn*) is to Yahweh himself (cf. Redditt [1995: 176]), the Lord God of Israel (Isbell [p. 59] misconstrues this figure as a human being of noble and honorable title; see further the single-character approach below).

The identity of the "messenger" or "angel of the covenant" has also generated considerable scholarly discussion. The eschatological context of Mal 3:1 with Malachi's apparent association of "the angel of the covenant" (*mal'ak habbĕrît*) with the "angelic forerunner" bearing Yahweh's name (*mal'āk . . . kî šĕmî bĕqirbô*) of the Exodus narrative (Exod 23:20–21) has led a majority of interpreters to conclude that "the messenger of the covenant" is an angelic or divine figure (but von Bulmerincq [1932: 350] and Mason [1977: 153] have noted that some commentators have identified Ezra the scribe as this messenger of the covenant). For example, Rashi understood this "angel of the covenant" as the divinely appointed angel responsible for avenging covenant breaking in Israel (cf. Cashdan [1948: 349]), while others have identified this personage as the guardian angel of the nation of Israel (so Lindblom [1962: 405, 421]; on Michael as one of the four archangels attending God and his role as the patron angel of Israel, see *ABD* 4:811).

Still others have assumed that the epithet was borrowed from the original Baal-Berith worshiped by the Shechemites and later subordinated to Yahweh as one of his servant angels (Judg 8:33; 9:4, 46; cf. J.M.P. Smith [1912: 63]; von Bulmerincq [1932: 345]). Most Christian interpreters have associated "the angel of the covenant" synonymously with "the angel of Yahweh," a distinct manifestation of the Hebrew deity in the OT/HB (e.g., J.M.P. Smith [1912: 63]; Baldwin [1972a: 243]; Verhoef [1987: 289]; Glazier-McDonald [1987a: 130–31]). If the specific function of "the angel of Yahweh" differs from that of Yahweh himself, such is not indicated in Mal 3:1.

More traditionally, at least in Christian biblical interpretation, it has been assumed that Malachi 3:1 makes reference to two distinct persons, one human (a "messenger" serving as a forerunner) and one divine (Yahweh himself, known by the titles of "The Lord" and "the messenger/angel of the covenant"; but see Petersen [1977: 43] who identified "my messenger" with "the angel/messenger of the covenant" as Yahweh's "covenant enforcer"). A variety of characters have been identified as fulfilling the role of Malachi's "forerunner," including Elijah, on the basis of Mal 3:23 [4:5], (cf. Cashdan [1948: 349]; the prophet Malachi himself, so Mason [1977: 152] following Elliger [1950: 197, 206]; the typological embodiment of the entire prophetic school, so Hengstenberg [2:1204–5]; or some unnamed "ideal figure," so S. R. Driver [1906: 318]; or even John the Baptist, so Henderson [1980: 456]). It should be noted that some early Jewish interpreters viewed the "messenger" figure as a heavenly or spiritual being, rather than a human being (e.g., the death angel, so Rashi). Typically, "The Lord" (*hāʾādôn*) and the unique epithet "the angel/messenger of the covenant" are considered synonymous titles for Yahweh by Christian interpreters (J.M.P. Smith [1912: 63]; Glazier-McDonald [1987a: 131–32]; see further Malchow [1984: 252–53]).

The single-character interpretation identifies the "my messenger," "the angel/messenger of the covenant," and "The Lord" as references to the same being by three different titles (e.g., Isbell [1980: 59] who misunderstands "The Lord" [*hāʾādôn*] as an honorific title of a noble person and regards the forerunner and the messenger as the same human being; cf. France [1982: 91 n. 31] who also tenders the impossible suggestion that all three epithets are titles for a human messenger of Yahweh).

According to Petersen (1977: 42–45), the "day of Yahweh" overtones in the fourth disputation establish the eschatological theme of the pericope. The NT commentary on Mal 3:1, pointing to John the Baptist as the "messenger" figure, interprets Malachi's eschatological projection on the basis of promise and fulfillment (cf. Matt 11:3, 10, 14; Mark 1:2; Luke 1:17, 76; 7:19, 27). The subsequent identification of Jesus Christ as "the angel of the covenant" in patristic literature fixed the traditional two-character reading of Mal 3:1 in Christian biblical interpretation (e.g., 1 Clement 23:5; cf. Calvin [1979: 569]; Pusey [2:486]). While this early church understanding of Mal 3:1 is accepted by Christian interpreters, it is necessary to admit the feasibility of Verhoef's (1987: 288) contention that John the Baptist represents the culmination of a "pyramid of forerunners." Wolf's (p. 124) suggestion that the identification of John the Baptist with Elijah "does not exhaust the full meaning of this prophecy" also merits careful consideration.

The later Jewish and early Christian interpretations notwithstanding, the pertinent question is what the prophet Malachi himself had in mind when he introduced these eschatological figures to postexilic Yehud. It seems likely that both the original writer and the original audience most naturally would have understood "my angel," "The Lord," and "the angel of the covenant" as titles for three separate divine beings (see Mullen [1980: 215] on "messengers" as "divine beings"). The first, "my messenger" is readily identified with the "the Angel of Yahweh" commissioned as Israel's "forerunner" in the covenant ratification ceremony at Mt. Sinai (Exod 23:20–21, 23). This divine person has "Yahweh's name in him" (Exod 23:21), so "my messenger/angel" represents an alter-ego or surrogate of some kind for Yahweh. It may be possible to explain the relationship of "the Angel of Yahweh" to Yahweh himself hypostatized in humanoid form (on hypostasis in the Ugaritic pantheon, see J. Gray [1957: 134]; and Mullen [1980: 268–69, 283]). The essence of Yahweh himself is visibly manifest in a personal presence (at times) of humanoid form, always in carefully prescribed roles (on the relationship of "the Angel of Yahweh" and Yahweh himself, see further, *ABD* 1:250).

Clearly, "The Lord" (*hāʾādôn*) is a title for Yahweh himself. It is possible that "the messenger/angel of the covenant" is not another distinct divine being, but rather a further manifestation of "the Angel of Yahweh" because this personage is also associated with the aftermath of the Israelite breach of the Sinai treaty as a covenant enforcer of sorts (Exod 32:34; 33:2; on the dual divine titles Sahru ["Dawn"] and Salimu ["Dusk"] for the manifestations of the planet Venus as the "morning" and "evening" star, see J. Gray [1957: 134]; Mullen [1980: 239]; and *ABD* 5:1150–51).

Alternately, the context of formal Temple entrance in Mal 3:1 may reflect the processional of deity in ancient mythology in which the deity enters his abode accompanied by angelic attendants (see *ABD* 1:252). Mullen (p. 210) notes that the messengers of Baal and Atirat are dispatched in pairs, apparently the case in Malachi as well (on the role of angels in the divine assembly of Yahweh, see *ABD* 2:215–17). If this is the case, then Malachi draws from the mythopoeic motif of the divine council or assembly in the ANE (cf. Petersen [1995: 209]). The imagery then becomes one of a divine processional into the Temple, with Yahweh himself flanked by two angelic retainers. The question remains whether these two personages are distinct divine beings or simply a dual representation of "the Angel of Yahweh."

As if the problems associated with the identification of the three figures of Mal 3:1 are not enough, the "covenant" the prophet specifies is also in question. Malachi may have in mind the long-established Mosaic covenant, the Davidic covenant, or even the covenant of Levi mentioned in the second disputation (note the "covenant" references in 2:4, 8, 10; cf. Malchow [1984: 253]). However, there are several reasons why it seems likely that Malachi has in mind the "new covenant" announced by Jeremiah and Ezekiel (Jer 31:31–34; Ezek 34:25; 36:26–28). First, Malachi's audience has already alluded to this new covenant in their dispute with the prophet over divine justice (see the NOTES on 2:17 above). Second, the eschatological context of the fourth disputation is firmly established. Third, even if the prophet spoke sarcastically of the people's expectant desire for divine intervention, such anticipation is difficult to explain if Malachi refers only to Yahweh's past covenant initiatives. Fourth, the allusion to Ezek 43:1–5 and the return of the divine presence to the Temple hints at the "new covenant" era.

3:2–4. Wells (p. 56) has identified the restoration community's demand for divine judgment as a *tragicomic* feature of human nature. The profound irony in such a demand is that God first targets those making the plea. Thus, the real issue of the fourth disputation is not God's *justice* (or *judgment*), but Israel's *purity*. Neither is the issue one of *universalism* (i.e., the worship of Yahweh by the nations, Mal 1:11) vs. *particularism* (i.e., the worship of Yahweh by Israel, Mal 3:2–4) as some commentators suggest (e.g., Chary [1969: 178]; Glazier-McDonald [1987a: 170]).

Rather, the heart of the matter is exactly that: hearts trained in faithful obedience to Yahweh offering pure worship to the God of creation and redemption.

This desired outcome of genuine worship offered to God by his people is accomplished through the difficult and painful process of *purification*. God's "spirit of judgment" and "spirit of burning, washing, and cleansing" transform the people of God into a holy community (cf. Isa 4:3–4; Zeph 3:11–13, 17; on the transformation of the human person in the eschaton, see Gowan [1986: 86–93]).

Here, Malachi's oracle calls to mind the entrance psalms and the "immense . . . *responsibility* which is laid upon the faithful believer" in preparing for worship by meeting the demands of Yahweh's character claims (Weiser [1962: 233]; cf. Pss 15; 24:3–6). The ultimate purpose of divine judgment is to "turn rebels into worshipers" (Tozer 1978: 217), that is why Malachi emphasizes the purification of the covenant community as an integral phase of the Day of Yahweh (on the relationship between personal piety and corporate worship, see Hill [1994: 12–23]).

3:5. The cynical plea for justice on the part of the believing remnant within the restoration community does not go unheard. God fully intends to serve as witness, judge, and executioner against the evildoers (cf. Mal 3:18). The defendants are the economically oppressed and socially disadvantaged: the widow, the orphan, and the alien or sojourner. These three social groups represent the "disenfranchised" and are often lumped together in legal and prophetic texts (e.g., Deut 24:19–21; Jer 22:3; Zech 7:10). They share a common bond in their helplessness and alienation. They also share a common heritage and destiny, in that the God who is their "maker" is also their "advocate" (cf. Ps 72:2, 4, 12).

Even this truth serves to indict the community of Yehud because in their selfish desire to hasten the Day of Yahweh, they too have trampled the rights of the "poor" through neglect and indifference (cf. Prov 14:21; 17:5; 19:17). The reality of divine judgment "is captured in the understanding that we need not perceive the mysteries" of theodicy; we need but accept God's love and forgiveness and learn compassion for the oppressed and the oppressor (R. W. Bailey [1977: 71]). In part, this explains the relationship between the twofold work of divine purification and divine judgment. Any appeal for divine justice must be tempered by the knowledge that at his epiphany God will judge all people, the wicked and the righteous. In view of this stark theological proposition, the question is better posed, "Where is the God of grace and mercy?"

The retort, "Where is the God of judgment?" (Mal 2:17), indicates that Malachi's audience expects the Day of Yahweh. They apparently anticipate the return of Yahweh to his Temple and a reinstallation of the divine presence in Jerusalem in fulfillment of Ezek 43:2–5; Hag 2:7; and Zech 8:3. In this regard, Malachi shares affinities with earlier prophetic voices announcing the reinstallation of the divine presence in Jerusalem and proclaiming justice for the righteous and judgment for the wicked (cf. Zeph 2:8–10; Joel 4:16–21 [3:16–21]).

Nevertheless, the book of Malachi also makes original contributions to OT/HB eschatology, most notably in developing the Day of Yahweh as a day of judgment for the evildoers *within* the ranks of the covenant people (cf. Verhoef 1987: 295), introducing the messenger (or angel) as a new eschatological figure who prepares the day of Yahweh's visitation (cf. Scalise [p. 410]), and advancing the notion of an eschatological ethic that provides signs of the "proleptic presence" of God's future rule (i.e., the prophet's exhortation to practice social justice corresponds with the biblical paradigm of what God is working toward in the eschaton, see Gowan [p. 125]).

However, this fourth disputation does not exhaust Malachi's eschatological interest because two questions remain: What does Yahweh expect of his people during the interim? And what will become of those who endure Yahweh's purification and judgment? The call to repentance in the fifth dispute answers the question of the community's response in the present (c. Mal 3:7), while the last dispute addresses the outcome of Yahweh's purification — the deliverance of the righteous in the Day of Yahweh (cf. Mal 3:17–18).

III. F. FIFTH ORACLE: CALL TO REPENTANCE (3:6–12)

3 ⁶"Indeed, I am Yahweh; I have not changed. And so you, O descendants of Jacob, you have not been destroyed. ⁷Since the days of your forefathers, you have spurned my statutes and you have not kept [them]. Return to me, so that I may return to you," Yahweh of Hosts has said.

But you say, "How can we return?" ⁸"Will anyone rob God? Surely you are robbing me!" But you say, "How have we robbed you?" "The tithe! The tithe tax! ⁹[So,] with the curse you are being cursed; yea, it is me you are robbing — the whole nation! ¹⁰Bring the full tithe into the [Temple] storehouse, so that there may be food in my house! Test me outright in this [thing]," Yahweh of Hosts has said; "[see] if I will not open for you the windows of heaven, and then I will pour out for you a blessing without measure. ¹¹I will repulse for you the devourer so that it may not ravage for you the produce of the land, and so the grapevine in the field may not be [utterly] barren for you," Yahweh of Hosts has said.

¹²"Then all the nations will call you happy. Indeed, you yourselves shall become a land of [his] favor!" Yahweh of Hosts has said.

The literary form of *prophetic disputation* persists throughout the book of Malachi (see the discussion of literary form in the introduction to the First Oracle above). This disputation speech is more complex than the previous disputations in that the oracle begins with a compound declaration ("I have not changed . . ." and "Return to me . . .") and includes a first and second round of *refutation* ("How shall we return? // "How are we robbing you?") and *rebuttal* ("But you are robbing me . . ." // "Bring the full tithe . . ."). Watts (1987a: 376) has classified Malachi's fifth oracle as an *assertive* type of "speech act" designed to both assure and persuade the audience/reader.

The MT marks paragraph breaks at 2:16 and 3:12 with the *pārāšâ sĕtûmâ* (the *sāmek* denoting the separation of smaller literary units), making Mal 2:17–3:12

subunit B of the Pericope III according to the literary divisions identified in the MT (see I. C. 4. Structure above).

Most commentators discern further microstructure (2:17–3:5 and 3:6–12) in this literary unit (2:17–3:12) on the basis of the emphatic adverb *kî* + formula of self-introduction (*'ănî YHWH*, cf. WO'C § 39.3.1d). Disagreement exists as to the clausal function of *kî* in this context: one position identifies *kî* as a subordinating conjunction in a logical sense ("for, because"; so Glazier-McDonald [1987a: 173]; NRSV), and the other prefers an emphatic understanding of *kî* ("indeed, truly"; so Verhoef [1987: 299]; Petersen [1995: 212]; NAB).

In either case, some coordination with the preceding disputation must be recognized; as Waltke and O'Connor (§ 39.3.4e) have cautioned, the two clausal uses of *kî* "should not be too strictly separated." VanGemeren (p. 204) considers 3:6–12 (i.e., the judgment of unfaithfulness to God) the chiastic complement of 2:10–16 (i.e., the judgment of unfaithfulness in marriage), both pivoting on the fulcrum disputation of the book promising the day of Yahweh's wrath (2:17–3:5).

Some versions of the LXX and certain biblical commentators propose alternative textual divisions, reconfiguring the fifth disputation by including Mal 3:6 [and in some cases v 7] as the conclusion of the fourth disputation speech (cf. von Bulmerincq [1932: 391] for a catalog of earlier scholars holding this view including Keil [2:461–62]; Packard [1902: 21]; J.M.P. Smith [1912: 66–67]; and more recently Laetsch [1956: 538]; and Kaiser [1984: 88]). See further the discussion of *kî* in the NOTES below.

Like the other oracles of Malachi, the fifth disputation includes a rhetorical question ("Will a man rob God?", 3:8a) and pseudo-dialogue ("But you say . . . ," 3:8b). The messenger formula ("Yahweh of Hosts has said") marks three distinct subunits in the disputation: the summons to repentance (v 7ab), the indictment and challenge (vv 7c–11), and the aftermath (v 12). In addition, the oracle possesses some degree of literary microstructure and contains numerous rhetorical devices. For instance, two balanced clauses make up verse 6, verse 7 features a play on the suffix pronouns ("you . . . me // me . . . you"), and incomplete reverse parallelism or chiasm occurs in 3:8–9 (with the inversion of *'ōtî*). Wendland (p. 118) has even identified a concentric (or chiastic) pattern unifying the entire disputation:

A introduction: divine premise, v 6
    B appeal to repent, v 7
        C indictment — robbing God, v 8
            D verdict — curse, v 9a
        C' indictment — robbing God, v 9b
    B' promise of blessing, vv 10–11
A' conclusion: vision of restoration, v 12

Further, Achtemeier (1986: 172) has noted role reversal in 3:8–9 as Yahweh puts Israel on the defensive with his counteraccusations (including syntactical variation in verse 9 for emphatic effect, ". . . it's me you are robbing!"). The combination of imperative verbs directed to Israel (*šûbû, hābî'û, běhānûnî*) and the first-person perfective and imperfective verbs describing the action of Yahweh (*šānîtî, 'āšûbâ, gā'artî*) depict the essence of covenant relationship between God and his people — a mutual *turning* to each other. Finally, the presence of God portrayed in the movement of Yahweh toward his people is heightened by the use of figurative language in verse 10 (i.e., God opening windows).

The integrity of the pericope has never been seriously challenged, although Sellin (1930: 610–11) suggested that 3:6–12 be placed after 1:2–5 because "Jacob" is the subject of both disputations. More recently, Redditt (1994: 247) denies any clear connection between Mal 3:6–7 and Mal 3:8–12 (cf. Wallis [1967: 232]). He prefers instead to theorize that 3:6–7 formed the original conclusion to the first disputation (1:2–5, because both pericopes address "Jacob") but was separated and misplaced in the process of redaction (cf. NJB; see further I. C. 2. Unity and 4. Structure above).

Rebuttals have been numerous and forceful, so much so that Sellin's hypothesis is now dismissed out of hand or ignored altogether (cf. Horst [1954: 272–73]; Verhoef [1972: 214]; Rudolph [1976: 282–83]; Glazier-McDonald [1987a: 173–74]). Generally speaking, a decided shift has occurred in the scholarly appraisal of the textual integrity of Malachi's oracles since the seminal work of von Bulmerincq (1926, 1932). Nearly a quarter of von Bulmerincq's commentary on Mal 3:6–12 was given to discussion of reconstructions of the MT by Köhler, Ewald, Wellhausen, Nowack, Marti, etc. (see von Bulmerincq [1932: 391–460]). Scholarly reconstruction of the MT of Malachi is much less radical now, so much so that Deissler (p. 316) can praise the faithful transmission of the text.

The textual apparatus of *BHK* proposed thirteen emendations of the MT (v 6, v 7, v 8 [5x], v 9, v 10 [2x], v 11, v 12 [2x]). This has been modified in the *BHS* to nine separate textual divergences (v 7 [2x], v 8 [5x], and v 9 [2x]). Only a handful of these variant readings warrant careful consideration; three are conjectural emendations and the others are based primarily on the LXX (prone to "loose paraphrasing" and "verbose expansions" in Mal 3:6–12, so J.M.P. Smith [1912: 45, 68]). Interpretive problems associated with Mal 3:6–12 hinge on the relationship of this disputation to the preceding oracle (2:17–3:5), one's understanding of the particle *kî* (3:6, whether causal or emphatic), and the nature of the parallelism deduced between the two verbs of the bicolon (3:6, *šnh* and *klh*). Pertinent variations of the MT introduced by the readings of the ancient versions are addressed in the NOTES below.

The fifth disputation is directed to the restoration community at large, leaders, priests, and people (especially the evildoers!). The essential message of this penultimate oracle is repentance, not tithing. God wants honest and genuine worship from his people, of which tithing is but a symbol. The prophet's summons to penitence (3:7) is in keeping with the oracular pattern of indictment, judgment, and call to repentance, with a *return* to God as the only logical response to the preceding threat of divine judgment (2:17–3:5).

The theme of *faithless* Israel connects the third and the fifth disputations, suggesting that violations of the marriage covenant are also among the indictments Yahweh has charged against his people (3:5). This call to repentance is directly related to the thesis of the opening disputation (1:2–5), because Yahweh's invitation to recalcitrant Israel to return to him in repentance issues from his great love and compassion for his people.

The purpose of the fifth disputation is to offer hope to postexilic Yehud by emphasizing Yahweh's immutability, countering the community's charge of capriciousness on God's part. Both in judging the sin of unrepentant Israel (3:6–7) and in rewarding the penitent and restoring covenant blessings to them, Yahweh has been just and ever consistent with his holy nature (3:11–12). It is at this point that Malachi touches universal aspects of the human experience, coping with unfulfilled promises, shattered dreams, and hope deferred.

NOTES

3:6 *kî.* Commentators are divided in their understanding of the emphatic adverb *kî* (cf. WO'C § 39.3.1d). If *kî* is a coordinating conjunction introducing a causal subordinate clause (cf. WO'C § 38.4), then the particle may be translated "for, because" (so Calvin [1979: 666]; Luther [Oswald 1975: 413]; Keil [2:461]; Baldwin [1972a: 245]; R. L. Smith [1984: 330]; Glazier-McDonald [1987a: 173]; cf. LXX *dióti,* Syr *mšl'd,* T *'ry,* NRSV "for").

However, if *kî* is a clausal adverb modifying the clause in itself, then the adverb may be translated emphatically "indeed, surely, truly" (cf. WO'C § 39.3.4). Such emphatic adverbs modifying clauses related to the act of speaking are *disjuncts* (cf. WO'C § 39.3.4b). Here the issue is the content of the utterance, permitting the rendering "indeed, surely" (so NAB "surely," V *enim;* cf. von Bulmerincq [1932: 392] who regarded *kî* as an "affirmative particle" [but left it untranslated, so NEB and NIV]; Rudolph [1976: 281] and NJB = "no"; Chary [1969: 268] = "yes"; and Verhoef [1987: 299] = "truly").

Other interpretive options have been proposed, including J.M.P. Smith (1912: 66) who read *kî* as an adversative ("but") and Dentan and Sperry (p. 1139) who deleted *kî* as an "artificial connector." Here the clausal *kî* is a *disjunct,* an emphatic adverb modifying the clause in itself. Since the referent is the content of the utterance, the translation "indeed" or "surely" is preferred. The messenger formula *'āmar YHWH ṣĕbā'ôt* in 3:5 (typically used in Malachi to begin and/or conclude disputations) and the independent pronoun *'ănî,* also used emphatically with YHWH after the adverb *kî,* confirm this reading. This does not deny that some coordination may exist between the fourth and the fifth disputations. They are related in theme (judgment) and Waltke and O'Connor (§ 39.3.4e) have noted the *emphatic* use of *kî* and the *logical* (or causal) use of *kî* are not to be "strictly separated."

'ănî YHWH. The combination of the independent pronoun (*'ănî*) and the divine name (*YHWH*) constitute the self-introduction formula, a formula by which a speaker reveals personal identity to an addressee by announcing his or her name (cf. Hals [1989: 362–63]). The self-introduction formula in Mal 3:6 is

understood alternately as an appositional construction ("I, Yahweh"; e.g., Glazier-McDonald [1987a: 173]; cf. NIV, NJB, NRSV) or as a predicate construction ("I am Yahweh," e.g., Calvin [1979: 666]; Henderson [1980: 458]; R. L. Smith [1984: 330]; cf. KJV, NEB). Given the placement of the self-introduction formula after the disjunct *kî* and before the first-person suffixing conjugation form *šānîtî*, the formula is better understood as a predicate construction (cf. *kî 'ănî YHWH* in Isa 43:3; 45:3; Jer 9:23 [24]; 24:7; Ezek 6:7, 10, 13; 7:4, 9).

The phrase is related to the predicate construction *'ănî YHWH* ("I am Yahweh") used liturgically in Lev 19:3, 4, 10, 12, 14, 16, 18, 25, 28, 30, 31, 32, 33, 36, 37 as a refrain marking legal pericopes (see von Rad [1962: 1:197]; cf. Wenham [1979: 263]). The self-introduction formula introduces the prophet's next disputation. More than a vestige of priestly terminology, this formula proclaims the identity of Yahweh much like *qādôš 'ănî YHWH* in Lev 19:2 (cf. Hartley [1992: 309]). The formula also confers upon Yahweh "the authority and right . . . to make known his will" to Israel, whether by gracious redemption (Exod 20:2) or by righteous judgment (Ezek 7:5, 27; 20:42; Childs [1974: 401]).

The contrasting independent pronouns in verse 6 (*'ănî // 'attem*) constitute an example of *logical structure* with finite verbs, involving *explicit antithesis* ("Yahweh" vs. "descendants of Jacob," WO'C § 16.3.2d). The initial position of the pronoun adds emphasis to the subject of each clause (GKC § 135a). See further the discussion of *'ănî* in 1:4 above.

lō' šānîtî. The verb *šnh* means "to repeat" (e.g., 2 Sam 20:10; Prov 17:9) or "to change" (Job 14:20; Prov 31:5). The use of *šnh* in Mal 3:6 is unique to the Haggai-Zechariah-Malachi corpus; however, the word occurs elsewhere in the Prophets only in Jer 2:36 (a description of "fickle" Judah!) and Jer 52:33 (Jehoiachin's release from prison in Babylonian captivity meant a "change" of garb). The suffixing form of *šnh* here conveys both the sense of the *indefinite perfective* ("I have not changed," so Verhoef [1987: 297]; Petersen [1995: 212]) and the *instantaneous perfective* ("I do not change," so R. L. Smith [1984: 330]; cf. WO'C § 30.5.1b, d).

The prophet's affirmation that Yahweh "has not changed" should not be construed primarily as a metaphysical statement, a theological commentary on the nature of God's being. Rather, Malachi attests the faithfulness of Yahweh to his covenant agreement with Israel. God has not changed the terms of the pact, but has remained constant in his oath of loyalty. It is for this reason that Israel has not been destroyed.

Waldman (pp. 543–44) supports a similar reading of verse 6 by extending the nuance of *šnh* ("to change") to "go back on one's word" or "renege" (or even "betray") on the basis of the Akkadian *enû* (adopted by Glazier-McDonald [1987a: 179–80]). While the issue of Yahweh "reneging" on or "honoring" his word is paramount, Waldman misses the intent of the self-introduction formula. The point ultimately is the identity or character of Yahweh in which his actions and responses toward Israel are rooted, not simply the action or response itself. The real issue is not so much Yahweh reneging on his word, as it is the person of Yahweh who is incapable of any such behavior (curiously Glazier-McDonald

[1987a: 178–79] expounds on the holy character of Yahweh implicit in the self-revelation formula and then proceeds to interpret *šānîtî* restrictively in the sense of reneging on the word of his covenant).

A further word critiquing the supposed parallel between the Akkadian *enû* and Mal 3:6 is warranted. The examples of the intransitive use of *enû* cited by Waldman are limited exclusively to Akkadian legal texts referring to written contracts and documents. While I grant Waldman and Glazier-McDonald the argument of the immediate and wider covenant context of Mal 3:6 (including mention of the Yahweh's "statutes," *mēḥuqqay*, 3:7), the prophet's chief concern is Israel's *violation* of Yahweh's covenant—not the *validation* of the document (cf. Ps 89:32–33 [31–32]).

Waldman also failed to note that in Akkadian literary texts, the sense of *enû* as "going back on one's word" is more clear because the verb *enû* is always accompanied by a verb of speaking (e.g., *qabû* or *zakāru*, "to speak" or even a noun like *awātu(m)/amātu(m)*, "word"; cf. *CAD* 4:175–76). The MT adheres to this pattern in Ps 89:35 [34] where Yahweh avers, "I will not invalidate my covenant, nor alter the utterance of my mouth" (*lō'-'ăḥallēl bĕrîtî ûmôṣā' śĕpātay lō' 'ăšanneh*).

Given the clear purpose of the self-introduction formula (with emphatic adverb *kî*), the very specific legal genre of this *enû* idiom ("renege") in Akkadian, and the lack of any complementary vocabulary referring to the speech act in Mal 3:6–12 (a literary text), Waldman's proposal to equate Malachi's use of *šnh* in verse 6 with the Akkadian *enû* idiom is dubious. It seems better to rely on the context of the disputation for the understanding that Yahweh "has not changed" with respect to his unwavering commitment to his covenant, nor has he changed the terms of that agreement.

wĕ'attem. The conjunction *waw* attached to a non-verb is *disjunctive*, an interclausal *waw* of the type where the scene or action shifts (WO'C § 39.2.3a, b). The clause describes both a contrast between "Yahweh" and "the descendants of Jacob" and the relationship of logical consequence ("I am Yahweh; I have not changed. And so, you, O descendants of Jacob . . . ," so Calvin [1979: 579]; Verhoef [1987: 297]; cf. NRSV, "therefore"; NIV, "so"; and Petersen [1995: 212], "moreover").

No consensus exists here among the commentators or the versions, because some render the *waw* as a simple copulative (e.g., LXX, V, Keil [2:461]; Baldwin [1972a: 245]; cf. NEB, NJB) and others read the conjunction with the adversative "but" (e.g., Rudolph [1976: 281]; R. L. Smith [1984: 330]; Glazier-McDonald [1987a: 173]; cf. NAB, "nor"). On the use of the independent pronoun involving *logical structure* with *explicit antithesis*, see WO'C § 16.3.2d.

bĕnê-ya'ăqōb. The expression "descendants of Jacob" designates the national entity or collective community of Israelites living in postexilic Yehud, who are literally *sons* of Jacob, the eponymous ancestor of Israel (so NAB, NEB, NJB; cf. *TDOT* 2:151). The plural *bānîm* can signify individuals of both sexes (*TDOT* 2:150), hence the rendering "children" (NRSV) or "descendants" (NIV). The NIV and NRSV construe the construct-genitive phrase *bĕnê-ya'ăqōb* as a vocative construction ("O descendants of Jacob"), because it stands in apposition to the second-person pronoun (*'attem*; cf. WO'C § 8.3d). I concur with this reading despite the lack of a preceding imperative verb characteristic of vocative constructions (cf. WO'C § 4.7d). The vocative here is in keeping with the emphatic purpose of the antithetical structure of the pronouns (*'ănî* and *'attem*; cf. Rudolph [1976: 282]) and the hortatory nature of the disputation (cf. *'ăhabtem bĕnê yiśrā'ēl*, "for so you love to do, O descendants of Israel," Amos 4:5).

Redditt (1994: 248) has resurrected Sellin's (p. 588) hypothesis that Mal 3:6–7 was originally the conclusion to the first disputation, because both address "Jacob." The issue of redaction in Malachi is broached in the introduction to this disputation (III. F.) and in I. C. 2. Unity, and 4. Structure above. On the name "Jacob," see the discussion of *ya'ăqōb* in the NOTES for 1:2 and 2:12 above, as well as the NOTES on *bēn* in 1:6; 3:3 above and 3:17, 24 [4:6] below.

lō' kĕlîtem. The verbal root *klh* can mean "perish, be destroyed" or "be consumed" (*BDB*: 477–78). The verb occurs in the Haggai-Zechariah-Malachi corpus only here and Zech 5:4 ("destroy," Meyers and Meyers [1987: 287]) and in the Twelve prophets only in Hos 11:6 ("finish off," Andersen and Freedman [1980: 585–86]) and Amos 7:2 ("devour . . . entirely," Andersen and Freedman [1989: xxxvii]). Malachi equates *klh* with divine judgment much like Zech 5:4, the wicked totally "consumed" (NRSV) or "destroyed" (NIV) by God's just wrath (cf. Ezek 22:31). Perhaps Malachi had in mind those earlier oracles announcing both Yahweh's intent to "finish off" Israel (*klh*, Isa 1:28; Jer 5:3; 16:4; Ezek 5:13; 6:12; 7:8; etc.) and Yahweh's reluctance to actually act so for the sake of his name (*klh*, Ezek 20:13; see vv 13–17). Indeed, Yahweh had not changed his posture toward Israel. Whether he judged their sin and preserved a remnant (Ezek 5:12–13) or threatened to judge them but relented (Exod 32:12; see v 14), Israel continued to exist as a sociopolitical entity and remained the people of God in Malachi's day. What greater demonstration of Yahweh's faithfulness to his covenant could the prophet offer?

The verb *klh* can also mean "to cease" or "to come to an end" (*BDB*: 477), permitting the alternative translation "nor do you cease to be sons of Jacob" (NAB; so NEB). This reading downplays *'attem* and *bĕnê-ya'ăqōb* as appositives and emphasizes the pun on the name "Jacob" with the verb *qb'* "to cheat" in a predicate construction (cf. Chary [1969: 268–69]; Mason [1977: 155]; and Deissler [1988: 332]; the LXX *pternízete* ["heel" or "cheat"] = Hebrew *'ōqĕbîm* from *'qb*). Still others have retained the appositive structure of *'attem bĕnê-yā'ăqōb* but read *klytm* (whether Qal stem or repointed as a Piel or Pual stem) as "cease, come to an end" with an implied object in keeping with the "lawbreaking" mentioned in verse 7 (see Glazier-McDonald's [1987a: 175–77] discussion of van Hoonacker; cf. Rudolph [1976: 282] and CHAL: 158, "do not come to an end = remain the same").

Emphasizing direct coordination between the fourth dispute (2:17–3:5) and the fifth disputation (3:6–12), J.M.P. Smith (1912: 68) understood *lō'* as emphatic *lā* and translated "you will *surely* be destroyed." However, Glazier-McDonald's (1987a: 177) criticism is apt here, in that such a reading makes the call to repentance in the fifth disputation meaningless. I am inclined to agree with Verhoef (1987: 300) who opted to render *klh* in verse 6 with "destroy" in-

stead of "cease" or "come to an end" because "the translation . . . stresses the fact
of God's unchangeableness as the reason for Israel's continued existence." Quite
apart from either translation (i.e., an explicit understanding of Israel as a perpetual covenant violator deserving judgment or an implicit understanding of Israel
as "unceasing cheats"), Baldwin's (1972a: 245) concession remains cogent: "The
fact is that neither God nor Israel had changed."

The symmetry of the bicolon in verse 6 and the LXX rendering of the MT
kĕlîtem with a form of the verb apéchō ("abstain, avoid" in middle voice instead
of the expected suntelḗō; cf. Zech 5:4, wĕkillattô // kaì suntelései) has spawned
numerous alternative (and sometimes inferior) translations of the MT of Mal
3:6b. The conjectured lî kullĕkem ("you sons of Jacob, you all belong to me") of the
BHK has been dismissed by J.M.P. Smith (1912: 69) and properly deleted from the
textual apparatus of the BHS. The difficulty of coordinating the verbs šnh and klh
in a parallel construction is especially manifest in the ancient versions.

The LXXB combines verse 6b with the first two words of verse 7a and paraphrases kaì humeîs hoí huioì lakòb, oùk apéchesthē apò tōn adikiōn tōn patérōn
humōn ("and you, sons of Jacob, have not abstained from the sins of your fathers"). The Syr deviates from the influence of the LXX ("you have not departed
from your injury," Kruse-Blinkenberg [1966: 104–5]); and T makes šnh transitive
by adding a direct object ("For I, Yahweh, have not changed my ancient covenant") and verse 6b introduces a pious expansion about those who believe divine
judgment is confined to life in this world (a jibe at Sadducean doctrine?; see the
discussion in Gordon [1994: 58–61]). Only the V renders verse 6 in a literal
fashion.

7. lĕmîmê 'ăbōtêkem. This construction combining the compound prepositions lamed and min + yôm is unique to 2 Kgs 19:25 and Mal 3:7 in the MT.
The temporal lamed and the locational min denote a terminus a quo, a point in
time when Israel began drifting away from a specified beginning point (WO'C §
11.2.10c, 11.2.11; cf. Verhoef [1987: 300]). The construct-genitive lĕmîmê with
'ăbōtêkem identifies this point in time as literally "from the days of your forefathers [or ancestors]" ("ever since," NIV, NJB, NRSV; "since," NAB).

Though deliberately ambiguous, the expression may refer more immediately
to the generation of the Babylonian Exile (cf. mîmê 'ăbōtênû, Ezra 9:7; J.M.P.
Smith [1912: 66] argued this position). More likely, given Malachi's penchant
for Deuteronomistic language, the reference is to that generation of Hebrews
who came out of Egypt but of whom God swore "they will not enter my rest" (Ps
95:11; cf. Deut 1:34; cf. Glazier-McDonald [1987a: 181–82] who reached a similar conclusion on the basis of Malachi's condemnation of intermarriage in the
third disputation [2:10–16] and Israel's apostasy at Baal of Peor [Num 25:18]).

sartem mēḥuqqay. Malachi uses the verb swr twice: once of the priests who
have "swerved" from the way of Yahweh (2:8), and again here of the community
that has "turned away" from Yahweh's covenant legislation. The one is simply a
natural consequence of the other, "misteaching" on the part of the priests encouraging covenant "misbehavior" on the part of the people. The root swr ("turn
aside") occurs elsewhere in the Haggai-Zechariah-Malachi corpus only in Zech
3:4 (where the angel of Yahweh removes the filthy garments from Joshua and

clothes him in clean apparel as a symbol of repentance and cleansing), Zech 9:7 (dealing with the reformation of Ashkelon and Gaza), and 10:11 (the *removal* of Egyptian political influence from the restored Yehud). The warnings of Deuteronomy against "turning away" (*swr*) from Yahweh share the context of the snare of idolatry (e.g., Deut 9:12, 16; 11:16, 28; 31:29). Perhaps this explains why the postexilic Israelites pleaded ignorance of the prophet's call to repentance, for they were not culpable of this kind of blatant religious apostasy. This combination of *swr* and *šmr* may well be another Deuteronomic convention (cf. Deut 17:19; 2 Kgs 18:6).

Given the distribution of the verb *swr* in covenant contexts, the word as used in Mal 3:7 connotes an attitude of rebellion and mutiny (Jer 6:28; Hos 7:14; cf. Andersen and Freedman [1980: 475–76]), willful rejection of divine instruction (Dan 9:5, 11), and deeds of apostasy and social injustice in violation of revealed covenant stipulations (Josh 23:6; Ps 14:3). Conversely, to turn aside (*swr*) from evil is basic to the way of godly wisdom and leads to the knowledge of God (Job 28:28; Prov 3:7; 16:6, 17). This is the first step toward genuine repentance (Jer 18:11; cf. Andersen and Freedman [1980: 134–35] on *swr*).

The suffixing forms *sartem* (and *šĕmartem* below) represent the *persistent perfective*, addressing a single situation that started in the past but continues until the present time (cf. WO'C § 30.5.1c). Malachi singles out this insidious covenant rebellion as the root cause of Israel's estrangement from Yahweh.

mēḥuqqay. The *ablative* sense of the preposition *min* designates movement "away from" a specified beginning point (i.e., "away from my statutes," cf. WO'C § 11.2.11b, d). The postexilic community has departed from the path marked out by Yahweh's statutes, choosing instead to follow another route demarcated by other statutes or none at all.

I disagree with Ringgren who understood *ḥōq* in Mal 3:7 and 22 [4:4] as a term for a "cultic regulation" (*TDOT* 5:146). Unlike the specialized meanings attributed to *ḥōq* in the so-called P strand of the Pentateuch (see *TDOT* 5:144), Malachi's use of the term in 3:7 and 3:22 [4:4] more closely approximates that of Deuteronomy and Deuteronomistic history. In this case, the legal terms like *ḥōq*, *mišpāṭ*, and *miṣwâ* have lost their technical meanings and are used to denote the law of Moses as a whole (cf. *TDOT* 5:145). This understanding of *ḥōq* in the more general sense of "torah" is supported by the legal context of the fourth disputation (as Malachi's indictment broadly cites both cultic regulations and issues of social justice, 3:4–5). The elliptical use of *ḥuqqay* as the implicit direct object of *šmr* in verse 7 (naming no specific cultic violation, but holding postexilic Yehud in contempt of covenant legislation in its totality) also supports this conclusion. Petersen (1995: 214) equates "statutes" (*ḥuqqay*) in Malachi with the covenant stipulations, whereas in Zechariah the word refers primarily to judgment — the covenant curses. Though influenced by the exilic prophet Ezekiel, the postexilic prophets favor the masculine form of the substantive (*ḥōq/ḥuqqîm*) in contrast to the prominence of the feminine form (*ḥuqqâ/ḥuqqôt*, 22x) in Ezekiel (Zech 1:6; Mal 3:7, 22 [4:4]; cf. *TDOT* 5:145–46).

Unlike the predilection of Deuteronomy for the third-person possessive pronoun "his statutes" (*ḥuqqāyw*, 4:40; 26:17; etc.), Malachi (like Ezekiel) prefers the first-person possessive pronoun "my statutes" (cf. Ezek 11:12; 36:27). The choice of the first-person possessive pronoun in these oracular texts may emphasize the divine authority vested in the law of Moses. R. L. Smith (1984: 330) separates (without explanation) *mēḥuqqay* from *ṡartem* and reads the word as the object of *šmr* in the second clause ("From the days of your fathers you have turned aside. My statutes you have not kept."). See further the discussion of *ḥōq* in 3:22 [4:4] below.

wĕlō' šĕmartem. The copulative construction *waw* + suffix conjugation after another suffixing form here serves in a hendiadys, representing two aspects of a complex situation (i.e., "rejecting" and "disobeying" God's statutes, cf. WO'C § 32.3b).

The verb *šmr* may mean "to watch, guard, observe, keep, etc." (*CHAL:* 377). Given the implied object *ḥuqqay* ("my statutes"), the verb *šmr* in this context means "keep" (so NAB, NEB, NIV, NRSV) or "observe" (so NJB) in the sense of a behavioral pattern of compliance or obedience to the word of God (cf. Ezek 11:12, *bĕḥuqqay lō' hălaktem ûmišpāṭay lō' 'ăśîtem*, "in my statutes you have not walked and my ordinances you have left undone"). The promise of divine blessing by the angel of Yahweh to the high priest Joshua contingent upon "keeping" God's requirements marks the only other place in the Haggai-Zechariah-Malachi corpus where *šmr* is associated with Israel's covenant obligations (*mišmartî tišmôr*, Zech 3:7; cf. *šmr* in 3:7b; 11:11).

The charge to "keep" or "observe" (*šmr*) the "commandments" (*miṣwôt*) and "statutes" (*ḥuqqîm*) of Yahweh pervades the book of Deuteronomy (more than 50 times). Curiously, the combination of *šmr* + the (feminine) accusative *ḥuqqôt* is more prevalent in Leviticus (18:4, 5, 26; 19:19, 37; 20:8, 22; cf. Deut 6:2; 11:1) than *šmr* + *ḥuqqîm* in Deut (4:40; 11:32; 16:12; 26:17; the pattern of Mal 3:22 as well).

The prophetic indictment of Israel for the failure to observe God's statutes and the exhortation to keep the divine ordinances are characteristic of Jeremiah and Ezekiel, more so than of Isaiah or the Twelve (e.g., Jer 16:11; 35:18; Ezek 11:20; 18:9, 19, 21; 36:27). One notable exception is Amos's indictment of Judah (a contested passage), "his statutes they failed to observe" (*wĕḥuqqāyw lō' šāmārû*, 2:4; cf. Andersen and Freedman [1989: 294, 306]). Ezekiel envisioned a time when the Davidic "servant" would instill obedience to the statutes of Yahweh in the "restored" Israel (*wĕḥuqqôtay yišmĕrû*, 37:24).

Both BHK and BHS propose inserting the cognate accusative *mišmartî* for the missing object after *šmr* (on the basis of Mal 3:14, *šāmarnû mišmartô*; cf. Zech 3:7). Others like Wellhausen (p. 210), J.M.P. Smith (1912: 74), and von Bulmer-incq (1932: 409) repointed the MT to account for the lacking direct object (*šĕmartum*, "you failed to keep *them*"; cf. Verhoef [1987: 301]). Glazier-McDonald (1987a: 182) has argued that this repointing of *šmr* is superfluous because *ḥuqqay* may serve as the gapped object of *šmr* as well (i.e., an example of *ellipsis* because the missing grammatical structure can be recovered from context, cf. WO'C § 11.4.3d). Similar examples of such gapping have been observed elsewhere in the disputations of Malachi (e.g., 1:3). The technique both reflects the dialogical nature of the oracles and the deliberate attempt to retain audience interest. See further the discussion of *šmr* in 2:7, 9, 15, and 16 above.

šûbû ʾēlay. The imperative form of the verb *šwb* conveys a sense of urgency, and places a demand for immediate and specific action upon the addressee (WO'C § 34.4). Holladay (1958: 185) included Mal 3:7 among the 164 instances of "covenantal" *šwb* in the OT/HB. By covenantal usage, Holladay (1958: 116) meant a passage expressing "a change of loyalty on the part of Israel or God, each for the other" (usually understood as "repentance" [Andersen and Freedman 1980: 645] or "a total reorientation toward Yahweh" [Wolff 1977: 49]). However, Holladay (1958: 120) insisted that the covenant usage of *šwb* was predicated upon the assumptions of Yahweh's covenant with Israel.

Basic to the idea of covenant was the initiative of Yahweh in establishing the treaty bond with Israel's ancestors (e.g., Judg 2:20). Therefore *šwb* here means "turn back to God (to whom one has a prior obligation"), thus reestablishing a former relationship (Holladay [1958: 120]).

The message of repentance was foundational to prophetic ministry (e.g., Isa 31:6; Hos 6:1), especially with the later prophets like Jeremiah (cf. 3:14, 22; 18:11; 25:5; 35:15) and Ezekiel (cf. 14:6; 18:30; 33:11; on the call to repentance supplanting the announcement of judgment in the transition of the prophetic-judgment speech to salvation oracle, see Westermann [1991: 205–6]). In addition, the "repentance" (*šwb*) motif, rooted in the "contingency" or "non-finality" of Yahweh's wrath (cf. Heschel [2:65]), lies at the core of Deuteronomistic histo-riography and theology (Deut 4:25–31; cf. von Rad [1966: 50]; Glazier-McDonald [1987a: 183]).

Holladay (1958: 118–19) explored the interesting bifurcation of *šwb* into two opposite meanings ("repent" and "become apostate"), concluding that the verb is a "kind of two-edged sword, cutting either way, depending upon one's point of view" (cf. Jer 4:1; Ezek 33:18). Andersen and Freedman (1980: 584–85) ob-served, however, that "turning" (*šwb*) from God in "willful and persistent viola-tion of his covenant is not the ultimate, unpardonable sin." God had proved his willingness to forgive and restore Israel to covenant fellowship should they turn to him in repentance. Rather, "refusal to repent was the ultimate sin"; and the restoration community was in danger of committing this unpardonable transgres-sion (Andersen and Freedman [1980: 585]). By way of macrostructure in the Twelve, it is interesting to note that in most manuscripts the collection begins with a call to repentance (Hos 14:2–3 [1–2]) and ends with the same prophetic appeal (Zech 1:3; Mal 3:7).

The preposition *ʾel* marks the direction of Israel's "turning" (WO'C § 11.2.2a). The verb *šwb* is one of motion and this is true for the word when it means "re-pent" in covenant contexts as well. True repentance involves "turning away from" evil and wrongdoing (Jer 25:5; Ezek 33:11) and "turning to" Yahweh (Isa 44:22; Hos 14:2–3). According to Andersen and Freedman (1980: 645) Israel's return from Babylonian captivity was symbolic of repentance. Perhaps the first-person possessive pronoun attached to the preposition was intended to correct Israel's misconception of the symbol. No magical or mechanistic relationship existed between Israel's habitation (and/or possession) of the land of covenant promise and the blessings of Yahweh's covenant. Yahweh's covenant still entailed a relationship between a people and their God — not a people and the land or Temple liturgy. "Return to *me*," says Yahweh through Malachi.

wĕ'āšûbâ 'ălêkem. The balanced bicolon *šûbû 'ēlay wĕ'āšûbâ 'ălêkem* inverts the pronouns ("you . . . me" // "I . . . you") and *šwb* "stands in parallelism with itself" (Holladay [1958: 51]; also true in Zech 1:3; Pss 68:23; 71:20; Eccl 12:7). Malachi's repetition of this call to repentance found in Zech 1:3 (minus one messenger formula) established continuity with the message of repentance enunciated by Haggai (1:12–14) and Zechariah (1:3–6; 7:8–11; 8:16–17; cf. Petersen [1995: 214]) and promoted the anticipation of the return of Yahweh's presence to the restoration community in the form of material blessings (Isa 8:3; Mal 3:10–12; cf. the discussion of *šwb* in Meyers and Meyers [1987: 93–94]; and Raitt [1971: 39]). According to Holladay (1958: 141), the couplet "Return to me, and I will return to you" advances "a plain statement of mutuality within covenant" (cf. *šûbû 'el-YHWH . . . wĕyāšōb 'el-happĕlêṭâ hanniš'eret,* 2 Chr 30:6).

The cohortative *'āšûbâ* has the nuance of purpose or result in the dependent clause ("*so that* I may return . . ." or "*then* I will return . . . ," WO'C 34.5.2). The return of Yahweh to Yehud is conditional, predicated by the prior return of Yehud to Yahweh (NEB, "If you will return to me, I will return to you . . ."; cf. JM § 116b). The disjunctive-*waw* contributes to the conditional relationship of *šûbû* + *'āšûbâ*, by shifting the scene to a "new participant" (WO'C § 39.2.3c).

Malachi's citation of Zech 1:3 suggests that the prophet recognized there was still an "imbalance" between the actions of the people and Yahweh's response (cf. Meyers and Meyers [1987: 123]). Israel had indeed returned to the land, but the tangible benefits of covenant relationship with Yahweh had not materialized, suggesting that the fault lay in Yahweh's failure to return to his people (cf. Mal 3:14–15).

The directional preposition *'el* + the plural second-person pronoun suffix underscore the reciprocity of covenant relationship (cf. *šûbâ 'ēlay,* Isa 44:22; *šûbû 'āday,* Joel 2:12). A change of heart in the restoration community will prompt a similar response in Yahweh as Israel's loving Father (Mal 1:2; 2:10; cf. Deut 7:12–13; Ps 89:34–35 [33–34]; Ezek 34:29–31; Joel 2:18–19). Raitt (p. 39) identifies Mal 3:7 as a Summons to Repentance, a distinct but subordinate element within a larger linguistic unit (although Raitt [p. 36] has overstated the "cultic accent" on optimism in Malachi's disputation, because the threat of judgment that characterizes the preexilic Summons to Repentance stands intact and precedes the Summons [cf. 3:5]).

The LXX translates *šwb* consistently in Zech 1:3 and Mal 3:7 with forms of *epistréphō,* whereas the V renders *converto* in Zech 1:3 and *reverto* in Mal 3:7.

'āmar YHWH ṣĕbā'ôt. See the discussion of this messenger formula in 1:4 above and verse 12 below. Petersen (1995: 213) notes that 4QXIIc reads YHWH *'ĕlōhîm.*

wa'ămartem bammeh nāšûb. On the reported speech formula introducing the audience's refutation of the prophet's words, see the discussion of *wa'ămartem bammâ 'ăhabtānû* in 1:2 above.

The more literal rendering of *bammeh* illuminates the verb *nāšûb* here (see also the discussion of *bammâ ʾăhabtānû* in the NOTES for 1:2 above). Malachi's audience essentially responds, "In respect to what (thing) shall we repent?" The restoration community protests innocence of any wrongdoing, assuming that their participation in the sacrificial rituals of the Temple liturgy sufficiently accounted for any guilt incurred as a result of chance misdeed (Mal 3:4; cf. Glazier-McDonald [1987a: 187] on Israel's habitual self-deception through "religiosity"). Holladay (1958: 141) quips, "This is the first time this question has been asked!"

On *šwb*, see further the discussion of the term in 2:6 above and 3:24 [4:6] below.

8. *hăyiqbaʿ*. The *hē'*-interrogative marks a polar question and functions rhetorically (WO'C § 40.3; cf. § 18.1c). The *hē'*-interrogative occurs in Mal 1:2, 8 [2x], 9, 13; 2:10 [2x]; and 3:8. See further the pertinent NOTES above.

The Qal prefixing form *yiqbaʿ* denotes the *nonperfective of desire* (i.e., expressing wish, desire, or possibility; WO'C § 31.4h). The verbal root *qbʿ* occurs in the MT only in Mal 3:8 [3x], 9 (LXX = *pternízō*) and Prov 22:23 [2x] (LXX deviates from the MT; cf. Scott [1965: 138] who read *qbʿ* ["rob"] in Prov 22:23 on the basis of Egyptian parallels), where the word is used in synonymous parallelism with *gzl* ("to take by force, rob," CHAL: 58). Both the BHK and BHS appeal to the LXX *ei pterniei* and read *hāyâʿăqōb* ("cheat, swindle, defraud"), understanding wordplay on the root *qbʿ* with the name *yaʿăqōb* ("Jacob") in verse 6 (so Wellhausen [1963: 210], Nowack [1922: 426], Marti [1904: 475], Sellin [1930: 612], von Bulmerincq [1932: 415], Chary [1969: 268], Mason [1977: 155], Deissler [1988: 333], NEB, NJB; cf. Gen 25:26; 27:36). Admittedly, the LXX consistently renders *ʿqb* with *pternízō* (prompting Holladay to suggest that *qbʿ* represents deliberate metathesis with *ʿqb* to avoid assonance, CHAL: 311).

However, one may legitimately ask whether the literary device of wordplay drives the textual emendation or whether overwhelming textual evidence necessitates emendation of the text. Three recensions of the LXX (α, σ, θ all read the verb *apostéreō*, "to rob, despoil"), V (*affigere*, "to injure, damage, ill-treat"), and Syr (*tlm*, "defraud") all support the MT *qbʿ* (suggesting that the ancient versions may reflect two text traditions, one reading *qbʿ* and the other *ʿqb*). The T *rgz* ("to anger") is ambiguous.

The MT has the advantage of being the more difficult reading (*lectio difficilior*), while the LXX *pternízō* may reflect the Hellenistic tendency toward typology (cf. Fishbane [1985: 412–13]). Glazier-McDonald (1987a: 188) has also noted that the force of the pun is diminished by the interruption of verse 7 and that neither is Malachi given to paronomasia. It is even possible that the deliberate use of *qbʿ* marks a type of "indirect" wordplay, in which the prophet teases the audience to ponder the implications of the combination *hăyiqbaʿ* + *qōbĕʿîm* with the earlier citation of *yaʿăqōb*. This would be more in keeping with a dialogical style intended to draw the audience ever more subtly and deeply into the thesis of the discourse.

I side with those affirming the correctness of the MT *qbʿ* and agreeing with Baldwin (1972a: 246) that the MT "has the advantage of a bluntness that rings true, and should be retained" (Rudolph [1976: 282]; R. L. Smith [1984: 331];

Verhoef [1987: 302–3]; Glazier-McDonald [1987a: 187–88]; so NAB, NIV, NRSV). Although it should be noted that a decisive judgment is not easily rendered and in the final analysis does not yield a significant difference in one's understanding of the text. The restoration community has been negligent with respect to payment of the tithe.

'ādām. The word meaning "man" or "mankind, humanity" occurs only here in Malachi, but elsewhere in the Haggai-Zechariah-Malachi corpus in Hag 1:11; Zech 2:8 [4]; 8:10 [2x]; 9:1; 11:6; 12:1; and 13:5 (although Maass has recommended emending 'ādām in Zech 9:1 and 13:5; cf. TDOT 1:82). Malachi uses the nonconventional collective 'ādām indefinitely to express the pronominal idea "someone, anyone" (WO'C § 7.2.1d; GKC § 139d; cf. hāya 'ăšeh-lō' 'ādām 'ĕlōhîm, "Will anyone craft gods for himself?" in Jer 16:20). The substantive 'ādām is a collective singular designating a class or a group (in this case "people, humankind").

'ĕlōhîm. Technically, 'ĕlōhîm is an epicene noun (i.e., "nouns used for a male or female animate," WO'C § 6.5.2). However, Waltke and O'Connor are quick to note that 'ĕlōhîm (and other grammatical forms for God) are masculine given the androcentric worldview of the HB (§ 6.5.3). I concur with their conclusion that "one cannot change or remove the masculine figurative representations of God without distorting the text of the Bible" (WO'C § 6.5.3b). Hence, I have retained "the prior gender" for God where appropriate in the translation of Malachi (cf. Achtemeier's [1988] sensitive and reasoned refutation of the feminist reading of 'ĕlōhîm in the Bible).

The divine name 'ĕlōhîm occurs in Mal 2:15; 3:8, 14, 15, 18, while the (disputed) construct 'ĕlōhê yiśrā'ēl and the construct 'ĕlōhê hammišpāṭ are found in 2:16 and 2:17 respectively. The epithet 'ĕlōhîm occurs only in combination with YHWH in Haggai (2:12 [2x], 14), while Zechariah utilizes the name both as a freestanding appellative and in combination with YHWH (Zech 6:15; 8:8, 23; 9:7, 16; 10:6; 11:4; 12:5, 8; 13:9; 14:5). Neither Haggai nor Zechariah employs the construct 'ĕlōhê (cf. Meyers and Meyers [1987: 442]; [1993: 115–16, 248–49, 296, 324, 331]). See further the discussion of 'ĕlōhîm in TDOT 1:267–84.

Grammatically, the noun 'ĕlōhîm is classified as a unique appellative and is used for the Hebrew deity Yahweh in an honorific or superlative sense (WO'C § 7.4.3b, 14.4b; more traditionally understood as the "plural of majesty," GKC § 124g). Implicit in Malachi's use of 'ĕlōhîm here is the sense of "God not man," "God of creation," and the "God of Israel" (cf. TDOT 1:273–82). The combination of 'ādām + 'ĕlōhîm in the first clause of the couplet in verse 8a elicits theological connotations of Yahweh's sovereignty as Israel's creator and suzerain and Israel's dependence and subservience to God as creature and vassal (cf. TDOT 1:83–87). The use of such theologically "loaded" terminology only serves to heighten the foolishness of engaging in the activity posed by the prophet's rhetorical question, "Will anyone rob God?"

kî. The adverb kî introduces an emphatic clause, dictating the translation "indeed" or "surely" after the rhetorical question of the preceding clause (WO'C § 39.3.4e; almost the nuance of an exclamation of immediacy with participles, cf. § 40.2.1b). The logical antithesis between the two clauses permits understanding *kî* in an adversative sense, "but" or "yet" (so NAB, NIV, NJB, NRSV; cf. Verhoef [1987: 303]). The NEB construes *kî* as a conjunction introducing a logical subordinate clause ("*that* you defraud . . ."; cf. the causal *dióti* of the LXX and *quia* of V). Both the content (ritual tithe) and the format (rhetorical question followed by declaration) of the disputation favor reading *kî* emphatically.

'*attem*. The independent pronoun has already been used to identify the people of postexilic Yehud in verse 6 above. Here '*attem* has a nominal function in relationship to the predicate participle *qōbĕ'îm* in the clause (WO'C § 37.6a). The emphatic force of the personal pronoun '*attem* ("you") has been retained throughout the translation. See further the NOTES on the use of '*attem* elsewhere in Mal 1:5, 12; 2:8; 3:1 [2x], 6, 9 [2x], 12.

qōbĕ'îm. The Qal participle refers to an ongoing state of affairs in present time, "you *continue* to rob me!" or "you are *still* robbing me!" (WO'C § 37.6d, e). After the pattern of *yiqba'* in verse 8 above, the BHK and the BHS propose '*ōqĕbîm* on the strength of the LXX *pternízete*. See further the discussion of *yiqba'* above. Though not prefaced by *hinnēh*, the emphatic *kî* serves to give the clause nearly the same force as the *exclamation of immediacy* ("*even now* you are robbing me!"; cf. WO'C § 40.2.1a).

'*ōtî*. Here the sign of the definite direct object ('*ēt*) with pronominal suffix marks the direct object (WO'C § 10.2.1c; with participle, cf. § 37.3b). The pronouns of the second clause move the discussion of the first clause from the indefinite (*anyone*) and generic (*God*) to the definite (*you* — postexilic Yehud) and the specific (*me* — i.e., Yahweh).

wa'ămartem bammeh. On the reported speech formula + the interrogative marker introducing an exclamatory question see the NOTES discussing this phrase in 1:2 and 3:7.

qĕba'ănûkā. The suffixing form here is a *recent perfective*, rendered as a simple past tense in English by use of the auxiliary verb "has/have" (WO'C § 30.5.1b). The context of the fifth disputation makes it clear that postexilic Yehud had interest only in the "here and now" (3:10–12). Again, BHK and BHS have proposed emending the MT to '*ăqabnûkā* on the basis of the LXX *epterníkamén se* to maintain the wordplay in verses 8–9 with *ya'ăqōb* in verse 6. See the discussion of *qb'* and '*qb* under *hăyiqba'* above.

hamma'ăśēr wĕhattĕrûmâ. The noun *ma'ăśēr* is unique to Malachi in the Haggai-Zechariah-Malachi corpus (only 3:8, 10) and denotes a "tithe" (2 Chr 31:5–6; Neh 12:44) or a "tenth-part" (Ezek 45:11, 14). The term belongs primarily to the technical vocabulary of Hebrew religious practice, a part of pentateuchal legislation prescribing appropriate offerings to Yahweh (Deut 12:6, 11, 17; 26:12; cf. the tithe of Abram to Melchizedek, Gen 14:20). The tradition of Jacob's dream at Bethel is generally understood to represent the origin of Israelite tithing to God (Gen 28:18–22 [E]; cf. von Rad [1961: 281]; ABD 6:579). According to Westermann (1987: 202), the reference is to the tithe of the harvest, a conditional levy of 10 percent imposed on the increase of produce (not capital).

The tithe was an offering presented to Yahweh as an act of worship acknowledging him as the Lord of the earth and the provider for Israel. The Torah required three tithes of Israel: the general tithe of the land given to the Levites (Lev

27:30–32; Num 18:21), the eating of a portion of the tithe in conjunction with the sacred meal consecrating the payment of the general tithe (Deut 14:23; cf. vv 22–27), and the tithe collected every three years for the poor (Deut 14:28–29; see Jagersma). According to Mayes (1979: 244–46), the Deuteronomic editor gives an "old" tithing law (Gen 28:22; Amos 4:4) a new context and a new meaning in Deut 14:22–29. The new context is the centralization of worship to a single sanctuary, and the new meaning is the humanitarian proviso of the Deuteronomic legislation (Deut 14:22–29). Levine (p. 450–51) understands the tithing law of Num 18:21 as the culmination of a long legal process resulting in the institutionalization of the Temple tax and the more careful specification of the recipients of that tax (namely, the priests in contradistinction to the Levites).

The context of the fifth disputation indicates that the prophet has the general tithe in mind, while the indictment of the fourth disputation intimates that the tithe for the poor may also be at issue (3:5; cf. Petersen [1995: 216]). Elsewhere in the Twelve Prophets the word appears only in Amos 4:4, but there the "tithes" are "special offerings promised on the eve of some hazardous enterprise or in a crisis" (Andersen and Freedman [1989: 430]).

těrûmâ. Like *ma'ăśēr*, this word is a liturgical term predominate in the legislation of the Pentateuch and the Temple vision of Ezekiel (58x of 71x). This term is also unique to the Haggai-Zechariah-Malachi corpus here in Mal 3:8. The word *těrûmâ* signifies a contribution, gift, or offering to Yahweh or his cult (Exod 25:2–3, Num 5:9; 31:29). This offering may be voluntary (Deut 12:6) or mandatory (Exod 29:27–28).

The two terms (*ma'ăśēr wětěrûmâ*) are paired in Deut 12:6, 11; 2 Chr 31:12 (note here the relationship between payment of the tithe and a surplus of foodstuffs); and Mal 3:8. If the worship scenario of Deut 12:6 and 11 has prompted Malachi's call for resumption of tithes and offerings, the *těrûmâ* here should also be understood in a general or representative sense (cf. Redditt [1995: 179]). In addition to the produce offerings of the land connoted by *ma'ăśēr*, *těrûmâ* extends the notion of offering to include gifts of material goods (e.g., construction supplies, garments), valuables (e.g., gold, silver, precious stones), personal services, booty, etc. (BDB: 929).

Glazier-McDonald's (1987a: 189) rendering of *těrûmâ* as "levy" assumes that Mal 3:8 refers to the "tithe of the tithe" or tithe tax prescribed in Num 18:26 and mentioned in Neh 10:38 (NJB "dues"; although her analysis is based on G. R. Driver's [1956] erroneous identification of the Hebrew word with the Akkadian *tarāmu*. See Milgrom [1991: 415] on the Akkadian *rêmu* and *tarīmtu* as cognates for *těrûmâ*). Petersen (1995: 216) also understands the phrase *ma'ăśēr wětěrûmâ* as the "general tithe" collected in regional storehouses and the "tithe tax" sent to Jerusalem to provision Yahweh's Temple (cf. J.M.P. Smith [1912: 74]). If the prophet's call for the reinstitution of the tithe is motivated by the stipulations of the so-called priestly source, then Malachi may have in mind the general tithe and the tithe tax. The context of Mal 3:8–10 and the appeal for the "full tithe" in verse 10 suggest the latter is the case.

The elliptical nature of the final verbless clause of verse 8 has prompted numerous textual emendations and exegetical interpolations. For instance, the LXX inserts *meth humôn eisin* and interprets "the tithes and offerings *are still with you*" (so von Bulmerincq [1932: 417]; R. L. Smith [1984: 301]), while Syr, T, and V all substitute the preposition *bêt* for the *hē'* of the definite article and read "*in* the tithes and offerings" (Calvin [1979: 666]; Luther [Owald 1975: 414]; Rudolph [1976: 281]; Verhoef [1987: 303]; Glazier-McDonald [1987a: 173]; so NAB, NEB, NIV, NJB, but NRSV "*in your* tithes and offerings"). I have opted to read the MT elliptically and emphatically; by virtue of its literary form the disputation tends toward ellipsis and prefers exclamation (governed by the emphatic adverb *kî*).

9. *bammě'ērâ 'attem nē'ārîm//'ōtî 'attem qōbě'îm.* The syntactical symmetry of the bicolon (object/pronoun subject/predicate participle) signals the currency of the community's plight. The nightmare of divine judgment is being played out even *now* in postexilic Yehud (cf. Petersen [1995: 212], "you are now being afflicted with a curse"). The emphatic position of the accusative in each clause calls attention to Yahweh as the God of "covenant curses" and the victim of "covenant crimes."

nē'ārîm. The verb '*rr* means "to bind with a curse" (KBL 1:91), although Speiser (1964: 24) has noted the difficulties with the translation "curse" (cf. JM § 82i on *nē'ārîm* as an Aramaising form). Elsewhere he has proposed that the basic meaning of '*rr* is "to restrain (by magic), bind (by a spell)" (cf. Speiser [1960]), preferring the rendering "to hold off, ban." Such a translation is awkward in Mal 3:9, so I have retained the traditional "curse" (recognizing the inadequacies of this understanding for the Hebrew '*rr*).

The verbal root '*rr* occurs in the Twelve only in Mal 1:14; 2:2; and 3:9 (see pertinent NOTES above). The Niphal participle functions as the predicate in the clause and describes an ongoing state of affairs ("you are being cursed"; cf. WO'C § 37.6c). The construction *bammě'ērâ . . . nē'ārîm* is an *internal* cognate accusative ("with the curse you are being cursed," cf. WO'C § 10.2.1g) and may be translated emphatically ("you are greatly cursed," so Verhoef [1987: 305]; cf. GKC § 117q).

bammě'ērâ. This substantive occurs in the MT only in Deut 28:20, 27; Prov 3:33; and Mal 2:2; and 3:9. Here *mē'ērâ* means "a misfortune which has already struck, and not in the sense of a curse formula or a word of curse" (*TDOT* 1:413). The noun is definite, but the cognate accusative is usually anarthrous (WO'C § 10.2.1g). I understand Malachi to be equating the experience of the postexilic community with "the curse," the covenant curses attached to the stipulations of the Mosaic treaty (Deut 28:15–57, especially v 45). Such a connection accords with the covenant theme of the prophet's message and accents the urgency of his call to repentance and covenant renewal in this disputation (cf. LXX *ápoblépontes . . . apoblépete*, "surely you have looked away"; and V *in penuria . . . maledicti*, "with want you are cursed"). According to Petersen (1995: 213), the reading of 4QXIIa (*wmr'ym 'tm r'ym*) may lie behind the LXX, but he prefers the MT as the more difficult reading.

The preposition *bêt* ("with") marks a (nonanimate) *instrumental* circumstance (WO'C § 11.2.5d). See also the NOTES on *hammě'ērâ* in 2:2 above.

wě'ōtî 'attem qōbě'îm. The repetition of this clause from verse 8 forms an envelope for the specific indictment demonstrating the validity of (and necessity for) the thesis of the disputation: postexilic Yehud must turn to Yahweh in repentance (v 6) because they have been (robbing) and they continue to rob God in the neglect of the tithes and offerings as stipulated in the Mosaic covenant (vv 8–9). Note too the juxtaposition of the initial rhetorical question of verse 8 ("will anyone rob God?") with the (disputed) final clause of verse 9 ("the nation — all of it!"). Both stand outside the *inclusio* and complement each other in a type of question-and-answer relationship.

The emphatic position of the definite direct object marker + pronominal suffix (*wĕ'ōtî*) underscores the primacy of Yahweh's role in the dispute and heightens the antithesis between the God of the covenant and the people (*'attem*, "you") of the covenant. See the discussion of this phrase in verse 8 above.

wĕ'ōtî. The *waw* here probably serves an epexegetical function, clarifying the sense of the preceding clause (WO'C § 39.2.4a, b). It has an emphatic sense ("yea") and may also compensate for the gapping of an initial conjunction in the opening clause of verse 9 (introduced by the preposition *bêt*, although this clause seems to be one of logical consequence as it relates to v 8, hence the insertion of ["So"] in the translation).

haggôy kullô. The word *gôy* means "people, nation" and when used generally of such groups, it implies a governmental structure and territorial holdings (*TDOT* 2:426–29). The term *gôy* used in the special religious (and pejorative) sense of "non-Israelite nation" has a wide distribution in the Haggai-Zechariah-Malachi corpus (Hag 2:7, 14, 22; Zech 1:15; 2:4 [1:21], 12 [8], 15 [11]; 7:14; 8:13, 22, 23; 9:10; 12:3, 9; 14:2, 3, 14, 16, 18, 19; Mal 1:11 [2x], 14; 3:9, 12). Here Malachi identifies Israel as *gôy*, much in the same vein as Hag 2:14 (in the context of a rebuke for impure sacrifice) and Zeph 2:1 and 9 (within a judgment oracle). The prophet's use of *gôy* may be two-edged satirically in equating Israel with the surrounding pagan nations (cf. Verhoef [1987: 306]; Glazier-McDonald [1987a: 192]) and hopefully as a reminder that Yahweh had reconstituted Israel as a *gôy* with its own governmental structure and territorial holdings (cf. *TDOT* 2:429–31).

kullô. The substantive *kōl* + pronominal suffix is an appositive of measure (WO'C § 12.3d; GKC § 127c; cf. *yiśrā'ēl kullōh*, 2 Sam 2:9; *hā'ām kullô*, Isa 9:8; *kol-bêt-yiśrā'ēl kullōh*, Ezek 11:15; *mĕnôrat zāhāb kullāh*, Zech 4:2). The Massora observes that Jeremiah, Ezekiel, and the Twelve prefer the spelling *kullōh* except in this instance. Even as *kullô* specifies *haggôy* more precisely, so the noun phrase *haggôy kullô* identifies the independent pronoun *'attem* in verses 8–9 more acutely. The fifth disputation was directed literally to "the nation — all of it!", not just the special categories of culprits indicted previously (i.e., the priests, 1:6–2:9; marriage covenant violators, 2:10–16; or those guilty of covenant justice infractions, 2:17–3:5). The whole nation is robbing God and therefore is subject to the curse of God.

The *BHS* conjectures *haggôy kullô* be emended to *hăgam kullô* and transposes the phrase at the end of verse 8. The ancient versions demonstrate some confusion over the expression as well. The LXX misunderstands the entire verse, here reading *klh* for *kōl* (*tò étos sunetelésthē*, "the year has come to an end") and in some cases joining the phrase to verse 10 (so θ). LXXS retains *haggôy* but translates *tò ĕthnos sunetelésthē* ("the nation has come to an end"; so T and LXXσ, which joins the phrase to verse 10 and understands it as a vocative). The V *gens tota* replicates the MT.

The MT is terse but understandable. The emphatic nature of the appositive *kullô* is consistent with the tone of the disputation, and the phrase *haggôy kullô* has its counterpart in *hamma'ăśēr wĕhattĕrûmâ* at the end of verse 8. In fact, it is quite possible that the conjectural emendation of the *BHS* is correct, because transposing the phrase *haggôy kullô* completes the thought of who must pay the tithes — "the whole nation." I have retained the MT order but posit the likelihood of the double-duty reading of *haggôy kullô*. Contextually, a portion of the prophet's audience has raised doubts about the justice of the divine penalty against the entire postexilic community. Given this perspective, the phrase *haggôy kullô* also makes good sense here in verse 9. The "whole nation" is both the subject for the imposition of the tithe (v 8) and the object of God's judgment (v 9).

10. *hābî'û 'et-kol-hamma'ăśēr.* The Hiphil imperative of *bw'* ("bring") bridges two imperatives in the disputation (*šûbû*, v 7 and *ûbĕḥānûnî*, v 10 below; cf. WO'C § 27.2b on Qal intransitive fientives in the Hiphil stem). Malachi's call to "bring the full tithe" constitutes a more pointed answer to the question posed by his audience in verse 8 ("How have we robbed you?"), countered by the prophet's cryptic response ("the tithe, the offering!") in verse 9.

The messenger formula *'āmar YHWH ṣĕbā'ôt* ("Yahweh of Hosts has said") accompanies the first and third verbs in the sequence, emphasizing the urgency of the prophet's call to repentance and challenging the postexilic community to examine pragmatically the benefits of a relationship of reciprocal faithfulness with God.

On the verb *bw'* (Qal stem, "come") in Malachi see 1:13 above and 3:1, 2, 19 [4:1], 23 [4:5], 24 [4:6] below. The Hiphil imperative form of *bw'* occurs elsewhere in the Twelve only in Amos 4:1, 4. Note that the LXX renders the Hiphil imperative of *bw'* with an aorist form of *eisphérō* ("you have brought").

The accusative *'et-kol-hamma'ăśēr* ("the whole tithe," NAB, NIV, or the "full tithe," JPSV, NJB, NRSV) suggests that the Israelites were withholding some portion of the tithe (probably due to economic constraints) but in character with behavior cited earlier in the offering of defective animals for sacrifice (1:8). On *kōl*, see further the NOTES on *kullô* in verse 9.

'el-bêt hā'ôṣār. The preposition *'el* conveys the sense of "goal" or "termination" ("into," WO'C § 11.2.2; see also the NOTES on *'el-hêkālô* in 3:1 above). The entire prepositional phrase serves as the indirect object of *hābî'û* ("Bring ..."). The LXX reads the third-person possessive pronoun *oîkō autoû* ("his house"), perhaps influenced by *'ôṣārô* in Deut 28:12. There is a parallel phrase in Zech 11:13 (*'el-hā'ôṣār*) if one accepts the widely recognized emendation *hā'ôṣār* ("the treasury") for the MT *hayyôṣēr* ("the potter"; see Meyers and Meyers [1993: 277–78]). The context of Zech 11:13 indicates the Temple "treasury" in this case is one of the storage rooms used specifically for housing precious metals, as a type of bank vault or depository.

The construct-genitive phrase *bêt hā'ôṣār* also occurs in Dan 1:2 ("his god's

treasury," Goldingay [1989: 5]) and Neh 10:39 [38] ("treasury," Williamson
[1985: 323]) and in each case refers to a temple storehouse. Depending on the
kinds of goods stockpiled, the 'ôṣār may have constituted "a wardrobe" (Jer
38:11) or an "arsenal" (Jer 50:25), an official "treasury" (cf. 1 Kgs 14:26; 15:18),
or simply some type of "warehouse" or "storehouse" (Joel 1:17). Here 'ôṣār is
better translated "storehouse" (so NAB, NIV, NJB, NRSV), because the supplies
were largely perishable agricultural goods housed for priestly consumption (as
opposed to precious metals, gemstones, and other nonperishables no doubt ware-
housed in the designated Temple treasury [so NEB] as a part of this storehouse
complex; cf. 1 Chr 9:26). Assuming Zerubbabel's Temple had a floor plan similar
to that of Solomon's Temple, these storerooms were auxiliary chambers surrounding the sanctuary proper (except for the entrance on the east side; cf. ABD
6:358, and see the diagram in Allen [1990: 231]). The bêt hā'ôṣār ("house of
supplies") was essentially an extended hallway divided into numerous rooms or
cubicles (lĕšākôt) for storage of tithes consisting of grain, wine, and (olive) oil
(Neh 10: 37–40 [36–39]; Solomon's Temple had thirty such rooms in each of
three stories of the auxiliary Temple storehouse, 1 Kgs 6:6–8; cf. Ezek 41:5–11).

wîhî ṭerep bĕbêtî. The waw is part of a volitional construction (imperative +
waw + prefix conjugation) with a consequential force "so that" (WO'C § 33.4,
34.6, 39.2.2). The prefix conjugation (of hāyâ) denotes the nonperfective of possibility, "so that there may be . . ." (WO'C § 31.4e). Here the LXX departs from
the MT (ĕstai hē diarpagē autoû, "there will be a plunderer in it").

Malachi equates the tithe with the word ṭerep, from the root ṭrp ("to tear [prey]
to pieces") with a derived meaning of "nourishment" in some contexts (TDOT
5:353). The word ṭerep occurs only here in the Haggai-Zechariah-Malachi corpus, but is used elsewhere to denote "food" generally, in Ps 115:5; and Prov 30:8;
31:15 (cf. R. L. Smith [1984: 331], "provisions"; Petersen [1995: 217], "fresh
food"). The expression "food in my house" refers to that share of the tithe used
to support the livelihood of the priests and Levites (Num 18:21–32).

The substantive + possessive pronoun bĕbêtî ("in my house") are frequently
used to indicate a building or a part of a building (as in bêt hā'ôṣār above, cf.
TDOT 2:111–12). During preexilic times bĕbêtî was sometimes used of Solomon's Temple (Jer 12:7; Ezek 23:39), and in the postexilic period the same expression was applied to Zerubbabel's Temple (Hag 1:9; Zech 1:16; 3:7). While
bêt (or more often bêt 'ĕlōhîm) does function as a synonym for hêkāl ("temple,"
e.g., 1 Kgs 6:3), Glazier-McDonald's (1987a: 195) observation that in later writings byt was the preferred term for identifying the Jerusalem Temple distorts the
truth. More accurately, bêt 'ĕlōhîm or bêt YHWH is predominant in the later
biblical writings (but note the use of hêkāl in Isa 44:28; 66:6; Jer 7:4; 24:1; 50:28;
51:11; Jonah 2:5 [4], 8 [7]; Hab 2:20; Hag 2:15, 18; Zech 6:12, 13, 14, 15; 8:9;
Mal 3:1).

The Jerusalem Temple was the site where Yahweh chose to place his name;
that is, the symbol of God's presence among and his suzerainty over them as his
elect people (1 Kgs 8:16, 20, 43–44; see ABD 6:359–60). The possessive pronoun
("my house") marks a series of three first-person pronouns in verse 10 contrasting

Yahweh and Israel and signifies the zeal Yahweh has for his sanctuary (cf. Isa 56:7; Jer 7:14–15; Hag 2:7, 9). The NAB, NEB, NIV, and NJB all translate quite literally (cf. "my House" in Meyers and Meyers [1987: 3, 108, 178]), while the NRSV reads "my sanctuary." The preposition *bêt* is used in a spatial sense, marking location ("in," WO'C § 11.2.5b).

ûběḥānûnî nā' bāzō't. The conjunctive *waw* joins the imperative clause with the preceding conjunctive-sequential clause, logically connecting the challenge to "test" God with the specific nature of the test (i.e., bringing the full tithe to Yahweh, cf. WO'C § 39.2.5).

The imperative form of the verb differs from the legislative nonperfective "in being more urgent or in demanding immediate, specific action on the part of the addressee" (WO'C § 34.4). The verb *bḥn* means to "test, try, prove" and occurs in the Haggai-Zechariah-Malachi corpus in Zech 13:9 (2x); and Mal 3:10, 15 (see *TDOT* 2:69–72; and the Excursus: Divine Testing below). I have translated the precative particle *nā'* emphatically ("outright") to heighten the sense of urgency conveyed by the three imperative verbs in the fifth disputation (cf. WO'C § 34.7). Biblical commentators are quick to note the extraordinary nature of Yahweh's request (e.g., Petersen [1995: 217]), a rare but not unique divine challenge in the OT/HB (cf. Redditt [1995: 180]).

The feminine demonstrative pronoun *zō't* specifies the exact nature of the "testing" called for in the volitional verb form (cf. WO'C § 17.3d on the demonstrative used for *direction of reference*). "Test me outright in this *thing*," that is, Yahweh says prove me in respect to the payment of the tithe. The masculine noun *hamma'ăśēr* ("tithe, tenth part," BDB: 798a) refers to the tithes and offerings generally and perhaps in an indefinite manner, thus accounting for the feminine demonstrative *zō't*. It is possible that the feminine demonstrative *zō't* anticipates the "blessing" (feminine *běrākâ*) in verse 10. Thus, Yahweh challenges Israel to test his faithfulness in providing the expected "blessing" when there is compliance with the obligations for payment of the full tithe (on the mystery of divine "testing" and "providing," see Brueggemann [1982c: 192–94]). The circumstantial use of the preposition *bêt* qualifies the realm of the verbal action (WO'C § 11.2.5e).

Excursus: Divine Testing

The root *bḥn* (Mal 3:10, 15) means to "test, try, prove" (used specifically of people) and is similar in meaning to the Hebrew *ḥqr* "to search," *nsh* "to test, try," and *ṣrp* "to smelt, refine, test" and almost always has religious connotations (cf. *TDOT* 2:69–72). The OT/HB indicates that God may "test" (*nsh*, Gen 22:1; Deut 8:2; *bḥn*, 1 Chr 29:17; Ps 17:3; Job 23:10) human beings, but in turn human beings are prohibited from "testing" God (*nsh*, Deut 6:16; cf. Weinfeld [1991: 346–47, 388]).

However, Malachi calls the postexilic Yehud to "test" (*bḥn*) God (3:10). By means of the divine invitation to test God, the prophet extends to the restoration community the opportunity to "prove" the faithfulness of God in keeping his covenant relationship (and covenant promises) with Israel by demonstrating their own faithfulness in obedience to the covenant stipulations regarding the tithe. Essentially, the Hebrews are summoned to affirm and approve their own faith in God and obedience to his covenant laws by reciprocating Yahweh's constant behavior (not simply proper "cultic conduct" as Glazier-McDonald [1987a: 194] contends, but in genuine humility and reverent worship with a "clean heart," Pss 51:10; 139:23–24).

Malachi's audience in their cynicism turns the table on the prophet by suggesting that the only ones who might "pass" such a test are the arrogant and the wicked, who appear to have flaunted their evil deeds before God and escaped divine judgment (bḥn, 3:15). Laetsch (p. 541) decried this as "a blasphemous perversion of God's challenge." Those who would sanction this testing of God from the posture of arrogance and covenant disobedience are sternly warned that God fully intends to distinguish the righteous from the wicked (Mal 3:18).

Frequently, the MT equates the Israelite testing and provocation of God (issuing from a posture of rebellion and unbelief) with the root nsh (e.g., Exod 17:2, 7; Pss 78:18, 41; 95:9), while the divine testing for purposes of judgment, purification, and character formation are usually connected with the root bḥn (cf. Jer 6:27; 9:7; 11:20; 12:3). Interestingly, God perceived the testing at Meribah as a bḥn experience, Ps 81:7, but the testing at Massah is described by the verb nsh (Deut 6:16; 33:8a), while the cognate verb ryb is applied to the episode at Meribah (Deut 33:8b). Clearly there is a complex of factors at work in the selection of the cognate verbs for "testing" (cf. TDOT 2:69–71).

According to Isa 48:10–11 God "refined" (ṣrp) and "tested" (bḥn) Israel for his own sake so that his holy name might not be profaned. However, this divine testing was also therapeutic, in that such testing prompted (or renewed) faith in God, diagnosing motive and attitude and exposing unbelief and rebellion (cf. Pss 17:3; 26:2; 66:10; 139:23). The NT claims it is not the healthy who need a doctor, rather the sick (Matt 9:12–13). Through testing God isolates our *illness* as a first step in the process of our *healing*.

The LXX consistently renders the Hebrew nsh with a form of the Greek word peirázein ("tempt, test, try"), while bḥn is nearly always translated with some form of dokimázien ("examine, prove, test"; but note 'etázein for bḥn in 1 Chr 29:17). This suggests that later Judaism discerned some theological distinction between the two terms in studying the question of God's testing of human beings. In fact, this assumption has its precursor in Ahaz's refusal to "test" (peirázein) God when the prophet Isaiah exhorted the Judean king to "prove" the word of God (Isa 7:12). The NT documents represent one completed stage (i.e., an early Jewish Christian perspective) of this developmental theology of divine testing.

According to the NT, God does not "test" (peirázein) anyone (Jas 1:13); nor should the faithful "test" (peirázein) God (1 Cor 10:9). Essentially, human beings bring this trial or test upon themselves by yielding to personal desires exploited by the Tempter (Jas 1:14–16; cf. Matt 4:3; 1 Cor 5:7). However, God does "test" the faith and deeds of God's faithful for the purpose of approving and purifying the faithful (dokimázein, 1 Cor 3:13).

God in his gracious providence is able to transform a given "trial" (peirázein) and its destructive potential for biblical faith into an experience that affirms and approves biblical faith and builds godly character (*dókimos/dokímion*, Jas 1:3, 12; 1 Pet 1:7; cf. Gen 50:20, "you intended evil against me, but God planned it for good"). This NT distinction between testing and provocation intended to disapprove or ruin biblical faith (*peirázein*) and testing designed to affirm and approve biblical faith both preserves human freedom and responsibility and at the same time confirms the goodness and sovereignty of God.

'āmar YHWH ṣĕbā'ôt. See the Notes on the messenger formula in 1:2, 4 above and verse 12 below.

'im-lō'. The particle *'im* ("if") may function as an interrogative (WO'C § 18.1c) or as a clausal conjunction (WO'C § 38.2d; cf. JM § 161f on the indirect question with *'im*). The combination of the conjunction *'im* and the negative particle *lō'* is unique to Mal 3:10 in Haggai-Zechariah-Malachi corpus, but the particle *'im* is found elsewhere in Hag 2:13; Zech 3:7; 4:6; 6:15; 11:12; 14:18; and Mal 1:6 (2x); and 2:2 (2x). The *'im-lō'* construction occurs frequently in the oracles of Jeremiah (15:11 [2x]; 22:6; 42:5; 49:20 [2x]; 50:45 [2x]), and Ezekiel (3:6; 5:11; 17:16, 19; 20:23; 33:27; 34:8; 35:6; 36:5, 7; 38:19).

The *'im-lō'* ("if not" or "whether or not") construction in Mal 3:10 is variously understood as an interrogative introducing a direct question (so NAB); emphatically as an abbreviated oath formula, serving as the apodosis of the protasis implied in the preceding imperative verb ("surely," so Glazier-McDonald [1987a: 196] [following J.M.P. Smith 1912: 72] and NJB; cf. GKC § 149, but contrast WO'C § 40.2.2b); as the protasis of a conditional clause with conjunctive *waw* joining a logically related clause (so Calvin [1979: 666]; G. A. Smith [1905: 368]; Chary [1969: 270]; Rudolph [1976: 281]; cf. LXX, KJV, NIV, NRSV); or as a true conditional clause made up of protasis (*'im-lō' 'eptaḥ . . .* , "if I will not open . . .") and apodosis (*wahărîqōtî . . .* , "and then I will pour . . .").

Mal 3:10d and 10e are best understood as a complete conditional clause for two reasons. First, the *waw*-relative + suffix conjugation introduce a consequential independent clause (the apodosis) following a conditional dependent clause (the protasis) with the *waw* serving as an *apodosis waw* (cf. WO'C § 38.2b). Second, reading a conditional clause properly interprets the intent of the divine testing (see the Excursus on "Divine Testing" above).

'eptaḥ. The verb *ptḥ* ("to open") occurs in the Haggai-Zechariah-Malachi corpus only four times (Zech 3:9; 11:1; 13:9; Mal 3:10). The literary anthropomorphism of God "opening windows" is overshadowed by the theological import of God's sovereignty in the realm of nature and the religious symbolism of rain showers "growing" righteousness among the people of Yahweh (cf. Zech 11:1; Isa 41:18; 45:8).

The nonperfective form of the verb *ptḥ* + the (negative) preposition *'im* introduce the protasis of a (real) conditional clause (cf. WO'C § 32.2.1, 38.2d). Malachi's use of *ptḥ* + *'ōṣār* + *šāmayim* clearly echoes the Deuteronomic blessing tied to covenant obedience, "Yahweh will open for you the goodness of his storehouse, to give the rain of your land in its season . . ." (Deut 28:12).

lākem. Grammatically the preposition *lamed* + pronominal suffix mark the indirect object of the nonperfective verb form 'eptaḥ ("I will open *for you* the windows of heaven"). The *lamed* of interest or (dis)advantage indicates the person(s) for or against whom an action is directed (WO'C § 11.2.10d). This same form, *lākem*, occurs five times in verses 10–11, always immediately following the verb. The repetition places heavy emphasis on the benefits Israel accrues from covenant relationship with Yahweh. The first two (v 10) statements affirm what Yahweh intends to do in postexilic Yehud, while the next three (v 11) describe preventative measures taken by Yahweh that will yield positive outcomes in the community. The use of the "ethical dative" (cf. WO'C § 11.2.10d) in series seems to be a demonstration of the statement made in the first disputation, "I have loved Jacob" (1:2).

'ēt 'arubbôt haššāmayim. The construct chain 'arubbôt haššāmayim serves as the direct object of the prefix-conjugation form 'eptaḥ. The Haggai-Zechariah-Malachi corpus employs the sign of the definite direct object without *maqqeph* in Hag 2:17; Zech 1:12; 8:9; 11:14; Mal 2:4; 3:10, and 23 [4:5]. On the particle 'ēt/ 'et-, see WO'C § 10.3 and the pertinent NOTES in 2:4 above and 3:23 [4:5] below.

The feminine noun 'arubbâ simply means a "vent" or an "opening," with specific identification contingent upon context (e.g., "window" [Isa 60:8] or "chimney" [Hos 13:3] of a house; or metaphorically of the "eyes" in Eccl 12:3). The phrase "windows of heaven" is a poetic expression for drenching rainfall (cf. NAB, NIV, NJB, "floodgates of heaven" ["the sky," JPSV]; NEB, "windows of the sky"; cf. LXX katarraktas toû ouranoû, "the sluices/torrents of heaven").

The construction 'arubbôt haššāmayim + the verb ptḥ is associated with the heavy rains unleashed as a part of the divine judgment in the great flood in Gen 7:11 and 8:2 (cf. 'arubbôt mimmārôm in Isa 24:18); whereas in Malachi the expression is construed as the divine blessing of abundant rain yielding bumper crops (cf. the response to Elisha's prediction of a glut of grain in the markets of Samaria, 2 Kgs 7:2, 19). The restoration community will experience the antithesis of Haggai's "weather report": "downpour" will displace "drought" in the forecast (Hag 1:6; 2:16, 19).

Some commentators continue to draw inferences regarding Hebrew cosmology from Malachi's reference to the "sluices of heaven" (so Glazier-McDonald [1987a: 196–97]). The notion that the ancient Hebrews understood the "firmament" (rāqî'a) of the heavens as a solid vault or shell encasing the earth is an intrusion of Hellenistic thought in pre-Christian Egypt through the LXX (sterérōma, Gen 1:6, 7, 8, etc.). The Hebrew rāqî'a is better rendered "expanse (of heaven," so NIV), not "dome (of heaven," so NRSV). G. J. Wenham (1987: 19–20) chides those who attempt to construct a *scientific* ancient Hebrew cosmology on texts employing *figurative* language. Further, the word firmament (rāqî'a) is used in synonymous parallelism with šāmayim ("heavens, expanse") in Ps 19:1, and the verb rq' primarily means to "stretch out" or "spread out" (often of solid materials by hammering; but in Job 37:18, God "spread out the skies" [rq' + šḥq]).

waḥărîqōtî. The waw-relative + Hiphil perfective nwq constitute a consequen-

tial independent clause, with the *waw* serving as an apodosis *waw* (cf. WO'C §
38.2b). The verb *nwq* occurs only in the Hiphil and Hophal stems and means "to
pour out, empty out, draw out" (*CHAL:* 339). The verb *nwq* is found in the
Haggai-Zechariah-Malachi corpus only in Zech 4:12 (meaning "empty [out],"
cf. Meyers and Meyers [1987: 256]) and Mal 3:10 ("and then I will pour out
. . ."). The rain is the tangible sign of God's blessing, and abundant produce is
the real proof of covenant blessing (what the people have been looking for [Hag
1:6; 2:16, 17, 19; cf. Joel 2:23–24], and that's what verse 11 promises).

lākem. The repetition of the indirect object continues the transition of the foil
between Yahweh and Israel by means of the pronouns "I" and "you." The prophet's condemnatory tone and antagonistic stance in verses 6–9 give way to promises of divine blessing in verses 11–12, mediated by the conditional clause of verse
10. See further *lākem* above in verse 10 and in verse 11 below.

běrākâ. The word is most always rendered "blessing," here not only in a bene-
dictory sense but also in an operative sense of good fortune (cf. *TDOT* 2:297–
300). The feminine noun occurs in the Haggai-Zechariah-Malachi corpus elsewhere only in Zech 8:13 and Mal 2:2 and elsewhere in the Twelve only in Joel
2:14 (in context, the promise of a blessing after repentance much like the fifth
disputation of Malachi). I have already discussed the Deuteronomic overtones of
Malachi's curse (see the NOTES on v 9 above). Not surprisingly, Malachi's promise of divine blessing has a similar parallel in the blessings/curses section of the
Mosaic covenant (cf. Deut 28:8).

The indefinite substantive functions as the (unmarked) direct object. I concur
with von Bulmerincq (1932: 439), Verhoef (1987: 308), and others who admit
that *běrākâ* here has both immediate and eschatological implications (contra Rudolph [1976: 284–85]). See the NOTES on *birkōtêkem* in 2:2 above.

'ad-běli-dāy. This phrase is unique to Malachi in the MT (cf. Ps 72:7, *'ad-běli*
yārēah, "until there is no moon"). The most literal rendering of the construction
comprised of preposition (*'ad*), negative particle (*běli*), and substantive (*dāy*) is
"until *there is* no sufficiency" (cf. Petersen [1995: 213], "a totally sufficient blessing"). The English versions read variously ("as long as there is need," NEB; "you
will not have enough room for it," NIV; "an overflowing blessing," NRSV, so
Verhoef [1987: 297]; "without measure," NAB; and "in abundance," NJB, so Rudolph [1976: 281]). Both T (*'d dtymrwn myst*) and Syr (*'dm dt'mrwn kdw*) translate "until you say, 'Enough!'" According to Gordon (1994: 119, 127), this expression is in general agreement with the explanation of the phrase given in the
Babylonian Talmud and Midrashim.

Likewise, commentators have offered numerous explanations of the phrase
(e.g., R. L. Smith [1984: 331], "until nothing is lacking"; J.M.P. Smith [1912:
73] and Glazier-McDonald [1987a: 198], "until there is no need"; Rabin [1955:
114], "until my power be exhausted"; Chary [1969: 270], "until exhaustion";
Laetsch [p. 538], "until there is no measure"). The interpretive crux is whether
God's blessing (*běrākâ*) is a direct reference to fructifying rainfall (i.e., until there
is no need for it) or an indirect reference to the by-products of that rainfall —
bountiful harvests (i.e., produce in abundance).

Given the covenant theme of Malachi and the prophet's appeal to the language of the Deuteronomic blessings and curses of the Mosaic covenant, the phrase is best understood as a reference to the overwhelming abundance of God's blessing (note the phrase *'et-habbĕrākâ ba'ăsāmekā* in Deut 28:8, "the blessing in your store[*houses*]"). Context supports this interpretation as well, because verse 11 calls attention to the produce of the fields and vineyards. The rain/fertility motif of divine blessing in Malachi is consistent with that of Joel 2:23, 26–27; 3:18 [4:18]; Hag 2:18, 19; and Zech 8:12; 10:1.

The negative particle *bĕlî* occurs in the Twelve only in Hos 4:6; 7:8; 8:7; and Zeph 3:6 (supplanted in later Hebrew by the negative *'ên* according to WO'C § 36.2.1g; cf. *mē'ên 'ôd* in Mal 2:13). The substantive *dāy* is found elsewhere in the Haggai-Zechariah-Malachi corpus only in Zech 14:16. On the preposition *'ad* see the NOTES on 1:4, 11 above.

11. *wĕgā'artî.* The *waw*-relative + suffix-conjugation form extend the future time aspect of the verb *g'r* initiated by the anticipatory (*casus pendens*) use of the *waw*-relative + suffix form after the prefix-conjugation in verse 10 (*'eptaḥ* + *wahărîqōtî*).

The verb *g'r* occurs in Mal 2:3 and 3:11 (establishing a contrast in that God earlier "rebuked" the offspring of the priests, but now he "rebukes" the locust from devouring the "offspring" or produce of the land) and elsewhere in the Haggai-Zechariah-Malachi corpus in Zech 3:2 (where Meyers and Meyers [1987: 186] note that *g'r* is almost always an anthropopathic term in prophecy, denoting a "divine invective against those who stand in the way of Yahweh's plan").

According to Caquot, the etymology of the root *g'r* suggests the translation "to scream, cry out," although the given context must establish a precise meaning for the word (*TDOT* 3:50). Traditionally, *g'r* here has been translated "rebuke" (Henderson [1980: 459]; J.M.P. Smith [1912: 73]; Laetsch [1956: 540]; Rudolph [1976: 281] ["threaten"?]; R. L. Smith [1984: 331]; so KJV, NRSV). Macintosh (p. 479) argued that *g'r* connotes the outworking of God's anger in the divine curse or invective so as to effect the "paralysis of the curse in its object" (i.e., "restrain," Calvin [1979: 666]; Glazier-McDonald [1987a: 199]; cf. NIV "prevent," NAB and NEB "forbid," and NJB "lay strict injunction").

Caquot has understood this "restraint" effected by the divine rebuke in a less passive sense, that by his "outcry" God repels or drives back the devourer (*TDOT* 3:52; cf. Holladay [1989: 147]). Given the emphasis on divine activity in the disputation, a more active rendering of *g'r* seems appropriate (hence the translation "repulse"; cf. Chary [1969: 270], "intervene against"). Verhoef (1987: 308–9) makes an interesting comment on the sequence of rainfall (v 10) that awakens the dormant locust eggs in the dry sands of the desert areas adjoining arable lands and Yahweh's "rebuke" of the locusts (v 11). See further the NOTES on *gō'ēr* in 2:3 above.

lākem. The repetition of *lākem* three times in verse 11 completes the transition begun in verse 10 from a pejorative use of the pronoun "you" for Israel to one of an affirming tone, emphasizing the nation as the recipient of Yahweh's benevolence. On the *lamed* of interest or (dis)advantage, see *lākem* below.

bāʾōkēl. The Qal participle *ʾōkēl* is a substantive functioning as the (prepositional) direct object (cf. WO'C § 37.2, 37.3, 10.2.1d). The form means "to devour, consume" in a wantonly destructive sense (cf. Glazier-McDonald [1987a: 199]). The definiteness of the construction with preposition *bêt* may specify a particular "devourer," and there is general agreement among commentators that Malachi is referring to the locust based on Joel's description of locust swarms as a "devouring" fire 2:5 (cf. Packard [1902: 32]; von Bulmerincq [1932: 445]; Rudolph [1976: 284]; Verhoef [1987: 308]; Glazier-McDonald [1987a: 198]; etc. [so NAB, NJB, NRSV]). However, both the NEB and NIV read "pests," while Wolf (p. 110) suggests that this devourer be equated with "the worm that eats the grapes" (based on Deut 28:39). Hence the more general term "devourer" may be more appropriate (cf. Petersen [1995: 218]; Redditt [1995: 180]). The Qal participle *ʾōkēl* occurs elsewhere in the Twelve Prophets as a substantive in Hos 9:4 and Nah 3:12, and as a predicate in Joel 2:5; Amos 6:4; Zech 7:6. The verb *gʿr* marks the recipient of the invective with preposition *bêt* in ten of fourteen OT/HB occurrences (*TDOT* 3:49).

wĕlōʾ-yašḥit. The *waw* is conjunctive-sequential in this case ("so that," WO'C § 39.2.2; cf. R. L. Smith [1984: 331]; Verhoef [1987: 308]; NRSV), not a copulative *waw* ("and," cf. Glazier-McDonald [1987a: 173]). The negative particle *lōʾ* introduces a compound negative result clause (with *wĕlōʾ-tĕšakkēl*, cf. WO'C § 38.3). The Haggai-Zechariah-Malachi corpus prefers exclusively the *scriptio plena* form of the negative particle *lōʾ* with interrogative *hēʾ* (see the NOTES on *hălōʾ* in 1:2 above).

The prefix-conjugation form of *šḥt* after the *waw*-relative + suffix-conjugation marks a modal *nonperfective of possibility* indicating a continuation of the future time aspect ("may not ruin," cf. WO'C § 31.4e). In the Piel stem *šḥt* means "wipe out, spoil, ruin" (*CHAL*: 366), and the verb occurs in the Haggai-Zechariah-Malachi corpus only in Malachi (2:8; 3:11, Piel stem; and 1:14, Hophal stem).

The vast majority of commentators and the contemporary English versions translate *šḥt* "destroy" (cf. Verhoef [1987: 308] "ruin"; NIV "devouring"). I prefer the understanding "ruin, ravage, lay waste" for *šḥt* here because contextually the postexilic community was not facing total destruction of their agricultural enterprise. Rather, Yehud had experienced extremely poor crop yields for a number of (successive?) harvest seasons (Hag 2:6; cf. Thompson [1980: 243, 358] on *šḥt* in Jer 12:10 ["laid waste"] and *šḥt* + *klh* ["destroy"?] in Jer 5:10).

lākem. The preposition *lamed* indicates interest or (dis)advantage, focusing attention on someone other than the subject or object (WO'C § 11.2.10d). While the preposition *lamed* + pronominal suffix grammatically mark the indirect object of *šḥt*, rendering the construction in English proves awkward ("it will not destroy for you"). I have construed *lākem* as a possessive ("your") with the object *ʾet-pĕrî hāʾădāmâ* (also for *wĕlōʾ-tĕšakkēl lākem* below; so all the English versions).

ʾet-pĕrî hāʾădāmâ. The combination of the nouns *pĕrî* ("fruit") and *ʾădāmâ* ("land, ground, soil," cf. *TDOT* 1:88–98) in a construct-genitive relationship is common in the OT and means literally "the fruit of the land" (cf. Gen 4:3; Deut 7:13; 26:2, 10; 28:4, 11, 18, 33, 42, 51; 30:9; Jer 7:20; Ps 105:35). The construct-genitive phrase functions as the direct object and indicates "the produce of the soil" (so NEB, NRSV), "the agricultural yield of the land" (cf. NAB, NIV "crops"), or "cultivated land" (*TDOT* 1:90–91).

The phrase *pĕrî hā'ădāmâ* is unique to Malachi in the Haggai-Zechariah-Malachi corpus, while the word *pĕrî* occurs in Zech 8:12 (a divine promise that the vine will yield its "fruit"; cf. Joel 2:22), and *'ădāmâ* appears in Hag 1:11; Zech 2:16 [12] (where *'ădāmâ* = *'ereṣ*, "land," in the sense of territorial holdings; as in 9:16 also); and 13:5 (where *'îš-'ōbēd 'ădāmâ* = "farmer," cf. Meyers and Meyers [1993: 381]). Malachi's forecast is a reversal of Haggai's description of postexilic Yehud as *ḥōreb . . . hā'ădāmâ* ("drought . . . on the land," 1:11).

The predominance of the phrase *pĕrî hā'ădāmâ* in Deut 28 suggests that the blessings and curses section of the Mosaic covenant shaped this disputation (see the NOTES on *bammĕ'ērâ* in verse 9 above). The phrase "the produce of the land" is probably symbolic of all cereal and vegetable agricultural produce.

wĕlō'-tĕšakkēl. The conjunctive *waw* + negative particle *lō'* introducing the second negative result clause in series carry an alternative force ("nor," cf. WO'C § 39.2.1b). On the negative particle *lō'*, see *wĕlō'-yašḥit* above.

tĕšakkēl. This prefix-conjugation form marks a *nonperfective of desire* denoting the desire or wish of the subject and continues the (modal) future time aspect established by *wĕlō'-yašḥit* (cf. WO'C § 31.4h).

The verb *škl* in the Piel stem means to "deprive, bereave, miscarry" and with respect to the agricultural capability of the land "fail to bear" (*CHAL*: 369). The verb is unique to Mal 3:11 in the Haggai-Zechariah-Malachi corpus (elsewhere in connection with the agricultural use of the land, cf. 2 Kgs 2:19, 21 [where drought causes the land to "miscarry"]; Ezek 14:15 [where wild animals "ravage" the land]).

In this instance the Piel *škl* is not transitive, but intensive, accounting for the adverb "utterly" in the translation (WO'C § 24.1; cf. Speiser's [1964: 90] discussion of the Piel factitive *yĕḥayyû* in Gen 12:12). The form *tĕšakkēl* is (third-person) feminine singular, with *haggepen* ("the vine[s]") serving as the subject of the verb. When the prophet declares that the vineyards will not be "utterly barren," he means exactly the opposite. The vineyards of Yehud will be "utterly fruitful," not a single vine will "miscarry."

haggepen baśśādeh. The prepositional phrase *baśśādeh* ("in the field") serves as an attributive adjective modifying the nominal absolute substantive *haggepen* ("the vine"; cf. WO'C § 8.3 and 14.3.1). The singular noun indicates a group or a class (i.e., "vines," so NEB, NIV; cf. WO'C § 7.2.2). The expression is unique to Mal 3:11 in the OT/HB, although *haggepen* occurs in the Haggai-Zechariah-Malachi corpus in Hag 2:19 and Zech 8:12 (see Meyers and Meyers [1987: 64–65, 423]; cf. *gepen bôqēq* ["a luxuriant vine"] in Hos 10:1 — but see the discussion of Andersen and Freedman [1980: 549–50]).

The word *gepen* means "grapevine" in 52 of 55 OT/HB occurrences, and the "vine in the field" is a reference to cultivated vineyards (perhaps symbolic of all fruit produce, cf. *TDOT* 3:57, 59). The word-pair *gpn* + *śdh* (Ugaritic *šd*) occur as a fertility motif already in Ugaritic (*TDOT* 3:55–56; cf. Isa 32:12). Hentschke

(*TDOT* 3:61) recalls, however, that everywhere in the OT/HB these symbols of fruitfulness are "clearly subordinated to the sovereign power of Yahweh."

'*āmar YHWH ṣĕbā'ôt.* See the NOTES on the messenger formula in 1:2, 4 above and verse 12 below.

12. *wĕ'iššĕrû.* The *waw*-relative + suffix (perfective) form following a suffix form mark a clause of logical consequence ("then . . . ," cf. WO'C § 32.2.3). Context dictates a continuation of the future time aspect established by the *waw*-relative + suffixing form in verse 11 (*wĕgā'artî*). The verb '*šr* ("to go") means "consider fortunate, call happy" in the Piel stem (KBL 1:97; see Janzen and *TDOT* 1:445–48). The verb '*šr* occurs in the Prophets only in Isaiah (1:17; 3:12; 9:15, 16 [2x]) and Malachi (3:12 and 3:15 where the arrogant are counted blessed because there is no divine justice according to Malachi's audience).

The English versions render this (somewhat awkward to translate) verb '*šr* variously ("call you blessed," NAB, NIV, NJB; "count you happy," NEB, NRSV). The sense here seems to be one of laud or praise for Israel as a nation blessed by God (Isa 61:9; cf. Pope [1977: 551] on '*šr* in Cant 6:9). More than pronouncing formal blessings on Israel, the nations count her happy given the bounty and prosperity of the land. This praising of Israel by the nations is "in harmony with election theology" (*TDOT* 1:447).

'*etkem.* The sign of definite direct object + the second-person pronominal suffix continue the emphasis on postexilic Yehud created by the repetition of '*attem* through the disputation. However, the pronoun continues the reversal of Israel's standing with Yahweh forwarded in verse 11 (*wĕgā'artî lākem*). The reversal of Israel's relationship to Yahweh from one of estrangement and alienation to one of reconciliation and endearment is contingent upon obstinate Israel's reversal in turning to Yahweh in repentance (v 7).

kol-haggôyim. Structurally, the phrase has its (somewhat) chiastic parallel in the emphatic *haggôy kullô* at the end of verse 9b (further indication that emendation of *haggôy kullô* is unwarranted). The inversion of *gôy* + *kōl* at the beginning of verse 12 lends dramatic effect to the reversal of Israel's fortunes predicted by the prophet (from "curse on the nation" in the opening of verse 9 to "blessed by the nations" here at the outset of verse 12).

Previously, Malachi had designated postexilic Yehud as *gôy* (v 9) because religiously and socially they were indistinguishable from the surrounding nations (*gôyim*). Verhoef (1987: 309) has commented that *kol-haggôyim* "is sometimes used in a hyperbolic sense to denote Israel's neighboring countries." If this is the case here, not only will the nations that formerly taunted and subjugated the people of Israel be obliged to acknowledge its "favored nation" status, but also Israel will finally fulfill its commission as the ensign of Yahweh's light and glory to the nations (*gôyim*, Isa 42:6; 60:3; 61:9, 11; 66:19).

kî-. The clausal adverb *kî* is a subordinating conjunction used in the logical sense "for" (so NAB, NEB, NIV, NJB, and NRSV) or "because of the fact that" (WO'C § 39.3.4e); although there is clearly overlap with the causal *kî* ("because"), the first clause formed with the *waw*-relative + suffix form (WO'C § 38.4a and § 32.2.3; cf. R. L. Smith [1984: 331]; LXX *dióti*). The causal *kî* is preferable because one situation (Israel emerging as a land of God's good plea-sure) constitutes the basis for another (all the nations calling Israel blessed).

tihyû 'attem. The simple nonperfective form of *hāyâ* continues the aspect of future time established by the preceding *waw*-relative + suffix form (cf. WO'C § 31.6.2). The emphatic use of the independent pronoun *'attem* with the second-person form of *hāyâ* involves *psychological focus,* connoting "strong emotional heightening" and "deep self-consciousness" (WO'C § 16.3.2e). The emphatic use of the independent pronoun *'attem* also continues the motif of reversal estab-lished in disputation (literally "you, *yes* you *Israel,* will become a land of *his* fa-vor" instead of a blighted land as you are currently [v 11]).

'ereṣ ḥēpeṣ. The indefinite construct-genitive phrase, used adjectivally as an attributive genitive (WO'C § 9.5.3a; cf. NAB, "delightful land," and NEB, "fa-voured land"), functions grammatically as an (unmarked) accusative (WO'C § 10.2.1) and is unique to Malachi in the OT/HB (cf. *wĕkol-gĕbûlēk lĕ'abnê-ḥēpeṣ* in Isa 54:12). Pending a return to Yahweh, Israel will become a "desirable" land, a land "graced" by God's material blessing (cf. JPSV, "the most desired of lands"). The word *'ereṣ* refers primarily to the land of covenant promise in a territorial sense, but the fate of the land and the people of Yahweh's covenant promise are really one as the independent pronoun *'attem* attests (see also the NOTES on *'ereṣ* in 3:24 [4:6] below).

The word *ḥēpeṣ* means "joy, delight" (KBL 1:340) and occurs in the Twelve Prophets only in Hos 8:8 ("enjoyment," Andersen and Freedman [1980: 482]) and Mal 1:10 and 3:12 (see *TDOT* 5:92–94). The phrase *'ereṣ ḥēpeṣ* has its coun-terpart in the construction *'ên-lî ḥēpeṣ bākem* (1:10).

Apart from repentance Yahweh takes no pleasure in Israel (1:10), but upon repentance Israel is restored as the land of (Yahweh's) delight (contra Edom as the "territory of evil," 1:4, or Moab "like a vessel of no value," Jer 48:38). As a name for Israel, "a land of favor" is probably a reference "to the land of God's pleasure, a land of wealth and magnificence because it is blessed by God (cf. Zech 7:14)" (*TDOT* 5:106). So while the nations would call Israel "blessed" or "happy" because of its bounty (vv 10–11), the prophet recognized that the land could be "favored" only because Yahweh was again God of the land (see *TDOT* 1:401–4; cf. Gordon [1994: 131–32] on the expansion "for you will be living in the land of the house of my *Shekinah* and will be fulfilling my will in it" in T).

'āmar YHWH ṣĕbā'ôt. The repetition of the messenger formula in the fifth disputation emphasizes the prophet's call to repentance and the promise of resto-ration as "the word of God" (vv 7, 10, 11, 12). See the NOTES on the messenger formula in 1:2, 4 above.

COMMENTS

The fifth disputation is a summons to repentance (v 7). The noneffect of this plea to "return to God" on the prophet's audience is all the more remarkable, in that the call to reorient allegiance to Yahweh is sandwiched between two disputations emphasizing themes of judgment and purification (2:17–3:5 and 3:13–21 [4:3]). Adapting Achtemeier's (1986: 172) outline of the book of Malachi as a courtroom drama, the fourth disputation constitutes a formal indictment (2:17–3:5), followed by the judge's verdict (3:6–12) and sentencing (3:13–21 [4:3]). In terms of setting, the three disputations shift from the eschatological future to the immediate present, and then back to the eschatological (near?) future.

Scalise (p. 413) has noted that Mal 3:6–12 is a disputation (about the tithe, vv 8–10) within a disputation (about the need for repentance, vv 6–7). Analyzed as a series of "speech-acts," the fifth disputation consists of a divine assertion ("I do not change," v 6) intended to reassure, a divine summons ("Return to me," v 7) meant to persuade, and a divine challenge ("Test me," v 10) designed to convince Malachi's audience (cf. Watts [1987a: 376–77]).

Also to be noted is the continuing movement of Yahweh toward his people, from an intermediary figure in the fourth disputation to the personalizing of the divine presence in the fifth. This dispute depicts *reversal:* in turning to God in obedience from disobedience, in threat ending with promise, in lack resulting in abundance, and in disgrace giving way to respect. The motif of reversal validates Wells's (pp. 57–59) observation that Mal 3:6–12 portrays a "crisis of hope" in the restoration community. This crisis of hope stems from the unhealthy preoccupation with the here and now, reaching its climax in 3:14, "What profit *is ours* because we have kept his command?"

3:6. The formula of self-introduction is important to understanding the prophetic word in the OT/HB (*'ănî YHWH*, "I Yahweh . . ." or alternately "I *am* Yahweh . . ."). According to von Rad (1966: 56), the formula is a symbol of divine presence within the Hebrew community and brands Israel as his possession. The formula also signifies God's authority and right, as Israel's sovereign, to dictate the terms of his will to the nation given his gracious behavior to them in the past (cf. Childs [1974: 401]).

Lastly, Zimmerli (1979: 176) has commented that the self-presentation formula is not only a revelatory word, but also a word that effects an event. In this case, the events are two: the possibility of repentance (v 7) and an invitation (rare in the OT; cf. R. L. Smith [1984: 334]; Scalise [1987: 414]) to experience restoration by testing God (vv 10–12; ultimately resulting in the certainty of divine judgment — this separation of righteous from the wicked was long overdue according to some in Yehud [3:17–18]). That Malachi's message was understood as such is evidenced by the reaction of some of the people who discussed the matter among themselves (3:16).

I am highly skeptical of the contention by Ahlström (pp. 26, 182–84) and Glazier-McDonald (1987a: 179) that the self-introduction formula "I YHWH" (*'ănî YHWH*) implies that God was demanding that the postexilic community turn away from the worship of other gods. There is scant evidence to support their reading of preexilic cultic prostitution into Malachi's use of "adultery" in his indictment of community sins (*n'p*, 3:5; cf. *TDOT* 4:100 on *n'p* as a more restrictive term for adultery than *znh*).

It seems more likely that Wells (pp. 41–42, 47) is correct in the assessment of postexilic Yehud as an assembly of "practical atheists" (whether in respect to Yahweh or any other deity; cf. Weinfeld [1991: 217]). The issue of religion (and idolatry) was subordinate to economic concerns. The practice of idolatry (perhaps implicit in the intermarriage of Hebrew and alien, 2:11) or any other religious activity appears to have been tempered, if not incited, by selfish materialism ("What do we profit?", 3:14). Bickerman (pp. 354–58) has admitted limited Babylonian religious influence among the first generation of Hebrew expatriates resettling Jerusalem; but he notes that it was the monotheists who won the ear of the Persian court. For all practical purposes, the Babylonian captivity immunized the Hebrews against "infectious idolatry."

Yahweh's declaration "I do not change" is a reference to the constancy of divine character that manifests itself in unswerving loyalty to his covenant word. God is not a man, a fallible and capricious human being prone to lie, change his mind, or renege on promises (Num 23:19; cf. Ps 77:11 [10] where the psalmist in his despair entertains the possibility that God has changed [šnh] but dismisses such an irrational notion after musing upon the "track record" of Yahweh's marvelous past deeds).

Israel's destiny and God's affirmation are entwined. Because Yahweh is unchanging in his character, his ancient covenant with Israel's forefathers still stands, along with his purposes to make Israel an ensign to the nations and an instrument of his universal kingdom (Achtemeier [1986: 186]). The psalmist recognized that Yahweh's wrath stings for but a moment, but his mercy and compassion last a lifetime (Exod 20:5; Ps 30:5). In view of Israel's legacy of covenant disobedience, the very fact that repentance and restoration remain a possibility gives testimony of God's gracious and enduring love for his people (cf. 1:2–5; see further Pilch and Malina [1993: 17–20] on the biblical social value of "Change").

7. Weinfeld (1991: 217–21) has documented the continuity between the preexilic and the postexilic "theology of repentance" (analyzing Deut 4:27–31; 30:1–10; 1 Kgs 8:44–53; Jer 29:12–14; Hos 5:15–6:1; and Neh 1:5–11). The basic OT/HB paradigm for renewing covenant relationship with Yahweh consists of a twofold pattern of "distress" (made manifest in numerous ways) and repentance or "(re)turning to God" (šwb). This distress, often called "trouble" (ṣārâ) or "evil" (rā'â), was perceived as divine wrath (cf. Weinfeld [1991: 219]). Only such distress could motivate Israel to turn to Yahweh in repentance (Deut 4:30). The process of repentance included searching for Yahweh (i.e., desiring to renew a relationship with him, Deut 4:29), seeking his face (in prayer, cf. Hos 5:15), confessing sin and guilt (1 Kgs 8:47–48), remembering Yahweh's covenant (Lev 26:42, 45), petitioning God to relent and reverse his anger and revive his people again (Ps 85:4), and returning (šwb) to Yahweh with a whole heart (Deut 30:2). Only then would God enact the covenant blessings and restore the fortunes of Israel (Deut 30:3; see further Pilch and Malina [1993: 178–80] on "Trust").

Weinfeld (1991: 220–21) has detected a stylized typology in the language of "returning to God," noting that the liturgical formulas of repentance are rooted in the penitential prayers of ancient Israel (cf. Pss 85:1–8; 106:40–46). Though tersely stated, Malachi's summons to "return to God" embodies this theology of repentance, including liturgical overtones in his use of words "spurn" (*swr*), "return" (*šwb*), and his call for payment of the "full tithe" (*kol-hamma'ăśēr*, v 10). Such a (re)turning to God in repentance requires abject humility, the acknowledgment of sin and guilt, and the open admission of human inability to remedy the situation. This humility implicit in Weinfeld's preexilic theology of repentance (in phrases like *wĕhēšîbû 'el-libbām*, "when they bring it [i.e., their sin] back to their heart") becomes a more explicit prerequisite for repentance in the postexilic period (note the use of *kn'* ["be humbled, humble oneself"] and '*nh* (II) ["to bow down, humble oneself"] in 2 Chr 32:26; 34:27; Isa 58:3, 5). R. W. Bailey (p. 78) has commented that "Malachi recognized the impudence of their spiritual pride" in the quip "How shall we return?" Whether through spiritual blindness or the pretense of religious ritual, the restoration community claimed no knowledge of sin or conceded any need for repentance. The prophet sensed the grave danger in this attitude, hence the urgency of his summons to repentance. As R. W. Bailey (p. 78) has aptly summarized, "He knew that their spiritual vision was dim, the root of the existence of the nation was shaky. The weakened religious life directly affected both moral and social conditions. It was essential that the people return to God."

8–10. Malachi's use of *'ādām*, "man" ("Will *anyone* rob God?", v 8) is instructive because the prophet is speaking of humanity universally (cf. *TDOT* 1:83–84). Malachi is appalled at the behavior of his fellow Hebrews, implying that not even the pagan Gentiles engage in such reprehensible activity. Theologically, the term *'ādām* "man (generically), person" connotes human dependence upon God as Creator of life and human responsibility to acknowledge God as Sustainer of the creature and servant (cf. *TDOT* 1:86). Thus, the divine curse is operative upon Israel at two levels: first, for failure to recognize the wellspring of life and all its possibilities; and second, for disobedience and insubordination to Yahweh as the beneficiaries of covenant privileges granted no other people on earth. The prophetic pronouncement of God's curse (v 9) on postexilic Yehud was a "reality check." The drought and pestilence, famine and poverty were more than just a string of "bad luck"; even this sequence of events was divinely appointed and pregnant with meaning for Israel.

Malachi's appeal for full payment of the tithe echoes the earlier rebuke of the priesthood for offering defective sacrificial animals (1:6–10; cf. J. J. Collins [p. 213]). Mason (1990: 253) has linked Malachi's concern for the tithing with Azariah the priest's claim that proper payment of the tithe yielded a surplus of produce (2 Chr 31:10), noting a characteristic in postexilic literature "that faithfulness to God is shown in faithful support of the temple cult." However, those who consider Malachi's message a retrogression to empty formalism and hollow ritual miss the point (cf. J.M.P. Smith [1912: 72]). Braun (1977: 302) objects to this reductionism, asserting that "obedient service to God does not embrace just a part of life. It is its total content."

The catalog of covenant violations in the fourth disputation indicates that the prophet grasps this principle (3:5). The point is that turning to God in spiritual renewal must *begin* somewhere; and practical obedience to the legislation regulating the tithe was deemed an appropriate first step in moving toward a relationship of fidelity with Yahweh because it necessitated a demonstration of faith in relinquishing already scarce staples given Persian taxation and drought conditions (cf. Mason [1990: 253]; and Scalise [1987: 414] who has remarked that the worthiness of the priests to receive the support tithe is not the question).

Laetsch (p. 539) has castigated the stingy Israelites of the restoration community as "chiselers." But cheating God in the payment of the tithe was merely a symptom of a more serious cancer, the failure to "fear" (*yr'*) Yahweh (cf. R. W. Klein [1986: 149]). Only by this posture of faith and reverence could the penurious community experience the wisdom of the adage that said, "there is one who scatters and adds more; but the one who withholds from what is due *tends* surely to want" (Prov 11:24; cf. McKane [1970: 435] on the relationship between enlightened self-interest and proper social concern, and Pilch and Malina [1993: 67–70] on the biblical social value of "Faith").

Clines (p. 209, appealing to de Vaux [2:380–81, 403–5]) has suggested that the tithe originated as a royal tax. It seems more likely that the payment of agricultural tithes reflects authentic pre-Deuteronomic religious custom (cf. McCarter [1980: 83]). The compact negotiated by Nehemiah with the later restoration community, which included a proviso regarding the tithe, indicates that Malachi's audience never responded to the challenge to "test God" (cf. Neh 10:29 [28]–39 [38]). The new system for collecting the tithes (i.e., traveling Levites who collected the "tithe of the soil" at rural depots) lends credence to this supposition (Neh 10:38 [37]; cf. Fensham [1982: 241] who holds that Hebrew practice was modeled after methods of Persian tax collection).

Brichto (pp. 104–5) has argued on the basis of 1:7–8 that Malachi rebuked the community for the quality of the tithe offered (inedible produce) not the quantity (so Glazier-McDonald [1987a: 192–93]). Brichto's analysis is faulty at several points, most notably in redividing and repointing the MT of Mal 3:9–10 apart from any manuscript evidence and in his assertion that *ṭerep* "does not constitute first-class food" (but see *TDOT* 5:353).

11–12. The grapevine is often a symbol of the prosperity of the land of Canaan in general, and in terms of covenant relationship it served as a tangible sign of the blessing of Yahweh (cf. *TDOT* 3:59). Prophetic visions of Israel's restoration frequently focus on the cultivation of the land, employing almost formulaic word pairs (e.g., "grapevine" and "fig tree," Joel 1:7; 2:22; Zech 3:10; or "grapevine" and "cultivated land," Isa 36:17; Zech 8:12; cf. Meyers and Meyers [1987: 423] on the symbolism of agricultural products in Hag 2:19 and Zech 8:12–13). In fact, the golden age of Israel under King Solomon is idealized as the era when Israel dwelt in safety, everyone under their own grapevine and fig tree (1 Kgs 5:5 [4:25]; cf. Ezek 36:29–30).

Hentschke has also identified a polemical use of the grapevine as a symbol of prosperity, in that the fruitfulness and abundance of the vine are distinctly subordinated to the sovereign power of Yahweh (*TDOT* 3:61). Jeremiah lamented over the vines of Moab because the "fruit" of gladness and joy had been

destroyed and replaced by shouts of travail as divine punishment for the insolence, haughtiness, and arrogance of the Moabites (Jer 48:28–33). Similar polemical overtones surface in Malachi's use of the grapevine as a foil for Israel's
pride in this dispute about the need for repentance.

The epithet "land of *his* favor" or "delightful land" for postexilic Yehud possesses important theological connotations. Foremost among them, Yahweh as
God of the land, the land as covenant inheritance for Israel, and the conditional
nature of Israel's possession of the land (cf. *TDOT* 1:401–5). Some commentators even see an echo of the Abrahamic covenant in the blessing of Israel by the
nations in Malachi's conditional promise (v 12; cf. Gen 12:1–3).

The gist of the prophet's dispute with the restoration community over repentance is *reversal*. As the people reverse their attitude and behavior in respect to
Yahweh's covenant, so Yahweh will reverse the experience of the people in the
land of covenant promise. The abundant yield of the grapevine and the copious
produce of the cultivated land attest to the favor of Yahweh and confer upon
Israel the status of blessed among the nations — no longer cursed (Zech 8:12–13;
cf. Meyers and Meyers [1987: 422–24] on Israel's reversal of fortunes contingent
upon their cooperation with Yahweh).

Baldwin's (1972a: 247) insight is cogent here, lest Malachi be misunderstood:
"Although the prophets spoke in material terms there were spiritual counterparts
to the fruits of the soil." The Hebrew wisdom tradition recognized that there were
both material and immaterial benefits affixed to generosity (Prov 11:25). Beyond
personal enrichment, Malachi expects a reversal in the community's lifestyle and
behavior — the repudiation of covenant violations like sorcery, adultery, false
oaths, and the gouging of the socially disadvantaged (Mal 3:5).

The same was true for Malachi's earlier contemporary Zechariah, who tied
the reversal of Israel's agricultural enterprise to speaking the truth, executing justice in the legal system, the pursuit of social harmony, and the demonstration of
personal integrity (Zech 8:16–17; cf. 7:9–10). Here Meyers and Meyers (1987:
428) have summarized that the prophet proclaims "the qualities of human behavior essential for a just and stable society."

One final caveat is necessary. R. L. Smith (1984: 334) aptly notes that the idea
of human beings testing God is rare in the OT/HB. Mal 3:6–12 is not an un-
restricted promise of material blessing to all who dutifully tithed the increase of
their produce (or income), as if God were little more than some kind of cosmic
slot machine. R. L. Smith (1984: 334) goes so far as to suggest that "it may be
that this passage in Malachi should be understood as a onetime, special act on
God's part to renew the fires of faith in an age of skepticism and indifference."
Perhaps this is so, although I am not sure that I want to limit the efficacy of God's
word in any age by a "knee-jerk" reaction to the abuses of what has become
known as "prosperity gospel" in contemporary American religion. However,
Smith's caution serves admirably as a warning to interpret Mal 3:6–12 carefully,
keeping in mind the covenant context of disputation, the community (vs. individualistic) orientation of the oracle, and the special circumstances peculiar to postexilic Yehud during the Persian period.

III. G. Sixth Oracle: Judgment and Vindication (3:13–21 [4:3])

3 [13]"Your words against me have been harsh," Yahweh said. But you have said, "How have we spoken against you?" [14]You have said, "It is futile to serve God! What profit [is there] because we have kept his charge, or because we have paraded mournfully before Yahweh of Hosts? [15]So now we consider the arrogant fortunate. Not only have those doing evil been built up, but also they have tested God and escaped."

[16]Then the fearers of Yahweh spoke together, each one with his companion. And so Yahweh took notice and listened. A book of remembrance was recorded in his presence, [enrolling] the fearers of Yahweh and those esteeming his name. [17]"They will be mine," Yahweh of Hosts said, "a prized possession during the day when I act. Then I will show compassion upon them, even as a man shows compassion for his son, the one who serves him. [18]Once again you will see the difference between a righteous person and a wicked one, between one who serves God, and one who has not served him."

[19 [4:1]]"For indeed, the day is coming, burning like an oven, when all [the] arrogant and all evildoers will be stubble. And this coming day will devour them," Yahweh of Hosts has said, "so that it will leave them neither a root nor a branch. [20 [4:2]]But a sun of righteousness will arise for you, those revering my name; and healing [is] in her wings. And so you will go out and you will frisk about like stall-fed calves. [21 [4:3]]And you will trample the wicked, indeed they will be ashes beneath the soles of your feet, during the day I am preparing," Yahweh of Hosts has said.

The literary form of *prophetic disputation* persists throughout the book of Malachi (see the discussion of literary form in the introduction to the First Oracle [1:2–5] III. B. above). This final oracle reflects the standard three-part disputation pattern of prophetic declaration, audience rebuttal, and prophetic refutation. However, the disputation is framed in a manner similar to that of the Fifth Oracle (3:6–12), offering a more complex series of charges and countercharges. Following the opening declaration ("Your words against me have been harsh," 3:13a), the disputation records two audience refutations ("How have we spoken against you?", 3:13b; and "What profit is it that we have obeyed . . . ?", 3:14) and two prophetic rebuttals ("You have said, 'It is futile to serve God,'" 3:13b; and "Once again you will see the difference between the righteous and the wicked," 3:18). Watts (1987a: 376–77) has identified Malachi's sixth oracle as a blend of several types of speech acts, including assertive speech of accusation intended to persuade (3:13–15), narrative report intended to elicit a response (3:16), assertive speech of assurance (3:17–18), and assertive speech of warning (3:19–21 [4:1–3]).

The paragraph divisions of the MT isolate three major literary units in the book of Malachi. The sixth oracle constitutes the third (3:13–18) and fourth

(3:19–21 [4:1–3] subunits of the third and final pericope (2:13–3:21 [4:3]) discerned in the MT, a treatise on the relationship of the people of the covenant to the God of the covenant (see I. C. 4. Structure above). I agree with those commentators who identify further microstructure in the oracle on the basis of the adverb "then" ('āz) used to introduce verse 16 and the shift from first-person assertion to third-person report in verses 16–18 (e.g., Calvin [1979: 667]; Mason [1977: 156–57]).

The last disputation of Malachi poses no textual problems of consequence, save the question of inserting ṣĕbā'ôt in the messenger formula introducing the oracle (3:13), as is the case in the LXXL, and wide-ranging conjectural emendations of the awkward phrase "those revering Yahweh and esteeming his name" (lĕyir'ê YHWH ûlĕḥōšĕbê šĕmô, 3:16). Significant divergences in the ancient versions are discussed in the NOTES below.

The LXX and V begin a new chapter at verse 19 [= 4:1], which has been adopted by all the modern versions (perhaps influenced by the pārāšâ sĕtûmâ [ס], the MT minor paragraph marker at the end of verse 18). The new chapter division misunderstands the interjection kî-hinnēh introducing verse 19 as disjunctive and thus interrupts the discourse directed to those who revere Yahweh's name (3:17–21; cf. 3:16). Wendland (p. 119) has noted that 3:13–18 is linked to 3:19–21 [4:1–3] by virtue of the fact that these verses "thematically satisfy the anticipation which was aroused in verse 18." In addition, these two sections of the final disputation are joined by a series of lexical connections, including the words "day" (yôm) and "wicked" (riš'â) and the phrases "doers of wickedness" ('ōśê riš'â, 3:15, 19 [4:1]) and "fearers of Yahweh" (yir'ê YHWH, 3:16, 19 [4:1]; cf. Nogalski [1993b: 193] who reaches to manufacture an inclusio to frame the beginning and end of the book with the repetition of riš'â in 1:4 and 3:15 and bēn in 1:6 and 3:17).

Apart from what some scholars have identified as the "occasional gloss" (e.g., sĕgullâ, "special possession" in 3:17; cf. J. M. P. Smith [1912: 84]), most commentators affirm the integrity of the final disputation. Redditt's (1994: 249; 1995: 155) hypothesis is representative of more recent trends supposing Mal 3:16–21 [4:3] to be the artifact of a later redactor who reworked the original message of the dispute (3:13–15 + 18?). The tight weave of both the thematic and literary structure of the pericope controvert this induction (cf. J. J. Collins [1984: 214] who dismisses as "inconclusive" arguments for the redaction of Mal 3:13–21 [4:3] due to the brevity of the oracle).

Wendland (p. 119) has outlined two distinct literary units in the sixth oracle: 3:13–18 and 3:19–21 [4:3]. The first section of the oracle is structured in an ABB'A' pattern demarcated by the envelope emphasizing "service" to Yahweh ('bd, 3:14, 18):

Yahweh is unjust (vv 13–15),
Yahweh took note (v 16),
Yahweh will spare (v 17),
Yahweh is just (v 18).

The second section demonstrates an XYX' schema, contrasting the fate of the wicked with the fate of the righteous:

the day of Yahweh is coming for the wicked (v 19 [4:1]),
the righteous experience healing and happiness (v 20 [4:2]),
the wicked will be crushed in the day of Yahweh (v 21 [4:3]).

This last oracle functions synthetically as a summary of the prophet's previous disputations that contrast the faithful with the faithless and call the people to repentance. The closing speech seeks to persuade Yehud to recognize that repentance is the only proper response to Yahweh's message, assures the righteous of justice in the day of Yahweh's visitation, and warns the wicked that divine judgment is inescapable.

The last disputation exhibits the hortatory style (terse and direct first-person speech) and recursiveness (the idea that Malachi's prophetic speeches evidence congruency in that they refer to themselves) characteristic of the prophet's previous oracles. Unlike the earlier speeches, the last disputation does not incorporate the rhetorical question as a response to the pseudo-dialogue. Instead, the prophet concludes with an exclamatory utterance (e.g., 3:18–21 [4:3]).

The sixth oracle contains numerous literary devices and rhetorical features, including partial chiasmus or inverted parallelism,

Yahweh is unjust + "serve God" + the wicked (3:13–15),
Yahweh is just + serve God + the wicked (3:18; cf. Wendland [1985: 119]),

synonymous repetition functioning as an inclusio ("those revering Yahweh," 3:16; cf. Wendland [1985: 119]), personification (ascribing human capabilities to the "day of Yahweh," 3:19), striking simile ("the day is coming, burning like an oven," 3:19 [4:1]) and metaphor ("they will be ashes under the soles of your feet," 3:21 [4:3]), and symbol employed as a visionary image ("the sun of righteousness," 3:20 [4:2]).

Like the fifth disputation, the sixth oracle is directed to the restoration community at large, leaders, priests, and people (both the righteous and the wicked, especially those whom R. W. Klein [1986: 150] called "latter-day Jobs," whose fate does not befit their faith). Fischer (p. 317) summarizes the basic message of Malachi's final disputation as a repetition of God's desire for honesty and fidelity. The key issues in the prophet's last oracle are the seeming triumph of wickedness over righteousness and God's apparent delinquency in judging sin within the community. The mercenary doubters of Yehud have complained that their personal piety yielded no tangible advantage. In fact, their experience in the "real world" showed that evildoers were actually the ones who had gained the upper hand.

Malachi concludes the disputation with an answer to the question of Yahweh's alleged mistreatment of the righteous within the restoration community. The coming Day of Yahweh will indeed vindicate divine justice, when the wicked are separated from the righteous by the fire of God's judgment. The essential purpose of this last disputation, then, is twofold. First, the prophet assures the righteous that Yahweh intends to dramatically demonstrate his justice in the life and times of postexilic Yehud. Second, the prophet warns the wicked they will face dire consequences on the day of God's visitation.

NOTES

3:13. *ḥāzĕqû 'ālay dibrêkem*. This uncommon phrase has been rendered fairly consistently by the biblical commentators and translators. For example, J. M. P. Smith (p. 76) adopts the reading of the KJV, "your words have been stout against me" (cf. Chary [1969: 270], *tendu*, "stiff"). The LXX translates the Hebrew *ḥzq* (Qal suffixing third plural) with the second masculine plural aorist *ĕbarýnate*, "you have pressed your words heavily upon me" (cf. V *valeo*, "your words have been strong against me"). Quite literally the stative verb *ḥzq* means "to be strong" (e.g., "the hand of Yahweh was strong upon me" [*wĕyad YHWH 'ālay ḥāzākâ*], Ezek 3:14). Mason (1990: 254) notes a certain irony in Malachi's use of *ḥzq*; elsewhere in postexilic literature the imperative *ḥzq* often appears as an exhortation to persevere in covenant faith. Malachi chides that the only way the people have been "strong" (*ḥzq*) is in their repining against Yahweh.

The verb *ḥzq* + the preposition *'al* signify that the words of the restoration community possessed their own measure of weight and authority (i.e., they stood against and prevailed over Yahweh's word; cf. Waldman [1974: 545–46]; and Glazier-McDonald [1987a: 208]). The verb *ḥzq* does not occur elsewhere in Malachi's oracles (on the root *ḥzq* in the Haggai-Zechariah corpus, see Meyers and Meyers [1987: 50, 419]). The suffixing form of *ḥzq* may be understood as a *persistent present perfective*, representing a situation that began in the past but continues in the present (WO'C § 30.5.1c).

'ālay. The preposition *'al* may be understood *metaphorically* indicating disadvantage for the object ("against," WO'C § 11.2.13c) or even in an *oppositional sense* ("over against," WO'C § 11.2.13f; cf. KBL 1:210). The adversarial tone of the dispute established in this initial declaration culminates in the pronouncement of Yahweh's judgment of the wicked on the day he chooses to act and demonstrate his justice (3:19-21 [4:1-3]).

The combination of *'al* + *dābār* elsewhere conveys a sense of "overruling" (2 Sam 24:4; 1 Chr 21:4; cf. NEB, NIV). This same combination of *'al* + *dābār* + *ḥzq* may even carry the meaning "to enforce upon" (1 Chr 21:4, so NJB; cf. NRSV "prevailed against"). This suggests that Malachi's audience not only spoke against Yahweh, but also sought to enforce their words (or theology?) upon him (cf. Andersen and Freedman [1980: 472] on "theological error that begins with a false opinion of Yahweh's character"). Given the foil of Yehud and Edom in Malachi's first disputation (1:2-5), the most interesting parallel is Ezekiel's indictment of Edom: "you have made your words impudent against me" (*wĕha'tartem 'ālay dibrêkem*, 35:13; cf. Zimmerli [1983: 227]).

dibrêkem. The plural form of the noun *dābār* + possessive pronoun means literally "your words" (so Verhoef [1987: 312]; Glazier-McDonald [1987a: 206]; NEB; NRSV; cf. NIV, NJB "things"). The reference is probably to the restoration community's indictment of Yahweh's justice in 2:17. The juxtaposition of the possessive pronouns for Yahweh ("me") and the people of Yehud ("you") continues the disputational tone established in the preceding speeches. The whining words that "wearied" Yahweh in the fourth disputation (2:17) now incite him to demonstrate the vigor of his divine justice (3:19–21 [4:1–3]). See further the discussion of *bědibrêkem* in 2:17 above.

'*āmar YHWH.* See the discussion of the messenger formula in 1:4 and 3:12 above. The BHS has proposed inserting *şěbā'ôt* at the end of the messenger formula after the LXXL, a harmonization prompted by the use of the phrase '*āmar YHWH şěbā'ôt* to conclude the fifth disputation (3:12; e.g., Petersen [1995: 221 n. b]). A study of the distribution of the messenger formula in Malachi suggests that the MT is the superior reading. The first and the last speeches are introduced by the shorter version of the messenger formula, '*āmar YHWH* (1:2; 3:13). Elsewhere Malachi uses the longer version of the messenger formula to open and close the second (1:6, 2:8), fourth (3:1, 5), and fifth oracles (3:13, 21 [4:3]). The third oracle (2:10–16) has no introductory messenger formula but concludes with the repetition of the formula ('*āmar YHWH 'ĕlōhê yiśrā'ēl*, '*āmar YHWH şěbā'ôt,* 2:16).

The use of the shorter messenger formula in 1:2 and 3:13 marks a type of envelope construction framing the six disputations. Interestingly, the variation of the messenger formula in 2:16 occurs at approximately the midpoint of the book. The epithet '*ĕlōhê yiśrā'ēl* included in the messenger formula is echoed in the reference to Israel in 1:5 and in the reference to God ('*ĕlōhîm*) in 3:18, perhaps denoting chiastic structure across the first, third, and sixth disputations (i.e., the beginning, middle, and end of the book). See further the discussion of the messenger formula in the NOTES on 2:16 above.

wa'ămartem. See the discussion of this form in 1:2 above. On the reported speech formula + the interrogative marker introducing an exclamatory question, see the NOTES on *wa'ămartem bammeh* in 1:2 and 3:7 above.

mah-[n]nidbarnû 'ăleykā. The interrogative *mâ* ("what?") introduces an exclamatory question ("How?", so NEB, NRSV; cf. WO'C § 18.3f), although contextually the literal "*What* have we spoken against you?" anticipates the prophet's response in verse 14 (so NIV, NJB; Rudolph [1976: 285]; R. L. Smith [1984: 335]; Glazier-McDonald [1987a: 206]; Verhoef [1987: 312]; Petersen [1995: 219]). I have retained the exclamatory force of the interrogative *mah-* because there seems to be an element of (feigned?) surprise in the reported speech of the audience. Baldwin (1972a: 248) has claimed that the community has spoken against Yahweh "unwittingly." On the form [*n*]*nidbarnû,* see the discussion of the *dagesh forte conjunctivum* after *mâ,* GKC § 37b.

By contrast, J.M.P. Smith (1912: 76) has charged that this question was not posed in good faith and that it implied a denial of Malachi's indictment and challenged the prophet to forward supporting evidence. The response of the righteous in verse 16 indicates that an accurate assessment of community motive probably lies somewhere between these two positions. No doubt the protest of innocence stemmed from a certain "religious posturing" on the part of community. However, the report of the consultation among the righteous after the prophet's rebuke indicates that at least some of Malachi's audience took his message to heart. The Haggai-Zechariah corpus prefers the interrogative *mah-*; whereas Malachi freely utilizes *mâ/mah-* along with *bammâ* (1:2; 2:17) and *bammeh* (1:7, 7; 3:7, 8). See further the discussion of *mâ* in 2:15 above and *mah-* in 3:14 below, and *'al* + *mâ* in 2:14 above.

[*n*]*nidbarnû*. The verb *dābar*, "to speak," denotes the activity of speaking, while the verb *'āmar*, "to say," most often requires the content of direct discourse (*TDOT* 3:98–99; cf. the notable exception in Cain's unspoken speech in Gen 4:8, supplied by the ancient versions S, LXX, Syr). As used here, *dābar* sums up the community's (ongoing?) conversation as a whole.

The Niphal stem *dbr* is rare, with two of the four OT/HB citations found in Mal (3:13, 16; cf. Ps 119:23; Ezek 33:30). Generally biblical interpreters have understood this Niphal form in a reflexive or reciprocal sense ("what have we said *among ourselves* . . . "), not in a passive sense (e.g., J.M.P. Smith [1912: 74]; Glazier-McDonald [1987a: 208–9]; cf. WO'C § 23.4e). Following Coats (1968: 24–25), R. L. Smith (1984: 337) takes *dbr* here to mean "rebellious murmuring" against Yahweh. This seems an overstatement, however. Dahood's (1970: 176) rendering of the Niphal *dbr* in Ps 119:23 with "gossip" or "slander" more closely captures the nuance of Malachi's intent. The restoration community does not deny that Yahweh has been the subject of their conversation (or gossip).

According to Calvin (p. 595), Malachi's audience has repeated their hypocritical speech about Yahweh with such frequency that they "acknowledge no fault" and respond "as though they wished to arraign the Prophet for having falsely charged them, inasmuch as they were conscious of no wrong." Yahweh is quick to offer supporting evidence given the community's challenge to demonstrate proof of their erroneous logic. See further the discussion of *nidběrû* in verse 16 below.

'āleykā. On the preposition of disadvantage see *'ālay* above. The possessive pronoun ("against *you*") attached to the preposition indicates that the reported speech is addressed directly to Yahweh, not to the prophet as Yahweh's agent (contra Calvin). The construction continues the confrontational tone of the disputation established earlier with *'ālay* ("against *me*").

14. *'āmartem*. On the reported speech formula, see the discussion of *wa'āmartem* above in verse 13. Curiously, no coordinating conjunction has been prefixed to the verb *'āmar*, marking disjunction between the interrogative of verse 13b and the prophet's answer in verse 14. von Bulmerincq (1932: 469) has linked this construction with the emphatic *hôga'tem* in 2:17.

šāwě' 'ābōd 'ĕlōhîm. The adjective *šāwě'* means "worthless, vain, without result" (*CHAL*: 361). The word occurs elsewhere in the Haggai-Zechariah-Malachi corpus only in Zech 10:2 (where *šāwě'* lies within the semantic field of *hebel*, "vain, empty"; cf. Meyers and Meyers [1993: 191]). Malachi uses *šāwě'* in a sense similar to that of Jer 2:30; 4:30; 6:29; and 46:11, where divine or human effort has been expended but no tangible results have been achieved (cf. the LXX *mátaios*, "useless, futile").

The infinitive '*ăbōd* functions nominally as the predicate of the clause, conveying the sense of a participle ("serving God *is* futile") or nonperfective finite verb ("to serve God *is* futile"; cf. WO'C § 35.5.1–3). Both the LXX and V read the Qal participle '*ōbēd* for the MT Qal infinitive '*ăbōd*, presumably to facilitate the understanding of the predicate construction.

The verbal root '*bd* ("to serve") in this context describes the service of proper worship of Yahweh and obedient behavior in keeping with Yahweh's covenant stipulations. The vassal or "servant makes no demands on his lord: he fears him instead" (Lindhagen [1950: 156]; cf. *THAT* 2:192–93). This conduct toward God is deemed useless for two reasons: first, the wicked go unpunished; and second, the righteous go unrewarded. J.M.P. Smith (1912: 76) has commented that such "commercial piety" was merely a sign of the times. Again, such thinking is quite logical if postexilic Yehud has assumed that a new covenant emphasizing individual responsibility has been implemented in the restoration community. See further the discussion of '*bd* in verses 17 and 18 below.

See the discussion of the divine name '*ĕlōhîm* in 2:17 and 3:8 above.

ûmah-[b]beṣaʿ. The conjunctive *waw* joins two clauses describing an interrelated situation (WO'C § 39.2.5). The ancient versions retain the conjunctive (e.g., LXX, T, V), while most modern English versions omit the coordinating conjunction "and" (e.g., NEB, NIV, NJB, NRSV; cf. NAB, "and what . . .").

See the discussion of the interrogative *mâ* under *mah-[n]nidbarnû . . .* in verse 13 above (cf. GKC § 37b on the *dagesh forte conjunctivum*). The combination of the interrogative *mâ* + the noun *beṣaʿ* occurs elsewhere only in Gen 37:26 (*mah-[b]beṣaʿ kî nahărōg 'et-'āhînû*, "What profit if we slay our brother?") and Ps 30:10[9] (*mah-[b]beṣaʿ bĕdāmî*, "What profit in my death [literally 'blood']?").

The noun *beṣaʿ* means "gain, profit, profitmaking" (*TDOT* 2:207). Originally, the Hebrew root *bṣʿ* was a technical term associated with the manufacture of carpets, literally meaning "to cut" or "to cut off" (i.e., a completed piece of woven material). Hence the derived meaning for *bṣʿ*, "to take one's cut, profit." Kellermann has demonstrated that "profitmaking" for its own sake is not illegal according to Hebrew thought (*TDOT* 2:207).

However, the word has been infused with pejorative connotations given the legal prescriptions prohibiting "unjust gain" (Exod 18:21; cf. Ps 119:36) and the prophetic indictments of "profit by oppression" (Isa 33:15b; Ezek 22:27; 33:31) and "greedy profiteers" (Isa 56:11; 57:17; Jer 22:17). The noun *beṣaʿ* is unique to Mal 3:14 in the Haggai-Zechariah-Malachi corpus, while the verbal root *bṣʿ* occurs in the corpus only in Zech 4:9 (with the meaning "complete," cf. Meyers and Meyers [1987: 251]).

The term *beṣaʿ* has neutral connotations in Mal 3:14. The issue in postexilic Yehud was not one of "illegal" gain or profit. Rather, the issue was one of correctly interpreting the blessings-and-curses theology of the Mosaic legal tradition (Deut 28). The righteous within the restoration community assumed their piety and obedience gave them claim to the goodness of God (cf. Job 41:11). Their misconceptions concerning divine punishment and reward are understandable if one recognizes that the people presume that the theology of "individual responsibility" promoted by the prophets Jeremiah (31:27–30) and Ezekiel (18:3) as part of Yahweh's new covenant was now operative. It is possible that the people of Yehud allude to Micah's promise (4:13) that Yahweh would bring the "profit" (*beṣaʿ*) of the nations to Zion after the Babylonian Exile in the reported speech of their response to Malachi. In fact, this belief that the new covenant order of individual responsibility has been ushered into community life prompts the discussion of divine justice in the fourth disputation (see the NOTES and COMMENTS on 2:17 above).

kî šāmarnû mišmartô. The clausal adverb *kî* functions as a coordinating conjunction and is used in a *logical* sense, "since, because" (WO'C § 39.3.4e).

The verbal root *šmr* means "to guard, to keep, to watch" (*CHAL:* 377). The context demands the understanding "to observe" in the sense of obey (see the discussion of *šmr* in 2:7, 9, 15, 16; 3:7). The suffixing form indicates the simple past (*recent* or *indefinite perfective* requiring the auxiliary "have"; cf. WO'C § 30.5.1b).

The noun *mišmeret* in combination with the verb *šmr* means to "keep an obligation" or "fulfill a requirement" (*CHAL:* 220). The phrase occurs commonly in pentateuchal legislation in a variety of contexts (Lev 8:35; 18:30; 22:9; Num 8:26; 9:23; see the discussion in Weinfeld [1991: 441]). Malachi employs the idiom with the meaning to fulfill a duty in a general sense after the fashion of Deut 11:1 (where the charge to be kept is the Torah of Yahweh, its decrees, ordinances, and commandments; *wĕšāmartā mišmartô wĕḥuqqōtāyw ûmišpāṭāyw ûmiṣwôtāyw*).

This association of the term *mišmeret* with the stipulations of Yahweh's covenant probably accounts for the reading of the plural *mišmarôt* in the ancient versions (LXX, T, V). The phrase has its parallel in the Haggai-Zechariah-Malachi corpus in Zech 3:7 as part of a conditional charge to the postexilic Levitical priesthood (*wĕʾim ʾet-mišmartî tišmōr*, "if you keep my service"; see Meyers and Meyers [1987: 195]). The prophet's audience contended that they had obeyed the law of God but had received no compensation for their loyalty.

wĕkî hālaknû qĕdōrannît. The *explicative waw* functions as a coordinating conjunction with an alternative force ("or"; cf. WO'C § 39.2.1b). On the clausal adverb *kî*, see the discussion of *kî šāmarnû mišmartô* above.

On the suffixing form *hālaknû*, see the discussion of *šāmarnû* above. The verbal root *hlk* means literally "to walk" (KBL 1:246–48; cf. NJB; R. L. Smith [1984: 335]; Glazier-McDonald [1987a: 206]) and is usually rendered "to go about (in mourning)" (so NAB, NIV, NRSV; cf. JPSV, "walking in abject awe . . ."). Elsewhere the conjoining of *hlk* + *qdr* is usually understood to connote the formal act of mourning the dead or ritual contrition for sin (Job 38:10; Pss 38:7 [6]; 42:10 [9]; 43:2; cf. Ezek 31:15). The combination of *šmr* + *mišmeret* + *hlk* suggests dependence on Zech 3:7, perhaps another example of Fishbane's (1985: 443–46) mantological exegesis.

The adverb *qĕdōrannît* is unique to Mal 3:14 in the OT/HB. The verbal root *qdr* may mean "be black, grow dark, darken, be unkempt, dressed in mourning attire" (*CHAL:* 313; cf. Arabic *qadira*, "to be black, dirty"). Most interpreters have associated the word with the customs and (dark) attire of mourning (e.g., G. A. Smith [1905: 370] ["walked in funeral garb"] or Verhoef [1987: 316]; cf. Job 30:28; Pss 35:13, 14; 38:7 [6]) or even the countenance of the mourner "darkened" by sackcloth and ashes (e.g., Henderson [1980: 460]; T inserts the preposition *bêt* and adds *nwḥ*, "go about *in* a sorrowful *spirit*").

Such (voluntary?) rites of mourning and penitence practiced in the restoration community are usually condemned as mere pretense (e.g., Laetsch [1956: 541]); but J.M.P. Smith (1912: 77) is less sure, noting that while *qĕdōrannît* "refers primarily to the outer garb and manner . . . [it] does not exclude a genuine inner grief." The pair of activities ("keeping" Yahweh's charge and "parading mournfully") suggest a cause and effect relationship that never materialized, perhaps because there was no "disinterestedness" on the part of the suppliants (see D. R. Jones [1962: 203]). It is possible to connect the MT *qĕdōrannît* to the root *qdd* ("to bow down") with only slight emendation (cf. LXX *eporeúthēmen hikétai*, "we have walked *as* suppliants" [i.e., humbly; cf. Syr *wdhlkn mkyk'yt*, "walked meekly"]). However, according to Baldwin (1972a: 248), "In this affirmation of virtue the more forcible expression is to be preferred."

Thomas (pp. 187–88) dissented, voicing support for an alternative reading based upon the Arabic *qadara* "to honor, to measure," assuming synonymous parallelism with *šāmarnû mišmartô* (cf. NEB, "behaved with deference"; Glazier-McDonald [1987a: 214], "walked earnestly"; and Petersen [1995: 219], "walked piously"). This view fails to recognize that the combination of *hlk* + *qdr* most often indicates mourning for the dead or penitence for sin. It also ignores the overwhelming support in the ancient versions for understanding *qĕdōrannît* as some form of self-abasement (LXX, Syr, T, V; cf. von Bulmerincq [1932: 475]). This reading also fits contextually with the fifth disputation (3:7) in which Malachi's audience asked "How shall we return?" The implication of the retort is that the community had repented before but this demonstration of penitent behavior yielded no tangible benefit (according to Cashdan [p. 353], Malachi addresses not the godless, but those who practiced forms of religion deficient in spirituality).

mippĕnê YHWH ṣĕbā'ôt. The complex preposition *mippĕnê* shows a frozen union between the noun *pānîm* and the preposition *min*. The construction functions syntactically as a preposition, linking the adverbial noun *pĕnê* to the verb *hlk* in a locative sense ("before"; WO'C § 11.3.1a). On the divine title YHWH *ṣĕbā'ôt*, see the NOTES in 1:4 above.

15. *wĕ'attâ*. The temporal adverb *'attâ* is a stative deictic, referring to the situation of speaking ("now," WO'C § 39.3.1h). The macrosyntactic word *'attâ* serves as an introductory and transitional signal in dialogue (WO'C § 38.1e). The coordinating *waw* is rendered variously (e.g., NIV = "but"; NAB = "rather") or simply omitted (e.g., NJB, NRSV). The *waw* is best understood as a conjunctive-sequential *waw* ("So now"; cf. WO'C § 39.2.2a).

'ănaḥnû mĕ'aššĕrîm zēdîm. The personal pronoun *'ănaḥnû* ("we") stands as the subject of the participial clause and identifies the prophet's audience in the reported speech of the final disputation. This independent pronoun is unique to Mal 3:15 in the Haggai-Zechariah-Malachi corpus, and the construction fits the

pattern of "selective-exclusive" force, drawing special attention to the subject or focus of the clause (WO'C § 16.3.3c). In this case, the personal pronoun ("we") singles out those in Malachi's audience who have criticized Yahweh's sense of justice (3:13; Ogden and Deutsch [1987: 108] suggest that the dispute reflects rival viewpoints within the community). Verhoef (1987: 317) is probably correct in understanding the intended audience as the restoration community in general (not only the hypocrites or the pious minority), especially those R. W. Klein (1986: 150) has described as "latter-day Jobs" whose current circumstance and faith are ill-matched with their faith in Yahweh (cf. Ogden and Deutsch [1987: 108], "this outpouring of an almost nihilistic view of the world is not a deliberate act, but rather a spontaneous expression. It points out the crisis of traditional faith and moral standards. In this respect it comes close to the passages in Job . . .").

The Piel participle *mě'aššěrîm* is usually translated "blessed" (so NAB, NIV) or "happy" (so NEB, NJB, NRSV). The verbal root *'šr* occurs elsewhere in the Haggai-Zechariah-Malachi corpus only in Mal 3:12 (see the discussion above). The participle is used as the predicate of the clause and describes an ongoing state of affairs (WO'C § 37.6a, d). The word *'šr* in this context means to "call blessed, happy" or "consider fortunate" in a laudatory sense (cf. Gen 30:13; Ps 72:17; Prov 31:28). Malachi's audience decried what they perceived to be the complete reversal of the divine justice paradigm: the righteous have been "cursed" and the wicked have been "blessed" (cf. Prov 11:21, "assuredly, the wicked will not remain exempt from punishment; but the offspring of the righteous will escape" [*mlṭ*]).

The adjective *zēdîm* means "insolent, presumptuous" (KBL 1:263) and occurs in Mal 3:15, 19 [4:1] and elsewhere in the prophets only in Isa 13:11 and Jer 43:2. Dahood (1965: 124) defines *zēdîm* concretely as "idols or false gods," that is, "those who presume to be God" (cf. Petersen [1995: 219], "the presumptuous"). The *zēdîm* are the impious and the arrogant, those who assume in their pride that their behavior is not subject to divine judgment. In the Psalms the *zēdîm* are those who stray from God's commandments (Ps 119:21) and flout his law (Ps 119:85). The adjective *zēdîm* is used as a substantive and functions syntactically as the accusative of specification (cf. WO'C § 14.3.2, 3). The LXX misread *zēr* for the MT *zēd*, translating *állotriós*, "stranger, foreigner, enemy."

gam-nibnû. The coordinating adverb *gam* has an emphatic force, "indeed" (NAB) or "clearly, plainly" (NIV = "Certainly"; cf. WO'C § 39.3.4d). Others have rendered the *gam . . . gam* construction as copulative coordination ("both . . . and"; note LXX *kaì . . . kaì* [= Syr]; cf. the causal construction of V, *siquidem . . . et*, "because . . . and") or disjunctive coordination (e.g., "not only . . . but *also*"; cf. Verhoef [1987: 312]; NRSV), although both prove less satisfactory.

The Niphal suffixing form of *bnh* means to "be built (up)" in a figurative sense (cf. *TDOT* 2:172). While some commentators render *bnh* literally ("built up"; e.g., Calvin [1979: 667]; R. L. Smith [1984: 335]; Glazier-McDonald [1987a: 206]), the context is one of economic advantage (or disadvantage), thus the more common rendering "prosper" (cf. Rudolph [1976: 286]; Verhoef [1987: 312]; so NAB, NIV, NJB, NRSV, but NEB reads "successful").

Theologically, the prosperity of the wicked is difficult for the righteous to bear because God is the one responsible for a man's good fortune (*TDOT* 2:173–74; cf. Job 22:23). Regrettably, the focus of the restoration community was material gain, not the intangible and spiritual "profit" of relationship with God Almighty (Job 22:23–28). See further the discussion of *bnh* in 1:4 above.

ʿōśê riš'â. The analog to the *zēdîm* ("proud, arrogant, presumptuous *ones*") is this construct-genitive ("doers of wickedness"). Meyers and Meyers (1987: 302–3) associated *riš'â* with the "wickedness of idolatry" in Mal 1:4; 3:15, 19 on the basis of the usage of *hāriš'â* ("The Wickedness") in Zech 5:8. However, the immediate context of Mal 3:15, 19 does not suggest the evil of idolatry. Rather, the prophet seems to have in mind the "wickedness" of rejecting Yahweh's law (Ezek 5:6) or even more specifically the "wickedness" of blaspheming God's justice (Ezek 33:19–20). The restoration community was apparently guilty of both, rebelling against Yahweh's Torah and speaking falsely about his execution of divine justice in the created order (cf. the LXX *poioûntes ánoma*, "law-breakers"). However, their behavior and speech were prompted by economic realities ("What profit . . . ?", 3:14), not a crisis in monotheistic ideology (note that the crux of the fifth disputation is the laxity of postexilic Yehud in respect to Yahweh's tithe, 3:8–10). See further the discussion of *gĕbûl riš'â* in 1:4 above and *ʿōśēh riš'â* in 3:19 [4:1] below.

gam. The coordinating adverb *gam* has an emphatic force and signals the final climax of the reported speech ("indeed, even"; cf. WO'C § 39.3.4d). The construction *gam . . . gam* is alternately understood as an intensive copulative ("see, yea see!"; GKC § 154a n. c). Verhoef (1987: 318) rejects the copulative reading of the LXX and Syr (so NAB, NEB, NIV, NJB, preferring instead a disjunctive rendering of *gam . . . gam* (so NRSV). I have opted for the latter understanding because the disjunctive reading better conveys the indignant outrage of the (hypothetical?) audience rebuttal.

bāḥanû ʾĕlōhîm. The verbal root *bḥn* occurs in the Haggai-Zechariah-Malachi corpus in Zech 13:9 (2x; cf. Meyers and Meyers [1993: 394]); Mal 3:10; and 3:15. The word means "to test, try, prove" and is used specifically of people and, according to Tsevat, almost always has religious connotations (*TDOT* 2:70–71). In a majority of the OT/HB occurrences *bḥn* expresses the concept of "divine examination and divine knowledge" (*TDOT* 2:70). Such is the case here, especially in respect to divine examination. However, in this context *bḥn* also connotes "human provocation" usually associated with the word *nsh*. The evildoers in the restoration community have "tested," in that their wickedness has both tried God's patience and challenged his justice (cf. Nah 1:2–3). Like the wicked envied by the psalmist, these rebels against Yahweh's covenant have assumed that God is either impotent and unable to mete out divine justice or that somehow they are immune to the effects of God's wrath (cf. Ps 73:4–12).

Laetsch (p. 541) is correct in noting that the intentional contrast between Mal 3:15 and Mal 3:10 "is a blasphemous perversion of God's challenge." The prophet Malachi had called the people to "test" God from the posture of humility, obedience, and faith. Instead these evildoers have challenged God from the vantage of insolence, disobedience, and unbelief. Rather than "testing" God, they have provoked him (NAB, "tempt . . . with impunity"; NIV, "challenge"; JPSV, "dared"). The LXX renders the MT *bḥn* with the verb *antitássesthai* ("to resist, fight against"), not the expected *dokimázein* or *etázein* ("to test, examine"). See the discussion of *bḥn* in 3:10 above and the Excursus: Divine Testing.

The divine name *'ĕlōhîm* is found in Mal 2:15, 16, 17; 3:8, 14, 15, 18. See the NOTES on 2:17 and 3:8 above.

wayyimmālēṭû. The Niphal nonperfective *yimmālēṭû* means "to escape" or more literally "get oneself to safety" (*CHAL:* 197; cf. NJB, "come to no harm"). The verbal root *mlṭ* occurs in the Haggai-Zechariah-Malachi corpus only in Zech 2:11 [7] and Mal 3:15. The *waw*-relative + prefix conjugation after suffix-conjugation forms may convey a present-perfect time structure ("have escaped"; cf. WO'C § 33.3.1c).

The restoration community contended with the prophet that the paradigm for divine deliverance had been inverted. Ezekiel had previously stated that cove-nant breakers cannot "escape" the judgment of Yahweh (*nimlāṭ*, Ezek 17:15). However, Malachi's audience argued that such "escape" was commonplace, per-haps having forgotten that Yahweh sometimes delivers (*nimlāṭ*) the guilty by means of the "clean hands" of the righteous (Job 22:30). Likewise, their assertion implied the converse must also be true: no longer are those who call on the name of Yahweh "delivered" (*yimmālēṭ*, Joel 3:5 [2:32]). Verhoef (1987: 319) has rightly acknowledged that these indeed are "harsh words" against Yahweh (cf. 3:13).

16. *'āz nidbĕrû yir'ê YHWH.* The temporal adverb *'āz* has a logical force, "then" (cf. WO'C § 39.3.4f; so V, NAB, NEB, NIV, NJB, NRSV). This adverb introduces a report modifying the discourse of verses 13-15 and supports the con-tention that the prophet addressed a diverse audience, including the righteous, the wicked, and those confused "latter-day Jobs." The insertion of this brief narra-tive is a unique feature among the prophet's six disputations (cf. Petersen [1995: 221-22] who notes that this strong temporal statement denotes a break in the dialogue of the disputations overall because after this the people of Yehud never again speak to Yahweh). After this final disputation, some from among the com-munity (i.e., those revering Yahweh) took the speeches seriously and deliberated over their meaning and possible implication for postexilic Jerusalem.

J.M.P. Smith (1912: 81), von Bulmerincq (1932: 490), and Sellin (p. 614) un-necessarily emend the MT *'āz* to *zeh* (or *zōh, zō't*) on the basis of the LXX *taûta* ("this, these things"). Although Glazier-McDonald (1987a: 217) incorrectly as-sumes that only the "righteous" make up the constituency addressed by the prophet, she is probably right to infer that the disputation has elicited some change of heart in the audience.

The Niphal suffixing form *nidbĕrû* is a reflexive construction in this context, and the sense of the plural tends to be distributive ("they spoke among them-selves"; cf. WO'C § 23.4b). The repetition of the Niphal stem links the form with [n]*nidbarnû* in verse 13, because some from the audience recognized "how they had spoken against Yahweh." Some commentators have reconstructed the con-tents of this discussion from verse 16b ("Then those revering Yahweh spoke to one another: *namely* 'Yahweh has considered, and he has listened *to us*'"; e.g., Luther

[Oswald 1975: 416]). Others have assumed the contents of this discussion were left unmentioned (e.g., Calvin [1979: 603]). I have sided with the latter position, in agreement with the English versions (NAB, NEB, NIV, NJB, NRSV).

The construct-genitive phrase *yir'ê YHWH* identifies the speakers in verse 16, "the fearers of Yahweh" (i.e., those who revere, honor, exhibit faith in Yahweh in a covenantal sense, cf. *TDOT* 6:296). This group of people is not to be equated with the "doers of evil" (*'ōśê riš'â*) of verse 15. Rather, they are to be contrasted with the wicked as mutual members of the prophet's audience (note that the LXX counts the "God-fearers" among the murmurers of the assembly). The (verbal) adjective (BDB: 431) *yir'ê* is used in an adjectival sense, and the construct-genitive *yir'ê YHWH* serves as the subject of the verb *nidbĕrû* (WO'C § 37.3b, 37.4; cf. 37.3c on the quasi-fientive stative participle of *yr'*).

The majority of commentators and English versions, however, understand the construction as a relative participle ("those *who* feared . . ."; so NAB, NEB, NIV, NJB, NRSV). I have retained the literalness of the construct-genitive phrase *yir'ê YHWH* as a quasi-technical term isolating a particular segment of the restoration community, those who had accepted the prophet's rebuke and "turned" (or now "returned") to Yahweh in response to Malachi's disputations (cf. Hanson [1986: 284] on the "God-fearers" as "the eschatological community remaining faithful to the Lord, and standing in readiness to serve as Yahweh's agents in restoring true worship, righteousness, and compassion in the land").

In this context, the word *yr'* connotes especially loyalty to Yahweh as the God of the covenant, moral response (proper conduct), obedience (to the revealed will of God), and right worship (*TDOT* 6:303, 306–13; cf. the "meek" of Isa 29:19 who experience joy in the Lord). According to Fuhs (*TDOT* 6:303), the polarity of *tremendum* ["fear"] and *fascinans* ["joy"] inherent in the numinous holiness of God explains why people react to the experience of God's presence with both fear and flight on the one hand and acceptance, trust, and joy on the other" (cf. Glazier-McDonald [1987a: 218–19]). See further the discussion of *yr'* in the NOTES for 1:6, 14; 2:5; 3:5 above and 3:20 [4:2]; 3:23 [4:5] below.

'îš 'et-rē'ēhû. In expressions of reciprocity the noun *'îš* ("man, person") is rendered with the distributive "each (one), each (other)" (KBL 1:43–44). The preposition *'et-* is comitative, marking companionship ("with," cf. WO'C § 10.3.1c). The preposition *'ēl* occurs in 4QXIIa instead of the MT *'ēt* (cf. Petersen [1995: 222 n. d]).

The noun *rēa'* may be translated variously as "friend, fellow, companion, neighbor" (*CHAL*: 342) and occurs in the Haggai-Zechariah-Malachi corpus in Zech 3:10 (*'îš lĕrē'ēhû*); 8:10 (*'îš bĕrē'ēhû*), 16 (*'îš 'et-rē'ēhû*), 17; 11:6; 14:13; and Mal 3:16. The idiom is literally rendered "a man with his fellow" and is used commonly to convey ideas of reciprocity and mutual exchange in personal interactions (cf. Meyers and Meyers [1987: 212]; see GKC § 91k on *rē'ēhû* as a collective singular). The combination of this idiom with the reflexive use of the Niphal stem (*nidbĕrû*) should be understood in an emphatic sense, denoting the sincerity and purposefulness of this dialogue among the "Yahweh fearers."

wayyaqšēb YHWH. The verbal root *qšb* means "pay attention, listen carefully" in the Hiphil stem (*CHAL*: 326). The word occurs elsewhere in the Haggai-

Zechariah-Malachi corpus in Zech 1:4 and 7:11. Like Mal 3:16, Zech 1:4 and 7:11 combine *qšb* + *šmʿ*. Zechariah applies the terms to the stubborn and disobedient ancestors of the postexilic community, echoing Jer 6:10, 17–19 (note the interplay of *qšb* + *šmʿ*) and Isa 42:23 (*yaqšib wĕyišmaʿ*).

Meyers and Meyers (1987: 401) correctly observe that *qšb* is a "verb of hearing." However, the literal translation "paid attention" (so Glazier-McDonald [1987a: 206]) is somewhat awkward in that it implies that Yahweh does not always pay attention, while the redundancy of the conventional "listened and heard" for *qšb* + *šmʿ* (so NIV; cf. R. L. Smith [1984: 335], "hearkened and heard"; and Verhoef [1987: 312], "heeded and listened") likewise suggests that Yahweh is a reluctant listener.

The NJB and NRSV "took note" better captures the sense of Yahweh's interest in the faithful (cf. Petersen [1995: 219], "listened carefully"). In contrast to those Hebrews of the preexilic period who refused to pay attention to the word of Yahweh, Yahweh readily notices and responds to the words of the righteous. The use of the covenant name Yahweh only serves to reinforce the relational dimension of the fear of the Lord. The *waw*-relative + prefixing conjugation following the suffix conjugation signify a (con)sequential event, "and so" (WO'C § 33.3.1d).

wayyišmaʿ. Context demands the translation "listen, hear" for *šmʿ*, and the prefixing conjugation with *waw*-relative following a similar form signifies a (con)sequential situation in the past (definite perfective, WO'C § 33.3.3). The verb *šmʿ* occurs in the Haggai-Zechariah-Malachi corpus in Hag 1:12; Zech 3:8; 6:15 [2x], 7:11, 12, 13; Mal 2:2; 3:16. The combination of *qšb* + *šmʿ* constitutes a poetic word pair in Psalms (5:3 [2]; 17:1; 61:2 [1]) and Proverbs (4:1; 7:24) and is sometimes understood as hendiadys (cf. NAB "listened attentively"; but this rendering interrupts the thread of discourse established by the series of *waw*-relative + prefixing conjugation forms, WO'C § 33.2.1c). See the NOTES for 2:2 above.

wayyikkātēb sēper zikkārôn lĕpānāyw. The Niphal nonperfective of *ktb* is unique to the Haggai-Zechariah-Malachi corpus. The form constitutes an example of the merging of the *middle* and *passive* in the Niphal stem, indicating "process" (WO'C § 23.2.2b). The *waw*-relative + nonperfective after a prefixing conjugation refer to a consequential present-time situation (the result of Yahweh's attentiveness to those "fearing" him; see *wayyišmaʿ* above).

According to Dahood (1970: 295), the verb *ktb* is sometimes used as a technical term for determining the fate of human being (cf. Ps 139:16). The metaphor of "the divine bookkeeper" is attested elsewhere in the Psalms (cf. Dahood [1968: 163]), but unlike Ps 69:29 [28] accounts are "entered" on the credit side of the ledger in Mal 3:16 (the [third-person singular] aorist indicative active *ĕgrapse* of the LXX has Yahweh himself writing the book). Malachi's divine register contrasts with that of the prophet Jeremiah (17:13) who warned that those "turning away" (*swr*) from Yahweh would be "enrolled in Sheol" (*bāʾāreṣ yikkātēbû*, see Holladay [1986: 501]; cf. Ezek 13:9 in Zimmerli [1979: 294–95]). See also the discussion of "heavenly books" in TDOT 7:380.

The construct-genitive phrase *sēper zikkārôn* ("book of remembrance") is unique to Mal 3:16 but has a parallel in Esth 6:1 (*sēper hazzikrōnôt*, "the book of records"). The phrase is often regarded a "Persianism" in Malachi (e.g., R. L. Smith [1984: 338]), but the concept of "heavenly books" is well documented in OT/HB and extra-biblical literature (cf. J.M.P. Smith [1912: 78]; Glazier-McDonald [1987a: 220]).

Nogalski (1993b: 207) has correctly recognized that this book of remembrance, following Persian tradition, is not only a catalog of names but also a record of events. However, he errs in identifying the book of remembrance in Mal 3:16 as the book of Malachi itself or even the Book of the Twelve. Nogalski has overlooked the key issue of the fifth disputation (Mal 3:6–12), namely that of reward (or better the lack of it!) for service to Yahweh by the righteous.

Verhoef (1987: 321) has more correctly understood the dynamic and all-inclusive nature of this "divine ledger." Yahweh's "book of remembrance" contains the names and an ongoing account of the words and deeds of the God fearers, a reminder of the righteous ones and what they have said and done (cf. Petersen [1995: 219], "a scroll memorializing"). Even as King Ahasuerus (Xerxes) remembered and rewarded the loyalty of Mordecai, God indeed intends to remember and reward the loyalty of the righteous (cf. Zimmerli [1979: 287]; Ogden and Deutsch [1987: 109]). It is this book of remembrance that will serve as the basis of Yahweh's winnowing of the righteous and the wicked promised in verse 18.

The frozen union of the noun *pānîm* ("face") with the preposition *lamed* (*lipnê*) is usually rendered "before" (WO'C 11.3.1). Here the complex preposition adds the (third masculine singular) object suffix and is understood most literally in a locative sense "before him" (i.e., Yahweh). Like *'md lpny* in Zech 3:1, *ktb lpnyw* is technical language referring to the Heavenly Court over which Yahweh presides (Meyers and Meyers [1987: 182]). This "book of remembrance" is written before Yahweh in the sense that the activity is carried out in this Heavenly Court "in his presence" (so NIV, NJB).

lĕyir'ê YHWH ûlĕhōšĕbê šĕmô. The balanced line consists of two dependent clauses joined by a conjunctive *waw*, each introduced with the preposition *lamed*. The masculine construct plural adjective is used as a substantive in apposition with the genitive function ("fearers of Yahweh"). On the adjective *yir'ê*, see further the discussion of *yir'ê YHWH* in the NOTES above. The preposition is a *lamed* of interest or "benefactive dative" ("for, on behalf of," WO'C § 11.2.10d).

The phrase *ûlĕhōšĕbê šĕmô* is unique to Mal 3:16 in the OT/HB. J.M.P. Smith (p. 78) emends the MT to read *ûlĕhōšĕ bišmô* ("those who take refuge in his name") following the LXX (*kai eulabouménois*, "and those revering . . .") because the construction "is a difficult and isolated Hebrew idiom and yields a rather weak sense" (Syr = *ûlĕšōbĕhê*, "and those praising . . .").

Glazier-McDonald (1987a: 222) has appealed to Gordis's (1976: 163) understanding of *hšb* as "esteem, regard highly" on the basis of Mishnaic Hebrew. This precise meaning for *hšb*, "value, esteem, regard," also occurs in the MT (e.g., Isa 13:7; 33:8; 53:3, 4; Job 41:19 [27]; cf. KBL 1:360, "respect, hold in high regard"). Mason (1990: 255) connects *hšb* with Gen 15:6 and translates "those who 'reckon' on God, that is who take his power and will to act into account" (cf. Petersen [1995: 219], "those who ponder his name").

Textual emendation here is unnecessary, so I concur with R. L. Smith (1984: 335, "value his name") and Glazier-McDonald (1987a: 206, "esteem his name") on the understanding of ḥšb (cf. NIV, "honor his name"). The clause serves as a foil with the "despisers" of Yahweh's name in Mal 1:6 (bôzê šĕmî). The conjunctive waw connects a pair of clauses and forms a hendiadys (WO'C § 39.2.5a). The Qal participle ḥōšĕbê has a relative use in the dependent clause serving as the indirect object of wayyikkātēb (WO'C § 37.5a).

The noun šēm ("name") occurs extensively in the Haggai-Zechariah-Malachi corpus (Zech 5:4; 6:12; 10:12; 13:2, 3, 9; 14:9; Mal 1:6 [2x], 11 [3x], 14; 2:2, 5; 3:16, 20 [4:2]). Malachi uses šēm exclusively in reference to Yahweh, and in verse 16d šēm is used in parallelism with the divine name YHWH. It is possible that the use of šēm in Malachi should be understood in a fashion similar to that of Zech 14:9 (YHWH 'eḥād ûšĕmô 'eḥād) where Yahweh is represented by "his name" to indicate the divine presence among his people. Meyers and Meyers (1993: 440) have observed allusions with cosmic implications in the message concerning the Jerusalem Temple. The eschatological shift in the final section of the last disputation (Mal 3:19–21 [4:2]) may suggest that Malachi intended the same focus on the Jerusalem Temple as the locus of the divine presence (and divine justice; cf. Mal 3:1). See further the NOTES on šĕmî in 1:6 above.

17. wĕhāyû lî 'āmar YHWH ṣĕbā'ôt. The relative waw + hyh has a deictic temporal function signifying future time (WO'C § 32.2.6c). The combination of the verb hyh + the preposition lamed is a periphrastic idiom for showing possession in BH (TDOT 3:372). Malachi has adapted the construction hyh + lamed of the covenant formula from the expected first-person form found in Hosea, Jeremiah, Ezekiel, and Zechariah to a third-person form for the sake of emphasizing Israel's privileged position in relationship to Yahweh (cf. TDOT 3:378–80). On 'āmar YHWH ṣĕbā'ôt, see the NOTES on 1:4 above.

layyôm. The temporal lamed ("in, during") indicates when Israel will belong to Yahweh as his special possession (WO'C § 11.2.10c). Malachi's appeal to "the day" may represent a cryptic borrowing from Ezek 30:2 (['ă]hāh layyôm, "Alas, for the day") and Joel 1:15 ('ăhāh layyôm, "Alas, for the day"). Both texts identify "the day" as the approaching "Day of Yahweh" (kî qārôb yôm [la] YHWH).

Israel remains Yahweh's "treasured possession" de jure, but during the Day of Yahweh the privilege and status concomitant with Israel's divine election will be manifest de facto. Yahweh's possession of Israel will be demonstrated in the dual activities of judging evildoers and blessing the righteous. The apparent absence of both initiated the complaints made by Malachi's audience in the last disputation. This "Day of Yahweh" is the theme of the fourth (2:17–3:5, especially 3:1–3) and the sixth disputations (3:13–21 [4:3], especially 3:19–21 [4:1–3]).

'ăšer 'ănî 'ōśēh. The relative pronoun 'ăšer introduces an attributive relative clause modifying layyôm (WO'C § 19.3a). The relative pronoun is best understood temporally after words of time (like yôm, WO'C § 19.3b; cf. V; Calvin [1979: 607]; Glazier-McDonald [1987a: 206]; NIV, NJB, NRSV). The independent pronoun 'ănî serves as the subject of the clause, following the word order of the identifying clause (subject-predicate, specifying the nature and character of "the day"; cf. WO'C § 16.3.3a). The verb 'śh literally means "to make, do, do work," but with *'ăšer* the word can mean "act" or "cause something to be done" (*CHAL*: 285).

Malachi's audience demanded divine intervention. The Day of Yahweh will see God "take action" (NAB; on the participle of *'śh*, see further the NOTES on 2:17 and 3:15 above and 3:19 [4:1], 3:21 [4:2] below). The participle *'ōśēh* functions as the predicate of the *identifying* clause and indicates the ongoing process of Yahweh's sovereign activity in preparing Israel and the nations for the day of his epiphany (Petersen [1995: 219], "on the day which I am creating" cf. WO'C § 37.6b). The Syr renders the MT *'śh* with *knwšy'*, "to gather, assemble" ("... on the day I assemble the people ...").

sĕgullâ. The word is unique to Malachi among the prophetic books of the OT/HB. The term is used in the Pentateuch (Exod 19:5; Deut 7:6; 14:2; 26:18) and the Psalms to describe the privileged status of the people of Israel (Ps 135:4). In two instances, *sĕgullâ* refers to unusual or special treasure acquired by royalty (Eccl 2:8; 1 Chr 29:3).

Weinfeld (1991: 368) equates *sĕgullâ* with covenant terminology and translates "treasured people" (*lĕ'am sĕgullâ*, Deut 7:6), on the basis of the Ugaritic *sglt* (used to connote a distinctive relationship between a Hittite suzerain and the vassal king of Ugarit). Greenberg (1951: 174) has proposed the derived meaning of "a dear personal possession, a treasure" for *sĕgullâ* by analogy to the Akkadian cognate *sikiltum* ("possession, acquisition," *CAD* 15:244–45). Greenberg's understanding of the word *sĕgullâ* as "private property" or "personal possession" better fits the context of Malachi's message. The prophet acknowledges Yahweh as sovereign over the *public* domain of the nations (1:5, 11, 14) but gives special recognition to Yahweh's sovereignty over Israel as his *private* domain.

In the Pentateuch (*lĕ'am*) *sĕgullâ* is paired with the parallel expression *'am qādôš* (Deut 7:6; 14:2; 26:18) or *gôy qādôš* (Exod 19:6). Significantly, Malachi narrows the understanding of the *sĕgullâ* from the nation as understood in the pentateuchal citations, to the righteous remnant of Israel — perhaps on the basis of this criterion of "holiness."

The English versions are in agreement in the rendering of *sĕgullâ* in Mal 3:17 (NEB = "my own possession," NIV = "treasured possession," NJB = "most prized possession," NAB and NRSV = "special possession"). The LXX *peripoiēsin* ("keep safe, preserve") has the sense of "acquisition" in this context. The Latin translation *peculium/peculiaris* (inherited or acquired "property") prompted the KJV translation "peculiar" for *sĕgullâ* in Exod 19:5; Deut 14:2; 26:18; Ps 135:4; and Eccl 2:8. Some commentators (e.g., Verhoef [1987: 312]), and a majority of the English versions assume the gapping of *lî* from the preceding clause and translate the possessive pronoun "my" with *sĕgullâ* (e.g., NEB, NIV, NJB, NRSV).

wĕhāmaltî 'ălêhem. The *waw*-relative + suffixing conjugation continue the consequential situation in future time introduced by the *waw*-relative + *hyh* at the beginning of verse 17 (WO'C § 32.2.3c). The form also has an epexegetical function in that this clause explains the leading situation introduced by *wĕhāyû* (WO'C § 32.2.3e). The eschatological orientation of the verse serves as a transition to the theme of the Day of Yahweh in the final section of the last disputation

(3:19–21 [4:2]). The construction of *ḥml* + preposition '*al* in Mal 3:17 follows that of Zech 11:5, 6 and Joel 2:18, a frequent pattern with this verb. Here the preposition '*al* governs the object of interest ("*upon* them," WO'C § 11.2.13c). The root *ḥml* occurs only in the Qal stem and is found in the Haggai-Zechariah-Malachi corpus in Zech 11:5, 6 and Mal 3:17 (2x). The verb *ḥml* means "to feel compassion, take pity" with the extended meaning "spare" (KBL 1:328; cf. *TDOT* 4:470–72) and is usually rendered "spare" in the English versions (so NEB, NIV, NJB, NRSV; but NAB "have compassion"). Meyers and Meyers (1993: 257–58) have noted that the word conveys both emotional response and tangible action, and "in three-fourths of its usages . . . it has a negative force" (i.e., someone, usually God, will not have compassion for someone else, often Israel in prophetic texts; e.g., Jer 13:14; Ezek 5:11). Malachi reverses that trend, echoing Joel 2:18, which relates Yahweh's restoration of Israel's fortunes as part of his compassionate reorientation to his people on the Day of Yahweh (see the discussion of *ḥml* in Wolff [1977: 61]; cf. Petersen [1995: 219], "act favorably").

The father-son motif + *ḥml* ascribed to Yahweh and Israel are unique to Malachi, perhaps borrowed from Ps 103:13 (utilizing *rḥm*, "show compassion"; but note Mal 1:6, "If I am a father . . ."). I have opted for the minority reading "have compassion" because it is the emotional response of Yahweh's compassion that prompts him to spare his people from the ordeal of judgment (Verhoef [1987: 323]; cf. Ezek 36:21 — note in this context that Yahweh has compassion on Israel for the sake of his own name). The LXX *airetiō* ("choose, appoint") conveys a sense of "divine election."

ka'ăšer yaḥmōl 'îš. The relative pronoun '*ăšer* + the preposition *kaph* introduce a comparative clause ("as," WO'C § 38.5). The Qal prefixing conjugation of *ḥml* is understood as a progressive nonperfective following the *waw*-relative + suffixing conjugation ("shows compassion," WO'C § 31.3b). The subject of the comparative clause ('*îš*, "a man") is an indefinite personal noun (WO'C § 13.8).

'*al-běnô hā'ōbēd 'ōtô.* The preposition '*al* governs the object of interest ("upon, for," WO'C § 11.2.13c). The dependent relative clause *hā'ōbēd 'ōtô* ("the one who serves him") functions as an attributive adjective modifying *běnô* ("his son"), hence the agreement in definiteness between *běnô* and *hā'ōbēd* (WO'C § 37.5a, b; cf. Crenshaw [1995: 149] on the anthropopathic language). The Qal participle '*ōbēd* occurs elsewhere in Mal 3:18, establishing a contrast between those who serve Yahweh and those who do not (see further the discussion of '*bd* in the NOTES for Mal 3:14, 18).

In this context the verb '*bd* means "to work" or "do service" in the sense of loyal obedience to an authority figure. The sign of the definite direct object + the object suffix ('*ōtô*) indicates the object or recipient of this faithful service, a man ('*îš*, i.e., the son's father). On the retention of the masculine gender of '*îš* and *běnô* ("a man . . . his son"), see WO'C § 6.5.3b (cf. NRSV, "parents . . . children").

The combination of *bēn* + '*ābad* occurs elsewhere only in Exod 4:23, where the meaning of "service" is one of formal worship of Yahweh. Such service in this context connotes a sense of submission to the will of the deity and compliance with his divine directives and is often used to describe the priestly ministry of the Levites (e.g., Num 18:21, 23). Tragically, Malachi indicts the Levites because they have abused their priestly station (2:8). Almost comically, the righteous among the prophet's audience presume such service to Yahweh is "unprofitable" (v 14). What the restoration community fails to appreciate is that ultimately Yahweh establishes the criteria by which "service" is evaluated (see the discussion of ʿābad in v 18 below).

18. wĕšabtem ûrĕ'îtem. The waw-relative + suffixing conjugation continues the consequential situation in future time introduced by the relative waw + hyh at the beginning of verse 17 (WO'C § 32.2.3c). The verb šwb is an auxiliary with rʾh and functions adverbially ("again," WO'C § 39.3.1b; see the NOTES on wĕnāšûb wĕnibneh in 1:4 above).

The conjunctive waw joins the auxiliary verb šwb and the verb rʾh and continues the consequential situation in future time of the waw-relative + suffixing conjugation (cf. the LXX kaì epistraphēsesthe, kaì ópsesthe, "and you will return, and you will see," so Syr).

The verb rʾh means literally "to see." In this context, it conveys the sense of "perceive or know" and with bên + lamed means to "see the difference between" (KBL 1:123). In Mal 1:5 the people of Yehud will see the downfall of Edom as a sign of Yahweh's covenant love, and now in 3:18 they will witness an even more personal demonstration of divine segregation of the righteous from the wicked. One wonders if the prophet also intends wordplay with šwb in 3:7, postexilic Yehud will "again see" when they "(re)turn" to Yahweh.

bên ṣaddîq lĕrāšāʿ. The preposition bên + lamed express an exclusive sense when used in paired phrases, marking distinction or class (WO'C § 11.2.6c). The pairing of bên + lamed in the following clause further emphasizes the distinction (or interval) between the classes of "righteous" and "wicked."

The adjective ṣaddîq is found only here in Malachi and is used as a noun or substantive (cf. WO'C § 14.3.3). The word is used in a moral sense, "righteous, upright" (in character) or "just" (in conduct, CHAL: 303; cf. Meyers and Meyers [1993: 126] on ṣaddîq in Zech 9:9). The adjective rāšāʿ occurs in the Haggai-Zechariah-Malachi corpus only in Mal 3:18, 21 [4:3] and may mean "guilty" (in a general legal sense) or a "transgressor" (in respect to conduct, CHAL: 347; cf. McKane [1986: 132] who translated rĕšāʿîm, "evildoers" in Jer 5:26). Both T and Syr render the MT collectives ṣaddîq and rāšāʿ with plural forms.

Malachi makes reference to those who are guilty before God on account of their transgressions, their wicked conduct. The words ṣaddîq and rāšāʿ are frequently found in parallel relationship in the OT/HB, especially in Psalms and Proverbs (44x; but the word pair occurs elsewhere in prophetic literature only in Ezek 21:8–9 [3–4] and Hab 1:4, 13). The English versions and most commentators (e.g., R. L. Smith [1984: 335]; Glazier-McDonald [1987a: 206]) ascribe definiteness to ṣaddîq and rāšāʿ, which serve as types or classes of people (i.e., "the righteous" and "the wicked"; but see Greenberg [1983: 84] and JM § 135c, 137i).

bên ʿōbēd 'ĕlōhîm. The Qal participle ʿōbēd has a relative use in the dependent clause (". . . one who serves God," WO'C § 37.5; see further the NOTES on *hā'ōbēd* in v 17 above). On the divine name *'ĕlōhîm*, see the NOTES for 2:15 and 3:8 above. These two dependent clauses (*bên 'ōbēd 'ĕlōhîm la'ăšer lō' 'ăbādô*) have their antecedent in *ûrĕ'îtem bên* (". . . you will see the distinction between . . .") and complete the antithesis established between the righteous and the wicked.

la'ăšer lō' 'ăbādô. The relative pronoun *la'ăšer* has a nominative function in the dependent clause (WO'C § 19.3a). The combination of the preposition *lamed* + the relative *'ăšer* is unusual, occurring elsewhere in the Twelve only in Amos 6:10 (cf. Hamilton [1990: 122]). Coupled with *bên*, the preposition *lamed* functions like a copulative *waw* ("between . . . *and* one who . . . ," KBL 1:123).

Dependent verbal clauses are sometimes negated with the (negative) adverb *lō'* (WO'C § 39.3.3a). The suffix conjugation form of *'bd* may be understood as a *persistent perfective*, representing a situation that started in the past but continues to the present (i.e., one who has not served God [and persists in that behavior]; cf. WO'C 30.5.1c). On the meaning of *'bd*, see the NOTES on *hā'ōbēd* in verse 17 above. It is the act (or non-act) of "serving" God (i.e., a posture of faithfulness, loyalty, and obedience to his commandments) that defines or characterizes a righteous person (or conversely, a wicked person). This repetition of *'bd* elucidates the analogy made to obedient children in verse 17. God will respond to the righteous in the same way a loving parent responds to an obedient child — with favor and reward.

19 [4:1]. *kî-hinnēh hayyôm bā'*. The combination of *kî* + *hinnēh* marks one of those instances when the logical force ("for") and the emphatic force ("indeed") of the clausal adverb *kî* should not be too strictly separated (WO'C § 39.3.4e). The adverb *kî* both introduces a temporal subordinate clause indicating *when* Yahweh will distinguish the righteous from the wicked (v 18; cf. NAB, "For lo," and NJB, "For look") and an emphatic pronouncement concerning the Day of Yahweh (NIV, "Surely"; cf. Petersen [1995: 219], "For indeed").

The linking of clausal adverb *kî* + emphatic particle *hinnēh* + participle is an announcement formula and is found elsewhere in the Haggai-Zechariah-Malachi corpus in Zech 2:13, 14; 3:9; and 11:16. The construction "indicates something that is about to happen" (Meyers and Meyers [1993: 283]) and "nearly always . . . has an ominous force, indicating Yahweh's intended punitive actions" (Meyers and Meyers [1987: 167]). One cannot help but wonder if Malachi also had in mind Ps 92:10 [9], where *kî-hinnēh* is repeated twice in conjunction with Yahweh's judgment of evildoers.

The subject of the clause, *hayyôm* ("the day"), is an equivalent here for the Day of Yahweh. The eschatological "day" of Yahweh's visitation brings both "disaster and deliverance" for Israel and the nations (*TDOT* 6:31). This Day of Yahweh is marked by the formula *bayyôm hahû'* in Zechariah (2:15 [11]; 3:10; 9:16; 12:3, 4, 6, 8, 9, 11; 13:1, 2, 4; 14:4, 6, 8, 9, 13, 20, 21). The phrase *hayyôm bā'* in Mal 3:19 echoes Zech 14:1 (*hinnēh yôm-bā' laYHWH*, "Indeed, a day belonging to Yahweh is coming"; cf. Meyers and Meyers [1993: 408–9]).

Malachi's use of *hayyôm* also has affinities to the prophet Ezekiel's warning concerning the destructive wrath of the Day of Yahweh (*hinnēh hayyôm hinnēh bā'â*, 7:10). Curiously, the outcome of Ezekiel's oracle against Judah is the recognition that "I [i.e., God] am Yahweh" (*yāda'* + *kî-'ănî YHWH*, 7:4, 9, 27). Yahweh's discerning judgment between the righteous and the wicked will demonstrate this as well (v 18).

According to Zech 3:9, the day of Yahweh's visitation will remove the guilt of the land of Israel "in one day" (or "the same day," *běyôm 'ehād*; cf. Meyers and Meyers [1987: 212]). Malachi's audience has indirectly requested this very thing by impugning Yahweh's justice (2:17). This direct reference to the Day of Yahweh in v 19 [4:1] completes the transition begun in verses 17–18 to the eschatological theme closing the final disputation. Verhoef (1987: 324) has remarked that there is "no reason whatsoever" for introducing a new chapter at this point given the topical continuity of the sixth disputation (as is the case in the LXX, V, and the English versions).

The particle *hinnēh* introduces a presentative *exclamation of immediacy* (WO'C § 37.6f, 40.2.1b; cf. GKC § 116p, "it is intended to announce an event as imminent, or at least near at hand [and sure to happen]"). The Qal participle *bā'* has a predicate function in the clause and approximates the future time aspect of the prefix conjugation (in this case a [con]sequential situation, WO'C § 37.7.2a). On *hinnēh* + *bā'*, see further the NOTES for 3:1 above, and on the *futurum instans* construction of *hinnēh* + participle, see the NOTES for *hinnēh 'ānōkî šōlēah* in 3:23 [4:5] below.

bō'ēr kattannûr. Both the verbal root *b'r* and the noun *tannûr* are unique to Mal 3:19 [4:1] in the Haggai-Zechariah-Malachi corpus. The verb *b'r* means "to burn, blaze up, consume, scorch" (KBL 1:145–46). A *tannûr* "is a fixed or portable earthenware stove, used especially for baking bread" (Andersen and Freedman [1980: 456]; cf. Redditt [1995: 184], "firepot" or "portable stove"). The Qal participle *bō'ēr* serves as the predicate of the adverbial accusative clause, describing the manner in which "the day *comes*" (cf. WO'C § 10.2.2e, 37.3b). The same form is used in connection with the Mt. Sinai theophany in Deut 4:11, 5:20 [23], and 9:15, perhaps an indication of the imagery Malachi desired to associate with the term.

The preposition *kaph* is used in a comparative sense ("as, like," WO'C 11.2.9b). The closest parallel to Malachi's use of *bō'ēr kattannûr* is *kěmô tannûr bō'ērâ* in Hos 7:4 ("like a burning oven"). According to Andersen and Freedman (1980: 456), "this destructive use of a *tannûr* (i.e., a furnace for destroying people in Ps 21:10 [9]) as an incinerator provides a symbol of divine judgment on the Day of Yahweh blazing like an oven" (such symbolism renders weak the NJB, "*glowing* like a furnace").

The LXXG inserts *kai phléxei autoùs* after the MT *bō'ēr kattannûr* ("and it will consume them"). The Syr inserts "my anger" before the MT *bō'ēr kattannûr*. The fact that this expression combining *bō'ēr* + *tannûr* occurs at the beginning of and again at the end of the Book of the Twelve is surely more than coincidental.

wěhāyû kol-zēdîm. The *waw*-relative + *hyh* have a deictic temporal function signifying future time, with the clausal *waw* indicating a *conjunctive-sequential* relationship (". . . the day comes *and* the arrogant *will be* . . . ," WO'C § 32.2.6c,

39.2.1d). The general quantifier *kōl* ("all, every") is used here emphatically in a universal distributive sense ("all" or "each one," WO'C § 9.5.3e, 15.6c).

The adjective *zēdîm* ("insolent *ones*") is found in prophetic literature only in Isa 13:11; Jer 43:2; and Mal 3:15, 19 [4:1]. Holladay (1986: 275) translates "insolent" but omits the disputed word *zēdîm* as a gloss in Jer 43:2 given its absence in OG. He has suggested that the intrusion of *zēdîm* in 43:2 is the result of a misreading of an early gloss noted in OG in Jer 42:17 (*kaì pántes oi allogenêis* = *wĕkol hazzārîm*). The reverse argument seems as plausible, with *kol-hā'ănāšîm wekol-hazzēdîm* original to the MT in Jer 42:17. Since the word *zēdîm* had been misconstrued as *zārîm* ("alien, foreigner") very early in the translation of the Hebrew into Greek, the phrase *wĕkol- hā'ănāšîm hazzēdîm* in Jer 43:2 was altered because *hā'ănāšîm hazzārîm* would have been nonsensical in context. All this is to say that Malachi's use of the clause *wĕhāyû kol-zēdîm* suggests dependence upon this reconstruction of Jer 42:17 (*wĕyihyû kol-hā'ănāšîm* [*wĕkol-hazzēdîm*]) or upon the MT of Jer 43:2 — given the prophet's penchant for phraseology from Jeremiah and Ezekiel. See further the NOTES for *zēdîm* in verse 15 above.

wĕkol-'ōśēh riš'â qaš. The juxtaposition of the phrases *kol-zēdîm* and *wĕkol-'ōśēh riš'â* with the single referent *qaš* marks hendiadys (cf. WO'C § 4.4.1b). See further the discussion of *kol-zēdîm* in the NOTES above, the discussion of *'ōśēh rā'* in the NOTES for 2:17 above, and *'ōśê riš'â* in the NOTES for verse 15 above.

The noun *qaš* is unique to Mal 3:19 [4:1] in the Haggai-Zechariah-Malachi corpus. The word is usually translated "stubble" (*CHAL:* 326), but more precisely the word describes grain chaff, stumps of grain stalks, straw stalks, or the like. The combination of "fire" + "stubble" is found several times in the OT/ HB, including Isa 5:24; 33:11; 47:14; Joel 2:5; Obad 18 (the burning of stubble is implied in Exod 15:7 and Nah 1:10).

Malachi's use of *qaš* reproduces the imagery of the Day of Yahweh portrayed in Joel 2:5. According to Allen (1976: 167), the linking of the key terms "fire" and "stubble" signifies "a far deeper level of theological content than appears on the surface. Over and over again, separately and together, they connote God's judgment of the wicked." There's a certain irony in Yahweh's use of Israel as a "fire" to consume the "stubble" of Edom (Obad 18), given Malachi's appeal to the overthrow of Edom as a sign of Yahweh's love for Israel (1:2–5) and the prophet's declaration that Yahweh will be the "fire" that consumes the "stubble" of Israel (3:19–21 [4:1–3]). Note that *qaš* is a metaphor, with no comparative preposition *kaph* as with the simile *kattannûr* ("*like* an oven").

wĕlihaṭ 'ōtām hayyôm habbā'. The *waw*-relative + suffix conjugation continue the sense of (near) future time established by the preceding construction *wĕhāyû* (see above). The verbal root *lht* in the Piel stem means "to devour, scorch" (*CHAL:* 173; on the uncompensated vowel in the middle weak Piel form see GKC § 64d). The word is unique to Mal 3:19 [4:1] in the Haggai-Zechariah-Malachi corpus and occurs elsewhere in the Twelve only in Joel 1:19 and 2:3, suggesting Malachi's dependence on Joel since the context is the Day of Yahweh in each case. According to Wolff (1977: 45), this phrase "does not portray a natural event, but rather can only be understood in light of the theophanic tradition in the Day of Yahweh formulations" (cf. *TDOT* 7:473–74).

The *nota accusativi* (or "sign of the accusative," *'ēt*) + the plural object pronoun ("them" [i.e., all arrogant ones and all evildoers]) mark the definite direct object of the transitive verb *lhṭ* (WO'C § 10.3.1a).

The phrase *hayyôm habbā'* serves as the subject of the verb *lhṭ* in the independent clause ("the *coming day* will consume them," Petersen [1995: 219]; but Redditt [1995: 184] construes the phrase as a temporal adverb with *kattanûr* ["oven"] serving as the subject of the clause). The definite article may indicate determination (especially since *hayyôm*, "the day," has been introduced earlier in the verse), thus the demonstrative translation "*this* coming day" (cf. KBL 1:235). The Qal participle *bā'* functions as an attributive adjective, explaining the agreement in gender, number, and definiteness (cf. WO'C § 14.3.1a, 37.4). See further the discussion of *hayyôm bā'* above.

'āmar YHWH ṣĕbā'ôt. See the NOTES on 1:4 above.

'ăšer lō'-ya'ăzōb lāhem. The relative pronoun *'ăšer* has a nominative function, referring to *hayyôm* as the subject of the clause ("the day . . . *which* will not leave them . . ."; cf. WO'C § 19.3). Here the relative particle also connects independent clauses and introduces a consequential clause ("*so that* it [i.e., "the day"] will leave them neither . . ."; cf. KBL 1:99; JM § 169.f).

The negative adverb *lō'* + *waw* is sometimes rendered with the disjunctive connectives "*neither* root *nor* branch" since the verb *'zb* governs a series of two alternative words (so NAB, NEB, NJB, NRSV; on the negative adverb *lō'*, see WO'C § 39.3.3). The verbal root *'zb* ("leave, abandon, leave behind," CHAL: 269) occurs in the Haggai-Zechariah-Malachi corpus only in Zech 11:17 and Mal 3:19 [4:1]. The NIV reads the Qal stem *ya'ăzōb* as a Niphal form (*yē'āzēb*) following the LXX aorist passive *hupoleiphthē* ("will be left to them"; cf. van Hoonacker [1908: 739]). The "fire" of divine judgment associated with the Day of Yahweh will be all-consuming, and destruction will be complete, leaving behind no trace of "vegetation" — only the residue of "ash" (v 21 [4:3]).

The preposition *lamed* signifies (dis)advantage, the indirect object of the verb *'zb*, and indicates those against whom the action is aimed: the evildoers within the restoration community (WO'C § 11.2.10d).

šōreš wĕ'ānāp. Both words are unique to Mal 3:19 [4:1] in the Haggai-Zechariah-Malachi corpus. After the clausal negative (*lō'*), *waw* + noun may have an alternative force ("or"). The word pair *šōreš* ("root", CHAL: 384) and *'ānāp* ("branch[es]", CHAL: 278) occurs elsewhere in the OT/HB only in Ps 80:10–11 [9–10] (a prayer for the restoration of Israel taking "root" in the land of covenant promise and spreading "branches" to the sea) and Ezek 17:8–9 (the allegory of the vine). Like the uprooted vine with withered branches in Ezekiel's allegory about the destruction of Jerusalem by the Babylonians, so the Day of Yahweh will utterly destroy the wicked — roots and branches until nothing remains. Malachi's audience will have their answer to the question concerning divine judgment of the wicked (2:17).

Wendland (p. 111) has identified verse 19d [4:1d] as a proverbial quotation from an unknown (contemporary?) wisdom source (cf. Andersen and Freedman [1989: 330] on Amos 2:9). Ogden and Deutsch (p. 111) trace the phrase "root and branch" to Phoenician and Ugaritic, as a variation of an ancient curse formula (cf. Cashdan [1948: 355]). The LXX, V, and Syr support the MT, while T reads "neither *son* nor *grandson*" (*br wbr br*; cf. Gordon [1994: 126] on the "stock-in-trade" translating of T).

20 [4:2]. *wĕzārĕḥâ*. The *waw*-relative + suffix conjugation continue the sense of (near) future time established by the preceding verbal constructions (WO'C § 32.3.6c, 39.2.1d; see the NOTES on *wĕhāyû* in v 19 [4:1] above). Given the contrast established between the evildoers in 3:19 [4:1] and the fearers of Yahweh in 3:20 [4:2], the *waw* is usually understood in an adversative sense "but" (so NAB, NEB, NIV, NJB, NRSV). The Qal stem *zrḥ* means "to rise, shine" (KBL 1:281) and is used to describe the sun (e.g., Jonah 4:8; Nah 3:17), a star (Num 24:17), light in general (Isa 58:10), and Yahweh's glory (Deut 33:2; Isa 60:2). The verbal root *zrḥ* is unique to Mal 3:20 [4:2] in the Twelve.

lākem yir'ê šĕmî. The preposition *lamed* marks a special variety of the *lamed* of interest, the *dativus ethicus* or "ethical dative" (WO'C § 11.2.10d). Although identifying the indirect object of *zrḥ* (". . . will rise *for you* . . ."), the construction indicates that someone other than the subject or object of the clause receives particular emphasis (in this case the righteous of Yehud).

The phrase *yir'ê šĕmî* modifies the pronoun ("you," plural), further specifying those who will benefit from the rising of the sun of righteousness (i.e., "fearers" or "reverers of my [Yahweh's] name,"; cf. JM § 121.1 on the nominal sense of the participle, "respectful of"). On *yir'ê YHWH*, see further the NOTES for verse 16 above. According to Hanson (1986: 284), the expression "fearers of Yahweh" has liturgical connotations and designates a group of people who have remained faithful to Yahweh and stand in readiness to serve as his agents in restoring covenant faith, righteous behavior, and true worship in Yehud. On *šĕmî* ("my name"), see further the NOTES for 1:6 above.

šemeš ṣĕdāqâ. The masculine noun *šemeš* ("sun"; cf. ABD 6:237–39) occurs in Mal 1:11, 3:20 [4:2] and elsewhere in the Haggai-Zechariah-Malachi corpus only in Zech 8:7. The construct-genitive phrase *šemeš ṣĕdāqâ* ("sun of righteousness") is unique to Mal 3:20 [4:2] in the MT. It is possible to understand the phrase as an attributive genitive, with the genitive form (*ṣĕdāqâ*) rendered as an adjective of the construct noun (*šemeš*, i.e., a "righteous" or "just" sun, following Calvin [1979: 617–18]; cf. WO'C § 9.5.3a). Alternately, the construct genitive phrase may be construed as either an epexegetical genitive or a genitive of association in which the genitive (*ṣĕdāqâ*) is characterized or explained by the construct noun (*šemeš*, cf. WO'C § 9.5.3c, h). The overwhelming majority of interpreters opt for this view (along with the LXX and V). Such a construction marks an example of gender concord, the absolute feminine noun *ṣĕdāqâ* controlling the phrase and explaining the feminine form of the suffixing conjugation *wĕzā-rĕhâ* (cf. WO'C § 6.6b). Technically, the construct genitive phrase *šemeš ṣĕdāqâ* is indefinite, "*a* sun of righteous(ness)" (cf. Petersen [1995: 219]).

The English versions render "*the* sun of righteousness/justice," assuming the phrase is a solar epithet for Yahweh (or a Christological title, so KJV ["the Sun of righteousness"]; cf. Calvin [1979: 618]; Luther [Oswald: 417]). Rather than a divine title, this phrase may be merely a figurative description of the eschatological day; the dawning of a new day ushering in an era of righteousness in which

Yehud will experience the complete reversal of current circumstances (see Gowan [p. 2] on the Israelite eschatological hope as "the end of evil"). Rudolph (1976: 289) notes that early Christians in Rome applied the title "sun of righteousness" to the *sol invictus*, commemorated on the 25th of December, explaining the date of Christmas Day.

The word *ṣĕdāqâ* is usually translated "righteousness" (so NEB, NIV, NRSV), but the sense is really that of "justice" as a characteristic of God the divine judge (*CHAL*: 303; cf. NAB, NJB, "sun of justice"). The context is one of divine judgment associated with the Day of Yahweh. The manifestation of a "sun of righteousness" on the Day of Yahweh will bring about the vindication of Yahweh's justice (Rudolph [1976: 289]), the restitution of "right order" within the community (Glazier-McDonald [1987a: 236]), and God's salvation for the pious remnant (Verhoef [1987: 329]). See further the NOTES on *šemeš* in 1:11 above.

Some commentators have attributed the phrase "sun of righteousness" to the influence of the Shamash cult of Babylonia (especially the concept of Shamash the sun god as the universal judge, cf. von Bulmerincq [1932: 533]; J.M.P. Smith [1912: 80]; Mason [1977: 158]; Petersen [1995: 224–25]; Weinfeld [1995: 28 n. 12]). Others associate the epithet with Canaanite ideology connected with solar characteristics ascribed to El Elyon (e.g., Glazier-McDonald [1987a: 236–37]). In a recent study, Taylor (pp. 211–16) dismisses the notion that the epithet "sun of righteousness" is evidence for an understanding of Yahweh as the sun in a postexilic solar cult. Rather, Taylor (p. 216) considers the solar epithet simply "a case of the use of figurative language for God."

Such figurative language is used elsewhere in poetic and prophetic literature to typify the blessing of Yahweh upon those to whom he raises his face "as an act of grace, so that the rays of his countenance (like the sun in its splendor) would shine upon them" (D. N. Freedman [1980: 233]). According to Knight (p. 42), light and salvation are synonymous in the OT/HB, "light being the sacramental sign of God's redemptive love." If this is the case in Malachi, the final disputation echoes the sentiments of the prophet's initial oracle, Yahweh loves Jacob (1:2–5).

Westermann (1969: 357–58) has observed that the theophanic language of Trito-Isaiah (that of Yahweh rising as a sun or a star, Isa 58:8; 60:2), nearly obliterates the older motif of ephiphany (that of Yahweh as victorious warrior, Deut 33:2; cf. Mayes [p. 398]). Given the context of judgment on the Day of Yahweh in Mal 3:13–21 [4:3], perhaps both images are symbolized in the solar epithet — the victory of Yahweh over evildoers and the glory of Yahweh's salvation rising like the sun upon the righteous in Israel.

It is possible that the source for Malachi's solar epithet, "sun of righteousness," was the winged sun disk pervasive in ANE iconography (so J. Gray [1974: 5]; see Figure 13 and Keel [pp. 28, 215–17]; cf. Petersen [1995: 225]). This icon depicting (falcon or eagle) wings against a full sun represented the guardianship of the deity, an emblem of divine effulgence as well as protection and blessing for those peoples overshadowed by the "wings" of the deity (see further M. S. Smith).

ûmarpē' biknāpehâ. The coordinating *waw* is a simple conjunctive ("*and* healing . . ."), rendered literally as such in the LXX and V (cf. Rudolph [1976: 286]; R. L. Smith [1984: 312]; Verhoef [1987: 336]). The English versions (NAB,

NEB, NIV, NJB, NRSV) and many commentators (e.g., J.M.P. Smith [1912: 80]; Glazier-McDonald [1987a: 206]; Petersen [1995: 219]) substitute the preposition *with* (healing . . ."), understanding the construction as a prepositional phrase or subordinate result clause modifying *šemeš ṣĕdāqâ*, cf. WO'C § 38.3). It seems more likely that the conjunction functions as an epexegetical *waw*, clarifying or specifying the sense of the preceding clause (and perhaps compensating for the gapping of the verb *zrḥ*, cf. WO'C § 39.2.4).

The substantive *marpē'* (I) means "healing, remedy" (*CHAL*: 216) and occurs in prophetic literature only in Jer 8:15, 14:19 [2x]; 33:6; and Mal 3:20 [4:2]. Malachi envisions the healing longed for by the prophet Jeremiah's audience (Jer 8:15, 14:19; the LXX and V support the MT *marpē'*).

According to Verhoef (1987: 329–30), the semantic domain of *marpē'* ("healing") is comprehensive (the opposite of disease, disaster, and trouble). The context of divine judgment in the sixth disputation suggests a meaning more akin to that found in Ps 107:20 ("rescue from ruin," *wĕyirpā'ēm wimallēṭ miššĕhîtôtam*). Based on the use of *marpē'* in Jeremiah, the "healing" anticipated for Yehud by Malachi included the physical reconstruction of the city of Jerusalem and environs (note that Malachi's oracles predate Nehemiah's activities by five decades), the spiritual rehabilitation of the people, and material prosperity based on economic and agricultural recovery in the land (Brueggemann [1991: 94]; cf. Andersen and Freedman [1980: 420] on the eschatological connotations of the verb *rp'*). This promise of healing in Jer 33:6 is connected with the "purification" of Israel (*thr*, 33:8; cf. Mal 3:3 above). Malachi's use of *marpē'* suggests dependence on Jer 8:15 and 33:6 and provides further support for the identification of the "covenant" announced by the messenger as the "new covenant" (Jer chaps. 31–33; see the NOTES on 3:1 above).

The preposition *bêt* (*biknāpehâ*) has a spatial sense ("in," WO'C § 11.2.5b). The feminine noun *kānāp* does occur elsewhere in the Haggai-Zechariah-Malachi corpus, with the meaning "wing(s)" (Zech 5:9) or "edge, fold" (of a garment, Hag 2:12; Zech 8:23). The word *kānāp* is most often translated "wings" in Mal 3:20 [4:2] (NEB, NIV, NRSV; cf. e.g., Glazier-McDonald [1987a: 238–40]). Some English versions (NAB, NJB) and biblical commentators (e.g., Chary [1969: 274]; Cashdan [1948: 355]; *TDOT* 7:230–31) equate the metaphorical reference to the wings of a bird with the therapeutic radiation of the sun and read "rays" instead of "wings" (but Verhoef [1987: 330 n. 29, citing Van der Woude] contends that the wings of a solar disk denote clouds, not sun beams). The note in JPSV reads "with healing in the folds of its garments" (perhaps influenced by Hag 2:12, *biknap bigdô*), while Syr substitutes "lips" for "wings" (cf. V *pinnis*, "feather/s, wing/s"). Dahood (1965: 107–8) documents the motif of a divine bird with great wingspan in Canaanite and biblical literature.

The phrase *ûmarpē' biknāpehâ* is unique to Mal 3:20 [4:2] in the MT and has proved difficult to interpret due to the complexity of the symbolism associated with solar disk iconography. The feminine singular possessive pronoun (-*āh*) attached to the dual construct form of *kānāp* is instructive, indicating Yahweh's "righteousness" (feminine *ṣĕdāqâ*) is the focal point of the vivid imagery.

Given the similarities of Malachi's figurative language to the icon of the ANE winged sun disk, it seems more likely the prophet intended direct correspondence with the winged feature of the symbol, rather than an indirect parallel with the rays of the sun (sometimes found on the symbol in the form of lines emanating from the sun representing beams of light). Even as the outstretched wings pictured on the solar disk ensured the protective presence of the deity for the king and all those under the shadow of the emblem in the ancient world, so too will the "wings" of Yahweh's "solar-like" righteousness overshadow those revering him and bring healing to postexilic Yehud (note the several poetic references to the protective "shadow" of Yahweh's "wings" [ṣēl + kānāp], Pss 17:8; 18:11 [10]; 36:8 [7]; 57:2 [1]; 61:5 [4]; 63:8 [7]; 91:4; cf. Deut 32:11; cf. Exod 19:4 recounting how Yahweh himself brought the Hebrews out of Egypt "upon eagles' wings" ['al-kanpê nĕšārîm]). Luther (Oswald 1975: 418) is correct to draw attention to the motif of divine protection associated with the symbol, because the righteous will no longer be trampled by evildoers (v 21 [4:3]; cf. TDOT 7:231). In fact, there will soon be a reversal of roles with the righteous supplanting the wicked as "victors."

wîṣā'tem ûpištem. The waw-relative + suffix conjugation (wîṣā'tem) introduce a consequential situation ("the sun . . . will arise . . . and so you will," (WO'C § 32.2.2). The waw also continues the sense of (near) future time established by the preceding verbal construction (wĕzārĕhâ above; cf. WO'C § 32.3.6c, 39.2.1d). The following waw-relative + suffixing conjugation (ûpištem) express a simple sequential situation (WO'C § 32.2.3c). The two verbs may be understood as hendiadys, representing two aspects of a complex situation ("you will come out leaping . . . ," or NEB, "break loose"; cf. WO'C 32.3b). I have retained the separate translation of the two verbs (yṣ' + pwš, "you will go out and you will frisk about") in an attempt to preserve the emphasis on the pronoun "you" (i.e., the God fearers) in the fifth and sixth disputations.

The verb yṣ' means, "go/come out, go/come forth," in the Qal stem (CHAL: 139–40, so JPSV, NJB, NRSV). The word occurs only here in Malachi's disputations. One wonders if the prophet's language here has been influenced by Zech 14:3 (or conversely?), depicting Yahweh "going forth" to fight against the nations (wĕyāṣā' YHWH . . . ; cf. Zech 14:8).

The Qal stem pwš means "frisk, paw the ground" (CHAL: 290) and is rare in the OT/HB (occurring only in Jer 50:11; Hab 1:8, and Mal 3:20 [4:2]). The word conveys a sense of carefree and energetic playfulness characteristic of tethered calves released to pasture in Jeremiah and Malachi (Holladay [1989: 417]; cf. JPSV 1962, NAB, and Glazier-McDonald [1987a: 206], "gambol"). The translation "stamp" (JSPV 1985) suggests a consequential situation in connection with 'ss ("trample," see NAB). The relationship of pwš ("paw the ground") and 'ss in v 21 [4:3] is not so much one of cause and effect, but rather the (simple) sequential outcome of divine judgment on the Day of Yahweh. The point of the imagery is that of the reversal of fortunes in postexilic Yehud and the vindication of the righteous.

kĕ'eglê marbēq. The preposition kaph is used in a comparative sense, describing comparison or correspondence ("as, like," WO'C § 11.2.9b). The noun 'ēgel ("bull-calf," CHAL: 264) is unique to Mal 3:20 [4:2] in the Haggai-Zechariah-

Malachi corpus (4QXIIa reads the singular *'ēgel;* cf. Petersen [1995: 220] n. e). The noun *marbēq* means literally "tying-place" (i.e., "stall," as the place where animals were fattened, BDB: 918) and functions as an adjective in the construct-genitive relationship with *'eglê* (WO'C § 9.5.3).

The translation "stall-fed calves," following McCarter (1980: 421), is preferable. The word occurs but three times outside Mal in MT: 1 Sam 28:24 (*'ēgel-marbēq*, literally the "fattened calf" belonging to the medium of Endor); Jer 46:21 (*kě'eglê marbēq*, metaphorically in reference to the mercenaries of Egypt); Amos 6:4 (*wa'ăgālîm mittôk marbēq*; cf. Andersen and Freedman [1989: 562–63] on the prophet's condemnation of Israel's "sumptuous consumerism" with respect to "calves from the stall").

The image depicted by the simile is that of well-fed calves, suggesting the prosperity of divine blessing (confirming the promise of 3:10 and overturning the lament of 3:14). Unlike the metaphor of the well-cared-for Egyptian mercenaries fleeing in terror in a time of danger (Jer 46:21), the portrayal in Malachi is one of carefree playfulness indicating peace and security (cf. Holladay [1989: 332]). The LXX interprets *moschária èk desmōn áneiména* ("calves loosed from fetters"), while Syr reads "calves of the herd" or "calves of the ox" (*min* + *bāqār* on the basis of the LXX *móschos,* "young bull"[?]; cf. V *vituli de armento,* "calves of the herd").

21[4:3]. *wě'assôtem rěšā'îm.* The *waw*-relative + suffixing conjugation represent a simple sequential situation (so NJB, NRSV; but NIV and Verhoef [1987: 312] understand a consequential situation, "then") and continue the sense of (near) future time established by the preceding verbal construction (WO'C § 32.3.3c; see the NOTES for *wîṣā'tem* above. The verb *'ss* occurs only here in the MT. The word means "to tread down, trample" (BDB: 779a). This understanding of the verbal root is derived from the Arabic *'ss* ("to go the rounds, trample, prowl"), and the masculine noun *'āsîs* ("sweet wine"; cf. Wolff [1977: 28–29]; Crenshaw [1995: 95]). On *rěšā'îm,* see the NOTES for *riš'â* in verse 19 above (3:19 [4:1]).

kî-yihyû 'ēper. A majority of interpreters and the English versions understand *kî* as a conjunction introducing the subordinate clause (*"for* they will be . . . ," e.g., Rudolph [1976: 286]; R. L. Smith [1984: 336]; Glazier-McDonald [1987a: 206]; cf. JPSV, NEB, NRSV). I side with the minority voice in reading *kî* emphatically as a clausal adverb ("surely, indeed," so Henderson [1980: 462]; Chary [1969: 274]; cf. WO'C § 39.3.4e). The emphatic rendering of *kî* is in keeping with the hortatory tone of the disputation, especially because the paragraph 3:19–21 [4:1–3] concludes the prophet's message to Yehud. Further, the clause beginning *kî yihyû 'ēper . . . ,* graphically announces the trenchant manner by which a distinction will be made between the righteous and the wicked (i.e., the one will trample the other, see v 18 above).

The Qal prefixing conjugation of *hyh* is a nonperfective form expressing specific future time contingent upon *wě'assôtem* ("and you will trample . . . indeed *they will be* . . ." (cf. WO'C § 31.6.2). The dramatic reversal in the fate of the righteous versus the wicked is underscored in the verbal subject pronoun ("*you* will . . . *they* will be . . .").

The noun *'ēper* may mean "dust" or "ash(es)" depending upon the context (cf. KBL 1:80; elsewhere the Hebrew idiom connects "dust and ashes" [*'āpār wā'ēper*] in a single phrase, Gen 18:27; Job 30:19; 42:6). The word occurs elsewhere in the Twelve only in Jonah 3:6. Given the message of the prophet's final oracle (especially *bō'ēr*, "burning" in 3:19 [4:1]), most commentators and the English versions translate "ashes" (e.g., Rudolph [1976: 286]; Glazier-McDonald [1987a: 206]; Petersen [1995: 219]; cf. JPSV, NAB, NEB, NIV, NJB, NRSV). A similar passage describing the judgment of Tyre utilizing *'ēš* ("fire") + *'ēper* ("ashes") is found in Ezek 28:18. The ancient versions consistently render *eper* with "ashes" (LXX *spodós*, V *cinis*, T *qiṭmā'*, Syr *qṭm*, etc.).

taḥat kappôt raglêkem. The preposition *taḥat* has a locational use, "under" (WO'C § 11.2.15). In 1 Kgs 5:17 [3] the phrase *taḥat kappôt raglāw* ("under the soles of his foot [*feet*]") pictures the subjugation of enemies by placing the foot on the neck of the vanquished foe (G. H. Jones [1984: 154]). Here the image is one of total conquest more than subjugation. The "wicked" are not subjugated by the "righteous," rather they are consumed by the "fire" of divine judgment (3:19 [4:1]). The destruction of the wicked by Yahweh in the day of his epiphany marks the victory of righteousness over evil, vindicating the "God-fearers" and erasing all doubts about God's justice.

The phrase *kappôt raglêkem* ("soles of your feet") is unique to Mal 3:21 [4:3] in the Twelve. In Second Isaiah the phrase (*kappôt raglayik*) occurs in connection with the worship of Yahweh by descendants of the former enemies of Israel in the "new" Jerusalem (Isa 60:14). Malachi's use of the expression *kappôt raglêkem* may be a veiled reference reinstating Israel's "covenant destiny" as outlined in Deut 11:24 (the divine promise of possessing all the land upon which they set foot [*kap raglêkem*] conditional upon their obedience to Yahweh's commandments). In either case, the phrase *kappôt raglêkem* appears to have eschatological connotations in Malachi. The LXX omits *kappôt* ("soles"; as dittography of *tḥt*, according to J.M.P. Smith [1912: 85]).

bayyôm 'ăšer 'ănî 'ōśēh. Here *bayyôm* ("in the day") is an equivalent expression for *bayyôm hāhû'* ("in that day"), the eschatological Day of Yahweh. Such a construction (i.e., *bayyôm* minus *hāhû'*) describing this divinely appointed "day" is unique to Malachi in prophetic literature. According to Botterweck (*TDOT* 6:28–31), the "Day of Yahweh" in postexilic prophecy continues the didactic tradition begun earlier in the prophets Zephaniah and Ezekiel. This didactic tradition "gradually becomes the nucleus around which crystallizes a complex eschatological drama" (*TDOT* 6:31; see further the discussion of *layyôm* [v 17] and *hayyôm* in [v 19] in the NOTES above).

The preposition *bêt* conveys a temporal sense in conjunction with the word of time (*yôm*, marking the actual time "when" Yahweh plans to act; cf. WO'C § 11.2.5c).

The relative pronoun *'ăšer* introduces an attributive (relative) clause modifying *bayyôm* (cf. WO'C § 19.3b on *'ăšer* as equivalent to "when" after words of time, so NIV, NJB). Because "the day" defines a *span of time* in which Yahweh will act more than a *point in time*, I have opted for the translation "during" (cf. *TDOT* 6:31).

The personal pronoun *'ănî* functions as the subject of the participle *'ōśēh* in the relative clause and involves *psychological focus* in the form of *self-assertion* (cf. WO'C § 16.3.2e). The distribution of the independent pronoun *'ănî* in the disputations confirms this emphasis on Yahweh's self-assertion; the word is found initially in oracles one (1:4, Yahweh's sovereignty over the nations) and two (1:6, 14; 2:9, Yahweh's sovereignty over Israel) and again in the Day of Yahweh oracles (five, 3:6, and six, 3:17, 21 [4:3]). The pattern also highlights the synergistic nature of covenant relationship with Yahweh, in that disputations one, two, five, and six all address the work or character of God in some way. Conversely, disputations three and four focus on human responsibility, namely repentance and social justice.

The Qal participle *'śh* in the relative clause is variously translated in the English versions ("act," NEB, NJB, NRSV; "take action," NAB; "do," NIV; "preparing," JPSV). The use of the participial form at the conclusion of the prophet's final disputation is significant for the audience of postexilic Yehud. In this case it seems that the participle indicates "a continuing state of affairs" in reference to present time (WO'C § 37.6e; or perhaps the so-called *futurum instans* denoting imminency, cf. § 37.6f). The prophet's final discourse would have little impact in bolstering the hopes of a beleaguered restoration community if the people were not assured that Yahweh was *even now* preparing this day of vindication and restoration for the faithful in Israel. On the participle *'ōśēh*, see further the NOTES for verses 15, 17, 19 [4:1] above.

'āmar YHWH ṣĕbā'ôt. The repetition of the word *yôm* (*hayyôm* in v 19a [4:1] and *bayyôm* in v 21c [4:3]) and the messenger formula in the same two verses forms an envelope construction framing the final pericope (vv 19–21 [4:1–3]) of the concluding disputation (3:13–21 [4:3]). The reversal of fortunes forecast for the righteous in the prophet's closing discourse constitutes a fitting capstone for Malachi's oracles, in that the assertion of Yahweh's covenant love for Israel made in the first disputation (1:2–5) will be demonstrated conclusively and finally in the "dramatic dénouement" of the Day of Yahweh (cf. Baldwin [1972a: 250]). On the messenger formula, see further the NOTES on 1:4 above.

COMMENTS

The prophet's concluding disputation addresses in reverse order the (hypothetical?) questions raised by the audience in the fourth and fifth oracles. The first question, "Where is the God of judgment?" (2:17), is answered directly in the bold declaration of divine judgment accompanying the imminent Day of Yahweh (3:19 [4:1]). The second question, ". . . who can stand at his appearing?" (3:2), finds its rejoinder in the affirmation that those who "fear" and "serve" Yahweh will be spared in the day of Yahweh's visitation (3:17–18).

Malachi's prioritizing of the two questions is important because the restoration community learned previously in the fourth disputation (2:17–3:5) that the coming Day of Yahweh will impact both the righteous and wicked. Therefore it was crucial for the prophet to offer some assurance of divine deliverance for the righteous, the segment of the community expressing doubt as to Yahweh's justice (i.e., "evildoers prosper . . . ," 3:15).

The sixth disputation forms a fitting conclusion to the prophet's message to postexilic Yehud for several reasons. Most significant, the opening and closing oracles of Malachi's message bridge the theological truth that "Yahweh has loved Jacob" (1:2). The reality of this divine election and love is obvious from the lessons of history, serving as the guarantee of the certainty of Yahweh's covenant love in the eschaton.

Next, the final discourse speaks to perhaps the most severe of all the questions posed by Malachi's audience, because they had seen little evidence to warrant continued covenant loyalty to Yahweh ("What profit is there . . . , 3:14). The Day of Yahweh brings the vindication of faith in the image of the "sun of righteousness" (3:20 [4:2]).

Finally, Malachi's last speech offers a remedy for what Wells (pp. 57–61) has described as the crisis of abandoned hope. The inhabitants of postexilic Yehud not only "robbed" God in neglecting the tithe (3:8), but also "robbed" themselves given their preoccupation with the temporal and tangible elements of life. The prophet sums up by challenging the community to appropriate the perspective of the Day of Yahweh, an outlook that trades the provisional "curse" of the present for the hope of the perpetual "blessing" of the future.

The carefully crafted argument of three literary subunits of the final disputation also contributes to the forcefulness of the prophet's concluding remarks, as Watts (1987a: 376–77) has observed. Malachi first accuses with the intent to persuade the audience to return to Yahweh (vv 13–15; cf. 3:7). He then consoles the "God-fearers" resident within the larger community by assuring them that Yahweh still loves "Jacob" (vv 16–18; cf. 1:2–3). Lastly, this agent of Yahweh closes his address to postexilic Yehud with the warning of divine judgment, confirming the earlier threat associated with Yahweh's visitation (vv 19–21 [4:1–3]; cf. 3:2).

The warning speech proves an effective, almost haunting, method for concluding the series of disputations because it accentuates the urgency of the hour for postexilic Yehud and leaves the issue of accountability to the prophet's message to the audience. Albeit a form of negative "operant conditioning," the threat of divine judgment historically functioned as one means by which Yahweh's prophets sought to motivate repentance in Israel (see Heschel [2:59–78] on the meaning and mystery of divine wrath).

In addition, all of the three subunits of the sixth disputation work together to unify this concluding discourse with the prophet's earlier speeches. The first literary subunit (vv 13–15) demonstrates immediate connections with the fifth oracle (3:6–12) in the repetition of the themes of "testing" (3:10) and "calling happy" (3:12). The second literary subunit calls attention to the audience rebuttal of the fourth oracle (2:17–3:5), "Where is the God of judgment?" (2:17). The God of judgment will distinguish between the righteous and the wicked (3:18). As already noted above, the third literary subunit (vv 19–21 [4:1–3]) echoes the themes of Yahweh's covenant love for Israel (stated in the first oracle, 1:2–5) and the Day of Yahweh introduced in the fourth oracle (3:1). Implicit throughout the final dispute is Yahweh's faithfulness, in contrast to Yehud's faithlessness (oracles two [1:6–2:9] and three [2:10–16]).

The final oracle is addressed to the same audience as the prophet's leading disputation, the postexilic community of Jerusalem in general (see the discussion of the one-group, two-group, and three-group audience hypotheses in I. C. 7. Message above). The community includes civil and religious leaders and the general populace, the pious, the pseudo-pious, and the impious (cf. Lindblom [1962: 406] and the heightening of the division of the Hebrew people into two groups during the postexilic period, the faithful and the apostates).

It is difficult to determine whether the audience rebuttal lamenting the lack of "profit" from serving God (3:14) represents a question of honest doubt raised by the pious of the community or an impudent jibe aimed at "organized religion" by the pseudo-pious and/or impious of Malachi's audience. Whatever the case, some of those among the pious and perhaps others among the doubters and skeptics took the prophet's invitation to heart and began to consider the matter earnestly. The closing statements of the second pericope (vv 16–17) are redirected to that subgroup of Malachi's audience.

The final pericope of the section (3:18–21 [4:1–3]) is addressed to the community at large, emphasizing the two essential constituencies of the community — the righteous and the wicked (after the pattern of earlier prophetic and wisdom traditions, e.g., Isa 3:10–11; 65:13–15; Hab 1:4; Ps 1:5; Prov 10:7; cf. D. R. Jones [1962: 203–4]). Unlike the report of the community-wide response to Haggai's appeal to rebuild Yahweh's Temple (Hag 1:14), only an unspecified number of "God-fearers" gave guarded attention to Malachi's message (Mal 3:16).

Postexilic Yehud has already spoken "harsh words" against Yahweh in the indictment of divine justice as demonstrated in the retribution principle (2:17). The two disputations are connected by the theme of divine judgment, the fourth oracle (2:17–3:5) emphasizing the purification of the community and the final oracle (3:13–21 [4:3]) threatening the great assize of the Day of Yahweh. Unlike the fourth disputation, however, the gravity of these charges against Yahweh prompts the prophet to respond as if Yahweh were speaking for himself. R. L. Smith (1984: 337) interprets this as "open rebellion," connecting the harsh words of Malachi's audience with the "murmuring" (equating *dābar* with *lwn* as a part of Coats's murmuring motif associated with the wilderness trek of the Israelites after the Exodus from Egypt).

This extreme stance is unwarranted for two reasons. First, the semantic range for *dābar* does include the meaning "rebellion," when the verb is coupled with the prepositions *bêt* or *'al* ("to speak *against*," KBL 1:210; cf. Num 21:5, 7; Ps 78:18). Nevertheless, the context of those citations employing *dābar* + *bêt* or *'al* as an idiom for rebellion invariably includes related terms, like *mrh* ("be refractory," Ps 78:17 [and note the use of *nsh* in v 18]) or *qsr* ("be impatient," Num 21:4 [followed by *ht'* in confession of sin in v 7]). Such is not the case in the context of *dābar* + *'al* in Mal 3:13. Second, interpreting *dābar* + *'al* as open rebellion assumes that Malachi addresses only the evildoers and the seditious within the community. Again, the context of Malachi militates against this understanding, especially in light of the prophet's challenge to "test" God from the posture of faith (*bḥn*, 3:10) and the reference to the "wicked" in the reported audience rebuttal (3:15). Indeed, the postexilic community was impatient given their plight (so Cashdan [1948: 353]), but it seems more likely that the response of the people was not a deliberate act of open rebellion. Rather, Baldwin (1972a: 248) and Ogden and Deutsch (1967: 108) are probably correct in assessing this verbal outpouring by the community as an "unwitting" and "spontaneous expression."

J.M.P. Smith (pp. 76–77) laments the fact that personal piety had degenerated into a commercial venture in postexilic Yehud. Glazier-McDonald (1987a: 214) even suggests that these acts of piety ("parading mournfully," v 14) were little more than a failed ploy to attract Yahweh's attention for the redress of their desperate situation. While the complaints about impoverishment no doubt betray a certain self-serving motivation for worshiping Yahweh, Mason correctly recognizes that a thread of honest doubt joins the questions posed by Malachi's audience in 2:17 and 3:13–15. It is entirely possible that the "righteous" within the community were attempting to excuse their negligence in paying the tithe, the prophet's contention in the previous disputation (3:8–9). The tithe constitued a tax on the increase of "capital," and Malachi's audience contends that they have garnered no "profit" (having assumed some direct correlation between religious practice and material prosperity). The scenario calls to mind Job's defense, indicting the wisdom and justice of God's sovereignty in order to protest his own innocence in respect to his predicament (Job 40:2).

The crisis of identity diagnosed in the opening disputation by Wells (pp. 46–48) resurfaces in the closing disputation. The postexilic community in Yehud awaited tangible evidence that Yahweh *still* "loved Jacob" (1:2–3). The expectations for the immediate implementation of Jeremiah's "new covenant" in postexilic Yehud fostered a new consciousness of individualism in the community. Unfortunately, a miscalculation of the application of the retribution principle to the evildoer (given the dynamics of the relationship of the "one" to the "many" within this covenant arrangement) caused a reversal in the community's values. According to Craigie (p. 245), "ordinary persons . . . abandoned ancient principles for a more empirical approach; since the arrogant and evil persons seem to prosper, without any response from God, why not join them?"

Glazier-McDonald's (1987a: 210–11) observations are cogent at this juncture, in that the harsh words of the people "should not be viewed as the symptom of an exhausted piety, but as the symptom of an anguished faith." The pious in Malachi's audience were attempting to ascertain their standing before Yahweh. Who are the "righteous"? Who are the "wicked"? If outward appearances were any indication, the answers to these questions are in doubt as the "God-fearers" evaluate their current experience.

This identity crisis, however, will be resolved by Yahweh in the day of his visitation. Absolute, and painfully clear, delineations will be made between the camps of the "righteous" and the "wicked" in Yehud (3:17–18). Here it appears that Malachi modifies Ezekiel's (21:8–9 [3–4]) pronouncement of Yahweh's intention to "judge" (*krt* = "cut off") both the righteous (*ṣādîq*) and the wicked (*rāšā ʿ*).

Malachi restricts Yahweh's judgment to the wicked in postexilic Yehud (3:19, 21 [4:1, 3]).

The litmus test by which Yahweh will assay the community is that of "fear" (*yr'*, 3:20 [4:2]), fear in the form of obedience to his covenant commands and genuine reverence in the worship response. It is worth noting that the theme of proper worship does connect the second (purified priestly instruction), fourth (purified ritual), and fifth (restoration of the tithe) disputations with the final discourse. The true covenant loyalty and worship Malachi intends is that outlined in Second Isaiah, the fast of social justice (Isa 58:6–9), the forsaking of personal pursuits for delight in Yahweh and his Sabbath (Isa 58:13) — then all will see Yahweh's love for Jacob (Isa 58:14).

Scalise (p. 415) aptly reminds us that the literary device of reversal, so prevalent in Malachi, culminates forcefully in the final disputation. Malachi's audience accused Yahweh of inverting the principles of divine justice in the fourth disputation, asserting that he "delighted" in evildoers (2:17). Now the community of postexilic Yehud is guilty of the very thing they (falsely) attributed to Yahweh (3:15). Likewise, Yahweh's servant offers the assembly the rare invitation to "put Yahweh to the test," so they might enjoy the overflow of his blessing (3:10); but Malachi's strident onlookers counter that this "test" is "rigged" in favor of the evildoers ("blessed" are the evildoers because they test God and escape, 3:15b).

Previously, the prophet announced Yahweh's condition for restoring prosperity to Yehud (the full tithe, 3:9–10), even predicting that the nations would ultimately pronounce a beatitude over Israel (3:12). Again, the people transpose the words of Malachi, articulating their own beatitude about the ungodly ("blessed" are the arrogant because they prosper, 3:15a). D. R. Jones (p. 204) comments that it was imperative that Malachi disentangle good and evil for his hearers because they were "not merely observing (as we must) the injustices of life, but glorifying them as conditions of the good life."

Malachi's final disputation is unusual in that it combines a third-person report (v 16) and a first-person speech by Yahweh (v 17) with the dialogical discourse (vv 13–15). The prophet's concluding oracle also shifts between two scenes, the earthly sphere of postexilic Yehud and the heavenly realm of Yahweh's abode. This fact, God's sovereign rule of the two realities, suggests an important clue for providing (at least) a partial answer to the question of theodicy raised by the pious skeptics in Malachi's audience.

Hebrew wisdom tradition was already probing the inscrutable question of human suffering, especially the suffering of the righteous. The sages accepted human suffering as a truism because the fall had rendered the created order "crooked" (Job 4:17; Ps 14:1–3; Eccl 1:13; 7:13). The solution was simply to put one's fate in the hands of Yahweh, since in his inscrutability he alone understands the mystery of human suffering (Job 36:26; 42:2; see the discussion of "Suffering" in *ABD* 6:219–25). Much like the sage, Malachi calls upon the restoration community to consider the end of the matter from the beginning and place their fate with Yahweh in view of the impending judgment of the Day of Yahweh (cf. Eccl 3:17; 8:12–13; 11:9).

In one sense, Malachi's solution to the (perceived) problems associated with divine retribution in this earthly reality has its counterpart in the psalmist's under-standing of the fate of the wicked (Ps 73:15–20). The righteous may gain limited perspective on the injustices of this life through contemplation of the heavenly reality, knowing that Yahweh is ultimately a just judge and the wicked will indeed perish (Ps 73:27–28). Notice also that, contrary to the perceptions of the assembly in postexilic Yehud, the divine reward of faith offered by Yahweh is not necessar-ily material (v 17). Yahweh's promise to the faithful is one of deliverance in the Day of Yahweh, not prosperity during the interim.

J. J. Collins (pp. 213–14) insists that "the book of remembrance" does not sug-gest salvation for the righteous beyond death, only healing in this life. By con-trast, Mason (1990: 255) understands the heavenly book in an eschatological sense, equating it with the record of those destined for life in the restored Jerusa-lem (Isa 4:3; cf. Cashdan [1948: 354] on the "book of remembrance" as the "book of all ages," the divine ledger of good deeds meriting future reward). While I am inclined to agree with Mason, the issue is not one of future versus immedi-ate reward, or a literal understanding of the "book of remembrance" versus a metaphorical one (cf. Scalise [1987: 416]), or even Yahweh's predetermination of human events (cf. Glazier-McDonald [1987a: 220]). Rather, the pressing con-cern for the prophet is that of offering some token of comfort and encouragement to righteous doubters of the restoration community. What postexilic Yehud really needs is the assurance that God has not forgotten them (cf. Petersen [1995: 225], the prophet "proffers good news to the righteous"). Yahweh's "book of remem-brance" affords such surety, certifying that the names of the righteous are perpet-ually in the forefront of his mind (cf. Verhoef [1987: 320] on the "book of remem-brance" as "active actualization"). On this more practical note, Mason (1990: 254) takes encouragement in the fact "that this preacher with a pastoral heart believes that God notes their 'fear' of him in his book, rather than their doubts." This affirms in a general way Heschel's (1:12) observation that behind the auster-ity of Yahweh's prophet is both love and compassion for humanity.

The language of the prophet in verse 17 abounds with intertextual echoes, "solemn and ... profound traditional terminology" according to Ogden and Deutsch (p. 109). Specific examples include the phrases "Lord of Hosts" (see the discussion in Ogden and Deutsch [1987: 107]), "the day when I act" (cf. Ezek 36:22, 32; Amos 9:12; Zeph 3:19), "as a man shows compassion for his son" (Deut 8:5; 32:5–6; Ps 103:13), and the word sĕgullâ ("special possession," Exod 19:5; Deut 7:6).

The reference to sĕgullâ is especially important, recalling Israel's covenant ex-periences with Yahweh and connoting their intimate relationship to him. Han-son (1986: 285) suggests that the term sĕgullâ ("special possession") was used to amplify the meaning of the phrase "fearers of Yahweh" (yir'ê YHWH), "propos-ing a radical new definition of what constituted the true people of God." In his efforts to isolate (or create?) the currents of social polarization between the cleric and laic elements of postexilic Yehud, Hanson probably overstates the case. The "fear of Yahweh" had always marked the true people of God, an attitude of rever-ence and actions of covenant obedience (cf. TDOT 6:306–9).

Given the association of *sĕgullâ* with the "kingdom of priests" and "holy nation" (Exod 19:6), it is unclear whether or not Malachi intends the citation as a further indictment of the Levitical priesthood. It is clear, however, that the equation of the righteous in Yehud with Yahweh's *sĕgullâ* signifies the renewal of covenant promises. Yahweh will provide the ultimate demonstration of his covenant love for Israel (1:2–3), he "will act as the 'father' he is and whose rights he has already claimed (1:6)" (Mason [1990: 255]). Malachi's association of the term *sĕgullâ* with the Day of Yahweh marks an original contribution to postexilic eschatology (cf. Glazier-McDonald [1987a: 225]).

The change in style in verse 17 from a third-person report about Yahweh's activity in verse 16 to a first-person speech by Yahweh is emphatic. According to Baldwin (1972a: 249), the literary shift accents Yahweh's compassion. Yahweh will have compassion on those who accept the prophet's rebuke and repent by returning to him in covenant obedience (3:7). As a consequence of Yahweh's compassion, the righteous are both delivered and pardoned in the approaching day of divine judgment (cf. Calvin [1979: 608–9]). The parent-child simile echoes the theology of Isaiah 40–55, where "attention is repeatedly drawn to the caring of God, who does not want his people to suffer any more" (Ogden and Deutsch [1987: 110]).

Increasingly, Malachi's audience experienced the blurring of theological truths and moral values. This inability to distinguish "good" from "evil" and "right" from "wrong" was not peculiar to postexilic Israel, for both Isaiah (5:20) and Micah (3:2) encountered the similar transposition of values. According to Glazier-McDonald (1987a: 228), the failure of Yahweh to act as the God of justice had obliterated the lines of distinction between the pious and impious. The fault lay not with Yahweh however, as Craigie (p. 246) notes: "a society may decide to abandon the distinction between good and evil, but God never abandons it." Rather, the fault lay with the restoration community (cf. the satirical plea in Isa 41:23 for the idols to "do good or do harm," so the people might know they are truly gods; apparently Malachi's audience could only recognize Yahweh at work in the "doing of good"). The malaise of postexilic Yehud was symptomatic of the "subtle crisis of secularism" (cf. Wells [1987: 41]). The combination of misteaching by the Levitical priesthood (2:8) and (apparently) a continued preoccupation with "materialism" as a sign of covenant blessing (3:14; cf. Hag 1:4, 6) resulted in this crisis of values. The Day of Yahweh will be an act of "values clarification," not one of "prosperity" versus "privation" with respect to material things, but "guilty" versus "not-guilty" in relationship to spiritual things (cf. Verhoef [1987: 324]).

The message of the concluding pericope of Malachi's final disputation is one of justice and judgment: justice in the vindication and restoration of the righteous and judgment in punishment and destruction of the wicked (3:19–21 [4:1–3]). This dual response of the prophet to postexilic Yehud serves as an answer to the question posed in 3:14 ("What profit in serving God?") and ultimately conveys the substance of the reply to the initial questions raised in the opening disputation ("How have you loved us?"). First, it is not futile to serve God because the God-fearers will survive the day of Yahweh's judgment as his special possession (3:20 [4:2]; cf. Scalise [1987: 416]). Second, Yahweh's love for Israel is manifest in this deliverance and in the reversal of fortunes in Yehud (3:21 [4:3]).

The fourth (2:17–3:5) and sixth disputations (3:13–21 [4:3]) are joined by the theme of divine judgment and the symbol of fire. Fire is often utilized to typify both the divine presence and divine judgment in biblical imagery (cf. Keel [1978: 183–86]). Scalise (p. 416) recalls that divine justice is a two-edged concept. Yahweh intends to purify the righteous in the refiner's fire of "testing" (3:2). Likewise, he proposes to incinerate the wicked in the (baker's?) oven of "destruction" (v 19 [4:1]). Part of the answer to theodicy in the sixth disputation lies in the truth of the prophet's indictment of the entire restoration community — the righteous are among the guilty as well. Important then, as it is now, is the fact that the emblems of God's presence and God's judgment are not mutually exclusive. Achtemeier (1986: 187) rightly emphasizes the verity of Yahweh's benevolent presence in the midst of the afflictions and sufferings of the righteous.

The "light" imagery associated with both "fire" and the "sun" are probably rooted in the language of the Psalms, not in the cosmic dualism of the Zoroastrian religion (so Mason [1990: 256]). Yahweh is depicted as "a sun" bestowing favor and honor in Ps 84:11, and there are numerous references to "light" in connection with the deliverance associated with Yahweh's theophany (cf. Glazier-McDonald [1987a: 235]). It is even possible that the reference contains an echo to the Aaronic blessing (Num 6:24–26), which would be appropriate given the rehabilitation of the priesthood envisioned by Malachi.

The application of the "rising sun" motif to Yahweh is fitting, because the sun god was deemed "the judge" among the gods in the pantheons of the ancients (Mason [1977: 158]; see further the discussion in Petersen [1995: 224–25] on the relationship of the image of the "sun" and the concept of "righteousness"). According to R. W. Klein (1986: 150), "the winged sun disk . . . is transformed into a symbol of God's great eschatological reversal." The "dawning" of Yahweh's presence in Yehud as the righteous judge puts to rest the lament of the assembly in 2:17, "Where is the God of judgment?" "This is a gospel for a people in conflict . . . it answers their complaint about God's apparently unfair retribution" (R. W. Klein [1986: 150]). The "sun" of Yahweh's justice emerges as a symbol of triumph because at his epiphany Yahweh will both judge the wicked and heal the righteous (I. G. Matthews [p. 34]; cf. D. R. Jones [1962: 205]). The Talmud interprets the sun as Yahweh's "weapon," a sword of judgment for punishing the wicked and leaving them without root in this world or branch in the world to come (b. 'Abod Zar 3b). By contrast the righteous are "healed" by and "revel" in the sun when Yahweh removes this weapon of both judgment and restoration from its sheath.

Both Mason (1977: 159) and R. W. Klein (1986: 150) struggle with the vindictive tone of the original ending of Malachi, contending that the final disputation provokes a disturbing uneasiness in the (ancient?) and modern reader. In part, Keil (2:467) understands the "treading down" of the wicked by the righteous as liberation from all oppression. Given this perspective, the thrust of the message is not so much one of the triumph of the righteous over the wicked, but the triumph of divine justice. Nevertheless, we must admit that the theophany of

Yahweh is awesome and terrible and the reality of Yahweh as divine judge is terrifying—such truths should be disturbing (Deut 7:21; Joel 2:11, 31; cf. Ogden and Deutsch [1987: 111]).

Malachi's prediction of "the eventual rehabilitation of the pious and the shameful end of the 'wicked' . . . refutes the suggestion that to serve God is meaningless" (Ogden and Deutsch [1987: 114]). In one sense, the final disputation constitutes a most fitting conclusion to the prophet's oracles because of the "amazing reversal" of fortunes for the righteous (Baldwin [1972a: 250]). Such reversal climaxes the literary motif of turnabout prominent throughout the book.

Theologically, the emphasis upon the retribution principle in the final disputation underscores the seriousness of divine threat and the certainty of divine promise mingled in the book. Malachi's concluding speech assures the pious of Yehud that Yahweh intends to root out the evil in his covenant community, thus establishing his people in faithfulness and righteousness in fulfillment of Zech 8:8. ·

The fact remains, however ungracious, that the prophet Malachi was at best a product of his age. The classical era of Yahweh's prophet as "vizier" had passed (cf. Petersen [1977: 6]). Malachi is a man of words only, feeding upon the ideas (and oracles) of his preexilic predecessors (cf. Lindblom [1962: 404]). Malachi can only *speak* about the future reversal of fortunes for Israel (cf. Petersen [1977: 8]). Little has transpired during the early Persian period of postexilic Israelite history to suggest the imminent fulfillment of Malachi's oracles. The assessment of the situation in Yehud some five decades later in the memoirs of Ezra and Nehemiah indicate that not much has changed. The prophetic visions of later Hebrew prophecy never materialized, creating a crisis of authority in the religious community and giving rise to the development of "apocalyptic eschatology" (cf. Hanson [1979: 16–31]).

III. H. APPENDIXES: APPEALS TO IDEAL OT FIGURES

Early commentators assuming the unity of Mal 3:22–24 [4:4–6] with the rest of the book included Luther (Oswald 1975: 419), Calvin (pp. 624 ff.), and Keil (2:469). Among the litany of more recent voices affirming the integrity of the concluding verses of Malachi are von Bulmerincq (1926: 136–39), Frey (pp. 180–83), Baldwin (1972a: 251), Childs (1979: 495), Glazier-McDonald (1987a: 244–45), and Verhoef (1987: 338; although others like Nowack [p. 428] and Sellin [p. 617] admit only 3:22 [4:4] as original to Malachi).[1] The hortatory style

---

[1]Although creative, von Bulmerincq's (1926: 221–24) unique hypothesis identifying Mal 3:22–24 [4:4–6] as fragments of a seventh disputation original to the prophet Malachi must be dismissed as fanciful speculation.

and thematic unity of these closing verses with the message of the book are most commonly cited as supporting evidence for understanding Mal 3:22–24 [4:4–6] as integral to the oracles of Malachi.

The integrity of Mal 3:22–24 [4:4–6] was questioned as early as Wellhausen (p. 211) and is now widely understood as an editorial summation of Malachi's messages appended to the book as a postscript. Commonly cited observations raising suspicions about the originality of these verses include the shift in literary form and style from disputation to admonition and curse; the discontinuity between the oracles of Malachi and the appendixes in message, theme, and tone (e.g., 3:22 [4:4] identifies the messenger of 3:1 by name and assigns the figure a different role in the eschaton, and the harshness of the appendixes seems to overshadow the message of exhortation and hope present in the oracles); and the Deuteronomic diction (e.g., the utilization of words and phrases like "Horeb," "all Israel," "law of Moses," etc.).

This postscript is usually regarded as an epilogue, but Petersen (1995: 232) rightly asks, ". . . to what is it an epilogue?" The literature on the book of Malachi proposes a variety of answers to the question, including an epilogue to the book of Malachi itself, or to the three anonymous "oracles" (Zech 9:1; 12:1; Mal 1:1), or to the Haggai-Zechariah-Malachi corpus, or to the Book of the Twelve, or to the Latter Prophets, or to the Former and Latter Prophets, or to the Torah and the Prophets, or even to the entire Hebrew Bible. The more prominent of these options are discussed below.

J. M. P. Smith (1912: 81), Elliger (1950: 205–6), Horst (1954: 275), Chary (1969: 276–77), and R. L. Smith (1984: 340–41) are among those scholars who recognize the appendixes of Malachi as secondary additions serving as a colophon or postscript to the book itself. Others identify the concluding verses of Malachi (3:22–24 [4:4–6]) as a postscript to the corpus of the Book of the Twelve (e.g., D. R. Jones [1962: 206]; Clark [1975: 40–41]; Deissler [1988: 337–38]; Coggins [1987: 84]; and Redditt [1994: 243]). It is also possible that Malachi's postscript constitutes an epilogue for the entire corpus of the Latter Prophets (i.e., Joshua-Malachi, e.g., Eissfeldt [p. 442]; Rudolph [1976: 291–93]; Schneider [1979: 148–51]; Fishbane [1985: 536]; Mason [1990: 238]; and B. A. Jones [1995: 59–63]).

Petersen (1995: 232–33) extends the linkage of Malachi's epilogue to the whole of the Hebrew Bible by assuming that Hos 14:10 [9] is also an epilogue. He argues that these two epilogues form a "canonical envelope" encasing the Book of the Twelve. In addition, the Hosean epilogue joins the Book of the Twelve with the Writings, while Malachi's epilogue connects the Latter Prophets with the Torah and the Former Prophets (cf. Andersen and Freedman [1980: 647–48] on the wisdom theme of Hos 14:10 [9]).

I have already acknowledged the concluding verses of the book of Malachi as an editorial conclusion (containing two postscripts, 3:22 [4:4] and 3:23–24 [4:5–6]) appended to the oracles of Malachi (I. C. 7. Message above). I admit that the appendixes may serve double duty, functioning as a summary to the book of Malachi and forming the conclusion to the Book of the Twelve (so Coggins [1987: 84]; cf. Clark [1975: 40–41] who understands Mal 3:23–24 [4:5–6] as a literary counterpart to Deut 34:10–12). For Clark, the appendixes of Malachi constitute a summary of the Prophets as enforcers of the Mosaic Law, with the first post-script identifying Moses as the first and greatest of the prophets and Elijah as the last of the prophets).

However, it seems odd that a later redactor would summarize Malachi's message so harshly, given the prophet's call to repentance and emphasis on the restoration of Israel as Yahweh's "special possession" (3:7, 17). Furthermore, the use of the oracular title *dĕbar-YHWH* in the superscription already works to join Malachi to Haggai and Zechariah as part of the Twelve, making this colophon somewhat redundant if it is a postscript for the collection of the Twelve Prophets.

It seems more likely that this appeal to the ideal figures of Moses and Elijah in the two appendixes of Malachi has significance for more than the book itself. The coupling of Moses and Elijah, personifications of the Hebrew legal and prophetic traditions, links these two basic theological building blocks of OT/HB thought. Thus, the two appendixes bridge two literary collections: the Primary History and the Latter Prophets. D. N. Freedman (1991: 42) has argued that this linkage is important for interpreting both collections because the Latter Prophets are supplemental to the Primary History, and the two anthologies were intended to be read together. If Petersen's (1995: 233) understanding of Hos 14:10 [9] and Mal 3:22–24 [4:4–6] is correct, then the Writings of the Hebrew Bible must be considered as a third anthology designed to be read along with the Former and Latter Prophets.

The appendixes of Malachi, then, may be construed as a deliberate effort on the part of a scribal editor or compiler to unite these two literary collections. The first appendix (3:22 [4:4]) appeals to Moses and connects the Hebrew prophetic tradition with the Law of Moses and the Hebrew legal tradition. The second appendix constitutes a conclusion "to the whole prophetic section of the canon by bringing the prophetic movement, typified by Elijah, into relationship with the Torah" (Mason [1990: 238]). It is entirely possible that the reference to Elijah points to both the Former and Latter Prophets, suggesting that the Primary History is now complete and has been divided into two major segments: Torah and Former Prophets. This division of the Hebrew Bible has been attributed to the editorial work of Ezra and Nehemiah (cf. D. N. Freedman [1991: 91–93]). If Ezra and Nehemiah were responsible for the postscript of Malachi, these verses may be appropriately dated toward the end of the fifth century B.C./E. (so Nogalski [1993b: 212]; and Redditt [1994: 249–50]).

Less convincing are those arguments citing Deuteronomistic overtones in Mal 3:22–24 [4:4–6] as evidence of editorial activity in the closing verses of the book (especially because the so-called D document virtually disintegrates given Polzin's [1976] typlogical analysis of biblical Hebrew; see the catalog of Deuteronomic stylistic features and vocabulary in J. M. P. Smith [1912: 85]; cf. Andersen and Freedman [1989: 328] on the "slippery" exercise of identifying Deuteronomic language).

More convincing are the textual, lexical, and structural arguments adduced for regarding Mal 3:22–24 [4:4–6] as secondary additions to the oracles of Malachi. For example, MT manuscripts consistently show a major paragraph break at 3:21 [4:3], and the Aleppo Codex separates 3:22–24 [4:4–6] markedly from the rest of the book in distinct columnar fashion. Additionally, the willingness of the earliest versions of the Hebrew Bible, and the earliest of the liturgical traditions associated with Malachi, to tamper with the arrangement of the closing verses of the book suggests that it was not considered part of the original (LXX manuscripts place 3:22 [4:4] after 3:24 [4:6], and the Masorah instructs a rereading of Mal 3:23 [4:5] after 3:24 [4:6]; see the NOTES on 3:22–23 [4:5–6] below). Moses, the key player in the Pentateuch and Israel's covenant mediator, resurfaces but twice in the Book of the Twelve (Mic 6:4; Mal 3:22 [4:4] and elsewhere in the Prophets only in Isa 63:11, 12 and Jer 15:1; cf. Dan 9:11, 13).

Surely this appeal to Moses at the conclusion of Malachi has significance beyond the prophet's own message? The prophet Elijah is conspicuous by his absence in the Latter Prophets section of the Hebrew Bible. This suggests that the reference to him here in the second appendix (Mal 3:23 [4:5]) not only joins the Latter Prophets (including the Book of the Twelve) to the Primary History, but also indicates that the Latter Prophets function as a commentary on the Primary History — especially the Former Prophets (cf. Freedman [1991: 36–41, 60–64]). Petersen (1995: 232–33) says that the epilogue represents a type of canonical integration implemented during the time when these books were being stylized into larger collections, signifying that no one section is superior to another but that all were intended to be read together. Finally, Clendenen's (1987: 6–7) study identifying the oracles of Malachi as *hortatory* discourse clearly demonstrates that the speech patterns begin and end with a statement of motivation, indicating that the anticipation of the coming Day of Yahweh (3:16–21 [4:3]) marks the end of Malachi's disputations. (See above I. C. 4. Structure).

1. Appeal to Moses (3:22 [4:4])

3 ²² ⁽⁴:⁴⁾Remember the Torah of Moses my Servant, whom I commanded at Horeb on behalf of all Israel — [the] statutes and [the] ordinances!

NOTES

3:22 [4:4]. The verse presents no textual problems and is rendered literally word for word in the ancient versions. Some LXX manuscripts (e.g., A, B, Q) and the Arabic transpose 3:22 [4:4] and 3:24 [4:6], presumably to avoid ending the book with the threat of a curse (although both the final disputation and the appendixes conclude with the threat of divine judgment).

zikrû. The Qal imperative of the root *zkr* ("to remember, mention, call to mind"; KBL 1:269–71) is unique in the Haggai-Zechariah-Malachi corpus. Elsewhere, this intellectual activity of remembering is associated with Israel's recollection of Yahweh's acts in history (e.g., Ps 105:5; Isa 44:21; 46:8, 9; etc.) and Israel's plea to God that he call to mind certain things (e.g., his covenant promises, Ps 111:5; deeds of righteousness, Neh 5:19; human hardship and suffering,

Ps 132:1; and even the impious [for purposes of judgment], Ps 74:22; cf. *TDOT* 4:64–82).

The combination of *zkr* + *tôrâ* occurs only here in the MT; the closest parallel is found in the prayer of Nehemiah (1:8; *zĕkār-nā' 'et-haddābār 'ăšer ṣiwwîtā 'et-mōšeh 'abdĕkā*). Eising cites five other passages where *zkr* is coupled with the law of God in its broadest sense (Exod 13:3; 20:8; Num 15:39; Pss 103:18; 119:52; see *TDOT* 4:68). The use of the imperative represents disjunction with the preceding disputation speeches; however, the imperative is also incorporated into the fifth oracle (*šûbû*, 3:7; and *hābî'û*, 3:10). Any attempt to label 3:22 [4:4] as an "appendix" solely on the basis of the shift from disputation to injunction overstates the case (cf. R. L. Smith [1984: 340]).

This codified legal instruction is described variously as "the Torah of Yahweh" (Exod 13:9; Isa 30:9; Amos 2:4; Ps 19:8; etc.), "the Torah of God" (Josh 24:6; Neh 8:18; 10:29; etc.), "the Torah of the Lord God" (2 Kgs 10:31; Neh 9:3), and even "the Torah of the Lord of Hosts" (Isa 5:24). There are also several references to the *tôrat mōšeh* (notably Josh 23:6; 1 Kgs 2:3; 2 Kgs 14:6; 23:25), occasionally found in context with *'ebed* (e.g., Josh 8:31, 32; Dan 9:11). The expression *tôrat mōšeh* is unique to biblical prophetic literature, and the phrase *tôrat mōšeh 'abdî* is unique to Mal 3:22 [4:4] in the OT/HB (but note *bĕtôrat mōšeh 'ebed-hā'ĕlōhîm*, Dan 9:11; cf. 9:13). See further the discussion of *tôrat-'ĕmet* in 2:6 above.

'ăšer ṣiwwîtî 'ôtô. The antecedent of *'ăšer* is in question. Following the V (*quam*), Ewald (1881: 86), von Bulmerincq (1932: 556–60), and Glazier-McDonald (1987a: 250) are among those commentators who understand *'ôtô* reflexively in conjunction with *'ăšer*. This more clearly identifies the double accusative of *ṣwh* (i.e., object of a person, *'ôtô* [= "Moses, my servant" since *'ôtô* is masculine singular and *tôrâ* is feminine] and object of a thing, *ḥuqqîm ûmišpāṭîm* ["statutes and ordinances"]), thus translating ". . . Moses my servant, "whom I commanded . . ."; cf. NJB "to whom . . . I prescribed"). Kruse-Blinkenberg (1967: 72) includes *kathóti* (for *'ăšer*) among those places where the LXX has incorrectly rendered the MT (cf. the expected *hós* in Mal 2:9).

More commonly, "the Torah of Moses" is understood to be the antecedent of *'ăšer* (translating "the Torah of Moses my servant, *that* I decreed . . ."; so G. A. Smith [1905: 372]; Chary [1969: 276]; cf. NAB, NEB, NIV, NRSV). While both are possible readings of verse 22, the construction in Malachi favors the traditional translation for two reasons. First, interpreting *'ôtô* reflexively fails to appreciate the use of *'abdî* as an honorary title used appositionally as an epithet for Moses and an integral component of the construct chain "the Torah of Moses my servant" (cf. Deut 34:5; Josh 1:2, 7, 13, 15; 8:31, 33; see the discussion in Boling and Wright [1982: 118]). Second, this reflexive construction of *'ăšer* + *'ēt* is uncharacteristic of the book of Deuteronomy and the Primary History in general, the very corpus that the first appendix of Malachi seeks to bridge with the prophetic corpus (note the combination *'ăšer* + *ṣiwwîtî* + *'ēt* in Deut 31:5, 29; Josh 7:11; 22:2; Judg 2:20; 2 Kgs 17:13; Jer 11:17, 22; cf. WO'C § 38.8d on subordination in the accusative frame with the relative conjunction *'ăšer*).

The verb *ṣiwwîtî* is derived from the root *ṣwh*, meaning "to command, to charge, to order, direct" and appears almost exclusively in the Piel stem in the OT/HB. Here *ṣwh* conveys the meaning "command" or "charge" in the sense of placing someone (i.e., Moses) under orders to execute or obligations to discharge. Thus, Moses is *charged* by Yahweh to *discharge* the demands of covenant relationship to Israel, imposing upon them the *charge* or duty to submit to Yahweh's authority and obey his teaching. The translation "whom I commanded" focuses attention on Yahweh as the source of this covenant instruction (rather than Moses as the mediator and explicator of Yahweh's Torah, cf. Deut 1:3, 5), because the purpose of the first appendix is to juxtapose the inherent authority of the Mosaic traditions in the Primary History with the prophetic traditions preserved in the Book of the Twelve and the Latter Prophets.

The verbal root *ṣwh* occurs elsewhere in the Haggai-Zechariah-Malachi corpus only in Zech 1:6 (see the COMMENTS below). The word predominates in the Pentateuch (245 of 496 times in the MT), with more than eighty citations in the book of Deuteronomy alone (and another 42 occurrences in the book of Joshua). Clearly, the word has Deuteronomic connotations and is used in the appendix to conjure up images of the Sinai/Horeb covenant and Mosaic legislation.

bĕḥōrēb. The place name Horeb occurs in the prophets only in Mal 3:22 [4:4]. The name occurs twelve times in the Pentateuch: three citations in the book of Exodus and nine in the book of Deuteronomy. The Hebrew *ḥōrēb* is derived from a root (*ḥrb* [I]) meaning "be dry, desolate" or perhaps (*ḥrb* [II]) "sword (shaped)" (cf. *TDOT* 5:150–54). Traditional pentateuchal source criticism has equated Horeb with the E (Elohist) and D (Deuteronomic) sources, and Sinai with the J (Yahwist) and P (Priestly) documents. Davies, citing Noth, has even suggested "Horeb" is a Deuteronomic (or later) expression (*ABD* 6:47).

At times the name Horeb functions synonymously as an alternate name for Mt. Sinai (Exod 33:6; cf. 1 Kgs 19:8, the story of Elijah's journey to Horeb, the mountain of God), and in other instances Horeb refers to the desolate region bordering Mt. Sinai (e.g., Exod 17:6; Deut 1:19; Ps 106:19). The dual names for the "mountain of God" may represent two separate traditions of the Exodus narrative (one employing the Semitic term "Horeb," with "Sinai" the name used by another people group?) or the twin peaks of a single mountainous complex (cf. *ISBE* 4:527). Early Christian tradition associated Mt. Sinai/Horeb with Jebel Musa in the southern Sinai peninsula (but on the location, see further the discussion and bibliography in *ISBE* 4:525–28; *ABD* 6:47–49).

'al-kol-yiśrā'ēl. The superscription of Zech 9:1 contains the phrase "all the tribes of Israel" (*wĕkol šibṭê yiśrā'ēl*; cf. Judg 20:2; 1 Sam 10:20; 1 Kgs 8:16; 2 Chr 6:5; etc.). According to Meyers and Meyers (1993: 95), "all the tribes of Israel" in Zech 9:1 represent the people and the geography of Yahweh's earthly inheritance (cf. *TDOT* 6:397–420). Given the development of the documentary hypothesis, commentators have recognized *kol-yiśrā'ēl* as Deuteronomic language used by the redactor of the Twelve Prophets (e.g., J.M.P. Smith [1912: 81]; Dentan and Sperry [1956: 1143]; R. L. Smith [1984: 340]; Glazier-McDonald [1987a: 250]; Redditt [1995: 185–86, 192]; but Baldwin [1972a: 251] objects); the phrases [*'el-*]*kol-yiśrā'ēl* (1:1; 5:1 [2]; 27:8; 29:1; 31:1; 32:45) and *kol-yiśrā'ēl* (11:6; 21:21; 31:7, 11 [2]; 34:12) predominate in the book of Deuteronomy.

'*al*. The preposition marks *advantage*, "on behalf of, for the sake of," highlighting the role of Moses as mediator between Yahweh and Israel (WO'C § 11.2.13c).

The phrase '*al-kol-yiśrā'ēl* is a Deuteronomistic description of Solomonic rule (1 Kgs 4:1, 7; 11:42; 12:20). Apart from a single reference to the rule of Baasha (1 Kgs 15:33), this designation for the people of Israel occurs only in postexilic literature (Neh 13:26; 1 Chr 11:10; 12:39; 14:8; 18:14; 28:4; 29:26; 2 Chr 9:30; 29:24; 30:1). For the Chronicler, '*al-kol-yiśrā'ēl* represented a formulaic and idealized understanding of a formerly fragmented Hebrew people now joined as one in unity given their covenant heritage and the common experience of worship before Yahweh in the Second Temple (on "all Israel" in the Chronicler, see Braun [1986: xxxv–xxxvii]). Hence, the language of Mal 3:22 [4:4] is Deuteronomistic only to the degree that postexilic editors and/or compilers deliberately selected vocabulary from Deuteronomy (and the Primary History) to cement the literary and theological relationship of the Latter Prophets with the Primary History by means of this first appendix.

Interestingly, D. N. Freedman (1991: 15) places Deuteronomy at the very center of the nine books of the Primary History. Thus, the nexus of Mal 3:22 [4:4] with the Primary History is the one book dominated by Moses, the central figure of that history. See also the NOTES and COMMENTS on *yiśrā'ēl* in 1:1; 2:11, and 16 above.

Like *kol-yiśrā'ēl*, the phrase [*ha*]*ḥuqqîm* *û*[*ham*]*mišpāṭîm* figures prominently in the language of Deuteronomy (e.g., 4:1; 5:1; 6:1; 12:1; etc.; cf. *TDOT* 5:139–47). The collocation of *ḥōq* and *mišpāṭ* is most often plural in Deuteronomy, signifying the collection of Mosaic legislation as a whole. The noun *ḥōq/ḥuqqîm* occurs in the Haggai-Zechariah-Malachi corpus only in Zech 1:6 and Mal 3:7, 22 [4:4]. Later postexilic writings show a preference for combining *ḥōq/ḥuqqîm* ("statute/s") with *miṣwā/miṣwôt* ("commandment/s," e.g., Ezr 7:11; Neh 9:13, 14; Ps 119:32–33, 47–48).

COMMENTS

Although *zikrû* is not coupled with another active verb, as is sometimes the case (cf. *TDOT* 4: 65–66), the use of the freestanding imperative here in Mal 3:22 [4:4] should be understood after the manner of *zkr* + '*śh* in Ps 103:18. That is, when the Bible enjoins someone to remember Yahweh or his word, it is an active cognitive commitment with behavioral outcomes. As Pedersen (1:106–7) observed, "When man remembers God, he lets his being and his actions be determined by him . . . to remember the works of Yahweh and to seek him, i.e., to let one's acts be determined by his will, is in reality the same." Eising has summarized that *zkr* "serves primarily to express an intellectual activity that is relational and personal" (*TDOT* 4:65). In verse 22 [4:4] the relational element is the Mosaic covenant and its implications for community life, while the personal component is Yahweh himself (implicit in the possessive pronoun attached to 'ebed, "my Servant").

The root zkr occurs elsewhere in the Haggai-Zechariah-Malachi corpus only in Zech 10:9 (affirming the "remembrance" of the person, work, and word of Yahweh and instructing the Israelites that this activity of remembering need not be hampered by site-specific restrictions) and Zech 13:2 (pointing to the eschaton when the names of idols will be "mentioned" no more; see the discussion in Meyers and Meyers [1993: 218, 370]). More directly related to Mal 3:22 [4:4] is the injunction of Josh 1:13 to "remember the word that Moses the Servant of Yahweh charged you . . ." (zākôr 'et-haddābār 'ăšer ṣiwwâ 'etkem mōšeh 'ebed-YHWH; on the use of the infinitive absolute as a word of command, see WO'C § 35.5.1).

The intent of the imperative zikrû in the first appendix is in conjunction with this "word of Moses," that corpus of materials recounting the received traditions of the Mosaic covenant (on dābār as a technical term for Mosaic law, see TDOT 3:117–18). Thus, while the command to obey Mosaic instruction remains paramount for the restoration community, the colophon serves primarily to append a later literary tradition (the Latter Prophets) to the earlier and already "inscripturated" tradition of the "Torah of Moses" (and the whole of the Primary History?).

The upshot of this union was the sanctioning of this prophetic corpus with same divine authority accorded to the "Torah of Moses."[2] It is certainly not outside the realm of possibility to speculate that after the completion of the Second Temple, there must have been some sort of "canonization" ceremony acknowledging the authoritative role of this literature in the restoration community. It seems only natural that the religious documents preserved and accumulated through the exilic period by the priestly and scribal guilds would be "formally" sanctioned now that the community had an official repository (cf. Ezra 6:13–22; Zech 8:9). The citation of Josh 1:13 in Neh 1:8 and the subsequent use of the motto "the book of the Torah of God/Yahweh" (bĕsēpēr tôrat hā'ĕlōhîm/YHWH) in later postexilic literature together suggest a literary collection formally recognized as the authoritative "Torah of Moses" (cf. Neh 8:8, 18; 9:3; 2 Chr 17:9; 34:13).

The delineation of the contents of this "Torah of Moses" is wide-ranging, from the entire Pentateuch (e.g., Mason [1977: 159]; Glazier-McDonald [1987a: 247]) to the book of Deuteronomy (e.g., G. A. Smith [1905: 372]) to the "lawbook" of Ezra (e.g., von Bulmerincq [1932: 554]) to the covenant code of Exodus 20–23 (Baldwin [1972a: 251]). Others dodge the question by claiming that the extent of the tôrat mōšeh cannot be assessed (so Horst [1954: 275]; Verhoef [1987: 338]).

The tôrat mōšeh in the context of this first appendix is best understood as a reference to the whole Pentateuch, an organic unity comprising the covenant stipulations, civil and ethical instruction, and narrative traditions associated with

---

[2]Boling and Wright (p. 125) acknowledge that sēper means a written document but consider the point moot in that the inscribed documents housed in the Ark of the Covenant and the oral teaching of the Levitical priesthood were vested with equal authority (p. 248).

Moses as Israel's lawgiver. Part of the response of the restoration community to the "crisis of authority" in this early postexilic period was to reconnect religious and civil leadership with the anthology of Mosaic covenant and legal tradition already codified and recognized as authoritative writ by the Hebrew constituency (according to Hengstenberg [2:1226], the divine nature of this "Law of Moses" is emphasized in the expressions "my servant" and "whom I commanded").

Malachi represents a shift away from earlier attempts by Haggai to root this authority in the Davidic covenant of dynastic kingship (cf. Hag 2:20–24). Zechariah and Malachi were phase one of this reorientation of community life around the Mosaic covenant (cf. Zech 1:6; 7:8–12; Mal 3:7), while the reforms of Ezra and Nehemiah may be viewed as phase two of an ongoing process to fill the vacuum of civil authority given the demise of the Davidic line (cf. Ezra 3:2; Neh 8:1, 14).

The more than coincidental parallels in character, covenant theme, and legal terminology between Mal 3:22 [4:4] and the land-grant ceremony of Josh 8:30–35 support this understanding of *tôrat mōšeh* as a collection of "inscripturated" documents (see Mason [1977: 159] [although I would qualify his understanding of "late stage" for this final form of the Torah]; cf. Hill [1988] on the Ebal ceremony as Hebrew land grant). The utilization of the phrase "the book of the Torah . . ." (*'et-sēper tôrat mōšeh*, Neh 8:1; *běsēper tôrat-YHWH*, Neh 9:3; 2 Chr 17:9; 2 Chr 34:14) may suggest the "canonization" of these documents as "Torah" or "Law of Moses" (cf. Clines [1984: 182]). It is worth noting, the translation, "'Treaty-Teaching," for *tôrat mōšeh* in the book of Joshua by Boling and Wright (p. 124) is also apropos for Malachi 3:22 [4:4] in that the prophets were the "covenant-consciousness" of Israel (cf. Craigie [1985: 248]).[3]

According to Boling and Wright (p. 118), "my servant" (*'abdî*) is an honorific title prominent in the Primary History (Genesis–2 Kings). This ancient title describes "the ideal role of the Israelite ruler in intimate relationship to Yahweh's supremacy" (Meyers and Meyers [1987: 68]). It is likely that Moses as "Servant of Yahweh" is paradigmatic for other Israelite patriarchs and heroes (cf. Deut 33:5), including Abraham (Gen 26:24), Isaac (Exod 32:13), Jacob (Deut 9:27), Joshua (Josh 24:29), David (2 Sam 3:18), and Isaiah (Isa 20:3). Zerubbabel is designated as Yahweh's *'abdî*, no doubt in anticipation of the restoration of Davidic rule in postexilic Jerusalem (Hag 2:23). However, such expectations were short-lived as evidenced by Zechariah's more opaque use of the title *'abdî* for another eschatological figure, not Zerubbabel (3:8; see the discussion in Meyers and Meyers [1987: 68–69, 202–4]).

The inclusion of the title *'abdî* for Moses in this first appendix accents the role ascribed to him by Hebrew tradition as Israel's lawgiver and specifically endows the Book of the Twelve, the Latter Prophets, and the Former Prophets with the

---

[3]Fishbane (1985: 536) has suggested that the purpose of the admonition to "remember the Torah of Moses" in 3:22 [4:4], which served as part of the coda to the entire prophetic corpus, was formulated as a safeguard against "antinomianism" spawned by unchecked "eschatological enthusiasm" on the part of certain later Hebrew prophets.

same divine authority accorded the "Torah of Moses." The weight and coherence of this conjecture is only strengthened by the blatant truancy of Moses in the books of the Latter Prophets (only Isa 63:11–12; Jer 15:1; Mic 6:4; and Mal 3:22 [4:4]).

Keil (2:470) steered the discussion concerning "the Torah of Moses my servant" in the wrong direction by noting that *'ăšer ṣiwwîtî 'ôtô* "is not to be rendered 'whom I charged . . . ,' for we do not expect any further explanation of the relation in which Moses stood to the law." Keil misunderstood the crisis of authority in postexilic Yehud. The restoration community did not abandon the emphasis of the preexilic period on the authority figure proper (cf. Josh 22:2, . . . *kol-'ăšer ṣiwwâ 'etkem mōšeh 'ebed YHWH . . .*). Rather, the postexilic period witnessed the redirection of this emphasis to the legacy of the authoritative figures of Israel's past — the authoritative tradition preserved in the literature attributed to these forefathers of covenant faith in Israel (cf. Mal 3:22 [4:4], . . . *tôrat mōšeh 'abdî 'ăšer ṣiwwîtî 'ôtô . . . ḥuqqîm ûmišpāṭîm*). This shift from person-based authority to a document-based authority in the Hebrew religious community was necessary given the reality of Persian suzerainty and the uncertainty of reinstating the Davidic dynasty. The vesting of this divine authority in the prophets as the rightful heirs of the Mosaic tradition through the *tôrat mōšeh* is readily observed in the combination of *ḥōq + ṣwh + 'ebed + nābî'* in Zech 1:6 (see Meyers and Meyers [1987: 96]; cf. Zech 8:9; Mal 2:6–8).

The issue related to the citation of "Horeb" here is not one of so-called pentateuchal sources with which Malachi may or may not have been familiar (cf. J. M. P. Smith [1912: 81]; von Bulmerincq [1932: 557]; Chary [1969: 276–77]; Mason [1977: 159–60]; Glazier-McDonald [1987a: 246–47]; Redditt [1995: 185]). It has been clearly demonstrated that Malachi was fully acquainted with the entire Pentateuch (see Dating the Oracles of Malachi above). Nor does the substantive *ḥōrēb* function simply as an introduction to the Elijah figure of the second appendix (Mal 3:23–24 [4:5–6]; cf. Glazier-McDonald [1987a: 247]).

Rather, the place name "Horeb" yokes the two appendixes of Malachi by connecting the ideal figures of Moses and Elijah with a site they had in common — the "mountain of God" (cf. Deut 5:2; 29:1; 1 Kgs 8:9; 19:8). Even as Horeb conjoins Moses and Elijah as paradigmatic prophets of Yahweh, so the two appendixes of Malachi serve to link great sections of the Hebrew canon they personify — the Torah and the Prophets. I have deliberately translated the preposition *bêt* with the somewhat ambiguous "at" to convey both the locative or spatial sense of the geographical site of Horeb and the temporal sense of an event (or better, a sequence of events in time, so NEB, NJB, NIV, NRSV; cf. WO'C § 11.2.5b, c). My point is to retain the historicity of the Horeb/Sinai covenant experience in opposition to those who "allege" that the Mosaic traditions are "literary fiction" (cf. Levenson [1985: 24]).

The use of *yiśrā'ēl* in the superscription to denote the whole remnant of the Hebrew nation has been documented above (see under 1:1). Its placement here by the scribal editor is consistent with that of the book of Malachi (1:1; 2:11, 16) and the postexilic prophets generally (cf. Zech 1:19; 8:13; 12:1). The reference to "Israel" in Zech 9:1 proves the exception with its emphasis on the geopolitical connotations of "Israel" (cf. the discussion in Meyers and Meyers [1993: 95, 168]). Verhoef's (1987: 339) suggestion that "all Israel" here refers to the various constituencies of the nation (i.e., tribes, leaders, men, women, etc.) runs counter to the intent of the appendix. True, the Israelite community is composed of special interest groups of various kinds; but the real point is the covenantal legacy that the restoration community in its totality shared with its preexilic precursor (i.e., all the generations of Israelites).

The phrase "all Israel" has several functions in this first appendix, foremost of which is connecting the oracular literature of the Latter Prophets with the legal and historical literature of the Primary History by using the "dialect of Deuteronomy" (cf. G. A. Smith [1905: 372]). The phrase *kol-yiśrā'ēl* connects Mal 3:22 [4:4] to Moses as covenant mediator at Horeb (Deut 29:1) but not primarily to emphasize the covenant theme in Malachi or chastise the "recalcitrant contemporaries" of the prophet (so Glazier-McDonald [1987a: 250–51]). Rather, *kol-yiśrā'ēl* is a reminder to the restoration community of its "covenantal continuity" with the preceding generations. The nationalistic expression may have been intended to bolster flagging spirits in a despairing postexilic Jerusalem and to exhort the people of Yahweh to adopt both the posture and practice of covenant obedience (note how the phrase *kol-yiśrā'ēl* is used "nationalistically" in later postexilic writings, e.g., Ezra 1:3; 8:25; Neh 7:73; 2 Chr 29:24; etc.; on "all Israel," see further Braun [1986: xxxv–xxxvii]). Perhaps more significant, the cacophony of "lexical echoes" to the Mosaic covenant in the first appendix acts to legitimize the theological commentary of Yahweh's prophets on the Torah of Moses.

The final lexical link between Mal 3:22 [4:4] and Deuteronomy is the word pair, "statutes and ordinances" (*ḥuqqîm ûmišpāṭîm*). Attempts have been made to distinguish *ḥōq* from *mišpāṭ*, either as "cultic law" versus "civil law" or "categorical law" contra "case law" (cf. *TDOT* 5:143; Baldwin [1972a: 251]). Ringgren maintains that such precise distinctions for the two technical legal terms are better observed in P rather than in D, but laments on the basis of the evidence that "the original meaning of terms . . . was soon lost, and the difference in meaning was only seldom observed" (*TDOT* 5:143).

The basic meaning "law" or "statute" for *ḥōq* and "judgment" or "ordinance" for *mišpāṭ* adequately services this reading of Malachi. Together the two constitute the essence of Yahweh's Torah (Deut 4:8, 44–45). Clearly, that is the understanding here: all the legislation of the Sinai covenant ascribed to Moses as Yahweh's mediator and lawgiver (Exod 19:6; 21:1; 24:3; Lev 18:26; Num 30:17; Deut 4:40; etc.) — not just "cultic regulations" (cf. *TDOT* 5:146). Here *ḥuqqîm* has a parenetic function similar to that found in Deuteronomy, an exhortation to adhere to the covenant ethic decreed by Yahweh (e.g., Deut 4:1, 5, 14). According to Köhler (pp. 204–5), the *mišpāṭîm* connote the "just claims of God" designed to maintain divine order and justice in creation, binding prescriptions essential to righteousness, even the very life of Israel (cf. Lev 18:5; Ezek 19:9; 20:11; on *mišpāṭ*, see further Hertzberg).

Meyers and Meyers (1993: 96) have recognized a similar Deuteronomistic linking of the Law and the Prophets in the use of *ḥōq* in Zech 1:6. They have argued that "reestablishing community law in the land was not a simple matter without the monarchy, and the prophetic missions of Haggai and Zechariah seem to authenticate both prophetic and pentateuchal tradition, which they understand to be [as] valid now and in the future, as they were in the past." The situation was no less true for the prophet Malachi or for the postexilic compilers of the Book of the Twelve. On *ḥōq*, see further the discussion in 3:7 above.

Those adhering to the authenticity of Mal 3:22 regard the verse as a summary statement of Malachi's message, a sober reminder that the people of Yehud remain under the unchanging authority of Mosaic law (e.g., Craigie [p. 248]; Verhoef [1987: 237–40]; Glazier-McDonald [1987a: 243–52]). These same scholars are quick to cite the continuity of theme between the oracles of Malachi and the first appendix (3:22 [4:4]), especially the theme of obedience to God's law. Achtemeier (1986: 196–97) actually tenders Mal 3:22–24 [4:4–6] as the prophet's last message, a "priestly torah" of mercy, echoing 1:2 ("I loved you, Yahweh has said") and a final "plea to his disbelieving and indifferent people."

Whether one views 3:22 [4:4] as an editorial addition or original to the oracles of Malachi, two essential teachings issue from the analysis of the verse. First, the vitality of the restoration community's religious life is dependent upon its capacity to "reidentify" with the past (cf. Isbell [1980: 77]). Israel's faith in the present tense and hope in the future tense was always conditioned by her ability (or inability) to "remember" the words and deeds of Yahweh in the past tense (Exod 13:3; 20:8; Deut 5:15; Ps 77:11; cf. Brueggemann [1982b: 14–39] on the role of *remembrance* in the Hebrew educational repertoire). The second is the centrality of the "Torah of Moses" to the existence of Israel. From Moses to Ezra and beyond, the law of God was "life and death, blessing and curse" for Israel (cf. Deut 30:15–20; on the importance of binding Yahweh's law to the people of Israel in the land of the covenant promise under the Mosaic covenant, see Hill [1988]).

2. Appeal to Elijah (3:23–24 [4:5–6])

3 ²³ [4:5]See! I am sending Elijah the prophet to you before the coming of the Day of Yahweh — the great and the terrible [day]! ²⁴ [4:6]And he will turn the heart of the forefathers toward the[ir] descendants and heart of the descendants toward their forefathers; or else [when] I come I will strike the land [with] a curse [for destruction].

NOTES

3:23 [4:5]. Due to the transposition of 3:22 [4:4] and 3:24 [4:6] in the LXX, 3:22–23 [4:5–6] follow 3:21 in the Greek versions (see NOTES on 3:22 [4:4] above). The verse poses no textual problems, apart from the insertion of *tòn thesbíten* ("the Tishbite") after "Elijah" in the LXX. No doubt a harmonization based on 1 Kgs 17:1; 21:28; 2 Kgs 1:3; etc. The other ancient versions (Syr, T, V) render the MT quite literally.

The particle *hinnēh* introduces a presentative *exclamation of immediacy*, and when coupled with a participle (here *šōlēaḥ*) the exclamation has the "nuance of vivid immediacy" (WO'C § 40.2.1b; cf. GKC § 116p, the *futurum instans*). The imminency connoted by the construction may be expressed by the English "Indeed!" or "See!" or even "Certainly!" This exclamation of immediacy also fits the category of *fuller exclamation* since the *hinnēh* clause helps define the material that follows (i.e., there is a direct link between Elijah's appearance and the arrival of "the Day of Yahweh" (cf. WO'C § 40.2.1c). The frequent utilization of the interjection *hinnēh* is a feature that the Haggai-Zechariah-Malachi corpus shares with the prophets Jeremiah and Ezekiel but not with the rest of the Twelve (Hag 1:9; 2:12; Zech 1:8, 11; 2:1, 5, 7, 13, 14; 3:8, 9 [2], 4:2; 5:1, 7, 9; 6:1, 12; 8:7; 9:4, 9; 11:6, 16; 12:2; 14:1). See further the discussion of *hinnēh* in 1:13; 3:1, 19, 23 and *hinĕnî* in 2:3 and 3:1 above.

'ānōkî šōlēaḥ lākem. This form of the independent pronoun is uncharacteristic of Malachi; the oracles prefer *'ănî* throughout (cf. 1:4, 6 [2], 14; 2:9; 3:6, 17, 21). J.M.P. Smith (1912: 85) has cited this variance as an indication of the secondary nature of 3:22–24 [4:4–6]. Glazier-McDonald (1987a: 252) objects, however, appealing to Ahlström's (pp. 8–11) study of *'ănî* and *'ānōkî* showing that they are used interchangeably in the Prophets. Nevertheless, her comparative study is compromised by the failure to examine the use of the two forms of this independent pronoun in disputed texts, as is the case for Mal 3:22–24 [4:4–6]. For example, Haggai and First Zechariah use *'ănî* exclusively (Hag 1:13; 2:4, 6, 21; Zech 1:9, 15 [2x]; 2:9; 5:2; 8:8, 11), whereas Second Zechariah prefers *'ānōkî* (11:6, 16; 12:2; 13:5 [2x]; except for the poetic Zech 13:9). Distinct patterns of preference are clearly discerned in the corpora of the postexilic prophets, suggesting more than Glazier-McDonald (and others who defend the integrity of Malachi's appendixes) care to admit. Scholars like von Bulmerincq (1932: 575) recognized no inconsistency between the first-person *'ānōkî* and the third-person *yôm YHWH*, noting that such shifts occur elsewhere (e.g., Zeph 1:17–18) and are to be attributed to "stock" phraseology.

The Qal participle *šōlēaḥ* occurs some sixteen times in the Haggai-Zechariah-Malachi corpus (Hag 1:12; Zech 1:10; 2:12 [8], 13 [9], 11 [15]; 4:9; 6:15; 7:2, 12; 8:10; 9:11; Mal.2:2, 4, 16; 3:1, 23 [4:5]). Mal 3:23 [4:5] (*hinnēh 'ānōkî šōlēaḥ lākem*) has its parallel in Mal 3:1 with the "messenger" who readies the way as Yahweh's "advanceman" (*hinĕnî šōlēaḥ mal'ākî*). Petersen (1977: 42) has recognized the intentional reworking of Exod 23:20 (*hinnēh 'ānōkî šōlēaḥ mal'ak . . .*) in Mal 3:1 and 23 [4:5] in Malachi's description of the eschatological "covenant enforcer." Glazier-McDonald (1987a: 132) mistakenly applies the parallel to Mal 3:1 and identifies the *mal'ak habbĕrît* as Yahweh himself. The phrase from Exod 23:20 (cf. Exod 33:2) more closely parallels Mal 3:23 [4:5] in grammatical form (identical three-word citation) and context (Yahweh sending a forerunner to do "preparatory work" — not Yahweh sending himself). The citation of Exod 23:20 in the second appendix only strengthens the argument for understanding Mal 3:22–24 [4:4–6] as a coda, forming a bridge between the Primary History (Torah + Former Prophets) and the Latter Prophets.

The exclamation *hinnēh* + participle constitute a type of messenger formula that anticipates a pronouncement or speech of some kind ("I am *about* to send . . ." or "I am *soon* sending . . ."; cf. Westermann [1991: 100–16]). The gist of this communication is found in the latter half of the second appendix (3:24 [4:6]; i.e., a message of reconciliation). Meyers and Meyers (1987: 167) have observed that this grammatical construction "nearly always . . . has an ominous force, indicating Yahweh's intended punitive actions." However, there are exceptions, including Zech 2:14 [10], which assures the Hebrew faithful that the event of Yahweh's coming is certain and soon. The *futurum instans* construction in Mal 3:23 [4:5] functions in a similar fashion.

The suffixed preposition *lākem* is noted in Mal 1:6; 2:3; 3:10 (2x), 11 (3x), 20, and functions here as the "*lamed* of indirect object" ("to you," cf. WO'C § 11.2.10d).

'et 'ēlîyâ hannābî'. The name *'ēlîyâ* ("my God is Yah[weh]") occurs only here in the Book of the Twelve and the Latter Prophets. This form of Elijah's name is uncommon, found outside Malachi in 2 Kgs 1:3, 4, 8 and 12 (but note the personal name *'ēlîyâ* in 1 Chr 8:27; Ezra 10:21, 26; apparently a later variation of the more common form of the theophoric name *'ēlîyāhû*, cf. Graesser). The more common long form of the name, *'ēlîyāhû*, predominates in the Elijah cycle (1 Kgs 17–2 Kgs 2). The LXX inserts *tòn thesbíten* ("the Tishbite") for the MT *hannābî'*, a harmonization with *'ēlîyāhû hattišbî* in 1 Kgs 17:1; 2 Kgs 1:3; etc.). In the narrative of the Former Prophets, Elijah is given the title "the prophet" (*hannābî'*, 1 Kgs 18:36; 2 Chr 21:12) and the title "his servant" (i.e., Yahweh, *'abdô*, 2 Kgs 9:36).

lipnê bô' yôm YHWH. The combination *hinnēh* (see above) + *bw'* + *yôm YHWH* are a recognized eschatological marker (cf. Meyers and Meyers [1993: 409]). Malachi uses *bw'* in eschatological contexts in 3:1 (*ûpit'ōm yābô' 'el-hêkālô,* "Then suddenly he will enter his temple . . ."; *ûmal'ak habbĕrît . . . hinnēh-bā',* "the messenger of the covenant . . . Indeed! He is coming . . .") and 3:2 (*'et-yôm bô'ô,* "the day of his coming"). The concluding verse of the second appendix also employs the verb *bw'* with eschatological connotations (see below, *pen-'ābô'*).

Parallel expressions for the "coming Day of Yahweh" occur in the Haggai-Zechariah-Malachi corpus in both First (2:14 [10], *kî hinĕnî-bā'*; and 3:8, *kî-hinĕnî mēbî'*) and Second Zechariah (9:9, *hinnēh malkēk yābô'lāk;* 14:1, *hinnēh yôm-bā' laYHWH;* and 14:5, *ûbā' YHWH 'ēlōhay*). The most common preexilic precursor of this prophetic phrase is *hinnēh yāmîm bā'îm* ("Indeed, days are coming"; cf. 1 Sam 2:31; 2 Kgs 20:17; Isa 39:6; Jer 7:32; etc.), signifying future divine judgment (e.g., Amos 4:2; 8:11) or future divine restoration of Israel (e.g., Amos 9:13; cf. Andersen and Freedman [1989: 422]). Elsewhere, the combination *hinnēh* + *bw'* + *yôm* introduce Yahweh's judgment against Babylon (*hinnēh yôm-YHWH bā'* . . . , Isa 13:9), while blends substituting *kî* (e.g., Jer 50:27, 31; Ps 37:13) and *'ăšer* for *hinnēh* are also attested (e.g., Ezek 21:30, 34). Most significant, the phrase *lipnê bô' yôm YHWH haggādôl wĕhannôrā'* mirrors Joel 3:4b [2:31b] (cf. 2:1, *kî-bā' yôm YHWH*). See further the discussion under *haggādôl wĕhannôrā'* below.

According to Preuss (*TDOT* 2:22, 34–36, 41), *bw'* is a relational word in theological contexts depicting either the movement of God to human beings or the entrance of people into the presence of God. Further, he has noted that *bw'* may signify Yahweh's approach to his people Israel (or any people) for purposes of judgment or salvation. Malachi uses both connotations associated with *bw'*: Yahweh's judgment (3:1–4) and Yahweh's salvation (3:19–20 [4:1–2]). In Mal 3:23 [4:5] *bw* has overtones of both judgment and salvation.

haggādôl wĕhannôrā'. The appositive construction indicates the categorization of *quality* or *character* of the lead word (in this case the construct chain "the coming of the Day of Yahweh"; cf. WO'C § 12.3c). Yahweh's epiphany will be both "great" and "terrible," that is, it will be awesome in magnitude and dreadful in outcome (cf. NAB, "Before the day of the Lord comes, the great and terrible day"; and NJB, ". . . before my day comes, that great and terrible day"). Most commentators and the majority of English versions read the compound appositive adjectivially, "the great and terrible day of Yahweh" (e.g., Verhoef [1987: 337]; Glazier-McDonald [1987a: 243]; so NEB, NIV, NRSV).

In addition to the combination of *gādôl* + *nôrā'* in the intertextual citation of Joel 3:4b [2:31b] and Mal 3:23b [4:5b], the same word pair may be found in Joel 2:11 (*kî-gādôl yôm-YHWH wĕnôrā' mĕ'ōd* . . .) and Mal 1:14 (*melek gādôl 'ănî* . . . *ûšĕmî nôrā'*). Similar phraseology describing Yahweh's eschatological day occurs in Jer 30:7 (*hôy kî gādôl hayyôm hahû'*) and Zeph 1:14 (*qārôb yôm-YHWH haggādôl*). The coupling of *gādôl* and *nôrā'* in the OT/HB is unusual but not rare, perhaps a Deuteronomic convention (Deut 1:19; 7:21; 8:15; 10:21; 2 Sam 7:23; 1 Chr 17:21; Dan 9:4; Neh 1:5; 4:8; 9:32; Joel 2:11; 3:4 [2:31]; Mal 1:14; 3:23 [4:5]; cf. *TDOT* 2:396), and according to Fuhs demonstrates the internal association of Yahweh's "holiness" and his "numinous nature" (*TDOT* 6:300). The LXX renders *nôrā'* by *epiphanēs* ("glorious").

Verhoef (1987: 338) and Glazier-McDonald (1987a: 251–52, 259–60) are among the more recent commentators defending the authenticity of the second appendix Mal 3:23–24 [4:5–6]). Both commentators vigorously underscore thematic and linguistic similarities between the appendixes of Malachi and the oracles of Malachi as evidence for the integrity of the coda. The linking themes are "the Mosaic law" and "the Day of Yahweh," and the key lexical connector is the word cluster comprised of *bw'* + *yôm* + *gādôl* + *nôrā'*. Curiously, on the relationship of Joel 2:31b [3:4b] and Mal 3:23b [4:5b], Glazier-McDonald (1987a: 253) places Joel's prophecy (ca. 515–500 B.C./E.) prior to Malachi (ca. 450 B.C./E.); yet she avers that "it is not . . . necessary . . . to posit [Malachi's] borrowing from Joel."

While a date for the book of Joel near 500 B.C./E. coincides with my typological analysis of later Hebrew prophets (see Appendix B), Glazier-McDonald's fervent defense for the genuineness of the appendixes will hardly bear the strain of careful scrutiny. The thematic continuity perceived in "the law" and "the Day of the Lord" is so general as to be true of almost any prophetic book. Likewise, lexical similarities between the oracles of Malachi and the appendixes are overshadowed by syntactical dissimilarities. For instance, the word pair *gādôl* + *nôrā'* in Mal 1:14 are predicate adjectives (cf. WO'C § 14.3.2), whereas they function as attributive adjectives in Mal 3:23 [4:5] (cf. WO'C § 14.3.1). Mal 3:23 [4:5] inverts the order of *bw'* + *yôm* found in Mal 3:2. Even the emphatic position of *haggādôl wĕhannôrā'* finds its complement in *ḥuqqîm ûmišpāṭîm* in 3:22 [4:4]. Finally, the amalgamation in one verse of a three-word citation from Exod 23:20, a six-word quote from Joel 2:31b [3:4b], the *futurum instans* construction of *hinnēh* + participle, and the reference to Elijah the prophet (unique to the Twelve here) defies coincidence.

I am inclined to agree with D. N. Freedman (1991: 50) on the initial collection of the Twelve Prophets concluding with Zechariah 8 and dating to the fourth year of Darius I (ca. 518 B.C./E.; Zech 7:1). I would include Joel in this original collection of Minor Prophets. The citation of Joel 2:31b [3:4b] in the second appendix of Malachi probably represents an example of Fishbane's (1985: 506–24) *mantological exegesis;* that is, the revision and adaptation of earlier oracular materials by a later prophetic tradition. The appeal in Mal 3:23 [4:5] to Joel 2:31b [3:4b] and the reference to Elijah the prophet ensure the authority and continuity of the apocalyptic vision for Israel seen by the earlier prophets, despite the modifications of those oracles by Second Zechariah and Malachi (e.g., the shift from the restoration of Davidic rule envisioned by Haggai to the hierocratic rule of Malachi, already intimated in Zechariah 3; cf. Meyers and Meyers [1987: 201]). The reference to the "Torah of Moses" in the first appendix (3:23 [4:4]) serves to temper the tendencies of this kind of mantological exegesis for "antinomian excess" (cf. Fishbane [1985: 524]).

It also seems that what Mosis describes as a typological significance for the phrase *gādôl wĕnôrā'* in Deut 1:19 and 8:15 applies equally to the usage in Mal 3:23 [4:5]. Even as the texts in Deuteronomy "do not have in mind the great wilderness any more than the actual historical region of the earlier wandering, but rather its quality as a place of trial and encounter with God" (*TDOT* 2:396), so too the appendixes of Malachi convey a certain typology about the quality of the "Day of Yahweh" as a time of trial and encounter with God. Note that such an understanding of this phrase advances the theological interface between the Latter Prophets and the Primary History promoted by the appendixes of Malachi.

3:24 [4:6]. The verse poses no textual problems in the MT. In addition to the transposition of 3:22 [4:4] and 3:24 [4:6] noted in 3:23 [4:5] above, Kruse-Blinkenberg (1967: 72) has noted the paraphrastic tendency of LXX here, incorrectly rendering *wĕhēšîb* (by *apokathístēmi* for the expected *eipstréphō* [i.e., "restore" for "turn back, convert"; cf. 3:7]), *bānîm . . . 'ăbôtām* (*anthrōpóu . . . plēsíon autoû* [i.e., "man" and "his neighbor" for "sons" and "their fathers"], including the change of noun number from plural to singular), and *ḥērem* (*árdēn* [i.e., "utterly" for "curse"]). The other versions (Syr, T, V) remain faithful to the MT. On Mal 3:22–24 [4:4–6] as an admonitory coda for the prophetic corpus, Fishbane (1985: 541) suggests that Deut 29:28 functions similarly for the Pentateuch (cf. Clark [p. 40] who connects Malachi's postscript with the colophon to the Pentateuch in Deut 34:10–12 on the strength of the reference to Moses as Israel's premier prophet).

wĕhēšîb. The verb *šwb* ("turn, return, go back," *CHAL:* 362–63) is a key term in the Haggai-Zechariah-Malachi corpus structurally (see Meyers and Meyers [1987: 123, 413]) and theologically (i.e., repentance as a response to prophetic preaching, cf. *ABD* 5:671–72). The root *šwb* occurs in Zech 1:3 (2x), 4, 6, 16; 4:1; 5:1; 6:1; 7:14; 8:3, 15; 9:8, 12 (2x); 10:9, 10; 13:7; Mal 1:4; 2:6; 3:7 (2x), 18, and 24 [4:6]. Here in 3:24 [4:6] *šwb* is a Hiphil perfective meaning "turn back" or "restore." This concept of repentance associated with *šwb* was a basic ingredient necessary for fidelity in the covenant relationship with Yahweh (cf. Deut 30:2–3, *wĕšabtā ʿad-YHWH . . . wĕšāb YHWH . . . ʾet-šĕbûtĕkā*). The idiom "turn the heart" may be rendered "reconcile" (JPSV; Petersen [1995: 227]). Petersen (1995: 231) rightly identifies the conflict as a generational one because "without the integrity between generations, Israel would not be Israel."

There is a certain irony in the use of *hēšîb* in the appendixes, because the ministry of restoring people to Yahweh had been a priestly function (*hēšîb*, Mal 2:6). Elijah had exercised important priestly functions, unchallenged by the established Levitical priesthood (e.g., building an altar and offering ritual sacrifice, 1 Kgs 18:30–40). Now an Elijah figure who is both priest and prophet (after the manner of Jeremiah and Ezekiel who were priests before they were prophets, Jer 1:1; Ezek 1:3) usurps that role to call both people and priests[!] to repentance. It is worth noting that the chief Elijah-figure in the NT, John the Baptist, was also by birth a priest (Luke 1:5). The actual ministry of restoration linked to the Elijah figure in the appendixes consists of reconciling parents and children (or an older generation with a younger one) by summoning the people to reject evil attitudes and practices and to obey God's statutes (Zech 1:3–6; note the elaborate parallels between the ministry of Elijah the Tishbite and the message of Malachi constructed by Childs [1979: 495–96]). This correlative offsetting of the peoples' return (*šwb*) to Yahweh and Yahweh's return (*šwb*) to his people in Zech 1:3, 4, 6, and 16 has implications for Mal 3:24 [4:6]. Meyers and Meyers (1987: 93–94) have observed that the repetition of *šwb* in Zech 1:3–16 enables God's prophet to "a) reveal God's promise of reciprocity; b) refer to the fact of the noncompliance with God's word of the preexilic generation; c) establish the important fact that a change of heart has occurred in the present generation . . . ; and d) anticipate the return of Yahweh to the community since the people have now turned toward him."

The citation of Zech 1:3 (*šûbû ʾēlay . . . wĕ ʾāšûb ʾălêkem*) in Mal 3:7 (*šûbû ʾēlay wĕ ʾāšûbâ ʾălêkem*) suggests that these same truths may be applied principally to Malachi's use of *šwb* in his fifth disputation (see Notes and Comments on 3:7 above). However, Meyers and Meyers (1987: 122–23, 413) are only partially correct when they aver that Yahweh *has returned* to the restoration community. Granted the people had obeyed (*šmʿ*) Haggai's message and revered (*yrʾ*) Yahweh in building the Second Temple (Hag 1:12); yet it seems that Zechariah's complementary message of spiritual renewal prompted at best a superficial *return* to Yahweh, since the oracles of both Second Zechariah (*bwʾ*, Zech 14:5) and Mal (3:7) promise the return (*šwb*) of Yahweh (cf. the warning in Zech 8:15–17 with the historical commentary in Zech 7:8–14 and note that these are the very covenant violations for which Malachi upbraids the community in his disputations, Mal 2:15–16; 3:5). Apparently, the people had not fully *returned* to Yahweh, perhaps due to their preoccupation with the economic benefits of covenant renewal (cf. Hag 1:6; Zech 8:10; Mal 3:10–11), nor had the *glory* (*kābôd*) of

Yahweh, symbolizing his covenant presence with his people, *returned* to the Second Temple. In fact, the Elijah figure must mediate the divine presence. In view of this, and given the messages of Second Zechariah and Malachi and the interpretive stance of the appendixes of Malachi, the early postexilic community was convinced that Yahweh had not yet come and the word of Zechariah (8:3) was still a promise — not a reality. The postscript of Malachi indicates that the overturning of the divine abandonment in conjunction with the Babylonian exile will take place in stages (Ezekiel 10; on the motif of divine abandonment, see Block [pp. 129–61]). The Elijah figure or forerunner announces the final installment of the eschatological plan ushering in the complete and permanent residence of Yahweh with his people (cf. Zech 8:3, 7–8; 9:8; 10:12; 13:9; 14:6; Mal 3:17).

lēb-'ābôt 'al-bānîm wĕlēb bānîm 'al-'ăbôtām. This phrase is unique to Malachi in the MT. The noun *lēb* occurs elsewhere in the Haggai-Zechariah-Malachi corpus in Mal 2:2 (2x); Zech 7:12; 10:7 (2x); 12:5, while the variant *lēbāb* is found in Hag 1:5, 7; 2:15, 18 (2x); Zech 7:10 and 8:17. According to Wolff (1974: 40–58) *lēb(āb)* is a complex Hebrew word and the most important term in all the vocabulary of OT/HB anthropology. He has cautioned that this word *lēb* must be understood *synthetically* as the locus of human feelings, desire, reason, and volition. The term *lēb* here carries all this "anthropological freight" and is to be understood synthetically, especially in respect to reason and will (cf. Joel 2:12–13). See also the discussion of *lēb* in the NOTES and COMMENTS for Mal 2:2 above.

'ābôt . . . bānîm . . . bānîm . . . 'ăbôtām. The noun *'āb* ("father") occurs in the Haggai-Zechariah-Malachi corpus in Zech 1:2, 4, 5, 6; 8:14; 13:3 (2x); Mal 1:6 (2x); 2:10 (2x); 3:7; and 3:24 [4:6] (2x). The word is gender specific in Zech and denotes the biological father of a child in Zech 13:3 and Mal 1:6. In Mal 2:10 God is understood typologically as the "father" of Israel (and all human beings) because he is the Creator. Elsewhere in the Haggai-Zechariah-Malachi corpus, the word connotes Israelite forefathers or ancestors. Despite ancient Israelite patriarchy, the understanding of *'ābôt* and *bānîm* here should not be restricted to males only since the audience of Malachi and the postscript (3:22–24 [4:4–6]) is all Israel. The use of *'ābôt* in Mal 3:24 [4:6] closely parallels that of Zech 1:2–6: the Hebrew ancestors of the restoration community who heard the oracles of the earlier prophets. Here Mason (1977: 161) has suggested that the deviation of the LXX from the MT at this juncture may reflect the influence of Hellenism on the younger generation, much to the horror of their parents.

Likewise, the plural *bānîm* ("sons") is better understood in this context as "children" or "descendants" similar to the usage in Isa 63:10; Jer 3:14, 22 (*šûbû bānîm*); Jer 4:22; 31:17 (*wĕšābû bānîm*); and Ezek 5:10 (*'ābôt + bānîm . . . bānîm + 'ăbôtām*). Rudolph's (1976: 293) suggestion (adopted by Glazier-McDonald [1987a: 254]) that "sons" in Hebrew families were the culprits responsible for social discord because they preferred Greek fashions fails to appreciate the typological nature of the postscript and misunderstands the implications that *hā'āreṣ* ("the land") has for the entire Israelite restoration community.

'al. The preposition *'al* may have a terminative sense of "to, unto" with some verbs of motion, as is the case here (*šwb*) and 2:2 (*śym*, also with *lēb*; cf. WO'C

§ 11.2.13b). The postscript uses '*al-bānîm* . . . '*al* '*ābôt* much like the construction '*al* + *lēb* in Ezek 14:3 and 38:10, connoting a process of "internalization" or "personalization" (of ideas, words, beliefs; cf. Zimmerli [1979: 300]). See the discussion of the preposition '*al* in 1:5, 7; 2:2 (2x), 3, 14 (2x), 16; 3:13 (2x), 17, 22 above.

pen-'*ābô*'. The telic particle *pen-* ("lest") is unique to the appendixes of Malachi in the Haggai-Zechariah-Malachi corpus. Here with the prefixing (nonperfective) the construction expresses contingency (cf. WO'C § 31.6.1c). This admonitory use of *pen* as a portent of divine judgment is especially common to the book of Deuteronomy (at least thirteen of the twenty-seven instances involving *pen* are directly or indirectly related to the threat of Yahweh's curse for covenant violations, usually with a second-person prefixing form of a verb; e.g., Deut 6:12, 15; 8:11, 12; etc.). According to Preuss (*TDOT* 2:27–30, 34–37), the use of *bw*' here not only foreshadows the coming judgment of the Day of Yahweh, but also intimates a complex of theological ideas associated with the Mosaic covenant and Israelite possession of the land of covenant promise. Interestingly, Yahweh indicated through Hosea that he would not come ('*ābô*') in wrath because of his great compassion (*nḥm*) for Israel (11:8–9; cf. Andersen and Freedman [1980: 590–91]).

wĕhîkkētî. The root *nkh* occurs in the Haggai-Zechariah-Malachi corpus only in Hag 2:17; Zech 9:4; 10:11; 12:4; 13:6, 7, and the Hiphil perfective form employed here means "to strike, hit, beat." The *waw*-relative continues the contingency of *pen-*'*ābô*', thus identifying the specific nature of the threat implicit in the warning '*ābô*' — Yahweh's intention to "strike the land" in his righteous judgment (WO'C § 32.2.1d). Apparently the restoration community in Jerusalem had already experienced this divine judgment in the form of natural calamities "striking" the land (Hag 2:17; see Andersen and Freedman [1989: 441–42] on *hikkētî* + *šiddāpôn* + *yērāqôn* as a "stock phrase" rooted in the curses of the Mosaic covenant in Amos 4:9; Deut 28:22; 1 Kgs 8:37 [= 2 Chr 6:28]; and Hag 2:17); and in that eschatological Day of Yahweh this judgment will become Israel's ally because he will "strike" Israel's enemies with plagues of blindness and madness ('*akkeh* . . . *battimmāhôn* . . . *baššiggā'ôn*, Zech 12:4).

'*et-hā*'*āreṣ ḥērem*. This phrase is cited by Waltke and O'Connor (§ 10.2.3d) as a double accusative of *direct object* + *means* (of instrument). The noun *hā*'*āreṣ* here does not mean the earth in a global sense, but "land" in a more restricted or territorial sense. Previously, von Bulmerincq (1932: 591) correctly observed that the reference to "forefathers" and "descendants" in 3:24ab [4:6ab] parallels the use of *hā*'*āreṣ*; thus, one cannot distinguish the territory of covenant promise from the people of the covenant who dwell in that land. The Haggai-Zechariah-Malachi corpus uses *hā*'*āreṣ* in similar fashion (e.g., Hag 2:4; Zech 7:5; 13:2; 14:10). The word '*ereṣ* occurs elsewhere in Malachi only in 3:12 (*kî-tihyû* '*attem* '*ereṣ ḥēpeṣ*; see the NOTES and COMMENTS on 3:12 above), where it also connotes "the land" within the borders of Israel.

Lohfink has argued that "ban" (cf. NEB), the usual translation of the word *ḥērem* (I) is misleading and the "action noun" is better rendered "object or person consecrated (for sacral use)" or "condemned for destruction," or even "curse" (by way of the LXX *anáthema*, so NIV, NJB, NRSV; cf. *TDOT* 5:188). This technical term occurs in the Twelve only in Zech 14:11 and the appendixes of Malachi (3:24 [4:6]). Elsewhere the word is attested in prophetic literature only in Isa 34:5; 43:28; and Ezek 44:29.

The combination of the verbs *ḥrm* + *nkh*, according to Lohfink, may be understood as *parallelism* (e.g., "exterminate" and "destroy") or *summation* (i.e., "utter destruction"; cf. *TDOT* 5:186–87). However, that is not the construction here (cf. WO'C § 27.4a on the denominative form of the abstract noun *ḥērem* in 1 Kgs 9:21). The noun *ḥērem* stands as the second object of the verb *nkh* and does not indicate the "summation of destruction" (cf. NAB). Rather, *ḥērem* specifies the nature of this divine judgment (i.e., it replicates the military motif with the sacral aspects of covenant relationship characteristic of the Hebrew conquest of Palestine as described by the Deuteronomistic historian[s], cf. *TDOT* 5:183–84) and the extent of Yahweh's *strike* (*nkh*) against the land — total destruction.

Again, Lohfink (*TDOT* 5:187) has noted that "the more the Hiphil of *ḥrm* becomes a synonym for verbs meaning 'destroy, exterminate,' the more it comes to refer only to human beings." If the converse is true, the Hiphil *hîkkētî* introducing *ḥērem* may refer primarily to the people of the land — not simply the physical features of the land — including the evidences of human cultivation and habitation. By contrast, Zech 14:11 informs us that upon Yahweh's victory over the enemies of Israel in the eschaton the land will never again be "devoted to destruction" (*ḥērem*; cf. Meyers and Meyers [1993: 448]).

COMMENTS

3:23 [4:5] The construction *hinnēh* + participle ("See!") may describe immediate circumstances or indicate a "long-term state of affairs" (WO'C § 37.6d). The combination of *hinnēh* + *šōlēaḥ* in this second appendix of Malachi corresponds to that of the first pattern, immediate circumstance. In fact, the appendixes of Malachi betray the dual eschatological interests of the postexilic era outlined by Hanson (1979: 209 ff., 280 ff.) as *hierocratic apocalyptic* and *visionary apocalyptic*. It is even possible that the appendixes of Malachi served to bridge the tensions between these two postexilic "theo-political" movements as much as they serve to join the Primary History and Latter Prophets as equally valid and authoritative religious anthologies. McCarthy (1963: 332) has identified this emotive use of *hinnēh* as the circumstance of *excited perception* — "where the emotional tone is so strong that we cannot treat the sentence as a simple statement of fact."

While "indeed" or "certainly" is an appropriate translation of *hinnēh* in this verse, I have opted to read "See!" because it captures both the sense of immediacy inherent in the grammatical construction and the need for personal awareness and involvement on the part of the audience (cf. NAB and NRSV, "Lo"; NEB and NJB, "Look"; NIV, "See"). To avoid blurring the distinction between *hinnēh* as an exclamation and a presentative introducing exposition (cf. WO'C

§ 40.2.1c), McCarthy (1963: 331) has encouraged grasping both the *feeling* and the *meaning* of the expression to appreciate the full force of the language. Marking *hinnēh* as a separate and complete thought ("See!") accentuates the exclamatory function of the particle and permits a more focused understanding of the exposition — the announcement of a messenger who ushers in the day of Yahweh.

The obvious grammatical and thematic similarities between Mal 3:1 and 3:23 [4:5] have incited considerable scholarly discussion as to the relationship of Yahweh's "messenger" (*mal'ākî*, 3:1) to "Elijah the prophet," as well as the identification of the Elijah figure. Even though the two texts are directed to different audiences (3:1 to the skeptics of Malachi's day and 3:23 [4:5] to the Hebrew covenant community of a later time period), the vocabulary, theme of divine judgment, and function of eschatological forerunner clearly demonstrate the relatedness of the two passages. Verhoef (1987: 340) neatly summarizes the interpretive options, whether two Elijah figures (e.g., a Christian understanding regarding the messenger of 3:1 as John the Baptist and the Elijah figure of the appendix as a "forerunner" of Christ's second coming, or the Jewish reading of 3:1 as an "angel" and 3:23 [4:5] literally as Elijah the prophet) or the more common approach of many modern interpreters maintaining that the messenger of 3:1 and the Elijah figure of 3:23 [4:5] are one and the same individual. Here I concur with Calvin (pp. 568, 627), and a host of interpreters in his wake, that the reference to "Elijah the prophet" in the appendixes is best understood as a clarification of the messenger figure introduced in 3:1 (cf. Eissfeldt [1965: 442]). See further the NOTES and COMMENTS on 3:1 above.

The identity of this Elijah figure constitutes a second interpretive problem. Obviously the LXX (note the textual variant, *tòn thesbíten*) and even some of the Jews of NT times (cf. Matt 17:10–11; Lk 1:17; Jn 1:21; although the Jewish writers of the NT understood the title "Elijah" in a figurative sense, e.g., Matt 17:12) assumed the literal appearance of the historical prophet Elijah, since he was translated into heaven in a miraculous way (2 Kgs 2:1–11; cf. Sir 48:10, which outlines the threefold ministry of Elijah in the eschaton as calming the wrath of God, reconciling parents and children, and restoring the tribes of Jacob).

Christian interpreters have diagnosed the Elijah figure variously as John the Baptist on the basis of NT teaching (cf. Baldwin [1972a: 252–53]; Verhoef [1987: 341]), the prophetic author of the book, Malachi himself (e.g., Petersen [1977: 42]), or even Yahweh (cf. Glazier-McDonald [1987a: 135–41]; but apparently confused, she reverses herself in 3:23 [4:5; see pp. 261–62] and appeals to the work of the messenger figure. See Malchow's [1989] review as well). Since the writings of Luther (Oswald [1975: 419]) and Calvin (pp. 627–28), most Protestant commentators have figuratively interpreted the Elijah figure as "a prophet in whom the spirit and power of Elijah are revived" — not the prophet Elijah reincarnate or resurrected (Keil [2:471]).

Not only do the two texts address different audiences, but these audiences also had different eschatological expectations. The earlier documents of the Haggai-Zechariah-Malachi corpus (i.e., Haggai and Zechariah 1–8) stressed the glory of the Second Temple in terms of the wealth of the nations flowing into the Temple treasury (Hag 2:7; cf. Zech 8:20–23). Zechariah 9–14 delays this "plundering of the nations" (and the subsequent glorification of the Second Temple) by embedding the event in the eschation — the coming Day of Yahweh (cf. Zech 14:14). Malachi further delays the event by introducing the forerunner figure who precedes the Day of Yahweh and shifts the means of Temple glorification from the wealth of the nations to the very presence of God (Mal 3:1). The specification regarding the messenger figure in the second appendix (i.e., Elijah the prophet) may have served as an exhortation intended to rekindle the community's hope in the promise of Yahweh's glorification given the dampening effects of the time delay and the equivocation of successive prophetic utterances.

The appeal to the idealized personages of Moses and Elijah in the appendixes along with the intertextual citations linking the Torah and Prophets by way of theological summary and even the spelling of the name Elijah (i.e., the more uncommon 'ēlîyâ for the expected 'ēlîyāhû) all suggest a typological approach to an interpretation of the postscript. The juxtaposition of the two ideal figures, Moses and Elijah, may be a conflation of two interrelated texts from the Primary History: Deut 18:15–22 (the forecast of a prophet *like* Moses) and 2 Kgs 17:13–14 (linking the prophetic ministry of Elijah to the stipulations of the Mosaic covenant; cf. Zech 1:6; 7:7). Indeed, Moses and Elijah are parallel "messengers of Yahweh" in that both were oracles of God, worked signs and wonders in his name, and encountered Yahweh in theophanic experiences at Horeb (Exod 4:8; Deut 5:2; 34:10; 1 Kgs 17:22–23; 19:8 ff.; 21:17; cf. Fishbane [1985: 373–74] on the typological function of Moses as a "legitimizer" of later prophetic tradition).[4]

In view of this, and given NT teaching, the Elijah figure of Malachi's appendixes is best understood in Christian interpretation typologically in the person and ministry of John the Baptist (see above I. F. 1. Malachi in the New Testament for extensive documentation of early church fathers making this identification, see Pusey [2:499–503]). Yet, Wolf's (pp. 124–25) caveat deserves a hearing because "the possibility remains that it [i.e., the identification of John the Baptist with Elijah] does not exhaust the full meaning of this prophecy." He has carefully observed that the gospel of Matthew hints that John was the Elijah figure in a limited way (11:14) and records Jesus predicting that Elijah not only "has come" but "is coming" — perhaps as one of the witnesses prior to the second coming of Christ in the vision of the Apocalypse (17:11; cf. Rev 11:3).

The sequence of events constituting the "Day of Yahweh" is compressed into an eschatological blur in the Haggai-Zechariah-Malachi corpus. However, the perspectives of the restoration prophets are consistent with the rest of OT/HB teaching on "that day," in that they conform to the general pattern of apostasy in Israel, followed by oppression and scattering by the nations as judgment for

---

[4] For Clark (pp. 67–68, 236) the promise of Elijah as "eschatological high priest" emerged from two currents of theological tradition: the servant of Yahweh motif of Second Isaiah and the portrayal of Moses as an eschatological prophet in Deut 18:15–19. The legacy of Moses as the *first* prophet preserved in the colophon to the Pentateuch (Deut 34:10–12) was blended with the legacy of Elijah as the *last* prophet in Malachi's colophon summarizing the message of the OT prophetic books (cf. Nogalski [1993b: 185]; and Redditt [1994: 249–50]).

breach of covenant, with Israel's subsequent repentance prompting God to regather the elect and restore the covenant blessings, while judging the nations for their exploitation of Israel (cf. ABD 2:84–85; Jacob [1958: 317–42]; and the Eschatological Scenario chart in Petersen [1977: 17]).

In the main, I am inclined to agree with Petersen ([1977: 14–15]) that the postexilic prophets represent a "deutero-prophetic" tradition expecting the future triumph of Yahweh but dependent upon the earlier classical prophetic literature. Further, Hanson (1979: 19–21) is probably correct in his assessment of the sociological tension between "vision" and "reality" spawning competing postexilic prophetic traditions: the "apocalyptic visionaries" (committed to a dramatic and revolutionary divine intervention in the human order) and the "hierocratic party" (political pragmatists content with their position as "brokers" in the contemporary power structures, the "theocratic prophets" for Petersen [1977: 8]).

The book of Malachi fits the general eschatological scenario of the apocalyptic visionaries as understood by Petersen and Hanson with the prophet's emphasis on the Day of Yahweh, divine judgment, and the restoration of the faithful (3:1–4, 16–21 [4:3]; cf. Clark [1975: 44–56] who marshals considerable documentation demonstrating the continuation of the "new exodus" motif of Second Isaiah in the restoration program of the postexilic prophets). Because Malachi modifies the eschatological teaching of Haggai and First and Second Zechariah (e.g., introducing the preparatory role of the *messenger* prior to the Day of Yahweh) and employs the apocalyptic message in an admonitory fashion (e.g., 3:19–21 [4:1–3]), the book fits both the exegetical and devotional rubrics created by Petersen (1977: 14) for deutero-prophetic literature. However, the appendixes of Malachi appear to illustrate a hybrid of visionary apocalypticism (e.g., the emphasis on the coming Day of Yahweh) and hierocratic pragmatism (e.g., the charge to remember the Torah of Moses). All this suggests that the later restoration Israelite community recognized the need for mediation of the two prophetic trajectories because nearly a century of Persian domination occasioned a demand for the nationalistic hope engendered by the apocalyptic agenda, while reality dictated finding security and stability in the only institutions the Israelites possessed—the Second Temple, the priesthood, and the Torah of Moses (see Fishbane [1985: 523–24, 535–36]).

Andersen and Freedman (1989: 521) have traced the earliest use of the phrase "Day of Yahweh" as a technical eschatological term to the "woe oracles" of the prophet Amos (5:18–20), noting two defining characteristics: darkness and reversal. The idea of Yahweh's eschatological day as a period of gloom, distress, destruction, and plague is amplified in the later prophets, to the degree that the concept develops into a leitmotif and a core tenet of OT/HB theology (see especially Zeph 1:14–18; Joel 4:9–16 [3:9–16]).

The use of the stock phrase "great and terrible" in the appendixes of Malachi no doubt assumes these multiple images associated with the Day of Yahweh: its imminent occurrence, ominous tone, forensic character, miraculous nature, and the reversal of fortune. The depiction of Yahweh's coming in the eschaton as a great and terrible day in Mal 3:23 [4:5] is a citation of Joel 2:11c and 3:4b [2:31b], where commentators have isolated direct ties between Joel's Day of Yahweh and the plagues brought upon Egypt by Yahweh, which precipitated the Hebrew Exodus (e.g., [Wolff 1977: 68]; Allen [1976: 100]; cf. 2 Sam 7:23//1 Chr 17:21), and are regarded (by Wolff) as heralds of theophanic activity against the nations. The Day of Yahweh is "great" because it constitutes the ultimate theophany; all the signs, miracles, and cataclysms of nature marking Yahweh's previous encounters with humanity were but pallid foreshadowings of this most dramatic and momentous intervention of Yahweh in the human sphere for the sake of his people Israel. The Day of Yahweh is "terrible" (so NAB, NEB, NJB, NRSV; NIV "dreadful") in that the encounter of the divine and the human most often induces fear and dread, even abject terror in the creature (cf. Exod 19:10–25; Judg 13:22; Isa 6:5).

The Day of Yahweh is also depicted as "terrible" because the aftermath of divine judgment, with its carnage and destruction, leaves survivors aghast and reeling in disbelief (cf. Isa 13:6–8; Lam 1:20; 2:11; Ezek 21:6–7). According to Jeremiah (30:7), this unprecedented Day of Yahweh is great (gādôl), even though it is a time of judgment and distress for Israel, because God will rescue his people from it—unlike the Babylonian onslaught of 587 B.C./E. (cf. Joel 4:16 [3:16], which also factors the deliverance of Israel into the schematic of Yahweh's day). In that sense, the postscript of Malachi is a message of covenant hope as much as it is a threat of divine curse (hence, the LXX interpolation "glorious" [èpiphanē] for "terrible" [hannôrā'] has some merit theologically).

The expression "the great and the terrible day" (haggādôl wĕhannôrā') fixes the typological context of the day of Yahweh as a time of divine testing, judgment, and reward for covenant obedience after the pattern of the Israelite post-Exodus desert trek experience (cf. Deut 1:19, 26; 7:12–16; 8:2; The phrase "the great and terrible . . ." is also applied to the forboding "moonscape" of the Sinai desert, home to a generation of Hebrews after the escape from Egypt [Deut 1:19]). Even as Moses served Yahweh as leader and prophet for Israel before the glory (kābôd) of Yahweh settled in the Tent of Meeting (Exod 40:34–38), so too the Elijah figure will serve Yahweh in a prophetic ministry of reconciliation before the (formal) return of Yahweh to his people (see Zech 8:1–3).

These adjectives from the parallel citation in Joel (3:4b [2:31b]) also establish the eschatological context of the Day of Yahweh for restored Israel as a day of an outpouring of God's spirit (Joel 3:1–2 [2:28–29]; cf. Num 11:16–25; Zech 12:10), celestial portents (Joel 3:3–4 [2:30–31]; cf. Hag 2:21), judgment for Israel's enemies (Joel 4:1–3; cf. Zech 12:1–9), and deliverance for the righteous of Israel (Joel 3:4 [2:32]; cf. Zech 13:1). The (continuing) delay of Yahweh's coming implicit in the introduction of the messenger figure as the forerunner of that event and the use of the idiom lipnê ("before") means that postexilic Yehud is still "bereft of the immediacy of the divine presence" (Fishbane [1985: 524]; cf. Petersen [1977: 40–41]). The appendixes of Malachi mitigate, in part, this eschatological crisis for the restoration community by asserting that the divine presence is manifest in "canonized" documents associated with the traditions of the ideal figures of Moses (i.e., Torah) and Elijah (i.e., Latter Prophets).

24 [4:6]. The basic meaning of the (Hiphil perfective) verb šwb is "to (re)turn, turn back, or bring back" (here the NAB, NIV, NJB, NRSV all read "turn"; cf.

Holladay [1958: 6–12]). The conjunction "and" (*waw*) is both a *conjunctive waw* in that it joins two clauses (WO'C § 39.2.5) and an *epexegetical waw* in that it serves to clarify or specify the sense of the preceding clause (WO'C § 39.2.4). The nonperfective *wĕqātaltî* construction (i.e., *waw* + suffix conjugation) after a predicate participle "represents an explanatory, imperfective situation" (WO'C § 32.2.5b). The verbal form here has the same anticipatory sense as the *wĕqātaltî* construction of 3:1 (*ûpinnâ*). However, although the postscript does clarify the identity of the "messenger of the covenant," it also weakens the force of immediacy connoted in the nonperfective construction by indicating the specific nature of the ministry of this messenger figure — effecting reconciliation implies that some interval of time must occur before the Day of Yahweh's epiphany.

The usage of the Hiphil perfective *hēšîb* in the postscript matches one of the definitions set forth by Holladay (1958) for the verb *šwb*: "motion back to a point of departure" (p. 87) with the "object a part of the body, either concretely or as an expression of the person" (p. 97). Specifically, Holladay (1958: 99) has placed this occurrence of *šwb* in a "covenantal context" and translates it "bring back." Human beings are the object of this "turning," thus it seems that Mal 3:24 [4:6] also fits Holladay's (1958: 89) category of ". . . motion, but with an implication of restoring to a relationship as well." The restoration of human relationships is but the by-product of the act or process of reconciliation (in this case accomplished by the messenger figure as the divine agent of reconciliation). Hence, I have chosen to render *šwb* in this context as "reconcile" (cf. NEB). Holladay's "covenantal" classification is appropriate because the restoration of human relationships is contingent upon personal repentance and "a change of loyalty on the part of Israel or God, each for the other" (1958: 116). The Hebrews of postexilic Yehud cannot effect a change in their loyalty to the religious heritage of their ancestors or each other until they consciously shift their allegiance back to Yahweh and the demands of his covenant.

The equation of the "heart" (*lēb*) with the person is an example of synecdoche. While contextually the postscript has the individual (or contemporary society) in mind, the word "heart" here especially connotes the affections that govern attitude and the disposition that informs volition — and ultimately shapes behavior. The messenger arranges no "truce" between warring parties. Rather, this Elijah figure interposes an "unconditional surrender" to Yahweh upon his audience and effects a complete reorientation in the operative worldview of the religious community.

Holladay (1958: 99) and Verhoef (1987: 342) are correct to emphasize the covenantal connotations of the term *šwb* in the context of the postscript. Those scholars understanding this ministry of reconciliation primarily as reform of the contemporary social order (especially at the microlevel of the family) are prisoners of the assumption that the postscript is original to Malachi (e.g., Rudolph [1976: 293]; Glazier-McDonald [1987a: 254]). In addition, they fail to recognize the typological nature of the coda with its appeal to ideal figures, representing Israel's covenant legacy with Yahweh, and the open-ended time frame for following through on the postscript's admonition and exhortation. At issue in Malachi's appendixes is the bonding of the current generation of postexilic Israelites to the

Mosaic covenant of their ancestors (cf. Jer 6:16 and the exhortation to return to the "ancient paths").

The call for reconciliation between the ancestors (lit. "fathers," ʾābôt) and the "descendants" (lit. "sons," bānîm) is really a call for covenant renewal with Yahweh, the "resolution of opposites" at the macrolevel in the sense of faithful ancestors versus faithless descendants (Petersen [1977: 44]; cf. Calvin [1979: 630–31]). "The present order must be reconciled with the previous state of things when God has entered into a covenant relationship with the 'fathers'" (Verhoef [1987: 342]; interestingly he notes that this interpretation accords better with Malachi's message than the "family discord" approach because the prophet consistently appeals to the past [2:10, 12; 3:4]).

I have elected to translate ʾābôt ("fathers") here with "forefathers" because the postscript specifically mentions two of the prominent patriarchal figures of earlier Israelite history, Moses and Elijah (and noting the English word "forefather" simply means "ancestor"). Mason (1977: 161) may be right in assuming that the conditions within the restoration community reflected in the postscript parallel those of Isaiah's era (3:5), but even there the context is one of covenant lawsuit and judgment for failure to execute social justice in the land (3:13–15). The same grim fate awaits this generation of Yahweh's elect (Mal 1:2–5) unless they heed the prophetic appeal to return to him (Mal 3:7).

The contingency introduced by pen- ("lest") does not apply to the epiphany of Yahweh, because "Yahweh's arrival is irrevocable" (Clark [1975: 35]; cf. Halévy [1909: 34] and von Bulmerincq [1932: 586] on the correct translation "when I come"). Rather, it is the curse of Yahweh that is revocable. Implicit here in the appendixes is Yahweh's capacity to change his mind and repent (nḥm) from following through on the threat of divine judgment in particular situations.[5] For example, Jeremiah reminded Judah of Yahweh's capability to "change his mind" and postpone or even waive divine judgment in response to Judah's repentance (18:8); and the survival of Nineveh hinges upon this very attribute of God (which drives the plot reversal in the book of Jonah), much to the chagrin of the prophet (3:9–10; 4:2; cf. Sasson [1990: 260–68]).

Andersen and Freedman (1989: 644–45) have observed that this "repentance" or relenting of judgment on God's part may occur under the following conditions: (1) as a reaction to specific events or developments in the human sphere, (2) in response to the intervention or intercession of a prophetic figure, and (3) in response to genuine and demonstrable repentance on the part of people. Given the citation of Joel 3:4b [2:31b] in the appendixes of Malachi, it is possible that the coda was intended to call Joel 2:14 to mind, offering (the restoration community?) the possibility of the substitution of a blessing for a curse in view of Yahweh's "change of mind."

This understanding of the Day of Yahweh may help to account for the desire of the expatriates only recently resettled in Jerusalem for the arrival of Yahweh's day. However, like the Israelites of Amos's era, postexilic Yehud also has a false

---

[5] See the extensive excursus "When God Repents" (including a comprehensive discussion of the verb nḥm) in Andersen and Freedman (1989: 638–79).

estimate of what this day of God will bring, hence the warning of a divine curse to conclude the postscript (cf. Andersen and Freedman [1989: 519–22]). Remarkably, this resolution of opposites accomplished by the Elijah figure within the restoration community prompts the same kind of reversal in the direction of the Day of Yahweh (cf. Wolff [1977: 68]). Yahweh will *return* to those who have *returned* to him (Mal 3:7).

The verb *nkh* may signify "striking" so as to kill (directly by a blow, Gen 4:15, *or* indirectly by plague, Exod 12:12) or punish (whether corporally, Exod 5:14, or by means of natural disaster, plague, war, etc., Exod 7:25; Josh 7:3; Amos 4:9). Here *nkh* possesses the connotation both to punish and even to kill. The context of covenant curse indicates that this divine judgment will occur primarily by means of natural calamity and plague (cf. Deut 28:27, 28, 35). The reality of this divine judgment is rooted in the memory of a series of natural disasters that "strike" (*nkh*) the early restoration community (prompting no "return" [*šwb*, reading the ancient vers. T and V]; Hag 2:17).

The covenant theme central to the prophetic books and the appeal to the ideal figures of Moses and Elijah in the appendixes of Malachi also suggest that *nkh* should be understood against the background of the Hebrew Exodus from Egypt under Moses's leadership (e.g., Exod 3:20; 12:12), the (blessings and) curses appended to the stipulations of the Mosaic treaty (e.g., Lev 26:24; Deut 28:22), and perhaps the miracles of Elijah ([?]; cf. 2 Kgs 2:8, 14).

The use of *nkh* in the postscript as a threat against postexilic Yehud may serve as a corrective for misperceptions generated by the apocalyptic visions of Second Zechariah. The Israelites themselves risked divine punishment as much as the enemies of Yahweh's people (Zech 12:4). Unlike Yahweh's earlier chastisement of postexilic Yehud with blight, mildew, hail (Hag 2:17), and locusts (Mal 3:11), which resulted in personal inconvenience and economic scarcity, the combination of *nkh* + *ḥērem* suggests the total destruction of the restoration community (recalling the destruction of Jerusalem by the Babylonians[?]; cf. Jer 21:6).

Elsewhere the combination of *nkh* ("strike") + *'ereṣ* ("land") refers to the people of a given land (e.g., Isa 11:4; Jer 43:11). This holds true for Mal 3:24 [4:6] because of the "dynamic" nature of the Mosaic covenant. Properly assessed, the Ebal ritual (Deut 27:1–26; Josh 8:30–35) was not a covenant-renewal ceremony or even an installment ceremony legitimizing Joshua as Moses's successor. Rather, the Ebal ritual constituted the "royal grant" clause of Israel's treaty with Yahweh (cf. Hill [1988]). As such, it was the instrument by which Yahweh authorized Israel to possess Canaan as his heir. The Ebal land-grant ritual completed the purpose of covenant renewal in the land of Canaan, the bonding of Yahweh's people Israel to the land of covenant promise under the jurisdiction of Yahweh's law.

The codas of Malachi recognize the fact that the divine curse effected for covenant violation inextricably applies to both the people and the land under Yahweh's suzerainty. The mention of "the land" here may be an allusion to the eschatological borders of Israel secondarily (cf. Meyers and Meyers [1993: 390]) but is to be considered primarily as an ellipsis for the Persian province of Yehud and the people living in that territory. If Malachi's postscript dates to the time of

Ezra and Nehemiah or later, it seems likely that the solidarity of postexilic Israel assumed by the word land (*hā'āreṣ*) reflects the interests of the Chronicler who understood that this new "unity was to be based on their common worship of Yahweh centered in the Jerusalem temple" (Braun [1986: xxxvii]).

Lohfink objects to the meaning "ban" for *ḥērem* as "false and misleading" (*TDOT* 5:188). Following the previous work of Meyers and Meyers (1993: 448) I have adopted Lohfink's definition, "curse," for the noun *ḥērem*: "the object or person consecrated . . . or condemned . . . ; the act of consecration or of extermination and killing" (*TDOT* 5:188). Others like de Vaux (2:260–61) actually equate *ḥērem* ("extermination, killing") with *'rr* ("curse") on the basis of the parallels between Judg 21:11 and 5:23. The word as used in this context with *bw'* and *nkh* possesses unmistakable military overtones, similar to the military motif for the Day of Yahweh developed in Joel and Zephaniah.

The only sacral connotations of the word "curse" (*ḥērem*) in Mal 3:24 [4:6] are those associated with Yahweh's righteous judgment of a nation consecrated to him in holiness by means of covenant relationship (Deut 7:26; Isa 43:28). The frequent distribution of both the verb and the noun in Deuteronomic passages strengthens the link the appendixes of Malachi develop between the Primary History and the Latter Prophets. The use of *ḥērem* may also serve as a foil, with Zech 14:11 as an antidote for spiritual complacency. Granted Yahweh's intention never again to designate Israel as *ḥērem* in the eschaton, that truth remained a prospect of the future; for the present Israel still lived in jeopardy of the divine curse affixed to the stipulations for covenant trespass.

By way of summary, the appendixes of Malachi function primarily as a "literary hinge" linking the two foundational corpora of the Hebrew Bible, the Law of Moses (as part of the Primary History) and the Latter Prophets. The postscript serves ancillary purposes as well: notably, identifying the messenger of the covenant (Mal 3:1), mediating the theological tension in the restoration community between the power of law and promise of prophecy (for a variation on this harmonization of divergent theological viewpoints, see Blenkinsopp [1977: 121–23]), and advancing the eschatological theme of the day of Yahweh by introducing the element of *praeparatio* (cf. Petersen [1977: 44]).

Craigie (p. 248) has condensed the meaning of the postscript of Malachi for postexilic Yehud into *retrospect* and *prospect*. Retrospect in the form of an exhortation based upon an appeal to the ideal figure of Moses. The exhortation reminded the people of the primacy of Mosaic Law for community life and encouraged that community to remain faithful to the legacy of Yahweh's covenant during (what had then become) an "interim" period of Hebrew history. Prospect in the form of an admonition based on an appeal to the ideal prophetic figure Elijah. The admonition was both a warning that "if the law is not fulfilled *in* the nation, it must be executed *upon* the nation" (Hengstenberg [2:1226]) and a pledge that the hope of a "restored" Israel projected in prophetic visions would indeed be realized. Together they composed a type of credo certifying the "canonized" scriptures of the Law and the Prophets as the source of authority and the witness of the divine presence for the restoration community.

APPENDIXES

◆

Appendix A: Von Bulmerincq's Categories for Dating Malachi

In his classic work on Malachi, von Bulmerincq (1926: 87–97) outlined the range of possibilities for the dating of Malachi's disputations under seven headings. This catalog is a representative sampling of positions taken by biblical scholars past and present on the date of the book of Malachi. For the sake of clarity I have modified von Bulmerincq's second category so that a distinction may be made in placing Malachi before Ezra, or after Ezra but prior to Nehemiah, assuming Ezra preceded Nehemiah.

1. Malachi contemporary with or prior to Haggai and Zechariah 1:8:
   Ewald (1875)
   Welch (1935)
   O'Brien (1990)
2a. Malachi before Ezra and Nehemiah:
   G. A. Smith (1905)
   Budde (1906)
   van Hoonacker (1908)
   Duhm (1911)
   J. M. P. Smith (1912)
   Kirkpatrick (1915)
   von Bulmerincq (1926)
   Nowack (1922)
   Sellin (1930)
   Pfeiffer (1941)
   Elliger (1950)
   Horst (1954)
   Oesterley-Robinson (1955)
   Rowley (1961)
   D. N. Freedman (1962, 1974, 1976, and 1991)
   Wellhausen (1963, Reprint)
   Eissfeldt (1965)
   Myers (1968)
   Fohrer (1968)
   Ackroyd (1970)

Clark (1975)*
Schneider (1979)
Hill (1981, 1982, 1983, and 1992)
van der Woude (1982)
Koch (1984)
Wanke (in Davies-Finkelstein 1984)
Craigie (1985)
Bullock (1986)
Drinkard (1987)
Glazier-McDonald (1987)
Yamauchi (1990)
Merrill (1994)
Berquist (1995)
Petersen (1995)

2b. Malachi after Ezra but prior to Nehemiah:
Dentan (1956)*
Neil (1962)*
Harrison (1969)
Bright (1981)*
Alden (1985)
Chisholm (1990)

3. Malachi during Nehemiah's first governorship:
Jones (1962)
Pusey (1977, Reprint)
R. L. Smith (1984)

4. Malachi between the first and second governorships of Nehemiah:
König (1893)
von Orelli (1897)
Archer (1974)
Mallone (1981)
Verhoef (1987)

5. Malachi during Nehemiah's second governorship:
Ewald (1875)
Hengstenberg (1956, Reprint)
Moore (1974, Reprint)
Wolf (1976)
Kaiser (1984)
Nogalski (1993b; or later in the book's final redaction?)
Redditt (1994; or later in the book's final redaction?)

6. Malachi contemporary with Ezra and Nehemiah:
Pressel (1870)
S. R. Driver (1922)
Laetsch (1970)
Keil (1975, Reprint)

* Dates Ezra after Nehemiah

Baldwin (1978)
Cook (1978)*
Calvin (1979, Reprint)
Henderson (1980, Reprint)
Newsome (1984)*
Ogden and Deutsch (1987)
Deissler (1988)
7. Malachi during the late Persian period or Hellenistic period:
Torrey (1898)
Winckler (1899)
Spoer (1908)
Holtzmann (1931)
Bosshard and Kratz (1990, in the book's final redaction)

APPENDIX B: TYPOLOGICAL ANALYSIS OF THE POSTEXILIC PROPHETS

In his book *Late Biblical Hebrew: Toward an Historical Typology of Biblical Hebrew Prose* (1976), Robert Polzin has attempted to classify and date several major stages of development in the Hebrew Bible on the basis of grammatical and syntactic features. By systematically applying these linguistic categories to selected texts, Polzin differentiated early biblical Hebrew from late biblical Hebrew on a relative chronological scale. The focal point of Polzin's research was the portion of the Hebrew Bible traditionally called the Priestly Document (or P). To establish the preexilic end of his continuum, Polzin utilized selections from the Pentateuch, the Court History, and the Deuteronomist. The postexilic segment of his continuum was keyed to the nonsynoptic portions of Chronicles, Ezra-Nehemiah, and Esther. By means of linguistic analysis Polzin both delineated the typological character and adduced a relative chronological relationship for his control and target corpora. Granted this fact, it seemed reasonable to assume that the typological methodology would yield criteria sufficient for the establishment of a relative dating scheme when applied to other texts as well. This analysis of the postexilic prophets is built upon just this premise. The nineteen diagnostic features of late biblical Hebrew (LBH) developed by Polzin for the typological analysis of biblical Hebrew prose are catalogued below according to Polzin's enumeration:

1. Polzin's (1976) Grammatical and Syntactic Diagnostic Categories

A. Features of Late Biblical Hebrew (LBH) not attributable to Aramaic influence
   1. Radically reduced use of *'et* with pronominal suffix

2. Increased use of 'et before noun in the nominative case: 'et emphatic

3. Expression of possession by prospective pronominal suffix with following noun, or šel plus noun

4. Collectives construed as plurals almost without exception

5. Preference for plural forms of words and phrases that earlier language uses in singular

6. Use of infinitive absolute in immediate connection with a finite verb of same stem almost completely lacking in Chronicler; infinitive absolute used as command not found at all in Chronicles

7. Chronicler's use of the infinitive construct with bĕ and kĕ

8. Repetition of singular word = Latin quivis (to express distributive)

9. Chronicler merging [i.e., a tendency to replace] third feminine plural suffix with a third masculine plural suffix

10. First-person singular imperfect [prefixing] with -āh (lengthened imperfect [prefixing] or cohortative) found but once in Chronicler's language

11. wayhî greatly receding in Chronicles and in later language

12. In appositional relationship, Chronicler prefering substantive before numeral and almost always in plural, contrary to older practice of putting number first

13. Chronicler showing increased use of infinitive construct with lĕ

B. Features of Late Biblical Hebrew (LBH) caused by Aramaic influence

1. Citing material and weight or measure, order often: material weighed or measured + weight or measure (+ number)

2. lĕ used often as mark of accusative

3. In min "from," nun often not assimilated before noun without article

4. Chronicler uses emphatic lĕ before last element of list

5. In attributive usage, rabbîm twice placed before substantive

6. Use of 'ad lĕ (for "up to, until")

2. Distribution of Linguistic Features in Control and Target Corpora

The following chart displays the distribution of linguistic features in Robert Polzin's control corpora and the additional corpora of prophetic books. It permits us to compare and analyze the typological character of each corpus. Polzin's grammatical and syntactic diagnostic categories (A.1–13 and B.1–6) are listed across the top of the chart. The various control and target corpora examined are registered down the column on the left side of the chart. A linear tabulation summarizing the typological character of each corpus may be found in Appendix B. 3 Typological Continuum of Control and Target Corpora Keys to the symbols and abbreviations used in the chart appear on page 399.

NOTES:

1. Refinement of the statistical analysis of the postexilic prophets has resulted in a modification of the typological profile of Haggai and Zechariah 1–8 (a

shift from a CBH feature to a unique feature in A.2) and Zechariah 9–14 and Malachi (a shift from a LBH feature to a CBH feature in A.7).

2. The identification of unique or LBH features in the control corpora of Jeremiah and Ezekiel is somewhat misleading, making chronological determinations based upon the linguistic evidence alone tenuous. For example, in category A.2 [Increased use of *'et* emphatic] Malachi yields 0 occurrences in 55 verses, Jeremiah but 2 occurrences in 1,362 verses, and Ezekiel only 5 occurrences in 1,273 verses — yet technically Jeremiah and Ezekiel demonstrate a typology different than that of Malachi. Similarly, in category A.3 (Expression of possession by prospective pronominal suffix) Malachi exhibits no examples of this feature in 55 verses, while Jeremiah yields one example in 1,362 verses — again demonstrating a slight degree of typological difference when compared to Malachi. In a third instance, Malachi, Jeremiah, and Ezekiel all show a reduction in the use of *wayhî* [A. 11]. However, since Malachi yields no examples of this feature, comparative analysis with the ratios of Jeremiah (30.8 per 1,000 verses) and Ezekiel (36.9 per 1,000 verses) is impossible.

3. Typological Continuum of Control and Target Corpora

Polzin's research may be summarized with the typological continuum of biblical Hebrew that he offered as a result of his systematic application of the nineteen aforementioned linguistic categories to the specified corpora. The expanded continuum of biblical Hebrew prose, including the target corpora of the postexilic prophets and the additional control corpora of Jeremiah, Ezekiel, Joel, and Jonah, is presented below. I have altered Polzin's continuum slightly, as I disagree with him on the placement of Ezr/N2 and Est/N1. I prefer to place Ezr/N2 before Chr since it yields fewer LBH features than does the Chronicler. I place Est/N1 (tentatively) before Ezr/N2 and Chr, based on the hypothesis of alternative language development in the Jewish community that remained in Babylon after the establishment of the restoration community in Palestine. In opposition to Polzin, I view Esther and the memoirs of Nehemiah not as late "archaizing" works, but as works of Babylonian origin or background. The classical biblical Hebrew features contained in these writings may not be deliberate archaizing tendencies of a later period, but features characteristic of the written language of the Jewish community remaining in Exile. I would say that the classical biblical Hebrew features *remain* in Est and N1, whereas Polzin has stated they *reappear*. Corpora with slashes are more or less homogeneous. (In fairness to Polzin, and this writer, I encourage the reader to carefully examine both Polzin's essay and my own full-scale adaptation of it.)

Typological Continuum of Biblical Hebrew

JE/CH/Dtr	Jer/Ezek	Pg	Hag/Zech/Mal/Jl/Jnh	Ps	Est/N1	Ezr/N2	Chr

{ ? }

{JE/CH/Dtr = Polzin's Classical Biblical Hebrew = CBH}

Polzin's Control Corpora

	A1	A2	A3	A4	A5	A6	A7	A8	A9	A10	A11	A12	A13	B1	B2	B3	B4	B5	B6
	✼	✼	✼	✼	✼	✼	✼	✼	✼	✼	✼	✼	✼	✼	✼	✼	✼	✼	✼
J E	p	p	p	p	p	p	p	p	p		p	p	p						
C H	p	p	p	p	p	p	p	p	p		p	p	p						
D t r	p	p	p	p	p	p	p	p			p	p	p	p					
	✼	✼	✼	✼	✼	✼	✼	✼	✼	✼	✼	✼	✼	✼	✼	✼	✼	✼	✼
P g	o	p	x	x	p	x	p	p	x		p	p	o	p					
P s	o	x	x	x	p	o	x	p	x		x	x	o	x					
C h r	x	x	x	x	x	x	x	x	x		x	x	x	x					
E z r			x	x	x	x	x	x	x		x	x		x					
N 2	x	x	x	x	x	x	x				x	x		x					
	✼	✼	✼	✼	✼	✼	✼	✼	✼	✼	✼	✼	✼	✼	✼	✼	✼	✼	✼
N 1	x	x	x	x	x	x	x	x	x		x	x	x	x					
E s t	x			x	x	x	x	x	x		x	x	x	x	x				

JE = Yahwist and Elohist strands*
CH = Court History*
Dtr = *Deuteronomistic material
Pg = Priestly base strand*
Ps = Priestly extensions*
Chr = Chronicles
Ezr = Ezra
N1 = Nehemiah (memoir portions)*
N2 = Nehemiah (non-memoir portions)*
Est = Esther

---

* See Polzin 1976: 88–103, 117–18 for a delineation of the contents of each corpora.

JE — 12 stable CBH features (contra A.1, A.2, A.3, A.4, A.5, A.6, A.7, A.8, A.9, A.10, A.11, A.12, A.13)

CH — 12 stable CBH features (contra A.1, A.2, A.3, A.4, A.5, A.6, A.7, A.8, A.9, A.11, A.12, A.13)

Dtr — 12 stable CBH features (contra A.1, A.2, A.3, A.4, A.5, A.6, A.7, A.8, A.11, A.12, A.13, B.1)

{Jer/Ezk..........Chr = Polzin's Late Biblical Hebrew = LBH}

Jer — 3 features of LBH are present (A.3, A.11, B.3); 13 features of CBH remain (contra A.1, A.5, A.6, A.7, A.8, A.9, A.10, A.12, A.13, B.1, B.2, B.4, B.5); 2 unique features appear (A.2, A.4)

Ezek — 4 features of LBH are present (A.2, A.3, A.11, A.13); 10 features of

Polzin's Target Corpora

	A1	A2	A3	A4	A5	A6	A7	A8	A9	A10	A11	A12	A13	B1	B2	B3	B4	B5	B6
	✻	✻	✻	✻	✻	✻	✻	✻	✻	✻	✻	✻	✻	✻	✻	✻	✻	✻	✻
H a g	p	o	p	x	p	x	x	p	p	x	p	p	x	p	*p*	*p*	-	-	-
Z 1	p	o	p	p	p	p	x	p	p	x	p	p	x	p	*p*	*p*	-	-	-
Z 2	x	p	p	p	p	p	p	x	p	*p*	x	p	o	p	*p*	*p*	-	-	-
M a l	p	p	p	p	p	x	p	p	p	*p*	x	p	o	p	*p*	*p*	-	-	-
	✻	✻	✻	✻	✻	✻	✻	✻	✻	✻	✻	✻	✻	✻	✻	✻	✻	✻	✻
J e r	p	o	x	o	p	p	p	p	p	p	*p*	x	p	p	p	*p*	x	*p*	-
E z k	p	x	x	o	o	p	p	p	p	p	o	x	p	x	p	*p*	*p*	*p*	-
J l	x	p	p	p	p	x	x	p	p	-	x	-	p	-	*p*	*p*	-	-	-
J n h	x	p	x	p	-	x	x	p	p	-	p	-	x	-	*p*	-	-	-	-

Target Corpora and Additional Prophetic Books

Postexilic Prophets
Jer = Jeremiah
Ezk = Ezekiel
Jl = Joel
Jnh = Jonah

Additional Prophets:
Hag = Haggai
Z1 = Zechariah 1–8
Z2 = Zechariah 9–14
Mal = Malachi

Key to Linguistic Features:

p = feature of classical biblical Hebrew (CBH)
p = feature of CBH in prophets, included for comparative purposes, not a part of Polzin's research
x = a feature of late biblical Hebrew (LBH)
x = a feature of LBH in prophets, included for comparative purposes, not a part of Polzin's research
x̲ = Polzin's LBH "archaizing" feature
o = unique feature

CBH remain (contra A.1, A.6, A.7, A.8, A.9, A.12, B.1, B.2, B.3, B.4, B.5); and 3 unique features appear (A.4, A.5, A.10)
Pg — 4 features of LBH are present (A.3, A.4, A.6, A.9); 7 features of CBH remain (contra A.2, A.5, A.7, A.8, A.11, A.12, B.1); 2 unique features appear (A.1, A.13)
Hag — 4 features of LBH are present (A.4, A.6, A.7, A.13); 8 features of CBH remain (contra A.1, A.3, A.5, A.8, A.9, A.11, A.12, B.1); 1 unique feature appears (A.2)
Zech/1 — 2 features of LBH are present (A.7, A.13); 10 features of CBH remain (contra A.1, A.3, A.4, A.5, A.6, A.8, A.9, A.11, A.12, B.1); 1 unique feature appears (A.2)
Zech/2 — 3 features of LBH are present (A.1, A.8, A.11); 9 features of CBH

remain (contra A.2, A.3, A.4, A.5, A.6, A.7, A.9, A.12, B.1); 1 unique
feature appears (A.13)

Mal — 2 features of LBH are present (A.6, A.11); 10 features of CBH remain
(contra A.1, A.2, A.3, A.4, A.5, A.7, A.8, A.9, A.12, B.1); 1 unique feature
appears (A.13)

Joel — 4 features of LBH are present (A.1, A.6, A.7, A.11); 9 features of CBH
remain (contra A.2, A.3, A.4, A.5, A.8, A.9, A.13, B.1, B.2)

Jonah — 5 features of LBH are present (A.1, A.3, A.6, A.7, A.13); 6 features of
CBH remain (contra A.2, A.4, A.8, A.9, A.11, B.2)

Ps — 8 features of LBH are present (A.2, A.3, A.4, A.7, A.9, A.11, A.12, B1); 2
features of CBH remain (contra A.5, A.8); 3 unique features appear (A.1,
A.6, A.13)

Est — 6 features of LBH are present (A.1, A.5, A.7, A.8, A.13, B.2); 6 features
of CBH remain (contra A.4, A.6, A.9, A.11, A.12, B.1)

N1 — 8 features of LBH are present (A.3, A.5, A.6, A.8, A.9, A.12, A.13, B.1);
5 features of CBH remain (contra A.1, A.2, A.4, A.7, A.11)

Ezra — 10 features of LBH are present (A.3, A.4, A.5, A.6, A.7, A.8, A.9, A.11,
A.12, B.1); no features of CBH remain

N2 — 10 features of LBH present (A.1, A.2, A.3, A.4, A.5, A.6, A.7, A.11,
A.12, B.1); no features of CBH remain

Chr — 13 features of LBH are present (A.1, A.2, A.3, A.4, A.5, A.6, A.7, A.8,
A.9, A.11, A.12, A.13, B.1); no features of CBH remain

Broadly speaking, the prophetic target and control corpora fall on the continuum between the CBH of Dtr and the LBH of Ps. The Pg corpus is usually dated
to the early exilic period, sometime between 600 and 550 B.C./E. depending upon
the source. If the Ps corpus dates to the activity of Ezra and Nehemiah in Jerusalem, then the prophetic corpora may be placed in a time frame ranging from ca.
600 to 450 B.C./E. Internal evidence (i.e., lexicography, date formulae, etc.) suggests that Jeremiah, Ezekiel, and Pg date to ca. 600–550 B.C./E. Typological profiles indicate that Haggai, Zechariah 1–8 and 9–14, Malachi, Joel, and Jonah are
to be dated within the same general time period (since the combination of LBH
and unique features in these texts falls between that of Polzin's Pg and Ps corpora). On the basis of internal evidence (literary style and form, lexicography,
date formulae, etc.) that general time frame for the postexilic prophets, Joel, and
Jonah is best placed near 500 B.C./E. (On the rationale for the chronological
relationships among the corpora on the Typological Continuum, see further Polzin: 85–122; and Hill 1981: 136–37; 1982: 128–32; and 1983: 82–86.)

APPENDIX C: INTERTEXTUALITY IN THE BOOK OF MALACHI

Vorster (pp. 18–19) classifies intertextuality as a subcategory of literary criticism investigating "the relationships between texts." Intertextual studies assume that the ancient writer, like any modern counterpart, made use of anterior texts, imitated others, and alluded to precursor and contemporary texts in the production of a document (Vorster 1989: 20; cf. Fishbane [1985] on "inner-biblical exegesis"). This listing of words and phrases does not necessarily presuppose the reliance of the book of Malachi upon the corresponding citation, nor does it attempt to distinguish categorically between an intertextual allusion and a quotation. The intent here has been simply to gather under one heading words, phrases, and clauses suggesting Malachi's interdependence with other portions of the OT/HB. This catalog of examples of intertextuality in Malachi is designed to supplement the study of intertextuality in Zechariah 9–14 by Meyers and Meyers (1993: 35–45). See the Notes and Comments in the commentary for discussion of additional single-word parallels not cited in this appendix.

1:3	אֶת־הָרָיוֹ שְׁמָמָה	וְאֶדוֹם לְמִדְבַּר שְׁמָמָה תִּהְיֶה (Joel 4:19 [3:19])
	'et-hārāyw šĕmāmâ	*wĕ'ĕdôm lĕmidbar šĕmāmâ tihyeh*
	". . . his [i.e., Esau's] mountains a wasteland"	"and Edom will become a desolate wilderness"

1:4	חֳרָבוֹת	כִּי־לְשַׁמָּה לְחֶרְפָּה לְחֹרֶב וְלִקְלָלָה תִּהְיֶה בָצְרָה (Jer 49:13)
	ḥŏrābôt	*kî-lĕšammâ lĕḥerpâ lĕḥōreb wĕliqlālâ tihyeh boṣrâ*
	". . . [the] ruins"	"for Bosrah will become a desolation, a disgrace, a ruin, and a curse")

1:6a	בֵּן יְכַבֵּד אָב	כַּבֵּד אֶת־אָבִיךָ (Exod 20:12)
	bēn yĕkabbēd 'āb	*kabbēd 'et-'ābîkā*
	"a son honors [his] father"	"Honor your father"

1:6b	הַכֹּהֲנִים בּוֹזֵי שְׁמִי . . . בַּמֶּה בָזִינוּ אֶת־שְׁמֶךָ	וַיִּבֶז עֵשָׂו אֶת־הַבְּכֹרָה (Gen 25:34)
	hakkōhănîm bôzê šĕmî . . . bammeh bāzînû 'et-šĕmekā	*wayyibez 'ēśāw 'et-habbĕkōrâ*
	"O priests, despisers of my name . . . How have we despised your name?"	"and Esau despised the birthright"

1:8   עִוֵּר לִזְבֹּחַ֫ . . . פִּסֵּחַ וְחֹלֶה   פִּסֵּחַ֫ אוֹ עִוֵּר . . . לֹא תִזְבָּחֶ֫נּוּ (Deut 15:21)

'iwwēr lizbōaḥ . . . pissēaḥ wĕḥōleh

pissēaḥ 'ô 'iwwēr . . . lō' tizbāḥennû

". . . a blind [animal] for sacrifice . . . a crippled or diseased [animal]"

"[the] crippled or blind . . . you shall not sacrifice . . ."

1:9a   וְעַתָּה חַלּוּ־נָא פְנֵי־אֵל   חַל־נָא אֶת־פְּנֵ֣י יְהוָה אֱלֹהֶ֫יךָ (1 Kgs 13:6)

wĕ'attâ ḥallû-nā' pĕnê-'ēl

ḥal-nā' 'et-pĕnê YHWH 'ĕlōhêkā

"And now [earnestly] entreat the favor of God"

"Entreat [earnestly] the favor of Yahweh your God"

1:9b   פְּנֵי־אֵל   פְּנִיאֵל (Gen 32:31 [30])

pĕnê-'ēl

pĕnî'ēl

"[the] face of God"

"[the] face of God"

1:9c   וִיחָנֵּ֫נוּ   פָּנָיו אֵלֶ֫יךָ וִיחֻנֶּ֑ךָּ (Num 6:25)

wîḥānēnû

pānāyw 'ēlêkā wîḥunnekā

"[so that] he may be gracious to us"

". . . his face to [shine upon] you, and be gracious to you"

1:9d   מִיֶּדְכֶם הָיְתָה זֹּאת   מִיָּדִ֞י הָיְתָה־זֹּ֣את לָכֶ֔ם (Isa 50:11)

miyyedkem hāyĕtâ zō't

miyyādî hāyĕtâ-zō't lākem

"from your hand this [thing] has come"

"from my hand this [thing] has come to you"

1:10a   מִי גַם־בָּכֶם֙   מִי בָכֶם (Hag 2:3)

mî gam-bākem

mî bākem

"who [even one] among you?"

"who among you?"

1:10b   וְלֹא־תָאִ֫ירוּ   יָאֵר יְהוָה (Num 6:25)

wĕlō'-tā'îrû

yā'ēr YHWH

"[so that] you would not kindle fire"

"may Yahweh shine . . ."; (cf. Fishbane 1985: 332–34)

1:11   כִּי מִמִּזְרַח־שֶׁמֶשׁ וְעַד־מְבוֹאוֹ   מִמִּזְרַח־שֶׁ֫מֶשׁ וּמִמַּעֲרָבָ֑ה (Isa 45:6)

kî mimmizraḥ-šemeš wĕ'ad-mĕbô'ô

mimmizraḥ-šemeš ûmimma'ărābâ

"from the rising of the sun to its setting"

"from the rising of the sun, and from the west"

מִמִּזְרַח־שֶׁ֫מֶשׁ עַד־מְבֹאוֹ (Ps 50:1)

mimmizraḥ-šemeš 'ad-mĕbō'ô

"from the rising of the sun to its setting"

ממִּזְרַח־שֶׁמֶשׁ עַד־מְבוֹאוֹ (Ps 113:3)

mimmizraḥ-šemeš ʿad-mĕbôʾô

"from the rising of the sun to its setting"

1:13	וַהִפַּחְתֶּם אוֹתוֹ	וְנָפַחְתִּי בוֹ (Hag 1:9)
	wĕhippaḥtem ʾôtô	*wĕnāpaḥtî bô*
	"and you sniff at it"	"and I blew it [away]"
1:14	כִּי מֶלֶךְ גָּדוֹל אָנִי	כִּי־יְהוָה . . . מֶלֶךְ גָּדוֹל
		עַל־כָּל־הָאָרֶץ (Ps 47:3 [2])
	kî melek gādôl ʾānî	*kî-YHWH . . . melek gādôl ʿal-kol-hāʾāreṣ*
	"for I am a great king"	"for Yahweh . . . [a] great king over all the earth"
2:2a	וְאִם־לֹא תָשִׂימוּ עַל־לֵב	וְלֹא־יָשִׂים עַל־לֵב (Isa 42:25)
	wĕʾim-lōʾ tāśîmû ʿal-lēb	*wĕlōʾ-yāśîm ʿal-lēb*
	"if you will not lay it to heart"	"but he did not lay it to heart"
		וְאֵין אִישׁ שָׂם עַל־לֵב (Isa 57:1)
		wĕʾên ʾîš śām ʿal-lēb
		"and no one lays it to heart"
		לֹא־שַׂמְתְּ עַל־לִבֵּךְ (Isa 57:11)
		lōʾ-śamt ʿal-libbēk
		"you did not lay it to heart"
		כִּי אֵין אִישׁ שָׂם עַל־לֵב (Jer 12:11)
		kî ʾên ʾîš śām ʿal-lēb
		"but no one lays it to heart"
2:2b	וְשִׁלַּחְתִּי בָכֶם אֶת־הַמְּאֵרָה	יְשַׁלַּח יְהוָה בְּךָ אֶת־הַמְּאֵרָה (Deut 28:20)
	wĕšillaḥtî bākem ʾet-hammĕʾērâ	*yĕšallaḥ YHWH bĕkā ʾet-hammĕʾērâ*
	"I will let loose upon you the curse"	"Yahweh will let loose upon you the curse"
2:3	וְזֵרִיתִי פֶרֶשׁ עַל־פְּנֵיכֶם	וְזֵרִיתִי אֶת־עַצְמוֹתֵיכֶם (Ezek 6:5)
	wĕzērîtî pereš ʿal-pĕnêkem	*wĕzērîtî ʾet-ʿaṣmôtêkem*
	"and I will spread offal upon your faces"	"and I will scatter your bones . . ."
2:7	כִּי־שִׂפְתֵי כֹהֵן יִשְׁמְרוּ־דַעַת	כִּי־אַתָּה הַדַּעַת מָאַסְתָּ וְאֶמְאָסְאךָ מִכַּהֵן לִי (Hos 4:6)

kî-śiptê kōhēn yišmĕrû-daʿat	kî-ʾattâ haddaʿat maʾastā wĕʾemʾāsĕʾkā mikkahēn lî,
"surely [from] the lips of the priest they safeguard knowledge"	"because you have rejected knowledge, I reject you from being a priest to me"

2:8

וְאַתֶּם סַרְתֶּם מִן־הַדֶּרֶךְ

wĕʾattem sartem min-hadderek

"but you yourselves have turned from the way"

(Exod 32:8) סָרוּ מַהֵר מִן־הַדֶּרֶךְ

sārû mahēr min-hadderek

"they have quickly turned from the way"

וְסַרְתֶּם מִן־הַדֶּרֶךְ

(Deut 11:28; 31:29)

wĕsartem min-hadderek

"and you [will] turn from the way"

2:10a

הֲלוֹא אָב אֶחָד

hălô ʾāb ʾeḥād

"surely there is one father?"

(Deut 32:6) הֲלוֹא־הוּא אָבִיךָ

hălô-hû ʾābîkā

"surely he is your father?"

כִּי־הָיִיתִי לְיִשְׂרָאֵל לְאָב (Jer 31:9)

kî-hāyîtî lĕyiśrāʾēl lĕʾāb

"because I have become a father to Israel"

2:10b

נִבְגַּד אִישׁ בְּאָחִיו לְחַלֵּל בְּרִית

bgd + ḥll + bĕrît

"act treacherously" + "profane" + "covenant"

עָבְרוּ בְרִית שָׁם בָּגְדוּ בִי (Hos 6:7)

ʿbr + bĕrît + bgd

"transgress" + "covenant" + "act treacherously"

2:11a

יְהוּדָה ... בְּיִשְׂרָאֵל וּבִירוּשָׁלָ[יִ]ם ... יְהוּדָה

yĕhûdâ ... bĕyiśrāʾēl ûbîrûšālā[yi]m ... yĕhûdâ

"Judah ... in Israel and in Jerusalem ... Judah"

אֶת־יְהוּדָה אֶת־יִשְׂרָאֵל וִירוּשָׁלָ[יִ]ם (Zech 2:2 [1:19])

ʾet-yĕhûdâ ʾet-yiśrāʾēl wîrûšālā[yi]m

"Judah and Israel and Jerusalem"

2:11b

וּבָעַל

ûbāʿal

"and he married"

וּלְאַרְצֵךְ בְּעוּלָה ... וְאַרְצֵךְ תִּבָּעֵל (Isa 62:4)

ûlĕʾarṣēk bĕʿûlâ ... wĕʾarṣēk tibbāʿēl

"and to your land 'married' ... and your land will be married"

2:11c

בַּת־אֵל נֵכָר

(Isa 56:3) בֶּן־הַנֵּכָר

bat-'ēl nēkār "the daughter of a strange El"	*ben-hannēkār* "[the] child of [the] foreigner"
	(Isa 56:6) וּבְנֵי הַנֵּכָר *ûbĕnê hannēkār* "[the] children of [the] foreigner"

2:12   מֵאָהֳלֵי יַעֲקֹב
mē'ohŏlê ya'ăqōb
"from the tents of Jacob"

(Zech 12:7) אֶת־אָהֳלֵי יְהוּדָה
'et-'ohŏlê yĕhûdâ
"to the tents of Judah"

2:13a   בְּכִי
bĕkî
"weeping"

(Joel 2:12) וּבִבְכִי
ûbbĕkî
"[and with] weeping"

2:13b   מֵאֵין עוֹד פְּנוֹת אֶל־הַמִּנְחָה
mē'ên 'ôd pĕnôt 'el-hamminḥâ
"no longer a turning to the
offering"

(Ezek 36:9) וּפָנִיתִי אֲלֵיכֶם
ûpānîtî 'ălêkem
"and I will turn to you"

(Ps 102:18 [19]) פָּנָה אֶל־תְּפִלַּת
pānâ 'el-tĕpillat
"he has turned to the prayer . . ."

2:14   בֵּינְךָ וּבֵין אֵשֶׁת נְעוּרֶיךָ
bênĕkā ûbên 'ēšet nĕ'ûrêkā
"between you and between the
wife of your youth"

(Isa 54:6) וְאֵשֶׁת נְעוּרִים
wĕ'ēšet nĕ'ûrîm
"the wife of [his] youth"

(Prov 5:18) מֵאֵשֶׁת נְעוּרֶךָ
mē'ēšet nĕ'ûrekā
"from the wife of your youth"

2:15a   וְלֹא־אֶחָד עָשָׂה
wĕlō'-'eḥād 'āśâ
"surely [The] One made
[everything]"

(Deut 6:4) יְהוָה אֶחָד
". . . YHWH 'eḥād*
"Yahweh is One"

2:15b   זֶרַע אֱלֹהִים
zera' 'ĕlōhîm
"[the] seed of God"

(Ezra 9:2) זֶרַע הַקֹּדֶשׁ
zera' haqqōdeš
"the holy seed"

2:16a   כִּי־שָׂנֵא שַׁלַּח
kî-śānē' šallaḥ
"Indeed, [The One] hates
divorce"

(Deut 24:3) וּשְׂנֵאָהּ . . . וְשִׁלְּחָהּ
ûśĕnē'āh . . . wĕšillĕḥāh
"and he hates her . . . and
divorces her"

2:16b

אָמַר יְהוָה אֱלֹהֵי יִשְׂרָאֵל

’āmar YHWH ’ĕlōhê yiśrā’ēl

"Yahweh, God of Israel, has said"

בְּה־אָמַר יְהוָה אֱלֹהֵי יִשְׂרָאֵל
(Jer 11:3; etc. [14x])

[kōh]-’āmar YHWH ’ĕlōhê yiśrā’ēl

"[thus] Yahweh, God of Israel, has said"

2:17a

כָּל־עֹשֵׂה רָע

kol-‘ōśēh rā‘

"everyone doing evil"

עָשָׂה + רָע
(Deut 4:24; 9:18; 17:2; 31:29)

‘āsâ + rā‘

"to do evil"

2:17b

טוֹב בְּעֵינֵי יְהוָה

ṭôb bĕ‘ênê YHWH

"good in the eyes of Yahweh"

וְהַטּוֹב בְּעֵינֵי יְהוָה
(Deut 6:18; cf. 12:25; 13:19[18]; 21:9)

wĕhaṭṭôb bĕ‘ênê YHWH

"[the] good in the eyes of Yahweh"

3:1

הִנְנִי שֹׁלֵחַ מַלְאָכִי וּפִנָּה־דֶרֶךְ לְפָנָי

hinĕnî šōlēaḥ mal’ākî ûpinnâ-derek lĕpānāy

"See! I am sending my messenger, and he will clear a way before me"

הִנֵּה אָנֹכִי שֹׁלֵחַ מַלְאָךְ לְפָנֶיךָ לִשְׁמָרְךָ בַּדֶּרֶךְ
(Exod 23:20)

hinnēh ’ānōkî šōlēaḥ mal’āk lĕpānêkā lišmorkā baddārek

"See, I am sending an angel before you, to guard you on the way"

וְשָׁלַחְתִּי לְפָנֶיךָ מַלְאָךְ
(Exod 33:2)

wĕšālaḥtî lĕpānêkā mal’āk

"and I will send an angel before you"

3:2

וּכְבֹרִית

ûkĕbōrît

"[cleansing] powder"

בֹּרִית
(Jer 2:22)

bōrît

"[cleansing] powder"

3:2–3

אֵשׁ + בֹּרִית + צרף + טהר

’ēš + bōrît + ṣrp + ṭhr

"fire" + "[cleansing] powder" + "to refine" + "to purify"

אֵשׁ + צרף + בחן
(Zech 13:9)

’ēš + ṣrp + bḥn

"fire" + "to refine" + "to test"

3:3

מְצָרֵף וּמְטַהֵר כֶּסֶף

mĕṣārēp ûmĕṭahēr kesep

"a refiner and purifier of silver"

וּצְרַפְתִּים כִּצְרֹף אֶת־הַכֶּסֶף
(Zech 13:9)

ûṣĕraptîm kiṣrōp ’et-hakkesep

"and I will refine them as one refines silver"

3:4

יְהוּדָה וִירוּשָׁלָ͏ִם

יְהוּדָה . . . בִּירוּשָׁלָ͏ִם (Zech 14:14)

	yĕhûdâ wîrûšālā[yi]m "Judah and Jerusalem"		*yĕhûdâ . . . bîrûsālā[yi]m* "Judah . . . in Jerusalem"

(Zech 14:21) בִּירוּשָׁלַם וּבִיהוּדָה
bîrûšāla[yi]m ûbîhûdâ
"in Jerusalem and in Judah"

3:7   שׁוּבוּ אֵלַי וְאָשׁוּבָה אֲלֵיכֶם אָמַר יְהֹוָה צְבָאוֹת

šûbû 'ēlay wĕ'āšûbâ 'ălêkem 'āmar YHWH ṣĕbā'ôt

"'Return to me and I will return to you,' Yahweh of Hosts has said"

שׁוּבוּ אֵלַי . . . וְאָשׁוּב אֲלֵיכֶם
(Zech 1:3) אָמַר יְהֹוָה צְבָאוֹת

šûbû 'ēlay . . . wĕ'āšûb 'ălêkem 'āmar YHWH ṣĕbā'ôt

"'Return to me . . . and I will return to you,' Yahweh of Hosts has said"

3:8   הַמַּעֲשֵׂר וְהַתְּרוּמָה

hamma'ăśēr wĕhattĕrûmâ

"the tithe and the tithe tax"

וְאֵת מַעְשְׂרֹתֵיכֶם וְאֵת תְּרוּמַת
(Deut 12:6)

wĕ'ēt ma'śĕrōtêkem wĕ'ēt tĕrûmat

"and your tithes and your contributions"

מַעְשְׂרֹתֵיכֶם וּתְרֻמַת
(Deut 12:11; cf. 2 Chr 31:12)

ma'śĕrōtêkem ûtĕrumat

"your tithes and [the] contributions"

3:9   בַּמְּאֵרָה

bammĕ'ērâ

"with the curse"

יְשַׁלַּח . . . אֶת־הַמְּאֵרָה
(Deut 28:20)

yĕšallaḥ . . . 'et-hammĕ'ērâ

"he will send the curse against you"

3:10a   אֶל־בֵּית הָאוֹצָר

'el-bêt hā'ôṣār

"into the Temple storehouse"

(Zech 11:13) בֵּית יְהֹוָה אֶל־הַיּוֹצֵר

bêt YHWH 'el-hayyôṣēr

"into the treasurey [at] the House of Yahweh"

3:10b   וּבְחָנוּנִי

ûbĕḥānûnî

"and test me"

(Zech 13:9) וּבְחַנְתִּים

ûbĕḥantîm

"and I will test them"

3:10c   אֶפְתַּח . . . אֶת אֲרֻבּוֹת הַשָּׁמַיִם

'eptaḥ . . . 'ēt 'ărubbôt haššāmayim

(Gen 7:11) וַאֲרֻבֹּת הַשָּׁמַיִם נִפְתָּחוּ

wa'ărubbôt haššāmayim niptāḥû

"I will open . . . the windows of heaven"

"and the windows of heaven were opened"

יִפְתַּח יְהוָה . . . אֶת־הַשָּׁמַיִם
(Deut 28:12)

yiptaḥ YHWH . . . 'et-haššāmayim

"Yahweh will open . . . the heavens"

3:11

פְּרִי הָאֲדָמָה

pĕrî hā'ădāmâ

"the produce of the land"

פְּרִי אַדְמָתְךָ (Deut 28:33, 42, 51)

[u]pĕrî [. . .] 'admātĕkā

"[and] the fruit . . . of your land"

3:14

שמר + מִשְׁמֶרֶת + הלך

šmr + mišmeret + hlk

"to keep" + "charge" + "to walk"

הלך + מִשְׁמֶרֶת + שמר
(Zech 3:7)

hlk + mišmeret + šmr

"to walk" + "charge" + "to keep"

3:16

קשב + שמע

qšb + šmʿ

"to pay attention" + "to hear"

שמע + קשב (Zech 1:14)

šmʿ + qšb

"to hear" + "to pay attention"

קשב + שמע (Zech 7:11)

qšb + šmʿ

"to pay attention" + "to hear"

3:17a

לַיּוֹם אֲשֶׁר אֲנִי עֹשֶׂה

layyôm 'ăšer 'ănî 'ōśeh

"during the day when I act"

אֲנִי עֹשֶׂה (Ezek 36:22, 32)

'ănî 'ōśeh

"I am [about] to act"

3:17b

סְגֻלָּה

sĕgullâ

"prized possession"

וִהְיִיתֶם לִי סְגֻלָּה (Exod 19:5)

wihyîtem lî sĕgullâ

"and you will be my prized possession"

לְעַם סְגֻלָּה (Deut 7:6; 14:2; 26:18)

lĕʿam sĕgullâ

"for a people, a prized possession"

3:17c

חמל + עַל

ḥml + ʿal

"show compassion" + "upon"

חמל + עַל
(Joel 2:18; Zech 11:5, 6)

ḥml + ʿal

"show compassion" + "upon"

3:17d

כַּאֲשֶׁר יַחְמֹל אִישׁ עַל־בְּנוֹ

כַּאֲשֶׁר יְיַסֵּר אִישׁ אֶת־בְּנוֹ
(Deut 8:5)

ka'ăšer yaḥmōl 'îš 'al-běnô
"even as a man shows
   compassion for his son"

ka'ăšer yěyassēr 'îš 'et-běnô
"even as a man disciplines his
   son"

כְּרַחֵם אָב עַל־בָּנִים (Ps 103:13)
kěraḥēm 'āb 'al-bānîm
"as a father has compassion for
   his children"

3:18

צַדִּיק + רָשָׁע

ṣaddîq + rāšā'
"righteous [one]" + "wicked
   [one]"

צַדִּיק + רָשָׁע
(Ezek 21:8–9 [3–4]; Hab 1:4, 13)
ṣaddîq + rāšā'
"righteous [one]" + "wicked
   [one]"

3:19a
[4:1]

כִּי־הִנֵּה

kî-hinnēh
"for indeed"

כִּי הִנְנִי (Zech 2:13, 14)
kî-hiněnî
"for indeed"

כִּי הִנֵּה (Zech 3:9; 11:16)
kî hinnēh
"for indeed"

3:19b
[4:1]

כִּי־הִנֵּה הַיּוֹם בָּא

kî-hinnēh hayyôm bā'
"For indeed, the day is coming"

הִנֵּה יוֹם־בָּא (Zech 14:1)
hinnēh yôm-bā'
"See! The day is coming"

3:19c
[4:1]

בער + תַּנּוּר

b'r + tannûr
"to burn" + "oven"

תַּנּוּר + בער (Hos 7:4)
tannûr + b'r
"oven" + "to burn"

3:19d
[4:1]

כָל־זֵדִים

kol-zēdîm
"all the arrogant"

הַזֵּדִים (Jer 43:2)
hazzēdîm
"the arrogant"

3:19e
[4:1]

קַשׁ

qāš
"stubble"

אֵשׁ . . . קַשׁ (Joel 2:5)
'ēš . . . qāš
"fire . . . stubble"

3:19f
[4:1]

וְלָהַט

lht
"devour"

לָהֲטָה (Joel 1:19; cf. 2:3)
lht
"devour"

3:20a
[4:2]

וּמַרְפֵּא בִּכְנָפֶיהָ

ûmarpē' biknāpêhā
"and healing is in her wings"

לְעֵת מַרְפֵּה (Jer 8:15)
lě'ēt marpēh
"for a time of healing"

אֲרֻכָה וּמַרְפֵּא (Jer 33:6)
... 'ărukâ ûmarpē'
"restoration and healing"

3:20b
[4:2]

כְּעֶגְלֵי מַרְבֵּק
kĕ'eglê marbēq
"like stall-fed calves"

עֵגֶל־מַרְבֵּק (1 Sam 28:24)
'ēgel-marbēq
"fatted calf"

כְּעֶגְלֵי מַרְבֵּק (Jer 46:21)
kĕ'eglê marbēq
"like fatted calves"

וַעֲגָלִים מִתּוֹךְ מַרְבֵּק (Amos 6:4)
wa'ăgālîm mittôk marbēq
"and calves from the stall"

3:21
[4:3]

תַּחַת כַּפּוֹת רַגְלֵיכֶם
taḥat kappôt raglêkem
"beneath the soles of your feet"

תִּדְרֹךְ כַּף־רַגְלְכֶם (Deut 11:24)
tidrōk kap-raglĕkem
"the soles of your feet tread"

3:22a
[4:4]

זִכְרוּ תּוֹרַת מֹשֶׁה עַבְדִּי
zikrû tôrat mōšeh 'abdî

"Remember the Torah of Moses
my servant"

זָכוֹר אֶת־הַדָּבָר אֲשֶׁר צִוָּה אֶתְכֶם
מֹשֶׁה עֶבֶד־יְהוָה (Josh 1:13)
zākôr 'et-haddābār 'ăšer ṣiwwâ
'etkem mōšeh 'ebed-YHWH
"Remember the word that Moses
the servant of Yahweh
commanded you"

3:22b
[4:4]

תּוֹרַת מֹשֶׁה
tôrat mōšeh
"the Torah of Moses"

בְּתוֹרַת מֹשֶׁה עֶבֶד־הָאֱלֹהִים
(Dan 9:11)
bĕtôrat mōšeh 'ebed-hā'ĕlōhîm
"in the Torah of Moses, the
servant of God"

3:22c
[4:4]

תּוֹרָה + מֹשֶׁה + עֶבֶד + צוה +
חֹק
tôrâ + mōšeh + 'ebed + ṣwh +
ḥōq
"Torah" + "Moses" + "servant"
+ "to command" + "statute"

חֹק + צוה + עֶבֶד + נָבִיא
(Zech 1:6)
ḥōq + ṣwh + 'ebed + nābî'
"statute" + "to command" +
"servant" + "prophet"

3:22d
[4:4]

עַל־כָּל־יִשְׂרָאֵל
'al-kol-yiśrā'ēl (See the discussion in NOTES and COMMENTS on
III. H. Appendixes: Appeals to Ideal OT Figures, pp. 363–90.)

3:23a
[4:5]

הִנֵּה אָנֹכִי שֹׁלֵחַ
hinnēh 'ānōkî šōlēaḥ
"See! I am sending ..."

הִנֵּה אָנֹכִי שֹׁלֵחַ (Exod 23:20)
hinnēh 'ānōkî šōlēaḥ
"See! I am sending ..."

3:23b [4:5]	בּוֹא יוֹם יְהֹוָה *bô' yôm YHWH* "the coming day of Yahweh"	הִנֵּה יוֹם־יְהֹוָה בָּא (Isa 13:9) *hinnēh yôm-YHWH bā'* "See, the day of Yahweh comes"
		הִנֵּה־יָמִים בָּאִים (Jer 7:32) *hinnēh-yāmîm bā'îm* "See, the days are coming"
		כִּי הִנְנִי־בָא (Zech 2:14 [10]) *kî hinĕnî-bā'* "for indeed, I am coming"
		כִּי־הִנְנִי מֵבִיא (Zech 3:8) *kî-hinĕnî mēbî'* "for indeed, I am bringing"
		הִנֵּה מַלְכֵּךְ יָבוֹא (Zech 9:9) *hinnēh malkēk yābô'* "See, your king comes"
		וּבָא יְהוָה אֱלֹהַי (Zech 14:5) *ûbā' YHWH 'ĕlōhay* "and Yahweh my God will come"
3:23c [4:5]	לִפְנֵי בּוֹא יוֹם יְהֹוָה הַגָּדוֹל וְהַנּוֹרָא *lipnê bô' yôm YHWH haggādôl wĕhannôrā'* "before the coming Day of Yahweh — great and terrible"	לִפְנֵי בּוֹא יוֹם יְהֹוָה הַגָּדוֹל וְהַנּוֹרָא (Joel 3:4 [2:31]) *lipnê bô' yôm YHWH haggādôl wĕhannôrā'* "before the coming Day of Yahweh — great and terrible"
3:24a [4:6]	שוב *šwb* "turn"	שוב (Deut 30:3; Zech 1:3, 4, 6, 16) *šwb* "[re]turn"
3:24b [4:6]	לֵב־אָבוֹת עַל־בָּנִים וְלֵב בָּנִים עַל־אֲבוֹתָם *lēb-'ābôt 'al-bānîm wĕlēb bānîm 'al-'ăbôtām* "the heart of the [fore]fathers toward the[ir] descendants, and the heart of the descendants toward their [fore]fathers"	אָבוֹת . . . בָּנִים . . . וּבָנִים . . . אֲבוֹתָם (Ezek 5:10) *'ābôt . . . bānîm . . . ûbānîm . . . 'ăbôtām* "parents . . . children . . . and children . . . their parents"

3:24c   נכה   (Deut 28:22) נכה
[4:6]   *nkh*   *nkh*
        "to strike"   "to strike"

3:24d   חֵרֶם   (Zech 14:11) וְחָרַם
[4:6]   *ḥērem*   *wĕḥērem*
        "a curse [for destruction]"   "banned for destruction"

Rare Vocabulary Items in Malachi

A catalog of those words, phrases, and clauses in Malachi occurring but once
elsewhere in the OT/HB.

וּכְבֹרִית   (*ûkĕbōrît*), "[and like] alkali [soap]" (3:2; Jer 2:22)

אֱלֹהֵי הַמִּשְׁפָּט   (*'ĕlōhê hammišpāṭ*), "the God of judgment" (2:17; Isa 30:18
[*'ĕlōhê mišpāṭ*])

לִפְנֵי בּוֹא יוֹם יְהֹוָה הַגָּדוֹל וְהַנּוֹרָא   (*lipnê bô' yôm YHWH haggādôl wĕhannôrā'*), "before the coming day of Yahweh, and terrible" (3:23 [4:5]; Joel 3:4)

מַלְאָכִי   (*mal'ākî*), "Malachi" (1:1; 3:1)

מִיֶּדְכֶם הָיְתָה זֹּאת   (*miyyedkem hāyĕtâ zō't*), "this [thing] came from your
hand" (1:9; Isa 50:11 [*miyyādî hāyĕtâ-zō't*])

וְנִיבוֹ   (*wĕnîbô*), "[and its] fruit" (1:12; Isa 57:19)

פְּנוֹת אֶל־הַמִּנְחָה   (*pĕnôt 'el-hamminḥâ*), "to turn to the offering" (2:13; Num
16:15 [*'al-tēpen 'el-minḥātem*])

פְּנֵי־אֵל   (*pĕnê-'ēl*), "face of God" (1:9; Job 15:4 [*lipnê-'ēl*])
qb', "rob"

קֹבְעִים   (*qōbĕ'îm*), "robbing" (3:8, 9)

וְקָרַבְתִּי אֲלֵיכֶם לַמִּשְׁפָּט   (*wĕqārabtî 'ălêkem lammišpāṭ*), "and I will draw near
to you for judgment" (3:5; Isa 41:1)

שׁוּבוּ אֵלַי וְאָשׁוּבָה אֲלֵיכֶם   (*šûbû 'ēlay wĕ'āšûbâ 'ălêkem*), "return to me, and I
will return to you" (3:7; Zech 1:3)
šḥt, "polluted, damaged"

מָשְׁחָת   (*mošḥāt*), "blemished [animal]" (1:14; Prov 25:26)

שֻׁלְחַן יְהֹוָה   (*šulḥan YHWH*), "the table of Yahweh" (1:7; 1:12 [*šulḥan
'ădōnāy*])

APPENDIX D: VOCABULARY RICHNESS IN THE BOOK OF MALACHI

On vocabulary richness in Malachi and the Haggai-Zechariah-Malachi corpus
see further von Bulmerincq 1926: 426–32; Hill 1981: 139–42; Radday (1973);
and Radday and Pollatschek (1980).

Vocabulary Unique to Malachi

The lexical items listed below include absolute and categorical *hapax legomena* identified in the book of Malachi.

'ss

וַעֲסוֹתֶם (wĕ'assôtem), "[and you will] tread down" (3:21 [4:3]; cf. KBL 2:860)

חֲבֶרְתֶּךָ (ḥăbertĕkā), "[your] marriage-partner" (2:14; cf. KBL 1:289)

מֻקְטָר (muqṭār), "incense" (1:11; cf. KBL 2:627)

nkl

נוֹכֵל (nôkēl), "act cleverly, cunningly, deceitfully" (1:14; cf. KBL 2:699)

ṣrp

מְצָרֵף (mĕṣārēp), "smelter, refiner" (3:2; cf. CHAL: 311)

qb', "rob"

קְבַעֲנוּךָ (qĕba'ănûkā), "[you] have robbed [me]" (3:8; cf. BDB: 867)

הֲיִקְבַּע (hăyiqba'), "[will anyone] rob?" (3:8; cf. BDB: 867)

קְדֹרַנִּית (qĕdōrannît), "unkempt, dressed in mourning attire" (3:14; cf. CHAL: 313)

ršš

רֻשַּׁשְׁנוּ (rušsašnû), "be shattered" (1:4; cf. CHAL: 347)

לְתַנּוֹת (lĕtannôt), "[for] jackals" (1:3; cf. BDB: 1072)

Nominal Constructions Unique to Malachi*

גְּבוּל רִשְׁעָה (gĕbûl riš'â), "[the] Territory of Evil" (1:4)

לֶחֶם מְגֹאָל (lehem mĕgō'āl), "defiled food" (1:7)

וּמִנְחָה טְהוֹרָה (ûminḥâ ṭĕhôrâ), "a pure offering" (1:11)

פֶּרֶשׁ חַגֵּיכֶם (pereš haggêkem), "offal of your feasts" (2:3)

בְּרִיתִי אֶת־לֵוִי (bĕrîtî 'et-lēwî), "my covenant with Levi" (2:4)

הַחַיִּים וְהַשָּׁלוֹם (hahayyîm wĕhaššālôm), "life [itself] and peace [itself]" (2:5)

בְּשָׁלוֹם וּבְמִישׁוֹר (bĕšālôm ûbĕmîšôr), "in peace and uprightness" (2:6)

מַלְאָךְ יְהוָה־צְבָאוֹת (mal'ak YHWH-ṣĕbā'ôt), "the messenger of Yahweh of Hosts" (2:7)

בְּרִית הַלֵּוִי (bĕrît hallēwî), "the covenant of Levi" (2:8)

נִבְזִים וּשְׁפָלִים (nibzîm ûšĕpālîm), "despised and abased" (2:9)

בְּרִית אֲבֹתֵינוּ (bĕrît 'ăbōtênû), "the covenant of our forefathers" (2:10)

בַּת־אֵל נֵכָר (bat-'ēl nēkār), "the daughter of a strange El" (2:11)

עֵד וְעֹנֶה ('ēd wĕ'ōneh), "witness or respondent" (2:12, reading עֵד for the MT עֵר)

בְּכִי וַאֲנָקָה (bĕkî wa'ănāqâ), "weeping and wailing" (2:13)

וְאֵשֶׁת בְּרִיתֶךָ (wĕ'ēšet bĕrîtekâ), "[and] the wife of your covenant" (2:14)

זֶרַע אֱלֹהִים (zera' 'ĕlōhîm), "[the] seed of God" (2:15)

*See further von Bulmerincq 1926: 429–31 for a tabulation of verb + noun constructions unique to the book of Malachi in the OT/HB.

וּמַלְאַךְ הַבְּרִית (ûmal'ak habběrît), "[and] the angel of the covenant" (3:1)

כְּאֵשׁ מְצָרֵף (kě'ēš měsārēp), "[like the] smelter's fire" (3:2)

וּכְבֹרִית מְכַבְּסִים (ûkěbōrît měkabběsîm), "[and like the] launderer's soap" (3:2)

וּמְטַהֵר כֶּסֶף (ûmětahēr kesep), "[and] a purifier of silver" (3:3)

וּכְשָׁנִים קַדְמֹנִיּוֹת (ûkěšānîm qadmōniyyôt, "[and like] the former years" (3:4)

עֵד מְמַהֵר ('ēd měmahēr), "an eager witness" (3:5)

בַּמְכַשְּׁפִים וּבַמְנָאֲפִים וּבַנִּשְׁבָּעִים לַשָּׁקֶר (bamkaššěpîm ûbamnā'ăpîm ûbannišbā'îm laššāqer), "[against] the sorcerers, [against] the adulterers, [against] those swearing falsely" (3:5)

לְמִימֵי אֲבֹתֵיכֶם (lěmîmê 'ăbōtêkem), "in the days of your forefathers" (3:7)

הַגּוֹי כֻּלּוֹ (haggôy kullô), "the whole nation" (3:9)

עַד־בְּלִי־דָי ('ad-bělî-day), "without measure" (3:10)

הַגֶּפֶן בַּשָּׂדֶה (haggepen baśśādeh), "the grapevine in the field" (3:11)

אֶרֶץ חֵפֶץ ('ereṣ hēpeṣ), "a land of delight" (3:12)

שֹׁרֶשׁ וְעָנָף (šōreš wě'ānāp), "a root nor a branch" (3:19[4:1])

INDEX OF AUTHORS

◆

Achtemeier, E. 28, 30, 33, 39, 210, 219, 227–28, 230, 233, 241, 255–56, 258, 269, 292, 304, 321–22, 362, 374
Ackroyd, P. R. 35, 67–68, 71, 72n.3, 73, 78
Adamson, J. T. H. 34, 36
Aharoni, Y. 61, 62n.2
Ahlström, G. W. 222, 255, 321, 375
Albright, W. F. 67
Alden, R. L. 17, 26
Allen, L. C. 208, 310, 347, 386
Alt, A. 67–68
Alter, R. 22, 25, 40, 40n2., 79n2.
Alter, R., and F. Kermode 25, 39–40
Andersen, F. I., and D. N. Freedman 24–25, 142–43, 147, 150, 152, 157, 165, 167, 182, 185–86, 202, 208–9, 211, 214–15, 225–27, 233, 250, 269, 271, 278, 281–84, 297, 299–301, 306, 318, 320, 329, 346, 348, 351, 353, 364–65, 376, 381, 385, 388, 388n.5, 389
Anderson, A. A. 281
Anderson, B. W. 286
Archer, G. L., and G. C. Chirichigno 86
Avigad, N. 70–71
Avi-Yonah, M. 61–62, 62n1., 65

Bailey, K. E. 218
Bailey, R. W. 50–51, 162, 164–66, 168, 220, 286, 290, 323
Baldwin, J. G. 5, 13n.3, 16, 20, 26, 29, 79–80, 85, 133, 140, 161, 164, 166–69, 173, 179, 184, 187–88, 190, 194, 200–1, 203, 205–7, 209, 213–15, 219, 221–24, 227–29, 234, 241, 243–45, 248, 253–55, 272, 280, 284–85, 287, 294, 296, 298, 303, 325, 330, 334, 355, 358, 361, 363, 368, 370, 373, 383

Barr, J. 235
Barth, C. 46, 48, 50
Bartlett, J. R. 78, 151, 153
Barton, J. 15n.5, 22
Bennett, T. M. 35
Bentzen, A. 13, 13n.1
Berlin, A. 195
Berquist, J. L. 41, 51, 53, 76
Bewer, J. A. 23
Beyer, B. E. 70
Bickermann, E. 322
Birch, B. C. 50, 283
Blenkinsopp, J. 19, 37, 206, 390
Block, D. I. 380
Boadt, L. 22, 36
Boecker, H. J. 36, 37n.4, 163
Boer, P. A. H. de 133
Boling, R. G., and G. E. Wright 207, 367, 370n.2, 371
Boman, T. 160
Bongers, H. A. 149
Bosshard, E., and R. G. Kratz 15n.1, 20–21, 20–21nn.1,2, 29, 146
Bossman, D. M. 47
Boston, J. R. 33nn.2,3
Botterweck, G. J. 151, 211, 354
Braun, R. L. 36, 40, 50, 163, 323, 369, 373, 390
Briant, P. 51, 66
Brichto, H. C. 160, 193–94, 256, 324
Bright, J. 19, 22, 61, 62n.1, 68, 72n.3, 73, 80
Brightman, F. E., and C. E. Hammond 91
Brown, M. L. 149
Bruce, F. F. 19
Brueggemann, W. 20n.1, 32, 33n.3, 37, 43n.3, 47–48, 50, 163, 311, 351, 374
Budde, K. 3, 143

415

Bulmerincq, A. von 77, 79n.2, 84, 155–56, 159, 161, 170, 185, 188, 191, 197, 199, 222–23, 230, 232, 238–39, 247, 274, 276, 282, 284, 287, 292–94, 300, 303, 307, 315, 317, 331, 334, 337, 350, 363, 363n.1, 367, 370, 372, 375, 381, 388

Calvin, J. 16, 133, 138, 145, 148, 155, 161–62, 165, 186, 188, 190, 193, 199, 207, 215, 224, 230, 233, 235, 237, 240, 243, 245, 247–48, 251, 253, 261, 274, 280, 285, 288, 294–96, 307, 313, 316, 327, 331, 335, 338, 341, 349, 361, 363, 383, 388
Cameron, G. 60
Cappellus, L. 155
Caquot, A. 316
Carmody, J., D. L. Carmody, and R. L. Cohn 49
Carroll, R. P. 34n.1, 46
Cashdan, E. 178, 180, 182, 185, 189–90, 216, 230, 245–47, 255–56, 287–88, 334, 349, 351, 358, 360
Cathcart, K. J., and R. P. Gordon 136, 231, 236
Charlesworth, J. H. 49
Chary, T. 14n.3, 133, 188, 204, 228, 232, 234, 245, 249, 269, 275, 282, 289, 294, 297, 303, 313, 315–16, 329, 351, 353, 364, 367, 372
Childs, B. S. 13, 13n.3, 16, 16n.2, 17, 20–21, 23, 45–47, 135, 137–38, 143, 265, 295, 321, 363, 379
Chittister, J. 23n.3
Clark, D. G. 364, 378, 384n.4, 385, 388
Clements, R. E. 14n.4, 47, 80
Clendenen, E. R. 21, 28–29, 34, 238, 260, 366
Clines, D. J. 65, 67, 69, 72n.3, 73, 75, 324, 371
Coats, G. 331, 357
Coggins, R. J. 19, 29, 45, 45n.4, 47, 78, 364
Collins, C. J. 249–50
Collins, J. J. 16n.1, 43, 48, 146, 223, 323, 327, 360
Cook, S. A. 51
Craigie, P. C. 45n.4, 47–48, 50–51, 163–64, 167–69, 220, 222–23, 241, 251–52, 255–56, 258, 358, 361, 371, 374, 390
Cranfield, C. E. B. 166
Crenshaw, J. L. 33n.3, 154, 343, 353
Cresson, B. C. 167, 169

Cross, F. M. 52, 72
Cross, F. M., and D. N. Freedman 154

Dahood, M. 176, 194–95, 197, 238, 331, 335, 339, 351
Davies, W. D., and L. Finkelstein 33n.3
Deissler, A. 17, 37, 186, 223, 249, 282, 293, 297, 303, 364
Dentan, R. C., and W. L. Sperry 35, 202, 210, 222, 287, 294, 368
Donin, H. H. 89
Drinkard, J. F. 80
Driver, G. R. 306
Driver, S. R. 23, 77, 79, 174, 190, 199, 215–16, 228–29, 234, 243, 245–47, 257, 288
Duhm, B. 287
Dumbrell, W. J. 142, 184
Durham, J. I. 189

Eichrodt, W. 147
Eiselen, C. F. 14n.3, 202, 215–16, 233, 243, 245, 251–52, 254
Eissfeldt, O. 19, 72n.3, 80, 190, 222, 364, 383
Elliger, K. 19, 23, 133, 167, 173, 188, 226, 275, 288, 364
Ellul, J. 51
Erlandsson, S. 134
Eskenazi, T. C. 68–69
Ewald, G. H. A. 250, 293

Fasol, A. 51
Fee, D. F., and D. Stuart 10–11
Fensham, F. C. 65, 67, 73, 324
Fischer, J. A. 36, 42, 162, 328
Fishbane, M. 172, 184, 303, 333, 364, 371n.3, 378, 384–86
Fishman, J. A. 82n.3
Foerster, W. 51
Fontaine, C. R. 225
France, R. T. 288
Freedman, D. B. 281
Freedman, D. N. 14, 14n.4, 21n.2, 22–23, 42n.1, 45, 47n.2, 50, 84, 138, 154, 157, 350, 365–66, 369, 378
Freeman, H. B. 36, 37n.5
Frey, H. 23, 363
Frye, R. N. 15n.5, 51
Fuller, R. 3–4, 234–35, 239, 241, 249

Garland, D. E. 51, 226, 242–43, 245, 258
Gehman, H. S. 138–39
Geldenhuys, N. 88

Gelston, A. 3, 6–8, 191
Gemser, B. 33n.2
Gesenius, W. 155
Gibson, J. C. L. 22
Glazier-McDonald, B. 10–11, 14n.3, 17,
   21, 24–26, 28, 36–38, 75, 78, 86,
   133–38, 144, 149, 155, 158–61,
   164, 167, 170, 173–74, 177–78,
   180–81, 183, 185–86, 188, 190,
   192, 194, 196–97, 199–202, 204–9,
   211, 213, 215, 219, 223–24, 227–
   30, 232–33, 235–38, 240, 243–53,
   255–57, 261–62, 264–66, 268–69,
   274–75, 278, 280, 282, 284, 287–
   89, 292–98, 300–1, 303–4, 306–8,
   310, 312–17, 321, 324, 329–31,
   333–35, 337–41, 344, 350–54, 358,
   360–63, 367–68, 370, 372–75, 377,
   380, 383, 387
Gloer, W. H. 51
Goldingay, J. 46, 310
Goppelt, L. 50
Gordis, R. 340
Gordon, R. P. 148, 184–85, 191, 218,
   298, 315, 320, 349
Gottwald, N. K. 23, 37, 75
Gowan, D. E. 290–91, 350
Graesser, C. 376
Graffy, A. 34–35, 35n.2, 36, 36n.3, 37n.4
Grant, R. M. 19
Gray, J. 50, 60, 79, 288–89, 350
Gray, S. W. 41, 50
Greenberg, M. 159, 342, 344
Grollenberg, L. H. 61
Gunkel, H. 23, 35
Gunkel, H., and J. Begrich 30

Halévy, J. 388
Hals, R. M. 294
Hamilton, V. P. 345
Hanson, P. D. 14n.4, 15n.1, 41, 47, 83,
   173, 338, 349, 360, 363, 382, 385
Harrison, R. K. 13n.3, 255–56
Hartley, J. E. 257, 295
Harvey, J. 31, 33
Hasel, G. F. 46
Hayes, J. H. 19, 22
Hayes, J. H., and J. M. Miller 62n.1
Hayes, J. H., and F. Prussner 46
Henderson, E. 133, 161, 199, 206, 213,
   215, 217, 227, 230, 237, 245, 250,
   252, 254, 279, 288, 295, 316, 334,
   353
Hendrix, J. D. 36, 39–41, 50, 173
Hengel, M. 5

Hengstenberg, E. W. 86, 288, 371, 390
Hermisson, H. J. 35
Hertzberg, W. 373
Heschel, A. J. 37, 153, 219, 301, 356, 360
Hessel, D. T. 50n.4
Hill, A. E. 24, 24n.1, 41, 53, 81, 82n.3,
   138, 162, 168, 290, 371, 374, 389
Hirsch, M. 5, 89
Hoftijer, J. 24, 24n.2
Hoglund, K. 51, 68, 73n.4, 74n.5
Holladay, W. L. 138–39, 153, 176, 197,
   208, 228–29, 252, 274, 280–81,
   301–3, 316, 339, 347, 352–53, 387
Holtzmann, O. 36, 37n.5
Hoonaker, A. van 14n.3, 155, 250, 253,
   297, 348
Horst, F. 19, 23, 33n.2, 133, 173, 188,
   204, 287, 293, 364, 370
House, P. R. 15n.5
Huffmon, H. 30–31
Hugenberger, G. P. 44, 243, 258
Hvidberg, F. F. 228, 232, 255

Ibn Ezra, A. 161, 182, 255, 287
Isaaksson, A. 243, 255
Isbell, C. D. 136, 140, 142, 226, 287–88,
   374

Jacob, E. 164, 167, 185, 385
Jagersma, H. 306
Japhet, S. 70
Jeffers, R. J., and I. Lehiste 82
Jemielity, T. 39, 173
Jones, B. A. 12–13, 364
Jones, D. C. 250
Jones, D. R. 197, 227, 229, 235, 245,
   255, 334, 357, 359, 362, 364
Jones, G. H. 354

Kaiser, W. C. 17, 20n.1, 26n.1, 27, 51,
   86, 260, 292
Kaufmann, Y. 17, 26n.1
Keel, O. 50, 350, 362
Keil, C. F. 86, 155, 188, 190, 199, 206,
   230, 233, 235–37, 240, 243, 245,
   249, 253, 255, 260, 262, 292, 294,
   296, 362–63, 372, 383
Kent, R. G. 53, 55
Keown, G. L. 50
Kikawada, I. M. 38
Kikawada, I. M., and A. Quinn 25, 79n.2
Kimchi, D. 182, 230, 287
Klein, G. L. 37
Klein, R. W. 3, 11, 41, 47, 50, 180, 199,
   204, 324, 328, 335, 362

Knight, G. A. F. 350
Koch, K. 45n.4, 49, 54, 76, 80, 84, 165
Kodell, J. 36
Köhler, L. 167, 293, 373
Krentz, E. 19, 22
Kruse-Blinkenberg, L. 3, 6–9, 154, 191,
  215–16, 232, 249–50, 298, 367, 378
Kuehner, F. C. 50

Labuschagne, C. J. 161
Laetsch, T. 13n.3, 17, 167, 206, 230,
  253, 269, 292, 312, 315–16, 324,
  334, 336
Laffey, A. L. 49, 256
LaPierre, D. 22
Lehmann, W. P. 82n.3
Lescow, T. 15n.1, 20n.1, 24, 29, 36–37,
  37n.4
Levenson, J. D. 50, 372
Levine, B. A. 151, 182, 191, 201, 306
Lewis, C. S. 286
Lindblom, J. 143, 150, 287, 357, 363
Lindhagen, C. 332
Lindsay, J. 78
Locher, C. 51
Long, B. O. 36
Longacre, R. E. 28
Longenecker, R. N. 5
Longman, T. 38, 40n.3
Luther, M. *See* Oswald, H. C.

McCarter, K. P. 3, 11, 180, 324, 353
McCarthy, D. J. 32, 33n.2, 382–83
McEvenue, S. E. 62n.1, 65, 68, 78,
  78n.1
Macintosh, A. A. 316
Mack, B. L. 38
McKane, W. 139, 160, 324, 344
McKenzie, J. L. 65, 241, 261, 266
McKenzie, S. L., and H. H. Wallace 27,
  42
McKnight, E. V. 22
Malchow, B. V. 11, 20–21, 260, 269,
  288–89, 383
Mallone, G. 50, 162, 164
March, W. E. 34, 37
Marcus, R. 210
Martens, E. A. 46
Marti, K. 23, 160, 192, 210, 223, 251,
  293, 303
Mason, R. 15n.5, 18–20, 26, 28, 35,
  35n.1, 36, 41–42, 45, 46n.1, 48, 78–
  80, 82n.3, 138, 152, 164, 167, 169,
  173–74, 184, 186–88, 203, 205–6,
  209–10, 216, 219, 222, 224–25,

227, 229, 231, 235, 243, 253, 256,
  260, 269, 283, 285, 287–88, 297,
  303, 323–24, 327, 329, 340, 350,
  358, 360–62, 364–65, 370–72, 380,
  388
Mathews, K. A. 82n.3
Matthews, I. G. 362
Mayes, A. D. H. 180, 250, 306, 350
Mays, J. L. 280
Mendenhall, G. E. 220
Merton, T. 40, 50n.4
Mettinger, T. N. D. 157
Meyers, E. M. 79n.2, 185, 206
Meyers, E. M., and C. L. Meyers 25, 61,
  62n.1, 66, 68–71, 75, 133–34, 137,
  139–40, 140n.4, 141–43, 147, 152,
  157, 159, 175–78, 182, 184, 189,
  191, 194–95, 198, 201, 203, 210,
  212–13, 225, 229–30, 233–35, 241,
  247, 249, 256, 265, 267, 269, 271–
  75, 277, 279, 282–83, 297, 302,
  304, 309, 311, 315–16, 318, 324–
  25, 329, 331–33, 336, 338–41, 343–
  46, 368, 370–73, 376, 378–79, 382,
  389–90
Milgrom, J. 201, 234, 238, 254, 257, 306
Moore, T. V. 12, 80, 133, 163
Morgenstern, J. 74n.5, 210
Muilenburg, J. 25, 38
Mullen, E. T. 140n.4, 147, 288–89
Müller, D. H. 188
Murray, D. F. 35, 37, 37n.5, 84n.5
Mussner, F. 43n.2
Myers, J. M. 69, 152, 166, 231, 242

Neusner, J. 90
Newsome, J. D. 45n.4, 50, 80
Nogalski, J. D. 13, 15n.1, 21n.2, 26, 75,
  80, 146, 172–73, 327, 340, 365,
  384n.4
North, R. 65, 73
Nowack, W. 23, 155, 192, 210, 251, 293,
  303, 363

O'Brien, J. M. 14n.3, 17, 21, 31–33,
  78n.1, 79, 82n.3, 83n.5, 173, 176,
  216, 228, 256, 276
O'Connor, M. 25, 157, 174
Ogden, G. S. 223, 226
Ogden, G. S., and R. R. Deutsch 174,
  176–77, 197, 211, 219, 223–24,
  228, 232, 235, 240–41, 245–47,
  251, 253, 255, 257–58, 335, 340,
  348, 358, 360–61, 363
Ollenburger, B. C. 46

Olmstead, A. T. 51–52, 60
Orelli, C. von 16, 234, 236
Oswald, H. C. 133, 138, 170, 230, 234,
    249, 266, 272, 276, 285, 294, 307,
    337–38, 349, 352, 363, 383

Packard, J. 160, 206, 215, 231, 237, 244,
    249, 251, 254, 260, 292, 317
Patterson, R. D. 34, 163
Paul, S. M. 198, 279
Peckham, B. 173
Pedersen, J. 369
Petersen, D. L. 4, 11, 13, 16, 33n.3, 36,
    41, 49n.3, 54, 68, 72, 75–77, 79–80,
    82n.3, 133–34, 138, 139, 152, 155,
    159, 161, 167, 170, 172–73, 178–
    82, 184, 186–88, 190–93, 196–200,
    202–11, 215, 217, 219, 223, 226,
    228, 231–32, 235, 237, 239–52,
    255, 260, 262, 265, 269, 274, 280–
    83, 286–89, 292, 295–96, 299, 302,
    306–7, 310–11, 315, 317, 330, 334–
    35, 337–40, 342–43, 345, 348–51,
    353–54, 360, 362–63, 364–66, 375,
    379, 383, 385–86, 388, 390
Pfeiffer, E. 26, 35, 35n.2, 37
Pfeiffer, R. H. 23
Pierce, R. 14, 23, 28, 40
Pilch, J. 40n.2, 174, 218
Pilch, J., and B. J. Malina 252, 268, 322,
    324
Plummer, A. 89
Pölger, O. 137n.1
Polzin, R. 21n.2, 22, 79n.2, 81, 82n.3,
    83, 211, 365
Pope, M. H. 191, 319
Provan, I. W. 178
Pusey, E. B. 80, 230, 288, 384

Rabin, C. 315
Rad, G. von 45n.4, 179, 295, 301, 305,
    321
Radday, V. T., and D. Wickman 239
Radday, V. T., and M. A. Pollatschek 13
Raitt, T. M. 302
Rashi (Solomon Ben Isaac) 16, 287
Redditt, P. L. 13, 15n.1, 20, 20n.1, 23,
    26, 35, 37, 41–42, 45, 47, 79–80,
    135, 152, 161, 172–73, 178, 191,
    207, 211, 217, 219, 223, 227, 229–
    30, 232, 234–35, 244–45, 255, 260,
    274–75, 281, 287, 293, 297, 306,
    311, 317, 346, 348, 364–65, 368,
    372, 384n.4
Rehm, M. 188–89

Reicke, B. 76
Rendsburg, G. A. 21n.2, 25, 79n.2
Richardson, P. A. 50, 91
Ringgren, H. 189, 224, 299, 373
Roberts, J. J. M. 178, 251
Robertson, D. 18–19, 22
Robinson, G. L. 16, 23, 36, 37n.5, 255
Robinson, J. 264
Rofé, A. 256
Rost, L. 66–67
Rowley, H. H. 73
Rudolph, W. 16–17, 36, 51, 68–69, 72,
    133, 135, 139, 155, 159, 161, 170,
    172–74, 178, 180, 186, 188, 190,
    194, 199–200, 203, 208, 215, 223,
    230, 232, 235, 239, 245–47, 249–
    50, 253, 255, 257, 269, 275, 282,
    293–94, 296–97, 303, 307, 313,
    315–17, 330, 335, 350, 353–54,
    364, 380, 387
Russell, D. S. 5
Ryken, L. 11, 40

Sanday, W., and A. C. Headlam 166
Sanders, J. A. 20–23, 23n.3
Sasson, J. M. 11, 24n.1, 83n.5, 89, 194
Scalise, P. J. 51, 290, 321, 324, 359–60,
    362
Schneider, D. A. 14, 14n.4, 19, 23, 81,
    364
Schreiner, S. 222, 230, 249–50, 253,
    256–57
Scott, R. B. Y. 51, 54, 139, 303
Sebök, M. 3
Segal, M. H. 155
Sellin, E. 20, 139, 173, 188, 190, 204,
    223, 226, 237, 251, 293, 297, 303,
    337, 363
Sellin, E., and G. Fohrer 20, 79, 222,
    242
Silva, M. 10–11
Smith, G. A. 133, 219, 222, 313, 334,
    367, 370, 373
Smith, J. M. P. 3, 5, 9–10, 16, 23, 26, 45,
    133, 150, 161, 167, 170, 178–79,
    181, 188, 190, 200, 202, 206–7,
    210, 212–13, 215, 217, 222, 226–
    28, 230, 232–33, 235–40, 243–44,
    248, 251–53, 257, 260, 275, 282,
    287–88, 292–94, 297–98, 300, 306,
    313, 315–16, 323, 327, 329–32,
    334, 337, 340, 350–51, 354, 358,
    364–65, 368, 372, 375
Smith, M. 68, 72
Smith, M. S. 350

Smith, R. L. 10–11, 14n.3, 23, 37, 47, 79, 86, 133, 139, 148–49, 152–53, 156, 158, 160–62, 166, 184–86, 188, 190, 192, 200, 206–7, 210, 213, 218, 230, 237–38, 240, 244, 246, 248–49, 255, 279–80, 294–96, 300, 303, 307, 310, 316–17, 319, 321, 325, 330–31, 333, 335, 339–41, 344, 350, 353, 357, 364, 367–68
Snyman, S. D. 146
Soulen, R. N. 19, 22
Speiser, E. A. 194, 307, 318
Spoer, H. H. 77
Steck, O. H. 134
Stern, E. 60–61, 62n.1, 68, 71, 231
Stolper, M. W. 51

Tate, M. E. 219, 255–56
Taylor, J. G. 350
Terrien, S. 46–47, 166
Thomas, D. W. 334
Thompson, J. A. 317
Tilley, W. C. 51
Tillman, W. M. 51
Torrey, C. C. 23, 155, 232, 243, 255
Tov, E. 3–4, 6, 11–12, 26
Tozer, A. W. 290
Tucker, G. M. 13n.2, 135–38, 138n.2, 140, 140n.5, 141, 143–44

Utzschneider, H. 19–20, 80, 172–73

VanGemeren, W. A. 45n.4, 47, 261, 292
Van Leeuwen, R. C. 15n.5, 33n.3
Vaux, R. de 324, 390
Verhoef, P. A. 5, 11, 13n.3, 17, 23, 26n.1, 29, 36, 50, 78, 80, 133, 135, 139–41, 147–49, 153, 155, 158, 160–62, 165, 170, 175, 178, 180–83, 186, 188, 190, 192, 197, 199, 201–2, 204, 206–7, 210, 213, 215, 217, 219, 222–23, 227–30, 232–34, 240–43, 245–46, 248–49, 251–53, 255–56, 258, 260, 269, 271–72, 274–76, 278, 285, 287–88, 290, 292–95, 296–97, 300, 304–5, 307–8, 315–17, 319, 330, 334–35, 336–37, 339–40, 342–43, 346, 350–51, 353, 360–61, 363, 370, 373–74, 377, 383, 387–88
Vermes, G. 184

Vriezen, T. C. 161, 165
Vuilleumier, R. 222

Waldman, N. M. 295–96, 329
Walhout, C., and L. Ryken 23n.3
Wallis, G. 36, 147, 165, 293
Walters, P. 233, 281
Waltke, B. K., and M. O'Connor 148, 150, 179–80, 248, 265, 282, 292, 294, 304, 381
Watts, J. D. W. 15n.1, 23, 46n.4, 145, 163, 172, 174, 222, 232, 236, 259–60, 266, 291, 321, 326, 356
Weinfeld, M. 159, 165, 198, 205, 209, 263, 311, 322–23, 333, 342, 350
Weiser, A. 18, 20, 187, 290
Welch, A. 84, 243
Wellhausen, J. 188, 192, 235, 251, 293, 300, 303, 364
Wells, C. R. 51, 163, 220, 256, 258, 285, 289, 321–22, 356, 358, 361
Wendland, E. 21, 25, 37–40, 40n.1, 161, 173, 260, 292, 327–28, 348
Wenham, G. J. 79n.2, 281, 295, 314
Westermann, C. 34, 34n.1, 37, 37n.4, 147, 150, 187, 198, 225, 232, 241, 255, 265–66, 280, 301, 305, 350, 376
Wevers, J. W. 201
Whedbee, J. W. 33n.3
Whybray, R. N. 79n.2
Widengren, G. 68
Williams, R. J. 156
Williamson, H. G. H. 53, 60, 66–72, 72n.3, 73, 310
Wilson, R. R. 80, 139
Wold, D. 257
Wolf, H. 36, 288, 384
Wolff, H. W. 210–12, 214, 241, 301, 343, 347, 353, 380, 386, 389
Woude, A. S. Van der 147, 173, 258, 351
Würthwein, E. 4, 26, 191

Yamauchi, E. M. 51–53, 62n.1, 66, 69, 73–74, 74n.5, 76
Yates, K. M. 51
Young, T. C. 52

Zimmerli, W. 159, 186, 189, 196, 203, 257, 282, 321, 329, 339–40, 381

INDEX OF SUBJECTS

◆

(Pages in **bold** indicate references to where the subject appears in the text of the book of Malachi rather than to its explanation.)

adultery 281
altar
 defilement of 170–71, **170**, 237
 "table of Yahweh" **170**, 177–79, 213,
  237–38, 268
 tears covering 221, **221**, 237–39, 253
 vain fires 171, **171**, 185
angel/messenger 144–45, **259**, 265, 269,
  286–90, 383
 Malachi as 16, 18, 87, 135–36,
  143–45
 priests as **171**, 212–13
angel of the covenant 87, **259**, 260, 265,
  269–71, 286–89
angel of Yahweh 136, 141, 144, 269,
  287–89, 298, 300
Artaxerxes I 51, 72, 72n.3, 73
Artaxerxes II 52, 72n.3

blessing **291**
 of Israel by the nations 325
 priestly 182, 199
 with respect to tithing **291**, 311, 315,
  324
 reversal of 335
 of the righteous on the Day of Yahweh
  291, 328, 341, 345, 360
blessings and curses 18, 217, 269, 285,
  332–333, 374
book of remembrance 49, 79, **326**, 339–
  40, 360
Book of the Twelve 45, 50, 146, 181,
  364, 366, 368

covenant
 Davidic 279, 289, 371
 of forefathers 42, 43, **221**, 227–28, 243

with Israel 145–70, 224–25, 231
with Levites 42, **171**, 197, 203–7, 209,
  211, 214–18, 220–21
of marriage 42, **221**, 223, 226, 229,
  240–46
as motif in Malachi 143, 220–21, 224,
  239
new 225, 270, 285, 289, 332–33, 351
Sinaitic 227–28, 367–77, 372
witness to 240–41, 280
of Yahweh profaned 227
curse
 on Edom (judgment against) **145**,
  151–160
 on priests 43, **171**, 198–200, 206
 with respect to tithing **291**, 307–8,
  323
 reversal of 388
 for social injustice 284
 striking the land **374**, 381–82, 389–
  90
 and violation of a vow **171**, 193–94
 on Yehud. See "cut off"
"cut off" 200, **221**, 233–236, 256–57,
  358

Darius I 51, 52–55, 56, 60, 69
dating the oracles of Malachi 51, 77–84
Day of Yahweh
 assurance of justice 328–39, 350, 355–
  63, **374**
 contributions to OT/HB eschatology
  49, 288–91, 384–90
 expressions for 376–77
 fate of the righteous and the wicked
  45, 341, 345–49, 352, 355–63
 purification of Israel 87, 271–78

Deuteronomistic diction 18, 45, 49, 186,
    196–97, 199, 227, 257, 263, 313,
    365, 368
disputation, as a literary form 34–37,
    145, 163
divine assembly 147, 288–89, 340
divorce
    in ancient translations 5, 8, 9, 249
    in Deuteronomy 5, 49, 249
    in Malachi 221, 222–23, 226–27, 229,
    232, 235–58, 240–59

Ebal "land-grant" ceremony 162, 371,
    389
Eber-Nahara 57–60, 61, 62, 65, 74–75
Edom 77–78, 145, 149, 151–60, 164,
    167–70
election, divine 47n.2
election, of Israel
    and the Day of Yahweh 341, 343
    and the "God of Israel" 251
    and God's love and hate 47, 150–53,
    164–68, 356
    in the NT 84
Elijah 374
    divine confirmation of 264
    as figurative messianic forerunner 50,
    87–88, 145, 288, 379–80, 383–89,
    390
    as ideal OT figure 365–66, 372, 390
    Jewish/Christian interpretations of
    145
    names for 376
endogamy 243
Esau 145, 149, 176
    Edomites identified with 149, 151–52,
    164
    etymology of 151
    in the *Haftarot* readings 89
    in the NT 84
    as the object of Yahweh's hate 152,
    166–68
eschatology 80, 376
    apocalyptic, emergence of 363
    Malachi's contributions to OT/HB
    49–50, 288–91, 361, 383–84
exogamy 229
    See also marriages, mixed
Ezra 16, 72–73, 136, 144–45, 287, 365

forerunner 50, 265, 287–88, 380, 383–84
    in Catholicism 91
    in Judaism and Christianity 145
    in the NT 86, 88

God, attributes of
    changeableness 166, 219–20, 388
    hate 145, 151–52, 166–69, 221, 250,
    251
    holiness 221, 230–31
    love 145, 146–47, 150–51, 165
    oneness 85, 224–25, 244–46
    unchangeableness 47, 291, 295, 322
God, theology of in Malachi 47
God, titles for 195–96
    Father 85, 170, 174, 175, 221, 224–
    25, 255, 302, 343, 380
    King 171, 175, 195–96
    Lord 84–85, 175, 190, 259, 268, 286–
    89, 360
    Master 84, 170, 174, 175, 232, 268
    The One 221, 244–47, 250, 255
    Yahweh of Hosts 29, 85, 145, 157,
    170–71, 195, 221, 236, 259, 291,
    326
governors of Yehud, Persian period
    71–72

Haggai 12, 14–15, 42, 48, 52, 56, 60, 70,
    75–76, 181, 272, 371, 374, 378
honor 170, 174–75, 196, 198, 218
Horeb 79n.2, 154, 366, 368, 372

individual responsibility, theology of 76,
    270, 333
intermarriage. *See* marriages, mixed
Israel 255
    "all Israel" 229–30, 366, 372–73
    divine election of 84, 166
    "the God of" 221, 251, 264–65
    "new Israel" 141–42, 229–30
    Yahweh's love for 145–70

Jacob 145, 221, 291
    "descendants of" 291, 296–98
    and the divine election of Israel 166
    in the *Haftarot* readings 89
    Israel/Yehud identified with 141, 146,
    149, 163–64
    in the NT 84
    reference to OT traditions about 151,
    176, 182, 185, 305
    "the tents of" 221, 235–36
    usage of the name 149, 303
Jerusalem 65–67, 72–73, 229–30,
    278–79
John the Baptist 12, 50, 86, 88, 90–91,
    145, 288, 379, 383–84

Joshua, the high priest 12, 70, 71, 181, 189, 203, 204, 206–207, 213, 298, 300
judgment 87
divine 153–54, 159
"the God of" 259, 264
God's relenting of 219–20
and purification 259–91
and vindication 326–63
justice, social 282–84, 286, 290–91

Levi(tes) 204–6, 216–18, 220–21, 276
life 171, 205–7

Malachi, the book
authorship 15–18, 45, 135–36, 144
contemporary influences 74–76
date 51, 77–84
integrity 19–21, 20n.1, 173, 260, 363–65, 375, 377
liturgical use in Judaism, Christianity, and Catholicism 88–91
message 41–45
in the NT 84–88
theology 46–51, 76, 80
Marathon, battle of 54–55, 74, 187
marriage covenant 43–44, 48–49, 221, 226, 229, 241–46
marriages, mixed 44, 75, 223, 228–29, 231–33, 240, 241, 255–59
messenger 16, 50, 85, 86–87, 91, 136, 144–45, 171, 212–13, 259, 265, 267, 286–90, 383, 387
messenger/angel. *See* angel/messenger
messenger formula 147, 157–58, 172, 176, 193, 196, 251, 253, 259–60, 292, 309, 330, 375
messenger of the covenant 44, 91, 267, 269–71, 273–75, 278
messenger of Yahweh 85, 171, 212–13, 269, 288
Moses 50, 365–74, 384
Torah of 299–300, 366, 367, 370–72, 374

Nehemiah 57, 71–73, 77, 80, 81, 365

offal 171, 201–3
offerings 170–71, 177–96, 220, 221, 236, 239–40, 259, 276, 277, 278–79, 306, 307, 308
oracle(s) 133–36, 133, 138–40
lawsuit oracles 29–33
oracular prose 24–26

peace 171, 205–7
priests
purified 265–77
rebuked 170–221

Qumran manuscripts 4, 6, 26, 209–10

remembrance 43n.2, 366–67, 369–70, 371n.3, 374
repentance, theology of 322–23
repentance and Divine testing 291–325
righteous, the 328–29, 332, 338–39, 344–45, 356–59
robbing God 291, 303, 305, 308

sacrifices. *See* offerings
seed 171, 200–1, 221, 246–48, 268
Sheshbazzar 56, 66–68, 69, 71
sorcery 281
statutes (of God) 204–5, 299–300, 369, 373–74
sun of righteousness 49, 79, 87, 91, 326, 349–50, 362

Tattenai 60, 69, 70, 74
Temple
closing the doors of 171, 184–85, 220
glorification of 383–84
Temple, Jerusalem (Solomon's) 55, 66, 75–76, 266, 268, 310, 341
Temple, return of the divine presence 154, 157, 259, 265–69, 289–90, 321, 341, 376, 379–80, 386, 390
Temple, Second (Zerubbabel's) 56, 268, 310, 379–80, 383–84
during the reign of Darius I 74, 75–76
Haftarah readings in 89
as the holiness of Yahweh 231, 238
preaching traditions of 35, 41–42, 210
restoration under
Nehemiah 73
Sheshbazzar 66–67, 68, 69
Zerubbabel 68–70, 69, 181, 193
Territory of Evil 145, 159, 169
testing, Divine 286, 291, 311–13, 325, 326, 336–37
tithe 44, 75, 79, 291, 293, 304–11, 323–25, 358

wicked, the 328–29, 334–36, 344–45, 347, 354, 356–69
widow and orphan. *See* justice, social

worship
  among the nations 187–88, 218–19
  true 41, 220–21, 289–90, 359

Yehud
  identified with Jacob 146
  organization and structure 61–65
  political and religious history 66–74

rebuke of by Yahweh 221–59
as The Holy Land/Holy Mountain
  169

Zechariah 12–15, 42, 56, 60, 70, 76,
  138, 371, 374
Zerubbabel 12, 53, 68–71, 75, 82, 181,
  371

INDEX OF SCRIPTURAL AND OTHER ANCIENT SOURCES

◆

OLD TESTAMENT
(With the Apocrypha)

Genesis
1:27   85, 244, 246
2:20–24   244, 246
3:15   241
4:3   317
4:15   389
7:11   314
9:2   175
12:1–3   325
14:20   305
15:6   340
18:27   354
19:21   181
21:17   269
22:1   166, 311
24:55   274
25:22ff   149, 166, 168
25:34   43, 152, 164,
            176
26:24   371
26:34–35   149, 152
28:20–22   194, 306
30:13   335
31:50   243
32:28   141
36:1ff   149, 151
43:3   240
45:11   272
49:1,28   149
50:20   313

Exodus
3:20   389
4:23   343
9:23–24   238
12:12   389
13:3   367, 374
15:7   347

15:11   196
15:17   154
17:2,7   312
17:6   79n.2, 368
18:8   191
18:21   332
19:6   166, 270, 342,
            361, 373
20:2   295
20:5   152, 322
20:7,16   282
20:12   43, 174, 175
20:14   226, 281
20:24   188, 189
21:21   272
23:20ff   87, 265, 269,
            287, 288, 375,
            378
25:2–3   306
25:30   178
29:8–9   276
29:27–28   306
29:37   238
29:44   213, 278
32:7   215
32:12   297
32:13   371
32:26–29   206
33:2   265, 289, 375
34:6–7   43, 182, 220
34:15–16   229
34:24   273
40:34–38   386

Leviticus
5:24[6:5]   282
7:15–16   178
8:35   333
8:36   135
10:2   207
10:11   213
14:11   275

17:6   238
18:4   300
18:26   373
18:29   257
19:2   295
19:13   282
19:15   181
20:2–5   229
20:6   281
22:3   207
22:17–20   194, 195
26:42,45   322
27:30ff   44, 79, 305–6

Numbers
1:7   67
6:23–27   39, 172, 182,
            184, 362
18:21ff   18, 79, 306,
            310, 344
20:12   43, 48
20:14   191
20:19   180
21:4   151
21:5,7   357
23:19   322
24:5   235
24:17   349
25:11–13   206
25:18   194, 298
28:2   178

Deuteronomy
1:1   79n.2, 141
1:19ff   368, 377,
            378, 386
1:34   298
3:10   209
3:11   149
4:11   346
4:21,38   154
4:24   273

Deuteronomy (*cont.*)
4:25ff   240, 263, 301
4:27–31   227, 322
4:37   165
4:40   299, 300, 373
5:2   372, 384
5:17[18]   281
5:18   226
6:4ff   225, 244
6:12,15   381
6:16   311, 312
7:3ff   44, 229, 243
7:6ff   43, 47, 342,
            360
7:12–13   302, 317
7:21   363, 377
8:2ff   166, 311, 386
8:5   360
8:19   240
9:12,16   214, 299
9:15   346
9:27   371
10:8–9   216
10:18   282, 283
11:1   300, 333
11:2   170
11:18   198
11:24   354
12:1   44, 369
12:6ff   79, 305, 306
12:25,28   263
12:29   233
13:19[18]   263
14:28–29   44, 283, 306
15:21   18, 43, 179,
            192
16:20   286
17:1   43, 179, 180,
            229
17:19   299
18:1ff   43, 79
18:10   281
21:9   263
21:21–23   194
24:1–4   5, 9, 49, 226,
            229, 249, 250,
            251, 257, 258
24:19–21   283, 290
27:19   284
28:1ff   48, 170
28:8   315, 316
28:12   309, 313
28:20ff   198, 199, 307
28:27,28,35 389
28:29   192

28:39   317
28:58   196
30:1ff   43, 44, 170,
            322
30:11   197
30:15–20   48, 247, 374
31:5,29   367
31:9ff   79, 141
31:29   215, 263, 299
32:4   244
32:6ff   43, 224, 255,
            360
32:12   232
33:2   349, 350
33:5   371
33:8ff   43, 204, 206,
            216, 312
33:10ff   173, 210, 216
34:10–12   364, 384

Joshua
1:13   370
2:2   372
8:30–35   367, 371, 389
23:6   299, 367
23:12   44

Judges
2:20   301, 367
2:22   166
5:5   207
8:33   287
9:23   226
13:21   272
13:22   386
21:11   390

Ruth
3:9   252

1 Samuel
2:31   376
3:21   272
6:5   198
7:13   162
13:13   197
15:22ff   48, 185
28:24   353

2 Samuel
2:9   308
3:18   371
7:23   382
20:10   295
24:4   329

1 Kings
4:1,7   369
5:4[4:24]   60
5:5[4:25]   324
6:31–32   184
8:37   381
8:44–53   310, 322
9:21   382
11:1–4   44
11:16   274
11:37–38   142
13:6   182
16:7,12   135, 143
17:1   5, 374, 376
18:30–40   379
19:1–10   262

2 Kings
1:3,4,8,12 376
2:1–11   383
2:14   264
2:19,21   318
9:25   138n.3, 139
10:4   272
13:2   197
17:13ff   135, 384
18:6   299
18:24   78
19:25   298
22:17   175
25:1   55

1 Chronicles
2:10   67
3:19   70
9:17–27   184
9:26   310
9:37   135
28:18   276
29:3   342
29:17   311, 312

2 Chronicles
2:6   279
18:16   175
21:12   376
30:6   302
31:5–6   305
31:12   306
32:26   323

Ezra
1:1–4   56, 66, 373
1:8ff   66, 67
2:1–2   68, 82, 142

2:25ff   61, 62
2:62   178
3:2ff   68, 371
3:8ff   56, 69, 70
3:12   76
4:1–5   65, 69
5:1–2   56, 68, 70
6:13–22   56, 70, 370
7:1–6   73, 280
7:8ff   57, 72, 72n.3
7:16   60
8:36   57, 65
9:1ff   44, 65, 73, 80,
     229
9:7   298
10:1   238
10:7   279
10:21,26   376

Nehemiah
1:1   57, 72
1:8   367, 370
1:11–2:10   73
2:1ff   57, 65, 72, 73
3:5,15,27   9, 13, 17–18,
     62
3:7ff   61, 78
4:8ff   65, 377
5:1ff   65, 73, 80
5:14ff   65, 72, 73, 75
5:19   366
6:2   62n.2
7:26   62
7:64   178
8:1ff   57, 72, 73,
     371
8:8   370
8:13–18   57, 73
9:30   135
10:1   73
10:28–39[29–40]   75,
     324
10:37–40[36–39]   306,
     310, 324
12:22   52
12:31,37   161
12:44   305
13:23ff   80, 258
13:26   369

1 Esdras
4:50   151

2 Esdras
1:40   17, 84

1 Maccabees
3:24   62

Sirach
48:10   50, 88, 383
49:10   12, 77
49:11   72, 73

Esther
1:1   61
6:1   49, 339
8:9   78

Job
6:29,30   208, 286
13:7   209
14:20   295
21:7   260
22:23   336
22:30   337
24:4   283
28:28   299
29:11   240
31:15   225
36:26   359
38:10   333
40:2   358
41:11   260, 332
42:2   359
42:6   354

Psalms
4:3   175
5:5ff   152, 208
11:5   152, 166
12:6[5]   238
13:1–3   286
14:1–3   299, 359
17:3   311, 312
18:29   184
21:10[9]   346
24:6   269
30:10[9]   332
31:7[6]   167
38:7[6]   333, 334
40:17[16]   161, 269
45:7[6]   209
47:3[2]   195, 196
50:1   186
50:10–11   190
51:4[2],9[7]   274, 275
51:10   312
67:2[1]   182
73:4–12   336
73:15–20   360
76:2   187

76:12   176, 194
77:11   322, 374
78:7–8   169
80:10–11[9–10]   348
84:11   362
89:35[34]   296
92:10[9]   345
95:3   195
95:11   298
102:18[17]   239
103:13   343, 360
106:33   261
107:20   45, 351
111:4   44
111:5   366
115:5   310
119:21   335
127:1   168
132:1   367
137:7ff   78, 149, 168
139:16   339
139:23–24   312
146:5   164
147:15   204

Proverbs
2:17   243
2:22   226
3:2   206
3:7   299
3:33   198, 307
4:1   339
5:18   44, 49, 241
8:32   217
10:21   211
11:21   335
11:24   324
11:25   325
14:21   290
17:15   263
25:26   195
30:8   310
31:5   295
31:10ff   44, 242

Ecclesiastes
2:8   342
3:17   359
7:9   248
12:7   302

Isaiah
1:1   179
1:17   319
1:25   273
1:29   249

Isaiah (*cont.*)
3:10–11   357
4:3–4   290, 360
5:20   361
5:24   347, 367
7:12   312
8:2   240
8:3   302
8:12,13   175, 176
9:8   308
10:2   283
11:4   209, 389
13:1   13n.1, 134, 137, 139
13:6–8   340, 386
13:11   335, 347
15:1   13n.1, 134, 137
19:4   175, 268
20:3   371
21:1   13n.1, 134
21:2   188
24:18   314
25:6   276
26:15   170
29:13   44, 185
29:19   338
30:18   264
34:5ff   151, 382
36:17   324
40:3   86, 266
41:8   47, 150
41:23   361
42:4,6   219, 319
42:5   225
42:23   339
43:1,7,15   41, 85, 166, 225
43:3   295
43:9–10   280
43:18   279
43:23,24   261
43:28   382, 390
44:22   44, 301, 302
44:28   310
45:1   54
45:23   227
47:6   189
48:10ff   47, 312
49:6,22   187
50:2   200
50:11   183
51:1–8   43
53:3   88, 340
54:12   159

54:14   278
56:3,6   233
56:7   311
56:11   332
57:19[18]   190
58:3ff   185, 323
58:6–9   350, 359
58:10   349
59:3   178, 209
60:2   273, 349
60:15   152
61:8ff   47, 247, 319
62:10ff   86, 266, 267
63:10   380
65:17–25   166
66:1–2   143

Jeremiah
1:1   213, 379
1:10   143
2:22   274
2:30   332
2:36   295
3:14ff   301, 380
4:4   274
5:3   297
5:10   317
5:26   344
6:7   253
6:8   152, 153
6:10,17–19   339, 388
6:20   240, 278
6:28   299
6:29ff   273, 274, 332
7:1–7   44, 282, 310
7:20   317
7:21ff   185, 251
8:12   228
8:14   240
9:7   166, 312
9:10   154, 155
10:6   187
12:2   208
12:11   198
13:14   343
13:16   198
14:19   351
15:1   366, 372
16:11   300
18:8   388
18:11   299
18:18   141, 213
19:7   279
20:8   253
21:6   389

23:10   281
23:33ff   134, 137, 138
29:12–14   322
29:23   280
30:7   377, 386
30:18   235
31:2   165
31:9   224
31:27–30   333
31:29ff   47, 76, 270, 285, 289
32:14   272
32:39   244
33:6   351
33:18   220
33:20–21   206
43:2   335, 347
46:21   353
48:10   193
48:38   320
49:7–22   43, 151, 153, 169
49:33   155
50:1   134, 135, 137, 142, 143
50:11   352
50:27,31   376
50:44–46   142
51:23   78
52:33   295

Lamentations
2:11   386
3:5   191
3:22,32   165
4:14   178

Ezekiel
1:1–3   137, 213, 379
1:25   161
3:14   329
4:12–15   201
5:6   336
5:10   380
5:17   198
6:5   201
7:11,23   252, 253
7:26   76, 213
8:1   55
11:15   308
12:19   253
13:9   339
14:3   381
14:15   318
16:50   228
16:59ff   48, 176

17:8–9   348
17:15   337
18:3ff   270, 285, 333
18:18   282
18:23,30–32 49
19:9   373
20:13   297
21:8–9[3–4] 344, 358
21:30,34   376
22:17–22   273
22:31   297
23:6   78
23:39   310
24:21   189
25:12–14   151, 153, 167
28:19,22   170
30:2   341
32:29   156
33:19–20   336
33:31   208, 332
34:4,16   180
35:1–15   151, 168, 169
36:9   239
36:21   343
36:22,32   360
36:25,33   275
36:29–30   324
37:24ff   66, 300
37:28   187
38:17   279
43:1–5   289, 290
43:27   186
44:13   204
44:16   178
45:11,14   305

Daniel
1:2   309
5:30–31   52, 56
9:5,11   299
9:11ff   366, 367
11:35   273
12:1   49

Hosea
4:4–6   173, 212,
             214, 316
5:7   226
6:1ff   48, 301
7:4   346
8:8   320
8:13   181
9:4   278, 317
9:9   215
9:15   152, 167, 250

10:1   318
11:1ff   44, 150, 166,
             174
11:6   297
11:8–9   381
12:8[7]   282
14:2   214
14:5   150, 256
14:9[8]   209
14:10[9]   364, 365

Joel
1:7   324
1:8   241
1:15   341
1:17   310
1:19   347
2:3,5   153, 317, 347
2:12ff   44, 219, 238,
             302, 380
2:14   315, 388
2:18   343
2:22   318
2:23,26–27   316
3:46[2:31b] 377, 378
             376, 377, 385,
             386, 388
4:1ff[3:1ff] 279, 386

Amos
1:5   233
2:4   215, 367
2:7   44, 227, 283
2:9   348
2:15   272
3:2   151
3:9   282
3:13   149
4:1,4   306, 309
4:2   376
4:5   297
4:9   381, 389
4:13   225
5:15   152, 167
5:18ff   271, 385
5:21   201
6:4   317, 353
9:11   279
9:12   360
9:13   376

Obadiah
1   142
10ff   78, 149, 151,
             153

13   167
17–21   168

Jonah
2:5[4],8[7] 310
2:10[9]   194
3:1   236
3:4   227
3:6   354
3:9–10   388
4:8   349

Micah
1:2   280
1:5   149
3:2   152, 361
3:10   209
3:11   213
4:5   166
4:13   333
5:11[12]   281
6:4   366, 372
6:6–8   18, 220
7:14,15   279
7:18–20   44

Nahum
1:1ff   13n.1, 44,
             134, 137, 142
1:2–3   336
1:10   347
3:6   201
3:12   317
3:17   349

Habakkuk
1:1   13n.1, 134,
             137, 138n.3,
             142
1:2ff   44, 252, 253,
             286
1:4ff   344, 357
1:8   352
1:13   226
2:12   209
3:17–19   164

Zephaniah
1:12   47
1:14ff   44, 377, 385
1:17–18   375
2:8–10   251, 290, 308
2:12   164
3:1   178
3:4   227, 230

Zephaniah (*cont.*)
3:6   316
3:11ff   48, 290
3:15   195, 266

Haggai
1:1ff   52, 56, 69, 70, 78, 134–35, 137, 140n.4, 143
1:4   274, 361
1:6ff   65, 75, 164, 315, 379
1:8   147, 181, 193
1:9ff   150, 191, 239, 266, 310, 375
1:12ff   69, 142, 302, 339, 375, 379
1:13   212, 267, 269, 375
1:14   248, 357
2:1ff   56, 69, 76, 135, 140n.4, 143
2:3ff   149, 150, 175, 183, 381
2:5   233, 272
2:6   317
2:7ff   54, 76, 188, 219, 290, 308, 311, 384
2:10ff   52, 140n.4, 176
2:12ff   162, 178, 230, 304, 351, 375
2:14   279, 308
2:15,18   268, 310, 380
2:17   44, 314, 381, 389
2:19   200, 316, 318, 324
2:20ff   53, 56, 70, 76, 236, 371
2:21ff   74, 169, 386
2:23   70, 147, 152, 239, 371

Zechariah
1:1ff   52, 56, 137, 140n.4
1:3ff   44, 147, 150, 156, 301, 302, 339, 379
1:5   160, 175, 264
1:6   149, 299, 368, 371, 372, 384

1:11   269, 274
1:12   159, 314
1:16   156, 267, 310, 373
1:19   142, 372
2:2ff   201, 229
2:9ff   150, 175, 273, 375
2:11ff   169, 219, 233
2:14ff   233, 267, 272, 345, 376
2:16ff   147, 230, 318
3:1ff   70, 76, 272, 340, 378
3:2   149, 200, 273, 316, 317
3:4ff   161, 210, 253, 298
3:5   152, 189
3:6   241
3:7   203, 204, 205, 207, 300, 310
3:8   339
3:9   313, 345, 346
3:10   324, 338, 345
4:2   308, 375
4:4,5,13   149, 268
4:7   209
4:9   332, 375
4:12   161, 236, 315
4:14   268, 272
5:4   281, 297, 298, 341
5:9   351
6:9ff   70, 140n.4, 239
6:15   43, 268, 304, 310, 339, 375
7:1ff   52, 56, 140n.4, 378
7:3,5   176, 222, 381
7:7ff   62n.1, 135, 274, 384
7:8ff   18, 76, 283, 371, 379
7:10   282, 283, 290, 380
7:14   153, 308, 320, 379
8:1ff   140n.4, 386
8:3ff   76, 156, 169, 230, 267, 290, 380
8:7   349, 375
8:8   43, 178, 363

8:9   256, 268, 310, 314, 370
8:12ff   200, 316, 318, 324, 325
8:13   142, 315, 372
8:16–17   48, 283, 302, 325
8:17ff   147, 152, 167, 281, 380
8:20–23   182, 188, 247, 268, 351, 384
9:1ff   13, 16, 133, 134, 135, 137, 138, 139, 140, 140n.4, 142, 169, 304, 364, 368, 372
9:6,10   233
9:9   344, 376
9:14   273
9:19   222
10:2   331
10:3   152, 194
10:9ff   49, 299, 370
11:5,6   343
11:10   234
11:13   309
11:14   142, 314
11:16   272, 345
11:17   256, 348
12:1ff   13, 133, 134, 135, 137, 138, 139, 140, 140n.4, 142, 304, 364, 372, 386
12:4   381, 389
12:6   49, 273
12:7ff   70, 214, 235, 386
13:1   44, 273, 274, 386
13:2   370, 381
13:9   49, 273, 275, 277, 311, 313, 336, 375
14:1   345, 375
14:8   279, 352
14:9   225, 341
14:11   49, 382, 390
14:14   277, 279, 384
14:16ff   166, 195, 201, 316
14:20   177, 230

Malachi

1:1   16, 133–45,
       364
1:2–3 84, 157, 163,
       164, 166, 258,
       356
1:2–5 20, 26, 27, 34,
       145–70, 172,
       176, 205, 347
1:3   6, 151–55,
       167, 220, 249,
       250, 383
1:4,5 7, 156–60, 162
1:5   160–62, 169,
       170, 196
1:6–2:9 26, 29, 80,
       170–221, 254
1:6–10 157, 173,
       187, 190
1:6–14 172, 187,
       193, 195
1:6   84, 174–77,
       179, 264, 341
1:7   85, 177–79,
       188
1:8   9, 177, 179–
       81, 220, 309
1:9   173, 181–83
1:10   183–86
1:11   85, 170, 186–
       89, 196
1:12   189–91
1:13   6, 21, 27, 173,
       191–93
1:14   26, 173, 178,
       193–96, 307
2:1–3 198, 205,
       219–20
2:1–9 172, 173,
       187, 223
2:1   173, 176,
       196–97
2:2   165, 175, 192,
       197–200, 307,
       315
2:3   9, 173, 177,
       200–3
2:4   177, 197, 203,
       204–5, 314
2:5   175, 205–8
2:6   156, 208–10
2:7   176, 189,
       210–13, 246
2:8   177, 213–16,
       281

2:9   9, 176, 179,
       181, 216–18
2:10–12 222–23, 246,
       255–57
2:10–16 26, 221–59,
       292
2:10   26, 85, 224–
       28, 234, 258
2:11   19, 21, 228–
       33, 238
2:12   27, 193,
       233–36
2:13–16 21, 222–23,
       254, 257–59
2:13   26, 177, 222,
       236–40, 266,
       316
2:14   232, 240–43
2:15   9, 243–49,
       258, 268
2:16   249–54, 291
2:17–3:5 26, 29, 248,
       253, 254,
       259–91
2:17   10, 26, 261–
       65, 269, 270,
       272, 285–86
3:1   86, 87, 239,
       246, 265–71,
       286–89, 310,
       375
3:2–3 277
3:2–4 289–90
3:2   87, 271–74
3:3   87, 165, 188,
       274–78
3:4   160, 278–79
3:5   87, 220, 265,
       279–85,
       290–91, 306
3:6–12 20, 21, 26, 27,
       223, 253,
       259, 291–
       325
3:6   259, 294–98,
       321–22
3:7   87, 156, 213,
       258, 298–
       303, 322–23,
       344, 371
3:8–10 323–24
3:8   10, 303–7,
       323–24
3:9   191, 198,
       307–309

3:10   181, 184,
       309–16
3:11–12 178, 324–25
3:11   182, 199,
       200, 316–19
3:12   27, 193, 291,
       319–20
3:13–21[4:3] 26, 253,
       326–63
3:13   7, 26, 157,
       329–31
3:14   165, 179,
       246, 331–34
3:15   159, 262,
       334–37
3:16   177, 274, 327,
       337–41, 366
3:17   234, 263,
       341–44
3:18   166, 169,
       312, 344–45
3:19[4:1] 26, 238, 262,
       345–49
3:20[4:2] 87, 177,
       349–53
3:21[4:3] 27, 263, 353–
       55, 365
3:22[4:4] 26, 174, 215,
       265, 299, 363,
       365, 366–74
3:22–24[4:4–6] 19, 21,
       27, 28, 29, 34,
       45, 363–66
3:23[4:5] 87, 88, 90,
       288, 374–78,
       382–86
3:23–24[4:5–6] 145,
       374–90
3:24[4:6] 156, 366,
       378–82,
       386–90

NEW TESTAMENT

Matthew
4:3   312
11:1–6 50
11:3ff 86, 288
11:7–15 50, 145
11:14 87, 384
17:9–13 88
17:10ff 87, 383, 384
19:11 49
23:3   85
23:23 48

Mark
1:2-8   50
1:2   86, 288
9:9-13   88
9:11-13   87
10:1-10   49

Luke
1:5   379
1:16-17   50
1:17ff   88, 288, 383
1:78   87
6:46   84
7:19ff   86, 288
12:48   48

John
1:21   383
3:28   86

Acts
6:3   48

Romans
3:1-4   84
9:6-7   166
9:11   166
9:13   43, 84, 166
13:4   48

1 Corinthians
3:12-15   49
5:7   312
6:16-17   242
8:6   85
10:9   312

2 Thessalonians
1:12   85

Hebrews
11:9,20-22   164
12:5-11   166
12:16-17   165

James
1:3,12   313
1:14-16   312
1:27   48
4:8   87

1 Peter
1:7   87, 313
4:17   286

2 Peter
3:4   262
3:10-12   49

Revelation
6:15-16   87
11:3   384
15:4   85
20:11-15   49

**RABBINIC
LITERATURE**

b. 'Aboda Zara, 3b
             362
b. Baba Batra, 15a
             12, 17
b. Giṭṭin, 90b   237, 251
b. Megilla, 15a   12, 17
b. Sanhedrin, 11a
             12
b. Sanhedrin, 22a
             237
b. Yoma, 9b   12
b. Zebaḥim, 62a   12

m. 'Eduyyot, 8.7   145

Targum (Jonathan) to
the Prophets
(TgNeb)   8, 16

DEAD SEA SCROLLS

4QXIIa   249, 397
4QXIIc   302
CDR 6:11   4

**OTHER ANCIENT
SOURCES**

Augustine
De civitate Dei   12
Confessiones, 1.1.1-4   41

1 Clement, 23:5   288

Constitutiones
Apostolorum,
   6.4.19   12

Cyprian, Didache
(Treatises)
9.22   144
4.35   12

Diodorus Siculus,
Bibliotheca historica,
19.95   78

Herodotus, Historiae
3.5ff   60
3.85-89   53
3.88-95   60
7.83   52

Irenaeus, Adversus omnes
haereses
3.11.4   145
4.17.5   144

Jerome
Corpus Christianorum
56A:901,903 145
76A:903   138
76A:906   174
76A:921ff   224, 235
76A:923   228
76A:924   237
Patrologia latina, 25:
   1541-42   16

Josephus
Contra Apionem,
   i.viii.3   12
Antiquitates Judaicae,
   xi.i.3[13-14]   69

Justin Martyr, Dialogus
contra Tryphonem
xli   219
xlix   145

Origen, In Johannem
Commentarius
2.17   12
6.13   12

Tertullian
Adversus Marcionem,
4.8.1   12
Adversus Judaeos,
5   145

INDEX OF
HEBREW AND OTHER
LANGUAGES

◆

See Appendixes C and D for citations of words using Hebrew font.

Hebrew
'āb 88, 174–75, 224, 227, 298, 380, 388
'ādôn 174, 175, 178, 190, 268, 287–88
'ādām 304, 323
'hb 42, 146–47, 148, 150–51, 165, 231
'āḥ 149, 226, 227
'mr 147–48, 156, 160, 262, 331
'āmar YHWH 19, 29, 140n.4, 147–48,
    157–58, 176, 193, 196, 251, 253,
    271, 284, 309, 320, 330, 341
'ănî YHWH 189, 292, 294–95, 321
'rr 42, 159, 193–94, 199, 307
'ărubbôt šāmayim 314
'šr 319, 335
'eḥād 224, 225, 244, 246
'ēl nēkār 231, 255–56
'ĕlōhîm 247–48, 264–65, 304
'ĕmet 208
'ên rā' 180
'ereṣ 320, 381, 389
'ēš 273
'ēšet nĕ'ûrekā 241, 249
'îš 338, 343
'ôṣār 309–10

bā'al 231–32
bārä' 85, 225
bēn 174, 276, 296, 343, 380
beṣa' 332
bĕrît 205–7, 215–16, 227, 243
bĕrākâ 315
bgd 8, 42, 226–27, 228, 241–42, 244,
    249, 254
bw' 267, 271, 272, 309, 376, 381
bzh 176, 179, 190–91, 216
bḥn 311–12, 336–37, 357
bnh 156–57, 158, 335
bō'ēr 346

bōrît 274
bqš 246, 268

g'l 178
gdl 161
gādôl 161, 187, 195–96, 377–78, 386
gādôl šĕmî 85, 187
gāzûl 192
gĕbûl 159, 162, 170
gôy 187, 196, 308–9, 319
g'r 200, 316

dābār 261, 329–30, 356
da'at 211–12
dbr 331, 337
dĕbar-YHWH 133–34, 136–41, 140n.4,
    143, 365
derek 214
dim'â 237

hălô' 148–49, 224
hyh 320, 341, 346, 353
hinnēh 200, 265, 271, 382–83
hlk 333
hrs 158

zbḥ 179–80, 195
zēdîm 335, 347
zkr 366–67, 369–70
z'm 159
zrḥ 201
zrḥ 349
zera' 9, 200–1, 247

ḥăberet 242–43
ḥag 201
ḥayyîm 206–7
ḥāmās 251–53

Hebrew (*cont.*)
ḥāpēṣ 263, 270
ḥēpeṣ 185, 320
ḥērem 381–82, 389, 390
ḥzq 329
ḥlh 181–82
ḥōleh 180, 192
ḥll 189, 227, 230
ḥml 343
ḥnn 182
ḥōq 299–300, 369, 373–74
ḥorbâ 156–57
ḥšb 340–41

ṭhr 189, 275
ṭerep 310
ṭôb 263

yg' 261, 262
yād 134–35, 142–43, 183, 185, 193, 240
ya'ăqōb 149, 150, 235, 296–97, 303
yd' 203, 226
YHWH ṣĕbā'ôt 7, 27, 29, 157–58, 193,
    196, 212–13, 236, 271, 284, 302,
    309, 327, 330
yĕhûdâ 228, 230, 278–79
yĕrûšālayim 229, 278–79
yiśrā'ēl 134, 141–42, 162, 170, 229, 368–
    69, 372–73
yôm 272, 341, 354
yôm bā' 49, 345–46, 348
yôm-YHWH 49, 54, 376
yṣ' 352
yr' 284, 338, 340, 349
yšb 274–75

kbd 174–75
kābôd 196, 198
kānāp 350–52
kappôt raglēkem 354
kî 156, 292, 294, 304–5, 319–20, 353
kî-hinnēh 327, 345–46
kōhēn 176, 197, 210
klh 293, 297–98, 308
ksh 237, 251–53
krt 233–34, 235, 256–57, 358
ktb 339

lēb 200
lĕbûš 251–53
lēwî 204–5, 215, 276

mlṭ 337
mal'āk 86, 135–36, 212–13
mal'āk 'ĕlōhîm/ YHWH 136, 212, 213,
    269

mal'ak habbĕrît 50, 86, 265, 269, 273,
    287, 375, 376
mal'ākî 13, 15–18, 134–35, 143–44, 265
ma'ăśēr 8, 10, 305–6, 309, 311
marpē' 350–51
māśśā' 13, 133, 136–41, 144
mĕ'ērâ 198–99, 307
mĕkaššĕpîm 281
melek gādôl 195
mĕmahēr 280
mĕṣārēp 273, 275
mizbēaḥ 177, 184, 237–38
minḥâ 185, 189, 192–93, 236, 239, 277,
    278
miṣwâ 196–97, 204
mišmeret 333
mišpāṭ 197, 264–65, 279–80, 284, 369,
    373
môrā' 175, 207
muqṭār 188

ngš 236, 277–78
n'p 281
naḥălâ 154, 168
nāśî' 67
nĕ'ūm-YHWH 150
nkh 381–82, 389–90
nôrā' 196, 377–78, 386
nsh 311–12, 336
nph 191
nś' 181, 202–3, 217

sĕgullâ 342, 360–61
sgr 184
swr 213, 298–99
sēper zikkārôn 79, 339–40

'ayin 160, 263
'ām 159, 216–17
'bd 331, 343, 345
'ebed 174, 371
'ēd 280
'ēr 234–35
'ôlām 160, 279
'md 272
'ōneh 234–35

'śh 229, 234, 236, 245, 262, 336, 341–42,
    347, 354–55
'ēśāw 149, 151
'šš 353

pnh 239, 266
pānîm 181–82, 217, 267, 334, 340
peḥâ 65, 67–68, 73, 77–79, 180–81

pen 381, 388
pereš 201, 203
pinnâ 86, 266
pissēah 180, 192
pth 313

ṣaddîq 344, 349
ṣĕdāqâ 278, 349–51
ṣwh 367–68

qb' 297, 303, 305, 307
qĕdōrannît 333–34
qōdeš 230–31, 238
qr' 158
qrb 180, 279–80
qšb 338–39

r'h 160, 344
rabbîm 209, 211, 212, 214–15
rā' 180
rṣh 181, 186
rāṣôn 239–40
rāšā' 344
rēa' 338
rîb 29–32, 83n.5
riš'â 336, 347
ršš 156
rûah 245, 248, 254, 272

śym 152, 155, 197–98, 200
śn' 150–52, 166–67, 237, 249–51
śāpâ 208, 210

šb' 281–82
šwb 87, 156–57, 210, 214, 301, 302,
    322–23, 344, 378–79, 386–87
škl 318
šālôm 206–7, 209
šlh 198–99, 203, 249–51, 265, 375
šēm 85, 173, 177, 187, 198, 207, 341,
    349
šĕmāmâ 153–54
šm' 197, 339
šmr 210–11, 217, 254, 300, 333, 348
šemeš 79, 186, 349–51
šnh 295, 298, 322
šēnît 236–37
šulhan 85, 178–79, 190

tannôt 5, 154–55
tannûr 346
tĕrûmâ 306
tô'ēbâ 228–29
tôrâ 208, 214, 215, 217, 370–71

Akkadian
am/[w]ātu(m) 296
arāru 193
enû 295–96
qabû 296
rašāšu 156
rêmu 306
sikiltu(m) 342
šaknu 65
tarāmu 306
tarīmtu 306
zakāru 296

Arabic
'ss 353
qadara 334
qadira 333
yâ 197

Greek
ággélos 136, 269
állótrios 335
anáthema 382
anoikodomēsōmen 157
apéileō 159
apéchō 298
dokimázien 312–13
dómata 155
ebarýnate 329
ekalýptete 237
exolethreúsei 233
epiblépein 266
epipháněs 377
epistréphō 302
epistrépsōmen 157
héōs 234
hyperánō 161
katéstraptai 156
kathiê itai 274
koinōnós 242
móschos 353
ômos 200
paratássō 159
peirázein 312–13
póa 274
poiéō 152
prosdéxetai 181
pternízō 303
seirēn 155
spodós 354
tássō 152
chōneúein 275

Latin
brachium 200
cinis 354
converto 302
destructi 156
dracones 155
herba 274
illud 181
onus 138
pinnis 351
reverto 302

super 161
valeo 329

Ugaritic
bġr.nḥlty 154
ḥālû' 149
la 197
sglt 342
'rb 278
šd 318